HANDBOOK OF ECONOMIC ORGANIZATION

Handbook of Economic Organization

Integrating Economic and Organization Theory

Edited by

Anna Grandori

Professor of Business Organization, Bocconi University, Italy

Edward Elgar
Cheltenham, UK • Northampton, MA, USA

Published by
Edward Elgar Publishing Limited
The Lypiatts
15 Lansdown Road
Cheltenham
Glos GL50 2JA
UK

Edward Elgar Publishing, Inc.
William Pratt House
9 Dewey Court
Northampton
Massachusetts 01060
USA

A catalogue record for this book
is available from the British Library

Library of Congress Control Number: 2012948840

This book is available electronically in the ElgarOnline.com
Economics Subject Collection, E-ISBN 978 1 78254 822 5

ISBN 978 1 84980 398 4 (cased)

Typeset by Servis Filmsetting Ltd, Stockport, Cheshire
Printed by MPG PRINTGROUP, UK

Contents

CONCLUSIONS

Contributors

Nicholas Argyres, Olin Business School, Washington University in St Louis, USA.

Margaret M. Blair, Vanderbilt University Law School, USA.

Giovanni Bonifati, Department of Communication and Economics, University of Modena and Reggio Emilia, Italy.

Richard M. Burton, Fuqua School of Business, Duke University, USA.

Massimo G. Colombo, Department of Management, Economics, and Industrial Engineering, Politecnico di Milano, Italy.

Li Feng, Department of Economics, Swedish University of Agricultural Sciences, Uppsala, Sweden.

Nicolai J. Foss, Copenhagen Business School, Denmark; and Norwegian School of Economics and Business Administration, Norway.

Bruno S. Frey, Warwick Business School, UK; and CREMA-Center for Research in Economics, Management and the Arts, Switzerland.

Victor P. Goldberg, School of Law, Columbia University, USA.

Anna Grandori, Department of Management and Technology and Center of Research on Organization and Management, Bocconi University, Milan, Italy.

George Hendrikse, Rotterdam School of Management, Erasmus University, Netherlands.

Jean-François Hennart, Center and Department of Organization and Strategy, Tilburg University, Netherlands; Faculty of Economics, University of Pavia, Italy; Queen's University Management School, UK; Department of Strategy and Organization, Singapore Management University, Singapore.

Geoffrey M. Hodgson, The Business School, University of Hertfordshire, UK.

Adelheid Holl, Center of Human and Social Sciences, Spanish National Research Council (CSIC), Madrid (ES), Spain.

Bruce E. Kaufman, Department of Economics, Georgia State University, USA; Centre for Workplace Organization and Wellbeing, Griffith University, Australia; and Work and Employment Research Unit, University of Hertfordshire, UK.

Peter G. Klein, Division of Applied Social Sciences, University of Missouri, USA.

Peter H. Kriss, Department of Social and Decision Sciences, Carnegie Mellon University, USA.

Karim R. Lakhani, Harvard Business School, USA.

Jan-Erik Lane, Department of Political Science, University of Freiburg, Germany.

Riccardo Leoni, Department of Economics 'H.P. Minsky', University of Bergamo, Italy.

Hila Lifshitz-Assaf, Harvard Business School, USA.

Siegwart Lindenberg, Department of Sociology, University of Groningen, Netherlands.

Joseph T. Mahoney, Department of Business Administration, College of Business, University of Illinois at Urbana-Champaign, USA.

Scott E. Masten, M.S. Ross School of Business, University of Michigan, USA.

Børge Obel, Interdisciplinary Center for Organizational Architecture, Aarhus University, Denmark.

Margit Osterloh, Warwick Business School, UK; and CREMA-Center for Research in Economics, Management and the Arts, Switzerland.

Ugo Pagano, Department of Economics, University of Siena, Italy; and Central European University, Hungary.

John Pencavel, Department of Economics, Stanford University, USA.

Phanish Puranam, London Business School, UK.

Ruth Rama, Center of Human and Social Sciences, Spanish National Research Council (CSIC), Madrid, Italy.

Marlo Raveendran, London Business School, UK.

Cristina Rossi-Lamastra, Department of Management, Economics, and Industrial Engineering, Politecnico di Milano, Italy.

Lorenzo Sacconi, Department of Economics, University of Trento and Econometica, Italy.

Ron Sanchez, Department of Innovation and Organizational Economics, Copenhagen Business School, Denmark.

Michael L. Tushman, Harvard Business School, USA.

Marco Villani, Department of Communication and Economics, University of Modena and Reggio Emilia, Italy.

Massimo Warglien, Department of Management, Università Ca' Foscari Venezia, Italy.

Roberto Weber, Department of Economics, University of Zurich, Switzerland.

Josef Windsperger, Department of Management, University of Vienna, Austria.

Todd R. Zenger, Olin Business School, Washington University in St Louis, USA.

INTRODUCTION

Economic organization as an object of study and as an emerging disciplinary field
Anna Grandori

AIMS AND SCOPE

This *Handbook of Economic Organization*, as the subtitle articulates, is an endeavor to integrate economics and organization theory in the explanation and design of economic organization. Its distinctive feature is in covering and providing greater unity to a leading interdisciplinary field that is attracting numerous researchers, and integrating insights from economics, organization theory, strategy and management, economic sociology and cognitive psychology. The very existence and expansion of a scientific community of this type indicates that the object of enquiry, something that in the course of being 'economic' is also 'organized', should not leave the analytical tools unaffected by the content. In particular, it signals that the conceptual apparatuses that have been constructed to analyze a different object – or a very particular type of economic organization – such as markets, can only partially shed light on the variety of forms of economic organization that are central in modern economies.

Originally, organization and 'administrative' science was an interdisciplinary science underpinned by other, more 'basic' and less applied social sciences, particularly economics, sociology and psychology. As one of its founding fathers (James D. Thompson) stated in establishing the first scientific review dedicated to the field, *Administrative Science Quarterly*, organization and administrative science should maintain the same links to basic social sciences as engineering and medicine have to the basic natural sciences. In the latter decades of the twentieth century, however, a process of 'Balkanization' of the organization field into various domains and dominions occurred, where theories returned to being heavily characterized by the 'mother disciplines' that, so to speak, 'directly invest' in the increasingly important and interesting field of economic organization. Models have flourished that are qualified as 'economics of organization', 'sociology of organization' and 'psychology of organization'. This theory proliferation phase has been very healthy in terms of providing new inputs and insights. However, its potential is going to remain underexploited if integration never occurs. The time is more than ripe for such integration efforts. In fact, the resources have matured, at the intersection of different research programmes on economic organization, and are well represented by the leading scholars who agreed to contribute to this volume. The authors are distinguished scholars at their productive peak in these fields, sharing an integrative stance in one way or another. In inviting the contributions, I made reference to an actual connected scientific network, if not a community proper: most contributors are linked by a history of cross-citation, participation in the same type of conferences and acknowledgement of each other's work. This is a loosely coupled community though, with a great deal of internal diversity and no single dominant paradigm. As such, it should yield maximum creative potential.

Furthermore, contributors have been invited to look at the future while taking stock of the past: each chapter not only represents the state of the art in a subfield, but also revisits foundational issues, offers some key new messages and original contributions, and identifies issues for future research. As a book 'role model' we had in mind a collection close in type and in the function of inspiring future research to March's 1965 *Handbook of Organizations*, rather than an encyclopedic model (which today is perhaps more common as a handbook template).

Since this Handbook focuses on economic organization and not on organization in general, the two core disciplinary fields brought into integration are organization theory, with its long tradition of interdisciplinary integration; and organizational economics, with its rich contribution delivered in recent decades by economics as applied to economic organization. Hence, 'economic organization' is here intended as both an object of enquiry and an emerging disciplinary field.

For the sake of clarity, this volume is not another handbook on the economics 'of' organization, where economics is intended as the discipline, providing theory and method, while organization is intended as the object of study (what is most often intended by the term 'organization(al) economics'). Other and excellent handbooks already exist with this approach, which are therefore to be considered different and complementary.

ITINERARY

Each chapter offers a journey into a specific field of economic organization (EO hereafter): from foundational issues, to key propositions, to research questions for the future. In a sense, so does the architecture of the volume when considered in its entirety: from foundations to models of EO formation and change, to the relations between different types of assets and EO, to the forms of EO.

The organization of each part was also inspired by (conjectured) problematic issues, as expressed in the call for contributions, in the form of quests for model extensions or of standing puzzles and dilemmas (represented in the titles of each part). The existence and importance of conjectured problems and questions have been substantially confirmed by the analyses offered by the chapters. The specific responses and contributions on each are summarized and discussed in the Conclusions, while here these are briefly illustrated together with the topics in order to provide a map for the journey.

Part I revisits the micro-foundations of EO in terms of modeling the knowledge, interest and rationality of economic actors. The conjectured need, and indeed the result, was largely to expand the prevailing models. Among the relevant extensions achieved are: an extension from the information processing and information costs foundations of EO to include knowledge and cognitive foundations; an extension of the model of motivation and interest beyond its identification with self-interest; and an extension of the portfolio of feasible and effective decision logics beyond (or between) the divide between a 'behavioral' and a 'rational' actor.

Part II burrows into the foundations of EO in the interacting and contracting between different actors. A most prominent extension prospected by the chapters in this part is on the notion of contracting. A first extension of the notion of contracting that emerges from this section is of a mechanism that is capable of regulating not only exchange relations, but also ongoing cooperative relationships and even communities, by establishing not only partnerships, but also condominium-like entities, including firms. In this sense, the section casts doubt on the validity of the currently common opposition between 'contract' and 'organization' (a doubt reinforced by various chapters in the other parts). The notion of contract is also expanded by reconnecting it to the wider Rawlsian notions of social contract and justice, as well as to its roots in communication and its linguistic artifact nature.

Part III offers models of the forces shaping the forms that EO, once established, is going to assume through processes of evolution and/or design. The section offers extensions such as models not only of 'adaptation' but also of 'exaptation' (that have been emerging in natural sciences as well, and are central to innovation); and from static to dynamic design models. Some notable reconciliations among long-lasting oppositions are also prospected: between Darwinian and Lamarkian evolution; and between design as an exercise in the comparative assessment of 'given' forms and, paraphrasing Simon, design as a science of the artificial concerned with 'the world as it might be'.

Parts IV and V analyze the relations between assets and EO. Some core dilemmas obtaining new analyses include: for human assets, the distinction between the assets and the actors entitled to possess and manage them; for technical assets, their status as exogenous and/or endogenous factors and, to the extent to which they play the role of independent variables, whether they act as enablers or determinants; and for human and technical assets, whether they are as distinct and different as is usually assumed.

The two sections jointly indicate that the role played by technical, human and social 'capital' needs to be revisited particularly in a knowledge-intensive, post-industrial economy. The chapters focusing on the governance of technical and human assets typically identify new dimensions, highlighted in the Conclusions, with respect to those considered in most current models. Broader notions emerge not only by giving greater consideration to variables of growing importance in reality, but also by addressing configurational issues such as the compatibility, complementarity and fungibility of the various practices and mechanisms to govern technical and human asset provision.

Finally, some defined forms of EO emerge from all the above processes and relations. Whether these can be qualified as discrete structural alternatives or as more continuous and overlapping combinations of mechanisms has certainly been one of my concerns for many years, but it seems that the contributions in this volume have gone even further than I expected in disentangling forms and reassessing their nature. This is certainly and predominantly what occurred with joint ventures and franchising, thanks to innovative ways of applying property rights theory in combination with organization theory. At the very least, the definition of each form, the boundaries between forms and the assessment of their distinctive functions and properties are restated, and the common notion that they can be positioned on some continuum is put under strain.

PART I

THE MICRO-FOUNDATIONS OF ECONOMIC ORGANIZATION: EXTENDING BEHAVIORAL ASSUMPTIONS ON KNOWLEDGE, INTEREST, AND RATIONALITY

1. Models of rationality in economic organization: 'economic', 'experiential' and 'epistemic'

Anna Grandori

This chapter reviews the models of decision-making relevant to economic organization, starting with the two main economic and behavioral paradigms. An original contribution will be the identification of a narrower and a wider account for each. It is then argued that, in the wider account, they need not be seen as rival 'paradigms' (only one of which is then seen as acceptable) but can be seen as alternative decision strategies (each with claims of effectiveness and efficiency under specified circumstances). Second, the chapter reviews recent research on decision-making in innovative settings which, as a whole, is seen as providing a third, missing model of decision-making that in the course of being 'heuristic' (oriented to empirical discovery) is also 'logically sound', hence arguably rational.

INTRODUCTION

The notion of rationality, in philosophy of knowledge and logic, is derived from 'reason' (*ratio, rationis*) and defined as: the principle governing knowing activities founded on logically sound procedures, on scientific method. The term 'rationality' thus refers to logically sound procedures in knowing activities.

The notion and models of rationality employed in economic sciences has come to be divided in two approaches, most often considered as two rival paradigms: the 'rational choice' approach typically assumed in the majority of economic models, rooted in the 'Savage paradigm' (Savage 1954); and the 'behavioral' approach typically assumed in the majority of organizational, behavioral and administrative science research, rooted in the 'Simon paradigm' (Simon 1947, 1955).

These two main types of approaches and groups of decision models – illustrated next – can be related to the general and philosophical notion of rationality indicated above by saying that the economic form of rationality is very concerned with 'the soundness of the logical procedures' employed in choice but not so much in knowledge construction (Shackle 1972); while the behavioral form of rationality is experiential and concerned with the methods of search employed to make sense of empirical data, but not so much with the logical soundness of those research methods.

This chapter offers a somewhat unconventional account of the field, that should be able to liberate decision-making research from the long-lasting divide and the many misunderstandings between the economic rational actor and the behavioral paradigms, thanks to the following contributions with respect to the current state of the art.

Two accounts – a narrower and a wider account – are reconstructed for each of the two main approaches to decision-making. It is argued that, in the wider accounts, they are not rival paradigms (only one of which is then seen as acceptable) but can be more properly considered alternative decision strategies (each with claims of effectiveness and efficiency under specified circumstances). Then a third, 'missing' model of decision making is identified (through a review of studies on innovative and knowledge-intensive decision making) that, in the course of being heuristic (oriented to empirical discovery) is also logically sound, hence arguably rational.

Simon began his seminal paper on economic and behavioral models of choice by observing that the 'economic man' is someone 'who in the course of being economic, is also rational'. The term 'economic' comes from *oikos* (house) and *nomia* (regulation, governance) – the governance of household, the principle of 'good administration': do not waste scarce resources, allocate them to their best uses (Douma & Shreuder 1992).

Being economic then means being concerned with best means and best ends, while being rational means to relate means and ends according to logically sound procedures. However, in a full picture, those procedures should not include only cost–benefit calculations, but also procedures for discovering the relevant resources and possible uses (Shackle 1972). In philosophy this is clear, and led to the distinction between instrumental rationality (how efficient is a means to an end) and epistemic rationality (how correct is a statement about reality: in particular about the cause–effect relations between means and their intended effects or ends) (Foley 1987).

The account provided here of the main models of rationality used in economic and behavioral science will pay attention to how they address these two aspects of rationality, often not clearly distinguished in available accounts, and indeed in available models too, of decision making in the economic sciences. A contribution of this chapter will in fact be to show how the divide between 'economic-rational models' and 'behavioral-heuristic models' can be significantly reduced if epistemic (knowledge-related) factors and utilitaristic (interest-related) factors are more clearly distinguished and recombined.

The account given of those two basic approaches also tries not to fall into the common trap of restricting and caricaturizing the 'rival' model in favour of the preferred one. As a result, two versions or accounts – a narrower and a broader (arguably better) account – are identified within each of the two traditions. This type of account is conducive to seeing more clearly how the two views can be considered not as rival paradigms, but as contingently effective decision strategies. The analysis of the two main available kinds of model in their broadest interpretation, and the consideration of discovery and knowledge-related aspects, as distinct from utilitaristic and economic aspects, will reveal that an interesting and rather uncharted territory lies between the two dominant groups of models. Various studies on problem solving and decision making in highly innovative and discovery-intensive fields are reviewed, that are not easily accommodated under the two available templates but do cluster together well, and give substance to a third group of models.

Accordingly, the analysis is organized in three main sections, respectively dedicated to economic models of the rational actor (in the two versions of 'omniscient' and statistical rationality); experiential models of rationality (in the two versions of behavioral and intendedly rational heuristics); and emerging epistemic models.

ECONOMIC MODELS OF RATIONAL CHOICE BETWEEN OMNISCIENCE AND STATISTICS

Simon's analysis of economic decision making, before contributing to define a new behavioral model of rational choice, started out by outlining the common components of any model of rational decision making. They are:

- a (alternatives, actions, options, causes);
- s (states of the world, contingencies, conditions);
- e (effects, consequences, outcomes);
- i (information on a, s, e);
- $U(e)$ (utility or value of consequences);
- eventually, probabilities attached to any of the other elements: $p(e)$ probability of consequences; conditional on the probabilities of conditions $p(s)$; and on the probability that an action a can be taken $p(a)$;
- eventually, a cost of experimentation and research term C_i can be added, representing the costs of information gathering.

Different forms of rationality can be defined as different configurations of those components. In the case of economic rational choice, the core requisite is a matrix of pay-off $U(a,s)$. Effects typically do not appear as an independent term, meaning that the causal nexus between actions and consequences is not seen as problematic. It is automatically linked to a and s. Eventually the utility of consequences is multiplied by their probability to obtain an expected utility (Feldman & Kanter 1965).

If nothing is known about the probability of each cell, it means that all alternatives have equal probabilities, given the state of knowledge (Luce & Raiffa 1958). In that sense, it is always possible to assign a 'starting' probability to each cell, to be eventually updated as new information becomes available, through Bayesian formulae. That is why a situation of uncertainty in which probabilities are truly unknown (Knight 1921) is one in which the set of possible a and s is not finite, or not enumerable or definable, and is considered a limiting condition for the applicability of an expected utility maximizing approach.

Two views or interpretations of those limiting conditions can however be distinguished in available accounts of rational choice. In a first view, the requirement of knowing the set of a and s has been interpreted in a strong way: they are objectively known, prediction of their consequences is pointwise and utility is cardinal. This view seems to lie behind the idea that rational choice implies 'omniscience'. Many behavioral scientists as well as many economists seem to believe that the admission that knowledge is not objective but fallible, and that actors do not have perfect foresight, amounts to abandoning the rational actor paradigm for accepting a bounded rationality assumption. Simon often used the word 'omniscient' to characterize the 'economic model of man'. Some economists endorsed such an extreme view of the rational actor: the conditions for rational choice have often been stated as 'all possible alternatives are considered' or 'all possible states of the world are conceived', or 'all possible contingencies are foreseen' or even 'with rational agents contingencies are never unforeseen, they are at worst indescribable' (Tirole 1999: 756). In that version, though, the rational actor model is only an 'ideal type' and is 'inapplicable' and 'unrealistic'.

Such an account of rational choice not only makes the model empirically impossible, but defines its conditions through statements that may be criticized for being logically impossible (and thus, arguably not rational) (Grandori 2010). According to philosophy of science and knowledge, in fact, a rational actor is not one pretending to hold infallible and complete knowledge (a logically impossible statement), but actually knows that there can be no such thing as complete and infallible knowledge (Russell 1948; Popper 1935 [1959]; Nagel 1963). As Nagel effectively pointed out (in an effort to defend economic science from the charge of being unrealistic) (1963: 214): a 'trivial way in which any statement can be said to be unrealistic is that it can never give a complete description of all the infinite aspects of any real objects or situation'.[1]

However, there is a second view, in which expected utility maximizing has another face. In the founding formulation of the rational choice model, Savage (1954) asserted 'the necessity of confining attention to, or isolating, relatively simple situations in almost all applications of the theory of decision developed in this book'. Economic models in practice do conform to this template, as they are usually very selective and stylized, considering very few alternatives and very few possible states of the world to be able to make utility-maximizing calculations, not models that take into account all possible dimensions of action, alternative actions and contingencies. In other words, in this account, utility-maximizing decision behaviors rest on stylized and simplified problems, not on omniscience. There are requisites though, as to when the stylized problem is an 'acceptable' model of the world, that Savage also specified. Savage asked the question: when is a problem model 'satisfactory'? He did not respond: when all possible alternatives and states of the world have been included. He responded that a problem model is satisfactory (acceptable) if the utility judgments over the alternatives and consequences within the 'small world' of the problem model do not change if transferred in the 'grand world' of reality: that is, a small world is a (statistically) representative partition of the grand world if the utility ordering of alternatives' consequences in the partition is the same as it would be in the grand world $[U'(e') = U(e)]$. It should be noticed that Savage's requisite has nothing to do with maximizing per se; it has to do with knowledge: the representational validity of the world model. Choosing actions so as to maximize U' is a further procedure.

In sum, in this second wider (statistical) account, the economic model of rational choice is a set of procedures or decision rules that:

- are applicable to simplified 'small worlds', rather than requiring an impossible complete knowledge (Savage 1954; Nagel 1963);
- can be defined as procedurally rational, but not substantively rational (in no possible world is there ever a guarantee of being 'objectively right', and pretending that this is so is irrational) (Popper 1935 [1959]);
- involve judgments, which may be frequency based or also subjective (such as 'subjective probabilities' and 'subjective utilities') (Luce & Raiffa 1958);
- are compatible with ordinal utility and ordinal comparisons among alternatives (Savage 1954; Sen 2002) rather than only with cardinal utility and pointwise prediction;

- may include learning, in the form of Bayesian rules (Oaksford & Chater 1998), rather than assuming that all decision inputs are known and given.

This second wider and statistical account is preferable, as argued, to the first strictly deductive 'ominiscient' account, as it is logically more consistent with the canons of logic and it is empirically more consistent with the practice of economics.

Even in this second account, though, there are limiting conditions for an expected utility-maximizing strategy being applicable. As argued, for expected utility-maximizing procedures of search, learning and choice being applicable, the core condition is that problems are finite, closed and structured: A and S should be statistically or logically definable and enumerable.[2]

This may be seen as a reason why, as pointed out by Shackle (1972), the main limit of the classic rational choice model, even in its broader definition, is that the notion of rationality employed is 'thin': restricted to meaning logical, consistent, deductively correct. In fact, a 'thick' and broader model, including logically sound methods for constructing knowledge – the epistemic side of decision making highlighted by Shackle – rests on logical procedures that have to do with improving the validity and reliability of knowledge, not with maximizing value.

Problems that can be defined in a sufficiently structured way, so that an expected utility-maximizing strategy is applicable, are not so rare though. They include decisions on production quantities with given prices, investments in listed stocks, resource allocation to a firm's divisions, optimization of production layouts and inventory levels.

EXPERIENTIAL MODELS BETWEEN BEHAVIORAL AND INTENDEDLY RATIONAL HEURISTICS

In Simon's writings, we can find two different arguments on why we need models of decision making based on bounded rationality (BR). In one view, bounded or limited rationality is a rival behavioral assumption with respect to complete knowledge or omniscience. In this view, rational choice is deemed unrealistic and practically and logically impossible. A second view is a 'contingent rationality' view: 'in many situations we may be interested in the precise question of whether one decision-making procedure is more rational than another' (Simon 1955: 112). There is a (meta) decision issue, then, on decision strategies: where problems are unstructured, decision making based on complete mapping (or a problem model that is a sufficient statistic for the real world) is inapplicable and a heuristic alternative becomes attractive (Beach & Mitchell 1978; Grandori 1984).

In closed, structured problems, the properties of different between decision strategies are not fundamental: a rule of choice based on a acceptability thresholds is quite compatible with utility theory (it is a particular case of choice with a utility function defined as a set of constraints). For example, in negotiations, 'reservation prices' or BATNAs (best alternatives to a negotiated agreement) play an analogous role to the more subjective and psychological notion of 'aspiration levels' (as Simon himself noticed, 1951: 104–105). Secondly, it has been shown that the actions deriving from *ex post* decision strategies based on experience, and optimal actions that might derive from *ex ante* decision strategies based on foresight, are likely to converge if the problem space is sufficiently regular and closed (Baumol & Quandt 1964; Aarts and Lenstra 1997). The difference becomes relevant in open, unstructured problems, with many, irregularly distributed peaks of possible results.

Two views or accounts of Simon's behavioral model of rational choice can be identified, though, as in the case of the economic rational actor model. And also in this case, the one which became more popular does not seem to be the best.

In the most common view, especially in the organization field, the model has been operationalized as the following set of procedures:

- Problem definition. Problems are defined as performance gaps vis-à-vis aspiration levels (AL).
- 'Pattern recognition'. Patterns or regularities are recognized in empirical data (such as the positions of pieces on a chess board) on the basis of their correspondence with a repertory of models stored in memory. Those judgments 'evoke relevant sets of alternatives' or moves (March & Simon 1958).
- 'Sequential search' for 'satisfactory' alternatives. Judgments of 'satisfaction' imply that the expected effects of alternatives can be evaluated, at least in ordinal terms, as equal or superior to aspiration levels (Simon 1955). Other acceptability rules were developed later which imply an even more limited amount of foresight, as they rest on the assumption that some aspects or attributes of the alternatives are reliable predictors of acceptable results – such as to eliminate alternatives not possessing those features (the 'elimination by aspect' heuristic) (Tversky 1972), or to accept only alternatives that differ marginally from formerly adopted ones ('bland alternatives') (March & Simon 1958).
- The search stopping rule is given by truncating the search as a 'satisfactory alternative' is found (Simon 1955).
- The search is made adaptive and 'intendedly rational' by aspiration level learning rules: AL are lowered/raised, or the subset of considered alternatives A' (within the set A of possible alternatives) is broadened/narrowed, as a function of the 'difficulty/easiness in finding' acceptable solutions (Simon 1955).

With respect to those decision procedures, subsequent developments have emphasized and added behavioral rules, and de-emphasized the 'intendedly rational' rules (or have mixed all of them together). For example:

- The principle of reinforcement. Decisions have been modeled as deriving from implementing actions drawn from a repertory based on the direct or vicarious experience of success/failure rates (Cyert & March 1963; Steinbrunner 1974).
- Local search. The principle of economizing on bounded rationality and of reducing risk in situations where effects are difficult to evaluate has been seen as the rationale behind the heuristics of searching for alternatives in the neighbourhoods of the currently implemented courses of action (Cyert & March 1963). This heuristic has become central in evolutionary economics and in the notion of routines (Stuart & Podonly 1996) as well as in the 'incrementalist' model of public decision making (Lindblom 1959; Davis et al. 1974).

● The 'logic of appropriateness'. If effects of actions are difficult to predict and even to evaluate *ex post*, actors are expected to shift to acceptability judgments based on conformity of actions to templates: what is appropriate for an actor of type X to do, in conditions Y (March 1994).

An important criticism raised about this group of BR models, by economists and scholars interested in performance, has been that all these decision strategies may be justified as effective and efficient, even as superior to complete mapping and choice of the best alternative, where there is an underlying ordinal judgment that the expected difference in benefits is low compared to the cost of search (Arrow 2004; Baumol 2004) – even if those costs and benefits cannot be evaluated pointwise. In other words, this observation reinterprets 'satisficing' and other models of boundedly rational behavior as hidden, possibly unconscious but eventually superior forms of maximizing behavior. The same could be said even about incremental models or random-choice and blind trial-and-error models (Cohen et al. 1976): if uncertainty is sufficiently high to make alternatives indistinguishable, then tossing a coin, or moving incrementally and observing the consequences before taking further action, is what rational choice procedures would also recommend (Cyert et al. 1978). Paradoxically, it is this most common behavioral version of heuristic decision making that, being so centered on saving cognitive effort, is more prone to be interpreted as a utility-maximizing model with the costs of search factored in.

In fact, in this version, bounded rationality has often been interpreted in economics as 'costly rationality' (Radner 2000), and used in its 'thin' version or even in a rhetorical function of acknowledgment of the existence of those costs in organizational economics (Foss 2003). In behavioral economics, bounded rationality has been still understood and operationalized as a set of behavioural heuristics, but it has been used and integrated into (rather than reduced to) classic economic rationality.

The notion of heuristics has been widely developed and used in behavioral decision theory (Kahneman et al. 1982) – an approach that, in turn, has been quite influential in the development of behavioural economics. The metholodogical stance in this tradition has been different and less antagonist toward economic rationality with respect to Simon's and the Carnegie School's stance. In the Tversky and Kahneman tradition, not only is there an interest in the assessment and effectiveness of decision procedures, but heuristics have typically been assessed in terms of deviance from the standards of statistical decision theory. Hence, the verdict has been predominantly negative: with respect to that template, commonly used heuristics are more sources of biases than effective or efficient methods of discovery (Kahneman et al. 1982). Even when the verdict is more positive, oriented to justify them in a more Simonian 'intended rationality' attitude (Gigerenzer et al. 1999), the very notion of heuristics in behavioral decision theory has come to indicate a form of minor, weak and 'fast and frugal' thought, a synonym for a shortcut or rule of thumb, although for possibly good reasons such as efficiency and the reduction of cognitive effort, rather than a form of logically sound reasoning. The repertoire of heuristics thus identified in behavioral decision theory has typically included those methods that methodology typically teaches not to use, that can and should be 'corrected': judging frequencies by 'availability', assigning probabilities taking into account representativeness, making estimates by 'anchoring', being overconfident in one's own hypotheses.

Another way to take into account the existence and importance of bounded rationality, while at the same time accommodating it within the frame of an enlarged view of economic rationality, widespread in behavioral economics, has been to enlarge the 'value-maximizing' approach by including behavioral parameters in utility functions, reflecting the many non-monetary, subjective and psychological factors which people usually give weight to (e.g. regret, identity, belongingness) (Bell et al. 1988; Akerlof & Kranton 2005); or risk attitudes different from risk neutrality and negative preferences assigned to uncertainty (Tversky & Kahneman 1981).

However, another version or interpretation of bounded rationality and a different notion of heuristics can be reconstructed. In this other version, the limits of rationality are limits of knowledge, and the type of reasoning involved cannot be accommodated in a subjective and more comprehensive value-maximizing approach. We have to draw on Simon's methodological writings (e.g Simon 1977; Simon et al. 1981), to find clearer concerns with problems of knowledge rather then information cost. For example, in his essay 'Does scientific discovery have a logic?' (1977), drawing on philosophers of science such as Pierce and Hanson, Simon puts center stage the heuristics of 'abduction'. Here, the notion of heuristics come closer to the meaning of the term in epistemology: methods of discovery that can and should be evaluated in terms of comparative efficiency, effectiveness and logical soundness. The studies by Simon and associates on human problem solving (Newell & Simon 1976) and scientific problem solving (Simon et al. 1981) have been used and revitalized in recent research on intendedly rational heuristics in complex, unbounded problems which have included pattern recognition-based 'abduction', 'cognitive representations' and analogic reasoning in the problem-solving processes of both scientists (Magnani et al. 1999) and strategy makers (Gavetti & Levinthal 2000; Gavetti et al. 2005; Gavetti & Warglien 2007).

In this version, decision behaviour is still economizing on costs of search and cognitive effort – it is intendedly instrumentally rational; but it is also, to some extent, intendedly epistemically rational, aimed at improving problem modeling. This latter component of BR does not involve judgments that can be related or reduced or translated into value maximizing, or even value satisficing, as they are judgments on how 'satisfactory' the model of the world, rather than the pay-off, is. As much as in the wider version of statistical decision theory *à la* Savage, decision making has a knowledge construction component, not only a cost and benefit component.

Once the need for knowledge construction heuristics is acknowledged, and the initial pattern recognition-based array provided by the experiential tradition is recalled, the door is open for exploring this terrain further. In fact, a much wider and much 'better' (more intendedly rational) repertoire of heuristics may be reconstructed, making use of the body of research available on decision making in innovative fields, where this issue is of paramount importance, as well as the body of work available in the methodology of research concerned with that issue.

However, even in its wider, more knowledge construction-oriented version – in which a 'positive'/effective rather than a 'negative'/biasing notion of heuristics is employed – experiential rationality may be qualified as intendedly rational in problems that are to some extent complex, but in which experience is available and sufficient for defining the needed acceptability parameters, in a resource-saving way. In fact, even in his methodological work, Simon qualifies his aim as one of detecting, through comparative assessment, 'efficient heuristics' for discovery. This logic is suited to solving moderately unstructured problems, such as finding a person fit for a role, or finding a law interpreting the observed movements of stock or raw material prices. What experiential rationality cannot do, even in this more extended version, is to proceed effectively rather than just efficiently, where experience is not a logically sound basis for knowledge and action or is not available (Bandura 1986; Felin & Zenger 2009). It cannot describe well, let alone guide effectively, discovery processes in which the main point is not to be efficient, or even 'fast and frugal', but to be insightful and possibly correct: processes like entrepreneurial discovery, the design of new products and services, the improvement of technologies, the formulation of strategies and business policies.

EMERGING EPISTEMIC MODELS: DECISION-MAKING IN INNOVATION PROCESSES

A fair amount of research is available on decision processes in areas such as entrepreneurship, technological innovation and strategy. The contribution of this section is to point out their commonalities and to use them for defining a 'third way', that may be called an 'epistemic' model of economic decision making. Studies on decision processes in the more innovative and knowledge intensive parts of the economy do in fact show a rich array of decision procedures and heuristics that differ interestingly from those contemplated in the two classic economic and experiential models, such as the following.[3]

Modeling

Which are the relevant variables and relations among them? Constructing a valid model of the problem at hand is a basic ingredient of logically sound reasoning where discovery is sought. In its strongest form, it involves theoretical abduction and the formulation of causal hypotheses on which kind of actions and states of the world may cause which effects (Bandura 1986; Magnani 2000; Felin & Zenger 2009). Those hypotheses may be generated by starting from effects (effects/benefits in search for causes/alternatives; ends in search for means; uses in search of resources) but also starting from antecedents or causes (alternatives/causes in search of beneficial effects; means in search of ends; resources in search of uses) (Saravasthy 2001; Henderson et al. 1999). Actually this second path is particularly attractive and effective in innovative problem solving and the discovery of new products and services, as a specific problem to be solved is not given.

Studies on decision making in new and innovative fields have repeatedly reported that problem models improve their representational capacity over time. For example, that was the case for the design and investment in information systems at the beginning of the information technology (IT) age: problems were initially modeled as technical investment issues, while the test of the consequences on organizational behaviors and on the complementary resources needed led to a redefinition and stabilization of problem modeling as a multivariate model including social, organizational and technical aspects (Grandori 1984). Gavetti & Rivkin (2007) provide an in-depth case study on the evolution of strategy-making logics of a new internet-based firm in a field that has these newness features. In that case too, problem models and decision strategies got upgraded over time. The authors report that managers declared that at the outset they 'didn't have a model to follow, as there was no such thing as advertising on the Internet at that time'. Hence, they did not focus on business planning, but on 'resources in search uses' – a 'piece of technology' that was licensed to companies for their use. The model or cognitive representation of themselves was to be a technology company. Later, following experimentation in marketing and advertising, that model was enriched and extended to a model of themselves as a 'techno-media' company. Decision strategies shifted from more exploratory effectuation to a more structured solving of diagnosed problems.

Recent studies on search in different conditions of uncertainty provide and clarify criteria for understanding when a problem model becomes 'acceptable'. Browne and Pitts (2004) review experiments on search stopping rules in design problems, in which problems are not given but have to be modeled. They single out from available descriptive research two types of stopping rules that have potential applications to these unstructured design-intensive and research-intensive problems: (1) stop when a predetermined threshold in the amount of evidence gathered is reached, or when a predefined list of items to be inquired about has been covered; or (2) stop when the marginal contribution of new information becomes small or negligible, or when the cognitive representation of the problem is stabilized and is no longer changed by further inquiry. In more uncertain, novel problems (with respect to available competences) strategies of the second type, based on the marginal representational stability of the model, prevailed.

Systematic Observation

Which is the relevant information to be gathered? In open problems, models and hypotheses can guide information gathering in an intendedly rational way. Model-guided sampling and data gathering is a logically sound heuristics – we all apply it in science, and nothing should prevent economic actors from doing the same (Kelly 1963). In fact, the type of search strategies that are followed in successful innovative entrepreneurial decision-making have been characterized as 'disciplined' and 'systematic' (Fiet 2002; Fiet & Patel 2008; Drucker 1985; Zander 2007), as research rather than search. For example, Zander (2007) reports historical evidence on 'how the inventive genius of Thomas A. Edison coincided with meticulous market analysis in the process of substituting incandescent light for gas illumination in New York City'. The documents report that Edison collected every kind of data about gas, then obtained information on the number of gas jets burning at each hour through a house-to-house survey, and collected some 24 books containing gas-light bills of consumers in the district, so as to be able to evaluate the economic feasibility of the substitution and to set a price.

In very new fields, there may be little accumulated knowledge for starting out with hypotheses on potentially successful actions. Again the analogy with research methods, in this case of the exploratory and 'grounded' kind, may be useful. It has in fact been often indicated that the discovery of opportunities for economic action can be best nurtured by scanning, alertness, curiosity and systematic field observation in search of clues, details, and peripheral or background structural phenomena that may lead to some innovative hypotheses (Kirzner 1979; Ginzburg 1979; Glaser & Strauss 1967). Interestingly, even in this data-driven rather than theory-driven research, the effective heuristics are almost the opposite of the local search and availability heuristics of the behavioral tradition: the observed and recommended behavior is to pay attention to the unusual, the faraway, the structural background and the apparently irrelevant in order to discover non-obvious opportunities.

Opportunistic Multipurposed Hypothesis Testing

Testing hypotheses involves a variety of methodological decisions on which part of the system of knowledge involved should be rejected and modified: the core hypothesis under test, conditions *ceteris paribus*, auxiliary theories implied in observation, and background knowledge (Lakatos 1970). Hypothesis testing is relevant in any knowledge construction process, and in economic decision making the 'opportunistic decision' on how to modify hypotheses is all the more relevant. In fact, in addition to interest in the 'truth', an interest in the pay-off is typically present, where the deciding economic and organizational organism can be conceived as a scientist, or scientific community, 'with self-interest' (Weick 1979). If the core hypothesis to be tested is the attainable pay-off, the possibility of changing the set of considered objectives, or the observation tools, or the domains of observation, or even the problem to be solved, without lowering the level of expected pay-off is therefore a precious heuristic (Grandori 1984).

Holding multiple objectives, coupled with the willingness to modify them, enhances the likelihood of finding solutions without reducing expectations. This way of proceeding has been described by Campbell (1960) as an 'opportunistic multipurposedness' of problem solvers, in particular of scientists, who in the course of trying to solve one problem end up in solving a different one. In economic action, this is all the more relevant, as the overall objective of actors may be to increase welfare, rather than to achieve particular targets and solve particular problems defined in substantive terms. In unstructured decision processes, in which multiple objectives and criteria are potentially relevant, a 'conjunctive' decision rule in which all constraints should be simultaneously satisfied is not very efficient and is error prone (Ballou & Pazer 1990). An alternative 'disjunctive choice rule' – achieve benefits on at least a subset of the matters and criteria, no matter which – is likely to be superior (Grandori 1984).

The value of treating objectives as hypotheses to be tested with logically sound methods has been particularly highlighted and developed in the field of public policy evaluation research (Chen & Rossi 1981). This field is explicitly devoted to developing applications of scientific research methods to discover the actual consequences, intended and unintended, of public policies, in order to evaluate results in the light of a revised set of objectives. Nothing, apparently, should prevent the application of a similar approach to business policies.

In fact, in the strategy field, descriptions of behaviors of this type are available, and even some conceptualizations of strategy making as a conscious 'hypothesis-driven approach similar to the scientific method' (Liedtka 2000). In particular, Liedtka also emphasizes the higher degrees of freedom available in conjecture development in decision-making 'concerned not with how things are but with how they might be – in short with design' (Simon 1969). Strategy making, as organization design, product design and much if not most innovative economic problem solving, belongs to this domain (Boland & Collopy 2004). We do not need (it would not be a heuristic passing an Occam's Razor test) to pose a further and different logic of discovery for situations in which the solutions sought are new and involve imagination and invention. In fact, authors such as Simon (1969), Hatchuel (2001), Lakatos (1976) and Shackle (1979) all worked at a theory of human problem solving applicable to design problems as well, although the nature of design problems and tasks may be characterized by some specific features: for example, they leave more room for opportunistic change of hypotheses and less room for experiential learning, and often require a shift from empirical to mental experiments. Liedtka summarizes the features of design processes in strategy, as well as in architecture from which she draws many examples, as 'abductive, hypothesis-driven, opportunistic and dialectical'; as any thought process that is both creative and logically sound, one would say.

The 'Logic of Robustness'

Rather than trying to foresee contingencies and looking for 'best' actions given the contingencies, devising actions that are robust no matter what the contingencies can be justified as a logically sound heuristic under high uncertainty (Grandori 2010). In fact, this logic of decision can be detected as a 'best pattern of thinking' in many decisions under strong uncertainty and risk (especially downside risk, possible damages), and natural hazards. For example, it is very difficult to predict in a pointwise fashion the timing, location and intensity of floods or earthquakes. The logically sound move is not to lower acceptability thresholds, or to take action based on very approximate data. The logically sound move is to prevent rather than predict, building actions and structures (e.g. dams, anti-seismic constructions) that would resist no matter what the contingencies. The analogous logic in the economic and social world would be to devise robust actions that would generate positive results irrespective of most conceivable environmental and behavioral contingencies. The strength of robust alternatives, in the social and economic world, is especially built on multifunctionality: they are artifacts and behaviors that have utility from many points of view under many states of the world. For example, in a famous analysis of 'robust action' by the Medici in Renaissance Florence (Padgett & Ansell 1993), the robustness of marriage ties was traced to the multifunctionality of the tie as seen by different actors and from different perspectives: patrimonial, legal, kinship and friendship ties.

A logic of robustness in crafting multifunctional artifacts is widespread in innovation processes. For example, in the design of the Millennium Park in Chicago, the highly creative, modern art outcome has been generated by a design process in which the position and role of artifacts in the garden, has been shifted to perform functions different from those initially hypothesized, and compatible with changing coalitions and aesthetic visions of the key players (Furnari 2009). It can be found in situations in which creative solutions to unexpected and new circumstances have to be found while simultaneously maintaining high reliability and minimizing risks and mistakes – as in unexpected conditions and emergencies in aeronautics or health care.[4]

Real Option Reasoning

This logic can figure among the heuristics for innovation, if intended as a strategy of committing resources to actions and projects, giving the possibility of deciding whether to invest further upon observation of the results of these experiments (Bowman & Hurry 1993; McGrath 1999; Kogut & Kutilaka 2001). The analogy with, and origination from, the notion of financial options does not imply that the 'wait and see', contingent value-maximizing logic of financial options should also necessarily be the logic if options are of a 'real' type (as has been maintained by some authors; e.g. Adner & Levinthal 2004). To the contrary, that difference may clarify what the difference is between financial and real options and what the logic is behind the latter. Real option reasoning is a (logically sound) heuristic for discovery, to the extent that it involves causal analysis, epistemic reasoning and manipulation of experimental conditions, rather than mere postponing an investment choice until the relevant state of the world has been observed. Conjecture making is implied in the selection of which projects to bet on in the first place, as well as in designing and managing them so as to generate desirable, expected consequences. For example, this logic is widely applied in early-stage investments in new ventures, through the practice of financing them in subsequent rounds: a 'make and see' rather than a 'wait and see' approach.

Pareto Improvements and Nash Improvements

Important middle-ground choice rules – between optimizing and satisficing – are available and have been described as characterizing intendedly rational decision making with partial knowledge of the world. In many situations, the frontier of maximum pay-offs cannot be known, either because the problem is unlimited, or because it depends on strategic interaction with other players who have no incentive to reveal their 'best alternatives' and acceptability thresholds. Exploration of the area above these thresholds is feasible, though, and may be guided by criteria of improvement rather than maximization (Grandori 2010). Negotiation is a type of intendedly rational decision making in which these decision criteria have been best explored (Raiffa 1982; Bazerman & Lewicki 1983). Offers are experiments, tested through counter-offers of different combinations and amounts of resources exchanged on each of them. Dominated packages and solutions are discarded and the Pareto superior ones are accepted. Nash improvements – packages and solutions for which the product of utilities on two orthogonal axes representing decision criteria or players is higher – provide a criterion for selecting more fair and balanced solutions (Grandori 1991).

It is also possible to detect, in the wide repertoire of negotiation rules, ways of deciding, in an intendedly rational way, when to stop the exploration process. Typically, exploration entails decreasing marginal returns, as more and more combinations are tried. Hence, the signal that further investment in exploration is not worthy is the drop in marginal improvements, becoming negligible or inferior to the cost of investment. In fact, negotiators are typically advised to signal that their reservation prices are approximating by decreasing the magnitude of concessions.

Those criteria are applicable also to a single decision maker, holding a variety of objectives or parameters that are not comparable or that they do not wish to reduce to a comparable format in order not to lose qualitative information. For example, decisions on industrial strategies involving trade-offs between, say, occupational levels or product quality and production costs; or choices among possible partners or collaborators entailing qualitatively different strengths and weaknesses; or choices among different product designs affecting markets shares, production costs and technological positioning in different ways.

CONCLUDING REMARKS

Taken together, all these 'best practices of thinking' that we may find in innovative decision processes seem to provide an array of logically sound heuristics for knowledge-generating, innovative decision making. This 'third' approach can be seen as complementing and bridging the economic rational choice models and the experiential and behavioral models, at present most often considered as distant and rival paradigms. The review and reconstruction of the basic forms of rationality relevant in economic organization conducted here suggests considering these three approaches as complementary. To think that all these forms of rationality are possible and effective under certain circumstances is quite important for understanding the links between them and the forms of economic organization they may support. In fact, an important (and much neglected) legacy that may be found (rarely) both in the BR tradition (Simon 1955) and in economic thought (Sah & Stiglitz 1985) is that a basic *raison d'être* of different types of economics organization – hierarchies, poliarchies and collectives – is that they deal with the fallibility of human knowledge in different ways and support different kinds of decision processes. Even in those contributions, the possibility that economic actors deal with the fallibility of human knowledge in a way similar to that of scientists is rather neglected. Connecting epistemic decision strategies with organizational architectures capable of sustaining them, and understanding their comparative effectiveness with respect to other structural alternatives in terms of valid knowledge construction under different circumstances, then stands out as a fruitful task for future research. As an example of this kind of implications, let me point out here at least that an epistemic approach to problem solving by problem shifting and hypothesis testing may be seen as the cognitive root of the emergence, in modern knowledge-intensive settings, of organizational architectures that are simultaneously decentralized and nearly undecomposable (Jones et al. 1997; Grandori 2009, 2013; Argyres and Zenger, Chapter 12 in this volume); that is, of a full range of decentralized and connected structural alternatives to both centralized and partially connected hierarchies and decentralized and disconnected poliarchies.

NOTES

1. Nagel was criticizing the type of defense that Friedman gave of the legitimacy of 'unrealistic assumptions' in economics, attacked by Simon. What is especially interesting for my argument is that Nagel concluded that 'unrealism' can be defended precisely because there can be no complete description of reality and no 'perfect foresight' of the world, and simplification is involved in any modelling.
2. Including logically finite but 'practically' infinite problems such as the game of chess.
3. The literature review here, and the grouping of studies to support and define an array of rational heuristics for discovery and innovation, builds on recent work published in Grandori (2010).
4. These situations have been characterized as 'distributed cognition' systems, in which human thought practices need to be reliable not only in themselves, but also in interaction with artifacts and tools incorporating their own heuristics (Hutchins 1995). For the system to be highly reliable, human cognition should be able to apply higher-order heuristics than machines and computers, rather than functioning

in a similar way – as many 'automatic pilot' disasters testify. Hutchins stressed the difference between human cognitive functions and the representational and computational functions also performed by computers, pointing out that because early cognitive scientists succeeded in infusing some information-processing procedures, discovered by studying humans, into computer programs: they came to believe that 'computers are made in the image of the human'. He counterargues that 'the computer was not made in the image of the person. It was made in the image of formal manipulation of abstract symbols. And the last 30 years of cognitive science can be seen as attempts to remake the person in the image of the computer' (p. 363).

REFERENCES

Aarts, E. and J.K. Lenstra (eds) (1997), *Local Search in Combinatorial Optimization*, New York: Wiley.

Adner, R. and D.A. Levinthal 2004 'What is *not* a real option: considering boundaries for the application of real options to business strategy', *Academy of Management Review*, **29**(1), 74–85.

Akerlof, G.A. and R.E. Kranton (2005), 'Identity and the economics of organizations', *Journal of Economic Perspectives*, **19**(1), 9–32.

Arrow, K.J. (2004), 'Is bounded rationality unboundedly rational? Some ruminations', in M. Augier and J.G. March (eds), *Models of a Man. Essays in Memory of Herbert A. Simon*, Cambridge, MA: MIT Press, pp. 47–56.

Ballou, D.P. and H.L. Pazer (1990), 'A framework for the analysis of error in conjunctive, multi-criteria, satisficing decision processes', *Decision Sciences*, **21**, 752–770.

Bandura, A. (1986), *Social Foundations of Thought and Action*, Englewood Cliffs, NJ: Prentice-Hall.

Baumol, W.J. (2004), 'On rational satisficing', in M. Augier and J.G. March (eds), *Models of a Man. Essays in Memory of Herbert A. Simon*, Cambridge, MA: MIT Press, pp. 57–66.

Baumol, W.J. and R.E. Quandt (1964), 'Rules of thumb and optimally imperfect decisions', *American Economic Review*, **54**, 23–46.

Bazerman, M.H. and R.J. Lewicki (eds) (1983), *Negotiating in Organizations*, Beverly Hills, CA: Sage.

Beach, L.R. and T.R. Mitchell (1978), 'A contingency model for the selection of decision strategies', *Academy of Management Review*, **3**, 439–449.

Bell, D.E., H. Raiffa and A. Tversky (1988), *Decision Making. Descriptive, Normative and Prescriptive Interactions*, Cambridge: Cambridge University Press.

Boland, R.J. and F. Collopy (2004), *Managing as Designing*, Stanford, CA: Stanford University Press.

Bowman, E.H. and D. Hurry (1993), 'Strategy through the option lens: an integrated view of resource investments and the incremental-choice process', *Academy of Management Review*, **18**(4), 760–782.

Browne, G.J. and M.G. Pitts (2004), 'Stopping rule use during information search in design problems', *Organizational Behavior and Human Decision Processes*, **95**, 208–224.

Campbell, D.T. (1960), 'Blind variation and selective retention in creative thought as in other knowledge processes', *Psychological Review*, **67**, 380–400.

Chen, H.T. and P.H. Rossi (1981), 'A multi-goal theory-driven approach to evaluation', *Evaluation Research*, **6**, 38–54.

Cohen, M.D., J.J. March and J.P. Olsen (eds) (1976), *Ambiguity and Choice in Organizations*, Bergen: Universitaetforlaget.

Cyert R.M. and J.J. March (1963), *A Behavioral Theory of the Firm*, New York: Prentice-Hall.

Cyert, R.M., M.H. DeGroot and C.A. Holt (1978), 'Sequential investment decisions with Bayesian learning', *Management Science*, **24**, 712–718.

Davis, O.A., M.A.H. Dempster and A. Wildavsky (1974), 'Toward a predictive theory of government expenditures: US domestic appropriations', *British Journal of Economics*, **9**, 587–608.

Douma, S. and H. Schreuder (1992), *Economic Approaches to Organizations*, Englewood Cliffs, NJ: Prentice Hall.

Drucker, P.F. (1985), 'The discipline of innovation', *Harvard Business Review*, **63**(3), 67–72.

Feldman, J. and H.E. Kanter (1965), 'Organizational decision making', in G. March (ed.), *Handbook of Organization*, Chicago, IL: Rand McNally.

Felin, T. and T. Zenger (2009), 'Entrepreneurs as theorists: on the origins of collective beliefs and novel strategies', *Strategic Entrepreneurship Journal*, **3**(2), 127–146.

Fiet, J.O. (2002), *The Systematic Search for Entrepreneurial Discoveries*, Westport, CT: Quorum Books.

Fiet, J.O. and P.C. Patel (2008), 'Entrepreneurial discovery as constrained, sytematic search', *Small Business Economics*, **30**(3), 215–229.

Foley, R. (1987), *The Theory of Epistemic Rationality*, Cambridge, MA: Harvard University Press.

Foss, N.J. (2003), 'Bounded rationality in the economics of organization: "much cited and little used"', *Journal of Economic Psychology*, **24**(2), 245–264.

Furnari, S. (2009), 'Mechanisms of aesthetic exaptation in architecture: how a beaux-arts garden evolved into an avant-garde art park'. Best Dissertation Award Paper, XXV EGOS Colloquium, 2–4 July, Barcelona.

Gavetti, G. and D. Levinthal (2000), 'Looking forward and looking backward: cognitive and experiential search', *Administrative Science Quarterly*, **45**, 113–137.

Gavetti, G. and J.W. Rivkin (2007), 'On the origin of strategy: action and cognition over time', *Organization Science*, **18**, 420–439.

Gavetti, G. and M. Warglien (2007), 'Recognizing the new: a multi-agent model of analogy in strategic decision-making', Strategy Unit Working Paper No. 08-028, available at http://ssrn.com/abstract=1022651.

Gavetti, G., D.A. Levinthal and J.W. Rivkin (2005), 'Strategy making in novel and complex worlds: the power of analogy', *Strategic Management Journal*, **26**, 691–712.

Gigerenzer, G., P.M. Todd and the ABC Research Group (1999), *Simple Heuristics that Make Us Smart*, Oxford: Oxford University Press.

Ginzburg, C. (1979), 'Spie. Radici di un paradigma indiziario', in A. Gargani (ed.), *Crisi della ragione*. Torino: Einaudi, pp. 57–106.

Glaser, B.G. and A. Strauss (1967), *The Discovery of Grounded Theory*, New York: Aldine Publishing Co.

Grandori, A. (1984), 'A prescriptive contingency view of organizational decision making', *Administrative Science Quarterly*, **29**, 192–208.

Grandori, A. (1991), 'Negotiating efficient organization forms', *Journal of Economic Behavior and Organization*, **16**, 319–340.

Grandori, A. (2009), 'Poliarchic governance and the growth of knowledge', in N. Foss and S. Michailova (eds), *Knowledge Governance*, Oxford: Oxford University Press.

Grandori, A. (2010), 'A rational heuristic model of economic decision making', *Rationality and Society*, **22**(4), 477–504.

Grandori, A. (2013), *Epistemic Economics and Organization. Forms of Rationality and Governance for a Wiser Economy*, London: Routledge.

Hatchuel, A. (2001), 'Towards design theory and expandable rationality: the unfinished program of Herbert Simon', *Journal of Management and Governance*, **5**(3–4), 260–273.

Henderson R., L. Orsenigo and G.P. Pisano (1999), 'The pharmaceutical industry and the revolution in molecular biology: interaction among scientific, institutional, and organizational change', in D.C. Mowery and R.R. Nelson (eds), *Sources of Industrial Leadership*, Cambridge: Cambridge University Press, pp. 267–310.

Hutchins, E. (1995), *Cognition in the Wild*, Cambridge, MIT: MIT Press.

Jones C., W.S. Hesterly and S.P. Borgatti (1997), 'A general theory of network governance: exchange conditions and social mechanisms', *Academy of Management Review*, **22**(4), 911–945.

Kahneman, D., P. Slovic and A. Tversky (eds) (1982), *Judgment under Uncertainty: Heuristics and Biases*, Cambridge: Cambridge University Press.

Kelly, G.A. (1963), *A Theory of Personality*, New York: Norton.

Kirzner, I.M. (1979), *Perception, Opportunity, and Profit: Studies in the Theory of Entrepreneurship*, Chicago, IL: University of Chicago Press.

Knight, F.H. (1921), *Risk, Uncertainty and Profit*, Boston, MA: Houghton Mifflin.

Kogut, B. and N. Kutilaka (2001), 'Capabilities as real options', *Organization Science*, **12**(6), 744–758.

Lakatos, I. (1970), 'Falsification and the methodology of scientific research programmes', in I. Lakatos and A. Musgrave (eds), *Criticism and the Growth of Knowledge*, Cambridge: Cambridge University Press.

Lakatos, I. (1976), *Proofs and Refutations. The Logic of Mathematical Discovery*, J. Worral and G. Currie (eds), Cambridge: Cambridge University Press.

Liedtka, J. (2000), 'In defense of strategy as design', *California Management Review*, **42**(3), 8–30.

Lindblom, C.E. (1959), 'The science of "muddling through"', *Public Administration Review*, **19**, 78–88.

Luce, R.D. and H. Raiffa (1958), *Games and Decisions*, New York: Wiley.

McGrath, R.G. (1999), 'Falling forward: real option reasoning and entrepreneurial failure', *Academy of Management Review*, **24**(1), 13–30.

Magnani, L. (2000), 'Theoretical abduction', in L. Magnani, *Abduction, Reason and Science. Processes of Discovery and Explanation*, Dordrecht: Kluwer Academic Publishers, pp. 15–52.

Magnani, L., N.J. Nersessian and P. Thagard (eds) (1999), *Model-Based Reasoning in Scientific Discovery*, Dordrecht: Kluwer Academic Publishers.

March, J.G. (1994), *A Primer on Decision Making*, New York: Free Press.

March, J.G. and H.A. Simon (1958), *Organizations*, New York: Wiley.

Nagel E. (1963), 'Assumptions in economic theory', *American Economic Review, Papers and Proceedings*, **53**, 211–219.

Newell, A. and H.A. Simon (1976), *Human Problem Solving*, Englewood Cliffs, NJ: Prentice Hall.

Oaksford, M. and N. Chater (eds) (1998), *Rational Models of Cognition*, Oxford: Oxford University Press.

Padgett, J. and C. Ansell (1993), 'Robust action and the rise of the Medici', *American Journal of Sociology*, **98**, 1259–1330.

Popper, K.R. (1935 [1959]), *Logik der Forschung* (The logic of scientific discovery), London: Hutchinson.

Radner, R. (2000), 'Costly and bounded rationality in individual and team decision making', *Industrial and Corporate Change*, **9**(4), 623–658.

Raiffa, H. (1982), *The Art and Science of Negotiation*, Cambridge: Cambridge University Press.

Russell, B. (1948), *Human Knowledge: Its Scope and Limits*, New York: Simon & Schuster.

Sah, R.K. and J.E. Stiglitz (1985), 'Human fallibility and economic organization', *American Economic Review*, **75**(2) Papers and Proceedings of the Ninety-Seventh Annual Meeting of the American Economic Association, pp. 292–297.

Saravasthy, S. (2001), 'Causation and effectuation: towards a theoretical shift from economic inevitability to entrepreneurial contingency', *Academy of Management Review*, **26**(2), 243–263.

Savage, L.J. (1954), *The Foundations of Statistics*, New York: Wiley.

Shackle, G.L. (1972), *Epistemics and Economics*, Cambridge: Cambridge University Press.

Shackle, G.L. (1979), *Imagination and the Nature of Choice*, Edinburgh: Edinburgh University Press.

Sen, A. (2002), *Rationality and Freedom*, Cambridge, MA: Harvard University.

Simon, H.A. (1947), *Administrative Behavior*, New York: Macmillan.

Simon, H.A. (1951), 'A formal theory of the employment relationship', *Econometrica*, **19**, 293–305.

Simon, H.A. (1955), 'A behavioral model of rational choice', *Quarterly Journal of Economics*, **69**, 99–118.

Simon, H.A. (1969), *The Sciences of the Artificial*, Cambridge, MA: MIT Press.

Simon, H.A. (1977), 'Does scientific discovery have a logic?' *Models of Discovery and Other Topics in the Method of Science*, Dordrecht, Netherlands and Boston, MA, USA: Reidel.

Simon, H.A., P.W. Langley and G.L. Bradshaw (1981), 'Scientific discovery as problem solving', *Synthései*, **47**, 1–27.

Steinbruner, John D. (1974), *The Cybernetic Theory of Decision*, Princeton, NJ: Princeton University Press.

Stuart, T.E. and J.M. Podolny (1996), 'Local search and the evolution of technological capabilities', *Strategic Management Journal*, **17**, 21–38.

Tirole, J. (1999), 'Incomplete contracts: where do we stand?' *Econometrica*, **67**(4), 741–781.

Tversky, A. (1972), 'Elimination by aspects: a theory of choice', *Psychological Review*, **79**(4), 281–299.

Tversky, A. and D. Kahneman (1981), 'The framing of decisions and the psychology of choice', *Science*, **211**, 453–458.

Weick, K.E. (1979), 'Cognitive processes in organizations', *Research in Organizational Behavior*, **1**, 41–74.

Zander, I. (2007), 'Do you see what I mean? An entrepreneurship perspective on the nature and boundaries of the firm', *Journal of Management Studies*, **44**(7), 1141–1164.

2. Motivation governance
Margit Osterloh and Bruno S. Frey

Motivation explains people's behaviour. It is therefore important to understand what induces individuals to work in what way. Standard economics (which has been adopted in many business schools) uses a one-dimensional concept of motivation. It essentially assumes that people are perfectly rational and are solely motivated in a selfish way. Based on the insights of psychological economics, this chapter argues, firstly, that people differ in their preferences with respect to pro-social orientations; secondly, that preferences are plastic and systematically susceptible to the design of institutions, working conditions and the quality of human interactions; thirdly, that individuals partly lack self-control in following their preferences; and fourthly, that preferences often are not known to the individuals and are wrongly interpreted. Applying the insights of psychological economics, we derive measures for motivation governance. Motivation governance consists of formal and informal organization designs aimed at influencing incentives in value-creating directions.

The chapter proceeds as follows. Firstly, motivation governance in standard economics is compared to the insights gained from psychological economics. The subsequent sections deal with heterogeneous preferences, in particular pro-social preferences, and plastic preferences. The chapter then engages in two little explored areas, bounded self-control and mistaken preferences, as discussed in happiness research.

MOTIVATION GOVERNANCE IN STANDARD ECONOMICS

For more than 30 years, standard economics has dominated business school research and economic research in dealing with human motivation (Gintis & Khurana 2006: 33). Although highly valuable in its capacity to explain competitive markets, it disregards empirical psychological insights almost completely (Frey & Benz 2004). The *Homo economicus* model treats individuals as utility maximizers who are rational, self-interested and self-controlled. The underlying motivational assumptions of standard economic theory can be typified by the following four assumptions (e.g., Frey 1992; Kirchgässner 2008):

1. There is a strict division between preferences (i.e., needs, values and utilities, which underlie motivation) and external restrictions. The individual's preferences are fixed and relatively enduring (Stigler & Becker 1977). Changes in individual behaviour are mainly a result of changes in restrictions. As a consequence, no analysis of the preferences is needed.
2. Individuals do not include other persons' preferences in their own preference function.
3. People act according to their preferences in a self-controlled way.
4. People know their preferences and interpret them correctly.

In addition, standard economics often adapts an even narrower version of the self-interested human being: individuals are assumed to maximize their own tangible interests, that is, their own pay-off in terms of money or goods (Camerer & Loewenstein 2004: 10). They are depicted to be solely motivated by tangible rewards and to avoid punishment.

As a consequence, motivation governance in standard economics is one-dimensional and simple. Motivation can only be fostered by variable pay-for-performance according to the relative price effect: the higher the price, the higher the effort. Empirically, such an effect has been confirmed for several cases, in particular for piece rate wages paid for simple jobs (Stajkovic & Luthans 1997). A much-quoted example is the field experiment of the personnel economist Lazear (2000) on the US company Safelite Glass: after changing from fixed hourly wages to piece rate, productivity increased by as much as 36 per cent (with an incentive effect of 20 per cent and a selection effect of 16 per cent), whereas the labour costs only rose by 9 per cent.

According to the message of standard economics, today in many companies variable pay-for-performance has caught on as the embodiment of modern management methods. The principle of piece rate wages has been transferred to all employment forms, for example to companies' middle and upper management (e.g., Bebchuk & Grinstein 2005; Rost & Osterloh 2009), government agencies (e.g., Bertelli 2006; Schneider 2007), and even to universities (Osterloh 2010). However, in contrast to piece rate work, these tasks are characterized by high complexity, a large scope of action and high interdependence with other employees. They cannot easily be measured by output indicators and be attributed to specific individuals. If employees nevertheless are paid according to the piece rate principle, dysfunctional effects appear, particularly if all people act in a selfish way. Three problems arise.

Firstly, a *Homo economicus* would have a strong incentive to respond only to those indicators that are easy to measure, because only those are relevant for his income. Not easily measurable parts of the tasks are disregarded, although they might be crucial to fulfilling the task as a whole. This effect is well known as the 'goal-displacement effect' (Merton 1940; Perrin 1998) or the 'multiple-tasking effect' (Ethiraj & Levinthal 2009; Holmstrom & Milgrom 1991; Kerr 1975). There is considerable empirical evidence for this effect (Staw & Boettger 1990; Gilliland & Landis 1992; Fehr & Schmidt 2004; Ordonez et al. 2009). For example, in the public service there are ambulances that concentrate on dealing with emergencies a short distance away so as to meet the goal to respond within eight minutes (LeGrand 2010). One step further is 'cream skimming' and 'gaming the system'. Empirical examples are chronically ill patients excluded from healthcare, teachers responding to evaluations by excluding bad pupils from tests (for empirical evidence in the United States, see Figlio & Getzler 2002), or putting lower-quality students in special classes that are not included in the measurement sample (Corley & Gioia 2000). These effects contribute to what is called the 'performance paradox': performance measures are manipulated and ultimately lose their ability to discriminate between good, average and bad performance (Meyer & Gupta 1994). These effects might explain why the impact on performance does not seem to have improved (e.g., Marsden & Belfield 2006), although in recent years variable pay-for-performance has been widely applied, and tools for output performance measurement have become more sophisticated.

Secondly, a *Homo economicus* would not contribute to a common good as long as his contribution is not measurable and remunerated individually. However, this is often the case with knowledge team work in which team members are in a good position to free-ride and have an incentive to do so (Osterloh & Frey 2000; Osterloh 2006; Frost et al. 2010). A social dilemma arises in which the actions of selfish and rational individuals lead to situations of collective irrationality (Dawes 1980; Miller 1992). Such an effect was found in a great number of situations when people realize that their individual contribution cannot be measured (Messick & Brewer 1983).

Thirdly, it has been shown that under certain conditions pay-for-performance undermines intrinsic work motivation, in particular the joy of fulfilling a particular task and the pro-social obligation to contribute to the community (see below). However, such a motivation is of great importance in a modern economy because it supports innovation and teamwork, and helps to fulfil tasks going beyond the ordinary (Frost et al. 2010).

Fortunately these problems – though ubiquitous – do not always arise, because the assumptions of standard economics do not hold under certain conditions, which are studied by psychological economics.[1]

THE VIEW OF PSYCHOLOGICAL ECONOMICS

Each of the key assumptions of standard economics is challenged by findings in psychological economics, which suggests that 'humans are dumber, nicer, and weaker than the homo economicus' (Thaler 1996: 227). Based on empirical evidence, psychological economics has developed a much richer understanding of the motivational characteristics of human beings. In particular, it has shown that individuals to a considerable degree are characterized by:

1. differences in their preferences (Andreoni 1990), including different extents of pro-social and selfish orientations (Meier 2006);
2. preferences which are plastic and systematically susceptible to the design of institutions, working conditions and the quality of human interactions (Ostrom 2000; Frey 1997);
3. bounded self-control in following their preferences (Rabin 1998; Frey & Benz 2004);
4. preferences that are not known to the individuals and are often wrongly interpreted (Ariely et al. 2006; Stutzer & Frey 2007).

Psychological economics has come to these findings by rigorously testing the assumptions of standard economics. Usually the following procedure is followed (Camerer & Loewenstein 2004):

1. identification of an assumption within the standard economic model;
2. identification of deviations from this assumption;
3. use of these deviations in order to generate an alternative hypothesis to the standard economic model;
4. construction of a behavioural economic model out of the alternative hypothesis;

5.   testing this model;
6.   development of new implications.

In this way psychological economics modifies the assumptions of standard economics step by step in order to develop an empirical foundation of the constructed models. At the same time, the standard economic model is used as a reference (Frey & Benz 2004; Rabin 2002). This procedure helps on the one hand to keep the comprehensiveness and elegance of the standard economic model. On the other hand, the economic model is increasingly based on an empirical foundation. This proceeding also explains the preference of psychological economics for laboratory experiments. They allow the isolation of individual variables and their modification under controlled conditions (Camerer & Fehr 2006). The disadvantage is the often missing external validity. For that reason, field experiments are more and more used (List 2006; Levitt & List 2009).

MOTIVATION GOVERNANCE IN PSYCHOLOGICAL ECONOMICS

As psychological economics is based on a much richer understanding of human motivation than standard economics, motivation governance in psychological economics is multidimensional and multifaceted (Frey & Osterloh 2002). We approach motivation governance by considering the four deviations of psychological economics compared to standard economics that are mentioned above.

Different Preferences

People differ in their preferences with respect to the extent of including selfish or pro-social orientations. In psychological economics, extrinsic and intrinsic preferences are distinguished that lead to different kinds of motivation. Extrinsic motivation is aimed instrumentally at activities not valued for their own sake. In contrast, intrinsic motivation is directed towards activities performed for their own sake rather than for any reward (Deci & Ryan 1985; Frey 1997; Osterloh & Frey 2000). According to Lindenberg (2001) extrinsic motivation is driven by the 'gain goal' to preserve and enhance one's resources. Intrinsic motivation is either driven by the 'hedonic goal' to feel good or by a 'normative goal' to act appropriately. The latter includes the well-being of others or pro-social preferences. Each goal competes to be in a person's cognitive foreground, thereby pushing the other goals into the background. When a goal is in the foreground, it governs what people like and dislike, what they attend to and what alternatives they consider (Lindenberg & Foss 2011).

Concerning pro-social preferences one of the most ubiquitous findings of psychological economics is that such motivation is much more prevalent than standard economic theory suggests (Meier 2006). For instance, a large body of research has accumulated on whether, when and why individuals contribute to the commons. Large-scale survey studies show that individuals contribute substantial amounts of money and time to public goods. In the United States (US) almost 70 per cent of all households make charitable contributions, exceeding one per cent of GDP (Andreoni et al. 1996). Pro-social behaviour is observed also in laboratory and field experiments. For example, it has been demonstrated that participants in the experiments invest up to between 40 and 60 per cent of their endowments in public goods (Fehr & Gächter 1998). Henrich et al. (2001: 77) conducted a series of ultimatum games in 15 societies around the world and came to the conclusion that 'the canonical model of the self-interested material pay-off-maximizing actor is systematically violated'.

Pro-social motivation is differentiated into altruism or reciprocity. Altruists benefit others unconditionally even at a personal cost (Fowler & Kam 2007). Reciprocists act conditionally, depending on the behaviour or intentions of others (Nyborg 2010). The pro-social behaviour of others is responded with one's own pro-social behaviour; selfish behaviour of others is responded to with one's own selfish behaviour.

Overall, in laboratory experiments, about 50 per cent of the test persons have been found acting in a reciprocal way, 20 per cent as altruists and 30 per cent as egoists (e.g., Andreoni & Miller 2002; Fischbacher et al. 2001). Field studies show a smaller proportion of altruists (Frey & Meier 2004). But such findings should be used with caution since the extent of pro-social behaviour is strongly dependent on the situation, which has an impact on which of the goals – the extrinsic gain goal or the two intrinsic goals – is prevailing.

As a consequence for motivation governance, employees have to be carefully selected. Above all, it has to be checked whether the job seekers are interested in the work to be performed or solely in the money that will come along with it. In all too many sectors of the economy, this task seems to have been neglected. In the financial sector, for example, many persons have been chosen whose only goal is to get as high a salary as possible. They therefore exhibit no loyalty to the firm and immediately accept any job that offers higher compensation (Frey & Osterloh 2012). Moreover, the recent financial market crisis shows that the prospect of huge salaries according to pay-for-performance criteria (which can be manipulated by the managers) has turned some of them from 'legends' (Hegele & Kieser 2001) into 'crooks' (Osterloh & Frey 2004; Osterloh et al. 2011). It also has been shown under pay-for-performance schemes that people who are most interested in money do self-select themselves into pay-for-performance jobs more frequently (Lazear & Shaw 2007).

Plastic Preferences

Preferences and motivations are not stable. The three goals – the extrinsic gain goal, the intrinsic hedonic goal and the intrinsic normative goal – differ in their strength (Lindenberg 2001). There can be a crowding-out or crowding-in effect of intrinsic motivation by external interventions which push the intrinsic goals into the background and the gain goal into the foreground. In particular, crowding-out effects can be activated by variable pay-for-performance or by external control if the following conditions hold (Deci & Ryan 2000; Frey & Jegen 2001):

1. the activity was originally intrinsically motivated;
2. the reward or control is interpreted as curtailing one's autonomy;
3. the extrinsic motivation generated by external rewards does not counterbalance the loss of intrinsic motivation.

There is extensive empirical evidence for the crowding-out effect. Firstly, there exist numerous laboratory experiments as well as meta-analyses of these experiments. They show that the effect is stronger with expected rewards than with unexpected ones, and stronger with pecuniary incentives than with symbolic ones (Deci et al. 1999; Heckhausen & Heckhausen 2006). Moreover, there is a stronger crowding-out effect with interesting activities than with less interesting, monotonous jobs (Weibel et al. 2010). Secondly, a number of field experiments support the crowding-out effect (see, e.g., Ariely et al. 2009; Frey et al. 1996; Frey & Götte 1999; Holmas et al. 2010).

Thirdly, some experiments also show how both the crowding-out and the price effect operate in conjunction. Pouliakas (2010: 618) and Weibel et al. (2010) show that a crowding-out effect can be compensated for by higher pay – but at a high cost compared to keeping or strengthening intrinsic motivation. This effect is well illustrated in a field experiment analysing the behaviour of school children voluntarily collecting money for cancer research (Gneezy & Rustichini 2000). The children reduced their efforts by about 36 per cent when they were promised a bonus of 1 per cent of the collected money, and raised their effort when they got a bonus of 10 per cent of the collected money. Fourthly, intrinsic motivation and job satisfaction can also be crowded out by external control, if this control is perceived as suspicious (Falk and Kosfeld 2006; Weibel 2007) or unfair (Long et al. 2011).

Finally, intrinsic motivation can be crowded out due to the free-riding of others. If free-riding takes place without sanctioning it, the pro-social motivation to cooperate in teams is undermined. The willingness to cooperate drops for everybody in the team if other team members are shirking (Fehr & Gintis 2007). In public-good games that mimic social dilemmas, a high number of participants contribute voluntarily in the first round to the common pool. When the participants realize that others are shirking, they reduce their contribution until after several rounds it is close to zero. As a consequence, organizations should guard and provide intrinsic motivation, in particular the normative intrinsic motivation, in order to make sure that employees do not free-ride but contribute to the common good.

Which measures for motivation governance can be derived from the insights of psychological economics in order to avoid crowding out intrinsic motivation and to crowd in intrinsic motivation? In general such interventions should: (1) be targeted to create an intrinsically rewarding job environment; (2) support employees' feelings of competence; (3) support employees' perception of esteem and relatedness by fair processes; (4) signal social norms; and (5) enable self-governance in teams to discipline free-riders. We discuss in detail seven mechanisms to foster intrinsic motivation.

Firstly, employees have to be paid a fixed compensation corresponding to their performance (Frey & Osterloh 2012). They must be given the signal that they are paid a good wage but that they are expected to work accordingly. Thus, a market wage has to be paid in order to be able to win and keep employees. After some time the compensation can be adjusted on the basis of a comprehensive evaluation of their work. This procedure avoids the crowding-out effect as well as the multiple tasking problem. At the end of the year, one can also distribute part of the profit to employees according to their contribution to overall performance rather than according to *ex ante* criteria. This measure strengthens solidarity with the company as a whole.

Secondly, intrinsic motivation can be enhanced through job design along several dimensions. The two most important dimensions are autonomy and task feedback (Gagné & Deci 2005). A job providing decision latitude enhances employees' self-determination and thereby strengthens interest and pride in the job. Task feedback, the degree to which the job provides clear information about performance levels, raises feelings of competence and empowers employees in their tasks. Three additional dimensions have been found to strengthen intrinsic motivation through raising perceived meaningfulness of the job (Hackman & Oldham 1980): variety (the degree to which a job requires the use of a number of different skills and talents); identity (the degree to which the job requires completion of a 'whole' piece of work or doing a task from beginning to end with a visible outcome); and significance (the degree to which the job offers opportunities to protect and promote the well-being of beneficiaries).

Thirdly, hierarchical control can be used to crowd in intrinsic motivation. Whereas this kind of control often undermines intrinsic motivation, there are two conditions under which the opposite holds. Empirical research demonstrates that hierarchical control is perceived as supportive if feedback is given in a constructive and timely way, and if caring guidance prevails (Weibel 2007). Hierarchical control that is executed for the sake of the community rather than for selfish interest is perceived to be legitimate. Field research shows that such benevolent, non-selfish monitoring leads to perceptions of organizational support and to higher pro-social motivation. Laboratory research (Fehr & Gintis 2007) demonstrates that people are more willing to contribute to a public good if a leader makes personal sacrifices.

Fourthly, awards and supporting forms of rewards foster intrinsic motivation if they bolster employees' feelings of competence and esteem. Awards play a special role in sectors where voluntary efforts are crucial, for example in academia, the arts, the military and public service (Frey & Neckermann 2008). It has been shown that the motivation of employees not getting an award is not reduced (Neckermann et al. 2008). Rewards in the form of monetary incentives also foster intrinsic motivation if they signal benevolence and a caring attitude and are presented with no strings attached (Kuvaas 2006).

Fifthly, procedural fairness furthers pro-social intrinsic motivation. Therefore, governance mechanisms need to be designed and executed in a fair way. The characteristics of governance mechanisms that lead to perceived procedural fairness can be summarized as participation, neutrality and being treated with dignity and respect (Tyler & Blader 2000). Participation gives employees a voice to choose between alternatives and to participate in devising the rules of cooperation. It has been empirically shown that participation furthers affective worker commitment and loyalty that can be regarded as a 'firm-specific utility' (Brown et al. 2011). Also, participation in political decision-making processes increases tax morale, which can be understood as the willingness to contribute to the community (Feld & Frey 2002; Frey & Torgler 2007). Neutrality refers to the extent to which employees feel that the company or their superiors make unbiased decisions. A precondition is the belief that individuals who set and sanction the rules do not allow personal advantages to enter into their decision-making. Lastly, governance mechanisms should signal dignity and respect to employees. All three characteristics of procedural fairness (participation, neutrality, and being treated with dignity and respect) are essentially unrelated to outcomes. Therefore, procedural fairness is crucial for situations that may lead to undesired results for the employees (Greenberg 1994).

Sixthly, people are highly sensitive to signals about socially appropriate behaviour. Such signals push the normative frame into the foreground and make individuals inclined to adhere to rules even if it is not in their own self-interest (Lindenberg & Foss 2011). Experiments suggest that participants were more willing to contribute to a common good if they were told that they were taking part in a 'community game' rather than in a 'Wall Street game' (Liberman et al. 2004; Reeson & Tisdell 2008). Subordinates who fill their own pockets with high salaries as well as 'pay-for-performance' schemes signal a 'Wall Street game'.

Seventhly, the punishment of free-riders fosters pro-social intrinsic motivation. In all kinds of communities some people free-ride. The willingness to contribute to the common good in a team declines drastically when contributors realize that others are shirking. Nobody wants to be a sucker. However, when free-riders can be punished, contributions are raised to the initial level, but only when punishment does not serve the self-interest of the punishers (Fehr & Rockenbach 2003). As a consequence, self-governance and peer control in teams, as opposed to control by superiors, is crucial. Sanctions by superiors are, in many cases, not considered to be unselfish. Also, team members often are in a better position than superiors to realize when peers are shirking. There are many examples that self-governance of commons is more efficient than hierarchical control with regard to counteracting shirking (Ostrom 2000).

Bounded Self-Control in Following One's Preferences

Individuals are often not able to stick to their long-term goals but fall prey to their desire for immediate satisfaction. Obvious examples are smokers who want to quit smoking, obese people who want to eat less, or workaholics who work more than is good for their health. They suffer from self-control problems. The phenomenon is called 'time-inconsistent preferences' or 'hyperbolic discounting' (O'Donoghue & Rabin 1999). Short-term and long-term preferences conflict with each other. These problems are also relevant in the sphere of work since they have an impact on employees' health, productivity and job satisfaction.

Which measures of motivation governance can be applied to mitigate bounded self-control? A common way is to commit oneself to institutions in order to get help when struggling to overcome weaknesses (Frey and Eichenberger 1991). But often this is not very successful. DellaVigna & Malmendier (2006) show that individuals choosing a monthly lump-sum contract with a health club in order to commit themselves in fact use the health club less than expected. In the end they pay 70 per cent more than they would have paid under a payment-per-usage scheme.

Libertarian or soft paternalism aims at skewing the decisions into the 'right' direction by a 'choice architecture', that is, by changing the context in a way that nudges individuals towards what is best for them in terms of their long-term-preferences (Thaler & Sunstein 2003). The authors use the following example: 'Consider the problem facing the director of a company cafeteria who discovers that the order in which food is arranged influences the choice people make . . . Putting the fruit before the desert is a fairly mild intervention. A more intrusive step would be to place the desserts in another location so that diners have to stand up and get a dessert after they have finished the rest or their meal' (Thaler & Sunstein 2003:175). Such measures are libertarian in the sense that people are free to do what they like. They are paternalistic in the sense that the choice architects try to influence people's decisions in order to support their long-term preferences.

However, there are objections to the idea of such a 'nanny' governance. It is argued that paternalism might unjustifiably 'take sides' in choosing to favour some personal interests over others. It ignores private solutions to the self-control problem. And it disregards the possibility of paternalists' failures (Whitman 2006). A pragmatic counter-argument is that there is choice architecture anyway. Organizational designs that frame decisions are inevitable, therefore the question is not whether to be paternalistic or not. Therefore 'results from the psychology of decision-making should be used to provide ex ante guidelines to support reasonable judgements' (Sunstein & Thaler 2003: 1166).

These problems could be mitigated if individuals can decide in a democratic way whether such paternalistic measures should be undertaken to serve as self-commitment. But it must be admitted that the problem of unwarranted 'choice architecture' may again appear with the presentation of the choice alternatives during the democratic process. As a consequence, libertarian paternalism is an interesting but disputable measure to overcome the lack of self-control among adults.

Unknown or Falsely Interpreted Preferences of Individuals

Standard economics relies on 'revealed behaviour': people always make choices leading to outcomes that maximize their utility. Individuals are assumed to be perfectly informed about what will bring them how much utility. This means that people do not make any systematic mistakes when making decisions. Possible errors are either randomly distributed, or if systematic mistakes occur, individuals correct them quickly by learning. This view has been criticized because 'it rules out – as a logical impossibility – any conflict between what man chooses to get and what will best satisfy him' (Scitovsky 1976: 4).

Standard economics thus simply assumes that people can successfully predict how they will feel about future outcomes. Many careful experiments and surveys have studied whether people are good at forecasting utility (reviews are provided by Loewenstein & Schkade 1999; Wilson & Gilbert 2003; Kahneman & Thaler 2006). They find that people are able to accurately predict whether an experience will primarily elicit good or bad feelings. In contrast, people often hold incorrect intuitive theories about the determinants of their happiness. They systematically overestimate the impact of specific life events on their experienced well-being with regard to intensity, as well as with regard to duration.

Standard economics is probably appropriate to explain the choices made by individuals for most goods and activities and for most situations. However, this is no longer the case when people have to make trade-offs between different activities, goods or options that differ systematically in the extent to which their future utility is affected. As a result, economic consequences differ from the predictions of standard economics (Stutzer & Frey 2008). When making a decision, some options, or attributes of options, are more salient than others, and are thus relatively overvalued. Consequently, people's experienced utility is lower than what they expected. Moreover, they consume different goods with different attributes and pursue different activities.

There are four major sources for systematic over- and undervaluation of choice options that can be distinguished (Stutzer & Frey 2008):

- the underestimation of adaptation;
- distorted memory of past experiences;
- the rationalization of decisions; and
- mistaken intuitive theories about the sources of future utility – in particular, the future utility of extrinsic goods is overestimated and that of intrinsic goods is underestimated.

The practical importance of misprediction is exemplified by a study on people's decisions to commute for a longer or a shorter time (Stutzer & Frey 2008). The decision to commute between place of work and place of living involves the trade-off between the salary or the quality of housing on the one hand, and commuting time on the other hand. Rational utility maximizers commute only when they are more than compensated for the costs of commuting. They should receive either a higher wage or more affordable or higher-quality housing. However, when people overestimate utility from goods serving extrinsic wants, they are expected to opt for too much commuting and then suffer lower utility according to their own evaluation. In a large panel data set for Germany, it is found that commuting is not fully compensated and that, on average, people who commute 22 minutes each way (sample mean) would need an additional 35 per cent of their monthly labour income to be as satisfied with their life as people who do not commute.

Which measures of motivation governance can be applied to mitigate systematic misprediction of happiness? In our view the most important measure is to inform individuals about the conditions under which future subjective well-being tends to be overrated and underrated. Practical examples are helpful because they are more easily remembered. Thus, for example, it should be communicated that buying a material good such as a flashy new car only raises happiness for a relatively short period of time. Thereafter, people get used to it and take its possession for granted. In contrast, individuals can be informed that relational goods, that is, having friends, acquaintances, a good family life and many social connections, do not wear out. Having them is a continual source of happiness. Such information helps individuals to learn to overcome errors in evaluations such as succumbing to the lure of materialistic possessions instead of a fruitful social life.

In contrast to some happiness scholars (e.g. Layard 2005; Frank 1999) we do not recommend that governments or firms engage in maximizing the happiness of the population or of their employees. This corresponds to a 'benevolent dictator approach' inconsistent with a democratic, liberal society. It provides politicians and executives with strong incentives to manipulate the happiness indicators (see, more fully, Frey and Stutzer 2006; Frey 2011). As the happiness indicators are based on surveys, there are many possibilities for such manipulation, for example by treating non-respondents or outliers in a way serving the politicians' and executives' goals, or simply by making up convenient data.

Also in firms, a policy to maximize happiness might strengthen incentives to manipulate happiness indicators. On the one hand, managers of firms may have an interest in diminishing misprediction as well as other sorts of behavioural anomalies leading to reductions in happiness. According to recent research (Oswald et al. 2010) happiness raises productivity. This relationship has long been studied in psychology. In particular,

Wright and Staw (1998), Boehm and Lyubomirsky (2008) and Amabile et al. (2005) show that happier persons are more efficient and creative. On the other hand, a firm's board should not simply ask the management to maximize the happiness of its employees. Once the employees are aware that the managers intend to raise their happiness in order to make them more productive, they have an incentive to answer in a strategic way. In particular, if they fear that the surveys capturing their happiness are not fully anonymous, they tend to report too-high happiness levels in order not to get into conflict with the management. In addition, managers have an incentive to manipulate the aggregate happiness indicator of their firm in order to satisfy their board. This can be done, for example, by deviating from a randomized survey or by disregarding the views of those employees suspected or known to be critical of the management. Therefore politicians as well as managers should be aware that the 'governance of happiness' may produce dysfunctional effects.

CONCLUDING REMARKS

The chapter shows that motivation governance has become a more difficult task once it is acknowledged that people's motivations are multidimensional and plastic. In contrast, standard economics conceives motivation in a one-dimensional way: more effort can be produced simply by raising the (relative) price or wage offered.

An important consequence for motivation governance is, firstly, to select employees carefully. Job seekers must be interested in the work to be performed, and not solely in the money that will come along with it. In all too many branches of the economy, especially in the financial sector, this task has been neglected. Pay-for-performance schemes are in line with employees who are most interested in money. Indeed, they self-select themselves into pay-for-performance jobs more frequently. Secondly, organizations should guard normative intrinsic motivation in order to make employees inclined to contribute to the common good. There exists an extensive repertoire of measures to do so, such as job design, procedural fairness, signalling of appropriate behaviour and punishment of free-riders. Thirdly, it is important to become aware of the limited measures of governance when it comes to mitigating bounded self-control and raising happiness. In these cases the most important measures are to inform individuals, for example, about the conditions under which future subjective well-being tends to be overrated and underrated. In particular, it has to be demonstrated that the gain in happiness produced by material goods wears off quite quickly, while relational goods can be a continually repeating source of happiness.

The new view of motivation based on insights from psychological economics makes it harder, but at the same time more challenging, to govern motivation in society as well as in particular organizations. We have pointed out ways in which this can be done with respect to heterogeneous preferences, their plasticity, as well as to bounded self-control and misprediction of future preferences. Research has only addressed some possibilities; much more needs to be inquired into in future work.

NOTE

1. We prefer the expression 'psychological economics' instead of 'behavioural economics' for two reasons. Firstly, economists had already examined human behaviour before this new field emerged. Secondly, Simon (1985) pointed out that the term 'behavioural' was misleading because it could be confounded with the behaviourist approach in psychology.

REFERENCES

Amabile, T.M., S.G. Barsade, J.S. Mueller and B.M. Staw (2005), 'Affect and creativity at work', *Administrative Science Quarterly*, **50**, 367–403.

Andreoni, J. (1990), 'Impure altruism and donations to public-goods – a theory of warm-glow giving', *Economic Journal*, **100**, 464–477.

Andreoni, J. and J. Miller (2002), 'Giving according to Garp: an experimental test of the consistency of preferences for altruism', *Econometrica*, **70**, 737–753.

Andreoni, J., W.G. Gale and J.K. Scholz (1996), 'Charitable contributions of time and money', unpublished.

Ariely, D., U. Gneezy, G. Loewenstein and N. Mazar (2009), 'Large stakes and big mistakes', *Review of Economic Studies*, **76**(2), 451–469.

Ariely, D., G. Loewenstein and D. Prelec (2006), 'Tom Sawyer and the construction of value', *Journal of Economic Behavior and Organization*, **60**, 1–10.

Bebchuk, L. and Y. Grinstein (2005), 'The growth of executive pay', *Oxford Review of Economic Policy*, **21**(2), 283–303.

Bertelli, A. (2006), 'Motivation crowding and the federal civil servant: evidence from the US Internal Revenue Service', *International Public Management Journal*, **9**(1), 3–23.

Boehm, J.K. and S. Lyubomirsky (2008), 'Does happiness promote career success?' *Journal of Career Assessment*, **16**, 101–116.

Brown, Sarah, Jolian McHardy, Robert McNabb and Kart Taylor (2011), 'Workplace performance, worker commitment and loyalty', Discussion Paper No. 5447 IZA, Bonn.

Camerer, C. and E. Fehr (2006), 'When does "economic man" dominate social behavior?' *Science*, 6 January, **311**(5757), 47–52.

Camerer, C. and G. Loewenstein (2004), 'Behavioral economics: past, present, future', in Colin Camerer, George Loewenstein and Matthew Rabin (eds), *Advances in Behavioral Economics*, New York: Princeton University Press, pp. 3–51.

Corley, K.G. and D.A. Gioia (2000), 'The rankings game: managing business school reputation', *Corporate Reputation Review*, **3**(4), 319–333.

Dawes, R.M. (1980), 'Social dilemmas', *Annual Review of Psychology*, **31**, 169–193.

Deci, E.L. and R.M. Ryan (1985), *Intrinsic Motivation and Self-Determination in Human Behavior*, New York: Plenum Publishing Co.

Deci, E.L. and R.M. Ryan (2000), 'The "what" and "why" of goal pursuits: human needs and the self-determination of behavior', *Psychological Inquiry*, **11**, 227–268.

Deci, E.L., R. Koestner and R.M. Ryan (1999), 'A meta-analytic review of experiments examining the effects of extrinsic rewards on intrinsic motivation', *Psychological Bulletin*, **125**(6), 627–668.

DellaVigna, Stefano and Ulrike Malmendier (2006), 'Paying not to go to the gym', *American Economic Review*, **96**(3), 694–719.

Ethiraj, S.K. and D. Levinthal (2009), 'Hoping for A to Z while rewarding only A: complex organizations and multiple goals', *Organization Science*, **20**, 4–21.

Falk, A. and M. Kosfeld (2006), 'The hidden costs of control', *American Economic Review*, **96**(5), 1611–1630.

Fehr, E. and S. Gächter (1998), 'Reciprocity and economics: the economic implications of homo reciprocans', *European Economic Review*, **42**, 845–859.

Fehr, E. and H. Gintis (2007), 'Human motivation and social cooperation: experimental and analytical foundation', *Annual Review of Sociology*, **33**, 43–64.

Fehr, E. and B. Rockenbach (2003), 'Detrimental effects of sanctions on human altruism', *Nature*, **422**, 137–140.

Fehr, E. and K.M. Schmidt (2004), 'Fairness and incentives in a multi-task principal–agent model', *Scandinavian Journal of Economics*, **106**, 453–474.

Feld, L. and B.S. Frey (2002), 'Trust breeds trust', *Economics and Governance*, **3**, 87–99.

Figlio, D. and L. Getzler (2002), 'Accountability, ability and disability: gaming the system', NBER Working Paper No. W9307 http://bear.warrington.ufl.edu/figlio/w9307.pdf.

Fischbacher, U., E. Fehr and S. Gächter (2001), 'Are people conditionally cooperative? Evidence from public good experiments', *Economic Letters*, **71**, 397–404.

Fowler, J.H. and C.D. Kam (2007), 'Beyond the self: social identity, altruism, and political participation', *Journal of Politics*, **69**(3), 811–825.

Frank, R. (1999), *Luxury Fever. Why Money Fails to Satisfy in an Era of Excess*, New York: Free Press.

Frey, B.S. (1992), *Economics as a Science of Human Behaviour*, Boston, MA: Kluwer.

Frey, B.S. (1997), *Not Just for the Money: An Economic Theory of Personal Motivation*, Cheltenham, UK and Brookfield, WI, USA: Edward Elgar.

Frey, B.S. (2011), 'Subjective well-being, politics and political economy', *Swiss Journal of Economics and Statistics*, **147**, 397–415.

Frey, B.S. and M. Benz (2004), 'From imperialism to inspiration: a survey of economics and psychology', in J.B. Davis, A. Marciano and J. Runde (eds), *The Elgar Companion to Economics and Philosophy*, Cheltenham, UK and Northampton, MA, USA: Edward Elgar, pp. 61–84.

Frey, B.S. and R. Eichenberger (1991), 'Anomalies in political economy', *Public Choice*, **68**, 71–89.

Frey, B.S. and L. Götte (1999), 'Does pay motivate volunteers?' University of Zurich, Institute for Empirical Research in Economics, unpublished.

Frey, B.S. and R. Jegen (2001), 'Motivation crowding theory: a survey of empirical evidence', *Journal of Economic Surveys*, **15**(5), 589–611.

Frey, B.S. and S. Meier (2004), 'Social comparisons and pro-social behavior: testing "conditional cooperation" in a field experiment', *American Economic Review*, **94**, 1717–1722.

Frey, B.S. and S. Neckermann (2008), 'Awards – a view from psychological economics', *Journal of Psychology*, **216**, 198–208.

Frey, B.S. and M. Osterloh (2002), *Successful Management by Motivation. Balancing Intrinsic and Extrinsic Incentives*, Heidelberg: Springer.

Frey, B.S. and M. Osterloh (2012), 'Stop tying pay to performance', *Harvard Business Review*, January–February, HBR's List of Audacious Ideas for Solving the World's Problems, pp. 4–5.

Frey, B.S. and A. Stutzer (2006), 'Mispredicting utility and the political process', in E. McCaffery and J. Slemrod (eds), *Behavioral Public Finance*, New York: Russel Sage, pp. 113–140.

Frey, B.S. and B. Torgler (2007), 'Tax morale and conditional cooperation', *Journal of Comparative Economics*, **35**, 136–159.

Frey, B.S., R. Eichenberger and F. Oberholzer-Gee (1996), 'The old lady visits your backyard: a tale of morals and markets', *Journal of Political Economy*, **104**, 193–209.

Frost, J., M. Osterloh and A. Weibel (2010), 'Governing knowledge work: transactional and transformational solutions', *Organizational Dynamics*, **39**, 126–136.

Gagné, M. and E.L. Deci (2005), 'Self–determination theory and work motivation', *Journal of Organizational Behavior*, **26**, 331–362.

Gilliland, S.W. and R.S. Landis (1992), 'Quality and quantity goals in a complex decision task: strategies and outcomes', *Journal of Applied Psychology*, **77**(5), 672–681.

Gintis, H. and R. Khurana (2006), 'Corporate honesty and business education: a behavior model', unpublished manuscript.

Gneezy, U. and A. Rustichini (2000), 'Pay enough or don't pay at all', *Quarterly Journal of Economics*, **115**(3), 791–810.

Greenberg, J. (1994), 'Using socially fair treatment to promote acceptance of a work-site smoking ban', *Journal of Applied Psychology*, **79**, 288–297.

Hackman, R.J. and G.R. Oldham (1980), *Work Redesign*, Reading, MA: Addison-Wesley.

Heckhausen, J. and H. Heckhausen (2006), *Motivation und Handeln*, Berlin and Heidelberg: Springer Verlag.

Hegele, C. and A. Kieser (2001), 'Control the construction of your legend or someone else will', *Journal of Management Inquiry*, **10**, 298–309.

Henrich, J., R. Boyd, S. Bowles, C. Camerer, E. Fehr, H. Gintis and R. McElreath (2001), 'In search of homo economicus: behavioral experiments in 15 small-scale societies', *American Economic Review*, **91**, 73–78.

Holmas, H., E. Kjerstad, H. Luras and O.R. Straume (2010), 'Does monetary punishment crowd out pro-social motivation? A natural experiment on hospital length of stay', *Journal of Economic Behavior and Organization*, **75**, 261–267.

Holmstrom, B.P. and P. Milgrom (1991), 'Multitask principal–agent analyses: incentive contracts, asset ownership, and job design', *Journal of Law, Economics, and Organization*, **7**, 24–52.

Kahneman, D. and R.H. Thaler (2006), 'Anomalies: utility maximization and experienced utility', *Journal of Economic Perspectives*, **20**(1), 221–234.

Kerr, S. (1975), 'On the folly of rewarding a, while hoping for b', *Academy of Management Journal*, **18**, 769–783.

Kirchgässner, G. (2008), *Homo Oeconomicus: The Economic Model of Behavior and Its Applications to Economics and Other Social Sciences*, Berlin and Heidelberg: Springer Verlag.

Kuvaas, B. (2006), 'Work performance, affective commitment, and work motivation: the roles of pay administration and pay level', *Journal of Organizational Behavior*, **27**, 365–385.

Layard, R. (2005), *Happiness. Lessons from a New Science*, London: Penguin.

Lazear, E.P. (2000), 'Performance pay and productivity', *American Economic Review*, **90**(5), 1346–1361.

Lazear, E.P. and K.L. Shaw (2007), 'Personnel economics: the economist's view of human resources', *Journal of Economic Perspectives*, **21**(4), 91–114.

LeGrand, Julien (2010), 'Knights and knaves return: public service motivation and the delivery of public services', *International Public Management Journal*, **13**(1), 56–71.

Levitt, Steven D. and John A. List (2009), 'Field experiments in economics: the past, the present, and the future', *European Economic Review*, **53**, 1–18.

Liberman, V., S.M. Samuels and L. Ross (2004), 'The name of the game: predictive power of reputations versus situational labels in determining prisoner's dilemma game moves', *Personality and Social Psychology Bulletin*, **30**(9), 1175–1185.

Lindenberg, S. (2001), 'Intrinsic motivation in a new light', *Kyklos*, **54**(2–3), 317–342.

Lindenberg, S. and N. Foss (2011), 'Managing joint production motivation: the rose of goal framing and governance mechanisms', *Academy of Management Review*, **36**(3), 500–525.

List, John A. (2006), 'Field experiments: a bridge between lab and naturally occurring data', *Advances in Economic Analysis and Policy*, **6**(2), Art. 8.

Loewenstein, G. and D.A. Schkade (1999), 'Wouldn't It be nice? Predicting future feelings', in D. Kahneman, E. Diener and N. Schwarz (eds), *Well-Being: The Foundation of Hedonic Psychology*, New York: Russell Sage Foundation, pp. 85–105.

Long, C.P., C. Bendersky and C. Morill (2011), 'Fairness monitoring: linking managerial controls and fairness judgements in organizations', *Academy of Management Journal*, **54**(5), 1045–1068.

Marsden, D. and R. Belfield (2006), 'Pay for performance where output is hard to measure: the case of performance pay for school teachers', *Advances in Industrial and Labor Relations*, **15**, 1–34.

Meier, S. (2006), *The Economics of Non-Selfish Behaviour: Decisions to Contribute Money to Public Goods*, Cheltenham, UK and Northhampton, MA, USA: Edward Elgar Publishing.

Merton, R.K. (1940), 'Bureaucratic structure and personality', *Social Forces*, **18**, 560–568.

Messick, D.M. and M.B. Brewer (1983), 'Solving social dilemmas: a review', in L. Wheeler (ed.), Beverly Hills, CA: Sage.

Meyer, M.W. and W. Gupta (1994), 'The performance paradox', *Research in Organizational Behavior*, **16**, 309–369.

Miller, G. (1992), *Managerial Dilemmas. The Political Economy of Hierarchy*, Cambridge: Cambridge University Press.

Neckermann S., R. Cueni and B.S. Frey (2008), 'Making them rich or proud? Managements' perspective on employee awards', Institute for Economic Research, University of Zurich.

Nyborg, K. (2010), 'Will green taxes undermine moral motivation?' *Public Finance and Management*, **10**(2), 331–351.

O'Donoghue, T. and Matthew Rabin (1999), 'Doing it now or later', *American Economic Review*, **89**(1), 103–24.

Ordonez, L.D., M.E. Schweitzer, A.D. Galinsky and M.H. Bazerman (2009), 'Goals gone wild: the systematic side effects of overprescribing goal setting', *Academy of Management Perspectives*, **23**, 6–16.

Osterloh, M. (2006), 'Human resources management and knowledge creation', in I. Nonaka and I. Kazuo (eds), *Handbook of Knowledge Creation*, Oxford: Oxford University Press, pp. 158–175.

Osterloh, M. (2010), 'Governance by numbers: does it really work in research?' *Analyse und Kritik*, **32**(2), 267–283.

Osterloh, M., and B.S. Frey (2000), 'Motivation, knowledge transfer, and organizational forms', *Organization Science*, **11**, 538–550.

Osterloh, M. and B.S. Frey (2004), 'Corporate governance for crooks. The case for corporate virtue', in A. Grandori (ed.), *Corporate Governance and Firm Organization*, Oxford, UK: Oxford University Press, pp. 191–211.

Osterloh, M., B.S. Frey and H. Zeitoun (2011), 'Corporate governance as an institution to overcome social dilemmas', in A. Brink (ed.), *Corporate Governance and Business Ethics*, Dordrecht, Heidelberg, London, New York: Springer, pp. 49–74.

Ostrom, E. (2000), 'Crowding out Citizenship', *Scandinavian Political Studies*, **23**, 3–16.

Oswald, A.J., E. Proto and D. Sgroi (2010), 'Happiness and productivity'. Mimeo, Department of Economics, University of Warwick.

Perrin, B. (1998), 'Effective use and misuse of performance measurement', *American Journal of Evaluation*, **19**, 367–379.

Pouliakas, K. (2010), 'Pay enough, don't pay too much or don't pay at all? The impact of bonus intensity on job satisfaction', *Kyklos*, **63**(4), 597–626.

Rabin, Matthew (1998), 'Psychology and economics', *Journal of Economic Literature*, **36**(1), 11–46.

Rabin, M. (2002), 'A perspective on psychology and economics', *European Economic Review*, **46**, 657–685.

Reeson, A.F. and J.G. Tisdell (2008), 'Institutions, motivations and public goods: an experimental test of motivational crowding', *Journal of Economic Behavior and Organization*, **68**(1), 273–281.

Rost, K. and M. Osterloh (2009), 'Management fashion pay-for-performance for CEOs', *Schmalenbach Business Review*, **61**, 119–149.

Schneider, M. (2007), 'Zielvorgaben Und Organisationskultur. Eine Fallstudie', *Die Betriebswirtschaft*, 619–637.

Scitovsky, T. (1976), *The Joyless Economy: An Inquiry into Human Satisfaction and Consumer Dissatisfaction*, New York: Oxford University Press.

Simon, H.A. (1985), 'Human nature in politics – the dialog of psychology with political science', *American Political Science Review*, **79**(2), 293–304.

Stajkovic, A. and F. Luthans (1997), 'A meta-analysis of the effects of organizational behavior modification on task performance', *Academy of Management Journal*, **40**, 1122–1149.

Staw, B.M. and R.D. Boettger (1990), 'Task revision: a neglected form of work performance', *Academy of Management Journal*, **33**, 534–559.

Stigler, G.J. and G.S. Becker (1977), 'De gustibus non est disputandum', *American Economic Review*, **67**, 76–90.

Stutzer, A. and B.S. Frey (2007), 'What happiness research can tell us about self-control problems and utility misprediction', in B.S. Frey and A. Stutzer (eds), *Economics and Psychology. A Promising New Cross-Disciplinary Field*, Cambridge: MA, pp. 169–195.

Stutzer, A. and B.S. Frey (2008), 'Stress that doesn't pay: the commuting paradox', *Scandinavian Journal of Economics*, **110**, 339–366.

Sunstein, C.R. and R.H. Thaler (2003), 'Libertarian paternalism is not an oxymoron', *University of Schiaco Law Review*, **70**(4), 1159–1202.

Thaler, R.H. (1996), 'Doing economics without Homo Economicus', in S.G. Medema and W.G. Samuels (eds), *Foundations of Research in Economics: How do Economists do Economics?* Cheltenham, UK and Brookfield, VT, USA: Edward Elgar, pp. 227–237.

Thaler, Richard H. and Cass R. Sunstein (2003), 'Libertarian paternalism', *American Economic Review (Papers and Proceedings)*, **93**(2), 175–179.

Tyler, T.R. and S.L. Blader (2000), *Cooperation in Groups: Procedural Justice, Social Identity, and Behavioral Engagement*, Philadelphia, PA: Psychology Press.

Weibel, A. (2007), 'Formal control and trustworthiness – never the twain shall meet?' *Group and Organization Management*, **32**(4), 500–517.

Weibel, A., K. Rost and M. Osterloh (2010), 'Pay for performance in the public sector – benefits and (hidden) costs', *Journal of Public Administration Research and Theory*, **20**(2), 387–412.

Whitman, Glen (2006), 'Against the new paternalism: internalities and the economics of self-control', Cato Institute Policy Analysis no. 563, February.

Wilson, T.D. and D.T. Gilbert (2003), 'Affective forecasting', in M. Zanna (ed.), *Advances in Experimental Social Psychology*, Vol. 35, New York: Elsevier, pp. 345–411.

Wright, T.A. and B.A. Staw (1998), 'Affect and favorable work outcomes: two longitudinal tests of the happy-productive worker thesis', *Journal of Organizational Behavior*, **20**, 1–23.

3. Cognition and governance: why incentives have to take a back seat

Siegwart Lindenberg

Can we get by with 'thin' notions of cognition and motivation as microfoundations for a theory of governance inside firms? This question is considered crucial for the development of the field and the answer given in this chapter is: no, we can not. The chapter takes Williamson's elaboration of an interest alignment approach with private orderings as one of the two prototypes of organizational governance. The underlying notions of cognition (as information impactedness) and motivation (as guile) are shown to be too thin to deal with the problems that arise in the kind of governance that gives pride of place to interest alignment, let alone to come up with solutions for alternative forms of governance. The chapter presents microfoundations that are much 'thicker' with regard to cognitions and motivation by focusing on overarching goals and by being informed by the state of the art in cognitive (social) psychology and sociology, neuroscience and evolutionary theory. It is shown that on the basis of such microfoundations, it is possible to pinpoint the shortcomings of the interest alignment approach (cum private orderings) and to formulate an alternative prototype of governance structures that is based on goal integration rather than interest alignment. A central feature deriving from the microfoundations that helped construct this prototype is that it is essential to base governance on the collaborative nature of organizations and on the precariousness of the collective orientation of their members.

INTRODUCTION

Organizations are social constructions in which a number of individuals pursue certain goals in a coordinated manner. Governance in organizations is comprised of ways to further this coordination. Why is it important to deal with cognitive issues when dealing with the internal functioning of organizations? There are basically two inter-related answers to this question. Firstly, in order to understand and possibly influence the governance structure of an organization in a proper way, one needs to have theory in place that can furnish the microfoundations for the processes that go on in organizations (Abell et al. 2008; Lindenberg 2003). Governance is the structured way in which individuals are brought to act in a coordinated way that furthers organizational goals, be these goals imposed or jointly established. It has become clear by now that microfoundations for theories that deal with goals must deal with an integration of cognitive and motivational aspects (Lindenberg 2006).

Secondly, some comparative institutional analyses, such as Williamson's approach based on a combination of bounded rationality and opportunism, did consider the joint effects of cognitions and motivations. However, so far, the underlying theory used could

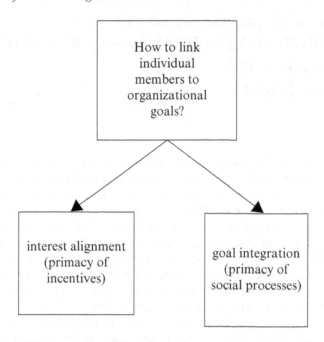

Figure 3.1   Two different ways to link individual to organizational goals

only deal with very thin notions of both cognition (as information impactedness) and motivation (as guile or opportunism).

In this chapter, I will focus on the currently most prominent approach to governance in organizations (which uses the thin notions of cognition and motivation) and I will contrast it with an approach in which the considerable variety of cognitive aspects (and their interrelations with motivations) and their dynamic interrelations are explicitly brought to bear. For this exposition, I make use of the fact that governance structures can be seen as layered sets of rules, procedures and practices. I will deal with two such layers. Firstly, there is the core set that specifies the main governance approach. Then there is the supportive belt (see Lakatos 1970), a second layer that is meant to supply support for the core and neutralize the most important shortcomings of the core. Governance structures should be compared with regard to both core and supportive belt.

Once 'organization' rather than 'market' has been chosen as mode of operation, it is an important issue all by itself how organizational goals come about (for example whether they are decided on by the leadership or jointly arrived at). However, given that there are organizational goals (no matter where they come from), an important question is how governance structures influence the link of individual members of the organization with organizational goals and thereby help to realize the actual coordination of individual efforts.[1] In this chapter, I will focus on this question.

What are the most important modes of governance for organizations? There are many modes of governance, but true to the important role played by goals, one can distinguish two prototypes of governance (see Figure 3.1). One way is to align the individual and organizational goals mostly by incentives that make self-interested behavior of the individual align with the realization of the organizational goals. A very different way is to integrate the goals of the individual with the goals of the organization, a process that may be called 'goal integration'. Here, social processes that help bring about and maintain goal integration have primacy over incentive instruments. Economists have argued forcefully that for governance, as for everything else, incentives have primacy. As Landsburg (1993: 3) puts it: 'Most of economics can be summarized in four words: "people respond to incentives." The rest is commentary.' And he goes on to say that a real economist insists on taking the principle seriously at all times. The question is not whether incentives have an effect but whether for purposes of governance they should have primacy. The goal integration approach would argue that for governance, social processes should have primacy and incentives have to take the back seat.

Of course, in the literature, one can find more modes of governance than just these two. For example, Nickerson and Zenger (2004) speak of 'consensus-based' hierarchy and contrast this to an 'authority-based' hierarchy. There is also the concept of 'network organization' (see for example Powell 1990; Van Alstyne 1997). However, I argue that consensus-based and network organizations are variants of the goal-integration mode of governance, not really separate types. For example, Nickerson and Zenger (2004) point to the importance of 'shared identity' for the consensus model, and when 'network organization' refers to an internal governance mode (rather than to interfirm governance), the important features mentioned are that people can trust each other to further common goals and that authority is not based on rank but on expertise (Van Alstyne 1997).

Before I can set out to deal with this issue, I have to introduce some microfoundational theory for the analysis of goal-related issues in governance. The crucial preliminary question is: what cognitive aspects are relevant when one deals with governance? In the following I will briefly expound goal-framing theory which focuses on overarching goals as the most important meeting ground for cognitive and motivational processes. The point will be that whenever aspects of norms and collective orientation play a role, it is especially important to pay close attention to cognitive processes. I will then compare the two approaches to governance and I will conclude with the message that in the light of insights into goal processes, social processes and incentive instruments are important, but that it is social processes that govern following rules, taking the initiative, and the sensitivity to incentives. An approach that is based on an assumed primacy of incentives cannot provide the instruments that are necessary to craft sustainable governance structures. Finally I will deal with the question: why do we see a lot more interest alignment than goal integration as forms of governance, if the former is inferior to the latter?

GOALS

On the basis of newer research in cognitive (social) psychology and sociology, neuroscience and evolutionary theory, one can safely say that any useful microfoundation for organizational processes must focus on the dynamics of goals. Goals are first and foremost cognitive phenomena. They are representations of desired states. But, at the same time, goals create links between the environment and motivational processes, so that they allow us to integrate the three components that are vital for microfoundations: environment, cognition, and motivation (Lindenberg 2006). The causal flows run between these three elements in all directions, from environment to goals to motivation, but also from motivation to goals and the perceived environment. Goals are the central element in this chain and so they seem to be the most promising focus for any microfoundational theory for organizations. The relevance of this kind of an approach lies in its ability to steer the elaboration of very concrete aspects of governance structures in a theory-driven way. Since there are so many goals, the crucial question is: what goals do we have to focus on for microfoundations of organizational behavior and governance?

Goal-Framing Theory

There can be many goals stored in the mind of an individual. However, for influencing behavior, it is necessary that a goal be activated ('focal'). Focal goals change according to situational cues and affordances and make the organism both selective with regard to inputs and prepared with regard to processing them, including differential expectations about the behavior of others. Therefore, goals are the most flexible form of functionality. This process of activation is often not deliberative and is quite automatic (see Bargh et al. 2001). Competing goals (say, those that have to do with the future and those that have to do with obligations) are inhibited to various degrees, so that the focal goal will capture most cognitive and motivational processes (see Gollwitzer and Bargh 1996; Kruglanski and Köpetz 2009; Marsh et al. 1998; Förster et al. 2005). Because there are almost infinitely many goals, microfoundations for organizational processes could not be specific enough if the most important goals cannot be identified. Goal-framing theory (Lindenberg 2001, 2008; Lindenberg and Steg 2007) does exactly that and in the following section, I will briefly introduce the most important features of this theory.

High-level (i.e. overarching) goals are so general that they 'set' the mind and control many different subgoals. A useful way to identify these goals is to take an evolutionary perspective. The functioning of goals most likely evolved with the development of the brain of primates and especially of human beings. Therefore, overarching goals should cover those aspects in life that take sustained and focused attention and are most pertinent to getting offspring into the gene pool (i.e. not just to have offspring but to have one's offspring survive to reproduce; see Cacioppo and Hawkley 2009): need fulfilment, acquiring and maintaining the means for need fulfilment, and fitting into the social context. The overarching ('high-level') goal concerned with need fulfilment is called 'hedonic', and it consists of the desire to maintain or improve the way one feels right now. Clearly there are many hedonic subgoals, depending on the needs that are to be fulfilled at the moment (hunger, sex, avoidance of pain and fear, affection, stimulation, economizing on effort, etc.) But they all share the overarching goal of improvement of maintenance of the way one feels. In order to engage in need fulfilment, one needs resources, and the goal concerned with this aspect is called 'gain' goal, consisting of the desire to maintain or improve one's resources. Again there are many subgoals, such as acquiring status or competence, and in more modern societies, also money. Surviving and raising offspring to an age when they can reproduce also requires intense social cooperation. The goal for this context is called the 'normative' goal and it concerns the desire to do what is appropriate according to group goals. Typical subgoals are to follow the situationally appropriate norms and rules, but also to cooperate with others in a joint effort to reach group goals. When one of these three goals is focal, it captures so many cognitive and motivational processes that it truly frames the situation. For this reason I speak of a 'goal-frame' to denote a focal high-level goal in combination with the cognitive and motivational processes that are activated by this goal. Each of the three goal-frames is linked to a particular neural system (Mendez 2009; Moll et al. 2005).

Balance: background goals and the a priori strength of goal-frames

Background goals Two important additional points have to do with the relation of these overarching goals to each other. Firstly, when one of the three is focal, the other two are not completely inhibited but pushed into the background to various degrees, thereby strengthening or weakening the relative weight of the foreground (focal) goal. More often than not, motivations are therefore mixed and it depends on the relative strength of the foreground and background goals what the final effect will be. When there is a conflict between focal and background goals, the focal goal will be weakened. For example, if focusing on enjoyable work comes at the expense of advancing in status, the hedonic goal-frame (foreground) and the gain goal in the background are incompatible. This only changes the goal-frame from a hedonic one to a gain goal-frame when the background goal has become stronger than the focal goal. Often, this is not the case and the conflict does not affect the orientation (the ordering of alternatives is still in terms of enjoyment of work, not in terms of status) but it may lead to the choice of less enjoyable (but also less status-incompatible) activities. Note that this is not just a cost–benefit effect. Foreground and background make a big difference for what information one is sensitive to, what plans one makes, and so on. When the hedonic goal is in the foreground, enjoyment, not status, will still be the major focus of selecting activities. Changes in enjoyment of activities will be much more keenly perceived than changes in status opportunities, and strategies selected will have to do mainly with enjoyment, not status. If goal-frame and background were reversed in this example, then the focus would be first and foremost on status aspects, with a reduction in activities that contribute to status but are highly boring or otherwise not enjoyable. Delegating such activities to others would be one way to deal with the conflict.

Compatible background goals strengthen the goal-frame. Thus, to stay in our example, activities that are enjoyable and help status advancement will be experienced as even more enjoyable. This may seem trivial, but such compatibility effects are vital for possible strategies to support a priori weaker goal-frames.

Different a priori strength The three goal-frames are not a priori equally strong. The hedonic goal-frame, being directly related to need satisfaction and thus being the most basic, is very likely to be a priori the strongest of the three goal-frames. In other words, in order to displace the hedonic goal from the foreground, the gain and normative goals must have additional supports. From an evolutionary perspective, the social context is there for the adaptive advantage of the individual and not the other way around. For this reason, the normative goal-frame is a priorily the weakest. The gain goal-frame, being linked to one's own resources, is in-between. In order to withstand the competition of conflicting hedonic goals, gain and normative goal-frames need to be supported by compatible goals in the background. In organizations, these supportive background goals are, in turn, often dependent on the governance structure.

INTEREST ALIGNMENT AS A PROTOTYPE OF GOVERNANCE IN ORGANIZATIONS

Because Williamson has worked out more explicitly than anybody else so far the core (basically a principal–agent perspective), its problems and its protective belt, I make use of his reconstruction of core, problems and protective belt. I present a prototypical view of the governance instrument, and that means that I do not describe what we find empirically but what theory says should be present or absent in order to achieve the desired governance results. In this sense, the prototypes presented here are theory-driven technologies.

The Core Set of Instruments for the Governance as Interest Alignment

Organizations can vary in the degree to which they require team work. But as Alchian and Demsetz (1972) have already stated long ago, the fact that organizations represent a separate governance problem at all derives from their being based on team work, even if the degree to which this is the case varies. However, Alchian and Demsetz (1972) then proceeded to analyze teams only from the point of view of team members' willingness to put effort into their (often) nonseparable tasks. In other words, they focus on the bilateral aspect of individual and organization, not on team work per se. Williamson also recognizes that teamwork is important in organizations. Yet, for the exposition of the core, he basically follows Alchian and Demsetz's (1972) bilateral lead. In this way, the approach remains dyadic: interest alignment as a form of governance is based on the view that an organization is a nexus of dyadic contracts. But the contracts are of a special kind: not exchange of money for goods and specific services but pay in exchange for willingness to accept 'fiat', that is, by being willing to be told what to do (Williamson 1985). With the help of employment contracts that make 'a priori' the centerpiece of governance, firms 'harmonize' bilateral exchanges that would otherwise lead to much haggling about what compensation is due for what kind of performance (Williamson 1981). In the approach of Alchian and Demsetz, typical for microeconomics before Williamson, cognitions are completely unproblematic (unbounded rationality) and motivation is simply maximizing behavior (see Lindenberg 2001). Williamson (1985) introduces slightly more refined (even though still very 'thin') notions of cognition and motivation. Human beings are boundedly rational and thus their cognitions are subject to what he calls 'information impactedness'. This means that people know too little to be able to trivialize the problems generated by the incompleteness of contracts. Thus researchers should not trivialize them either. In addition, Williamson sharpens the neoclassical motivational assumption by explicitly taking an extreme form of incentive-driven calculativeness as the default form of motivation. For him, a realistic view of human nature is self-interest seeking with guile, including the 'calculated efforts to mislead, distort, disguise, obfuscate, or otherwise confuse' (Williamson 1985: 47). Pro-social tendencies such as kindness, sympathy, solidarity and the like have no place in this view. Williamson goes on to stress that 'to the extent that such factors are acknowledged, their costs, rather than their benefits, are emphasized' (Williamson 1985: 391). This means that people are not restrained by norms or laws except when norms and laws affect their instrumental outcomes. In terms of goal-framing theory, it is clear that

Williamson assumes an extremely strong gain goal-frame (with no effects of background goals) to be the default (see also Stout 2011).

On the basis of these refinements, Williamson can now focus on the considerable incompleteness of the employment contract, especially with regard to things like the 'adequate' effort level. Given that incentives are seen as the major human motivator, the incompleteness of the employment contract need to be addressed by more or less explicitly stated incentives (both positive and negative; see also Hart 2008) that supposedly make the individual choose to behave self-interestedly in a way that also positively contributes to the realization of organizational goals.

The core thus consists of a contracted 'a priori' that is embedded in incentives that align the employee's interest with organizational goals. As a governance instrument, the core of this approach focuses entirely on the gain goal-frame.

Problems with the core of interest alignment

Core institutions are the bare bones of a governance approach. In practice it needs additional arrangements that deal with the most important shortcomings of the core: the protective belt. What are the shortcomings in this case? In a great advance over previous dealings with the core, Williamson has identified important problems concerning the core. They have to do with problems related to asset specificity, disputes and weak incentives, all three being problems that he identified as arising from specific situations in organization as opposed to markets. First of all, contrary to markets, organizations depend to various degrees on skills and knowledge that is specific to the particular firm (Williamson calls this 'human asset specificity'). This limits re-employment of labor and creates an interest in both management and labor to safeguard the employment relation from arbitrary termination (Williamson 1985). The protective belt thus has to provide such safeguards.

Secondly, because of the specificity of human assets in combination with the incompleteness of contracts, disputes (with guile) are likely and they cannot easily be solved in court. As Williamson (1996: 155–156) acknowledges himself, fiat may be invoked for 'good causes' as well as for 'bad causes', and the latter, if perceived as such by employees, easily lead to disputes that absorb valuable human resources for unproductive purposes. Employees too will use guile to haggle where incompleteness of contracts is high. Courts cannot easily distinguish between good and bad reasons for haggling and thus the protective belt has to provide 'in-house' means for resolving disputes.

Thirdly, alignment problems are different for different tasks (Bonner et al. 2000). There are tasks that allow proportional compensation, such as piece rate. However, in modern organizations (whether in the private or public sector), tasks that lend themselves to direct proportional compensation (such as production and clerical tasks) have become rare. Instead tasks that require a considerable degree of intelligent effort in terms of judgment, choice, problem solving and response to novel situations have invaded virtually all layers of an organization. Such tasks are difficult to monitor and thus create high metering costs. For this reason, they do not lend themselves to schemes that create strong alignment of performance and compensation. This allows only weak incentives inside organizations, which potentially exacerbates the danger of the incompleteness of contracts. The protective belt thus also has to provide solutions for achieving alignment with weak incentives.

The Protective Belt for Incentive Alignment

Firstly, with regard to the problem of avoiding the possibility of arbitrary termination, the protective belt should contain more job security for employees with higher human asset specificity. However, it must also contain the necessary training opportunities to build up and keep up the firm-specific skills and knowledge.

Secondly, concerning the importance of dispute resolution, special arrangements are needed. In conjunction with employment contracts, fiat can greatly reduce haggling. However, things can go wrong and fiat will not be accepted. Threat of dismissal is not a viable way to enforce fiat because organizations need to offer job security to employees with firm-specific assets. Appealing to the courts is also no solution because courts are not well equipped to settle disputes about internal organizational affairs. Thus, the organization must create internal 'private' orderings that are coupled with forbearance: grievance procedures, careful negotiations and renegotiations of the contracts, and labor unions as 'voices' for the employees.

Thirdly, weak incentives create special motivational problems and ask for special solutions in the protective belt. Since pay-for-performance cannot be uniformly applied, other incentive schemes must fill the gap. The most important tool to keep individuals motivated is to offer career opportunities in an internal labor market. This solves a number of motivational and selection problems. Even though incentives are weak (in the sense that they are not strictly contingent), there is the possibility to judge performance more globally and to reward good performance with promotion. In addition, the human asset specificity can be cumulatively built up. Even more importantly, given these kinds of reward, employees should gain by being willing to share firm-specific knowledge and skills with other employees and thus be motivated to do so.

All the problems are mitigated if the interest alignment approach is linked to positive reputational effects of managers. Choosing to work for an organization, employees should be able to base their decision on the reputation of the organization about how employees are treated. Knowing this, managers will then use their discretionary power (fiat) with an eye to such reputational effects (Williamson 1985: 261). They will devise formal and informal rules and procedures that are focused on creating order, mitigating conflict and realizing mutual gain (Williamson 1985: 240ff; Williamson 2002).

Problems not solved by protective belt for interest alignment

There are a number of important problems of both core and protective belt that had not been identified, let alone dealt with by Williamson. Others have provided incisive criticisms of the core and the protective belt (see for example Grandori 2004). In many ways, the present critique elaborates these criticisms in the light of the dynamics of overarching goals. Thereby, it is possible to gauge the possibility that the approach can be repaired by additional private orderings versus the possibility that it contains a fatal flaw in terms of goal management.

First of all, there is the empirical problem that even 'global' incentive schemes that target overall performance do not work very well as tools for interest alignment (Bonner et al. 2000; Weibel et al. 2010). In addition, incentive schemes tend to produce perverse effects because the governance structure emphasizes a gain goal-frame and therefore strategic behavior when important resources (such as promotions) are involved. In other words, even with the protective belt, the approach furthers strategic behavior by employees while at the same time the protective belt is meant to mitigate such behavior in the face of weak incentives. Why is this so?

The basic answer is that in any approach that puts a primacy on incentives, there will also be a primacy of monitoring for the sake of using the incentives. With this primacy, all the inherent problems of monitoring when tasks are largely inseparable will conspire to undermine the workings of interest alignment. Even for global incentive schemes (needed for promotion decisions), it is necessary to monitor performance in some way. For that purpose performance indicators will be chosen that lend themselves to measurement. However, for the tasks that require intelligent effort, performance indicators necessarily cover only a selection of activities. Since employees under this regime are in a gain goal-frame, they will also focus on those tasks that are monitored rather than those that are relevant for the realization of organizational goals (Meyer and Gupta 1994). Another source of perverse incentive effects is the possibility that employees focus on changing the incentive schemes or their application in favor of their own advancement or reward. Thereby valuable time and attention is siphoned away from essential tasks and performance indicators are corrupted (Milgrom and Roberts 1988; Smith 1995). These problems are not solved by the measures suggested by Williamson.

Career rewards are particularly important because they are both motivators and selection mechanisms. However, they are also highly problematic, because the global performance indicators are by and large linked to comparative rather than absolute standards, which puts a premium on competition. For all employees, the emphasis on competition for promotion will lower the relative strength of the normative goal-frame even more. By design, success in terms promotion is uncertain in tournaments. True, the hierarchical tournaments are able to select people who can perform well under competitive stress. For these winners, the scheme helps stabilize the gain goal-frame, which helps to keep a high sensitivity for incentive instruments, and it will thereby stem the dangers of sliding into a hedonic goal-frame with its high sensitivity to effort and other negative aspects of work that make one feel worse. However, the problems of indicator behavior and influence attempts are certainly not solved by tournaments. If anything, a stronger gain goal-frame will make these problems larger. In addition, the willingness to share promotion-relevant knowledge and to cooperate with others (who are actual or potential competitors) is lowered by a strengthened gain goal-frame.

For the losers (and there are likely to be many due to the pyramidal structure of the internal labor market), the picture looks quite different. At best, they will slide into a hedonic goal-frame with an emphasis on direct rewards such as social approval from colleagues and avoiding disapproval by refusing to compete against these colleagues (Lindenberg 1996). For many, the hedonic goal-frame will also strengthen the focus on those imperfections of the monitoring of global performance that have hedonic implications (such as feelings of unfairness). Because monitoring in organizations with regard to tasks that require intelligent effort is chronically difficult and incomplete, and because the causal attribution of effects to individual performance in teamwork is also chronically difficult, the dispensation of rewards and punishments used in promotion schemes will be likely based on a considerable degree of attributional errors. Among the losers, this is likely to produce feelings of being treated unfairly. They are likely to feel frustrated. Because monitoring and causal attribution are highly incomplete, people are also likely to feel undervalued. They see their efforts not rewarded, see others' lack of effort falsely rewarded, see themselves falsely punished for things they believe they have not done, etcetera. A shift toward the hedonic goal-frame is likely to create lack of meaning, a short time horizon with procrastination, and even goals of revenge, getting even, aggression and sabotage. Indeed, such feelings have been identified as a major cause of deviant behavior in organizations (Ambrose et al. 2002). Grievance procedures cannot compensate for the failures of performance assessments and causal attributions about who did what and who is worthy of being promoted. When monitoring is difficult, grievance procedures are not likely to rectify what has not been observed but should have been, or what has been observed as 'fact' but was mistaken. At best, they can create a feeling of being heard, of pointing to the gaps in the maze of assessment, and the psychological satisfaction that derives from not feeling completely powerless. Note that it is not the imperfections of the global performance assessment per se that is the culprit; rather it is the combination of the assessment with the competitive nature of tournaments.

This leaves a heavy psychological burden on issues of dignity and equity concerns to redress the perverse motivational effects. What place do such concerns have in this kind of governance structure? In an optimistic mood, Williamson believes that the zone of indifference, which is supposedly part of the employment contract, might not really create common goals ('goal sharing'), but it will create acquiescence, and that this might suffice (Williamson 1985: 249). Does it really suffice? Quite clearly, it does not suffice. Attention to aspects of collective orientation is lacking in every aspect of the suggested governance instruments. For example, Williamson explicitly mentions 'relational teams' where tasks are not well separable (i.e. where asset specificity is high and the ability to monitor is low). However, true to the dyadic contracting approach, he can say nothing about the functioning of teams. Teamwork in organizations necessitates intelligent effort with regard to cooperation and coordination on the micro level. When is it necessary to consult others? How are binding decisions in the team taken? Who is responsible for completing certain activities? How often and when will one meet to discuss issues relating to the common goals? Mathieu and Rapp (2009) point to role clarification as one of the most important aspects of this kind of team design, but what is important is clearly not just the clarification of the individual roles but especially the interplay of roles for the realization of the common goals. For this interplay, a certain orientation towards collective goals is necessary. Simon criticized Williamson for ignoring this aspect (Simon 1997: 263). The difficulty in bringing such 'team spirit' effects about by interest alignment is made even bigger by the fact that: (1) the governance is established to govern the individual, thereby focusing on the bilateral employment contract rather than on the jointness of the tasks; (2) interest alignment is linked to the presumption that employees will shirk and deceive the principle unless kept from doing so by appropriate incentives and private orderings. Both aspects emphasize the centrality of the gain goal-frame. This emphasis makes team spirit very unlikely. There is good evidence that people in a gain goal-frame tend to assume that others are likely not to cooperate (Van Lange 1992). In turn, if one expects others not to cooperate, one is more likely not to cooperate oneself (Fischbacher et al. 2001).

Williamson is quite mute about how these issues could be dealt with in an interest alignment approach. Paraphrasing Barnard, he claims that 'cooperation is jointly determined by social factors and incentive alignment . . . Informal organization facilitates communications, promotes cohesion, and serves to protect the personal integrity and self-respect of the individual against the disintegrating [sic] effects of formal organization' (Williamson 1985: 6). He covers such aspects with the term 'dignitary values' but what he really means becomes clear when he later adds that 'the firm will engage in considerable social conditioning to help assure that employees understand and are dedicated to the purposes of the firm . . . Effective adaptation in a cooperative team context is especially difficult and important to achieve. A sense that management and workers are "in this together" furthers all of those purposes' (Williamson 1985: 247). Here, the importance of a collective orientation (and thus a normative goal-frame) is clearly acknowledged, but how this might come about remains a mystery. He openly admits that he has no solution to offer other than pointing to the importance of finding one. 'I originally intended to include a discussion of dignitarian values and how they influence economic organization. The effort was not successful, however' (Williamson 1985: 44n). Yet, he finds that 'the importance of deepening our knowledge of economic organization in dignitary respects is enormous', and he adds in a footnote to this remark that 'the calculative orientation that economists bring to bear advantageously on other matters may be a disability on this' (Williamson 1985: 405).

Microeconomic theory only deals with gain goal-frames, leaving out the other two overarching goals and the cognitive and motivational effects surrounding these goals. Investigating the validity of the single gain-frame model of microeconomics in 15 very different societies around the world, Henrich et al. (2001: 73) conclude that this model 'is not supported in any society studied'. This point is also driven home by Alchian and Woodward (1988) who reviewed Williamson's *Economic Institutions of Capitalism* and concluded: 'We believe it is important to recognize the forces of ethics, etiquette, and "proper, correct, reasonable, moral, etc." standards of conduct in controlling business relationships.' However, 'we don't know enough about how such "moral" forces operate to say more than that they exist and should not be ignored in seeking an understanding of how the economic institutions of capitalism, or any other -ism, evolve and operate . . . Whatever the emotive language, "decent" behavior saves resources and enables greater welfare' (p. 77).

In short, when we are equipped with the insights about how goal-frames work and we look at an approach to governance that relies mainly on incentive instruments, we see that such an approach cannot adequately deal with the drawbacks of a single-minded focus on a gain goal-frame. From the point of view of the interest alignment approach, both the massive sliding into a hedonic goal-frame and the consequences of governance that fails to support (or even drives out) a normative goal-frame can only be vaguely registered as more or less mysterious negative side effects of the 'calculative approach'. Since overarching goals are not considered at all, there is also no way to trace the consequences of emphasizing the gain goal-frame from the start of the employment relationship.

GOAL INTEGRATION AS A PROTOTYPE OF GOVERNANCE IN ORGANIZATIONS

For the goal-integration approach, organizations are social constructions that focus on collaborative efforts, about getting things done together that could not have been done alone. Organizations are thus seen a nexus of joint productions (Lindenberg & Foss 2011) rather than a nexus of bilateral contracts. Joint production is a very special kind of phenomenon. It is a complex productive activity that involves heterogeneous but complementary resources and a high degree of task and outcome interdependence. In this reconstruction of the goal integration approach, I will make explicit use of goal-framing theory in order to highlight the potential contribution that close attention to such cognitive (and concomitant motivational) processes can serve for our understanding of governance in organizations.

What is meant by 'goal integration' is that the organizational goals and the goals of the individual are integrated rather than 'aligned'. As we will see, this integration consists in both fostering a normative goal-frame and fostering a motivation for joint production that draws on this goal-frame. In the past, there have been prominent suggestions about goal integration. Simon had already observed that governance consists to a large extent in influencing the premises of decisions. He claimed that 'the organization trains and indoctrinates its members. This might be called the "internalization" of influence, because it injects into the very nervous system of the organization members the criteria of decision that the organization wishes to employ' (1957: 103). He also stated that 'appropriate attention to . . . organizational identification substantially changes the theory of the firm and, consequently, theories of the economy' (Simon 1997: 263). This comes down to a suggestion of using goal integration for the theory of the firm, albeit with the wrong instruments ('indoctrination'). More recently, the economists Akerlof and Kranton (2005: 28) concur by pointing to the importance of modeling the employees' attachment to a firm and motivations to act in the firm's interest by means of the concepts of identity and identification; and they conclude that 'we see identity as the next step in the evolution of the economic modeling of organizations'. Earlier, March and Olsen (1989, 1995) had already suggested that organizations make certain identities salient because people operate by the 'logic of appropriateness' and will take the courses of action that fit with the identity that has been made salience. What is appropriate is specified by institutionalized rules (covering duties, rights, routines, roles, informal obligations, and standard operating procedures). 'Individuals come to define themselves in terms of their identities and to accept the rules of appropriate behavior associated with those identities. They seek the competencies required to fulfill their identities' (March and Olsen 1995: 38). All of these suggestions on goal integration come more or less close to using what is called a 'normative goal-frame' in goal-framing theory. However, even though 'decision premises,' 'identity', 'identification' and 'logic of appropriateness' seem to hint at aspects of overarching goals, none of these concepts is linked to a theory about the workings of such goals, of the way they compete, of the precariousness of the normative goal-frame, and of the importance of dealing specifically with joint production in addition to normative or rule-related ways of acting.

A normative goal-frame pertains to collective goals. However, not all collective goals are about joint production in the sense of a productive activity that involves heterogeneous but complementary resources and a high degree of task and outcome interdependence. A normative goal-frame could foster a strong sense of solidarity or tight cohesion, with passive individuals being governed by the collective. Yet, joint production is not the same as strong solidarity or tight cohesion, with passive individuals being governed by the collective. Also identification with the organization as a whole and its goals is not enough. Rather, the motivation to participate in joint production is coupled with a special kind of normative goal-orientation in which members of an organization perceive the environment differently than they do in purely 'communal' or independent action. Being part of a joint endeavor is seen as having one's own role and responsibilities vis-à-vis this endeavor. This involves sharing of cognitions about the relevant tasks, interdependencies, timing and possible obstacles to smooth coordination in terms of joint goals. Goal-related actions from others are mutually anticipated and cognitively coordinated with regard to temporal and spatial aspects of cooperation (Higgins & Pittman 2008; Sebanz et al. 2006). Rather than being absorbed by routine behavior, they engage in problem-solving, and being heedful of their and others' contribution to the collective goals (Weick & Roberts 1993), they try to assist others to do their bit (Tomasello et al. 2005) but also to sanction them if they do not (Ostrom et al. 1992). In ambiguous situations team members will not wait to be instructed but will take the initiative (De Dreu et al. 2008; Wrzesniewski & Dutton 2001). In short, realizing that one is involved in a joint endeavor mobilizes a focus on behavior that furthers the joint endeavor (Wageman 1995). Management of these integrated cognitive and motivational processes can thus be taken to be the central point of departure for a theory of governance that is devoted to value creation in situations of task and outcome interdependence.

The Core Set for the Governance as Goal Integration

For joint production motivation, the core can be said to consist of means to establish a normative goal-frame and to link this goal-frame to joint production motivation via task and team design. Let me briefly elaborate.

Since the primacy lies with the orientation towards the collective, the starting point consists of embedding social processes rather than the establishment of incentive schemes. The first important tool for establishing a normative goal-frame in organizations is to make sure that all members of the organization are 'in this together', jointly trying to realize common goals. This can be done by making collective goals salient from the start. Starting out with an emphasis on a gain goal-frame makes it difficult if not impossible to get people into a normative goal-frame later on (see for example Six and Sorge 2008; Wielers 1997). When employees are involved in joint decision-making in the organization, this is likely to help make collective goals salient (Hyman and Mason 1995). However, it is also possible that as employees join the organization, they are socialized right away into viewing the organizational context as one of reaching collective goals even if they are not involved in joint decision-making (just as a new member of an orchestra would be drawn into the existing collective orientation). This is quite different from a dyadic contractual approach, in which the first thing is the focus on the bilateral relation of the organization to the employee. An interest alignment approach introduces the new employee to cues that point to a very different context than a collective orientation. How sensitive people are to such cues can be gleaned from an experiment by Liberman et al. (2004). They identified a Prisoner's Dilemma game for their subjects as either a 'community game' (with a focus on a normative goal-orientation) or a 'Wall Street game' (with a focus on a gain goal orientation). In the former case, around 70 percent of the subjects cooperated; in the latter case, it was only 33 percent. The identification of what the game is about made all the difference (see also Pillutla & Chen 1999), because it is linked to a shift in the overarching goal.

Secondly, once the normative goal-frame is established, it needs to be linked to joint production. This means that individuals need to see what they can do for the realization of the common goals, rather than waiting passively for instructions or simply copying the behavior of others. There thus has to be an additional ingredient that creates this link between the normative goal-frame and joint production. For this to happen, employees must be embedded in functional interdependence with others (Lindenberg 1997). In other words, task and team designs must clearly be dedicated to joint production. There is no room to go into the design features in detail here (see Lindenberg and Foss 2011) but a few pointers may suffice. In order to serve this linking function, the functional connections of tasks and goals (within and between teams) must be objectively established and subjectively easy to recognize. In other words, the game must obviously be one of interdependent production. And plans for dealing collectively with problems that arise for reaching the common goals (such as delays, breakdowns of machines, conflicts, etc.) must be worked out on the basis of aiding joint production rather than social goals (such as harmony or avoiding blame).

A third important ingredient for linking a normative goal-frame to joint production is to hold employees individually accountable, even though it is a collective effort. An individual should clearly be aware of playing a responsible role in the interdependent realization of common goals.

Problems with the core for the governance as goal integration
There is first of all the problem of establishing collective goals of the entire organization rather than of the local team or department. When employees indentify only with a lower-level entity, we get subgroup egotism and fragmentation (see Shamir et al. 1998). Conversely, if we just get identification with the whole without individual accountability, we are likely to get 'organization men' (Whyte 1956) for whom loyalty, submission and impression management are the central focus and who develop little individual intelligent effort and creativity directed at the common goals (Bernthal & Insko 1993), and who are susceptible to fall pray to 'social loafing' (Karau & Williams 1993; Sundaramurthy & Lewis 2003). How can this be solved?

A second major problem of is the precariousness of the normative goal-frame. It tends to decay (Andreoni 1988; Fehr & Gächter 2002) unless it receives continuous support. In this respect, it is not enough to foster collective identification. How can this be done?

A third major problem is authority. Organizations need an authority structure. However, it is known from previous research that a feeling of being controlled can reduce the motivation to commit oneself to the work itself (Deci et al. 1999). This would also negatively affect joint production motivation. How can the negative aspects of authority structures be avoided?

The Protective Belt for Goal Integration

The first problem I identified above was that of establishing identification with collective goals of the entire organizations. In order to achieve identification with the highest-level collective goals, it is necessary to use symbolic management that is directly focused on identification. Effective ways of such symbolic management include a societally valued mission for the entire firm (such as IKEA's 'creating a better everyday life for the many') (Ashforth et al. 2008), and of the 'celebration' of the large collective entity in periodic face-to-face rituals (Islam & Zyphur 2009). In addition, it is important that the leadership, and not just the local supervisors, are driven by joint production motivation, because employees' commitment to the firm as a whole seems to be very sensitive to signals that betray what goal-frame leaders of the organization have (see Mühlau & Lindenberg 2003; Six et al. 2010). Any signal that profitability (for the firm or for the individual high-level managers) is a goal by itself rather than a by-product of joint production will undermine identification of employees with the highest-level collective goals of the firm. Another important instrument to bolster identification is to maximize the individual employee's understanding of the way functional connections of tasks and goals (within and between teams) work in practice, with all their difficulties and constraints. If the employee cannot understand how they affect others in the organization, and if they cannot distinguish between other people's difficulties in executing their tasks from their unwillingness to do so, the identification is likely to remain with local teammates whose tasks, goals and constraints are more transparent. Useful ways to achieve transparency in this regard are job rotation (Lindenberg 1993) and cross-training, in which employees are trained in the duties of other employees (Marks et al. 2002).

The second major problem that the protective belt has to solve is the stabilization of the precarious normative goal-frame and to foster the individual accountability. Here, additional support of the goal-frame from the background is crucial (Lindenberg and Steg 2007). As mentioned above, background goals can weaken but under special circumstances also strengthen the goal-frame. In this way, rewards can play an important supportive role without displacing the normative goal-frame. Following collective goals can be made individually rewarding in some way. This means that in addition to establishing goal integration by fostering a collective orientation, collective and individual goals must be literally linked within the person itself. This can be done by focusing on gain and hedonic background goals. For this purpose, some kind of contingency for such rewards must be present. From goal-framing theory, three important pointers can be derived on dealing with contingent rewards without driving employees into a gain goal-frame. Firstly, because in joint production monitoring individual performance (and thus accountability) is difficult, performance assessment should be focused not only on outcomes but especially on process (Lerner & Tetlock 1999). Losing time for one's own project by being called to help at various times with some urgent projects of others is different from not being willing to cooperate, even though the outcome may be the same in both cases (Perlow 1999). When supervisors have good information on both outcomes and process, the individual can be held accountable and good reasons can be distinguished from bad reasons for having done or not having done something. Secondly, the contingent rewards (both hedonic and gain) must be modest (compared to the non-contingent rewards), because otherwise they would not remain in the background and would take over as goal-frame. Very prominent contingent pay will drive the normative goal into the background in favor of the gain goal. Lavish hedonic rewards in terms of perks (office space, fancy car, expense account) will also drive the normative goal into the background in favor of the hedonic goal. Thirdly, the contingent individual rewards should express the link to joint production. This means that the rewards must be explicitly given as recognition for one's contribution to joint production. This makes it necessary to create language and procedures that link accountability to individual contributions to the common goals. This may be a costly investment, but it is necessary to have individual rewards and have them in such a way that they do not displace the normative goal.

Since joint production is based on interrelated teamwork, there should also be (modest) gain and hedonic rewards for group performance. Again, this should be given as recognition for the contribution to common goals a higher organizational level than the group itself.

A third major problem with the core is the authority structure and the obvious possibility that employees feel controlled, losing their motivation to work jointly for the common goal. In order to deal with this problem, the protective belt has to establish an authority structure that is not based on property rights or contractual fiat but on functional legitimation. In other words, rather than fiat or power, authority should ideally be linked to superior insight on what is needed for the realization of common goals (Lindenberg 1993). Directing others then comes down to directives in the service of realizing common goals, rather than giving orders (fiat). Conflicts can then best be resolved in the same spirit: what is best for realizing the common goals, not who has the power to silence resistance (see Alper et al. 2000; Behfar et al. 2008). This will also make spillovers from task into relational conflicts less likely (Simons & Peterson 2000), because conflict will mainly be based on technical problems rather than status problems or problems of defensive egos (Wittek 1999; Simons & Peterson 2000; Sherman and Cohen 2006).

Problems not solved by protective belt for goal integration
The protective belt just described is quite difficult to establish because it takes slow instruments, such as creating identification with collective goals, building a transparent task and team structure, building functional legitimacy, and creating an intricate reward structure linked to recognition for contributions to collective goals. All these elements take time to establish and take effort to maintain. After all, the normative goal-frame is the a priori weakest overarching goal. This difficulty and time-intensive establishment of the integral governance structure is itself a considerable disadvantage if time is of the essence. Compared to quicker ways to motivate people (say, with incentives, see below), it may seem awkward and cumbersome. In addition, of all the difficulty of establishing such a core and protective belt, the most difficult element will be the reward structure. It needs very careful calibration. Both too much emphasis on reward and too little will come down to the same thing. Too much emphasis will make the gain goal-frame take over, too little will erode the normative goal-frame in favor of the gain or hedonic goal-frames. Calibrating the reward structure is therefore the major challenge in setting up and maintaining this kind of governance structure. But ultimately, as with many things that take a great deal of investment (such as a good partnership), time may not be of the essence but long-run sustainable profitability would be.

CONCLUSION

Organizations are all about joint production which, in turn, rests on common goals (Lindenberg and Foss 2011). Can joint production be governed without members of the organization seeing it as joint production? This is the crucial question that concerns cognitions in organizations. In this chapter it has been seen that prototypes of organizational governance instruments can be analyzed with the aid of goal-framing theory in which integrated cognitive and motivational processes are explicated in terms of the dynamics of overarching goals. The three overarching goals are the gain goal (focused on resources), the hedonic goal (focused on the way one feels) and the normative goal (focused on appropriate behavior). Governance instruments determine which of the three overarching goals dominates (i.e. is the 'goal-frame'). Such instruments can be decomposed into core elements and protective belts. The dominant approach in the literature features a core that focuses on interest alignment with a primacy on incentive instruments. Problems with the core are supposedly tackled by the protective belt. Williamson's contribution to specifying the protective belt for incentive instruments embedded in contractual 'fiat' is still the state of the art. Yet, as Williamson admits himself, the underlying notions of cognition (as information impactedness) and motivation (as guile) is much too thin. For this reason, the protective belt runs into problems that cannot be analyzed let alone solved within a framework that only deals with one goal-frame (the gain goal-frame). The biggest problem is that the primacy of incentives creates both a primacy of a gain goal-frame (thus no normative goal-frame, no cognitions of joint production) and a concomitant primacy of monitoring performance for the administration of incentives (even if the incentives are weak). By definition, monitoring individual performance in team structures is difficult and can be fraught with unintended negative consequences that undermine the intended effects of the incentive instruments. Most importantly, the primacies of incentives and of monitoring make it virtually impossible to foster a collective orientation and motivation for joint production. There is no way this shortcoming can be repaired by staying within the interest alignment approach, since a strong gain goal-frame inhibits normative goals. Within an incentive alignment approach, there is no way to make the goal-frame weak enough to prevent it from crowding out normative goals. Even though Williamson says that 'cooperation is jointly determined by social factors and incentive alignment' (Williamson 1985: 6), the social factors can simply not be 'added' to social relations among members who are constantly pushed into a strong gain goal-frame by incentive alignment instruments.

The contrasting prototype of organizational governance (the goal integration approach) puts the primacy with social processes that establish a collective orientation up-front and that foster (by work and team design) a motivation for joint production with individual accountability. Individual and group rewards are important in bringing this about, but they must be couched explicitly as rewards for reaching the common goals. This can be achieved because rewards can be administered in such a way that they remain background goals, rather than displace the normative goal-frame in the foreground. Authority structures that are based on expertise rather than fiat also help stabilize the joint production motivation by avoiding the negative hedonic reactions to being controlled.

This analysis also has implications for the field of comparative institutional analysis.

Once it was a great advance to distinguish between markets and hierarchies (Williamson 1975). However, from the point of view of considering the dynamics of overarching goals, this distinction says little about how governance actually works. It says much more about how it should work if there were only a gain goal-frame (admittedly with the cognitive limitations of bounded rationality). Then useful additional forms were introduced by pointing to network and consensus forms of governance (Powell 1990; Nickerson and Zenger 2004). However, again, these concepts were not descriptive of how governance actually works. Rather they suggest that governance could either function wholly within a gain goal-frame or wholly within a normative goal-frame. Goal-frames however are dynamically interdependent. If one is interested in how governance actually works, one needs to trace the dynamic interdependence of the goal-frames and for that one needs microfoundations that take seriously the role of cognition in all kinds of organizations.

If it is true that the interest alignment approach faces huge problems of sustainability of linking the individual employees to organizational goals, the crucial question is why we see so much more use made of interest alignment than of goal integration in the empirical world. If joint production is not necessary, a market will do better than an organization. But if it is necessary, one has to deal with it in the context of governing organizations. After all, the most important kind of motivation in an organization is a motivation to operate in collaborative contexts. Because the incentive alignment approach cannot deal with this, ultimately there must be a long-term efficiency loss to this approach. However, long-term efficiency is often not what guides decisions about governance. Due to the difference in a priori strength of the goal-frames, it is much easier and quicker to establish and maintain a gain goal-frame than a normative goal-frame, and this holds even more for a normative goal-frame that is conducive to joint production motivation. Thus, if the short term is prevalent, the use of incentive tools will always appear handier and quicker. When things go wrong, as they must, repair is again handier and quicker by using additional incentive tools than by establishing the cumbersome basis for joint production motivation. In addition, incentive tools have gained considerable legitimacy. There seems to be a self-reinforcing loop: short-term prevalence favors incentive tools; which, in turn, increases the importance of disciplines dealing with incentive tools (such as microeconomics); which, in its turn, legitimizes the short-term prevalence and the tools used to govern it. This should not distract from the main conclusion that follows from this chapter: to the degree that longer-term interests come to prevail, quick-fix governance will lose its attractiveness, and scientific disciplines will become prominent that provide the underpinnings for governance tools of goal integration. Such tools are necessarily based on microfoundations that deal with the dynamics of overarching goals and thus with the interactive effects of cognitions and motivation.

NOTE

1. As I will argue later, the way organizational goals are established can affect aspects of governance. But for sake of clarity, it is better to ignore this possibility at first and only introduce it later.

REFERENCES

Abell, P., T. Felin and N.J. Foss (2008), 'Building microfoundations for the routines, capabilities and performance link', *Managerial and Decision Economics*, **29**, 489–502.

Akerlof, G.A. and R.E. Kranton (2005), 'Identity and the economics of organizations', *Journal of Economic Perspectives*, **19**, 9–32.

Alchian, A. and H. Demsetz (1972), 'Production, information costs, and economic organization', *American Economic Review*, **62**, 772–795.

Alchian, A. and S. Woorward (1988), 'The firm is dead; long live the firm. A review of Oliver E. Williamson's *The Economic Institutions of Capitalism*', *Journal of Economic Literature*, **26**, 65–79.

Alper, S., D. Tjosvold and K.S. Law (2000), 'Conflict management, efficacy, and performance in organizational teams', *Personnel Psychology*, **53**, 625–642.

Ambrose, M.L., M.A. Seabright and M. Schminke (2002), 'Sabotage in the workplace: the role of organizational injustice', *Organizational Behavior and Human Decision Processes*, **89**, 947–965.

Andreoni, J. (1988), 'Why free ride? Strategies and learning in public goods experiments', *Journal of Public Economics*, **37**, 291–304.

Ashforth, B.E., S.H. Harrison and K.G. Corley (2008), 'Identification in organizations: an examination of four fundamental questions', *Journal of Management*, **34**, 325–374.

Bargh, J.A., P.M. Gollwitzer, A. Lee-Chai, K. Barndollar and R. Trötschel (2001), 'Automated will: nonconscious activation and pursuit of behavioral goals', *Journal of Personality and Social Psychology*, **81**, 1014–1027.

Behfar, K.J., R.S. Peterson, E.A. Mannix and W.M.K. Trochim (2008), 'The critical role of conflict resolution in teams: a close look at the links between conflict type, conflict management strategies, and team outcomes', *Journal of Applied Psychology*, **93**, 170–188.

Bernthal, P.R. and C.A. Insko (1993), 'Cohesiveness without groupthink', *Group and Organization Management*, **18**, 66–87.

Bonner, S.E., R. Hastie, G.B. Sprinkle and S.M. Young (2000), *Journal of Management Accounting Research*, **12**, 19–64.

Cacioppo, J.T. and L.C. Hawkley (2009), 'Loneliness', in M.R. Leary and R.H. Hoyle (eds), *Handbook of Individual Differences in Social Behavior*, New York: Guilford, pp. 227–239.

Deci, E.L., R. Koestner and R.M. Ryan (1999), 'A meta-analytic review of experiments examining the effects of extrinsic rewards in intrinsic motivation', *Psychological Bulletin*, **125**, 627–668.

De Dreu, C.K.W., B.A. Nijstad and D. van Knippenberg (2008), 'Motivated information processing in group judgment and decision making', *Personality and Social Psychology Review*, **12**, 22–49.

Fehr, E. and S. Gächter (2002), 'Altruistic punishment in humans', *Nature*, **415**, 137–140.

Fischbacher, U., S. Gächter and E. Fehr (2001), 'Are people conditionally cooperative? Evidence from a public goods experiment', *Economics Letters*, **71**(3), 397–404.

Förster, J., N. Liberman and E.T. Higgins (2005), 'Accessibility from active and fulfilled goals', *Journal of Experimental Social Psychology*, **41**, 220–239.

Gollwitzer, P.M. and J.A. Bargh (eds) (1996), *The Psychology of Action: Linking Cognition and Motivation to Behavior*, New York: Guilford Press.

Grandori A. (2004), 'Reframing corporate governance: micro foundations, governance mechanisms and institutional dynamics', in A. Grandori (ed.), *Corporate Governance and Firm Organization*, Oxford: Oxford University Press, pp. 1–7.

Hart, O. (2008), '*Economica* Coase Lecture: Reference points and the theory of the firm', *Economica*, **75**, 404–411.

Henrich, J., R. Boyd, S. Bowles, C. Camerer, E. Fehr, H. Gintis and R. McElrcath (2001), 'In search of homo economicus: behavioral experiments in 15 small-scale societies', *American Economic Review*, **91**(2), Papers and Proceedings of the Hundred Thirteenth Annual Meeting of the American Economic Association, 73–78.

Higgins, E.T. and T.S. Pittman (2008), 'Motives of the *human* animal: Comprehending, managing, and sharing inner states', *Annual Review of Psychology*, **59**, 361–385.

Hyman, J. and B. Mason (1995), *Managing Employee Involvement and Participation*, New York: Sage.

Islam, G. and M.J. Zyphur (2009), 'Rituals in organizations: a review and expansion of current theory', *Group Organization Management*, **34**, 114–139.

Karau, S.J. and K.D. Williams (1993), 'Social loafing: a meta-analytic review and theoretical integration', *Journal of Personality and Social Psychology*, **65**, 681–706.

Kruglanski, A.W. and C. Köpetz (2009), 'What is so special (and non-special) about goals? A view from the cognitive perspective', in G.B. Moskowitz and H. Grant (eds), *The Psychology of Goals*, New York: Guilford Press, pp. 27–55.

Lakatos, I. (1970), 'Falsification and the methodology of scientific research programmes', in I. Lakatos and

A. Musgrave (eds), *Criticism and the Growth of Knowledge: Proceedings of the International Colloquium in the Philosophy of Science*, Cambridge: Cambridge University Press, pp. 91–196.

Landsburg, S.E. (1993), *The Armchair Economist. Economics and Everyday Life*, New York: Free Press.

Lerner, J.S. and P.E. Tetlock (1999), 'Accounting for the effects of accountability', *Psychological Bulletin*, **125**, 255–275.

Liberman, V., S.M. Samuels and L. Ross (2004), 'The name of the game: predictive power of reputations versus situational labels in determining prisoner's dilemma game moves', *Personality and Social Psychology Bulletin*, **30**, 1175–1185.

Lindenberg, S. (1993), 'Club hierarchy, social metering and context instruction: governance structures in response to varying self-command capital', in S. Lindenberg and H. Schreuder (eds), *Interdisciplinary Perspectives on Organization Studies*, Oxford: Pergamon Press, pp. 195–220.

Lindenberg, S. (1996), 'Short-term prevalence, social approval and the governance of employment relations', in J. Groenewegen (ed.), *Transaction Cost Economics and Beyond*, Boston, MA, USA; Dordrecht, Netherlands; London, UK: Kluwer, pp. 130–146.

Lindenberg, S. (1997), 'Grounding groups in theory: functional, cognitive, and structural interdependencies', *Advances in Group Processes*, **14**, 281–331.

Lindenberg, S. (2001), 'Intrinsic motivation in a new light', *Kyklos*, **54**, 317–342.

Lindenberg, S. (2003), 'The cognitive side of governance', *Research in the Sociology of Organizations*, **20**, 47–76.

Lindenberg, S. (2006), 'How social psychology can build bridges to the social sciences by considering motivation, cognition and constraints simultaneously', in P.A.M. Van Lange (ed.). *Bridging Social Psychology: The Benefits of Transdisciplinary Approaches*, Hillsdale, NJ: Erlbaum, pp. 151–157.

Lindenberg, S. (2008), 'Social rationality, semi-modularity and goal-framing: what is it all about?' *Analyse und Kritik*, **30**, 669–687.

Lindenberg, S. and N. Foss (2011), 'Managing joint production motivation: the role of goal-framing and governance mechanisms', *Academy of Management Review*, **36**(3), 500–525.

Lindenberg, S. and L. Steg (2007), 'Normative, gain and hedonic goal frames guiding environmental behavior', *Journal of Social Issues*, **65**, 117–137.

March, J.G. and J. Olsen (1989), *Rediscovering Institutions: The Organizational Basis of Politics*, New York: Free Press.

March, J.G. and J.P. Olsen (1995), *Democratic Governance*, New York: Free Press.

Marks, M.A., M.J. Sabella, C.S. Burke and S.J. Zaccaro (2002), 'The impact of cross-training on team effectiveness', *Journal of Applied Psychology*, **87**, 3–13.

Marsh, R.I., J.L. Hicks and M.L. Bink (1998), 'Activation of completed, uncompleted, and partially completed intentions', *Journal of Experimental Psychology: Learning, Memory, and Cognition*, **24**, 350–361.

Mathieu, J.E. and T.L. Rapp (2009), 'Laying the foundation for successful team performance trajectories: the roles of team charters and performance strategies', *Journal of Applied Psychology*, **94**, 90–103.

Mendez, M.F. (2009), 'The neurobiology of moral behavior: review and neuropsychiatric implications', *CNS Spectr.*, **14**, 608–620.

Meyer, M.W. and V. Gupta (1994), 'The performance paradox', *Research in Organizational Behavior*, **16**, 309–369.

Milgrom, P. and J. Roberts (1988), 'An economic approach to influence activities in organizations', *American Journal of Sociology*, **94**, Supplement, S154–179.

Moll, J., R. Zahn, R. de Oliveira-Souza, F. Krueger and J. Grafman (2005), 'The neural basis of human moral cognition', *Nature Reviews Neuroscience*, **6**, 799–809.

Mühlau, P. and S. Lindenberg (2003), 'Efficiency wages: signals or incentives? An empirical study of the relationship between wage and commitment', *Journal of Management and Governance*, **7**, 385–400.

Nickerson, J. and T. Zenger (2004), 'A knowledge-based theory of the firm: the problem-solving perspective', *Organization Science*, **15**, 617–632.

Ostrom, E., J. Walker and R. Gardner (1992), 'Covenants with and without a sword: self-governance is possible', *American Political Science Review*, **86**, 404–417.

Perlow, L. (1999), 'The time famine: toward a sociology of work time', *Administrative Science Quarterly*, **44**, 57–81.

Pillutla, M.M. and X.P. Chen (1999), 'Social norms and cooperation in social dilemmas: the effects of context and feedback', *Organizational Behavior and Human Decision Processes*, **78**, 81–103.

Powell, W. 1990. 'Neither market nor hierarchy: network forms of organization', *Research in Organizational Behavior*, **12**, 295–336.

Sebanz, N., H. Bekkering and G. Knoblich (2006), 'Joint action: bodies and minds moving together', *Trends in Cognitive Science*, **10**, 70–76.

Shamir, B., E. Zakay, E. Breinin and M. Popper (1998), 'Correlates of charismatic leader behavior in military units: subordinates' attitudes, unit characteristics, and superiors' appraisals of leader performance', *Academy of Management Journal*, **41**, 387–409.

Sherman, D.K. and G.L. Cohen (2006), 'The psychology of self-defense: self-affirmation theory', in M.P. Zanna (ed.), *Advances in Experimental Social Psychology*, San Diego, CA: Academic Press, pp. 183–242.

Simon, H. (1957), *Administrative Behavior. A Study of Decision-Making Process in Administrative Organizations*, 2nd edn, New York: Free Press

Simon, H. (1997), *Models of Bounded Rationality. Volume. III: Empirically Grounded Economic Reason*, Cambridge, MA: MIT Press.

Simons, T.L. and R.S. Peterson (2000), 'Task conflict and relationship conflict in top management teams: the pivotal role of intragroup trust', *Journal of Applied Psychology*, **85**, 102–111.

Six, F. and A. Sorge (2008), 'Creating a high-trust organization: an exploration into organizational policies that stimulate interpersonal trust building', *Journal of Management Studies*, **45**, 857–884.

Six, F., B. Nooteboom and A. Hoogendoorn (2010), 'Actions that build interpersonal trust: a relational signalling perspective', *Review of Social Economy*, **68**(3), 285–315.

Smith, P. (1995), 'On the unintended consequences of publishing performance data in the public sector', *International Journal of Public Administration*, **18**, 277–310.

Stout, L.A. (2011), *Cultivating Conscience: How Good Laws Make Good People*, Princeton, NJ: Princeton University Press.

Sundaramurthy, C. and M. Lewis (2003), 'Control and collaboration: paradoxes of governance', *Academy of Management Review*, **28**, 397–415.

Tomasello, M., M. Carpenter, J. Call, T. Behne and H. Moll (2005), 'Understanding and sharing intentions: the origin of cultural cognition', *Behavioral and Brain Sciences*, **28**, 675–735.

Van Alstyne, M. (1997), 'The state of network organization: a survey in three frameworks', *Journal of Organizational Computing and Electronic Commerce*, **7**, 83–151.

Van Lange, P.A.M. (1992), 'Confidence in expectations: a test of the triangle hypothesis', *European Journal of Personality*, **6**, 371–379.

Wageman, R. (1995), 'Interdependence and group effectiveness', *Administrative Science Quarterly*, **40**, 145–180.

Weibel, A., K. Rost and M. Osterloh (2010), 'Pay for performance in the public sector – benefits and (hidden) costs', *Journal of Public Administration Research and Theory*, **20**, 387–412.

Weick, K.E. and K. Roberts (1993), 'Collective mind in organizations: heedful interrelating on flight decks', *Administrative Science Quarterly*, **38**, 357–381.

Whyte, W.F. (1956), *The Organization Man*, New York: Simon & Schuster.

Wielers, R. (1997), 'The wages of trust: the case of child minders', *Rationality and Society*, **9**, 351.

Williamson, Oliver E. (1975), *Markets and Hierarchies: Analysis and Antitrust Implications*, New York: Free Press.

Williamson, O.E. (1981), 'The economics of organization: the transaction cost approach', *American Journal of Sociology*, **87**, 548–577.

Williamson, O.E. (1985), *The Economic Institutions of Capitalism*, New York: Free Press.

Williamson, O.E. (1996), 'Revisiting legal realism: the law, economics, and organization perspective', *Industrial and Corporate Change*, **5**, 383–420.

Williamson, O.E. (2002), 'The lens of contract: private ordering', *American Economic Association Papers and Proceedings* (May), 438–443.

Wittek, R. 1999), *Interdependence and Informal Control in Organizations*, Amsterdam: Thela Thesis.

Wrzesniewski, A. and J.E. Dutton (2001), 'Crafting a job: revisioning employees as active crafters of their work', *Academy of Management Review*, **26**, 179–201.

4. Knowledge governance: meaning, origins and implications
Nicolai J. Foss

This chapter addresses the distinctiveness of knowledge governance as an emerging field in economic organization. Specifically, it is only rather recently that organizational economists and organizational scholars have begun to systematically treat knowledge as more than just an additional constraint on the maximization problem. Knowledge can be subject to transacting, organizing and governing and can be influenced in terms of its growth, change, composition, and so on by the deployment of governance structures and mechanisms. The various ways in which knowledge and organization are intertwined are discussed, and it is suggested that a key explanatory purpose of knowledge governance is the explanation of heterogeneous firm-level capabilities. Other frontier issues, notably the inclusion of the governance of beliefs and cognitions in the knowledge governance project, are also discussed.

INTRODUCTION

Assumptions about the knowledge held by individuals have been an integral part of the economics of organization and governance since its inception. Thus, Knight (1921) tied the entrepreneur's judgment concerning the use of scarce resources to meet highly uncertain future consumer demands closely to the existence of the business firm (cf. Foss & Klein, Chapter 22 in this volume), and Coase (1937) placed the epistemics of acting under uncertainty centrally in his analysis of firm organization (Langlois 2007). The huge body of work in organizational economics that has been accumulating since the beginning of the 1970s has placed assumptions about how well agents individuals process knowledge (cognitive assumptions) and how they can gain access to knowledge (epistemic assumptions) (Goldman 1978) center stage.[1]

Given the impressive pedigree of work that somehow links knowledge and economic organization, what sense can we make of the often-voiced complaint that organizational economics theories somehow 'neglect knowledge', expressed with different force and in different ways by many economists and management scholars (Demsetz 1988; Winter 1988; Kogut & Zander 1992; Grandori 1997, 2001a, 2001b; Grandori & Kogut 2002)? Moreover, in what sense is 'knowledge governance' something distinctive? The overall purpose of this chapter is to answer these questions.

I shall specifically argue that it is only rather recently that organizational economists and organizational scholars have begun to systematically treat knowledge in a 'thick' manner – specifically, as something that is not just an additional constraint on the maximization problem, but can be subject to transacting, organizing and governing and which can be influenced in terms of its growth, change, composition, and so on by the deployment of governance structures (Williamson 1996) and mechanisms (Grandori 1997). In fact, this is (one interpretation of) what is meant by 'knowledge governance' (Foss 2007). Thus, much of the impetus behind the recent interest in knowledge governance has emerged from the critique of organizational economics on the part of those who endorse the 'knowledge-based view of the firm' (in its various incarnations). The critics argue that organizational economics tend to treat production knowledge as essentially homogenous across firms in an industry, flying in the face of a reality of differential capabilities. Echoing Richardson (1972), these writers argue this matter because differential capabilities are determinants of economic organization (notably the boundaries of the firm) on a par with (or perhaps even more important than) such determinants as asset specificity, frequency and uncertainty (e.g., Langlois 1992; Jacobides & Winter 2005). As Argyres et al. (2012) note, a number of prominent organizational economists – including Holmström and Roberts (1998) and Williamson (1999) – have, somewhat surprisingly, accepted this argument. However, as Argyres et al. also note, the knowledge-based view gives complete explanatory primacy to capabilities, and fails to acknowledge that governance structures and mechanisms may antecede capabilities. In fact, a key explanatory purpose of knowledge governance may indeed be the explanation of heterogeneous firm-level capabilities. I end by discussing this and other frontier issues, notably the inclusion of the governance of beliefs and cognitions in the knowledge governance project.

WHY 'KNOWLEDGE GOVERNANCE'?

Origins

The origins of knowledge governance are manifold. In their *Organization Science* dialogue on the 'knowledge and organization' nexus, Grandori and Kogut (2002) point to influences such as the growth of knowledge literature in the philosophy of science, the vast body of work on technology transfer, the organizational learning literature, and evolutionary economics. This pedigree supplies the 'knowledge' part. In terms of the 'governance' part, knowledge governance is nourished by the fields of organizational design theory and organizational economics (Grandori 2001a; Foss 2007).

In a broader context, 'knowledge' has been all the rage for more than a decade in a number of fields in management studies (e.g., Grandori & Kogut 2002; Eisenhardt & Santos 2003). Thus, a 'knowledge movement' that cuts across traditionally separate disciplines in management research has emerged. The strategy field has a number of approaches that place (firm-level) knowledge (e.g., capabilities and competences) center stage (e.g., Grant 1996; Spender 1996; Kogut and Zander 1996); the international business field is in the process of developing a view of the multinational corporation as a knowledge-based entity (Tallman 2003); network ideas that stress connections between knowledge nodes, often based on sociological notions of network ties (Granovetter 1973), are becoming increasingly influential (Kogut 2000; Ghoshal & Tsai 1998; Tsai 2001, 2002); and, of course, knowledge management has become not only a huge body of literature, but also a widespread organizational practice (Easterby-Smith and Lyles 2003; Spender 2005). What unites these ideas is the notion that the management and governance of knowledge of whatever kind has become a critical issue for competitive dynamics, international strategy, the building of resources, the boundaries of firms and many other issues.

The Context: New Phenomena in Need of Explanation

The origin of knowledge governance as an emerging field may also be seen in the context of a number of new *explananda* for organizational research that became increasingly visible with the advent of a number of tendencies that are often summarized under the rubric of the 'knowledge economy' (Foss 2005). Among these tendencies is the increasing importance of human capital inputs, immaterial assets and scientific knowledge in production, the increasing importance of immaterial products, the need to control in-house an increasing number of technologies (even if product portfolios are shrinking) (Brusoni et al. 2001), and in general to tap an increasing number of knowledge nodes, not just through internal but also through an increasing number of alliances and network relations with other firms as well as public research institutions. These tendencies are often seen as profoundly impacting economic organization and competitive advantages (Adler 2001). However, the mechanisms through which this takes place are not always transparent, and part of what knowledge governance is up to may be understood as an attempt to theorize such mechanisms.

Much emphasis has been placed on the strongly growing importance of human capital as a driver of changes in economic organization (e.g., Rajan & Zingales 2001). In management research the increasing importance of human capital has been reflected in notions of 'knowledge workers' and 'knowledge-intensive firms' (Starbuck 1992), that is, 'organizations staffed by a high proportion of highly qualified staff who trade in knowledge itself' (Blackler 1995: 1022). According to a prominent argument, such firms may be differentiated from 'traditional' firms in terms of organizational control by relying less on direction through the exercise of authority, eschewing high-powered performance incentives, and embracing 'culture' and 'clan' modes of organizational control. According to some this is more akin to a revolution than a gradual evolution; as Zingales (2000: 1641) argues:

> in 1994 a firm like Saatchi and Saatchi, with few physical assets and a lot of human capital, could have been considered an exception. Not anymore. The wave of initial public offerings of purely human capital firms, such as consultant firms, and even technology firms whose main assets are the key employees, is changing the very nature of the firm.

Virtually all of those who have written on the subject agree that tasks and activities in the knowledge economy need to be coordinated in a manner that is quite different from the management of traditional manufacturing activities. However, there is considerable divergence in the accounts of what exactly are the changed coordination requirements in the knowledge economy. Thus, some argue that 'traditional' coordination mechanisms such as price, authority, routines, standardization, and so on will diminish in relative importance, because knowledge-intensive production requires the increased use of mechanisms such as trust, communication, community, democratic procedures, and so on that can better cope with the particular metering problems and exchange hazards that are characteristic of knowledge transactions (e.g., Ghoshal et al. 1995). These scholars typically also argue that the increasing reliance upon cross-functional processes, extensive delayering, and empowerment reflect an aim to create highly specialized and motivated units by means of extensive delegation of discretion. Cross-functional processes substitute for hierarchy in the coordination of tasks. Scholars promoting this view will tend to see the boundaries of firms blurring and employment relations undergoing dramatic change as a result of knowledge networks increasingly cutting across the boundaries of the firm and participative governance being increasingly adopted. Others take a more hard-nosed and less rosy view of the ongoing changes in economic organization. An important part of the tendencies constituting the knowledge economy are an intensification of competition as industry boundaries are eroded, and as internationalization and liberalization increase. In response to such competitive pressures, as Adler (2001: 220) points out, 'firms are fine-tuning their management structures and planning processes, demanding greater accountability at every level, and enforcing more discipline in the planning and execution of operations'. As Zenger and Hesterly (1997) note, improved methods of cost allocation, more widespread use of IT and better measures of input and output performance have decreased the costs of monitoring employees and organizational units, in turn promoting a tendency to smaller organizational units that face more high-powered incentives.

With respect to the boundaries of the firm, many management scholars argue that trust-based ('community'-based) forms of organization emerge that can better handle 'innovation tasks' (idem.). Others point out that 'the buffering functions of management are devolving to the mechanisms of modularity and the market – informational decomposition, flexibility and risk spreading' (Langlois 2003: 376). This does not necessarily imply that the boundaries of firms blur; rather, firms specialize and disintegrate. Also, while a modular system often internalizes knowledge-intensive transactions in modules, it is entirely consistent with innovative efforts (Langlois & Robertson 1995). Thus, the information and knowledge richness associated with innovative efforts does not necessarily imply trust, rich information and knowledge transfer between firms, and so on.

In sum, the emergence of the knowledge economy has given rise to a rich debate on the nature of the knowledge-based drivers of changing economic organization, as well as how economic organization influences knowledge processes. Theorizing the underlying mechanisms may be seen as the essence of knowledge governance.

Meaning

The term 'knowledge governance' seems to have been first used by Grandori (2001a). She offers a series of examples of 'governance mechanisms' (a possible second terminological innovation) that support such processes as knowledge sharing and integration. Thus, decision rights, routines, rewards, modes of communication and so on are governance mechanisms that can be combined in multiple ways across governance structure and influence various knowledge-related processes via their effects on individuals' knowledge sharing, creating, integrating, and so on, behaviors. This conceptualization treats 'knowledge' as a dependent variable, endogenous to governance. However, no explicit definition of knowledge governance (as a new field or a new construct) is proffered. In Grandori's 'dialogue on organization and knowledge' with Bruce Kogut

(Grandori & Kogut 2002: 225), she explains that an important way in which knowledge approaches have contributed 'is in providing a new contingency factor for understanding organizational arrangements, as well as to suggest new ways to conceive the nature of organizational contingencies. Knowledge complexity, differentiation, specialization, complementarity, and interdependence are emerging as important contingencies affecting effective organization and governance solutions.' This treats knowledge (characteristics) as an independent variable, driving governance.

There is, of course, nothing wrong in treating 'knowledge' as both dependent and independent variables. Thus, some knowledge assets may effectively be thought of as exogenous; for example, capabilities take time to change. Other aspects of knowledge may be thought of as endogenous, and partly influenced by exogenous knowledge variables; for example, outcomes of knowledge integration processes in a firm may be constrained (or facilitated) by the capabilities that are controlled by the firm. Moreover, in a dynamic analysis, one period's exogenous variables may be taken to be next period's endogenous variables. Thus, capabilities may be taken as exogenous in the short run; however, they are obviously endogenous in the longer run.[2]

Nevertheless, for heuristic purposes it makes sense to distinguish knowledge governance with knowledge treated as an exogenous variable, and knowledge governance with knowledge treated as an endogenous variable. Given this, knowledge governance in the former sense may be defined as a sustained attempt to uncover how knowledge transactions (which differ in their characteristics) and governance mechanisms (which differ with respect to how they handle transactional problems) are matched, using economic efficiency as the explanatory principle. This is how knowledge governance is explicitly defined in Foss (2007), and more implicitly in, for example, Silverman (1999) and Nickerson and Zenger (2004), all papers that take their primary cues from organizational economics (particularly transaction cost economics). However, much of the capabilities perspective as it applies to governance issues also adopts the 'knowledge governance with knowledge treated as an exogenous variable' approach. Specifically, capabilities writers adopt a 'capabilities first' heuristic according to which capabilities have explanatory primacy relative to governance considerations, and can, for the purposes of explaining economic organization (typically, the boundaries of the firm), be taken as exogenous (e.g., Kogut & Zander 1992; Madhok 1996).

We may also think of a knowledge governance approach in which 'knowledge' is endogenous in the sense that the focus is on how governance structures and mechanisms influence knowledge-related behaviors, such as individual knowledge sharing, integration, creation, forgetting, and so on. Much management research in organizational theory, international business, strategic management, knowledge management and technology strategy has adopted such an approach (without calling it 'knowledge governance'). Team theoretical work in organizational economics may also qualify as a knowledge governance approach in this sense, as the focus in team theory is on how the design of communication channels and the allocation of decision rights influence organizational outcomes, such as the rate of approval/rejection of innovation projects (i.e., knowledge creation) (Marschak & Radner 1972; Sah & Stiglitz 1985, 1986; Garicano 2000). Economics work on human capital in labor economics and on entrepreneurship also has a bearing on knowledge governance (for details, see Foss & Mahnke 2003).

KNOWLEDGE GOVERNANCE WITH EXOGENOUS KNOWLEDGE

Capabilities and Economic Organization

While knowledge governance is positioned in the broad 'knowledge movement' (Eisenhardt & Santos 2003; see also Grandori & Kogut 2002), in historical and substantive terms it owes much to the long-standing capabilities critique of organizational economics. Capabilities theorists put forward that capabilities ideas hold the key to understanding organizational heterogeneity – a key issue in strategic management and other management research fields – while organizational economics is largely silent about this issue. To the extent that such heterogeneity matters to economic organization – notably, the boundaries of the firm – the capabilities view therefore holds explanatory primacy.

The first contribution in the research literature to make use of the 'capabilities' terminology in the context of understanding economic organization and to make the above arguments was Richardson (1972). Drawing on Penrose (1959), Richardson (1972: 888) argues that explaining the 'division of labour between firm and market' requires that we place the 'elements of organisation, knowledge, experience and skills' center stage. In a footnote, he mentions Coase's (1937) explanation of the boundary costs in terms of the relative costs of using firms versus markets as basic coordination modes, and adds that the 'explanation that I have provided is not inconsistent with his but might be taken as giving content to the notion of this relative cost by specifying the factors that affect it' (Richardson 1972: 888n).[3]

Partly because the capabilities idea did not catch on in management research and economics until the end of the 1980s, the discussion lay dormant for almost two decades. However, it was revitalized in 1988 in important contributions by Demsetz (1988) and Winter (1988). Both argued that the economics of the firm neglected firm-specific knowledge and how it shapes the boundaries of the firm. Later papers by Kogut and Zander (1992, 1996), Madhok (1996), Connor and Prahalad (1996) and others aggressively argued that economic organization was fully explainable in capabilities terms, and that no use needed to be made of the notion of opportunism (or moral hazard, or misaligned incentives in general; for a critique of this position, see Foss 1996). This position seems to have been abandoned in favor of an argument that capabilities ideas and organizational economics are complementary in an additive manner. In such an understanding, for example, capabilities theory informs us about which resources are needed to position in an industry and compete in certain ways, while organizational economics informs us about the optimal sourcing and organization of such resources. Such an understanding of the relation between the two perspectives is explicit or implicit in much work over the last decade or so (e.g., Argyres 1996; Silverman 1999). It may have been given legitimacy among those who subscribe to organizational economics by the fact that Williamson (1999) seemed to endorse it. Arguments that stress the additive complementarity of different theories are often made in management research (e.g., Mahoney & Pandian 1992). Note, however, that accepting the argument that complementarity obtains in an additive manner is implicitly a call for giving up theory development in the intersection of capabilities theory and organizational economics; in fact, it is a denial that there is a meaningful shared domain of application, because it implies that the relevant theories address different *explanandum* phenomena. Therefore, they are not theoretical rivals.

Capabilities First

However, some work has explored relations of complementarity that goes beyond the additive in greater detail. Such work recognizes that there is a meaningful zone of overlap between the capabilities view and organizational economics. In contrast to earlier contributions it is recognized that the theories are not rival, or additive, but that the variables identified in the different approaches may be seen as interacting in an essential manner. For example, Mayer and Argyres (2004) and Argyres and Mayer (2007) conceptualize transacting (i.e., contracting) as a learned capability. Learning in a contractual relation reduces transaction costs; as a result changes in contract terms can be observed that are not explainable in terms of changes in asset specificity but rather in terms of learning and capability. In early work that also stressed genuine complementarity, Langlois (1988, 1992) argued that transaction costs may moderate the link from the capability distribution in an industry to vertical scope. Specifically, he argued that under dynamic conditions firms may not be able to access the services they wish to access; suppliers may not understand what exactly is required of them. Such communication costs (Langlois calls them 'dynamic transaction costs') may drive boundary decisions in dynamic environments (see also Teece 1977), while the more conventional transaction costs of transaction cost economics drive boundary decisions in more static environments.[4] In Langlois's approach, capabilities are primary; transaction costs enter as a moderating force. Although written from a transaction cost perspective, the Mayer and Argyres papers also exemplify the dominance of capabilities: their argument assumes that learning and capabilities drive governance, rather than the other way around

The dominance of the 'capabilities first' heuristic is arguably caused by a prevalent conception that capabilities ideas remain our best shot at a theory of organizational heterogeneity and that they encapsulate heterogeneous resources, routines, coordination mechanisms, identity, and so on. 'Capabilities' is a much richer construct than, say, 'asset specificity'. Organizational economics has typically not emphasized organizational heterogeneity, which has not traditionally been seen as either part of the *explanans* or the *explanandum* phenomena of organizational economics. Thus there is little in, for example, Williamson (1996) or Hart (1995) that suggests why firms should be heterogeneous with respect to how they organize production and conduct transactions. Because the capabilities construct is first and foremost designed as an encapsulation of organizational heterogeneity, it has played essentially no role in mainstream organizational economics.

Dimensionalizing Knowledge and Identifying Knowledge-related Exchange Hazards

While arguments linking capabilities and economic organization have often been made in the management literature, the notion of 'capability' is, however, a macro-construct that easily suppresses the fine grain of the mechanisms that link knowledge and economic organization.[5] In contrast, the transaction, the contract or the individual agent are units that are more easily identified, dimensionalized and given to empirical measurement. Indeed, the absence of a clear unit of analysis has been highlighted as a source of confusion in the knowledge movement (Williamson 1999). Is it routines (Nelson and Winter 1982), or dynamic capabilities (Teece et al. 1997), or practices (Spender 2005), or knowledge assets (Winter 1987)?

Disciplines, fields or approaches are not necessarily characterized by unique units of analysis. Thus, the existing diversity when it comes to addressing knowledge in organizations may simply reflect that different research problems are involved. In general, what is the preferred unit of analysis should depend on the relevant research problems. The unit may thus differ depending on whether the focus is, for example, on knowledge sharing, integration or creation inside the firm, or how knowledge that, in some sense, resides on the firm level impacts firm boundaries. Knowledge governance issues are inherently multi-level and require multi-level theory and empirics. Moreover, the relevant units of analysis may differ, depending on the explanatory purpose at hand.

That being said, however, some units of analysis seem to be more generally applicable than others. Perhaps the most generally applicable unit of analysis for the kind of problems that knowledge governance seeks to solve is the knowledge transaction, that is, the transfer of an identifiable 'piece' of knowledge from one actor to another (Contractor & Ra 2002). Most knowledge governance issues seem somehow reducible to this transactional level. This also holds for macro arguments that posit that the boundaries of the firm are shaped by the firm-level idiosyncratic knowledge (e.g., Kogut & Zander 1992), for such arguments implicitly appeal to mechanisms involving knowledge transfer that ultimately turn on individuals (e.g., Langlois 1992). More generally, knowledge processes, such as knowledge sharing, integration and creation, are reduceable to (sequences of) knowledge transactions.

Taking the knowledge transaction as the unit of analysis obviously has the added benefit of linking up with organizational economics and an established framework for linking transactions to alternative kinds of organizing. However, the way of dimensionalizing transactions that has become dominant in organizational economics, namely the transaction cost economics triad of frequency, uncertainty and asset specificity, seems incomplete for the purposes of dimensionalizing knowledge transactions (cf. also Grandori 2001a; Heiman & Nickerson 2002; Nickerson & Zenger 2004). It is not clear how dimensionalizing a knowledge transaction in these terms assists the understanding of, for example, knowledge sharing where transactional problems may be caused more by the degree of codification of the relevant knowledge than its 'uncertainty' (whatever that might mean in the specific context). The knowledge-based literature has not been very successful with respect to forwarding, theoretically, dimensionalizations of knowledge.[6] An exception is the Winter (1987) taxonomy, which has been the basis for much subsequent empirical work (e.g., Kogut & Zander 1993; Simonin 1999; Grandori & Kogut 2002, and which presents the the dimensions of tacitness versus explicitness, system quality versus stand-alone, teachability versus non-teachability, and complexity versus non-complexity. Although these dimensions have usually been applied to more aggregate knowledge constructs (such as routines and capabilities) in the empirical literature, they may also be used to characterize knowledge transactions. Other dimensions may be relevant. For example, scholars working from a transaction cost economics perspective have suggested adding 'appropriability' as a relevant dimension (e.g., Oxley 1997), and Contractor and Ra (2002) suggest adding how 'novel' the knowledge is (knowledge with a higher degree of novelty is more costly to contract, absorb, assimilate, integrate, and so on).

In the context of knowledge governance, the implications of dimensionalizing the unit of analysis are that the costs of sharing, integrating and creating knowledge vary systematically with the relevant dimensions, and that the deployment of governance mechanisms to curb such costs should take this into account. Thus, along the same lines of reasoning as in standard transaction cost economics, knowledge transactions give rise to organizational hazards and costs depending on how they score in terms of the above dimensions. For example, in the context of sharing knowledge, knowledge transactions that are characterized by explicitness, stand-alone, high teachability, non-complexity are less costly to govern than knowledge transactions that score opposite on these characteristics. Transactions (in the context of knowledge sharing) that involve knowledge that is new, tacit, has significant system-quality, is hard to teach, and so on, are associated with cost of transmitting the knowledge from sender to receiver, (measurement) costs of ascertaining the extent to which knowledge has been shared, (monitoring) costs of inspecting input performance, and other well-known organizational costs. This treats governance as endogenous to knowledge characteristics. However, it is also possible to consider the reverse causality.

KNOWLEDGE GOVERNANCE WITH ENDOGENOUS KNOWLEDGE

Governance Driving Knowledge: The Economics of the Firm

Williamson (1985) admits that transaction cost economics 'freezes' technology, at least as a heuristic starting point. This would seem to rule out the possibility that governance can antecede knowledge in the sense that the choice of governance structures and the deployment of governance mechanisms within those structures influence the amount, type, quality, and so on of the knowledge that is shared, integrated, created, and so on. However, one should not confuse heuristic assumptions with substantive theory. In fact, classical organizational economics has right from the beginning identified many theoretical mechanisms that have the potential to link governance and knowledge (although, as we shall see, that potential has mainly been realized in management research).

Thus, Alchian and Demsetz (1972) argued that a key purpose of the 'specialized surrogate market' of the firm is to gain superior (relative to other firms) knowledge about productivities, and the efficient matching of employees and activities. Thus, the existence of the firm is directly linked to the ability to gain and deploy superior knowledge. A similar argument can be derived from Williamson et al.'s (1975) point that an advantage of intra-firm labor allocation is that it can take advantage of costly-to-communicate rating information. Alchian (1984) stressed the relational rents stemming from improved information gained by repeated association. Such rents rooted in superior knowledge may give rise to opportunistic haggling that is best controlled within the firm. Sah and Stiglitz (1985) explained how organizational structures may be conceptualized as structures for evaluating projects, and different structures will yield different evaluation outcomes. Thus, the knowledge-related activity of evaluating, for example, innovation projects is directly linked to internal organization. Jensen and Meckling (1992) examine how delegation of decision rights influence the utilization of locally held knowledge, which places knowledge utilization center stage. Many papers in agency theory have explicitly linked organizational practices, such as the up-or-out mechanism, to human capital accumulation (Prendergast 1993).

A succinct way of understanding 'governance' is that it is the formal and informal allocation of decision (or property) rights and the mechanisms that enforce such rights (Jones 1983). This rights allocation and the accompanying enforcement mechanisms constitute the distribution of authority, the attributes of governance mechanisms, organizational structure, and other aspects of formal organization, but clearly also relates to, for example, social ties and networks inside firms. An allocation of property rights is also an allocation of incentives (Barzel 1997), including incentives to search for knowledge, share knowledge, accumulate human capital, leverage knowledge capital, and so on. Moreover, property rights influence bargaining powers (Hart 1995). Thus, the allocation of property rights, in terms of both overall governance structures (i.e., the allocation of ownership rights) and the governance mechanisms inside those structures (which specify the allocation of, e.g., decision rights) would be expected to influence knowledge processes. For example, the specification of income rights in a governance structure directly influence how much each participating individual appropriates of the value created by interaction in the relevant governance structure. Appropriation matters to knowledge processes, for example, because employee incentives to search for, share, create and integrate knowledge are influenced by how much they can appropriate.[7]

Thus, several theoretical mechanisms link governance and knowledge. It is true that organizational economics has refrained from making a major issue of why such mechanisms should work differently in different firms (in this sense, the capabilities critique is valid). However, it is not at variance with organizational economics to posit that managers face different constraints, or have different utility functions, and will therefore make different choices. Neither is it inconsistent with organizational economics to posit that such choices are path-dependent (Williamson 1996; Argyres & Liebeskind 1999). Thus, the mainstream economics of the firm has a huge potential to deal effectively with knowledge governance issues. However, so far, rather few organizational economists have risen to the challenge (but see, e.g., Garicano 2000).

Governance Driving Knowledge: Beyond the Mainstream Economics of the Firm

In contrast, the exploration of knowledge governance has been thriving in management research. Thus, different branches of management research provides examples of work in the 'governance driving knowledge' vein, such as work relating to how multinational corporations leverage human resource management systems to promote knowledge transfer between subsidiaries (cf. Minbaeva et al. 2003); research into how governance mechanisms are deployed to knowledge-based strategic alliances (Mowery et al. 1996; Oxley 1997); work on the governance of human capital-intensive organizations (Child & McGrath 2001; Teece 2003); the organizational antecedents to the absorption of knowledge held by outside stakeholders (Foss et al. 2011); the link between control of knowledge assets and the appropriation of surplus from relations (Coff 1999; Coff & Blyler 2003); the provision of rewards to knowledge workers (Osterloh & Frey 2000; Reinholt et al. 2011); and the impact of job design and communication on the motivation to share knowledge (Foss et al. 2009). This research stream took off at the end of the 1990s, as the emerging knowledge movement in management research made contact with scholars who worked on organizational structure, design and human resources (HR) issues, often from a partly economics-based perspective.

Thus, in an early and influential paper Osterloh and Frey (2000) examine how knowledge transfer is influenced by organizational design. They identify a number of exchange hazards that beset internal knowledge transactions, argue that the transfer of tacit knowledge cannot be accomplished by contracting, and point out that it is difficult to sanction employees for holding back tacit knowledge. Therefore, the management of individual motivation becomes central. Firms have access to mechanisms (that markets do not) to manage intrinsic motivation, such as participation which signifies agreement on common goals and raises employees' self-determination, thereby strengthening intrinsic motivation and personal relationships. In turn, this allows for establishing psychological contracts based on emotional loyalties, which in turn raise the intrinsic motivation to cooperate. In contrast, too heavy-handed use of market-like incentives may crowd out intrinsic motivation. This chapter is one of the first of an increasing number of papers that link governance and knowledge processes in an explicit multi-level argument through the mediating effect of employee motivation (e.g., Gottschalg & Zollo 2007; Minbaeva et al. 2003; Foss et al. 2009).

Nickerson and Zenger (2004) seek to combine transaction cost economics and complexity theory (Simon 1962; Kauffman 1995) in the explanation of how alternative organizational forms influence the efficient production of valuable knowledge. The unit of analysis for knowledge generation is a specific problem, the value of which is determined by the values in the array of possible solutions and the cost of discovering a particularly valuable problem. The solution to complex problems is assumed to represent unique combinations or syntheses of existing knowledge. Problems differ according to their decomposability. Decomposable problems involve limited interaction, whereas non-decomposable problems involve extensive interaction. This has important implications for the type of searching for a solution. Non-decomposable problems require individuals to share their specialized knowledge, which raises knowledge-related exchange hazards. Three distinct governance structures and their suitability for problems with differing characteristics are examined: markets, authority-based hierarchies and consensus-based hierarchies. Briefly, markets are ideally suited when problems are decomposable and directional search is desired; consensus-based hierarchy creates high organizational costs and should only be adopted when the benefits for consensus are high, which is for problems that are highly complex and non-decomposable; finally, authority-based hierarchy is superior to markets in supporting heuristic search, but inferior in supporting directional search. The authors propose that authority-based hierarchies are best suited to a range of problems that are moderately complex.

Nickerson and Zenger's (2004) reasoning is an ingenious adaptation of fairly standard transaction cost economics. As such it relies on the notion of 'discrete structural alternatives' (i.e., the three Williamsonian governance structures). In contrast, Grandori (1997, 2001a) analyzes the various kinds of governance mechanisms that govern the transfer, sharing and integration of knowledge between and within firms. She concludes that the portfolio of mechanisms that are effectively employable between firms to link nodes of specialized knowledge can hardly be distinguished from those mechanisms employable within firms. An implication of her discussion is a denial of the strong emphasis on discrete governance structures in transaction cost economics. This is exactly contrary to the thrust of the Nickerson and Zenger (2004) discussion which builds off the Williamsonian emphasis on discrete governance structures that embody fixed constellations of governance mechanisms. Through a series of practical examples of knowledge governance, Grandori argues that various kinds of governance mechanisms are typically not specific to governance structures.[8]

One future development path for knowledge governance lies in opting for higher micro-specificity than is contained in the notion of governance structure. Governance structures can indeed contain different kinds of governing mechanisms in ways that may differ significantly across different manifestations of the 'same' structure. This also means that it is hard to make clear predictions regarding how exactly governance structures drive knowledge processes. A more fine-grained approach is to explore the various ways in which governance mechanisms combine to drive knowledge processes and what are the relations of complementarity and substitutability between governance mechanisms in this process. Such an undertaking will call on the skills and insights of organizational behavior and human resource management scholars.

THE FURTHER REACHES OF KNOWLEDGE GOVERNANCE: DEALING WITH BOUNDED RATIONALITY AND ITS RAMIFICATIONS

Epistemic and Cognitive Assumptions in Organizational Economics

The conjecture that animates knowledge governance is that it is possible to bring knowledge considerations into the corpus of established organizational economics and organizational design in a 'thick' manner, in the sense of dealing substantially with phenomena like tacit knowledge, differential capabilities and learning; phenomena that are not easily aligned with the standard economics paradigm of asymmetric and imperfect information.

However, such integration takes place on several levels. One is the level of empirical research where such integrative efforts may be a matter of throwing a couple of knowledge-related variables into otherwise entirely standard designs derived from, say, transaction cost economics. Another one is the level of theoretical inquiry. Here the situation is quite different. It is arguable that a concern with the role of knowledge in the context of economic organization may necessitate a re-evaluation of a number of the fundamental assumptions that are often used to guide theory-building in the economics of organization (e.g., Bayesian and game-theoretical foundations).

Organizational economics makes strong assumptions about the cognitive powers of agents. Like virtually all of formal, mainstream economics, it assumes cognitive homogeneity, correctness and constancy: agents hold the same, correct, model of the world, and that model does not change. These assumptions are built into formal contract theory (i.e., agency theory and property rights theory) through the assumption that payoffs, strategies, the structure of the game, and so on are common knowledge. Bounded rationality is occasionally invoked as a necessary part of the theory of the firm, particularly by Williamson (1985, 1996), but most of the contracting problems studied in the modern theory of the firm require only asymmetric information (Hart 1990). Indeed, bounded rationality seems to serve little function beyond justifying the assumption that contracts are incomplete (Foss 2001). Likewise, because of the Bayesian underpinning of game-theoretic contract theory, Knightian uncertainty, or any notion of open-endedness or indeterminacy, has no role to play.

Because of these epistemic and cognitive assumptions, there is little or no role for governing knowledge in the wider sense of the governance of cognitive representations, including defining heuristics for dealing with Knightian uncertainty (Grandori 2001b, 2010). However, as Phelps (2006: 13) observes:

> work on contracts has posited, explicitly or implicitly, that the parties to a contract share identical 'rational expectations,' since they have the identical model of the world. Work in that vein does not fit in a theory of capitalist economies, in which views are never homogenous and may be wildly diverse.

Demsetz (1988) argues that organizational economics suffers from a fundamental asymmetry: knowledge for the purpose of decision-making is assumed to be scarce (as in agency models with their reliance on asymmetric information), while knowledge for the purpose of production is free. Demsetz argues that taking scarce production knowledge into account implies a different theory of firm boundaries (roughly akin to what was discussed above as the capabilities view). However, the problem is deeper than Demsetz posits: standard theories assume that knowledge may be costly, but decision-making is free in the sense that, equipped with sufficient knowledge, decision-makers can always compute an optimal solution to any decision problem. This is also reflected in the idea that differences in beliefs among individuals can be completely explained by differences in information and that individuals are not only (fully) rational in the sense of being capable of maximizing expected utility, but also ascribes such rationality to others. These tenets are contradicted by the notion of bounded rationality and its various ramifications.

Bounded Rationality and Economic Organization

An important aspect of knowledge in the context of economic organization is bounded rationality, which not only speaks to the efficiency with which decision-makers process knowledge (Marschak & Radner 1972; Garicano 2000), but also to issues of cognitive representations in complex and uncertain environments (Gavetti & Levinthal 2000; Grandori 2001b; Hatchuel 2001). Furubotn (2001: 136) explains that:

> [g]iven the cognitive restrictions that constrain each individual and the costly nature of information, a decision maker can have only *partial* knowledge of the full range of options known to the society as a whole. He can no longer be assumed to know everything about existing technological alternatives, the characteristics and availability of all productive inputs, the existence and true properties of every commodity in the system, etc.

In the context of the theory of the firm, we cannot reduce the relevant decision problem to combining known inputs into known outputs in a transaction cost minimizing manner.

If decision-makers know only a small subset of the many possible input combinations and cannot perfectly foresee future preferences, 'the individual devising the firm's policies has to act as a true entrepreneur rather than as a manager routinely implementing clear-cut marginal rules for allocation' (Furubotn 2001: 139). The formation of cognitive representation in the form of setting direction, defining missions, and so on becomes crucial, as does making sure that a process of organizational learning takes place within this cognitive framework (Witt 1998). Entrepreneurs also form cognitive representations about which assets they need to secure the services from, the major contractual hazards associated with such procurement and the most effective ways of protecting against such hazards. This suggests that the same transaction might be governed very differently, as human agents may hold heterogeneous cognitive representations (see Argyres & Liebeskind 1999; Furubotn 2002; Mayer & Argyres 2004).

Many proponents of bounded rationality have tended to model economic actors as hard-wired to choose certain courses of actions: 'behavioralists tend to assume that agents are (1) hard-headed rule followers or (2) pre-programmed satisficers *ab ovo*' (Langlois & Csontos 1993: 118). Others have argued that Knightian uncertainty also has the effect of turning decision-makers into 'hard-headed rule followers' (e.g., Heiner 1983). However, as Foss and Klein (Chapter 22 in this volume) argue, building on Knight (1921) and Mises (1949), there is a more positive side to bounded rationality and uncertainty, namely the formation of judgment. Judgment represents a novel conjecture regarding the use of resources for servicing preferences, resides in the head of an entrepreneur (or in the heads of the members of an entrepreneurial team), is difficult to communicate, and so on. This creates barriers to exchange, and to capture profit from his judgment the entrepreneur must deploy it in the context of his own venture, and hire employees who can work based on their derived judgment.

Governing Cognitions

Whereas the link in the Knightian story is from judgment to governance, governance also influences cognitions. Thus, Lindenberg (2003; see also Grandori 1997; Lindenberg & Foss 2011) argues that the governance of motivation – for example, to share, create and integrate knowledge – is first and foremost the governance of cognition.

Lindenberg's argument fundamentally derives from bounded rationality, because with standard assumptions on cognition, there is fundamentally nothing to 'govern' as individuals are cognitively alike. He applies the insight from (social) cognition research that mental constructs have to be activated in order to affect behavior, and that goals are particularly important mental constructs in which cognitions and motivations are intricately intertwined (e.g., Kruglanski & Köpetz 2009), in the construction of a theory of 'goal-framing'. Briefly, overarching goals combine cognitive and motivational elements. When they are focal (i.e., when they are activated at the moment), such goals 'frame' a situation by steering important cognitive processes in the service of the focal goal, a process in which motivation expresses itself though cognitions. More concretely, goals (and especially overarching goals) govern what we attend to; what concepts and chunks of knowledge are being activated; what alternatives we consider; what information we are most sensitive about; and how we process information (Lindenberg & Foss 2011). For example, goals may be directed towards what is 'appropriate' (the normative goal-frame). Or, they may have hedonic orientations (the hedonic goal frame) or be oriented towards personal gain (the gain goal-frame). Cues in the environment can drastically affect goals, thereby creating shifts in cognitions and motivations and the way they interact. Governance structures would have to be specifically constructed to deal with this interaction because it creates constraints on virtually all governance mechanisms.

Lindenberg and Foss (2011) systematically address how governance mechanisms affect goals. For example, they argue that authority structures that stress fiat or control rights as basis for the legitimacy of orders and instructions are likely to weaken the normative goal-frame in favor of a gain or hedonic goal-frame, and that group rewards that emphasize the contribution to common goals on a higher organizational level than the group itself support a normative goal-frame. Although this perspective is framed as a general one, applicable to all forms of organization, it is arguable that it is particularly applicable to the understanding of knowledge governance in organizations. The governance of knowledge raises distinct motivational, incentive and coordination problems in organizations, because of the difficulties of defining well-defined performance measures for knowledge sharing, integration, creation, and so on, and because of the importance of stimulating not just autonomously motivated behaviors, but, more specifically, behaviors that are intrinsically motivated (and thus conducive to creativity and learning) and socially motivated (and thus conducive to knowledge sharing efforts).

The goal framing perspective addresses different kinds of motivation, deriving from different cognitions, that are all in different ways important to knowledge governance. In particular, the perspective recognizes that undertaking different kinds of knowledge-related efforts require different motivations, and therefore different governance instruments. Thus, creative knowledge-creating behaviors may require a dominance of hedonic goal-frames are associated with intrinsic motivations, while the sharing of knowledge may require the dominance of the normative goal-frame that is more strongly associated with pro-social motivations.

CONCLUSIONS

In this chapter I have provided a characterization of the emerging field of knowledge, differentiating between two knowledge governance streams: a stream that endogenizes knowledge and identifies governance structures and mechanisms as relevant antecedents, and a stream that reverses this causality. The former stream owes much to certain currents in the theory of the firm, notably team theory and transaction cost economics, and to contributions to management research in organization, strategic alliances, product development and international business. The latter stream owes more to the capabilities view of the firm. This interpretation and account complements earlier accounts of knowledge governance, notably Grandori and Kogut (2002) and Foss (2007). To progress, however, the knowledge governance view needs to go beyond the notions of agency, motivation and cognition associated with its source theory. In particular, knowledge governance ultimately means more than the efficient organization of knowledge-related transactions, activities or behaviors: it also means governing the cognitions of individuals, and therefore the knowledge that is pragmatically applied to make sense out of situations and what should properly be done in those situations. Although the knowledge governance approach has historically developed from the economic theory of the firm, organizational design perspectives, the capabilities view and knowledge management, in the future knowledge governance will benefit from closer liaisons with cognitive science and the micro-organizational behavior literature.

NOTES

1. For example, agency theory and its game-theoretical foundations make several explicit, and often quite extreme, assumptions on these domains (e.g., shared common priors, common knowledge, specific assumptions about what exactly is asymmetric information) (Foss & Stea 2011). Equilibrium outcomes in terms of contracting, levels of monitoring, and so on are crucially dependent on what exactly is assumed about knowledge in these models. More generally, asymmetric information, ignorance about future contingencies, and ambiguity concerning contract terms ('bounded rationality') are invoked to explain imperfect and incomplete contracting, ownership patterns and incentive design.
2. While organizational economics suggests that both 'knowledge' (e.g., human capital investments) and 'governance' (e.g., ownership patterns) are chosen simultaneously (as in Hart 1995), and thus both are choice variables, the choice itself may still be constrained by pre-existing capabilities. For example, some human capital investments make sense, given the business that the firm is in, while others do not.
3. Unlike most subsequent research, Richardson explicitly dimensionalizes capabilities (in terms of the extent to which capabilities in adjacent stages of the value chain are 'similar' and 'complementary') and argues that the resulting taxonomy has direct implications for the boundaries of the firm. Thus, he argues that similar and highly complementary capabilities should be organized by a firm, while dissimilar but highly complementary capabilities give rise to hybrid organizational forms, and dissimilar and complementary capabilities are best organized by the market.
4. In a related later paper, Jacobides and Winter (2005) build a model of industry evolution that ostensibly studies the co-evolution of firm capabilities and the costs of transacting and organizing. However, in spite of the announced co-evolution of transaction costs and capabilities, in actuality capabilities have explanatory primacy in this paper, as indeed in the rest of the literature on capabilities and transaction costs. Thus, capabilities and learning directly influence transaction costs, rather than the other way around; while the capabilities view and organizational economics are both part of the same theoretical edifice, the foundation consists of capabilities ideas.
5. As Argote and Ingram (2000: 156) noted, to the extent that there has been progress in studying knowledge as the basis of competitive advantage, 'it has been at the level of identifying consistencies in organizations' knowledge development paths and almost never at the level of human interactions that are the primary source of knowledge and knowledge transfer'. In contrast, organizational economics is unabashedly methodologically individualist, and therefore seeks to highlight action and interaction in the explanation of governance.
6. The many studies of inter-firm imitation and intra-firm knowledge transfer (e.g., Maritan & Brush 2003) tend to develop dimensions of, say, capabilities in an inductive manner, and the explicit or implicit dimensionalizations differ from study to study.
7. For example, social ties and networks are important for understanding the links between knowledge and superior returns, not just because of their potentially beneficial effects on returns, but also because such ties and networks grant legitimacy to the claims that employees may make on rents (Coff & Blyler 2003).
8. The extent to which this is a critical point against, for example, transaction cost economics is open to debate. See, for example, Anderson and Gatignon (1986) for the same point, but made from the perspective of transaction cost economics.

REFERENCES

Adler, P.S. (2001), 'Market, hierarchy, and trust: the knowledge economy and the future of capitalism', *Organization Science*, **12**, 215–234.
Alchian, A.A. (1984), 'Specificity, specialization, and coalitions', *Journal of Institutional and Theoretical Economics*, **140**, 34–49.

Alchian, A.A. and H. Demsetz (1972), 'Production, information costs, and economic organization', *American Economic Review*, **62**, 772–795.

Anderson, E. and H. Gatignon (1986), 'Modes of foreign entry: a transaction cost analysis and propositions', *Journal of International Business Studies*, **17**(3), 1–26.

Argote, L. and P. Ingram (2000), 'Knowledge transfer: a basis for competitive advantage in firms', *Organizational Behavior and Human Decision Processes*, **82**(1), 150–169.

Argyres, N. (1996), 'Evidence on the role of firm capabilities in vertical integration decisions', *Strategic Management Journal*, **17**, 129–150.

Argyres, N.S. and J.P. Liebeskind (1999), 'Contractual commitments, bargaining power, and governance inseparability: incorporating history into transaction cost theory', *Academy of Management Review*, **24**(1), 49–63.

Argyres, N.S. and K.J. Mayer (2007), 'Contract design as a firm capability: an integration of learning and transaction cost perspectives', *Academy of Management Review*, **32**, 1060–1077.

Argyres, N., T. Felin, N.J. Foss and T. Zenger (2012), 'The organizational economics of organizational capability and heterogeneity: a research agenda', *Organization Science*, **23**, 1213–1226.

Barzel, Y. (1997), *Economic Analysis of Property Rights*, Cambridge: Cambridge University Press.

Blackler, F. (1995), 'Knowledge, knowledge work and organizations: an overview and interpretation', *Organization Studies*, **6**, 1021–1046.

Brusoni, S., A. Prencipe and K. Pavitt (2001), 'Knowledge specialisation, organizational coupling and the boundaries of the firm: why firms know more than they make?' *Administrative Science Quarterly*, **46**(4), 597–621.

Child, J. and R. McGrath (2001), 'Organizations unfettered: organizational form in an information intensive economy', *Academy of Management Journal*, **44**, 1135–1148.

Coase, R.H. (1937), 'The nature of the firm', *Economica*, **4**, 386–405.

Coff, R. (1999), 'When competitive advantage doesn't lead to performance: resource-based theory and stakeholder bargaining power', *Organization Science*, **10**, 119–133.

Coff, R. and M. Blyler (2003), 'Dynamic capabilities, social capital, and rent appropriation: ties that split pies', *Strategic Management Journal*, **24**, 677–686.

Connor, K.R. and C.K. Prahalad (1996), 'A resource-based theory of the firm: knowledge versus opportunism', *Organization Science*, **7**(5), 477–501.

Contractor, F.J. and W. Ra (2002), 'How knowledge attributes influence alliance governance choices', *Journal of International Management*, **8**, 11–27.

Demsetz, Harold (1988), 'The theory of the firm revisited', *Journal of Law, Economics and Organization*, **4**, 141–161.

Easterby-Smith, M. and M.A. Lyles (eds) (2003), *Handbook of Organizational Learning and Knowledge Management*, Oxford: Blackwell Publishing.

Eisenhardt, K.M. and F.M. Santos (2003), 'Knowledge-based view: a new view of strategy', in A. Pettigrew, H. Thomas and R. Whittington (eds), *Handbook of Strategy and Management*, London: Sage.

Foss, N.J. (1996), 'Knowledge-based approaches to the theory of the firm: some critical comments', *Organization Science*, **7**, 470–476.

Foss, N.J. (2001), 'Leadership, beliefs and coordination', *Industrial and Corporate Change*, **10**, 357–388.

Foss, N.J. (2005), *Strategy and Economic Organization in the Knowledge Economy: The Coordination of Firms and Resources*, Oxford: Oxford University Press.

Foss, N.J. (2007), 'The emerging knowledge governance approach', *Organization*, **14**, 29–52.

Foss, N.J. and V. Mahnke (2003), 'Knowledge management: what does organizational economics contribute?' in M. Easterby-Smith and M. Lyles (eds), *Handbook of Knowledge Management*, Oxford: Basil Blackwell.

Foss, N.J. and D. Stea (2011), 'The principal's theory of mind', Working Paper.

Foss, N.J., K. Laursen and T. Pedersen (2011), 'Linking customer interaction and innovation: the mediating role of new organizational practices', *Organization Science*, **22**, 980–999.

Foss, N.J., D.B. Minbaeva, T. Pedersen and M. Reinholt (2009), 'Encouraging knowledge sharing among employees: how job design matters', *Human Resource Management*, **48**(6), 871–893.

Furubotn, E.G. (2001), 'The new institutional economics and the theory of the firm', *Journal of Economics Behavior and Organization*, **45**(2), 133–153.

Furubotn, E.G. (2002), 'Entrepreneurship, transaction-cost economics, and the design of contracts', in E. Brousseau and J.M. Glachant (eds), *The Economics of Contracts: Theories and Applications*, Cambridge: Cambridge University Press.

Garicano, L. (2000), 'Hierarchies and the organization of knowledge in production', *Journal of Political Economy*, **108**(5), 874–904.

Gavetti, G. and D. Levinthal (2000), 'Looking forward and looking backward: cognitive and experiential search', *Administrative Science Quarterly*, **45**(1), 113–137.

Ghoshal S. and W. Tsai (1998), 'Social capital and value creation: the role of intra-firm networks', *Academy of Management Journal*, **41**, 464–476.

Ghoshal, S., P. Moran and L. Almeida-Costa (1995), 'The essence of the megacorporation: shared context, not structural hierarchy', *Journal of Institutional and Theoretical Economics*, **151**, 748–759.

Goldman, A.J. (1978), 'Epistemics: the regulative theory of cognition', *Journal of Philosophy*, **75**, 509–523.

Gottschalg, O. and M. Zollo (2007), 'Interest alignment and competitive advantage', *Academy of Management Review*, **32**(2), 418–437.

Grandori, A. (1997), 'Governance structures, coordination mechanisms and cognitive models', *Journal of Management and Governance*, **1**, 29–42.

Grandori, A. (2001a), 'Neither hierarchy nor identity: knowledge governance mechanisms and the theory of the firm', *Journal of Management and Governance*, **5**, 381–399.

Grandori, A. (2001b), 'Cognitive failures and combinative governance', *Journal of Management and Governance*, **1**, 252–260.

Grandori, A. (2010), 'A rational heuristic model of economic decision making', *Rationality and Society*, **22**, 477–504.

Grandori, A. and B. Kogut (2002), 'Dialogue on organization and knowledge', *Organization Science*, **13**, 224–232.

Granovetter, M.S. (1973), 'The strength of weak ties', *American Journal of Sociology*, **78**(May), 1360–1380.

Grant, R.M. (1996), 'Towards a knowledge-based theory of the firm', *Strategic Management Journal*, **17**, 109–122.

Hart, O.D. (1990), 'Is "bounded rationality" an important element of a theory of institutions?' *Journal of Institutional and Theoretical Economics*, **16**, 696–702.

Hart, O.D. (1995), *Firms, Contracts, and Financial Structure*, Oxford: Oxford University Press.

Hatchuel, A. (2001), 'Towards design theory and expandable rationality: the unfinished program of Herbert Simon', *Journal of Management and Governance*, **5**, 260–273.

Heiman, B. and J.A. Nickerson (2002), 'Towards reconciling transaction cost economics and the knowledge-based view of the firm: the context of interfirm collaborations', *International Journal of the Economics of Business*, **9**, 97–116.

Heiner, R.A. (1983), 'The origin of predictable behavior', *American Economic Review*, **73**, 560–595.

Holmström, B. and J. Roberts (1998), 'Boundaries of the firm revisited', *Journal of Economic Perspectives*, **12**, 73–94.

Jacobides, M.G. and S.G. Winter (2005), 'The co-evolution of capabilities and transaction costs: explaining the institutional structure of production', *Strategic Management Journal*, **26**(5), 395–413.

Jensen, M.C. and W.H. Meckling (1992), 'Specific and general knowledge, and organizational structure', in L. Werin and H. Wijkander (eds), *Contract Economics*, Oxford: Blackwell.

Jones, G.R. (1983), 'Transaction costs, property rights, and organizational culture: an exchange perspective', *Administrative Science Quarterly*, **28**, 454–467.

Kauffman, S. (1995), *At Home in the Universe*, Oxford: Oxford University Press.

Knight, F.H. (1921), *Risk, Uncertainty, and Profit*, New York: August M. Kelley.

Kogut, B. (2000), 'The network as knowledge: generative rules and the emergence of structure', *Strategic Management Journal*, **21**, 405–425.

Kogut, B. and U. Zander (1992), 'Knowledge of the firm, combinative capabilities, and the replication of technology', *Organization Science*, **3**, 383–397.

Kogut, B. and U. Zander (1993), 'Knowledge of the firm and the evolutionary theory of the multinational corporation', *Journal of International Business Studies*, **24**, 625–645.

Kogut, B. and U. Zander (1996), 'What firms do? Coordination, identity, and learning', *Organization Science*, **7**, 502–518.

Kruglanski, A.W. and C. Köpetz (2009), 'What is so special (and non-special) about goals? A view from the cognitive perspective', in G.B. Moskowitz and H. Grant (eds), *The Psychology of Goals*, New York: Guilford Press.

Langlois, R.N. (1988), 'Economic change and the boundaries of the firm', *Journal of Institutional and Theoretical Economics*, **144**, 635–657.

Langlois, R.N. (1992), 'Transaction cost economics in real time', *Industrial and Corporate Change*, **1**(1), 99–127.

Langlois, R.N. (2003), 'The vanishing hand: the changing dynamics of industrial capitalism', *Industrial and Corporate Changes*, **12**(2), 351–385.

Langlois, R.N. (2007), 'The entrepreneurial theory of the firm and the theory of the entrepreneurial firm', *Journal of Management Studies*, **44**, 1107–1124.

Langlois, R.N. and L. Csontos (1993), 'Optimization, rule-following, and the methodology of situational analysis', in U. Mäki, B. Gustafsson and C. Knudsen (eds), *Rationality, Institutions, and Economic Methodology*, London: Routledge.

Langlois, R.N. and P.L. Robertson (1995), *Firms, Markets, and Economic Change: A Dynamic Theory of Business Institutions*, London: Routledge.

Lindenberg, S. (2003), 'The cognitive side of governance', *Research in the Sociology of Organizations*, **20**, 47–76.

Lindenberg, S. and N.J. Foss (2011), 'Managing motivation for joint production: the role of goal framing and governance mechanisms', *Academy of Management Review*, **36**, 500–525.

Madhok, A. (1996), 'The organization of economic activity: transaction costs, firm capabilities and the nature of governance', *Organization Science*, **7**, 577–590.

Mahoney, J. and J.R. Pandian (1992), 'The resource-based view within the conversation of strategic management', *Strategic Management Journal*, **13**, 363–380.

Maritan, C.A. and T.H. Brush (2003), 'Heterogeneity and transferring practices: implementing flow manufacturing in multiple plants', *Strategic Management Journal*, **24**, 945–960.

Marschak, J. and R. Radner (1972), *The Economic Theory of Teams*, New Haven, CT: Cowles Foundation and Yale University Press.

Mayer, K. and N. Argyres (2004), 'Learning to contract', *Organization Science*, **15**, 394–410.

Minbaeva, D., T. Pedersen, I. Björkman, C. Fey and H.J. Park (2003), 'MNC knowledge transfer, subsidiary absorptive capacity, and HRM', *Journal of International Business Studies*, **34**, 586–599.

Mises, L. von. (1949), *Human Action: A Treatise on Economics*, New Haven: Yale University Press.

Mowery, D.C., J. Oxley and B. Silverman (1996), 'Strategic alliances and interfirm knowledge transfer', *Strategic Management Journal*, **17**, 77–91.

Nelson, R.R. and S.G. Winter (1982), *The Evolutionary Theory of the Firm*, Cambridge, MA: Harvard University Press.

Nickerson, J. and T. Zenger (2004), 'A knowledge-based theory of the firm: the problem-solving perspective', *Organization Science*, **15**(6), 617–632.

Osterloh, M. and B. Frey (2000), 'Motivation, knowledge transfer and organizational form', *Organization Science*, **11**, 538–550.

Oxley, J. (1997), 'Appropriability hazards and governance in strategic alliances: a transaction cost approach', *Journal of Law, Economics, and Organization*, **13**, 387–409.

Penrose, E.T. (1959), *The Theory of the Growth of the Firm*, Oxford: Blackwell.

Phelps, E.P. (2006), 'Further steps to a theory of innovation and growth – on the path begun by Knight, Hayek, and Polanyí', Paper for the 2006 ASSA meetings.

Prendergast, Canice (1993), 'Role of promotion in inducing specific human capital acquisition', *Quarterly Journal of Economics*, **108**, 523–534.

Rajan, Raghuram G. and Luigi Zingales (2001), 'The influence of the financial revolution on the nature of firms', Wirtschaftspolitische Blatter, **48**(6), 635–641.

Reinholt, M., T. Pedersen and N.J. Foss (2011), 'Why a central network position isn't enough: the role of motivation and ability for knowledge sharing in networks', *Academy of Management Journal*, **54**, 1277–1297.

Richardson, G.B. (1972), 'The organisation of industry', *Economic Journal*, 883–896.

Sah, R. and J.E. Stiglitz (1985), 'The theory of economic organizations, human fallibility and economic organization', *American Economic Review, Papers and Proceedings*, **75**, 292–297.

Sah, R. and J.E. Stiglitz (1986), 'The architecture of economic systems: hierarchies and polyarchies', *American Economic Review*, **76**, 716–727.

Silverman, B.S. (1999), 'Technological resources and the direction of corporate diversification: toward an integration of transaction cost economics and the resource-based view', *Management Science*, August, 1109–1124.

Simon, H.A. (1962), 'The architecture of complexity', *Proceedings of the American Philosophical Society*, **106**, 467–82.

Simonin, B.L. (1999), 'Transfer of marketing know-how in international strategic alliances', *Journal of International Business Studies*, **30**, 463–490.

Spender, J.C. (1996), 'Making knowledge the basis of a dynamic theory of the firm', *Strategic Management Journal*, **17** (Winter Special Issue), 45–62.

Spender, J.C. (2005), 'Review article: an essay of the state of knowledge management', *Prometheus*, **23**(1), 101–116.

Starbuck, W. (1992), 'Learning by knowledge-intensive firms', *Journal of Management Studies*, **29**, 713–741.

Tallman, S. (2003), 'The significance of Bruce Kogut's and Udo Zander's article, "Knowledge of the firm and the evolutionary theory of the multinational corporation"', *Journal of International Business Studies*, **34**, 495–497.

Teece, D.J. (1977), 'Technology transfer by multinational firms: the resource costs of transferring technological know-how', *Economic Journal*, 242–261.

Teece, D.J. (2003), 'Expert talent and the design of (professional services) firms', *Industrial and Corporate Change*, **12**, 895–916.

Teece, D.J., G. Pisano and A. Shuen (1997), 'Dynamic capabilities and strategic management', *Strategic Management Journal*, **18**, 509–534.

Tsai, W.P. (2001), 'Knowledge transfer in intra-organizational networks', *Academy of Management Journal*, **44**(5), 996–1004.

Tsai, W.P. (2002), 'Social structure of "coopetition" within a multiunit organization', *Organization Science*, **13**, 179–190.

Williamson, O.E. (1985), *The Economic Institutions of Capitalism*, New York: Free Press.

Williamson, O.E. (1996), *The Mechanisms of Governance*, Oxford: Oxford University Press.

Williamson, O.E. (1999), 'Strategy research: governance and competence perspectives', *Strategic Management Journal*, **20**, 1087–1108.

Williamson, O.E., M.L. Wachter and J.E. Harris (1975), 'Understanding the employment relation: the analysis of idiosyncratic exchange', *Bell Journal of Economics*, **6**, 250–278.

Winter, S.G. (1987), 'Knowledge and competence as strategic assets', in D. Teece, (ed.), *The Competitive Challenge*, Cambridge, MA: Ballinger, pp. 159–184.

Winter, S.G. (1988), 'On Coase, competence, and the corporation', *Journal of Law, Economics, and Organization*, **4**(1), 163–180.

Witt, Ulrich (1998), 'Imagination and leadership: the neglected dimension of an evolutionary theory of the firm', *Journal of Economic Behavior and Organization*, **35**, 161–177.

Zenger, T.R. and W.S. Hesterly (1997), 'The disaggregation of US corporations: selective intervention, high-powered incentives, and molecular units', *Organization Science*, **8**, 209–222.

Zingales, L. (2000), 'In search of new foundations', *Journal of Finance*, **55**, 1623–1653.

PART II

THE CONSTITUTION OF ECONOMIC ORGANIZATION BETWEEN INTERACTING AND CONTRACTING

5. Contracts: coordination across firm boundaries
Victor P. Goldberg

Contracts between firms involve a projection over the future. In this chapter I analyze some of the problems that arise in contractual relationships and some of the mechanisms that parties have developed to cope with these problems. An overarching problem is what has been labeled opportunism and, in particular, the problem of hold-up. While the contractual interaction might be as simple as a straight-forward promise to deliver some well-defined commodity at a future date, the more analytically interesting contracts involve adaptation as new information becomes available. Contracts often involve a form of 'real option'; that is, rather than spell out what should happen in all future contingencies, the contract gives one or both parties the option to make decisions (including abandonment or termination) as new information becomes available. One governance device is to give one party the power to make decisions as new information arrives. The party that values flexibility the most would be given the power to make the decision and it would be confronted with a 'price' reflecting the counterparty's reliance.

While economists often model contracts in a principal–agent form with the agent posing a problem of moral hazard, the more interesting problems concern double-sided moral hazard. That is, the outcomes depend on the behavior of both parties. An additional set of problems arises when the subject matter of the contract cannot be defined at the outset, for example the construction of a state-of-the-art plant or production of inputs for a product that is still being designed.

Back in the days when I was a graduate student, the theory of the firm was not really a theory of the firm at all. The firm in those days did not even merit being labelled a 'black box'. Something out there equated marginal cost to marginal revenue and then kind of disappeared so that we could focus on the market. Ronald Coase's classic paper (Coase 1937) got us to theorizing about firms. A theory of the firm that captures how and why firms are organized as they are is going to be pretty empty if it is to explain all firms. A theory of the state that applies equally to the United States, Luxemburg and Belize will either be so unwieldy as to be unworkable or so superficial as to be uninformative. So too with a theory of the firm that applies equally to General Motors, a biotech startup and a small retail store. That does not mean that we cannot say something interesting about any of these. But it does mean that an overarching theory capturing them all is probably not worth pursuing.

Likewise, a theory of contracts. In the economic modeling in the old days the world was characterized by zero transaction costs or, what amounts to the same thing, complete contingent contracts. Under either formulation, the structure of the contracts was irrelevant. The structure does matter, however, if transaction costs (whatever that might mean) are positive or contracts are incomplete. But that does not tell us much. A 50-year shopping center lease with an anchor tenant has little in common with the sale of 1000 bushels of wheat for immediate delivery.

Rather than attempting an overarching theory, I propose a toolkit, a set of concepts that, strung together creatively, will explain particular relationships. One approach, which I am eschewing, is to set up a classification scheme and then to use the theory to demarcate the classes. Williamson (2002), for example, uses concepts like asset specificity to classify transactions on a continuum from simple market-mediated transactions, to relational contract, and finally integration by ownership.[1] This approach has proven fruitful, but I am reluctant to pursue it for two reasons. First, the boundaries between the archetypes are porous. Transactions that one might predict to take place within organizations can take place between firms; and vice versa. But even if the boundaries were sharply delineated, that only tells us why things are in various boxes, but does not necessarily tell us how and why things work within those boxes. The concepts with which I am concerned cut across those boundaries. I will ignore the boundary questions and confine my attention to contracts between independent entities. Still, I should note that many of the problems (and solutions) that arise across firm boundaries would arise within firms as well; commission pricing, for example, is used in both contexts. I am not saying that mine is a better concern, only that it is a different concern.

Over three decades ago I suggested three concepts that would be useful in understanding contract structure:

> First, people are not omniscient; their information is imperfect and improvable only at a cost. Second, not all people are saints all of the time; as the relationship unfolds there will be opportunities for one party to take advantage of the other's vulnerability, to engage in strategic behavior, or to follow his own interests at the expense of the other party. The actors will, on occasion, behave opportunistically. Third, the parties cannot necessarily rely on outsiders to enforce the agreement cheaply and accurately.[2]

I would modify that list today by including adverse selection in the first category; moral hazard, hold-up and rent-seeking in the second; and verifiability in the third. To this I would now add adaptation to change. Parties might want to rely on the continuation of a relationship and still maintain the ability to adapt as new information becomes available. The allocation of the decision rights will be important. A contract might grant one party the right to decide but at a 'price' that reflects the other party's concerns; or the contract might set up a more elaborate governance mechanism, a committee perhaps, with a voting mechanism; or it might simply rely on a third party – a mediator or arbitrator.

Some, perhaps most, economists have a Pavlovian response to questions of contract structure: it must be risk aversion. I find that unhelpful, especially when dealing with contracts between sophisticated firms with access to reasonably competent counsel. Publicly traded corporations should be risk neutral since their owners, the shareholders, can deal with risk by diversifying their portfolio. Even if the corporate actors were risk averse, there would be no reason to believe that attitudes toward risk would affect the structure of any particular contract if the contract were one of many in a firm's portfolio. Ultimately, the question is whether invoking risk aversion is helpful in understanding the contract or whether it gets in the way. My experience has been that it is the latter. Consider, for example, the fact that most publicly traded corporations carry liability insurance. The standard response of most economists would be that this must reflect the risk aversion of management and that, because of moral hazard, the accident rate (and therefore costs) would be increased. A double whammy for the shareholders. If instead we ask why a firm might carry liability insurance regardless of risk attitudes, a different picture emerges. One possible reason is that the insurer provides valuable services. For example, it might be the most efficient provider of inspection services. In that case, the purchase of insurance might have the effect of reducing the net costs of accidents. I will return to the analysis-without-risk-aversion shortly.[3]

Contracts are not zero sum. The parties expect that by entering into a contract they will be better off. In expectation the contract creates value. However, the parties are not necessarily focused on the joint gains – their concern is what is in it for them. Their focus on value division can result in the pie being smaller than it otherwise might have been. An employee might shirk, a borrower might take negative expected value projects. To constrain this behavior the employer or lender will have to impose restraints and/or incur the costs of monitoring.

Consider what seems to be a fairly simple case, the renting of space in a mall to a retailer. If the lease period is too short, the retailer risks being held up at the renewal stage. The more site-specific investment it makes, the more vulnerable it would be at that stage. Increasing the lease period raises other problems. The longer the time period, the greater the likelihood that the rent will be out of line with current market conditions. I will note other problems with a long lease, but first I want to consider problems arising from a discrepancy between the current price and market price and how parties might contractually cope with the problem. If the rent is well below market rate, the mall might try to reduce services or otherwise make life miserable for the tenant either to save costs or to encourage renegotiation. The tenant's protection from this can be specific contractual language: 'thou shalt maintain quality standard X'. But X might be hard to define; moreover, the definition must reflect the verifiability if a dispute were to arise. Or the retailer could rely on the fact (if it be a fact) that the mall cannot fine-tune such behavior; reducing maintenance or security services would affect multiple tenants, some of whom have rents closer to the current market rates. If, on the other hand, the rent were well above market rate, the retailer could act in a manner that would make the mall less attractive, hurting other tenants – a classic 'externality'. Hurting other tenants would hurt the mall owner in two ways. Firstly, its revenue from other tenants might be a function of their revenues; secondly, if it has to bring in new tenants, the rent it could ask would be implicated.

Typically, part of the rent in retail leases is a function of sales. That has two positive features. Firstly, it is an imperfect indicator of market conditions – it reduces the gap alluded to above. Secondly, it provides some incentive for the lessor to provide services that will result in increased sales. Since both parties contribute to the outcome, both have to be incentivized. The retailer's interest in maximizing profits is in tension with the lessor's interest in its sales revenue. The lease could try to bring the two closer by imposing constraints on the retailer (for example, requiring minimum hours of operation). Of course, if sales revenues are to be a component of the rent, the lessor would require some means of assuring accuracy of sales reporting.

What if the retailer's business dried up? Suppose that it had, for example, been selling compact disks. Could it shift to another line of business, one that competed with that of another tenant? If it were allowed to sublease, would there be any restrictions? Alternatively, what if the opportunity cost of the space increased because the mall operator found a more attractive tenant? Could it evict the sitting tenant? Could the tenant just say no? Or might the mall operator have the right to terminate subject to paying a fee? The lease has to embody mechanisms for adapting to such changes. In Calabresi–Melamed terms, the right to evict (or the tenant's right to stay) is a property rule, while the right to evict subject to paying compensation is a liability rule.[4] A fairly common arrangement would give the tenant property protection, but at the same time give it the obligation for making payments for the duration of the lease. If it wanted out, the lease might give it the right to sublet subject to the lessor's approval 'which could not unreasonably be withheld'. The tenant would remain as a guarantor of the sublessee's payments. But this is far from the only solution. We can be reasonably certain that a lease would not give either party the right to terminate without cost; except at specified intervals. The cost would reflect the *ex ante* balance of the value to the one party of the option to terminate against the cost of the other party if that option were exercised.

The problems are exacerbated if we consider the lease with the anchor tenant, typically a large department store. A significant role for the anchor tenant is bringing customers to the mall; and these customers will ultimately spend money in other parts of the mall. The mall owner pays for that service indirectly in the form of a reduced rental rate. Indeed, the value of the marketing services can be so high that the anchor tenant's rent could be nominal or even zero. Because the location-specific investment of the anchor tenant is so high, these leases are for very long periods, typically over a quarter-century. A lot can change over the life of such a long lease. One device for dealing with the long time period is to give the tenant a series of renewal options, for example, a 20-year lease with five five-year options to renew.

If the neighborhood deteriorates or a new highway diverts traffic away from the mall, the anchor tenant might find even a zero price to be too high. Could it simply shutter its store, leaving the mall with a large vacancy? Would it have to guarantee the mall that it would maintain a minimum level of sales or activity? If so, how would it define that level, given that the issue would probably not arise for decades and that its ability to reach a contractually defined level might be impacted by the mall operator's decisions? To further complicate things, suppose that the anchor tenant opened a new outlet in a nearby mall and then shuttered this store, but continued to pay the nominal rent. Would that justify the mall owner's terminating the lease?[5]

I could go on, but the basic points I want to make are threefold. Firstly, even for this reasonably common instance, there are a lot of really hard problems. Secondly, by and large people have worked out the various trade-offs. Thirdly, both the problems and the tools for coping with them recur in other contexts. It is this last point that I want to pursue.

Contingent compensation arrangements, like the percentage lease, are common. Oil leases typically pay the owner a royalty (often one-eighth). Apparel licensees typically pay a minimum fee plus a royalty on sales above the minimum. Book royalties take the same form. Top Hollywood talent receive gross profits contracts which give them a share of the film's revenues offset against a fixed fee. Many franchise arrangements include a percentage of sales as part of their obligation to the franchisor. Plaintiff lawyers' contingent compensation is usually a fraction of the recovery. Salesmen are paid on commission. Auction houses take a percentage of the sale price. The contract between a biotech firm and a pharmaceutical company will typically include milestone payments triggered by certain events (like identification of a promising molecule) and royalty payments if the product reaches the market.

Why all this sharing? Giving away a share of revenue acts as a tax on effort, which suggests that all of these arrangements would be inefficient. How does the sharing create value rather than destroy it? In the lease discussion I noted two possible roles for the sharing rule: imperfectly tracking market conditions and aligning incentives. True, the retailer's incentive might be weakened by the tax, but the mall owner's enhanced incentive more than makes up for that. A good short-hand term for the situation in which outcomes depend on the efforts of both parties is 'double-sided moral hazard'. Both parties contribute to the outcome and both have to be motivated.

That does not explain all contingent compensation arrangements, but it is a start. Another form of explanation rests on imperfect information. If parties disagree about the potential value of as asset (for example, a film proposal, a book manuscript), they can pave over the difference by making a portion of the compensation depend on the actual outcome. If a seller has greater knowledge of the value of an asset than the buyer – an adverse selection problem – one solution is to make a portion of the seller's compensation depend on the subsequent performance of the asset. For example, the sale of a private business might make a portion of the price a fraction of the sales volume in the first one or two years after the sale (an earnout). None of these mechanisms is perfect; the earnout, in particular, is subject to manipulation by the buyer to the extent that it can divert sales to the post-earnout period. My point is that there are plausible explanations for why sharing arrangements might create value, and that for these explanations it is not necessary to invoke risk aversion of one of the parties. Indeed, some sharing arrangements come with 'no-cross-collateralization' clauses, which would make no sense if risk aversion or risk-pooling were the motivating factor.

Because the future is uncertain, there is value in maintaining the ability to adapt as new information becomes available. While some of the information relates to exogenous factors like the weather, market conditions, changes in input prices, and so forth, some is endogenous. For example, a buyer learns about the reliability of a supplier (regarding quality, timely performance, ability to innovate or willingness to make accommodations).

The making of a movie provides a good example of the significance of adaptation as new information becomes available. Movie studios take options on the projects, typically at a modest fee. If the project progresses far enough the studios, in effect, take options on the talent in the form of 'pay or play' clauses. With these clauses the talent promises to set aside a time period to make a particular film; the studio, however, maintains flexibility by reserving the right not to make the film at all or to make the film without using the talent. The price of this option would not be modest. The price would depend on the significance of the talent and, implicitly, the talent's reliance (the opportunity cost of the time set aside). For significant talent, this would typically take the form of the fixed fee (which for major artists could be in the range of $20 million).[6]

Successful movies often beget sequels. But success is hard to predict. So, usually the studio would wait until the first movie is successful before committing to making a second. It would have the right at its sole discretion to decide on whether a sequel should be made. In effect it maintains an option to abandon (or a 'real option'). But it faces a problem. If the film did turn out to be successful, and if a particular artist was an essential element in the later projects, that artist would have substantial bargaining leverage. One obvious device for coping with this problem is to include in the initial contract with the artist the terms for any sequel. Experience suggests that any such contractual constraints will be only partially successful in restraining the renegotiation. A more extreme response to the problem is to eschew the option to abandon and instead film the sequels at the same time as the original, as was done in the *Lord of the Rings* trilogy. That this route is so rarely taken attests to the value of the option to abandon.

The simplest form of adaptation to change is to enter into short-term or spot contracts. The buyer and seller enter into a contract; after it is performed each is free to enter into another one with this party or anyone else. At the opposite extreme are constitution-like agreements – for example, a condominium agreement that establishes a governance mechanism, voting rules, and rules for amending the agreement. In between are a wide variety of devices.

A typical biotech agreement with a large pharmaceutical company (Big Pharma), for example, would vary the governance mechanism over the course of the agreement. In the first exploratory phase, the pharmaceutical company has a passive governance mechanism, the option to abandon if the project seems unpromising. As the project progresses and information becomes available, a more responsive governance mechanism is needed. Typically, a joint committee is created to determine the direction in which the research should proceed. If the committee failed to agree, their dispute would be kicked upstairs. If the higher-ups could not resolve the dispute, then the agreement would specify a method for resolving the dispute, which might, but need not, entail a legal remedy. The threat of disappointing one's superiors is, most likely, a stronger sanction than the legal remedy. As the project moves from the research to the development stage, Big Pharma bears the future costs of testing and marketing (which typically dwarf the costs in the research and development stage), and decision-making and effort shift to it. Decisions as to testing, pursuing patents and marketing would be entirely in its hands. In the event that it chose to abandon the project, the agreement might give the biotech firm the right to pursue the project with other Big Pharma firms, perhaps with some compensation attached.[7]

One way of dealing with changing circumstances is to grant one party the discretion to adapt, but to confront it with a 'price' reflecting the costs the counterparty would incur from granting that discretion. The pay-or-play clause alluded to above is one example. Generally, if X values discretion by more than it costs Y to grant that discretion, there is room for a deal. The 'price' of the discretion will be determined by the bargaining skills of the party. That price can take many different forms.

Consider an agreement for the simultaneous development of a coalmine and an adjacent power plant. If the coalmine has poor access to any other potential users, it would require some assurance that it could receive enough money to make development of the mine worth while. The power plant would want an assured source of supply and would like the flexibility to adjust its level of output as demand conditions change. There are a number of mechanisms for achieving this. To achieve both the assurance and flexibility, the buyer would get a requirements contract which says, in effect, you agree to provide whatever we ask for, as long as we can use it at this plant. But, how to compensate the seller for granting that discretion? It could, after all, be stuck with a billion-dollar hole in the ground and no takers for its coal.

One possibility, seldom used, would be an upfront payment by the buyer. A variant on that would be a stand-by charge, a fixed payment per time period, say a month. Requiring the buyer to take a minimum amount, either in defined time periods or over the life of the agreement would provide some assurance. A take-or-pay clause (which says you pay whether or not you take) is a variation on requiring payment for a minimum. Again, the agreement could be for a particular time period or for the entire life of the agreement. There is one big difference between a standby and a minimum quantity type of arrangement. Under the former, the buyer pays the contract price from the first unit on top of the standby fee. Under the latter, the buyer pays a zero price for each unit until the minimum is reached. That is, the buyer agrees to pay the contract price times the minimum as a lump sum, regardless of whether it takes anything. The marginal price, the price per unit actually taken, is zero until the minimum is reached. These arrangements can be further complicated by allowing for some inter-temporal flexibility in the form of 'make-up' clauses (If you took less than the minimum in period 1 you can take more than the minimum in period 2 and use that to offset the shortfall of the previous period).

The seller's variant on the requirements contract is a full output clause. If, for example, a manufacturer produced a waste product that has some potential value (examples would be petroleum coke, a by-product of coking at an oil refinery, and day-old bread which could be used in the production of breadcrumbs or animal feed), it would not want disposal of that product to inhibit its production decisions for its primary products. The less storage capacity it had on hand, the more it would value a promise to remove the product promptly so that it might avoid the costs entailed by slow removal, perhaps a plant shutdown. A buyer with substantial capacity could promise to take the output, and if its capacity were sufficient, the cost it would incur from granting such flexibility would be negligible. If, however, it would incur costs, perhaps in the form of special equipment or increased warehouse space, it could price the discretion by imposing a minimum or maximum quantity or other restrictions.[8]

While the previous discussion emphasized the implicit pricing of discretion, it could also be priced directly, at least in the short run. The closer the delivery date, the more costly it will be for the seller to adjust. So, for example, in its agreement with a contract manufacturer, Apple could increase or decrease the quantity without penalty if it were to give satisfactory advance notice (60 days). With only 30 days' notice it could adjust the quantity by 25 percent, still with no premium. If Apple required even greater flexibility, then it would be responsible for any overtime charges and vendor premiums. Apple could cancel any purchase order with 30 days' notice, provided that it reimburse the manufacturer for costs reasonably incurred.[9]

An extreme form of flexibility is to make an agreement backward-enforceable, but not forward-enforceable. That is, the agreement sets out a set of terms that will be incorporated into every transaction once it takes place, but there is no promise that any future transactions will be made. Many automobile franchise agreements took this form prior to legislative intervention.[10] If a dealer ordered a car and the manufacturer agreed, then all the terms of the agreement would be incorporated; but the manufacturer made no promise that it would ever accept an order. It would maintain the right to terminate the dealer instantly and without compensation. The manufacturers rarely found it necessary to exercise that right, but it gave them a powerful tool for influencing the performance of the dealers.

Contract law labels such agreements illusory and they are unenforceable; while some are illusory by drafting accident, others are illusory by design. The General Motors–Fisher Body contract that has been the subject of vigorous academic debate was illusory, my suspicion is by design.[11] A modern example of a deliberately unenforceable agreement is a Kellogg agreement with one of its suppliers:

> Kellogg generally encourages its employees to obtain required goods and services from suppliers who have entered into formal agreements with Kellogg, and Kellogg agrees to use reasonable efforts to communicate the existence of the Agreement to such employees with a general need to obtain the products and Services within the scope of this Agreement.[12]

Why do it? Neither party's reliance on the continuation of the agreement involves relation-specific capital or technology. Kellogg's reliance takes the form of finding competent, reliable suppliers; but it maintains the ability to multiple-source, thereby avoiding hold-up problems and allowing it to obtain current market prices. And it preserves the option to abandon.

The previous discussion concerned adjustment of the obligation – making a movie, producing a drug, determining the level of output – as new information became available. If the performance of a contract is to take place over time, then something has to be said about price. Contracts for the sale of defined goods over a long time period will usually include some price adjustment mechanism. This is another instance in which the casual invocation of risk aversion obscures the analysis. A price adjustment mechanism could reduce the wasteful, excessive searching for private information. If prices would be adjusted mechanically in subsequent years, there would be less incentive to expend resources to produce information of future market conditions. Secondly, if there was a substantial gap between the contract and market prices, the disadvantaged party need not take it lying down. It can attempt to renegotiate the contract, perhaps by engaging in value-reducing acts by, for example, 'working to the rules' or putting forth a strained interpretation of the contract language. If the probability of wasteful behavior increases as the contract–market gap widens, price adjustment rules that are expected to narrow that gap become increasingly attractive. My earlier example of a commercial lease with rent that is well above the market rate is illustrative. There are many things the tenant can do (or threaten to do) that would impose costs on the landlord.

There are a lot of mechanisms available for adjusting price within a long-term contract. All are imperfect. Their relative costs and benefits will determine which, if any, the parties should choose. The easiest way to adjust the price is to index. Indexing has the advantage of being mechanical and generally non-manipulable. The disadvantage of indexing is that the index might track market conditions poorly. One way to allow the contract to track market conditions is to permit the buyer to solicit outside offers, with the seller having the right of first refusal (or to meet competition). The buyer could solicit bids from outside sources and if it were to receive a bona fide bid below the contract price, the supplier would be given the option to match. The likelihood that parties to a long-term contract would use some variation on a meeting competition clause for price adjustment would depend upon the availability of alternative suppliers, for it would not make sense if there were significant relation-specific investments. Meeting competition clauses are sometimes deployed even if the product is not a homogeneous commodity. For example, the General Motors–Fisher Body contract had such clauses for each party, notwithstanding the variability of automobile bodies.[13] Likewise, Apple had a similar arrangement with a supplier, despite the differences between Apple products and other computers.[14]

Negotiation is, of course, always an option. Even if the contract explicitly utilizes one of the methods mentioned in the previous paragraph or unambiguously states that the contract is a fixed price agreement, one party could propose that the price be renegotiated. The contract could explicitly establish the conditions under which renegotiation is to take place. It could require renegotiation at fixed intervals or have it triggered by specific events (for example, a rise in a price index of more than 20 percent). 'Gross inequity' or 'hardship' clauses call for renegotiation if the contract price is too far out of line, but typically do not spell out the criteria for determining when a gross inequity exists, or what to do if it does exist. The parties could agree to renegotiate in good faith and determine what would happen if the negotiations break down. The failure to negotiate a new price could result in continued performance at the current price, termination, mediation or arbitration, and so forth. The downside of renegotiation, of course, is that one party could behave opportunistically, taking advantage of the counterparty's vulnerability.

If the subject matter is poorly defined, the likelihood that the parties would opt for some variant of cost-plus pricing increases. This notwithstanding the well-known flaws of cost-based pricing: poor incentives on cost control and gold-plating. Lawyers pricing by the billable hour are, in effect, using a variety of cost-based pricing, although the prices they name (say, $150 per hour for a paralegal) bear little resemblance to costs. Complex construction projects also have a significant cost-based price component. The contract might specify a price and a mechanism for pricing 'change orders'. Since the parties cannot rely on the external market to price the change order, they will typically resort to a cost-based solution. As the expected share of the change orders in the final cost of the project increases, the contract becomes more cost-based. In a significant class of cost-based contracts the features of the output are not known at the time of contracting. A supplier might, for example, promise to make parts for future models of a car even though that car has not yet been designed. In markets with rapid technological change in which the characteristics of the output and the inputs are changing, cost-based pricing is common. The aforementioned Apple contract is illustrative. For each new product Apple's supplier would propose a unit price quote based on a number of expected cost components: non-recurring engineering and tooling costs; direct labor cost; cost of procured material; packaging costs; product warranty costs; and profit. The labor cost would be estimated *ex ante* and adjusted *ex post*. The unit price quote would be adjusted to take into account the utilization rate. For procured material, the supplier would pass through any cost reductions including rebates and discounts.

In this chapter my concern has been the problems inherent in coordinating behavior across organizational boundaries and the mechanisms for coping with them. I use 'coping' advisedly. There is, I think, a tendency of academics to overpromise, to 'solve' problems. My goal is more modest. I have emphasized the problem of adapting to changed circumstances, in particular the trade-off between reliance and flexibility and the allocation of decision making between the parties. I have emphasized one feature that recurs in many contexts. One party is granted the decision-making authority, but it is confronted with a price reflecting the costs that flexibility imposes on the counterparty. Because the prices are often implicit, identifying them and how the decision maker's discretion is constrained can be a difficult task

Other problems – especially moral hazard, adverse selection, hold-up and rent-seeking – have played only a subsidiary role. I have also downplayed the role of extra-legal mechanisms, notably reputation. That reduced role is primarily due to space constraints. The non-role of risk aversion, however, was deliberate. If we are to understand the structure of contracts, then we should tie our hands, metaphorically, and vow not to invoke risk aversion as an explanation.

NOTES

1. See also Hart & Moore (1990).
2. Goldberg (1980).
3. See Goldberg (2009).
4. Calabresi and Melamed (1972).
5. For a case in which this happened, see *Oakwood Village LLC v. Albertsons, Inc.*, 104 P.3d 1226, 514 Utah Adv. Rep. 10, 2004 UT 101.
6. For more on pay or play clauses, see Goldberg (2006, Ch. 15).
7. See Gilson et al. (2009).
8. For more on quantity adjustment, see Goldberg (2006, Ch. 5).
9. Fountain Manufacturing Agreement between Apple Computer, Inc. and Sci Systems, Inc. (May 31, 1996). http://contracts.onecle.com/apple/scis.mfg.1996.05.31.shtml
10. See Kessler (1957) and Macaulay (1966).
11. See Goldberg (2008).
12. Complaint, Kellogg v. FPC, Appendix Exhibit 1. Agreement for the Purchase of Goods. The case is being litigated on other grounds.
13. 'In the event that the FISHER COMPANY shall manufacture and sell to third parties automobile bodies similar in grade to those furnished to GENERAL MOTORS at or about the same time but at a price less than the amount paid by GENERAL MOTORS therefore, namely: the cost of said bodies and (17.6%) Seventeen and Six Tenths Per Cent in addition thereto, then said GENERAL MOTORS shall be obligated to pay for such similar grade of automobile bodies made at or about the same time only the price charged by the FISHER COMPANY to third parties, and any over-payment in respect thereto shall be refunded by the FISHER COMPANY.'
    'If the price to be paid by GENERAL MOTORS for automobile bodies manufactured by the FISHER COMPANY substantially exceeds the general average market price of similar grade automobile bodies manufactured by other persons, firms or corporations, GENERAL MOTORS shall have the right to place its orders for automobile bodies elsewhere, unless the FISHER COMPANY agrees to fill the order given it by GENERAL MOTORS at a price not in excess of such general average market price of similar grade automobile bodies manufactured by such other persons, firms or corporations, if said price be available to GENERAL MOTORS for its requirements.'
14. 'SCI hereby warrants that at no time will the prices charged Apple for any Product under this Agreement exceed the prices offered other customers on similar terms and conditions' (Article 10.7).

REFERENCES

Calabresi, Guido and A. Douglas Melamed (1972), 'Property rules, liability rules and inalienability: one view of the cathedral', *Harvard Law Review*, 85, 1089–1128.
Coase, Ronald (1937), 'The nature of the firm', *Economica, N.S.*, 4(November).
Gilson, Ronald, Charles Sabel and Robert Scott (2009), 'Contracting for innovation: vertical disintegration and interfirm collaboration', *Columbia Law Review*, 431–502.
Goldberg, Victor (1980), 'Relational exchange: economics and complex contracts', *American Behavioral Scientist*, 23(January), 337–352.
Goldberg, Victor (2006), *Framing Contract Law: An Economic Perspective*, Cambridge, MA: Harvard University Press.
Goldberg, Victor (2008), 'Lawyers asleep at the wheel? The GM-Fisher Body contract', *Industrial and Corporate Change*, 17, 1071–1084.
Goldberg, Victor (2009), 'The devil made me do it: the corporate purchase of insurance', *Review of Law and Economics*, 5, 541–553.

Hart, Oliver and John Moore (1990), 'Property rights and the nature of the firm', *Journal of Political Economy*, **98**(6), 1119–1158.

Kessler, Friedrich (1957), 'Automobile dealer franchises: vertical integration by contract', *Yale Law Journal*, 1135–1190.

Macaulay, Stewart (1966), *Law and the Balance of Power: The Automobile Manufacturers and Their Dealers*, Russell Sage Foundation.

Williamson, Oliver (2002), 'The theory of the firm as governance structure: from choice to contract', *Journal of Economic Perspectives*, **16**(3), 171–195.

6. The enterprise as community: firms, towns, and universities
Scott E. Masten

At a very broad level, firms and municipalities share a number of features. Among other things, both are self-governing entities that make investments and purchase, produce, and distribute goods and services, sometimes, but not always, for an explicit price. Yet towns and firms are perceived as being governed differently: Whereas municipalities are governed democratically, the archetypal firm is viewed as an autocracy. The sharp contrast conventionally drawn between 'autocratic' firms and more 'democratic' entities like towns and cooperatives is misleading, however. As Henry Hansmann (1988) has pointed out, traditional business corporations are, in essence, lender cooperatives, organizations over which investors exercise democratic control. From this perspective, the issue becomes less one of whether communities or enterprises are democratically governed but who gets to vote. This chapter explores the role and limitations of democratic governance and the factors that contribute to the dominant forms of governance observed in political and commercial settings. Following an overview of the functions of democracy, I discuss some of the distinctive and common features of town and firms. I then present evidence on the extent of faculty participation in decision making in American (United States) colleges and universities and discuss the origins and possible reasons for the existence of and observed variations in democratic governance in academic institutions. I conclude that a primary function of democratic governance is protecting the interests of parties for whom markets and contracts are least effective and discuss the implications of this function for the governance of business enterprises.

INTRODUCTION

At a very broad level, firms and municipalities share a number of features. Both are self-governing entities that make investments and purchase, produce, and distribute goods and services, sometimes, but not always, for an explicit price. In their corporate forms both have common origins in medieval Europe, where states granted charters establishing associations whose existence did not depend on the identities of, and thus could outlive, their members. Such long-lived organizations required means of adapting to change in both their membership and environment, procedures for which were, and continue to be, provided by the entity's 'constitution' – its charter, bylaws, or articles of incorporation, as the case may be. Towns and firms also employ parallel internal administrative structures: boards (city councils, boards of directors) and executives (mayors, chief executive officers), supported by administrative staff, overseeing operational divisions.

Their shared origins and similar legal and organizational structures notwithstanding, towns and firms are perceived as being governed differently. Whereas municipalities, like larger political units such as provinces and nations, are governed democratically, the archetypal firm is characterized as an autocracy, with formal authority over the organization's operations consolidated in the owner or owners' agent. Indeed, the peremptory authority of management is often cited as the distinguishing property of internal organization in the theory of the firm. In the words of Milgrom and Roberts, 'what most distinguishes any centralized [business] organization is the authority and autonomy of its top decision makers or management – that is, their broad rights to intervene in lower level decisions and the relative immunity of their decisions from intervention by others' (Milgrom and Roberts 1990: 79; see also Coase 1937; Simon 1951; Williamson 1975).

Outside of the occasional jejune paean to one-party autocracy (e.g., Friedman 2009), almost everyone agrees that democracy is preferred to dictatorship as a system of government. At the same time, advocacy of democracy in the workplace is largely confined to a radical fringe. Yet exceptions to the general rule do exist. At the geopolitical level, governments – including nations philosophically predisposed toward democracy such as colonial Britain or the United States (US) during the Cold War – have frequently exhibited a preference for dealing with client states ruled by an autocrat who could be more easily controlled or, if necessary, replaced than could a democratic government. On the commercial side, business enterprises such as professional service partnerships, producer and consumer cooperatives (some of which are large enough to appear in the Fortune 500 list of industrial corporations), and commodity and financial exchanges are or have been, to one degree or another, governed democratically (see Hansmann 1988; Pirrong 1999).

The sharp contrast conventionally drawn between 'autocratic' firms and more 'democratic' entities such as towns and cooperatives is misleading, however. As Henry Hansmann (1988) has pointed out, traditional business corporations are, in essence, lender (or investor) cooperatives. The difference in governance between traditional business firms, on the one hand, and worker, producer, or consumer cooperatives, on the other, is simply a matter of which set of patrons – investors, workers, suppliers, or customers – have legal control of the organization. Because some means of arriving at collective decisions (i.e., voting rules) will be needed regardless of which group of patrons is in charge (the exception being single-owner enterprises such as sole proprietorships), whether it is better to assign control to one set of patrons instead of another – or possibly to share control among two or more patron classes – will depend, in part, on the benefits and limitations of collective decision making and how those vary with the attributes of patrons and transactions. In this analysis, the predominance of investor democracy among commercial enterprises is the result of generally greater hazards of contracting for capital than with input suppliers, workers, and customers combined with arguably greater difficulties of the latter three groups in exercising effective collective control (Hansmann 1988: 277–284, 301; Williamson 1987).

Following the proceeding logic, municipalities are no longer so clearly more democratic than business corporations (cf. Grandori 2013). After all, municipal employees have no more right, by virtue of their employment alone, to vote in municipal elections or on local referenda than do company employees to vote in board elections or on bylaw amendments. Much as corporations restrict voting rights to shareholders, cities restrict local voting rights to citizens, typically individuals who satisfy particular residency requirements. In principle, this need not be the case, however; voting rights could, at least theoretically, be based on criteria other than residency: land ownership, birth, or employment, for example. Indeed, municipalities need not be democratic at all. Cities and towns could be (as they have been at various times and locations) operated as departments of national (or provincial) governments by administrators appointed by the central (possibly though not necessarily democratically elected) government. Alternatively, residential communities might be run as for-profit enterprises that contract with residents, as do landlord-owned apartment complexes, some of which easily exceed many towns and villages in population. In between are communities that combine private ownership and democratic governance: residential cooperatives, in which tenants collectively own and manage rental properties, and condominiums and gated communities, in which commercial firms own and manage common areas exterior to owner-occupied dwellings (Hansmann 1991).

The broad purpose of these examples is to challenge conventional presumptions about the 'natural' domain of democratic governance and to motivate an exploration of the role and limitations of democratic governance and of the factors that contribute to the dominant forms of governance observed in political and commercial settings. I begin in the next section with a brief overview of three functions ascribed to democracy in the literature, followed by a look at some of the distinctive and common features of town and firms. I then provide evidence on the extent of faculty participation in decision making in American colleges and universities and discuss the origins and possible reasons for the existence of and observed variations in democratic governance in academic institutions. I conclude with some thoughts on the implications of the discussion for the governance of ordinary business enterprises.

THE FUNCTIONS OF POLITICAL GOVERNANCE

The political economy literature has identified three main functions of democratic governance: preference aggregation; political agent incentive alignment; and securing political bargains (see Shepsle 1993). Voting as a means of aggregating preferences (*à la* Arrow 1963 [1951]) is well understood, and its use is commonly associated with situations where discrete actions or policies affect multiple individuals, giving decisions a public-good nature. Less generally familiar, the political incentive-aligning function of democracy derives from agency theory to posit that, because acquiring and applying policy-relevant expertise is costly, political actors will only develop and use 'the knowledge required for effective decision-making' if they possess the ability to influence outcomes acquired through voting rights (Gilligan 1993: 325). To the extent that the quality of decisions will be better if decision authority is allocated to those who are best informed, an implication of this theory is that voting authority will be most valuable if allocated to those 'with demonstrable expertise' (Gilligan 1993: 338).

Finally, democracy's role as a commitment device – which is at the heart of democratic philosophy dating back at least to Montesquieu, James Madison, and Alexander Hamilton, and which has more recently been developed and extended by North and Weingast (1989) and Weingast and Marshall (1988), among others (see Miller 1997) – starts from the premise that, like economic transactions, political bargains seek to create joint surpluses but are subject to reneging and appropriation hazards that can prevent deals from being reached or otherwise result in inefficient outcomes. Thus, in the relations between a government and its citizens, both ruler and ruled stand to benefit from private investment stimulated by a 'bargain' limiting the wealth that the state can appropriate from its citizens. Similarly, politicians stand to gain from striking deals with each other, as when legislators trade votes in pursuit of the majorities necessary to enact legislation benefiting their respective local constituents (e.g., Buchanan and Tullock 1962). But without adequate assurances that others will, when the time comes, uphold their end of the bargain, citizens may be reluctant to make investments and legislators to expend the political capital necessary to achieve joint surpluses (North and Weingast 1989; Weingast and Marshall 1988).

Two aspects of political exchange ostensibly complicate the task of securing agreements among political actors. Firstly, because no independent third party with the power to compel performance exists to which political transactors can appeal to enforce their agreements, political bargains must be self-enforcing. Secondly, because the sanctions that an individual can impose on a defecting ruler or fellow legislator are typically small, 'self' enforcement of political bargains often requires collective action – mass revolts, protests, boycotts and the like. Carrying out such actions requires coordination: while the success of an insurrection depends on attracting sufficient participation, the cost to an individual of participating in an unsuccessful action (including the possibility of imprisonment or execution) can be severe. To overcome the private disincentive to participate, would-be insurgents must settle on the definition, and find a way of communicating the occurrence, of an infraction and the appropriate responses thereto.

Constitutionally prescribed democratic decision rules, according to this view, enhance confidence in governmental policies relative to autocracy in two ways. Firstly, democracy broadens the interests of the government: democratic governments are less likely than autocratic ones to infringe individual property and political interests to the extent those interests are represented in legislatures (North and Weingast 1989; McGuire and Olson 1996). Secondly, constitutions promote the self-enforcement of political bargains by defining and communicating limits on decision-making authority (e.g., Hardin 1989; Weingast 1993; Kandori 1992). By defining the set of eligible voters and applicable vote thresholds, constitutions and bylaws also determine both whose interests are protected and the degree of commitment to the status quo. Other things being equal, rules establishing more 'veto points' – parties or groups with the power to block a proposal – enhance commitment but, in doing so, also make it more likely that some actions with positive expected net benefits will be delayed or blocked. Thus, simple majority rule, which requires acquiescence by only half of enfranchised voters, affords protection to the majority but leaves minority interests exposed to expropriation by a dominant coalition. A unanimity rule, by contrast, assures that all voters' interests are respected but would also often make change all but impossible to accomplish. Intermediate between unanimity and majority rule in the number of veto points established, bicameral and presidential governments – which require ratification of proposals by multiple, independently elected bodies – and supermajority requirements represent efforts, within this framework, to strike a balance between the competing demands for flexibility and commitment in political decision making.

Against these benefits are many well-known drawbacks of democracy. Democratic decision making is widely disparaged as slow, cumbersome, and inefficient. Frequent criticisms include policy incoherence; lack of accountability; capture by special, entrenched, or ideological interests; and an inherent propensity to preserve the status quo to the extent of fostering 'gridlock' (e.g., Fiorina 1996: 85–87; Krehbiel 1996: 9; Pfiffner 1991: 44–46). By contrast, autocracy affords the authority and flexibility to act unilaterally and decisively in times of crisis or opportunity. In the language of the theory of the firm, hierarchical governance affords executives the authority to respond to changing circumstances in 'an adaptive, sequential fashion' (Williamson 1975: 25). The merits of allocating decision authority to a particular group will depend on both how severe these costs are and which of the functions of democracy are most important.

DISTINGUISHING FIRMS AND TOWNS

The modern separation of political and commercial spheres makes it easy to overlook the fact that the distinction between municipal and commercial activity was not always so clear. According to McCall (2011: 534), medieval jurists applied the Latin word *universitas*, denoting an association or corporate body existing independently of its members, in common to 'towns, universities, religious communities, and guilds' and, eventually, to for-profit businesses. Many modern European cities, moreover, had distinctly commercial origins: when European trade began again to flourish during the late-medieval Commercial Revolution (roughly the eleventh to fourteenth centuries), it was common for kings and lords to issue charters for the establishment of marketplaces, which included among their powers the rights to raise taxes, mint coins, and 'establish a court (which practically included the right to specify the law) to the owner of the market' (Bindseil and Pfeil 1999: 741). For much of this time, the only security afforded merchants in these marketplaces was the interest of the owners (typically abbots or lords) who stood to gain from the collection of rental fees, customs, and tolls as well as from increased business for their tenants (Britnell 1981: 221; Kadens 2004: 49).

The success of these early marketplaces under the authority of a lord illustrates the capacity of communities to thrive and prosper without the support of democratic institutions. Marketplaces that failed to provide an attractive environment 'perished, because no traders attended the market' (Bindseil and Feil 1999: 745). What, then, if anything, did the later introduction of local democracy contribute? All three functions of democratic governance probably play a role in the allocation of political authority. But some would appear to play a more important role than others. For example, an implication of the political incentive alignment theory, as noted earlier, is that affording community members voting rights will be more valuable where, other things the same, members are better informed or can acquire information at lower cost (Gilligan 1993). But it is hardly plausible that the average citizen is better informed about local government expenditures and programs – much less governmental policies at the national level – than about matters related to his or her own workplace. Moreover, the negligible power to influence outcomes accruing to an individual vote in a large community eliminates any meaningful incentive. Yet members of large political communities, but not members (employees) of smaller 'commercial communities' (firms), possess voting rights, suggesting that incentive alignment is not a pivotal function of democracy in this context.

Voting for purposes of preference aggregation is potentially more important. Inasmuch as the principal function of governments is the provision of public goods, some means of arriving at a collective decision about appropriate levels will be needed, and voting serves that purpose (if imperfectly). The case for democratic governance in the provision of *local* public goods is far weaker, however. Firstly, as Demsetz (1968) and Coase (1974) long ago observed, the existence of public goods does not necessitate public production; municipalities in theory can, and in practice often have, contracted with private firms for the provision of local public goods (see, for example, Masten 2011). In acting as a central contracting agent, a town stands in relation to citizens much as a firm stands in relation to its employees, suppliers, and customers.

A town operating as a contracting agent does still have to decide what level of public goods to procure on behalf of its citizens, for which voting is one mechanism. Comparison of the activities of towns and firms again suggests the limitations of this rationale for democratic governance. The focus on bilateral transactions in both transaction cost and agency theories has obscured the fact that cost considerations typically make it uneconomical to tailor characteristics of a firm's products and operations to individual suppliers, workers, or customers. Every product is a multidimensional array of attributes; think, for example, of the many specifications comprising an automobile: horsepower, transmission, shape, interior materials, and so on. But efficiencies of mass productions imply that even such basic product features as color and size will be offered in only a limited range. Even contract terms are often standardized and nonnegotiable. (Try negotiating variations in the terms of your cell phone contract.) When a firm chooses its product mix, it does so for all customers, some of whom may have preferred a different combination of product attributes. Similarly, for job characteristics: every job consists of a multidimensional array of attributes – work hours; line speed; work conditions such as safety, temperature, noise, and lighting; even location – many of which cannot be changed for one employee without doing so for all. To the extent that decisions with respect to job and product characteristics affect all workers and customers, they represent local public goods just as much as the availability of parks or the quality of local schools. Yet customers are not given the opportunity to vote on the colors in which cars or ties are available or what line of products the grocer stocks; nor do employees (except perhaps in union shops) vote on job attributes.

The reason that consumers generally do not vote on product characteristics, despite their public nature, is that firms have an incentive to provide combinations of product attributes and price that approximate the efficient combination or, at a minimum, that yield a result at least as good as what a 'democratic' process would achieve. The same is arguably true of job characteristics: employers have an incentive to offer a combination of workplace conditions that balance their appeal to employees with their cost; an employer providing unattractive work conditions would either have to pay higher wages or suffer higher worker turnover.

The potential for competition among communities to yield efficient provision of local public goods was, of course, precisely the point of Tiebout (1956). As long as there exist sufficient numbers of providers relative to the heterogeneity of individuals, competition among communities for residents should provide something approaching the efficient level of local public goods without the need for democratic local government. Municipal corporations could just as well be business corporations, with profit-maximizing managers and directors replacing vote-maximizing mayors and city councils. The longevity of medieval marketplaces and modern apartment complexes suggests that these enterprises yielded satisfactory production of local public goods despite the lack of democratic governance.

A central feature of the preceding illustrations, however, is mobility. Consumers can, for most purchases, switch producers fairly easily. Changing employers is typically more costly than changing suppliers but, depending on occupation and location, is often a feasible and reasonably common practice. Residential mobility generally costs less for renters than for homeowners; relocating to another country may be very costly if not impossible. These examples suggest a general pattern: the strength of preference for democratic governance appears, at least in rough terms, to correlate inversely with mobility. Consumer and labor cooperatives are rare; landlord-owned apartment complexes are far more common than residential cooperatives; democracy dominates, in Western countries, at the municipal level as well as above. An increased demand for democracy as mobility decreases could be a response to inefficient levels of public good provision or to greater appropriation risk, however. Discriminating between the two functions requires a more detailed inquiry.

COMMUNITIES OF SCHOLARS

American universities provide an interesting setting to explore the functions and limitations of democratic governance. Firstly, like firms, universities offer services for a price and compete with each other in both input and output markets. In governance respects, however, academic institutions often resemble governments more than commercial enterprises, with faculty exercising authority, either directly or through elected representative bodies, over important institutional decisions. Secondly, the large number and variety of American colleges and universities makes it possible to explore differences in governance among institutions. The United States is home to more than 2000 four-year colleges and universities, approximately one-third of which are public (state-owned) institutions and two-thirds are private, mostly non-profit institutions (although the number of for-profits has recently been growing).[1] In addition to public versus private status, institutions differ in their 'mission' (teaching versus research institutions, for example), affiliations (religious versus secular), and quality and selectivity: The higher education market in the US is highly stratified in the quality of both students and faculty.[2]

Control of American universities has long been a subject of controversy and contention. Officially, ultimate authority in most universities resides in university boards analogous to boards of directors in corporations. Members of such boards frequently decry their lack of practical authority, however. Typical is the complaint of José Cabranes, a US federal judge and former general counsel of Yale University with experience on several university boards (Cabranes 2007: 957):

> [M]ore than thirty years as a trustee of private universities in the United States leads me to this simple conclusion about the governing boards of such institutions: These governing boards govern very little. Except for approving annual budgets submitted by the university administration in omnibus form and supporting projects by their financial largesse, trustees play no role, or a very limited role, in major decisions that shape and define the vital purposes of a university.

They play no role in deciding who will teach students, or what they will be taught, or shaping programs of research and related activities using the university's resources.

Interestingly, university administrators also claim a lack of power, complaining that 'provosts and presidents are constrained from both above [by boards] and below [by faculty] by decisions that are not under their control' (Fethke and Policano 2012: 172, 176), while faculty increasingly bemoan the centralization of decision-making authority accompanying the 'corporatization' of universities (e.g., Andrews 2006).

A pair of surveys of faculty and administrators conducted in 1970 and 2001 provides a more detailed picture of how decision-making authority is actually distributed in American institutions of higher education. Specifically, the surveys asked representatives of participating institutions to classify for each of 15 areas of decision making the extent of actual faculty and administrator authority as follows:[3]

- 'Administrator Determination': decisions or actions over which administrators have unilateral authority.
- 'Faculty Determination': decisions or actions over which 'the faculty of an academic unit or its duly authorized representatives have final legislative or operational authority with respect to policy or action'.
- 'Joint Action': decisions or actions that 'formal agreement by both the faculty and other components of the institution' and are subject to 'veto by any component'.

Each of the surveys received responses from over 800 institutions. Figure 6.1 summarizes graphically the average levels of faculty participation reported by responding institutions across decision areas. Two features immediately stand out: firstly, that faculty at American colleges and universities exercise significant authority over a range of decisions and secondly, that faculty authority increased on average in all decision areas between 1970 and 2001. Figure 6.1 also suggests that the amount of faculty versus administrator authority tends to vary with relative expertise: on average, faculty have more authority on matters relating to the curriculum and degrees while administrators have more authority on decisions involving budgetary matters, for example. Interestingly, faculty also have significant authority in faculty appointments and tenure decisions, especially in the 2001 when faculty had veto authority in approximately 70 percent of responding institutions, but had authority over individual salaries in fewer than 20 percent of institutions in 2001 and only 6 percent in 1970, even though hiring, promotions, and individual salary determination all involve the evaluation of faculty merit. Such large discrepancies in the authority to set salaries compared to hiring and tenure decisions are hard to reconcile on the basis of expertise alone.

Authority over specific decisions (direct democracy) is less important, of course, to the extent that parties effectively participate in the selection of those who do make decisions. Figure 6.1 shows that faculty had selection or veto power over department chair appointments in 54 percent of responding institutions in 2001 (up from 22 percent in 1970) but had such authority over dean appointments in only a third of institutions in 2001 (up from 14 percent in 1970). Moreover, where faculty did possess formal authority over administrator appointments, it was predominantly in the form of Joint Action.

The 2001 survey did not inquire about faculty authority in the appointment of

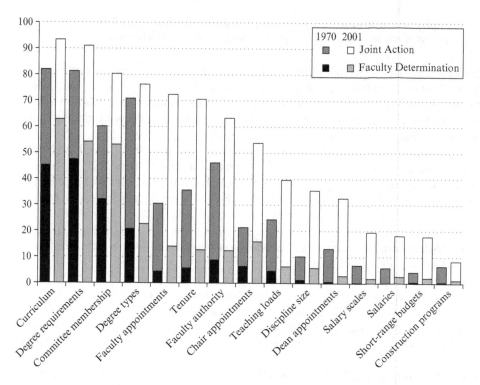

Sources: 1970: Report of the Survey Subcommittee of Committee T (1971) 2001: Kaplan (2002).

Figure 6.1   Faculty authority in university decisions, 1970, 2001 (% of institutions)

presidents, but the 1970 survey indicated that faculty participated in the selection of presidents in fewer than 10 percent of institutions, almost always in conjunction with other authorities (Masten 2006: 666). Thus, whereas professors had significant control over membership on the faculty through their authority to hire, promote, and dismiss faculty, they had little formal authority over the selection of top administrators, who generally serve at the pleasure of, and thus act as agents of, governing boards. Boards at public universities may be appointed by governors or legislatures or elected by the population at large. At private universities, however, boards of trustees are mostly self-perpetuating: Brown (2007) reports that trustees at private universities are selected by the trustees themselves over 90 percent of the time. Even among universities with religious affiliations, 72 percent of board membership is self-perpetuating, with only 24 percent of trustees selected by a religious body. The six trustees of the Harvard Corporation, which owns Harvard University, elect themselves for life terms.

The summary figures presented in Figure 6.1 have two limitations. Firstly, the overall averages reported potentially conceal significant variation among universities in the amount of faculty authority in decision making. Secondly, although the total number of responding institutions in each survey was similar (826 and 882), the samples do not perfectly overlap. To provide a sense of the variation among institutions and a more accurate picture of how given institutions changed over time, I extracted the approximately

Table 6.1   Institutions by type and affiliation (intersection 1970–2001 surveys)

Type	Private	Public	Religious
University	19	65	16
LA plus	45	121	64
Liberal Arts	19	30	128
Specialized	10	5	–

520 institutions appearing in both the 1970 and 2001 surveys. Table 6.1 shows the distribution of those institutions by type – research universities, 'LA plus' (liberal arts colleges offering some graduate degrees), liberal arts colleges, and specialized institutions – and affiliation – private, public, or religious. Table 6.2 reports average levels of faculty participation in decisions over which faculty either have full authority or veto power, that is, the sum of responses for Faculty Determination and Joint Action, for those institutions.

The first two columns of Table 6.2 contain the overall averages for each decision area for 1970 and 2001, respectively. Consistent with the full-sample comparisons depicted in Figure 6.1, faculty authority increased on average between the two surveys. The remaining columns report the corresponding averages for selected institution types and affiliations. Comparisons of the 1970 and 2001 responses for each of the specific institution types generally show similar patterns of increasing faculty authority. For the most part, the 19 private research universities in both surveys maintained the highest levels of faculty authority, with reductions in reported faculty authority only over decisions concerning types of degrees offered, dean appointments, and the faculty's role in campus governance. Perhaps the most striking changes were the sizeable increases in faculty participation at liberal arts colleges (both public and private), Catholic institutions, and to a lesser extent, public research universities, institution categories that had significantly less faculty governance than did private research universities in 1970 (Masten 2006). Overall, the evidence indicates that these other institution types have approached and, in many decision areas, largely caught up with their private university counterparts in the 30 years between the two surveys.

What explains the prevalence of faculty authority in American colleges and universities and the variation in that authority among institutions and over time? One possibility is that faculty simply have a greater taste for control than other types of employees. Arguments based on tastes are difficult to refute, but casual observation of faculty attitudes toward committee and administrative work does not lend itself to this explanation. Another, more plausible explanation is that faculty control reflects the need to draw on the often highly specialized expertise of faculty on academic matters such as course content, degree requirements, and professional evaluation, decision areas in which, as noted above, faculty possess the greatest authority.

Strictly speaking, faculty expertise explains why administrators would want to consult faculty on relevant matters but does not by itself explain why faculty have authority for those decisions; it is in fact common for administrators to draw on the specialized knowledge and judgment of faculty through consultation on decisions for which administrators retain full authority (see Masten 2006; Kaplan 2002). What formal authority offers that consultation alone does not is increased confidence that faculty will receive

Table 6.2 Incidence of faculty governance (determination or joint action), 1970 and 2001

Decision areas	All		Priv. Univ.		Pub. Univ.		Priv. LA		Pub. LA		Catholic	
	1970	2001	1970	2001	1970	2001	1970	2001	1970	2001	1970	2001
1 Faculty appointments	00.31	00.75	00.67	00.78	00.41	00.81	00.52	00.72	00.09	00.57	00.34	00.77
4 Tenure	00.35	00.74	00.73	00.73	00.46	00.79	00.48	00.60	00.10	00.54	00.48	00.73
6 Curriculum	00.82	00.94	00.97	00.98	00.88	00.98	00.94	00.98	00.72	00.87	00.65	00.91
7 Degree requirements	00.82	00.94	00.98	00.96	00.89	00.96	00.99	10.00	00.78	00.83	00.60	00.86
9 Types of degrees offered	00.72	00.78	00.99	00.73	00.80	00.82	00.91	00.83	00.49	00.63	00.52	00.71
12 Relative staff sizes of disciplines	00.09	00.35	00.08	00.22	00.08	00.32	00.18	00.40	00.00	00.29	00.14	00.32
13 Programs for buildings and other facilities	00.07	00.08	00.07	00.06	00.03	00.07	00.11	00.09	00.12	00.09	00.09	00.08
15 Appointments of academic deans	00.13	00.33	00.28	00.17	00.20	00.36	00.14	00.32	00.03	00.37	00.05	00.30
16 Appointments of department chairmen	00.21	00.57	00.28	00.33	00.29	00.54	00.28	00.36	00.04	00.51	00.24	00.60
17 Faculty salary scales	00.05	00.20	00.06	00.09	00.02	00.16	00.05	00.17	00.03	00.19	00.09	00.21
18 Individual faculty salaries	00.06	00.20	00.00	00.12	00.11	00.31	00.01	00.12	00.00	00.20	00.10	00.16
19 Short-range budgetary planning	00.03	00.17	00.00	00.13	00.03	00.15	00.06	00.15	00.10	00.19	00.04	00.19
21 Average teaching loads	00.23	00.42	00.30	00.45	00.22	00.53	00.35	00.48	00.11	00.44	00.27	00.39
25 Authority of faculty in governance	00.46	00.64	00.53	00.46	00.56	00.70	00.25	00.66	00.32	00.57	00.37	00.55
27 Membership . . . senate committees	00.60	00.83	00.70	00.70	00.67	00.87	00.62	00.85	00.53	00.81	00.58	00.73

a return on their time and effort advising the university by providing the ability to, at a minimum, block (veto) unfavorable actions. More generally, shared governance helps to secure bargains between faculty, administrators, and institutional boards, and with students, alumni, and public and private donors to the extent their interests are represented on boards or in the administration. Because faculty and administrators (or other patrons or 'stakeholders') place different relative values on research, teaching, service to the institution, facilities, athletics, and a host of other activities and attributes of universities, opportunities exist for mutually beneficial bargains in which, for example, administrators offer to compensate faculty for forgone research opportunities (and thereby promotion and alternative job prospects) in exchange for service on university committees. Such bargains are subject to reneging hazards, however, while the complexity and subtlety of academic responsibilities and the need to accommodate changes in demand and resources make contracting ineffective (Milgrom and Roberts 1992: 127–129). Academic bargains, like political ones, must therefore be largely self-enforcing. Like democratic institutions generally, faculty governance promotes the security of bargains by expanding the set of transactors with veto power and by providing a relatively verifiable criterion by which to judge the legitimacy of decisions: that proposals receive the explicit consent of designated individuals or groups before being implemented.

My analysis of differences in decision-making authority among universities in 1970 showed variations in the allocation of authority to be broadly consistent with this commitment function of faculty governance (Masten 2006). Faculty authority in general, and joint action in particular, were most prevalent in large, selective, 'full-service' research universities, where, because of greater specialization, heterogeneity was likely to be greatest and mobility least. The greater tendency toward autocratic governance in state and Catholic-affiliated institutions, meanwhile, was consistent with the need to protect the interests of external patrons on whom the institution was dependent for resources or support. The reason for the increase in faculty authority overall, but especially at state and Catholic institutions, between 1970 and 2001 seen in Figure 6.1 and Table 6.2 has yet to be determined, but possible factors include an increase in emphasis on research, making these institutions more like research universities in character, and declining state support for higher education and decreasing influence of religious authorities, representing a reduction in the interests of these external patrons.

The history of emergence of faculty governance in the United States provides further support for the commitment function of democratic governance in higher education. Until late nineteenth century, the typical institution of higher learning in the US consisted of a small denominational college. Because the curriculum was standard and static, faculty could be as well: there was little academic specialization, with each professor expected to be a 'jack-of-all-disciplines' (Veysey 1965: 142). Meanwhile, control resided in the president and outside governing boards composed mainly of clergy, and the 'administration' consisted solely of the president, who typically doubled as a teacher.

The emergence and governance of the modern American university can be traced to two major events. The first was a decision by the US Supreme Court in 1819, ruling against the state of New Hampshire in what is known as the Dartmouth College case, which gave private universities constitutional protection from state authority by removing a state's ability to revoke an institution's charter. As a result, for the first time in the US or elsewhere, private universities and colleges gained assurance of the right to operate without interference by the state. Having lost the ability to influence how colleges used resources, legislators became understandably reluctant to provide private colleges with public funds. States that wanted to promote particular programs or directions were now obliged to set up universities of their own. Whereas only two state universities (Georgia, founded in 1785; and North Carolina, in 1789) existed prior to 1819, nine additional state universities were founded in the 25 years following the decision: Virginia (1825), Indiana (1828), Michigan (1837), Missouri (1839), Mississippi (1844), Iowa (1847), Wisconsin (1848), Minnesota (1851), and California (Berkeley, 1855).

The second, and arguably more significant, factor was the introduction, toward the end of the century, of research as a significant function of universities. As scholarships increased and became more specialized, it became increasingly difficult for any individual to understand and evaluate contributions to all fields. In contrast to the days of the small college president who was able to teach the entire curriculum, the relative competence to evaluate performance in the age of scientific research shifted from the administration to the faculty. Lacking the necessary expertise, presidents and boards were forced to rely increasingly on the judgment of faculty as to academic merit. At the same time, the addition of research and increasing specialization also increased the heterogeneity of faculty, reducing mobility and increasing conflicts both among faculty and between faculty and administrators. Organizational arrangements that can be traced to these developments include: (1) the decentralization of decision making authority to academic departments; (2) the emergence of large administrative bureaucracies; and (3) an expansion of faculty control and corresponding contraction of the influence of governing boards and presidents over university operations (Veysey 1965; Duryea 1973: 29).

CONCLUSION

Issues associated with the allocation of decision authority are much bigger than this chapter can encompass. My more modest aim has been to challenge some conventional assumptions about the functions and domain of democratic governance by drawing some parallels and contrasts between firms and communities and by providing some more detailed information on the decision making of American universities that suggests that faculty governance arose as a means to help secure academic bargains following the emergence of research as a significant function of universities. Left unexplained is why democratic governance has not been more widely used to address commitment problems in employment settings more generally. Agency theorists have long noted that an employer's inability to commit not to revise compensation schemes limits its ability to elicit effort and firm-specific investments from employees (e.g., Gibbons 1987, 1998). In fact, the conditions alleged to motivate democratic governance in political and academic settings could be argued to characterize most traditional employment relations: In the typical firm: (1) the effort and investments employees are willing to make depend on the credibility of promised rewards; (2) contingent contracting is impractical (and seldom observed); (3) multiple employees interact with a single employer, and the sanctions that an individual employee can exact on a reneging employer (other than quitting) are generally few and relatively minor; and (4) many job attributes have the form of local public goods. Yet employee governance in business firms analogous to faculty governance in universities is rare.

Two factors would appear to contribute to this outcome. On one side, the existence of an important class of external patrons (the firm's owners) on whom the organization is dependent for capital and whose interests (protection of investments against appropriation by insiders and overall maximization of long-run returns) may not align with the short-term interests of the firm's employees favors autocratic control. On the other is the arguably greater availability of alternative employment opportunities and, thus, greater mobility in commercial than academic settings, which would tend to reduce the need for protections offered by democratic governance. As Holmstrom has put it: 'the very fact that workers can exit a firm at will and go to other firms, and that consumers and input suppliers and other trading partners can do likewise, limits the firm's ability to exploit these constituents [and] makes it feasible for the firm to go about its business of setting "internal rules of the game" in a relatively unfettered fashion' (Holmstrom 1999: 90). But even conventional business firms, he adds, 'feel . . . pressures to be democratic and nonpartial when exit is costly for [their] members': 'Democracy is a costly governance procedure, but it appears to be the best one available when [as in the case of governments] exit is precluded' (Holmstrom 1999).

NOTES

1. Another approximately 2000 institutions offer associate (two-year) degrees (Chronicle of Higher Education 2010).
2. For a discussion of the reasons for and implications of quality stratification in American higher education, see Masten (1995).
3. The surveys further subdivided the Administrator Determination category based on the extent to which faculty played an advisory role in administrator decisions (Consultation, Discussion, or None). The 1970 survey covered an additional 16 decision areas not covered by the 2001 survey. See Masten (2006) for more detail on definitions and decision categories.

REFERENCES

Andrews, James G. (2006), 'How we can resist corporatization,' *Academe*, **92**(3), available at www.aaup.org/AAUP/pubsres/academe/2006/MJ/feat/andr.htm.

Arrow, Kenneth (1963 [1951]), *Social Choice and Individual Values*, 2nd edn, New York: Wiley.

Bindseil, Ulrich and Christian Pfeil (1999), 'Specialization as a specific investment into the market: a transaction cost approach to the rise of markets and towns in Medieval Germany, 800–1200', *Journal of Institutional and Theoretical Economics*, **55**(4), 738–754.

Britnell, R.H. (1981), 'The proliferation of markets in England, 1200–1349', *Economic History Review*, **34**(2), 209–221.

Brown, William O. (2007), 'Determinants of university board structure', paper presented at the International Society for New Institutional Economics Annual Meeting, Reykjavik, Iceland, 22 June, available at http://www.isnie.org/assets/files/papers2007/brown.pdf.

Buchanan, James M. and Gordon Tullock (1962), *The Calculus of Consent*, Ann Arbor, MI: University of Michigan Press.

Cabranes, José A. (2007), 'Myth and reality of university trusteeship in the post-Enron era', *Fordham Law Review*, **76**, 955–979.

Chronicle of Higher Education (2010), '2005 Carnegie classification of institutions of higher education by classification category and control', *Almanac of Higher Education, 2010–2011*, available at http://chronicle.com/article/2005-Carnegie-Classification/123998/.

Coase, Ronald H. (1937), 'The nature of the firm', *Economica N.S.*, **4**, 386–405.
Coase, Ronald H. (1974), 'The lighthouse in economics', *Journal of Law and Economics*, **17**(2), 357–376.
Demsetz, Harold (1968), 'Why regulate utilities?', *Journal of Law and Economics*, **11**, 55–66.
Duryea, E.D. (1973), 'Evolution of university organization', in James A. Perkins (ed.), *The University as an Organization*, New York: McGraw Hill, pp. 15–37.
Fethke, Gary C. and Andrew J. Policano (2012), *Public No More: A New Path to Excellence for America's Public Universities*, Stanford, CA: Stanford University Press.
Fiorina, Morris P. (1996), *Divided Government*, 2nd edn, Boston, MA: Allyn & Bacon.
Friedman, Thomas (2009), 'Our one-party democracy', *New York Times*, 9 September.
Gibbons, Robert (1987), 'Piece-rate incentive schemes', *Journal of Labor Economics*, **5**, 413–429.
Gibbons, Robert (1998), 'Incentives in organizations', *Journal of Economic Perspectives*, **12**, 115–132.
Gilligan, Thomas W. (1993), 'Information and the allocation of legislative authority', *Journal of Institutional and Theoretical Economics*, **149**, 321–341.
Grandori, Anna (2013), *Epistemic Economics and Organization. Forms of Rationality and Governance for a Wiser Economy*, London: Routledge.
Hansmann, Henry (1988), 'The ownership of the firm', *Journal of Law, Economics, and Organization*, **4**(2), 267–304.
Hansmann, Henry (1991), 'Condominium and cooperative housing: transactional efficiency, tax subsidies, and tenure choice', *Journal of Legal Studies*, **20**(1), 25–71.
Hardin, Russell (1989), 'Why a Constitution?' in B. Grofman and D. Wittman (eds), *The Federalist Papers and the New Institutionalism*, New York: Agathon Press, pp. 100–120.
Holmstrom, Bengt (1999), 'The firm as a subeconomy', *Journal of Law, Economics, and Organization*, **15**, 74–102.
Kadens, Emily (2004), 'Order within law, variety within custom: the character of the medieval merchant law', *Chicago Journal of International Law*, **5**(1), 39–65.
Kandori, Michihiro (1992), 'Social norms and community enforcement', *Review of Economic Studies*, **59**, 63–80.
Kaplan, Gabriel E. (2002), *Preliminary Results from the 2001 Survey on Higher Education Governance*, unpublished report presented to Committee T of the American Association of University Professors, Washington, DC, 15–16 February.
Krehbiel, Keith (1996), 'Institutional and partisan sources of gridlock: a theory of divided and unified government', *Journal of Theoretical Politics*, **8**, 7–39.
Masten, Scott E. (1995), 'Old school ties: financial aid coordination and the governance of higher education', *Journal of Economic Behavior and Organization*, **28**(September), 23–47.
Masten, Scott E. (2006), 'Authority and commitment: why universities, like legislatures, are not organized as firms', *Journal of Economics and Management Strategy*, **15**(3), 649–684.
Masten, Scott E. (2011), 'Public utility ownership in 19th-century America: the "aberrant" case of water', *Journal of Law, Economics, and Organization*, **27**(October), 604–654.
McCall, Brian M. (2011), 'The corporation as imperfect society', *Delaware Journal of Corporate Law*, **36**, 509–575.
McGuire, Martin C. and Mancur Olson, Jr. (1996), 'The economics of autocracy and majority rule: the invisible hand and the use of force', *Journal of Economic Literature*, **34**(1), 72–96.
Milgrom, Paul and John Roberts (1990), 'Bargaining costs, influence costs, and the organization of economic activity', in J. Alt and K. Shepsle (eds), *Perspectives on Positive Political Economy*, Cambridge: Cambridge University Press, pp. 57–89.
Milgrom, Paul and John Roberts (1992), *Economics, Organization and Management*, Englewood Cliffs, NJ: Prentice-Hall.
Miller, Gary J. (1997), 'The impact of economics on contemporary political science', *Journal of Economic Literature*, **35**, 1173–1204.
North, Douglass C. and Barry R. Weingast (1989), 'Constitutions and credible commitments: the evolution of the institutions of public choice in 17th century England', *Journal of Economic History*, **49**, 803–832.
Pfiffner, James P. (1991), 'Divided government and the problem of governance', in J.A. Thurber (ed.), *Divided Democracy: Cooperation and Conflict between the President and Congress*, Washington, DC: Congressional Quarterly Press.
Pirrong, Stephen Craig (1999), 'The organization of financial exchange markets: theory and evidence', *Journal of Financial Markets*, **2**, 329–357.
Report of the Survey Subcommittee of Committee T (1971), *AAUP Bulletin*, Spring, 69–124.
Shepsle, Kenneth A. (1993), 'Political institutions and the new institutional economics: comment', *Journal of Institutional and Theoretical Economics*, **149**(1), 347–350.
Simon, Herbert A. (1951), 'A formal theory of the employment relationship', *Econometrica*, **19**, 293–305.

Tiebout, Charles, (1956), 'A pure theory of local expenditures', *Journal of Political Economy*, **64**(5), 416–424.
Veysey, Lawrence R. (1965), *The Emergence of the American University*, Chicago, IL: University of Chicago Press.
Weingast, Barry R. (1993), 'Constitutions as governance structures: the political foundations of secure markets', *Journal of Institutional and Theoretical Economics*, **149**, 286–311.
Weingast, Barry R. and William J. Marshall (1988), 'The industrial organization of Congress; or, why legislatures, like firms, are not organized as markets', *Journal of Political Economy*, **96**, 132–163.
Williamson, Oliver E. (1975), *Markets and Hierarchies*, New York: Free Press.
Williamson, Oliver E. (1987), 'Corporate finance and corporate governance', *Journal of Finance*, **43**(3), 567–591.

7. Ethics, economic organization and the social contract

Lorenzo Sacconi

This chapter introduces a notion of an ethical social norm that integrates its description as a self-sustaining regularity of behavior with the normative meanings of the statements by which a norm is formulated in the moral language. This definition is applied to organizational ethics where the main problem – abuse of authority – is identified with the help of a critical reading of new-institutional economic theory of the firm. Given a game-theoretical definition of an institution, it is then shown that only by integrating it with the social contract as shared mode of reasoning may the process of convergence to the beliefs system that backs an equilibrium institution be started. Thus the chapter illustrates the egalitarian social contract as both an impartial justification for organizational constitutions and as an equilibrium selection device. It is shown that equilibrium selection through the social contract solves the problem of legitimization of authority in the organizational relation between a non-controlling stakeholder and the entrepreneur or the management of a firm, holding hierarchical authority over the stakeholder. The result is a fiduciary relation between a stakeholder (the trustor) and the owner, director or manager (the trustee) based on fair distribution of the cooperative surplus. This is the basis for the explanation of corporate social responsibility, understood as an extended model of organizational governance that generalizes to all the possible ownership forms of the economic organization, giving credit to the idea that social responsibility is an overarching social norm in the field of organization governance

INTRODUCTION

By an ethical social norm is meant a norm pertaining to ethics in both its normative and descriptive understandings. From a normative perspective, a norm is a rule of behavior derivable from a principle which is commonly understood as universalizably prescriptive by agents, and whereby they decide to abide by the same rule of behavior. Descriptively, a norm is a regularity of behavior which is normally followed by members of a given action domain for most of the time, when they expect that others will also follow it.

Normatively, the social responsible model of organizational governance is the result of the stakeholders' social contract under the moral assumptions of impersonality, impartiality and empathy. Stakeholders agree to select such a governance structure as part of the organization constitution (an economic institution) that they join in order to escape from a mutually destructive 'state of nature'. Solution of the surplus distribution problem is egalitarian (or maximin). This is a consequence of Binmore's reconsideration of Rawls's maximin principle in a game-theoretical context (Binmore 1989, 1991, 2005). This result is replicated in the chapter by reference to a simple repeated game (the trust game), among a non-controlling stakeholder and the firm's management or entrepreneur. In this case, given an already defined structure of ownership over the physical assets of the firm, the stakeholder grants authority to the entrepreneur only because such authority is exercised in accordance with a principle of fair distribution of the utility surplus.

All this depicts social responsibility owed to the organization's stakeholders as a normative model of multi-fiduciary organization governance. But the distinctive feature of this approach is that the normative social contract theory also works as part of an explanation of how a social norm of organizational governance may be selected, and how it may come to evolve until it establishes itself as one of the main institutions in a given action domain. Institutions are hence defined in game-theoretical terms as equilibria supported by belief systems.

The chapter shows that the social contract explains the emergence of a 'social responsibility' norm in the domain of organizational governance, and how the equilibrium selection process leading to such an institution may be started. This is intrinsic in the social contract theory as a theory of agreement on a set of rules which also entails that each agent expects that the same rule is accepted and expected to be accepted by all other participants. But it also means that the fair social contract must select an equilibrium point which is a feasible way to implement the agreement reached through the social contract.

This double functioning of the social contract as justification for, and explanation of, an institution's emergence corresponds to the definition given here of ethics and organizational ethics. Descriptively, I accept the social scientist's understanding of ethical norms. But I also show that this cannot work unless the description includes the operation of a normative judgment which is prescriptive and universalizable, and able to override any other reason to act. In fact, inasmuch as the social contract is a normative principle that entails agreement on a solution for cooperation and coordination problems, it gives rise to a system of beliefs and mutual expectations about reciprocal behavior which induces convergence to an equilibrium.

ETHICS AND SOCIAL NORMS

Economists, as well as social and organization theorists, often understand ethics as a domain of social norms performing pro-social functions that are self-sustaining and thus do not require external enforcement to be complied with. Pro-social functions are typically identified in the facilitation of cooperation and coordination among individuals in both organizational contexts – wherein authority relations are legitimized and hence their acceptance is facilitated by compliance with moral codes – and the markets, where individuals cooperate through imperfect contracts assisted by norms of business ethics. Ethical norms, moreover, are seen as self-sustaining because they induce incentives to conform with the regularity of behavior that gives them a behavioral content. This inducement of motivations to conform is simply explained by the mutual expectation that other members of the same action domain will behave similarly. A notion of reciprocity – either instrumental or intrinsic – is part of this explanation, so that conformity depends on the expectation of reciprocal behavior. When reciprocity is instrumental, conformity is seen as each agent's self-interested best response to the shared expectation that every other agent will also conform.

Normally, those who accept this perspective on ethics do not claim to have considered its normative contents, and they frankly admit that their analysis is entirely descriptive and does not purport to give any moral justification in favor of intentional action conforming with a particular norm. At best, adhesion to a social norm is explained intentionally in terms of enlightened self-interest given common (or more realistically 'shared') knowledge of other player adherence. This is a fully respectable tradition of thought traceable back to David Hume (1739 [2000]). Since the work of David Lewis, it has led to the growing contribution of game-theoretical models to the understanding of social norms, conventions, and the like (Lewis 1969; Schotter 1981; Sugden 1986; Young 1998; Skyrms 2004; Bicchieri 2006). However, despite the honest admission that its intent is merely to 'describe' ethics, an explanation of how ethical norms actually work that completely disregards the normative content and meaning of these norms seems somewhat paradoxical.

Is it really possible that the cooperative and coordinative functions discharged by ethical norms can be explained without any reference to the content of normative judgments and the meanings of the linguistic utterances by which ethical norms are expressed? Can the effectiveness of these functions be completely indifferent to the normative content of norms, that is, independent of their content in terms of commands, obligations, rights or permissions – as if the same functions could be performed for whatever obligation, right or duty affirmed, and whatever the reasons justifying them? The self-enforceable nature of ethics itself, which is a basic tenet of this descriptive perspective, is grounded in the idea that mutual expectations of reciprocal compliance – often complemented by self-interest (as in Lewis 1969; Schotter 1981; Sugden 1986, but clearly not in Bicchieri 2006), but without reference to any intrinsic normative reason as to why a norm should be adhered to – are enough to explain norm compliance. Again, the argument must work as if the merit of the purported command, right or duty were completely indifferent. Indifference regards not only the agent's first-person reasons to act but also the formation of their expectation concerning why other agents should act in accordance with the norm or why they should expect conformity from each other (which in general will depend on higher-level expectations: an agent expects reciprocity and conformity from others precisely because they expect that others will also expect conformity from them).

This, in fact, is the distinctive characteristic of Lewis's social conventions of pure coordination. No intrinsic reason disposes us to obey one convention amongst others if they perform exactly the function of permitting us to achieve the same goal or objective, or to satisfy the same value through coordination. In this case, the sole reason for conforming with one convention among others is the expectation that others will do the same. Here, however, emerges the deep difference with respect to ethical norms that do not perform a merely pure coordinative function but also give us reasons to make a choice among different ways to carry out cooperative endeavors based on terms of value like well-being, fairness, rightness or the equitable distribution of some cooperative surplus, and so on. When reasons to convince other interacting agents to forego their individual incentives to pursue their individually preferred outcomes in order to join a common mutually beneficial plan of action (but not necessarily as good for them as their most preferred alternative) are at stake, and also when reasons are needed for agreeing on one among many possible cooperative plans, each characterized by a different distribution of benefits and none of them completely individually irrational (in the sense that they could not be sustained by any equilibrium point), then the content of ethical norms in terms of justice, fairness, equality, righteousness, duties, or otherwise social wellbeing, typically seems to matter (for a definition of ethical norms that modifies the one given by Lewis, including normative acceptance, see Pettit 1990; see also Donaldson and Dunfee 1999).

As a matter of fact, the description of ethics provided thus far also seems insufficient once attention is paid to the work of philosophers who have tried to describe the common characteristics of ethical judgments expressed through the use of moral language. One may recall, for example, that from a meta-ethical perspective Richard Hare (1963, 1981) set the conditions whereby statements, expressed through sentences constructed according to the linguistic rules on utterance formation, may have 'moral meaning'. Ethical statements from this meta-linguistic perspective are 'prescriptive', 'universalizable' and 'overriding'. Note that this too is a description of how moral statements work (how they acquire their meaning in accordance with how we regularly use the language), without commitment to any specific ethical intuition or normative theory in particular. The first condition is that any sentence stating an ethical norm is a prescription, that is, we understand it as a guide to action. Thus, describing the functioning of ethical norms without reference to how we understand their prescriptive meanings seems to be wrong. The second condition – universalizability – is that, in order for any sentence stating a prescription to be understandable (and effective to our action) as an ethical norm, it must pass the universalization test. This is a minimal requirement of consistency, but it excludes for example the typical contingent explanation of conventions according to which we abide by a norm only because we find ourselves in a particular context wherein a given outcome happens to be 'focal' owing to the contingent reciprocal beliefs of anyone about anyone. The utterance of a norm is understood as ethically prescriptive when it is unconditional on specific contexts and can be reformulated in abstract and universal terms. It can thus be extended from an initial case of application – to which the utterance referred – to all the situations that are invariant with respect to the initial one only in regard to the normatively meaningful characteristics (maybe a certain relation between two or more variables). But these situations may well differ from each other in regard to any other contingent facts, things or individuals described by the relative sentences (for example, the names of persons occurring as variables in a relation that has 'prescriptive' meaning may freely vary). Thus the only way in which the explanation of norm compliance as exclusively based on mutual expectations can be rendered consistent with the description of how ethical norms work in language is to state that the norm which we understand as universally prescriptive is 'abide by other persons' expectations about you in whatever context' (i.e., 'do always what others expect from you or believe you will do' – in other words, 'pure conformism'), without any anchorage in the different prescriptive contents (norms) that expectations may have case by case. However, many of us may not understand statements only about what others expect us to do as universally prescriptive.

The last condition – overridingness – imposes some consistency between prescriptive utterance and behavior by requiring that we understand as truly universally prescriptive only norms that we carry out in practice through our actual behavior. This condition may be too strong, because it does not allow any room for 'weakness of the will' – a not-irrelevant psychological phenomenon. If any discrepancy between utterances about values that we understand as universally prescriptive and our choices must be excluded, we are perhaps obliged to discard some of the most intuitively significant moral sentences as void of moral meaning. Nevertheless, this is a condition of realism and genuineness of ethical statements that reminds us that we cannot understand as really universally prescriptive a norm which, after due reflection on all the alternatives, proves psychologically impossible to put consistently into practice (see also Griffin 1998). This relates to self-enforceability. Since an ethical norm that we truly find meaningful is a motive that overrides any other motive – after the agent's entire set of reasons, incentives and motivations has been considered – it will be revealed as effectively guiding our practical behavior. Such a norm does not need any external enforcement for it to be put into practice: it emerges (so to speak) 'spontaneously' from overall consideration of all the motives for action. Summing up, in order to say that a moral norm overrides any other reason or incentive to act, the repertoire of motivations that we consider must at least include various sentences whose content is the universally prescriptive meanings of alternative norms.

Moreover, normative ethics theories are also part of the picture. If overriding universally prescriptive norms surface in our intuitive judgments and behavior, normative theories of ethics can be seen as systematic kinds of argumentation from which such judgments are entailed and that are in accordance with an entire class of intuitively normative statements. Alternative normative ethics theories have thus a 'quasi-empirical' content. Each of them accords with a class (not necessarily the same) of sentences with intuitive universalizable prescriptive meanings. At the same time – insofar as it is normative – each theory tries to deny our initial intuitions about the universalizable prescriptive meaning of certain sentences that disagree with it. It is therefore impossible to explain how a behavior conforming with a norm emerges to perform coordination and cooperative functions without reference to a prescription that can be accounted for in terms of some normative ethics theory. Consequently, principles rationalized by a normative theory, besides providing reasons to justify actions, can also be seen as causal factors of the initial formation of those systems of mutually consistent (normative) expectations usually invoked to explain why an ethical norm is obeyed (in this chapter, for example, norms will emerge from agents' normative and predictive beliefs in so far as these expectations are shaped by principles of the social contract).

All these considerations suggest that, in order properly to explain how ethical norms perform their pro-social function in the market or organizations, and are 'spontaneously' complied with – even if mutual expectation of conformity may be very important – reference must necessarily be made to the normative reasons to act that are contained in some universalizable ethical judgment usually rationalized by a normative theory. And it will be expressed by some sentence from which a prescription follows which is the normative content of a behavior regularity.

ORGANIZATIONAL ETHICS

Ethical norms, as described in the previous section, will be now applied to economic organizations. They have two roles to play here. Firstly, by means of explicit normative prescriptions they provide arguments in favor (or against) existing or potentially alternative organizational arrangements, in particular with regard to the allocation among the organization's members of authority and the right to make discretional decisions affecting surplus distribution. In this way, organizational ethics suggests criteria with which to choose governance models for the organization, and principles for their strategic management and decision-making. Ethical theory is taken as the basis for deriving prescriptive and universalizable statements that are then employed to decide whether certain forms of authority allocation can be accepted and hence are morally legitimized forms of organizational authority.

The second role of organizational ethics is to ensure that the legitimate arrangement of organization authority and the governance structure are implemented through a self-enforceable ethical social norm. In other words, it must verify whether moral legitimization coincides with enough de facto legitimization, sufficient to give rise to a stable enough organizational relationship. This can come about if the organization's moral norm justifying a given arrangement of organizational authority proves to be the basis for a self-enforceable social norm, and if a decision mechanism is identified through which that social norm can be come into being and evolved until its complete establishment.

Accordingly, the main problem of organizational ethics can be retrieved by a critical reading of the new-institutional theory of the firm (Williamson 1975, 1986). In this perspective, the main problem of economic organization is preventing the opportunism that may occur when contracts are incomplete and the parties to the contract undertake specific investments whose outputs, due to the gaps in the contract, can be expropriated by those who hold control over essential decision variables needed for the success of other agents' investments. This position (usually understood as having control over the firm's physical assets, that can be used in the investment, but which may also consist in controlling some cognitive ability that may be essential to its success) puts its holder in a position to hold up the investor in order to reap as large a part as possible of the surplus engendered by their investment. The solution is to allocate authority to the party responsible for the investment, giving them control over the decision variable able to condition the investment's success (this usually means giving them ownership of the firm's physical assets).

However, as soon as the organization of the firm increases in complexity, the apparent efficiency of this solution breaks down and becomes less than a second-best optimum. Assume that specific investments are multiple, so that many investments can only obtain a surplus when they are made in the same organization with others, and that some cognitive resources, even if not necessarily idiosyncratic, are essential for valorization of other cognitive resources possessed by members of the organization; and finally assume that these resources or investments are complementary, so that the reduction of one of them may prejudice the value of the others (Sacconi 2000; but see also Aoki 1984, 2010).

The hierarchical governance structure that allocates all the residual decision control to one party is less than second-best in these situations because it is evident that having ownership and residual control legitimates appropriation of the entire surplus generated by the firm. But by predicting that their investment will remain unremunerated with any part of the organization surplus, and that the importance of a cognitive asset will not be recognized at the level of the governance structure, non-controlling stakeholders will recognize that there is no reason to invest in the use of their idiosyncratic, essential or complementary cognitive assets. This is quite clear in inter-temporal models (see Grossman & Hart 1986; Hart & Moore 1990). Once the control structure is settled at time 1, then specific investments that are non-contractible and unforeseen events that open the possibility for essential decisions favorable to the valorization of investment (but are also non-contractible) occur at time 2. Finally, at time 3 a bargaining session takes place where the distribution of residual decision rights is relevant because they settle the bargaining status quo which conditions negotiation of the surplus division after investments have been made, but the decision essential for their valorization has still to be taken. The status quo entails a threat of exclusion from the firm for those parties who are not protected by residual control but have carried out a specific investment or have invested their cognitive resources in cooperative and complementary modes. The controlling party will threaten non-controlling stakeholders with exclusion if they do not agree that the decision variable has been resolved favourably for investments, only if all the surplus will be appropriated by the controlling party. The distribution will thus reflect an imbalance of rights in the governance structure. But it is evident that if the non-controlling stakeholders are provident and risk averse, even if they are not perfectly rational and able to forecast future events, at time 2 they will reduce their specific investments and their effort in employing their complementary cognitive assets in proportion to their expectation of being expropriated. The result cannot but be an inefficient solution. What is important to note here is that the inefficiency must be imputed to the expectation of being unfairly expropriated borne by stakeholders who have legitimate claims to participate in the surplus distribution. Organizational inefficiency reflects expectations of unfair treatment. Abuse of authority results thus the main problem, and organizational ethics comes to the fore. Ethics comes before efficiency.

Note that, in the incomplete contract model with inter-temporal structure and *ex post* bargaining, inefficiency follows from sub-investments anticipated at the second stage of the model and in some sense from a remarkable amount of cognitive skill and prudency on the part of non-controlling stakeholders. But in the real world it is much more likely that the judgment of being treated unfairly will have a negative effect on the level of surplus. For example, even if this may seem irrational, non-controlling stakeholders (especially consumers or employees) may reject the bargaining proposal backed by the exclusion threat. This may occur precisely because of a fairness judgment, as observed in many experiments on ultimatum games (even if in the case considered the strong party settles the exit option unilaterally while the agreement is left to emerge from bargaining). Secondly, disloyal behavior may occur also in a later phase of the game, after the *ex post* bargaining has been concluded. Disloyal behavior (especially by employees) may be undertaken by non-controlling stakeholders in the organization who are advantaged by an asymmetry of information in the implementation stage of the *ex post* renegotiated bargain. Consider, in fact, that complementarity of cognitive resources typically occurs in teams where the members' productivities are interdependent and inseparable from one another, so that separate monitoring of a single member's output does not yield much information about their productivity, which depends on the effort put into complementary resources by other team members. Since productivity is inseparable, a team member can always disclaim their responsibility for a reduced output by claiming that other team members are responsible.

Central to organization ethics, therefore, is the issue of unfairness in surplus distribution due to unilateral authority allocation. Its central concern is to put forward principles of justice acceptable to both controlling and non-controlling stakeholders, and which are able to provide assurance about the principle of justice compliance sufficient to induce them to make optimal effort and an efficient level of investment in their idiosyncratic or complementary assets. Principles of justice in the distribution of surplus also affect the surplus production – as typified by cooperation problems where mutual advantage from joint action and distributive conflict on the surplus distribution are simultaneously present.

A fair balance in the surplus distribution reflects a balance in the stakeholders' rights. A typical solution considered in this chapter is the one related to the intuitive idea of the 'firm social responsibility' owed to the non-controlling stakeholders. It is the responsibility of a corporate board of directors, which is appointed by the owners, to balance the owners' residual right of control and claim or right to the surplus with duties owed to non-controlling stakeholders. These commit the board to allocation and distribution policies that allow non-controlling stakeholders to have a fair share of the cooperative surplus.

This duty corresponds to a constraint on the shareholders' claim to appropriate the entire surplus resulting from the stakeholders' cooperation. It should be clear that this parallels a solution of the organizational authority legitimization problem discussed at the beginning of this section. Authority is legitimated when stakeholders, typically the non-controlling ones, accept it as the best solution of a cooperation problem among them. When the corporate governance structure is arranged in such a way that non-controlling stakeholders can participate in a fair share of the firm's surplus, they may accept the authority relation as the best solution of their cooperative and coordination problems. They thus agree to enter the authority relation because it satisfies their independent reason to act defined in terms of a claim of justice (Raz 1985; McMahon 1989; Sacconi 2000). In this case authority is provided with moral legitimization.

THE SOCIAL CONTRACT AND THE EMERGENCE OF SOCIAL NORMS IN THE DOMAIN OF ORGANIZATIONAL GOVERNANCE

This and the following two sections explain how the social contract of the firm (Sacconi 2000, 2006a, 2006b, 2007, 2010a, 2010b) can be understood as the source of emerging social norms in the domain of organizational governance which satisfies the definition of ethics given in section 2 and able to solve the problem quoted in section 3.

Social norms are in fact nowadays deemed no less important for corporate and organizational governance in general than legal norms. In fact, these two types of norms are complementary (Stout 2006, 2011). Since the adoption of certain contracts or statutes at the corporate level is to some extent voluntary, social norms may be seen as drivers of the voluntary adoption of one or another legal model (e.g., shareholder vs. stakeholder oriented). Moreover, even if a legal system makes some legal constraints and principles in corporate governance mandatory, it largely depends on social norms whether the legal constraints will be actually followed and whether adherence will spread at societal level. Certain legal institutions of organization governance, such as fiduciary duties, may or may not be established in a given context according to how social norms of trust are shaped at societal level. For example, if bridging social capital and trustworthiness in a given society were very low, assigning the fiduciary duties of autonomous trustees an important role in organizational governance could be pointless (Macey 2008).

Social norms are even more important for the economic rather than legal analysis of institutions because modern economists understand them as 'conventions' (again see Schotter 1981; Sudgen 1986; Young 1998; Posner 2000). Conventions are coordination game equilibria that may endogenously emerge from repeated strategic decisions among players participating in a given domain of interaction. They are stable and self-enforceable once a system of mutually consistent expectations has formed that sustains the common belief that all participants will maintain behavior consistent with the norm. Because of their self-enforceability and incentive compatibility, conventions are the kind of institutions that economists like more, that is, 'spontaneous orders' (Hayek 1973; Sugden 1986).

Hence, the gist of this section is that, once complementarity with the law has been recognized, and assuming that no mandatory laws are obstructing the emergence of a model of organizational governance based on social responsibility, the endogenous beliefs, motivations and preferences of economic agents such as companies and their stakeholders become the essential forces driving the implementation of the model. In game-theoretical terms, the normative model is implementable in equilibrium. This is also the basis for the widely accepted view that 'corporate social responsibility' (for an account of this issue see section 6) implementation is mainly a matter of voluntary self-regulation of self-enforceable principles and norms. Thus, its implementation may rest primarily on soft laws, social standards, code of ethics, voluntary adoption of contracts, provisos and statutes, all of which are self-sustaining norms constraining 'from within' the discretion of corporate directors and managers (Wieland 2003; Sacconi 2006a).

The best way to integrate social norms into the emergence and stability of organizational governance models is to resort to Aoki's (2001, 2010) account of institutions. Institutions 'are not rules exogenously given by the polity, culture or a meta-game' but 'rules created through the strategic interaction of agents, held in the minds of agents and thus self-sustaining' (Aoki 2001: 11). An institution is 'a self-sustaining system of shared beliefs about a salient way in which the game is repeatedly played' (Aoki 2001: 11). The content of shared beliefs is 'a summary representation (compressed information) of an equilibrium in a repeated game' (Aoki 2001: 11). Thus, the salient feature of the equilibrium played has a symbolic representation inside the agents' minds and coordinates beliefs that in their turn induce behaviors and their replication over time.

Cognitive components (i.e., beliefs deriving from compressed mental representations of salient aspects of ongoing equilibrium play) and behavioral components (i.e., the iterated play of a given set of equilibrium strategies) are interlocked in a recursive scheme (Aoki 2010; also see the inner circle of Figure 7.1). The starting point is cognitive, and it consists in pattern recognition whereby given situations of interaction are framed as games of a certain form wherein players are expected to reason in a given quasi-symmetrical way. At step two, this framing of the situation induces players to entertain quasi-converging beliefs about a certain mode of playing the game. Thus, at

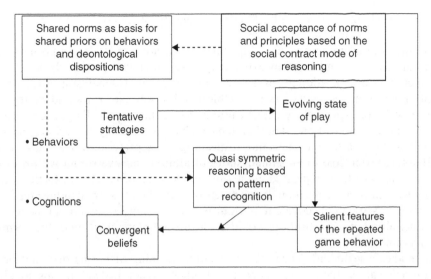

Figure 7.1 Aoki's modified diagram representing the recursive process of institution formation

step three, on passing from beliefs to the players' actual behavior, each player adopts a tentative strategy based on the belief that others will also adopt strategies consistent with the aforementioned mode of behavior. Hence, in step four, strategies clash and some of them prove to be more successful and based on a better prediction. By trial and error, therefore, strategies converge towards an equilibrium of the game. This may be construed as an evolutionary result because the mode of playing attracts more and more players through iterated adaptation to the other players' aggregate behaviors in the long run. At each repetition, however, this evolving equilibrium is summarily represented in its salient features by a compressed mental model resident in the players mind so the fifth step concluding the circle is again cognitive.

This circle can be recursively iterated so that the ongoing equilibrium mode of playing is repeatedly confirmed by beliefs that translate into equilibrium behaviors, which are represented summarily by mental models, and so on. At some point, this belief system reaches a nearly complete state of 'common knowledge' (Lewis 1969; Binmore and Brandenburger 1990) about how players interact. The resulting equilibrium is an institution: a regularity of behavior played in a domain of interaction and stably represented by the shared mental model resident in all the participants' minds. It is essentially equivalent to the notion of a social norm as a 'convention'.

However, a limitation is apparent in this understanding of institutions, and it concerns the normative meaning of an institution. Institutions in the above game-theoretical definition only *ex post* tell each player what the best action is. Once the players share the knowledge that they have reached an equilibrium state, then playing their best replies is actually a prescription of prudence that confirms the already established equilibrium. Thus, institutions tell players only how to maintain the existing, already settled, pattern of behavior. They say nothing *ex ante* about how agents should behave before the mental representation of an equilibrium has settled and a self-replicating equilibrium behavior has crystallized. Institutions only describe regularity of behavior and are devoid of genuine normative meaning and force.

Here the notion of ethics as not only stable social norms but also as norms satisficing moral meaning conditions, as explained above, enters the picture. In fact, institutions including organizational governance contain norms (Donaldson 2012), such as constitutional principles, laws, statutes, ethical codes, standard rules and shared social values, which are expressed by explicit utterances in the players' language concerning values, rights and obligations. These statements have a primarily prescriptive meaning, and if individuals attribute them moral meaning, such prescriptions are also universalizable (i.e., extensible to all similar states of affairs) and overriding with respect to alternative prescriptions expressed in the same context (Hare 1981). Norms thus defined literally have normative meaning independently of the fact that they induce replication of an already settled collective equilibrium behavior. Thus, a second component of a proper definition of an institution should be the mental representation of the normative meaning of norms.

This makes a great difference. The normative meaning of norms does not depend on knowledge about the ongoing behavior of other players. Instead, norms are able to justify and give first-place reasons for shared acceptance of a mode of behavior addressing all the participants in a given interaction domain before it has been established as an equilibrium point. A norm gives intentional reasons to act independently on the evolutionary benefits of adaptation in the long run because when an individual or a group of agents in a given action domain initiate an institutional change, it cannot stem from the pressure of evolutionary forces, which unfold their attraction only in the long run. Instead, a norm enters the players' shared mental model (Denzau and North 1994) of how the game should be played, shapes the players' reciprocal disposition to act and their default beliefs about common behaviors, and hence becomes the basis for their first coordination on a specific equilibrium. In other words, it works as the first move in a process of equilibrium selection that activates the recursive process outlined by Aoki (2010). According to a line of theorizing in behavioral game theory, because a norm has been (cognitively) commonly accepted it may affect both dispositions to act (preferences) and expectations (default beliefs about how other players behave), so that the norm becomes a game equilibrium (Grimalda and Sacconi 2005; Sacconi 2007, 2011; Sacconi and Faillo 2010; Sacconi et al. 2011).

This equilibrium selection function of norms is deployed in two contexts: (1) within a well-defined game, where an old equilibrium path (old institution) has been abandoned for whatever reason and a new equilibrium path (new institution) has to be reached; and (2) when the underlying action domain changes because environmental or technological changes have occurred, or some further action opportunity is simply discovered by players, so that achieving a new equilibrium is necessary.

In these contexts, 'the point is that some symbolic system of predictive/normative beliefs precedes the evolution of a new equilibrium and then becomes accepted by all the agents in the relevant domain through their experiences' (Aoki 2001: 19). The key point is, therefore, to explain how a norm (basis for a system of normative beliefs) becomes acceptable by agents before the relevant equilibrium behavior is settled through rational best response, evolution or other behavioral mechanisms such as reciprocity and conformism. What is required is a collective mode of reasoning (cognition) able to explain how a normative mental model arises before any evolutionary pressure has operated in that direction, and on the basis of which a norm may become commonly accepted in a not yet equilibrium state. Therefore, what is needed is a cognitive mechanism of justification for norms that can operate in a similar way in many different contexts, so as to be able to produce a social norm that adapts to diverse situations.

The best justificatory account for the *ex ante* shared acceptance of norms is the social contract model. Contractarian norms result from a voluntary agreement in a hypothetical choice situation that logically comes before any exogenous institution is superimposed on a given action domain, or before any institution has yet emerged. Thus, a norm arises only because of the voluntary agreement and adhesion of agents, even before it is established as an evolutionary equilibrium. To define the agreement, any social contract model sets aside threats, fraud and manipulation – resources that would render the parties substantially unequal in terms of bargaining power – and considers all the agents as equal in respect to their rational autonomy, so that many of their arbitrary differences are placed under a veil of ignorance. Although a long tradition of different contractarian models could be cited (to exemplify one of the main lines of thought in the social contract tradition, consider Hobbes 1651 [2010]; Buchanan 1975; Gauthier 1986; Hampton 1987; for applications of the social contract model to enterprises see also Keeley 1988; Vanberg 1992; Sacconi 2000), the main reference here is to the Kantian model of the social contract developed by John Rawls (1971).

By introducing the social contract as the cognitive mechanism by which a norm may be accepted and become a shared mental model, Aoki's recursive model can be reformulated. The inner circle of Figure 7.1 is retained. What is new (as shown in the upper part of Figure 7.1) is that the pattern derives from a shared social norm that categorizes the game as the domain of application of some more general principle. From this categorization it follows that some shared idea of the players' disposition to act (preferences) and common beliefs can be applied in the case under examination. In turn, the social norm derives from social contract reasoning (see Figure 7.1) employed by players in order to agree on basic principles and norms when equilibrium institutions are not already established.

THE SOCIAL CONTRACT AS AN EQUILIBRIUM SELECTION DEVICE

The Rawlsian Maximin Principle Vindicated

This subsection applies Binmore's (2005) game-theoretical vindication of the Rawlsian social contract to the organization stakeholders' interactions (see also Sacconi 2010b). It gives the basic model of how the social contract (a normative ethics principle) not only justifies an institutional model of organizational governance but also provides a source for its selection as a social norm – that is, as an institution in a revised Aoki's sense. Equilibrium selection has been a growing body of literature over the last three decades in game theory (Harsanyi & Selten 1988; Binmore 1987, 1988) from the perspective of how player may interactively solve their uncertainty on how their counterparties are going to play a non-cooperative game with multiple equilibria and hence to calculate the correct

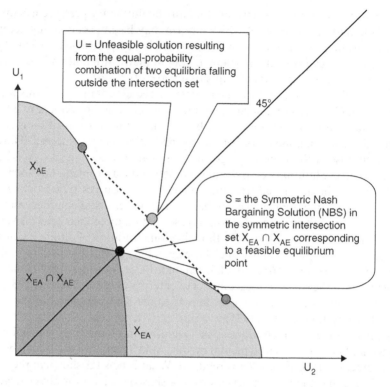

Figure 7.2   The Binmore–Rawls egalitarian solution

and stable best response. What characterizes Binmore's contributions to the social contract theory (Binmore 1989, 1991, 2005) is that an *ex ante* approach to the selection of
repeated play equilibria in (evolutionary) non cooperative games is justified.

Assume that two stakeholders, a poor worker (Eve) and a rich proprietor of means of
production and capital (Adam) meet in a 'state of nature' structured as a non-cooperative
game. Assume that they repeatedly play the same game resulting in a wide set of feasible
outcomes. The 'state of nature' precedes the institution of any legal artifice such as the
'corporation' under which they could form a regulated team. In Figure 7.2 the convex
and compact pay-off space X_{EA} corresponds to the outcome set of the state of nature
repeated game. Let these outcomes be all equilibria of the repeated game (i.e., when one
player chooses their component of one of these strategy combinations the other has no
incentive to deviate from it by changing his strategy component).

Then assume that before agents engage in the relevant interaction (e.g., a largely
incomplete contract), they want to agree *ex ante* on the selection of one of these possible
equilibrium points or outcomes. This may be seen as agreeing on a social norm, singling
out what they should be entitled to by playing their roles under a formal organization.
This distributive norm is a skeletal constitution for the organization that the agents
would be prepared to enter. Since the constitution must be fair, impartiality and impersonality of the agreement are required. Taken together, these assumptions are the 'veil of
ignorance' hypothesis. In other words, each agent makes their decision 'as if' they were

ignorant about their true identity, so that in order to reach a deliberation they take in turn the positions of each possible participant in the game.

In this context, impersonality means that acceptance of the solution must not depend on personal and social positions. Thus, players should select a solution that cannot be affected by the symmetrical replacement of social roles and personal positions with respect to individual players. Technically, Figure 7.2 depicts this replacement by the symmetric translation of the initial pay-off space X_{EA} with respect to the Cartesian axes representing the utility of player 1 and player 2, respectively. Thus, under the initial pay-off space X_{EA}, player 1 will have all the possible pay-offs of Eve, and player 2 all the possible pay-offs of Adam. But under the translated pay-off space X_{AE}, roles are reserved and player 1 will then get Adam's possible pay-offs and player 2 will get Eve's possible pay-offs. Moreover, Figure 7.2 illustrates that each player, when taking the other's perspective, exercises perfect empathetic identification. That is, when player 1, who under X_{EA} was Eve, thinks to be Adam under X_{AE}, this player is able to reproduce exactly the same pay-offs that player 2 experienced when the player was Adam.

Impartiality means that the players must agree on an outcome under the hypothesis that the reciprocal replacement of positions works in such a way that each stakeholder has an equal probability of finding themselves in the position of each of the possible two roles. Equal probability explains how the solution may not change under the symmetrical translation of the pay-off space with respect to the players' utility axes. Take an outcome x_{EA} that by replacing personal positions may realize in two non-coinciding ways (x_{EA} itself and x_{AE}). To make this outcome acceptable requires taking the expected value of an equal probability distribution over the two realization ways: $\frac{1}{2}x_{EA} + \frac{1}{2}x_{AE}$. This would identify a point in the space that is invariant under the players' positions replacement (i.e., an egalitarian solution residing on the bisector).

However, this construction is not meant to be an excessive idealization. Agents retain awareness that the solution must be an equilibrium of the original game. That is, the solution must be a collective behavior that the parties know is self-enforceable and incentive-compatible once they think that they all are playing it. This is a requirement of realism of the agreed solution: agents cannot afford to agree *ex ante* on a solution if it is not incentive-compatible *ex post* (beyond 'the veil of ignorance'). The reason is simple. Admit that the impartial solution proves *ex post* not to be an equilibrium of the original game (does not belong to the original pay-off space of the 'state of nature' game). Hence, the player who *ex post* would be most favored by returning to a solution belonging to the initial equilibrium set would simply deviate to an equilibrium strategy.

Consequently, the stability condition requires that the *ex ante* solution (agreed behind the 'veil of ignorance') must correspond to an outcome that under the players' place-permutation would nevertheless belong to the *ex post* equilibrium set. In other words, the selected outcome must be an equilibrium (say) either if player 1 takes the position of Adam (and player 2 respectively the position of Eve) or in the opposite case when their identification is reversed (player 2 occupies Adam's position, whereas player 1 takes Eve's position), and all the more so when an equally probable combination of the two identifications is taken.

What has been just set is a new feasibility condition. Owing to the state of nature game's assumptions, only equilibria of the original pay-off space X_{EA} are feasible. Any further outcome – potentially subject to agreement – would be wishful thinking because no *ex post* equilibrium would exist that could implement it (see point U in Figure 7.2). Adding the conditions of impersonality and impartiality further restricts feasible outcomes to the symmetric intersection $X_{EA} \cap X_{AE}$ of the two pay-off spaces generated by symmetrical translation of the original space, which is a proper subset of the initial outcome (equilibrium) set $X_{EA.}$ as shown in Figure 7.2. This is a symmetrical pay-off space wherein any bargaining solution necessarily falls on the bisector, which is the geometrical locus of egalitarian solutions (where parties share the bargaining surplus equally). Note that this result takes for granted an egalitarian status quo preceding the agreement, but this assumption too is a consequence of the veil of ignorance.

In particular, players resort to the Nash bargaining solution (NBS), which is the most widely employed solution for bargaining games (Nash 1950). It prescribes picking the point of the efficient (north-east) frontier of the pay-off space (representing the outcomes set of possible agreements) where the product $\Pi(u_i - d_i)$ of the utilities u_i of players ($i = 1, 2$), net of utility d_i associated with their status quo, is maximal. Assuming that the players bargain according to the typical rationality assumptions of game theory (Harsanyi 1977), and given that the feasible outcome set is the symmetric intersection sub-space $X_{EA} \cap X_{AE}$, the NBS is by assumption egalitarian and selects the point S of Figure 7.2.

The striking result of this construction is that the minimal requirement of social justice (impersonality and impartiality) becomes compatible with realism and *ex post* stability in an interaction where players are free to choose according to their preferences. Freedom of choice and incentive compatibility does not require relinquishing the moral demands of social justice. On the contrary, it entails that the solution must be egalitarian and must coincide with the Rawlsian maximin distribution, even within an originally asymmetrical set of possible outcomes. Thus, given a real-life set of possible outcomes reflecting possible inequality between the participants, the solution falls on the equilibrium that most favors the worst-off player, which in most cases is the egalitarian distribution.

'Organization Social Responsibility' as Norm Selected by the Social Contract in a Trust Game

To give more concreteness to the foregoing exemplification of the organization social contract, consider now a strategic interaction between a non-controlling stakeholder A (i.e., an employee with a specific investment at stake) and a controlling stakeholder B (the entrepreneur or the manager) taking the form of a trust game (TG) (see Figure 7.3). By entering the relationship, the trustor (player A) accepts (trusts) the authority of the trustee (player B). On the contrary, by not entering, he refuses to take a subordinate position in the relationship with B. Moreover, by entering, A invests idiosyncratically in the relationship. The trustee is an authority who can abuse some discretionary power. Once the trustor has entered, the trustee may choose between abuse and no-abuse. No-abuse would maximize the two players' joint pay-off and also the Nash bargaining product in the outcome space, but abusing for a self-interested trustee is strictly dominant. Thus, in the one-shot TG, a self-interested trustee will always abuse, and hence the unique equilibrium solution of the game is (no-entrance, abuse).

However, the TG game is played repeatedly. On considering repeated strategies and their average outcomes, many possible equilibria exist. These include the original (no-entrance, abuse), the perfectly fair (entrance, no-abuse), plus all the possible pairings of

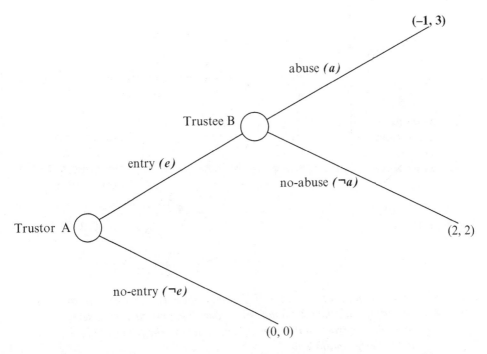

Figure 7.3   The stakeholder–entrepreneur/manager/owner Trust Game

entrance with mixed strategies combining abuse and no-abuse up to a limit probability of two-thirds and one-third, respectively. Indeed, the entire dashed region of the pay-off space in Figure 7.4 is filled with possible equilibrium points of the repeated TG.

Given so many equilibria, many possible conventions would emerge from reciprocal coordination. In particular, the trustee has a 'conformity problem' with a social norm of fair treatment consisting in the Nash bargaining solution (NBS) (by which B equally shares the surplus). If the firm is run to the fair reciprocal advantage of both stakeholders, only the equilibrium coinciding with the NBS can emerge. By contrast, a model of organizational governance consistent with a purely shareholder-value maximization approach would justify the equilibrium corresponding to the Stackelberg solution.

Application of the Binmore–Rawls theory of equilibrium selection based on the *ex ante* social contract is starkly simple in this case (see also Sacconi 2010b). The idea to study the rise of corporate culture in a repeated trust game was originally presented in Kreps (1990); for the use of this game to illustrate business ethics see Sacconi (2000). However both these contributions focused on the existence of fair equilibria and role of general principles when the game is played under unforeseen contingencies and bounded rationality; and neither of them discussed in depth the equilibrium selection problem.

Figure 7.5 illustrates the symmetric translation of the repeated TG pay-off space with respect to the player utility axes U_A and U_B, which consists of its rotation around the north-west boundary of the initial space X_{AB}. The symmetrical intersection subset $X_{AB} \cap X_{BA}$ reduces to the rotation axis itself, that is, no more than a line segment (along the bisector) consisting of all the egalitarian distribution. By simply adding basic strong

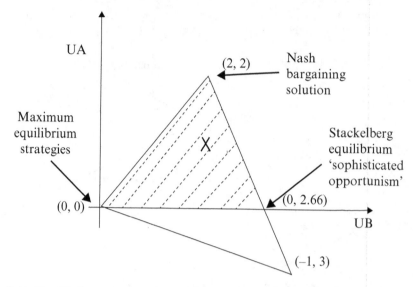

Figure 7.4   Equilibrium set of a repeated TG, even if there is an egalitarian solution coinciding with the maximum Nash bargaining product, in absence of the social contract equilibrium selection device, the firm would select the Stackelberg equilibrium

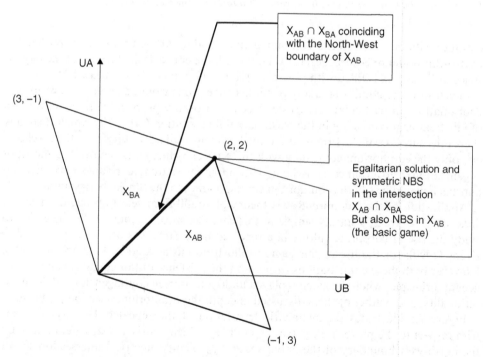

Figure 7.5   The repeated TG with symmetrical pay-off space translation, and the egalitarian solution

Pareto optimality (i.e., agreeing on solutions that permit mutual improvements for all, if available) directly leads to choosing the equilibrium point consistent with the NBS of the original game (2, 2), which is also its egalitarian (and maximin) solution. To put it differently, the intersection set coincides in this case with the bisector where all the egalitarian pay-off distributions reside, and by simple application of Pareto optimality we may choose the best for all egalitarian solution, which is identical with the maximum Nash bargaining product. Nevertheless, once the egalitarian solution was selected, it would be incentive-compatible and stable. This is an abstract representation of an organization ethical norm endogenously emerging from the non-controlling stakeholder versus entrepreneur or manager interactions aided by the social contract reasoning. Under such a norm, the trustee behaves as if she owed the trustor (stakeholder) fiduciary duties of fair treatment. This norm is called 'organization social responsibility' (OSR) owed to the organization stakeholders.

A MULTI-FIDUCIARY AND MULTI-STAKEHOLDER MODEL OF THE ORGANIZATIONAL GOVERNANCE

When the subject of organizational ethics is studied with reference to today's real world, what is encountered is the ever growing phenomenon of corporate social responsibility (CSR) and its generalization to the social responsibility of productive organizations in general. Firms, business organizations, but also cooperatives and non-profits, are increasingly considered to be subject to commitments such as discharging socially responsible practices and programs to the benefit of the organization's stakeholders. Management and reporting standards are redefined as being centered on all the stakeholders' interests and not merely on those of the shareholders. Such practices, programs, management and reporting standards are seen as ethical and as involving rational and purposeful action of those who are in a position of authority toward the organization's stakeholders.

To gain a proper understanding of the global CSR movement requires questioning in depth the nature of organizations as social and economic institutions. On the battleground of organizational governance models, CSR denotes a movement that strives to affirm a social norm advocating an extension of the range of obligations owed by firms and productive organization to all their stakeholders. Thus the CSR movement is the main example of emergence (even if not the only one) of the social norm that in more abstract and skeletal terms is called a norm of organizational social responsibility (OSR) owed to the organisation stakeholders.

To be more precise about the basic principle of this norm, CSR – so understood – has been defined as a model of extended organization governance whereby those who run firms, such as entrepreneurs, directors and managers, have responsibilities that range from fulfillment of their fiduciary duties towards the owners to fulfillment of analogous fiduciary duties towards all the firm's stakeholders (Sacconi, 2006a, 2006b, 2007, 2010a)

Two terms must be defined for this definition to be clearly understood. The first term is 'fiduciary duties'. The assumption here is that a subject has a legitimate interest but is unable to make the relevant decisions, in the sense that they do not know what goals to pursue, what alternative to choose, or how to deploy their resources in order to satisfy their interest. The trustor therefore delegates decisions to a trustee empowered to choose actions and goals. The trustee may thus use the trustor's resources and select the appropriate course of action. For a fiduciary relationship to arise, the trustor must possess a claim (right) towards the trustee. In other words, the trustee directs actions and uses the resources made over to them so that results are obtained that satisfy the trustor's interests. These claims (i.e., the trustor's rights) impose fiduciary duties on the agent who is invested with authority (the trustee) that they are obliged to fulfill. The fiduciary relationship applies in a wide variety of instances such as teacher–pupil relationships and many others. In the corporate domain, the relationship is between the board of a trust and its beneficiaries, or between the board of directors of a joint-stock company and its shareholders, and then more generally between management and owners. The term 'fiduciary duty' means the duty or responsibility to exercise authority for the good of those who have granted that authority and are therefore subject to it (Flannigan 1989).

The second term is 'stakeholders'. This term denotes individuals or groups with a major stake in the running of the firm and who are able materially to influence it (Freeman 1984; Freeman & McVea 2001; Freeman et al. 2010; Donaldson and Preston 1995; Evan & Freeman 1993; Freeman & Velamuri 2006; Clarkson Centre 1991; Clarkson 1995). However, from an economist's point of view, most relevant to defining stakeholders is the following distinction between two categories: stakeholders in the strict sense, and stakeholders in the broad sense.

'Stakeholders in the strict sense' are those who have an interest at stake because they have made specific investments in the firm, such as in the form of human capital, financial capital, social capital or trust, physical or environmental capital, or for the development of dedicated technologies. Such investments may substantially increase the total value generated by the firm and are made specifically in relation to that firm so that their value is idiosyncratically related to the completion of the transactions carried out by or in relation to that firm. These stakeholders are reciprocally dependent on the firm because they influence its value, but at the same time depend largely upon it for satisfaction of their well-being prospects (lock-in effect). By contrast, 'stakeholders in the broad sense' are those individuals or groups whose interest is involved because they undergo the 'external effects', positive or negative, of the transactions performed by the firm, even if they do not directly participate in the transaction, so that they do not contribute to or directly receive value from the firm.

One can thus appreciate the scope of the firm's stakeholder responsibility defined as an extended form of governance: it extends the concept of fiduciary duty from a mono-stakeholder setting where the sole stakeholder relevant to identification of fiduciary duties is the owner of the firm, to a multi-stakeholder one in which who run the firm owes fiduciary duties to all its stakeholders. This was exactly the result that was derived in the abstract through the stakeholder or owner (or manager) trust game above.

This normative model of a firm's responsibility toward its stakeholders can be extended to any form of business firm and productive organization with legal personality, which makes it an institutional 'person' partly insulated from its individual members and constituencies. Hence it is not necessarily tied to the particular cases of publicly owned companies or family-controlled capitalist corporations. It could be equally applied to a cooperative company where some stakeholders (for example consumers) own the firm and are thus obliged to permit extension of the fiduciary duties of the cooperative's managers to workers, capital lenders, suppliers, local communities, and the like. Or it could be applied to a law firm organized as a limited liability partnership or a professional association, where a few senior partners, who hold residual control rights, occupy the same position that, in the definition of CSR as far as the social responsibility toward stakeholders is concerned, is taken by managers, entrepreneurs or directors.

In all these cases, there is a category of stakeholders who control the organization through ownership constituted by a residual control right and a claim right on the residual (profit) (Hansmann 1996). Moreover it appoints the board of directors and managers. Under each of these ownership forms, authority, legitimately assigned to the owner category, may be abused. In fact, organizational authority entails by definition that the authority has at their disposal a sphere of discretion wherein *ex ante* non-contractible decision variables are placed and hence withdrawn from the discipline of an *ex ante* established detailed rule or contract. These discretionary decisions affect the possibility of non-controlling stakeholders to profit from their specific investments and their cognitive assets employed in a complementary and hence mutually advantageous way. Even though there are numerous ownership forms, the underlying problem – abuse of authority – is therefore recurrent (as stated above), and cannot be solved as long as the governance structure is focused only on design of the ownership and control rights of a particular stakeholder category. Therefore the organization stakeholder responsibility (OSR) requires the controlling stakeholder (if in a managerial position) or the management appointed by them to discharge extended fiduciary duties toward non-controlling stakeholders.

Note that in the public company case the corporate control exerted in general by shareholders is very weak. The corporate governance powers exercised by managers and directors is in many respects autonomous and seems to exercise a large part of the actual residual control right. Different schools of thought see this contingency in very different ways. According to supporters of the principal–agent model (for example Jensen and Meckling 1976; but see also Macey 2008 and Jensen 2001), who affirm 'shareholder primacy', this relative independence of managers carries the risk of managerial opportunism and self-dealing behavior. Hence they suggest curbing it through corporate governance engineering, such as the design of incentive contracts (stock options, etc.) and contestable control mechanisms such as hostile takeovers – whose aim is to provide positive incentives and negative sanctions so as to align the managers' interests with those of the shareholders. Other corporate governance theorists (e.g. Blair & Stout 1999; Stout 2011; but also Elhauge 2005; Gelter 2009) see this relative autonomy as the true manifestation of the nature of a 'corporate actor' which is not constrained to serve solely the interests of its shareholders but must pursue whatever goals the cooperative bargaining solution amongst stakeholders assigns to it (Aoki 1984; Sacconi 2000, 2006a, 2006b). Thus the directors are legitimately entitled to operate as the stewards of the corporation and as trustees of the stakeholders whose well-being depends on the company's conduct and that contribute to the company's success. In particular, Blair and Stout (1999) defend the idea that the board of directors plays the role of an impartial hierarchy mediating among the different corporate stakeholders in order to prevent reciprocal opportunism (especially abuse of authority on the part of the controlling shareholders) and favoring their mutually beneficial cooperation. As regards the publicly owned corporation, the socially responsible model of the economic organization, based on the idea of extended fiduciary duties toward strict and broad sense stakeholders, concurs with this corporate governance doctrine and seeks to provide it with a deep contrarian-ethics foundation and also with the idea that it may be supported by an evolving stable ethical norm based on the stakeholders' 'social contract'.

However, it is noticeable that the idea of an economic organization run by a board of directors or an entrepreneur exercising control rights without being the ultimate proprietor of the firm and owing extended fiduciary duties to all the stakeholders is not restricted to this case alone, and the public company is not the only or best example. Another case could be a state-controlled corporation (where the uninformed shareholder is the government), but an even better example is provided by large non-profits – for example a private university or a hospital run by a foundation. Although in these cases there is no subject who exercises ownership in its complete sense, because nobody is legitimately identifiable as the 'residual claimant', there are nonetheless managers and directors who are invested with a substantial part of the twofold definition of ownership, that is, they may exercise residual control over discretionary *ex ante* non-contractible decisions and hence are endowed with authority (Hansmann 1996). They are therefore also able to abuse this authority both in the self-dealing sense and by running the organization so as to give an unfair benefit to some stakeholder with which they have privileged relationships. Also this case perfectly enters the domain of application of the multi-stakeholder and multi-fiduciary governance model of the economic organization, once it is taken for granted that 'owner' in the strict sense in the foregoing definition is an empty category. Indeed, these organizations can be taken perhaps as the historical first manifestation of the very idea of social responsibility of the organizational governance toward all the organization's stakeholders (see Aoki 2010).

END REMARKS AND CONCLUSIONS

The main result of this chapter may be restated as follows: in general, in a context of constitutional choice concerning the firm's governance structure where two (or more) differently endowed stakeholders confront one another in a 'state of nature', it can be shown that an egalitarian constitution of the firm is agreed (for this general result see also Sacconi 2010b). By 'constitutional choice' is meant the selection of an admissible subset of the stakeholders' 'state of nature' strategies, that if unconstrained would allow them to undertake any opportunistic behavior in their contractual relationships. Under the ethical assumption of the veil of ignorance, however, they reach agreement on a constitution of the firm such that they make a final allocation of pay-offs which is identical to the best egalitarian distribution of the cooperative surplus among those feasible for the constitutional choice. In other words, they accept the firm's constitution that allows an equal distribution of the surplus which is as good as possible for both (or all) the players. Egalitarian solutions are monotonically ordered in terms of growing mutual benefits, or symmetric Nash bargaining products, so that the constitution admitting the best feasible egalitarian solution will be chosen (Sacconi 2010b).

But what is really essential to the novelty of the result is that the egalitarian constitution is not only the outcome of cooperative bargaining. It is also the result of an equilibrium selection device, which ends up with a (self-sustaining) Nash equilibrium.

Therefore, further to the support given to the multi-stakeholder organizational governance presented in the previous section, there are important consequences of the results set out in this chapter, and especially in the section on 'The social contract as an equilibrium selection device', for the fields of new institutional economics, law and economics, and organization design. Firstly, it is received wisdom that when incentive compatibility is required, the optimal design of economic organizations must set aside fairness as an 'idealistic' requirement and seek only some 'second-best' level of efficiency. Moreover, it has been argued that adhering to fairness as the primary value would entail that all the parties involved are doomed to a strictly Pareto-inferior position (Kaplow and Shavell 2002); that is, fairness would condemn everybody to faring worse. As I have shown, on the contrary, requiring incentive compatibility in terms of an equilibrium condition entails exactly the opposite. Equality comes first, and only on 'second thoughts', within the set of egalitarian solutions (that satisfy the basic ethical requirement of the veil of ignorance), can Pareto dominance be used to choose the best egalitarian solution in terms of general acceptance and mutual benefit (for further analysis of this point see also Sacconi 2010b).

Secondly, libertarian new-institutional economists and social philosophers, following Hayek, often argue that distributive justice is a 'mirage' which must be eschewed if the tenets of liberty and the endogenous stability of institutions (as if they could emerge as spontaneous orders) are to be maintained. But after my analysis this seems not to be the truth.

If a libertarian is mild – that is, if they accept the minimum morality contained in the idea of an original position from where the endogenous selection of an equilibrium point is framed by the 'thought-experiment' of agreeing to consider the decision in terms of exchangeable positions among the players – then only an egalitarian solution can follow. Endogeneity of the outcome, understood as a spontaneous order, is fundamental; in addition to the veil of ignorance. And both are consistent with the idea that the decision is taken from a 'state of nature' (original position) perspective. Given these premises, one may only look for the best (Paretian) egalitarian solution among the feasible outcomes.

The emphasis by libertarians on spontaneous orders entails not introducing the hypothesis of a *deus ex machina* able to enforce whatever artificial common plan the participants may agree to from the *ex ante* perspective. On the contrary, only agreements with which they can comply by dint solely of their individual strategies are regarded as feasible. According to a libertarian, the state cannot be invoked to expand the set of possible agreements beyond those that can emerge from endogenous interaction. Even on admitting all this, however, a choice under the veil of ignorance entails that the solution must be the best (Pareto-superior) egalitarian solution compatible with feasibility.

It is the relinquishment of some efficiency, not equality, that as a matter of logic the libertarian view entails. As far as self-enforceability of institutions is required, fairness cannot be eliminated from the original position perspective (under the veil of ignorance), while efficiency is constrained by the impossibility of assuming that any whatever constitutional agreement will be enforced. This largely changes the perspective of organization design. If business organizations are seen as orders that must first be self-sustainable and self-regulated – for example through soft laws or self-regulation – before being enacted by mandatory law and becoming part of the (state-enforced) legal system, fairness should be the first requirement of a good design.

REFERENCES

Aoki, Masahiko (1984), *The Cooperative Game Theory of the Firm*, Cambridge: Cambridge University Press.

Aoki, Masahiko (2001), *Toward a Comparative Institutional Analysis*, Cambridge, MA: MIT Press.

Aoki, Masahiko (2010), *Corporations in Evolving Diversity*, Oxford: Oxford University Press.

Bicchieri, Cristina (2006), *The Grammar of Society: The Nature and Dynamics of Social Norms*, Cambridge: Cambridge University Press.

Binmore, Ken (1987), 'Modelling rational players, part I', *Economics and Philosophy*, **3**, 179–214.

Binmore, Ken (1988), 'Modelling rational players, part II', *Economics and Philosophy*, **4**, 9–55.

Binmore, Ken (1989), 'The social contract: Harsanyi and Rawls', *Economic Journal*, **99**, 84–106.

Binmore, Ken (1991), 'Game theory and the social contract', in R. Selten (ed.), *Game Equilibrium Models II, Methods, Morals, Markets*, Berlin: Springer Verlag.

Binmore, Ken (2005), *Natural Justice*, Oxford: Oxford University Press.

Binmore, Ken and Adam Brandenburger (1990), 'Common knowledge and game theory', in Ken Binmore (ed.), *Essays in the Foundation of Game Theory*, Oxford: Basil Blackwell, pp. 105–150.

Blair, Margaret M. and Lynn A. Stout (1999), 'A team production theory of corporate law', *Virginia Law Review*, **85**(2), 247-331.

Buchanan, James M. (1975), 'The limits of liberty: between anarchy and Leviathan', Chicago, IL, USA and London, UK: University of Chicago Press.

Clarkson Centre for Business Ethics (1991), *Principles of Stakeholder Management*, Joseph Rotman School of Management, University of Toronto, Canada; reprinted 2002 in *Business Ethics Quarterly*, **12**(2), 257–264.

Clarkson, M.C. (1995), 'A stakeholder framework for analyzing and evaluating corporate social performance', *Academy of Management Review*, **20**(1), 92–117.

Denzau, Arthur and Douglass C. North (1994), 'Shared mental models: ideologies and institutions', *KIKLOS* **47**(1), 3-31.

Donaldson, Thomas (2012), 'The epistemic fault line in corporate governance', *Academy of Management Review*, **37**(2), 256–271.

Donaldson, T. and T.W. Dunfee (1999), *Ties that Bind; A Social Contract Approach to Business Ethics*, Boston, MA: Harvard Business School Press.

Donaldson, Thomas and Lee E. Preston (1995), 'The stakeholder theory of the corporation: concepts, evidence, and implications', *Academy of Management Review*, **20**(1), 65–91.

Elhauge, Einer (2005), 'Sacrificing corporate profit in the public interest', *NYU Law Review*, **80**(3), 733–869.

Evan, William M. and R. Edward Freeman (1993), 'A stakeholder theory of the corporation: Kantian capitalism', in Tom L. Beauchamp and Norman E. Bowie (eds), *Ethical Theory and Business*, Englewood Cliffs, NJ: Prentice Hall, pp. 97–106.

Flannigan, Robert (1989), 'The fiduciary obligation', *Oxford Journal of Legal Studies*, **9**(3), 285–294.

Freeman, R. Edward (1984), *Strategic Management: A Stakeholder Approach*, Boston, MA: Pitman.

Freeman, R. Edward, Jeffrey R. Harrison, Andrew C. Wicks, Bidhan L. Parmar and Simone De Colle (2010), *Stakeholder Theory: The State of the Art*, Cambridge: Cambridge University Press.

Freeman, R. Edward and John McVea (2001), 'A stakeholder approach to strategic management', in Michael A. Hitt, R. Edward Freeman and Jeffrey S. Harrison (eds), *The Blackwell Handbook of Strategic Management*, Oxford: Blackwell, pp. 189–207.

Freeman, R. Edward and S. Ramakrishna Velamuri (2006), 'A new approach to CSR: company stakeholder responsibility', in A. Kakabadse and M. Morsing (eds), *Corporate Social Responsibility (CSR): Reconciling Aspiration with Application*, New York: Palgrave Macmillan, pp. 9–23

Gauthier, David (1986), *Morals by Agreement*, Oxford: Clarendon Press.

Gelter, Martin. (2009), 'The dark side of shareholder influence: managerial autonomy and stakeholder orientation in comparative corporate governance', *Harvard International Law Journal*, **50**(1), 129–134.

Griffin, J. (1998), *Value Judgment. Improving Our Ethical Beliefs*, Oxford: Oxford University Press.

Grimalda, Gianluca and Lorenzo Sacconi (2005), 'The constitution of the not-for-profit organization: reciprocal conformity to morality', *Constitutional Political Economy*, **16**(3), 249–276.

Grossman, Sanford J. and Oliver Hart (1986), 'The costs and benefit of ownership: a theory of vertical and lateral integration', *Journal of Political Economy*, **94**(4), 691–719.

Hampton, J. (1987), *Hobbes and the Social Contract Tradition*, Cambridge: Cambridge University Press.

Hansmann, Henry (1996), *The Ownership of the Enterprise*, Cambridge, MA: Harvard University Press.

Hare, Richard M. (1963), *Freedom and reason*, Oxford: Oxford University Press.

Hare, Richard M. (1981), *Moral Thinking*, Oxford: Clarendon Press.

Harsanyi, John C. (1977), *Rational Behavior and Bargaining Equilibrium in Games and Social Situations*, Cambridge: Cambridge University Press.

Harsanyi, J.C. and R. Selten (1988), *A General Theory of Equilibrium Selection in Games*, Cambridge, MA: MIT Press.

Hart, Oliver and John Moore (1990), 'Property rights and the nature of the firm', *Journal of Political Economy*, **98**(6), 1119–1158.

Hayek, Fredrick A. (1973 [2010]), *Law, Legislation and Liberty*, Chicago, IL: University of Chicago Press.

Hobbes, Thomas (1651), *Leviathan: Or the Matter, Forme, and Power of a Common-Wealth Ecclesiasticall and Civill*, Ian Shapiro (ed.), New Haven, CT: Yale University Press.

Hume, David, (1739 [2000]), *A Treatise on Human Nature*, David Fate Norton and Mary Norton (eds), Oxford: Oxford University Press.

Jensen, Michael C., (2001), 'Value maximization, stakeholder theory, and the corporate objective function', *Journal of Applied Corporate Finance*, **14**(3), 8–21.

Jensen, Michael C. and William H. Meckling. (1976), 'Theory of the firm: managerial behavior, agency costs and ownership structure', *Journal of Financial Economics*, **3**(4), 305–360.

Kaplow, L. and S. Shavell (2002), *Fairness versus Welfare*, Cambridge, MA: Harvard University Press.

Kaufman, Allen (2002), 'Managers' double fiduciary duty: to stakeholders and to freedom', *Business Ethics Quarterly*, **12**(2), 189–213.

Keeley, Michael (1988), *A Social-Contract Theory of Organization*, Notre Dame, IN: University of Notre Dame.

Kreps, David (1990), 'Corporate culture and economic theory', in Alt J. and K. Shepsle (eds), *Perspective on Positive Political Economy*, Cambridge: Cambridge University Press.

Lewis, David. (1969), *Convention. A Philosophical Study*, Cambridge, MA: Harvard University Press.

Macey, Jonathan R. (2008), *Corporate Governance*, Princeton, NJ: Princeton University Press.

McMahon, Christopher (1989), 'Managerial authority', *Ethics*, **100**(1), 33–53.

Nash, John F. (1950), 'The bargaining problem', *Econometrica*, **18**(2), 155–162.

Pettit, Philip (1990), 'Virtus normativa: rational choice perspectives', *Ethics*, **100**, 725–755.

Posner, Erik A. (2000), *Law and Social Norm*, Cambridge, MA: Harvard University Press.

Rawls, John (1971), *A Theory of Justice*, Oxford: Oxford University Press.

Raz, Joseph (1985), 'Authority and justification', *Philosophy and Public Affairs*, **14**(1), 3–29.

Sacconi, Lorenzo (2000), *The Social Contract of the Firm: Economics, Ethics and Organization*, Berlin: Springer Verlag.

Sacconi, Lorenzo (2006a), 'CSR as a model of extended corporate governance, an explanation based on the economic theory of social contract, reputation and reciprocal conformism', in Fabrizio Cafaggi (ed.), *Reframing Self-regulation in European Private* Law, Dordrecht: Kluwer Law International, pp. 289–346.

Sacconi, Lorenzo (2006b), 'A social contract account for CSR as extended model of corporate governance (Part I): rational bargaining and justification', *Journal of Business Ethics*, **68**(3), 259–281.

Sacconi, Lorenzo (2007), 'A social contract account for csr as extended model of corporate governance (Part II): compliance, reputation and reciprocity', *Journal of Business Ethics*, **75**(1), 77–96.

Sacconi, Lorenzo (2010a), 'A Rawlsian view of CSR and the game theory of its implementation (Part I): the multistakeholder model of corporate governance', in Lorenzo Sacconi, Margaret Blair, R. Edward Freeman and Alessandro Vercelli (eds), *Corporate Social Responsibility and Corporate Governance: The Contribution of Economic Theory and Related Disciplines*, Basingstoke: Palgrave Macmillan, pp. 157–193.

Sacconi, Lorenzo (2010b), 'A Rawlsian view of CSR and the game theory of its implementation (Part II): fairness and equilibrium', in Lorenzo Sacconi, Margaret Blair, R. Edward Freeman and Alessandro Vercelli (eds), *Corporate Social Responsibility and Corporate Governance: The Contribution of Economic Theory and Related Disciplines*, Basingstoke: Palgrave Macmillan, pp. 194–125.

Sacconi, Lorenzo (2011), 'A Rawlsian view of CRS and the game theory of its implementation (Part III): conformism and equilibrium selection', in Lorenzo Sacconi and Giacomo Degli Antoni (eds), *Social Capital, Corporate Social Responsibility, Economic Behavior and Performance*, Basingstoke: Palgrave Macmillan, pp. 42–79.

Sacconi, Lorenzo and Marco Faillo (2010), 'Conformity, reciprocity and the sense of justice. How social contract-based preferences and beliefs explain norm compliance: the experimental evidence', *Constitutional Political Economy*, **21**(2), 171–201.

Sacconi, Lorenzo, Marco Faillo and Stefania Ottone (2011), 'Contractarian compliance and the "sense of justice": a behavioral conformity model and its experimental support', *Analyse & Kritik*, **33**(1), 273–310.

Schotter, Andrew (1981), *The Economic Theory of Social Institutions*, Cambridge: Cambridge University Press.

Skyrms, S. (2004), *The Stag-Hunt and the Evolution of the Social Structure*, Cambridge: Cambridge University Press.

Stout, Lynn A. (2006), 'Social norms and other-regarding preferences', in John N. Drobak (ed.), *Norms and the Law*, Cambridge: Cambridge University Press, pp. 13–35.

Stout, Lynn A. (2011), 'New thinking on shareholder primacy', working paper, School of Law, UCLA.

Sugden, Robert (1986), *The Economics of Rights, Co-operation and Welfare*, Oxford: Basil Blackwell.

Vanberg, V.J. (1992), 'Organizations as constitutional systems', *Constitutional political Economy*, **3**(2), 223–253.

Wieland, Joseph (ed.) (2003), *Standards and Audits for Ethics Management Systems - The European Perspective*, Berlin: Springer Verlag.

Willamson, Oliver (1975), *Market and Hierarchies*, New York: Free Press.

Williamson, Oliver (1986), *The Economic Institutions of Capitalism*, New York: Free Press.

Young, Peyton H. (1998), *Individual Strategy and Social Structure, an Evolutionary Theory of Social Institutions*, Princeton, MA: Princeton University Press.

8. Language and economic organization
Massimo Warglien

In this chapter, two broad perspectives on organization and language are reconstructed. The first perspective focuses on language in organizations: how language is used in organizational settings. This includes economic modeling and experimental work, both inspired by Arrow's influential notion of 'organizational code', but also more qualitative field work on language games organizations play. The second perspective focuses on organizations as language. Moving from Searle's view that institutions are at the heart a fact of language, two main issues are explored: the combinatorial (generative) nature of organizational processes and forms, and recursion as a fundamental organizing principle. Despite its apparent fragmentation, the study of organization and language appears mature for integrative efforts that may help to reconsider how language shapes organizational life.

INTRODUCTION

Language is ubiquitous in organizations. It permeates virtually all organizational phenomena. It is hard to imagine any form of human organization without language supporting it. Yet, despite language pervasiveness – or maybe for its taken-for-grantedness – research on organization and language is still a largely underdeveloped province of organizational studies. It mostly consists of an unsystematic set of theoretical principles and empirical observations, and of research streams hardly communicating with each other. Writing a handbook chapter on information and language is thus a peculiar challenge, since the matter lacks the organization and the set of generally understood principles and regularities that make a 'handbook spirit'.

This chapter has no pretense to provide a complete map of a rather scattered territory, but instead suggests a simplified organization of select research around a few thematic principles. First of all, I make a distinction between 'language in organizations' and 'organization as language'. The former clearly aims at studying how language is used within organizations and how it interacts with important aspects of organizational life. The latter indicates that organizations can be analyzed as language phenomena; or more weakly that organization and language share important structural features.

The study of 'language in organizations', in turn, has been undertaken under fairly different points of view, reflecting different theoretical commitments from loosely coupled communities of researchers. In his chapter, I will focus on two main perspectives. The first one belongs to a tradition ascribed to the influential book by Arrow (1974) on *The Limits of Organization* – although dating back at least to March and Simon (1958). It focuses on the analysis of 'organizational codes', that is, of how organizations structure information representation in order to enhance coordination effectiveness and efficiency. This tradition of research, at the crossroads of information economics and models of bounded rationality, emphasizes the advantages deriving from organizational information-handling, while considering also its potential negative side-effects. Recently, research on organizational codes has received renewed attention both in modeling and empirical efforts, reported below.

A second major thread of research on how language is used in organizations addresses the interactions of language and action patterns in organizations. If research on codes is mainly dealing with semantic issues of meaning representation, this research addresses a sort of organizational language pragmatics. Studies in this field are often grounded in the (second) Wittgenstein's concept of 'language games' (Wittgenstein 1953), or in the theory of speech acts (Austin 1962; Searle 1969). The fundamental point from this stream of research is that in organizations 'people do not use language primarily to make accurate representations of perceived objects, but, rather, to accomplish things' (Alvesson and Kärreman 2000: 137). The same piece of 'code' can be used for very different purposes. Research in these areas mostly focuses on the reconstruction of such different usages and how they integrate in larger units of discourse, as reported below.

As Searle (1995) has repeatedly argued, however, language is not just instrumental in human institutions; it is the stuff of which institutions are made. This leads to the section of this chapter focusing on organization as language. Most of it deals with issues related to the broader grammatical aspects of organizing. Two classical structural features of grammar are especially relevant to analyzing organizations. The first one is the combinatorial (or 'compositional') nature of language, and its associated generative capacity; that is, the capacity to generate potentially infinite new combinations. The second, associated aspect is the recursive nature of language: the fact that linguistic entities can be embedded within themselves, generating self-similar structures. Recent research has investigated how the combinatorial and recursive aspects of organizing generate the variety of organizational forms and action patterns, and may help to solve the puzzle of organizations as intentional agents. Finally, I suggest avenues for a possible conversation among the different research communities populating this vital but still fragmented research area.

Any attempt to selectively map a loosely structured research field is bound to leave out important domains of analysis. I chose to neglect fundamental contributions that, while highly relevant for the study of organization and language, are addressing core issues that find more easily home in other organizational research domains. It was an especially painful choice to leave aside the rich set of contributions to the semiotic analysis of organizational culture (Barley 1983; Fiol 1989, 2002), which is much contiguous to the themes in this chapter, and that would deserve an autonomous treatment. Also, issues of organizational narrative and storytelling (Boje 1991, 1995; Czarniawska 1998), that deal with higher levels of discourse organization, were left out with regret. Reasons of space, and the focus of this Handbook on integrating economic and organization theory, determined the choice of issues in this chapter.

ORGANIZATIONAL CODES

In general, a code is a system of symbols assigned to represent some information, which is shared or agreed between a sender and a receiver. The use of 'code' as a way to characterize information representation in organizations is associated to Kenneth Arrow's seminal book on *The Limits of Organization* (Arrow 1974). While the concept of 'code' in Arrow is clearly inherited from communication theory (Shannon 1948), its use diverges from the original, since 'different bits of information, equal from the viewpoint of information theory, will usually have very different benefits and costs' (Arrow 1974: 38). Arrow's analysis introduces two fundamental assumptions: individuals have limited information processing abilities, and from an individual point of view acquiring a code is an irreversible investment. These two assumptions have major implications for understanding how code affects organization.

Codes are relevant in organization because 'much of the information received is irrelevant' (Arrow 1974: 53). Reducing the costs of handling irrelevant information is a fundamental task for organizations: codes arise to enhance the efficiency of communication within organizations. One may see an organizational code as a specialized language employed within an organization. Of course, a code can work only if it is adopted on both sides of a communication channel, by both sender and receiver. Thus, organizations have to invest in codes shared by their members, who in turn have to invest in learning them. Shared codes considerably enhance the coordination capabilities within organizations while making communication efficient. Yet, their nature of irreversible investment generates some peculiar implications.

Firstly, efficiency comes at the cost of potential information loss. Information that can be relevant might never be channeled through the organization. Organizational codes limit the 'agenda' of organizations, the items that are considered relevant for decision making. Of course, a well-designed code should capture the information which is more relevant to the organization; but even in this case, new issues may arise, criteria of relevance may change, and thus a code may act as a barrier preventing the acquisition and processing of information of significant decision-making value.

Secondly, organizational codes generate path dependence. A code may be generated to respond to specific circumstances, but its nature of irreversible investment will freeze the effect of those circumstances and carry it on to new contexts, since changing a code is costly. Furthermore, changes in codes might disrupt coordination if they are not simultaneously adopted by anyone in a given organization. As a result, codes will become firm specific, depending on the time and the context of their original creation, and rather rigid over time.

Arrow's analysis has been greatly influential. However, most subsequent analysis of organizational communication has focused more on issues of information channel design (Radner 1993; Bolton and Dewatripont 1994; Christensen and Knudsen 2010), while Arrow's analysis of organizational languages or codes has not been developed until recently, when the design (or spontaneous emergence) of codes has become the object of significant theoretical and experimental developments.

On the theoretical side, much attention has focused on the degree of coarseness of organizational codes. How coarse a code is has obvious implications for organizations. Think of the degree of 'coarseness' of a code as the categories agents use to classify situations, objects, actions, and so forth. Clearly, agreeing on broader categories when classifying a specific object is easier than agreeing on finer ones. At the same time, finer categories are more informative. Thus, a fundamental problem of design is to deal with the trade-offs between the informativeness and the coordination advantages associated to a given degree of coarseness of a code.

Crémer et al. (2007) preserve Arrow's original assumption that an organization can design its own code, and develop a simple formal model of code optimization from which remarkable properties follow. The basic set-up is made of two agents – say a salesman and an engineer – that serve clients demanding a solution to a distribution of (finite) problems. The salesman, given bounded rationality, has an upper limit k of problem categories into which to classify problems. The organization has to design a code made of k 'words' (each word stands for a category) that allows the salesman to transmit to the engineer information on the class of the problem presented by a client; in other words, the code is an organizational lexicon of problems. In turn, the engineer has to work out a diagnosis of the problem before solving it, and the less precise the word, the more costly the diagnosis activity. The optimal code is thus a code that minimizes such diagnosis costs, given the k limitation.

An immediate implication of the set-up is that an optimal code will assign less frequent events to 'broader' words (i.e. to coarser categories), while keeping more precise words to label more frequent problems. Furthermore, under conventional assumptions of convexity of the diagnosis cost function, coarser categories will be used less frequently.

Increasing the number of salesmen has an interesting (and somehow surprising) consequence. Imagine that there are an engineer and two salesmen, that have to communicate the category of problems presented by two different groups of clients carrying different distributions of problems. Despite the differences in the environments the two salesmen face, the optimal code will be the same for both of them (and contain k words). Thus, organizations will tend to 'standardize' their language against the variety of environments ('no dialects'), while saturating their agents' cognitive capacity. Furthermore, the resulting code will be the one you might expect if a single agent had to face the total distributions of both salesmen; and will reproduce the properties mentioned in the paragraph above.

Some of the most interesting implications however arise if organizations are left free to decide simultaneously both their code and their organizational structure, given the environment they face. Consider now two different services A and B, each consisting of an engineer and a salesman, and each facing a potentially different client environment. If problem distributions are different for the two client populations, optimal codes for A and B will also be different. At the same time, A and B might have an interest to collaborate if clients' rate of arrival is uncertain, in order to optimize the use of productive capacity, represented by the engineer's available time. When will it be convenient to integrate A and B, and what will be the implications for the organizational code? The predictions of the model are that integrated forms should prevail as the cost of each diagnosis decreases, the homogeneity of the two client distributions increases, and the synergy between the two services increases. The code of the integrated units will be, as above, the same for both. Thus, the distribution is that the relative disadvantage of using a more 'generic' common code for both units will be offset by lower unitary diagnosis cost (since the cost of 'imprecision' will accordingly diminish), by greater homogeneity of demand populations (which implies that the distance between the separate codes should be lesser), and (obviously) by greater synergy between the services.

Hierarchy can be introduced as vertical communication with separate local codes. Rather than integrating via horizontal communication, services A and B could preserve separate, specialized languages and hire a hierarchical 'translator' that receives messages from one unit and translates it to the other one. Crémer et al. (2007) show that hierarchical integration will prevail in cases intermediate between those implying prevalence of separation or horizontal communication; in particular, for values of the diagnosis (+ translation) cost which are intermediate between the high costs favoring separation and the low costs favoring integration by horizontal communication.

The theory can be used to formulate some interesting predictions, that contrast with those based on incentive considerations, as in conventional agency models. A good example is predicting the impact of information technology on organization. As information technologies reduce the cost of using imprecise categories by decreasing diagnosis costs, the prediction of the model is that one should observe increasing centralization of information and decentralization of decision making. Centralization of information is favored by an increase in links across and within firms by the means of both hierarchy and common codes at the expense of separation. And horizontal, decentralized coordination spreads as a substitute for hierarchy. Both predictions find ample support in the evidence over organizational changes induced by the diffusion of ICT.

Similar concerns animate Wernerfelt's (2004) model of organizational languages. Just like Crémer et al. (2007), Wernerfelt is interested in the implications of coarse coding, for example the use of some broad partition of the states of the world in communication (and thus the use of 'imprecise' words). Differently from Crémer et al., however, Wernerfelt does not assume that an organization can design an optimal language, but instead looks at the set of codes that can be supported in equilibrium in a coordination game. The context is that of a team (thus, there are no conflicting interests) where members have to coordinate in allocating resources and each member has a privately known valuation of the resources. Communication is costly, so the team has to solve the trade-off between coordination advantages and communication cost. The main result of Wernerfelt's model is that here will be multiple equilibria, some of which are inefficient. Furthermore, equilibria in which different groups of members use different codes may exist if the importance of the 'local' group coordination exceeds the advantages of inter-group coordination. The model has implications for both inter- and intra-firm phenomena. On the one hand, the model implies that stable differences in firms internal languages may be a source of inter-firm differences in an industry; on the other one hand, heterogenous environments may raise difficulties for intra-firm coordination due to the internal code differences they induce.

In parallel to the renewed interest in modeling organizational code, and independently from it, there has been a recent stream of experimental literature looking at the emergence of codes in coordination games played in the laboratory. Very much in Arrow's spirit, this literature emphasizes the efficiency of codes, their effects on coordination, and their specificity and history-dependence. At the same time, it is concerned with the emergence of coordination equilibria rather than code design, and opens new windows onto the internal structure of code. It also demonstrates the wide applicability of experimental methods in such field of research.

Weber and Camerer (2003) investigate a simple experimental paradigm derived from research on psycholinguistics (Clark & Wilkes-Gibbs 1986). In the basic set-up, sender–receiver pairs of subjects have to develop a common system of verbal expressions (in natural language) to represent ('denote') single objects out of larger collections of them. For example, a sender must enable the receiver to find a single picture representing a scene of office life out of a collection of 20 pictures of similar subject. Players have a common interest, being rewarded for mutual success. Cost considerations can be added by introducing rewards for faster communication, providing incentives for the emergence of shorter codes. Thus, pairs of subjects have to solve the fundamental expressive trade-off between efficiency and clarity of communication (Martinet 1964). Long descriptions make it easier to individuate single pictures and succeed in coordination, but are too costly. Shorter description are more efficient but risk to miss their communicative goal.

Camerer and Weber show that, within each pair, stable and efficient codes tend to emerge with experience; the duration of each element of the code evolves along classical learning curves. At the same time, codes tend to present substantial path-dependence, being highly pair-specific. As a result, attempts to match subjects coming from different pairs generate substantial breakdowns in performance, due to differences in the codes developed by each pair and to inertia in adapting to the new organizational setting. Besides these results, that confirm the basic Arrow (1974) predictions, Weber and Camerer (2003; see also the subsequent Feiler and Camerer 2010) can extend their framework to an experimental analysis of the causes of mergers failure, by considering the effects of integrating individuals coming from different organizational codes in preexisting pairs. Taking organizational codes as metonymies for organizational cultures, they show how individuals facing the perspective of a merger tend to systematically underpredict the impact of structural change on the speed of adaptation of the code (and consequently on organizational performance).

Selten and Warglien (2007) develop a different experimental paradigm, looking at the development of artificial languages in pairs of subjects facing a coordination game, in which they have to agree on a code to denote geometric figures composed combinatorially out of a set of constituent features. The use of an artificial language (made out of arbitrary signs) allows a stricter control of the cost of communication and of the structure of the language being generated. Furthermore, Selten and Warglien compare how different environments affect the nature of the language generated. This allows for establising some new results. On the one hand, the endogenous emergence of roles is demonstrated. The need to attain efficient code with little coordination failure often leads to the spontaneous establishment of asymmetric roles, where one member of the pair is assuming the role of the designer of the code, while the other member follows. This supports the idea that even in pure self-organizing contexts code design may emerge as an effective answer to the need to achieve linguistic coordination. The most interesting results, however, concern the internal structure of the code. Selten and Warglien observe that whenever subjects have to deal with often repeating sets of figures (stationary environments), efficient but idiomatic, structureless codes tend to emerge. However, when dyads of subjects face ever-changing sets of figures, they tend to develop grammar-like language structures that allow for capturing the combinatorial structure of the figures and express it in a rule-based, compositional language. When a figure will be seen only once, there is no room for idiomatic codes learned through repetition. Subjects need to find ways to express objects seen for the first (and last) time and make their expression understandable to others. When *ex post* adjustment is not possible, some sort of '*ex ante*' flexible coordination rule has to be found. The result corrects the somehow pessimistic conclusions of Arrow (1974): once one looks at the internal syntactical structure of language, its combinatorial, generative capabilities can to some extent correct the inertia and rigidity that may be suggested by a look at its lexical aspects only.

Language Games, Speech Acts and Organizational Pragmatics

Research on codes addresses a very simplified view of organizational language: its basic lexical aspects, or how elementary 'units of meaning' represent single entities such as objects or events. Indeed, very little is said about the internal structure of organizational languages (with the possible exception of Selten and Warglien, looking at conditions favoring the emergence of compositional proto-grammars), nor about the way language is actually used 'in action': what could be broadly labeled the 'pragmatics' of organizational language.

A fairly differentiated thread of research has tried to address the latter issue – how language is used in organizations – by looking at more qualitative evidence and building on conceptual, verbal theorizing. Being often radically critical of economic thinking and adverse to what is often (mis-)labeled as 'positivistic research', this stream has unfortunately rarely sought interaction with the literature on organizational codes (the same applies symmetrically to the latter). As an unfortunate result, there has been no effort to integrate the results of both, although, as I will argue later, there might be important opportunities for dialogue and cross-fertilization.

If economic thinking on organizational language has been much leveraged on a view of codes as representations, much research on language in action has taken as a reference point Wittgenstein's (1953) concept of a 'language game'. Originally, the concept of language games was meant to convey the move from a view of meaning as 'representation' to a perspective on meaning as use. As is well known, Wittgenstein never gave an explicit definition of language games, as an expression of his late preference for the use of 'family resemblances' between concepts rather than definitions based on necessary and sufficient conditions. Instead, he provided examples and suggested general properties associated to such examples, the foremost being that language games are 'part of an activity, or form of life' (Wittgenstein 1953: 12). In a similar vein, researchers have suggested and analyzed examples of language games played in organizational context. I will briefly refer here to three such examples: the leadership game, managerial ambiguity and the use of linguistic 'war games' in competing organizations.

In his essay on leadership as a language game, Pondy (1978) submits the concept of leadership to one of those 'therapeutical' language analyses characteristic of the late Wittgenstein style. In particular, Pondy notices that since behaviors are observable, while meaning is not, leadership studies have overemphasized the nature of leadership as influence on behaviors, underestimating its nature of a language game that engages a leader in influencing meanings – how people perceive and conceive the nature of their activity, the problems they face, their sense of identity. As a matter of fact, Pondy claims, much leadership acts are language acts, that affect behaviors only through the mediation of the meaning creation process: 'the real power of Martin Luther King was not that he had a dream, but that he could describe it, that it became public, and therefore accessible to millions of people' (Pondy 1978: 230). It is thus the use of language subtleties that makes leadership effective. For example, by articulating in words the inarticulate, tacit feelings of a group, a leader can transform such feelings in a social fact, as many successful orchestra conductors are able to do. By recognizing this aspect of leadership one can understand a fundamental issue of leadership, the possibility to induce surprise while being understood at the same time; generating new meaning implies a mixture of novelty and the common ground that makes understanding possible. Moreover, leadership is open-ended: one cannot understand the open-ended nature of leadership acts without referring to the generative property of language, its ability to generate a potential infinity of new, understandable expressions – a point that will be developed later in this chapter.

Astley and Zammuto (1992) analyze in a similar vein the inherent ambiguity of managerial language. In their own words, 'organizations are created and sustained as managers engage their surroundings through the use of linguistic codes and conventions that define appropriate patterns of social activity. Corporate language categorizes and structures organizational context, define organizational boundaries, and provides a framework within which action unfolds.' (Astley and Zammuto 1992: 449). Why should managers demonstrate a preference for linguistic ambiguity rather than adhering to rules of clarity and unambiguity like, for example, scientists? Astley and Zammuto argue that ambiguous language responds to the fact that managers have to face inconsistent demands while producing a sense of order and direction. Ashley and Zammuto illustrate their claims by the example of managerial language in organizations trying to recover from bankruptcy (Ertel et al. 1991). The language game managers have to play during recoveries from Chapter 11 bankruptcy is that of creating a sense of (new) direction while reassuring constituents that their concerns are addressed. Thus, their statements must be equivocal to be compatible with a variety of interpretations. The nature of organizations as a political coalition of heterogenous interests (Cyert and March 1963) forces management to provide an ambiguous language.

It has often been claimed that the language of conflict can shape our perception of other players in a game (McNamara et al. 1999). Schelling (1960) has strikingly remarked that while our vocabulary is rich in words designating common interest or adversarial relationships, there are no words to designate the relation between players when motives for conflict and cooperation coexist. While we have a rich lexicon for partners or for opponents, how are we to designate someone who is a partner and an opponent at the same time? Devetag and Warglien (2008) provide experimental evidence of the inherent difficulty in representing the coexistence of conflicting and common motives on simple 'mixed motives' games, and relate it to basic linguistic constraints. Rindova et al. (2004) analyze how organizational language can trap organizations in extreme conflict and competition – in 'war language games'. Using the 'cola wars' of the 1980s as a leading example, Rindova et al. (2004) show how the use of a war language in competition creates an 'enemy mindset' in which organizational actors and stakeholders are increasingly mobilized in an effort to destroy the competitor, using all available competitive 'weapons'. Typical effects of the war language game are attribution errors (declines in performance are attributed univocally to aggressive moves of the competitor); focus of attention on competition with the rival, disregarding other factors; greater emotional involvement in rivalry; and the legitimation of aggressive moves. Once started, a war language game becomes self-reinforcing, triggering a sequence of retaliation moves that locks both rivals in the interpretation of behavior of the other as merely aggressive. Thus, Rindova et al. (2004) argue that rivalry in industry can depend not only upon the structural conditions of an industry, but also the (history-dependent) dynamics triggered by the language games organizations engage in.

It is common to associate language games and speech acts. However, while language games tend to conflate meaning and use (Bach 2006), the notion of speech acts (Austin 1962; Searle 1969) tends to separate them, making a clear difference between the meaning of words and what a speaker can make with words (the speech act). Examples of speech acts are commands or excuses. In a way, the notion of a speech act directs attention to what is represented in a code. One particular type of speech act, performatives, has attracted the most attention of organizational theorists interested in language. According to Austin (1962), a performative is a sentence which does something in the world rather than describing something about it. Examples include a promise, a sentencing to jail or a nomination to an organizational position.

Perhaps the most influential use of the category of performative speech acts for organizational analysis is Winograd and Flores's (1986) attempt to define organizations as networks of commitments, and to suggest design strategies for organizational communication on the grounds of such definition. Flores and Ludlow (1976) analyze 'what do people do in an office' and find the prevalence of two types of performatives: directives, expressing desire that an action be performed ('I would like you to go immediately to the headquarters'); and commissives, expressing commitments to perform an action ('I promise to deliver the report tomorrow morning'). Flores and Ludlow suggest that 'organizations exist as networks of directives and commissives' (p. 102), a point that might suggest a strong similarity with a contractualistic view of organizations as systems of mutual promises. However, the emphasis on a contract-like relationship is somehow integrated by the centrality of notion of breakdown: things happen all the time that make contractual-like relationships fail, and organizational (and managerial) action is mostly concerned with repairing such breakdowns through conversations (linguistic interactions) that trigger new networks of directives and commissives. Thus, Flores and Ludlow (and later Winograd and Flores) suggest a sort of conversational counterpart to the modern theory of the firm, where managerial conversations are the fundamental organizational answer to the inherent incompleteness of ordinary networks of work commitments.

Speech acts theory has been employed in the analysis of different organizational issues. Ford and Ford (1995) analyze the change process in organizations as a phenomenon that occurs within organizational communication (rather than being just supported by it). They claim that in different phases of the change process different types of performative speech act are prevalent. For example, phases in which the process focuses on understanding are characterized by assertives (commitments to bring about evidence about assertions), while performatives and commissives (see above) play a major role when action for change (focus on bringing intended change results) is called for. Ford and Ford also describe in conversational terms how breakdowns in the change process may happen and what can cause them. Donohue and Diez (1985) study the use of conversational directives in work negotiation in relation to different parameters characterizing the negotial process. Cooren (2004) analyzes the production and use of texts in organizational contexts, and explores the type of actions that can be performed by texts by using Searle's classification of speech acts.

Among speech acts, declarations (Searle 1969) have special relevance for the investigation of the relationships between language and organization. They are speech acts whose content is brought into existence by the very performance of that act. The legal founding of a company, the nomination of a chief executive officer (CEO), the bankruptcy declaration are such kind of speech acts. In an insightful analysis of such speech acts, John Searle (1995) points to some fundamental properties of declarations that have broad implications for theories of institutions (see also Hodgson 2006). First of all, what kind of 'fact' is created by a declaration? A declaration attributes to a person or a thing a function – a function that is not 'naturally' associated to the person or thing. For example, being a piece of printed paper does not imply being money. When John is nominated Dean, he is attributed functions (legal rights he can exert, decisions to make, etc.) that are not originally associated to John as such. Thus, declaring a Dean or a CEO is performing a constitutive rule (Searle 1995) of the type 'X counts as Y in C', where C is the context within which the attribution of function ('counts as') is defined. The second relevant property of the 'fact' created by a declaration is that it is an 'institutional' fact as long as the function attributed to X can be performed only if there is a collective agreement or acceptance in some constituency. If nobody (or even not enough persons) in a community does recognize to that piece of paper the attribution of money, it ceases to perform such function. The third important element of Searle's analysis is the claim that institutional facts are inherently language-dependent. This is due not only to the fact that constitutive rules are almost universally performed through some linguistic medium. More deeply, a constitutive rule has by itself a linguistic nature, since the attribution of function is a symbolic act that imposes a status on X by a marker, a symbolic element that make it possible to add to X its institutional status.

While this short summary of Searle's analysis can hardly do justice to its breadth and depth, it should suffice to illuminate a fundamental point: a formal organization, as any institution, cannot come into existence and be reproduced without constantly relying on institutional facts of a linguistic nature. Organization is language, a point that will be further developed in the next section.

ORGANIZATION AS LANGUAGE

Generative Rules for Organizing

An often-cited Karl Weick definition is that organizing is a 'consensually validated grammar for reducing equivocality by means of sensible interlocked behavior' (Weick 1979: 3). The analogy between language and patterns of actions has deeper roots (often gone unnoticed) in Chomsky (Miller and Chomsky 1963; see also Skvoretz and Fararo 1980). The challenge to look at grammar as a model for organizational phenomena has been taken up by a thread of research which has emphasized that organizing can be considered as a language, with its lexicon and its syntactical rules.

In a series of important contributions, Brian Pentland (Pentland 1992, 1995; Pentland and Rueter 1994) has explored how processual aspects of organizations can be analyzed in terms of explicit grammatical models. After Chomsky, modern linguistics has been emphasizing the generative nature of grammar: its capability to generate a potentially infinite set of (correct) sentences out of finite elements. By specifying structural constraints over admissible sentences, grammars 'describe a set of possible outcomes, not an individual outcome'. Pentland has suggested a basic description of the elements of an organizational grammar, applying it to organizational processes, that can be considered the organizational equivalent of a sentence. First of all, Pentland (1995) suggests mapping the lexical components of a grammar to the 'moves' in an organizational process. The concept of a 'move' is derived from Goffman (1981). Moves are acts (not just 'speech acts') that 'have a distinctive unitary bearing on some set or other of the circumstances in which participants find themselves' (Goffman 1981: 24). For example, in a software support organization (Pentland 1992) moves can be 'assign', 'transfer', 'refer', and so on. Secondly, syntactical aspects can be identified. Pentland (1995) suggests two types of syntactical elements: syntactic constituents and syntactic constraints. In linguistics, syntactic components are subunits of the sentence structure (such as noun phrases or verb phrases. Sentences are obtained as combinations of such constituents. Pentland notes that 'syntactic constituents provide a way of describing the structural features of a pattern without elaborating it down to the specifics of the lexicon' (Pentland 1995: 545). March and Simon's (1958) 'performance programs' or Nelson and Winter's (1982) routines are suggested to be the organizational syntactic constituent. Like language ones, they can be combined and nested together in larger units. Constraints over admissible combinations, however, are provided by grammatical rules. Example of such constraints are: institutional structures (e.g. institutional constraints on access to resources), technological structures (that affect possible combinations of actions in interaction with artifacts), coordination structures (interdependencies between individuals' actions that constrain their combinations, such as sequential constraints *à la* Thompson 1967) and cultural structures (constraining appropriate behavior). In an analysis of a customer service center providing support to users of a software product, Pentland and Rueter (1994) offer an example of how a grammatical analysis of organizational processes could be performed, demonstrating the empirical viability of his approach. The case analyzed is especially interesting because, on the surface, it displays a great variety of behaviors; something apparently far from a routinized process. However, once 'moves' are coded and their sequences are analyzed in the light of a grammatical model, strong regularities emerge. By using a testing method based on work by Olson et al. (1994), Pentland and Rueter show that most observed sequences of moves can be 'rewritten' in terms of the rules of a simple grammar made of a limited number of rules.

The issue of generativity takes center stage also in the contribution of Huseyin Leblebici (2000; see also Salancik and Leblebici 1988). However, in Leblebici's approach the focus shifts from moves and routines to transactions and forms. The problem addressed by Leblebici is how to explain the generation of the variety of existing organizational forms (and how new forms can come about). Rooting his approach in the institutionalist tradition, Leblebici shifts the unit of analysis to transactions (which in turn have a sort of 'morphology' constrained by the nature of the goods object of transaction). Generative rules should help to understand how sets of patterned transactions (forms) can be organized. Four rules are suggested, that considerably overlap with those defined in Pentland's approach, but are framed in ways more consonant to the view of the firm as a 'nexus of contracts' (while the former is clearly akin to behavioral theories of the firm). Rules of causal order establish constraints over sequences or groupings of activities. Rules of membership define who can be party to a transaction. Rules of allocation determine responsibilities and rights among member parts. Finally, rules of social discourse provide socially validated templates for modes of organizing (e.g. categories of organization forms such as 'fast food' or 'elementary school'). Since these rules are subject to continuous social evolution, their change provides opportunities for innovation in forms. On the grounds of this conceptual structure, Leblebici sketches an analysis of the diversity of forms of governance structures based on the generative properties of rules of allocation. Different forms of governance result from different combinations of duties, power, liabilities and obligations, and other rights and obligations among parties, according to rules that are derived from an analytical classification of legal relations between transacting parties.

The Recursive Constitution of Organization

A feature of language strictly associated to generativity is recursivity: the possibility to nest propositions within larger propositions, as in 'I think that you are guessing what I am thinking'. Recursivity is a more general capability of human cognitive systems, maybe its most characteristic signature; Hauser et al. (2002) actually claim that it is what makes humans unique. It is the same principle that allows us to bootstrap on the ability to add 1 to a natural number to generate an infinite set of natural numbers. Organizational hierarchical architectures, subsystems nested within other subsystems, are clearly children of recursion (Simon 1962). Indeed, the two fundamental abstract metaphors that allow us to think about hierarchy (and represent it) – the tree and the nested boxes – are recursive.

The recursive nature of language can help us to better understand one enduring puzzle of organizational discourse: how agency can be attributed to organizational entities. Organization theorists have always been oscillating between two ontological statuses of organizations. On the one hand, organizations have been viewed as actors with their own identity and intentionality; on the other hand, organizations have often been reduced to interactions among interdependent individuals. The first view is perhaps the most diffused, especially in classical organization theory, but also the most problematic. The nature of the organization as an actor that can decide, commit itself, adapt to a fragmented environment or even be proud of itself, is far from obvious. Of course, there is a set of legal constitutive facts (an instance of Searle's declaratives) that provide juridical personality to organizations. But an organization is more than its juridical status. It has to reproduce itself each day through its participants' behavior. Once more, Searle's principle of 'X counts as Y in C', can help us to understand how language creates and reproduces multiple levels of agency by (recursive) function attribution.

This is the core of Robichaud et al.'s (2004) analysis of the constitution of organizations as actors through discourse. The challenge they face is how the intrinsically 'multivocal' and pluralistic nature of organizations as systems of individual actors can coexist and be reconciled with the univocal view of organizations as actors. In their view, recursivity is the key feature of language allowing the emergence of organizations as autonomous entities. They claim that the constitution of organizations as actors is based on the recursive embedding of levels of agency through discourse. Organizations persist and reproduce themselves through the mediation of language interaction – 'organizational conversations'. The basic idea is that since conversations can 'embed' other conversations, collective agency is the result of recursively embedding the participants of a conversation in a new discursive entity (e.g. a group) of a higher level. For example a 'group' embeds the linguistic interactions among its participants by shifting to a higher level of discourse. This is possible because in a conversation participants can refer not only to each of them, but also to the relation among them established by the conversation. Thus, an 'us' level can be established. This process can only be successful in constituting a collective level of agency, however, as long as one individual can talk not only about a group, but talk for it, standing in a 'counts as' relationship with the new entity. More plainly, a collective entity can emerge not only where it is possible to refer to it, but also when 'there is a voice to represent it', instantiating the agency of the higher-level entity (see also Callon and Latour's 1981 theory of macro-actors). For example, union representatives can speak on behalf of a group of employees, but once single employees become 'the group' and someone can speak for the group, the single employees are 'black-boxed' in the new entity, that now can make commitments, be frustrated or accept. It is important to stress that the new entity does not need to be legally represented; it is enough that it is consensually represented in language, that all participants can identify as the 'group'. The legal declaration is just a special case of this broader process of linguistic constitution of a collective entity.

Robichaud et al. (2004) illustrate this framework by analyzing how in an encounter between a mayor and citizens the 'city as actor' increasingly becomes institutionalized at an autonomous level able to act, judge and listen, in a process that allows a shift from the level of personal stories carried to the encounter by participants to a more abstract representation of a 'voice translating many voices' in which 'individual voices will echo in the distance, as a ghostly presence' (Robichaud et al. 2004: 629). This allows the mayor to re-establish himself as the representative of the citizens' voice rather than a polemical interlocutor of their complaints.

While the evocative language of Robichaud et al. (2004) may look distant from the abstract language of economic thinking, it addresses issues that have become relevant in the recent economic debate. What makes us able to reason in terms of collective entities? Theories of team reasoning (Sugden 1993; Bacharach 1999) have recently stressed the power of reasoning in terms of collective entities to favor coordination. For example, Bacharach informally characterizes team reasoning in this way: 'when each member of a group works out what to do by putting themself in the position of an imaginary manager and determining the action which the manager would prescribe for them, they "team reason"'. Robichaud et al. (2004) provide a first effort to understand how language shapes the emergence of such collective entities and their collective recognition and legitimation at multiple levels, and how we can imagine that such an entity 'reasons'.

SOME CONNECTIONS

The lack of interaction among different research threads is one of the major factors hampering the emergence of 'language and organizations' as a field with a recognizable agenda and a shared sense of key research questions. In particular, economic, typically formal views of organizational language and more cognitively, semiotically, typically qualitatively oriented ones have substantially ignored each other, with a great loss of opportunities for intellectual progress. Yet, a more productive disciplinary dialogue is mature and timely. I briefly suggest three examples pointing in this direction.

Language and Cognitive Representations in Organizations

The literature on organizational codes has been often trapped in an oversimplified view of 'meaning' as simple reference to states of the world. More qualitative views of language in organizations have stressed how language contributes to the way organizations interpret or make sense of their environment: how language contributes to organizational cognition, and vice versa. The two views are not irreconcilable. A richer cognitive characterization of organizational codes is possible without losing formal rigor. For example, models of code 'coarseness' (Crémer et al. 2007; Wernerfelt 2004) provide a first step towards a richer characterization of how categories are represented in codes (Jäger and van Rooij 2007) and how they affect interactive behavior (Mullainathan et al. 2008). Similarly, the role of context and metaphors in shaping how agents jointly construct meaning through language has often been emphasized in sense-making views of organizations. Without losing the richness of their content, these cognitive factors can be represented formally in ways that make them amenable to the modeling of interaction (Warglien and Gardenfors 2011); for example, one could represent and model how the manipulation of contextual cues affects the capability of two organizational agents to reach a 'meeting of minds' over the interpretation of a given situation.

Modeling Language Games in Organizations

Attempts to model language games – and bridge semantics and the pragmatics of language use – have been blooming in recent years (Benz et al. 2006; Parikh 2010). They might provide interesting ways to connect qualitative, interpretive studies of language use in organizations to formal models of communication. As seen above, field studies have repeatedly highlighted how ambiguity increases in organizational language as multiple constituencies with diverging interests exert their pressure over management (Astley and Zammuto 1992). This observation clearly resonates with a well-known result in the literature on communication in game theory: as agents' interests diverge, the better-informed agent will send increasingly noisy (uninformative) signals to the less-informed one (Crawford and Sobel 1982). More recent developments in modeling language games can further contribute to explain how games of ambiguity work, for example by analyzing how agents disambiguate ambiguous signals (Parikh 2010). Of course, introducing behaviorally informed views of game playing might further enhance our understanding of the use of language in organizations. For example, taking into account cognitive difficulties in representing mixed-motives games (Schelling 1960; Devetag and Warglien 2008) can help to understand how the 'war language games' described by Rindova et al. (2004) may effectively tilt organizational members members towards greater competitive aggressiveness. More generally, field research on organizational language can greatly enrich our view of the language games organizations play, while (possibly behavioral) game-theoretical models of such games can refine our understanding of agents' strategies and the equilibria of such games.

Incomplete Contracts in the Light of Language

The notion of contractual incompleteness has been playing a central role on the stage of the debate on the economics of organization for several decades. In the recent theoretical debate, there has been a remarkable shift of attention towards the cognitive and behavioral aspects related to incomplete contracts (Tirole 2009; Hart & Moore 2008; Fehr et al. 2011). This has led to closer attention being paid to the flexibility inherent to incomplete contracts, and to the role of contracts as 'reference points', as well as to the fact that contracts might be 'too complete', not too incomplete. I suggest that attention to the semantic and pragmatic issues involved in contracting might provide a useful complement to such perspectives.

For example, traditionally the literature has focused on incompleteness as related to the insurgence of 'observable but unverifiable states of the world'. This constrains the analysis to a very specific form of legal 'truth gaps' in the semantics of the contract. However, from the perspective of this chapter, it is clear that the different forms of contractual incompleteness are to a large extent related to semantic and pragmatic issues. In other words, and unsurprisingly, contracts happen to share most of the common 'imperfections ' of the natural language in which they are written (and as in language, such imperfections may be virtues as well as defects). This would reveal a complex typology of form of contractual indeterminacy (Varzi and Warglien, n.d.), some of which are not really incompleteness but correspond instead to forms of overdeterminacy (e.g. to a form of 'truth gluts' that are dual to the classical forms of underdeterminacy).

When obligations and state of the world are not quantifiable or anyway not quantified in contracts, contractual elements are expressed in lexical terms that are usually evaluated in terms of categories (e.g. 'stewing chicken'). In turn, categories have prototypes against which belonging to a category is established. The role of such prototypes as reference points provides important elements for understanding much of the informal agreement and shading processes that surround incomplete contracting (Fehr et al. 2011), as well as legal resolution of contractual disputes (see the classic Frigaliment Imp. vs. B.N.S. Int'l Sales). Furthermore, contracts themselves are usually written on the basis of default templates (Tirole 2009) that are usually molded on prototypical situations. Economic analyses of categorization and decision making (Mullainathan et al. 2008) might find a promising field of application in the analysis of incomplete contracts, and enrich the cognitive dimension of contract theory.

Finally, analyses of organizational speech acts have suggested that organizations are regulated by networks of commitments and promises (Winograd and Flores 1986) that share important similarities with incomplete contracts. Understanding how these commitments and promises are negotiated and maintained, and how their breakdowns are faced, might provide important comparative elements with the way in which incomplete contracts are negotiated, maintained and repaired. There are large dialogue opportunities between formal theories and field work that might shed new light on the continuum of forms of 'directives and commissives' that weave organizations and markets together.

CONCLUDING REMARKS

In a recent comment Brandenburger and Vinokurova (2012) have suggested that time seems ripe for 'work in what might be called "organizational linguistics"'. This chapter has tried to map some of the research that might feed such work. The relative fragmentation of such literature may lead us to underestimate how much has already be done, and its potential impact on classical issues in research on economics and organization. Most of the current research on organizations and economics still implicitly considers language as a neutral veil on organizational decision making. New insights may be gained by removing this assumption and by starting to look into the deep effects of language on the nature of organizational life.

REFERENCES

Alvesson, M. and D. Kärreman (2000), 'Varieties of discourse: on the study of organizations through discourse analysis', *Human Relations*, **53**, 1125–1149.
Arrow, K.J. (1974), *The Limits of Organization*, New York: Norton.
Astley, W.G. and R.F. Zammuto (1992), 'Organization science, managers, and languages', *Organization Science*, **3**, 443–460.
Austin, J.L. (1962), *How To Do Things with Words*, Cambridge, MA: Harvard University Press.
Bach, K. (2006), 'Speech acts and pragmatics', in M. Devitt and R. Hanley (eds), *Philosophy of Language*, Oxford: Blackwell, pp. 147–167.
Bacharach, M. (1999), 'Interactive team reasoning: a contribution to the theory of co-operation', *Research in Economics*, **53**, 117–147.
Barley, S. (1983), 'Semiotics and the study of occupational and organizational cultures', *Administrative Science Quarterly*, **28**(3), 393–413.
Benz, A., G. Jager and R. van Rooij (eds) (2006), *Game Theory and Pragmatics*, Basingstoke: Palgrave Macmillan.
Boje, D. (1991), 'The storytelling organization: a study of story performance in an office-supply firm', *Administrative Science Quarterly*, **36**(1), 106–126.
Boje, D. (1995), 'Stories of the storytelling organization: a postmodern analysis of Disney as "Tamara-Land"', *Academy of Management Journal*, **38**(4), 997–1035.
Bolton, P. and M. Dewatripont (1994), 'The firm as a communication network', *Quarterly Journal of Economics*, **104**, 809–839.
Brandenburger, A. and N. Vinokurova (2012), 'Comment on "Toward a behavioral theory of strategy"', Organization *Science*, **23**, 286–287.
Callon, M. and B. Latour (1981), 'Unscrewing the big Leviathan: how actors macro-structure reality and how sociologists help them to do so', in A. Cicourel and K. Knorr- Cetina (eds), *Advances in Social Theory and Methodology. Towards an Integration of Micro- and Macro-Sociologies*, Boston, MA: Routledge & Kegan Paul, pp. 277–303.
Christensen, M. and T. Knudsen (2010), 'Design of decision making organizations', *Management Science*, **56**(1), 71–89.
Clark, H.H. and D. Wilkes-Gibbs (1986), 'Referring as a collaborative process', *Cognition*, **22**(1), 1–39.
Cooren, F. (2004), 'Textual agency: how texts do things in organizational settings', *Organization*, **11**(3), 373–393.
Crawford, V. and J. Sobel (1982), 'Strategic information transmission', *Econometrica*, **50**, 1431–1451.
Crémer, J., L. Garicano and A. Prat (2007), 'Language and the theory of the firm', *Quarterly Journal of Economics*, 373–407.
Cyert, R.M. and J.G. March (1963), *A Behavioral Theory of the Firm*, Englewood Cliffs, NJ: Prentice-Hall.
Czarniawska, Barbara (1998), *A Narrative Approach to Organization Studies*, Thousand Oaks, CA: Sage.
Devetag, G. and M. Warglien (2008), 'Playing the wrong game: an experimental analysis of relational complexity and strategic misrepresentation', *Games and Economic Behavior*, **62**(2), 364–382.
Donohue, W. and M. Diez (1985), 'Directive use in negotiation interaction', *Communication Monographs*, **52**(4), 305–318.
Ertel, P., G. Koury and J. Sokol (1991), 'The turnaround at StorageTek', in A.G. Bedeian and R.F. Zammuto (eds), *Organizations: Theory and Design*, Hinsdale, IL: Dryden Press.

Fehr, E., O. Hart and C. Zehnder (2011), 'How do informal agreements and renegotiation shape contractual reference points?' NBER Working Paper, 17545.

Feiler, L. and C.F. Camerer (2010), 'Code creation in endogenous merger experiments', *Economic Inquiry*, **48**(2), 337–352.

Fiol, C.M. (1989), 'A semiotic analysis of corporate language: organizational boundaries and joint venturing', *Administrative Science Quarterly*, **34**, 277–303.

Fiol, C.M. (2002), 'Capitalizing on paradox: the role of language in transforming organizational identities', *Organization Science*, **13**(6), 653–666.

Flores, F.J. and J. Ludlow (1976), 'Doing and speaking in the office', in G. Fick and R. Sprague (eds), *Decision Support Systems: Issues and Challenges*, Laxenburg: IIASA, pp. 99–118.

Ford, J. and L. Ford (1995), 'The role of conversations in producing intentional change in organizations', *Academy of Management Review*, **20**(3), 54–570.

Frigaliment Imp. vs. B.N.S. Int'l Sales, 190 F. Supp 116—S.D.N.Y. 1960.

Goffman, E. (1981), *Forms of Talk*, Philadelphia, PA: University of Pennsylvania Press.

Hart, O. and J. Moore (2008), 'Contracts as reference points', *Quarterly Journal of Economics*, **123**, 1–48.

Hauser, M.D., N. Chomsky and W.T. Fitch (2002), 'The faculty of language: what is it, who has it, and how did it evolve?' *Science*, **298**, 1569–1579.

Hodgson, G. (2006), 'What are institutions?' *Journal of Economic Issues*, **40**(1), 1–25.

Jäger, G. and R. van Rooij (2007), 'Language structure: psychological and social constraints', *Synthese*, **159**, 99–130.

Leblebici, H. (2000), 'Allocation of rights and the organization of transactions: elements of a generative approach to organizing', *Journal of Management and Governance*, **4**, 149–168.

March, J.G. and H.A. Simon (1958), *Organizations*, New York: Wiley.

Martinet, A. (1964), *Elements of General Linguistics*, London: Faber & Faber.

McNamara, R.S., J.G. Blight, R.K. Brigham and T.J. Biersteker (1999), *Argument Without End: In Search of Answers to the Vietnam Tragedy*, New York: Public Affairs.

Miller, G.A. and Chomsky N. (1963), 'Finitary models of language users', in R.D. Luce, R.R. Bush and E. Galanter (eds), *Handbook of Mathematical Psychology*, Vol. 1, New York: Wiley, pp. 419–491.

Mullainathan, S., J. Schwartzstein and A. Shleifer (2008), 'Coarse thinking and persuasion', *Quarterly Journal of Economics*, **123**, 577–619.

Nelson, R. and S. Winter (1982), *An Evolutionary Theory of Economic Change*, Cambridge, MA: Belknap Press.

Olson, G.M., J.D. Herbsleb and H. Rueter (1994), 'Characterizing the sequential structure of interactive behaviors through statistical and grammatical techniques', *Human Computer Interaction*, **9**, 427–472.

Parikh, P. (2010), *Language and Equilibrium*, Cambridge, MA: MIT Press.

Pentland, B.T. (1992), 'Organizing moves software support hot lines', *Administrative Science Quarterly*, **37**(4), 527–548.

Pentland, B.T. (1995), 'Grammatical models of organizational processes', *Organization Science*, **6**, 541–556.

Pentland, B.T. and H.H. Rueter (1994), 'Organizational routines as grammars of action', *Administrative Science Quarterly*, **39**, 484–510.

Pondy, Louis R. (1978), 'Leadership is a language game', in M. McCall and M. Lombardo (eds), *Leadership: Where Else Can We Go?* Greensboro, NC: Center for Creative Leadership, pp. 87–98.

Radner, Roy (1993), 'The organization of decentralized information processing', *Econometrica*, **61**(5), 1109–1146.

Rindova, V., M. Becerra and I. Contrado (2004), 'Enacting competitive wars: actions, language games, and market consequences', *Academy of Management Review*, **29**, 670–687.

Robichaud, D., H. Giroux and J.R. Taylor (2004), 'The metaconversation: the recursive properties of language as a key to organizing', *Academy of Management Review*, **29**(4), 617–634.

Salancik, G.R. and H. Leblebici (1988), 'Variety and form in organizing transactions: a generative grammar of organization', in N. DiTomaso and S.B. Bacharach (eds), *Research in the Sociology of Organizations*, Vol. 6, Greenwich, CT: JAI Press, pp. 1–32.

Schelling, T. (1960), *The Strategy of Conflict*, Cambridge, MA: Harvard University Press.

Searle, J.R. (1969), *Speech Acts: An Essay in the Philosophy of Language*, London: Cambridge University Press.

Searle, J.R. (1995), *The Construction of Social Reality*, New York: Free Press.

Selten, R. and M. Warglien (2007), 'The emergence of simple languages in an experimental coordination game', *Proceedings of the National Academy of Sciences of the United States of America*, **104**, 7361–7366.

Shannon, C.E. (1948), 'A mathematical theory of communication', *Bell System Technology Journal*, **27**, 379–423.

Simon H.A. (1962), 'The architecture of complexity', *Proceedings of the American Philosophical Society*, **106**, 467–482.

Skvoretz, J. and T.J. Fararo (1980), 'Languages and grammars of action and interaction: a contribution to the formal theory of action', *Behavioral Science*, **25**, 9–22.

Sugden, R. (1993), 'Thinking as a team: towards an explanation of non-selfish behavior', *Social Philosophy and Policy*, **10**, 69–89.

Thompson, J.D. (1967), 'Organizations in action: social science bases of administrative theory', New York: McGraw-Hill.

Tirole, J. (2009), 'Cognition and incomplete contracts', *American Economic Review*, **99**(1), 265–294.

Varzi, A.C. and M. Warglien (n.d.), 'Indeterminate contracts and semantic indeteminacy', unpublished manuscript.

Warglien, M. and P. Gärdenfors (2011), 'Semantics, conceptual spaces and the meeting of minds', *Synthese*, **184**.

Weber, R. and C. Camerer (2003), 'Cultural conflict and merger failure', *Management Science*, **49**(4), 400–415.

Weick, K.E. (1979), *The Social Psychology of Organizing*, Reading, MA: Addison-Wesley.

Wernerfelt, B. (2004), 'Organizational languages', *Journal of Economics and Management Strategy*, **13**(3), 461–472.

Winograd T. and F. Flores (1986), *Understanding Computers and Cognition: A New Foundation for Design*, Norwood, NJ: Ablex Publ Corp.

Wittgenstein, L. (1953), *Philosophical Investigations*, New York: Macmillan.

PART III

THE SHAPING OF ECONOMIC ORGANIZATION BETWEEN DESIGN AND EVOLUTION

9. Organizational adaptation and evolution: Darwinism versus Lamarckism?
Geoffrey M. Hodgson

An ongoing debate within organization studies concerns the roles of individual adaptation and competitive selection in the evolution of populations of firms. On one side, Michael Hannan and John Freeman (1989) emphasize the role of selection and stress the de facto limits of individual firm adaptability. Conventionally their 'selectionist' position is described as 'Darwinian', whereas opposing views that emphasize adaptability are described as 'Lamarckian'. It is argued here that this labelling is misconceived. Darwin himself believed in the Lamarckian inheritance of acquired characters. Even if Lamarckian inheritance occurs, evolution requires selectionist mechanisms as well. And for detailed reasons the application of the Lamarckian notion to organizational evolution is problematic. By contrast, abstract Darwinian principles do apply, and Darwinism emphasizes adaptation and development as well as selection. The careful use of properly defined Darwinian principles not only helps to avoid earlier pitfalls but also fruitfully guides ongoing enquiry.

INTRODUCTION

Researchers into organizations have long debated the relative importance of individual-level adaptation versus population-level selection in explaining changes in industry characteristics.[1] To a large degree this is a matter of empirical investigation. It cannot be resolved in an a priori manner.

This chapter addresses this literature, without bringing further empirical evidence to bear. Instead, the main contention is that the debate within organization studies over the processes of change has been confused by the use of inexact and misleading terminology, particularly in regard to the terms Lamarckism and Darwinism. In turn, this state of confusion has prevented the use of abstract principles from general evolutionary theory that have been developed since the 1980s, in both the philosophy of biology and evolutionary economics (Hull 1988; Hodgson 2002; Stoelhorst 2005, 2008; Stoelhorst and Huizing 2006; Hodgson and Knudsen 2006a, 2010b; Aldrich et al. 2008; Pelikan 2010). These principles are often described as 'generalized Darwinism'.

The much more restrictive and historically inaccurate use of the term 'Darwinian' by many organizational researchers has proved to be a barrier to the adoption of generalized Darwinian principles and consequent insights. Furthermore, the false dichotomy between Lamarckism and Darwinism may have deterred investigation into intermediate positions involving the necessarily relationship between adaptation and selection.

The aim of this chapter is to clear up the terminological confusion and to indicate briefly how the principles of generalized Darwinism can be useful as an overall framework for helping to understand organizational evolution. They also add to the research agenda by framing the issues involved in explaining empirical outcomes. After summarizing the confusion in the next section, this chapter establishes that Darwinism and Lamarckism are not mutually exclusive. It then shows that for the Lamarckian label to be meaningful – temporarily leaving aside the question of its validity – a distinction between genotypes (more generally, replicators) and phenotypes (more generally, interactors) is required. The next section argues that while something remotely similar to Lamarckian inheritance may occur in social evolution, the label is misleading. And social evolution, as argued below and elsewhere (Veblen 1899; Campbell 1965; Hodgson and Knudsen 2010b), is Darwinian. Contrary to widespread belief, Darwinism embraces rather than excludes such phenomena as learning and adaptation. The chapter shows that organizational adaptation or development cannot be ignored, especially in a fully fledged Darwinian theory. It then explores some applications of the Darwinian framework. A final section concludes the chapter and points to some implications of the argument.

AN UNRESOLVED DEBATE CONFOUNDED BY CONFUSING TERMINOLOGY

Historically, social scientists have had a very uneasy relationship with Darwinism (Degler 1991). Worries about 'social Darwinism' and misleading portrayals of Darwinian selection as 'blind' have helped to dissuade social scientists from addressing Darwinian principles. While Darwinism has been abused in the past, many contemporary worries turn out to be groundless.[2]

Partly because of fears about Darwinism, and partly because of a belief in the appropriateness of the other label, many prominent social scientists including Jack Hirshleifer (1977), Herbert Simon (1981), William McKelvey (1982), Richard Nelson and Sidney Winter (1982), Robert Boyd and Peter Richerson (1985), Friedrich Hayek (1988) and J. Stanley Metcalfe (1994) have described social or economic evolution as 'Lamarckian'. In some of these cases the 'Darwinian' label is even ignored or dismissed.

The dispute within organization science over the relative importance of adaptation and selection (Baum 1996), and the extent to which firm routines can change in individual firms, is sometimes described as a contest between 'Darwinian' and 'Lamarckian' conceptions of organizational change (Usher and Evans 1996). The seminal work of Michael Hannan and John Freeman (1989) is described as 'Darwinian' because it stresses industry-level selection and gives a low estimate for the possibilities of individual organizational adaptation.[3]

According to Van de Ven and Poole (1995), the Darwinian evolution of organizations means that traits are inherited through intergenerational processes, whereas Lamarckian evolution means that traits can be acquired within the lifetime of an organization through learning and imitation. Many works actually agree with this distinction and promote Lamarckian evolution over Darwinian ideas, without much detailed consideration of the nature of either form of evolution.

DARWINISM AND LAMARCKISM ARE NOT MUTUALLY EXCLUSIVE

John Wilkins (2001) portrays 'Lamarckism' as an ambiguous term with three prominent and different meanings:

1. The first meaning of Lamarckism is the notion that acquired characters can or will be inherited. Jean Baptiste de Lamarck (1984 [1809]) promoted this idea, but it was not original to him.
2. A second strong theme in the writings of Lamarck – which he developed rather than originated – is that evolution leads to greater complexity. This idea has today grown beyond its Lamarckian associations.
3. A third use of the Lamarckian label entails an emphasis on will, choice or volition in the process of evolutionary change. But Lamarck himself emphasized neither will nor volition, and their association with Lamarck originates from his hostile critic Georges Cuvier (Boesiger 1974; Burkhardt 1977).

Taken literally, the first sentence of the third meaning of Lamarckism is uncontroversial and does not exclude Darwinism. Although human mental capacities are more highly developed, most living organisms anticipate, choose and strive for prefigured goals. These intentional factors play a role in biological as well as social evolution. It is when these anticipative and purposive capacities are assumed to have somehow appeared without cause and independently of an evolutionary process that the third meaning becomes problematic. Yet this extraordinary version of the third meaning is as far from Lamarck himself as one could imagine.

In its uncontroversial form, the third meaning acquires more bite when it is combined with the first meaning of Lamarckism above: volition thus becomes part of the mechanism by which new characteristics are developed and acquired. The third meaning says nothing about inheritance, which is the key element in the first meaning.

The volitional acquisition of characteristics is often contrasted to the allegedly 'blind' or random mutations in some versions of Darwinism. But Darwin himself never wrote of random mutations, and in principle core Darwinian principles are broad enough to accommodate both contrasting accounts. Furthermore, volition and randomness are neither mutually exclusive (think of the stock market) nor are they strictly necessary for Darwinian evolution to occur.

Contrary to a widespread view, Lamarckism and Darwinism are not mutually exclusive. This is confirmed by inspection of the following definitions of these terms:

- Darwinism is a general theoretical framework for understanding evolution in complex population systems, involving the inheritance of replicator instructions by individual units, a variation of replicators and interactors, and a process of selection of the interactors in a population.
- Lamarckism (after Lamarck 1984 [1809]) is a doctrine admitting the possibility of the (genotypic/replicator-to-replicator) inheritance of acquired (phenotypic/interactor) characters by individual organisms or entities in evolutionary processes.
- Weismannism (after Weismann 1889) is a doctrine denying the possibility of the

(genotypic/replicator-to-replicator) inheritance of acquired (phenotypic/interactor) characters by individual organisms or entities in evolutionary processes.

Lamarckism and Weismannism are clearly mutually exclusive. But Darwinism is logically compatible with each of them. In fact, Darwin himself promoted the possibility of the Lamarckian inheritance of acquired characters in successive editions of the *Origin of Species.* Darwin himself was a Lamarckian. After Darwin's death and the publication of August Weismann's (1889) work, biologists gradually became persuaded that the inheritance of acquired characteristics does not occur with biological organisms.

LAMARCKISM REQUIRES DARWINISM AND THE GENOTYPE–PHENOTYPE DISTINCTION

Not all acquired characters are beneficial. We become old and infirm. Accidents lead to injuries. Prominent cases of acquired characteristics include injuries and other impairments. But, for species to evolve, the effects of such deleterious acquired characters must be restricted. We need to account for the existence of sufficiently tight limits that disallow inheritance of useless and injurious characters. Accordingly, Lamarckism depends on the Darwinian principle of selection in order to explain why any disastrous propensity to inherit acquired impairments does not prevail. As Richard Dawkins (1986: 300) argues, 'the Lamarckian theory can explain adaptive improvement in evolution only by, as it were, riding on the back of the Darwinian theory'. Lamarckism, if valid in any particular domain, depends on Darwinian mechanisms of selection for evolutionary guidance.

Lamarckism involves the inheritance of acquired characteristics. Inheritance means more than merely 'passed on'. A dog catches fleas and passes some of them to another dog. Is that Lamarckian inheritance? If so, the fleas must be regarded as an acquired character and their jumping from one animal to another must be treated as inheritance. Similar arguments must apply to a host of other phenomena such as catching a cold and contagious laughter. All those processes would qualify (misleadingly) on similar grounds as Lamarckian.

But almost all biologists now deny that acquired characters can be inherited genetically and they reject Lamarckism. None of them would see the phenomena described in the previous paragraph as a challenge to the current consensus in biology. I am not saying that what is true in biology must be also true in social evolution. The point is different. As David Hull (1982) points out, more must be added to make the Lamarckian claim meaningful. Inheritance must be distinguished from infection or contagion. An extra ingredient must be the genotype–phenotype distinction or a relevant equivalent. It is only with such a distinction that inheritance can be properly defined and distinguished from catching colds or fleas.

The genotype–phenotype distinction was introduced in biology in the twentieth century, long after the deaths of Lamarck and Darwin. But it is necessary to understand this issue. Any infection or contagion affects the phenotype, not the genotype. By contrast, the Lamarckian inheritance of acquired characters means that a development in a phenotype can affect its own genotype, by some presumed internal process. We know in biology that this generally does not happen (with the possible exception of epigenesis), but that is not the point. We need to establish the difference in principle between Lamarckian inheritance and contagion. In biology this becomes clear by reference to the concepts of genotype and phenotype.

The genotype is a mechanism for storing and passing on information. It guides the development and behaviour of the phenotype, in interaction with its environment. The phenotype is an entity that hosts the genotype. Several authors suggest the term replicator as a generalization of genotype, and interactor as a generalization of phenotype (Hull 1988; Brandon 1996). These conceptual generalizations are important when we address the question of the possible existence of social entities hosting equivalent information-retaining and developmental mechanisms. As generalizations they would apply to social as well as biological evolution.

Replicators are conditional, program-like bits of information, held by an entity (interactor).[4] A genome is an example of a replicator. But there are other replicators, such as routines in organizations (Nelson & Winter 1982), which also hold information and guide behaviour. Developing the work of others, Hodgson & Knudsen (2010b) regard a replicator as consisting of information, held by an interactor that can represent adaptive solutions to problems and guide its development. Replication and inheritance are treated as synonyms.

The replicator–interactor distinction is a conceptual advance that helps develop the evolutionary programme in economics and organization studies. There is some confusion in Nelson and Winter's (1982) classic work because routines carry inheritable instructions (like genotypes or replicators) and are also the actual expression of these instructions (like phenotypes or interactors). After it has become clear that the key role of routines is to retain and pass on inheritable instructions, we can now focus on how these instructions trigger developmental processes and thereby become expressed in particular entities. This is important because it allows social scientists to study the learning processes that are situated within a broader selection environment.

Following Hull (1988), Hodgson and Knudsen (2010b) define an interactor as a relatively cohesive entity that hosts replicators and interacts with its environment in such a way as to lead to changes in the population of interactors and their replicators. Social organizations are obvious candidate replicators.

In this section it has been established that the distinction between replicator/genotype and interactor/phenotype is essential to understand the meaning of the Lamarckian hypothesis of acquired character inheritance. I now turn to question its veracity in social evolution: does Lamarckian inheritance exist at this level, involving social mechanisms rather than genes? To answer this question we have to look more closely at possible social interactors and replicators.

IS LAMARCKIAN INHERITANCE MEANINGFUL IN SOCIAL EVOLUTION?

In order to consider the possibility of Lamarckian inheritance in social evolution the replicators and interactors in the social domain must first be identified. Lamarckian social evolution would require social replicators (not biological replicators such as genes) that were affected by the acquired character of its interactor.

We need to look for capacities to store and replicate knowledge – mechanisms that act as social and organizational replicators. The mechanisms involved are very different from the gene. Richard Dawkins (1976) proposed the 'meme', which led to a claimed 'science' of 'memetics'. But the meme idea ran into problems, partly because no consensus emerged on its definition, other than to hint vaguely that memes were ideas. By treating social information as simply ideas, meme enthusiasts raised but ignored the ancient philosophical problem of relating the ideal to the material and of mind to matter. Without such a reconciliation the mechanisms of meme-replication and storage are elusive. But unless we have some notion of how the information is stored and replicated the meme concept is almost useless in practice.

Can memetic evolution be Lamarckian? As Hull (1982) points out, the passing of memes (if regarded like Dawkins as replicators) from person to person would not be the inheritance of acquired characters because the ideas themselves have been defined as replicators and not characteristics. But one of the problems with the meme concept is that when it is applied it is often unclear whether it is a replicator or an interactor.

Ideas are either replicators or (features of) interactors. If they are features of interactors then the spreading of ideas from one interactor to another is an example of contagion, not Lamarckism. If ideas are replicators, then (as pointed out above) their diffusion is the copying of replicators rather than acquired characters. This again is not Lamarckism.

Over 100 years ago, American pragmatist philosophers such as Charles Sanders Peirce (1878), William James (1890) and John Dewey (1922) reached a solution to the philosophical problem of reconciling ideas with an evolutionary process involving matter. They regarded psychological habits as the foundation and preconditions of ideas. For pragmatists, habits are acquired dispositions that serve as the basis of belief (Peirce 1878). Pragmatist psychology and philosophy are undergoing a revival today (Joas 1993), and they are supported by experimental and neurological evidence indicating that our underlying habitual dispositions are at work well before we make conscious decisions (Hodgson 2010). The American institutional economist Thorstein Veblen (Camic and Hodgson 2011) was strongly influenced by pragmatism and he argued accordingly that habitual and instinctive dispositions were the foundation of all social institutions.

Habits are the most elementary replicators of social evolution. Habits are learned dispositions to behave in a particular way in particular circumstances. They are hosted by individuals (their interactors). Further examples of social replicators include routines, which refer to dispositions within organizations to carry out sequences of actions. Routines are hosted by organizations as their interactors, and in turn are built on the habits of the individuals involved.

Consider the replication (copying) of habits. Someone teaches us a new language. We imitate and repeat. We are corrected. This goes on until our responses are ingrained in habit. Gradually the knowledge of the language is transferred from one person to another. The replicators are replicated. But note that the process of habit replication relies on behavioural imitation. (The way in which habits of thought are copied is more complex; it relies on language and is discussed in Hodgson and Knudsen, 2010b: 138–139.) In all cases of habit replication, the mechanism of replication goes through the interactor. Unlike genes in biology, there is no direct copying from replicator to replicator.

At first sight this seems very Lamarckian, because as we repeat the behaviour of our teacher and we develop the appropriate habits, our acquired behaviour (copied from another) gets encoded in our own habits. Our habit replicators change because we acquire a behavioural characteristic. Hodgson and Knudsen (2006a, 2006b, 2010b) admit that this Lamarckian link (from our behaviour to our habit) does exist.

But the indirectness of habit replication creates problems for the Lamarckian story. The Lamarckian link (from our behaviour to our habit) is a causal cul-de-sac. All it does is ensure that we retain the capacity to repeat the behaviour. The Lamarckian link plays no part itself in the inheritance process. This is very different from any imagined Lamarckian process in the biological sphere, where replicators get copied directly. That is another reason why the Lamarckian description in the social sphere is misleading rather than strictly wrong. Ironically, the Lamarckian concept is more appropriate for the biological sphere, despite its invalidity in that domain. Similar arguments apply to the replication of organizational routines, because that process too is grounded on the replication of individual habits (see Hodgson and Knudsen 2006a, 2006b, 2010b).

There are additional arguments why Lamarckian inheritance, if it existed, would be limited. The introduction of too much Lamarckian influence would mean that much cognitive and extraneous noise would interfere with the tried and tested information in the replicators. In Hodgson and Knudsen (2008, 2010a, 2010b) we show that the generation of complexity in an evolving system depends critically on the minimization of copy error. Too much Lamarckian meddling with genotypes and replicators would mean too much response to the accidental and superficial, rather than the enduring properties of the environment. Crucial information would be lost and the growth of complex outcomes would be more difficult.

The misleading claim by some social scientists that social evolution is Lamarckian is a distraction from the compelling conclusion that it is Darwinian, and that generalized Darwinian ideas can be helpful in understanding the processes. By contrast, Lamarckism does not provide an adequate evolutionary framework and it is a red herring, notwithstanding the existence of processes in social evolution that seem very superficially to be like Lamarckism.

Having identified replicators and interactors in the social domain, the claim is that social evolution is Darwinian, in the sense that the principles of selection, variation and inheritance apply to social entities and processes. Darwin himself conjectured that this was the case and the proposition has been discussed by a number of authors for over 150 years (Hodgson and Knudsen 2010b). The idea that social evolution is Darwinian does not mean that social evolution is determined solely by biological phenomena. By contrast, social evolutionary processes and entities are identified. The proposition that social evolution is Darwinian also does not mean that social evolution is similar in detail to, or analogous to, biological evolution. Instead it means that there are ontological communalities between biological and social evolutionary processes at a very abstract and general level. The fact that Newton's laws of motion apply to billiard balls, spacecraft and planets does not mean that these entities are similar. And no analogy is invoked. The identification of distinct social replicators and interactors is a key step in elaborating the proposition that abstract Darwinian principles apply to evolution in both nature and society.

EVO-DEVO: EMBRACING BOTH SELECTION AND ADAPTATION

Avoiding the pitfalls of slavish imitation or reductionism, we can learn still more from biology. Highly relevant in the dispute concerning the relative roles of selection and adaptation in organizational studies is the famous 'evo-devo' dispute in biology concerning the relative roles of development, selection and genotypic transmission (Wimsatt 1999; Stadler et al. 2001; Baguñà and Garcia-Fernàndez 2003). This debate has reminded biologists that selection, development and adaptation are intertwined and inseparable processes. Darwin himself did not put a one-sided emphasis on selection, so Darwinism must embrace development and adaptation as well.

Consistent with the outcome of this debate, Hodgson and Knudsen (2010b) claim that replication, development, adaptation and selection are all essential features of evolution in population systems. Consideration of their relative roles is an empirical as well as a theoretical matter, but the outcome would not make any of these features inessential. In any meaningful system, both selection and adaptation are bound to occur.

Selection occurs because organizations differ both in their inherent characteristics (Nelson 1991) and their local environments. Some firms go bankrupt. Some are so successful that their routines are copied by other firms. Others lead to successful spin-offs (Dahlstrand 1998). In principle, such differential success and replication amounts to selection, according to its technical definition (Price 1995; Hodgson and Knudsen 2010b). Bankruptcy is an example of subset selection. Spin-offs involve 'generations' and an entwined process of inheritance, and can represent successor selections. Selection – in one or another of these senses – is a major reason for changes in the overall profile of a population of organizations. But it does not imply that selection as a process always leads to improvement or efficiency. As in biology, selection can lead to suboptimal outcomes (Gould 1980; Hodgson 1993, Ch. 13).

Turning to adaptation, in the organizational studies literature it typically refers to a change in a specific organization rather than an environmental or other change. For Daniel Levinthal (1992: 432) 'adaptation is defined to have occurred when an organization changes its strategy, structure or some other core attribute to fit some new environmental contingency'. More narrowly, for Ross Brennan and Peter Turnbull (1999: 182): 'Adaptations can be defined as behavioural modifications made by one company, at the individual, group or corporate level, to meet the specific needs of another organisation.' Although this focuses appropriately on organizational change, it overly restricts adaptations to serving the undefined 'needs' of another entity.

A further complication is that the concept of adaptation has acquired different meanings in biology and organization studies. In biology, adaptation refers to change in a whole population, including population changes resulting from natural selection. In organization studies and business economics it has shifted its meaning to changes performed by any one organization, to refer to the process or outcomes of adjustment of the characteristics of an individual organization in a given environment. These different meanings complicate the growing use of ideas from biology to help understand processes of organizational change (Hodgson and Knudsen 2010b).

It is not easy to clear up this terminological mess, but I suggest the following solution. When addressing organizations and their strategic dilemmas, the primary issue is the capacity of an organization to change, in a manner that improves its performance by some appropriate criterion, and increases its chances of survival.

Organizations are more than the sum of their individual members. They involve structured interactions between individuals. The capacity of any organization to change – even a small firm – depends on structured internal relations and does not depend on the intentions or attributes of individuals alone. The study of organizational adaptability is much about internal structures and procedures and their capacity to enable appropriate change. The internal culture of the firm is intimately connected to those structures and procedures, as well as to the values and beliefs of individuals (Schein 1996; Sørensen 2002). It is vital – and more meaningful – to focus on the strategies, structures and procedures within the organization.

We may define organizational adaptability as the capacity of an organization to change its strategies, structures, procedures or other core attributes, in anticipation or response to a change in its environment, including changes in relations with other organizations. The resulting adaptations do not necessarily improve performance, but they are generally intended by some criterion to do so.

Here a link may be forged with the growing literature in evolutionary economics on routines (Nelson and Winter 1982; Cohen and Bacdayan 1994; Cohen et al. 1996; Becker 2008). Routines are defined as organizational dispositions to energize conditional patterns of behaviour within organizations, involving repeated sequential responses to cues that are partly dependent on social positions in the organization (Hodgson 2008). Establishing a routine in a firm means building or using internal relations and positions that enable repeated sequential behaviours. These in turn help to develop particular habits and other specific conditional dispositions among individuals. Routines, in short, are replicators within organizations (Hodgson and Knudsen 2010b).

We must not overlook the amount of adaptation that does occur in reality. After all, the move from a single-person firm to an enterprise of three or four members involves a considerable amount of organizational development and adaptation, especially in complex and changing environments. Furthermore, given rapidly changing circumstances – new entrants, new technologies, new products, changing government policies – most firms are required to adapt to some degree, on an almost continuous basis, or face extinction.

The argument in the preceding paragraph finds a close parallel in the evo-devo literature in biology. Those that emphasized the development (devo) side of the story pointed out that while a changing gene-pool is the ultimate record of evolutionary change in biology, selection does not operate directly on genes themselves. Selection operates on the entities that genetic replicators guide through development in an environmental context. The objects of selection are interactors and as a result there are changes in the population of hosted replicators. The two faces of selection are unavoidably connected by a developmental and adaptive process, which depends on both the replicators and how they express themselves in a particular environment. Similar remarks apply to organizations and the replicators (habits and routines) that they host. While changing habits and routines are the ultimate record of economic development, selection operates directly on organizations and individuals, which are outcomes of development in particular contexts.

As noted above, the relative importance of adaptation and selection can only be discovered by empirical enquiry. But the generalized Darwinian framework shows that both processes are unavoidably present to some degree in biological or social evolution. Furthermore, even if the possibilities for individual firm adaptation are limited, small differences in adaptive capacity from firm to firm may be crucial for survival. Consequently, even if much industrial change results from selection, the development of individual firms cannot be ignored in explanations of change or in the formulation of business strategies.

Consequently, some reconciliation may be possible between the organizational ecology literature, with its stress on selection and highly limited adaptation, and the business strategy literature, with its stress on the need for adaptability (Chaffee 1985; McKee et al. 1989; Mintzberg and Quinn 1991).

UNDERSTANDING ORGANIZATIONAL EVOLUTION

Although the Lamarckian red herring has diverted many scholars from appreciation of the Darwinian character of social evolution, it has eventually helped us understand the importance of the replicator–interactor distinction, which in turn enhances our appreciation of the informational nature of the processes involved.

The adoption of the replicator–interactor distinction is not only important to clear up terminological confusion, it is also vital to understand the processes of business evolution. There are theoretical reasons why replicators are relevant in the social domain. Just as biological evolution has led eventually to organisms of greater sophistication and complexity, so social and economic evolution is marked by an even more rapid increase in the complexity of technology and institutions in a relatively short period of human history.

In fact, rapidly increasing complexity is one of the most dramatic features of social evolution. In a few thousand years humans have evolved from primitive hunter-gatherers to inhabitants of complex civilizations. In a few hundred years we have seen the rise of capitalism and an explosion of scientific and technological knowledge. In a few decades we have observed a new phase of globalization and the evolution of complex business organizations and networks.

In general terms, it is important to understand the necessary conditions under which complexity is enhanced in evolving systems. The most basic and important condition is the existence of replicators that can store and copy information to instruct and guide the development of their host entity (Hodgson and Knudsen 2008, 2010a, 2010b). Another essential requirement is that copy error during replication is minimized. By contrast, both reading and developmental errors – which occur when using information from a source copy – do not corrupt the original information and are generally less serious. If the original information remains intact and is copied faithfully, then it might be retrieved. But if replication over time leads to the loss of information from the original, then it is gone forever. This argument suggests that replicators and faithful replication underlie the manifestly increasing complexity of social evolution. Some enduring of fidelity in the copying of this key information is a necessary condition for the evolution of complexity. Misleading claims that social evolution is 'Lamarckian' have obscured this.

With social and economic evolution the advance of complexity depends upon similar conditions. In a world of complexity and uncertainty, designed solutions to economic and business problems are difficult and risky. While some planning and guidance is desirable and unavoidable, we have to rely enormously on tried and tested knowledge.

Many successful firms do this. Over one-third of all retail sales in the United States pass through chain organizations (Winter and Szulanski 2001). Most successful chains expand by imposing a single organizational template on all chain outlets, including those that are franchized (Bradach 1998). Similar replication strategies are found in firms when they develop new production plants in different locations. All these cases involve the strategic replication of habits and routines, replicating through a series of business units.

Such replication often tolerates little creative embellishment or modification. Consider Intel's 'Copy Exactly' factory strategy. This ramps up production quickly by copying everything at the development plant – the process flow, equipment set, suppliers, plumbing, manufacturing clean room and training methodologies. Everything is selected to meet high-volume needs, recorded, and then copied exactly.

Other prominent examples of firms that try to stimulate growth by reducing copy error include (Knudsen and Winter, n.d.): McDonald's, Burger King, Pizza Hut, Kentucky Fried Chicken, Holiday Inn, Novotel, Hilton (various brands), Marriott (various brands), Bank of America, Wachovia, HSBC, Merrill Lynch, Starbucks, Cosi, Office Depot, Staples, Borders, Barnes & Noble, Ikea, The Bombay Company, Benetton and Gap.

Business replication strategies that minimize copy error have become widespread through a combination of trial and error, and competitive selection weeding out firms with less successful policies. The theoretical argument above may help to explain the otherwise puzzling observation that many firms base growth strategies by cloning existing arrangements as exactly as possible.

Given the existence of social replicators such as habits and routines, it is necessary to understand the manner and degree in which these organizational replicators change. There might be fixed routines for adaptability, in which case an organization may be adaptable but have fixed 'genetic' recipes for adaptation. A pressing question for the business strategists is to what extent habits and routines can be changed, and if so, how. The evidence suggests that they are generally difficult to change; executives who try top-down change with insufficient regard to underlying habits and routines are courting failure (Kolb 2002; Stadler 2007; Hodgson 2011). Because so much information held in habits and routines is tacit and inaccessible, business leaders cannot fully understand the knowledge stored in organizations (Nonaka and Takeuchi 1995). This makes radical change from the top risky, and suggests that business strategies should be cautious and responsive to the opinions of workers in organizations.

Researching the 'genetics' of social evolution involves understanding the psychological and neurological mechanisms involved in these social processes, including a deep appreciation of how social structures and positions enable the retention of knowledge that relates to coordinated activity within organizations or teams.

CONCLUSIONS

Labels matter. So too do the understandings associated with these labels. An ongoing dispute within organization science shows that the deployment of not only misleading labels, but also correct labels with inadequate understandings, can prevent the development of an overarching conceptual framework. This inclusive framework can not only accommodate differing empirical assessments of the relative importance of selection and adaptation, but also provide the conceptual structure for the development of detailed theories of organizational and industrial evolution (Stoelhorst and Huizing 2006). That framework is known as generalized Darwinism. Contrary to the many misunderstandings surrounding the 'Darwinian' label, generalized Darwinism does not uphold that organizational development or adaptation are unimportant.

Whether true or false, simply to understand the claim that social evolution is Lamarckian requires something like the genotype–phenotype distinction. The importance of this distinction remains, notwithstanding the fact that the Lamarckian claim turns out to be a red herring. After the conceptual mess is cleared up and the Darwinian character of social evolution is established, it has been shown here that the implied conceptual framework is useful in at least the following respects:

- It underlines the need to identify social replicators (such as habits and routines) and interactors (organizations) and it emphasizes the crucial role of social replicators in retaining and helping to pass on knowledge.
- Because replicators play a crucial role in the development of social interactors (organizations), and evolutionary selection acts directly upon organizations, the replicator–interactor framework emphasizes the importance of both developmental adaptation and competitive selection in social evolution. It undermines attempts to dichotimize these processes, and helps to reconcile insights from organization studies, organizational ecology and business strategy. These Darwinian insights help to integrate different research programmes.
- The replicator–interactor framework is useful for helping to understand processes leading to greater complexity in social and business systems. A general theoretical argument underlines the importance of the copying fidelity of replicators in evolution. This also may help us to understand why so many successful business firms insist on exact copying of business routines when they establish or franchise new plants or outlets.
- The emphasis on the importance of social replicators and their capacity to store information leads to the conclusion that radical strategic change from the top carries high risks. Because of its largely tacit nature, business executives can understand only a small part of the knowledge held in organizations. Leadership and entrepreneurship are important but overemphasized. Successful business strategy must involve employees at every level of the organization.

Although it has precedents going back to the late nineteenth century (Hodgson and Knudsen 2010b, Ch. 1), we are only at the beginning of this modern Darwinian research programme in the social sciences, and these are just a few of the possible insights that may emerge. The acceptance of Darwinian principles combined with the discovery of the specific mechanisms involved in biology led to an explosion of productive research in biology that continues today. By using generalized Darwinian principles in the social domain, combined with a detailed understanding of the psychological and social mechanisms involved in the retention and replication of information in social organizations, we may be on the brink of a substantial expansion of our understanding of organizational evolution.

NOTES

1. This chapter draws on several joint works with Thorbjørn Knudsen. Thanks are also due to David Gindis and Anna Grandori for comments on an earlier draft. See Hodgson (forthcoming) for an extended discussion of the implications of the approach.
2. For example, much of the rhetoric against 'social Darwinism' turns out to be attacking a largely mythological and inappropriately described invention of the critics (Bannister 1988; Hodgson 2004, 2006). Furthermore, Darwin himself acknowledged intentionality and never regarded evolution as random or blind. See also Hodgson and Knudsen (2010b) for criticism of other misguided rejections of Darwinism.
3. To add further confusion, Reydon and Scholz (2009) have recently argued that the work of Hannan and Freeman (1989) and McKelvey (1982) is not 'Darwinian' because it lacks an adequate explanation of organizational diversity. If true, this would not mean that this work was un-Darwinian, but simply that their Darwinian account was incomplete. Incomplete Darwinism does not disqualify the Darwinian label: it means that more work must be done within the Darwinian framework. For the Darwinian label to be unwarranted the approach would have to be incompatible with Darwinism. This is not the case.
4. Information here means a code or signal, as stored and manipulated by computers and present in DNA. A message has 'information content' when its receipt causes some action (Shannon and Weaver 1949). With social evolution it is essential to bring meanings and interpretations into the picture. But at first general principles of Darwinian evolution are established.

REFERENCES

Aldrich, Howard E., Geoffrey M. Hodgson, David L. Hull, Thorbjørn Knudsen, Joel Mokyr and Viktor J. Vanberg (2008), 'In defence of generalized Darwinism', *Journal of Evolutionary Economics*, **18**(5), 577–596.

Baguñà, Jaume and Jordi Garcia-Fernàndez (2003), 'Evo-devo: the long and winding road', *International Journal of Developmental Biology*, **47**, 705–713.

Bannister, Robert C. (1988), *Social Darwinism: Science and Myth*, 2nd edn, Philadelphia, PA: Temple University Press.

Baum, Joel A.C. (1996), 'Organizational ecology', in Stewart R. Clegg, Cynthia Hardy and Walter R. Nord (eds), *Handbook of Organization Studies*, London: Sage, pp. 77–114.

Becker, Markus C. (ed.) (2008), *Handbook of Organizational Routines*, Cheltenham, UK and Northampton, MA, USA: Edward Elgar.

Boesiger, Ernest (1974), 'Evolutionary theories after Lamarck and Darwin', in Francisco J. Ayala and Theodosius Dobzhansky (eds), *Studies in the Philosophy of Biology*, London, UK and Berkeley and Los Angeles, CA, USA: Macmillan and University of California Press, pp. 21–44.

Boyd, Robert and Peter J. Richerson (1985), *Culture and the Evolutionary Process*, Chicago, IL: University of Chicago Press.

Bradach, Jeffrey L. (1998), *Franchise Organizations*, Boston, MA: Harvard Business School Press.

Brandon, Robert N. (1996), *Concepts and Methods in Evolutionary Biology*, Cambridge, UK and New York, USA: Cambridge University Press.

Brennan, Ross and Peter Turnbull (1999), 'Adaptive behaviour in buyer–seller relationships', *Industrial Marketing Management*, **28**, 481–495.

Burkhardt, Richard W., Jr (1977), *The Spirit of System: Lamarck and Evolutionary Biology*, Cambridge, MA: Harvard University Press.

Camic, Charles and Geoffrey M. Hodgson (eds) (2011), *Essential Writings of Thorstein Veblen*, London and New York: Routledge.

Campbell, Donald T. (1965), 'Variation, selection and retention in sociocultural evolution', in H.R. Barringer,

G.I. Blanksten and R.W. Mack (eds), *Social Change in Developing Areas: A Reinterpretation of Evolutionary Theory*, Cambridge, MA: Schenkman, pp. 19–49.

Chaffee, Ellen-Earle (1985), 'Three models of strategy', *Academy of Management Review*, **10**(1), 89–98.

Cohen, Michael D. and Paul Bacdayan (1994), 'Organizational routines are stored as procedural memory – evidence from a laboratory study', *Organization Science*, **5**(4), 554–568.

Cohen, Michael D., Roger Burkhart, Giovanni Dosi, Massimo Egidi, Luigi Marengo, Massimo Warglien and Sidney Winter (1996), 'Routines and other recurring action patterns of organizations: contemporary research issues', *Industrial and Corporate Change*, **5**(3), 653–698.

Dahlstrand, Åsa Lindholm (1998), 'Growth and inventiveness in technology-based spin-off firms', *Research Policy*, **26**(3), 331–344.

Dawkins, Richard (1976), *The Selfish Gene*, Oxford: Oxford University Press.

Dawkins, Richard (1986), *The Blind Watchmaker*, Harlow: Longman.

Degler, Carl N. (1991), *In Search of Human Nature: The Decline and Revival of Darwinism in American Social Thought*, Oxford, UK and New York, USA: Oxford University Press.

Dewey, John (1922), *Human Nature and Conduct: An Introduction to Social Psychology*, 1st edn, New York: Holt.

Gould, Stephen Jay (1980), *The Panda's Thumb: More Reflections in Natural History*, New York: Norton.

Hannan, Michael T. and John Freeman (1989), *Organizational Ecology*, Cambridge, MA: Harvard University Press.

Hayek, Friedrich A. (1988), *The Fatal Conceit: The Errors of Socialism. The Collected Works of Friedrich August Hayek, Vol. I*, William W. Bartley III (ed.), London: Routledge.

Hirshleifer, Jack (1977), 'Economics from a biological viewpoint', *Journal of Law and Economics*, **20**(1), 1–52.

Hodgson, Geoffrey M. (1993), *Economics and Evolution: Bringing Life Back Into Economics*, Cambridge, UK and Ann Arbor, MI, USA: Polity Press and University of Michigan Press.

Hodgson, Geoffrey M. (2002), 'Darwinism in economics: from analogy to ontology', *Journal of Evolutionary Economics*, **12**(2), 259–281.

Hodgson, Geoffrey M. (2004), 'Social Darwinism in Anglophone academic journals: a contribution to the history of the term', *Journal of Historical Sociology*, **17**(4), 428–463.

Hodgson, Geoffrey M. (2006), *Economics in the Shadows of Darwin and Marx: Essays on Institutional and Evolutionary Themes*, Cheltenham, UK and Northampton, MA, USA: Edward Elgar.

Hodgson, Geoffrey M. (2008), 'The concept of a routine', in Markus C. Becker (ed.), *Handbook of Organizational Routines* Cheltenham, UK and Northampton, MA, USA: Edward Elgar, pp. 3–14.

Hodgson, Geoffrey M. (2010), 'Choice, habit and evolution', *Journal of Evolutionary Economics*, **20**(1), January, pp. 1–18.

Hodgson, Geoffrey M. (2011), 'Organizational evolution versus the cult of change', *Corporate Finance Review*, January–February, **16**(1), 5–10.

Hodgson, Geoffrey M. and Thorbjørn Knudsen (2006a), 'Why we need a generalized Darwinism: and why a generalized Darwinism is not enough', *Journal of Economic Behavior and Organization*, **61**(1), September, pp. 1–19.

Hodgson, Geoffrey M. and Thorbjørn Knudsen (2006b), 'Dismantling Lamarckism: why descriptions of socio-economic evolution as Lamarckian are misleading', *Journal of Evolutionary Economics*, **16**(4), 343–366.

Hodgson, Geoffrey M. and Thorbjørn Knudsen (2008), 'Information, complexity and generative replication', *Biology and Philosophy*, **43**(1), 47–65.

Hodgson, Geoffrey M. and Thorbjørn Knudsen (2010a), 'Generative replication and the evolution of complexity', *Journal of Economic Behavior and Organization*, **75**(1), 12–24.

Hodgson, Geoffrey M. and Thorbjørn Knudsen (2010b), *Darwin's Conjecture: The Search for General Principles of Social and Economic Evolution*, Chicago, IL: University of Chicago Press.

Hull, David L. (1982), 'The naked meme', in Henry C. Plotkin (ed.), *Learning, Development and Culture: Essays in Evolutionary Epistemology*, New York: Wiley, pp. 273–327.

Hull, David L. (1988), *Science as a Process: An Evolutionary Account of the Social and Conceptual Development of Science*, Chicago, IL: University of Chicago Press.

James, William (1890), *The Principles of Psychology*, 2 vols, 1st edn, New York, USA and London, UK: Holt and Macmillan.

Joas, Hans (1993), *Pragmatism and Social Theory*, Chicago, IL: University of Chicago Press.

Knudsen, Thorbjørn and Sidney G. Winter (n.d.), 'An evolutionary model of spatial competition'.

Kolb, Darl G. (2002), 'Continuity, not change: the next organisational challenge', *University of Auckland Business Review*, **4**(2), 1–11.

Lamarck, Jean Baptiste de (1984 [1809]), *Zoological Philosophy: An Exposition with Regard to the Natural History of Animals*, transl. by Hugh Elliot from the 1st French edn. of 1809, Chicago, IL: University of Chicago Press.

Levinthal, Daniel A. (1992), 'Surviving Schumpeterian environments: an evolutionary perspective', *Industrial and Corporate Change*, 1, 427–443.

McKee, Daryl O., P. Rajan Varadarajan and William M. Pride (1989), 'Strategic adapatability and firm performance: a market-contingent perspective', *Journal of Marketing*, 53(1), 21–35.

McKelvey, William (1982), *Organizational Systematics: Taxonomy, Evolution, Classification*, Berkeley, CA: University of California Press.

Metcalfe, J. Stanley (1994), 'Evolutionary economics and technology policy', *Economic Journal*, 104(4), 931–944.

Mintzberg, Henry and Quinn, James Brian (1991), *The Strategy Process: Concepts, Contexts, Cases*, Englewood Cliffs, NJ: Prentice-Hall.

Nelson, Richard R. (1991), 'Why do firms differ, and how does it matter?' *Strategic Management Journal*, 12, Special Issue, 61–74.

Nelson, Richard R. and Sidney G. Winter (1982), *An Evolutionary Theory of Economic Change*, Cambridge, MA: Harvard University Press.

Nonaka, Ikujiro and Hirotaka Takeuchi (1995), *The Knowledge-Creating Company: How Japanese Companies Create the Dynamics of Innovation*, Oxford and New York: Oxford University Press.

Peirce, Charles Sanders (1878), 'How to make our ideas clear', *Popular Science Monthly*, 12, 286–302.

Pelikan, Pavel (2010), 'Evolutionary developmental economics: how to generalize Darwinism fruitfully to help comprehend economic change', *Journal of Evolutionary Economics,* online.

Price, George R. (1995), 'The nature of selection', *Journal of Theoretical Biology*, 175, 389–396.

Reydon, Thomas A. and Markus Scholz (2009), 'Why organizational ecology is not a Darwinian research programme', *Philosophy of the Social Sciences*, January, 1–25.

Schein, Edgar H. (1996), 'Culture: the missing concept in organization studies', *Administrative Science Quarterly*, 41(2), 229–240.

Shannon, Claude E. and Warren Weaver (1949), *The Mathematical Theory of Communication*, Chicago, IL: University of Illinois Press.

Simon, Herbert A. (1981), *The Sciences of the Artificial*, 2nd edn, Cambridge, MA: MIT Press.

Sørensen, Jesper B. (2002), 'The strength of corporate culture and the reliability of firm performance', *Administrative Science Quarterly*, 47(1), 70–91.

Stadler, Bärbel M.R., Peter F. Stadler and Günter P. Wagner (2001), 'The topology of the possible: formal spaces underlying patterns of evolutionary change', *Journal of Theoretical Biology*, 213, 241–274.

Stadler, Christian (2007), 'The four principles of enduring business success', *Harvard Business Review*, July–August, 62–72.

Stoelhorst, Jan Willem (2005), 'The naturalist view of universal Darwinism: an application to the evolutionary theory of the firm', in John Finch and Magali Orillard (eds), *Complexity and the Economy: Implications for Economic Policy*, Cheltenham, UK and Northampton, MA, USA: Edward Elgar, pp. 127–147.

Stoelhorst, Jan Willem (2008), 'The explanatory logic and ontological commitments of generalized Darwinism', *Journal of Economic Methodology*, 15(4), 343–363.

Stoelhorst, Jan-Willem and Ard Huizing (2006), 'Why the adaptation–selection debate is misconstrued: a Darwinian view of organizational change', *Sprouts: Working Papers on Information Systems*, 6(16), http://sprouts.aisnet.org/6-16, retrieved 14 March 2011.

Usher, John M. and Martin G. Evans (1996), 'Life and death along Gasoline Alley: Darwinian and Lamarckian processes in a differentiating population', *Academy of Management Journal*, 39(5), 1428–1466.

Van de Ven, Andrew H. and Marshall Scott Poole (1995), 'Explaining development and change in organizations', *Academy of Management Review*, 20(3), 510–540.

Veblen, Thorstein B. (1899), *The Theory of the Leisure Class: An Economic Study in the Evolution of Institutions*, New York: Macmillan.

Weismann, August (1889), *Essay upon Heredity and Kindred Biological Problems*, Edward B. Poulton, Selmar Schonland and Arthur E. Shipley (eds), Oxford: Clarendon Press.

Wilkins, John S. (2001), 'The appearance of Lamarckism in the evolution of culture', in John Laurent and John Nightingale (eds), *Darwinism and Evolutionary Economics*, Cheltenham, UK and Northampton, MA, USA: Edward Elgar, pp. 160–183.

Wimsatt, William C. (1999), 'Genes, memes, and cultural heredity', *Biology and Philosophy*, 14(2), 279–310.

Winter, Sidney G. and Gabriel Szulanski (2001), 'Replication as strategy', *Organization Science*, 12(6), 730–743.

10. Exaptation in innovation processes: theory and models

*Giovanni Bonifati and Marco Villani**

In this chapter we present a contribution to a theory of exaptation phenomena in innovation processes. We first define exaptations and discuss some related conceptual issues. In order to contribute to the development of an exaptation-based view in the economics of innovation, in the remaining sections we propose a theoretical framework and simulation models for the study of the processes of exaptation. We relate exaptation phenomena at different levels of organization and provide a framework for their analysis. Next we argue that in innovation theory an exaptation-based perspective can be considered, at least potentially, an alternative to the 'adaptation through selection' perspective. We then represent and clarify the theory presented above, by means of two agent-based simulation models. In the first model, exaptation occurs through the exchange of artefacts and information between two agents. In the second model many agents are producers and consumers of thousands of artefacts and are able to introduce innovations. The latter model is explicitly designed to simulate the emergence of recurrent patterns of interactions, and their changes, as consequence of locally introduced innovations. A final section concludes the chapter.

EXAPTATION: DEFINITIONS AND CONCEPTUAL ISSUES

In evolutionary biology the term 'exaptation', coined by Gould and Vrba (1982), refers to those characters that are useful for survival but that were not selected for this purpose. Exaptations contribute to survival thanks to the process by which features developed for others reasons are used by an organization of which they are part. Feathers, for example, were not selected for flying, and cannot therefore be said that they are adapted for this use. Originally, feathers had the function of thermoregulation. Later they were co-opted by birds for flying. In other words, feathers were exapted for a purpose different from the original one, through a process that has made them 'apt' for such use (Gould 2002: 1232). So, feathers are apt for flying in virtue of their 'ex' form: they are 'ex-apt'. Note that the feathers for flying are the result of a (unintentional) process of change, a process in which all the structural conditions necessary for the new functionality are developed.

In socio-economic systems, an exaptation can be defined, in very general terms, as a result of a process through which an initial attribution of a new functionality to existing outcomes of human activity – whether they are artefacts, organizations, scientific achievements or cultural models – leads to new outcomes. In socio-economic systems the attribution of a new functionality can be intentional or unintentional. In any case, what is relevant to examine is the process by which the initial attribution of a new functionality leads to new outcomes. In other words, in socio-economic systems, as in the biological ones, a change in functionality is embedded in new outcomes only at the end of a process (see below).

In this chapter we refer the above definition of exaptation to artefacts with the aim of examining the emergence of new artefacts through exaptation processes. In the present section, we report some examples of new artefacts resulting from processes of exaptation and we face some conceptual issues arising from the relationship between exaptation and innovation.

Exaptations as a Ubiquitous Characteristic in Innovation Processes

According to Gould (2002: 1270–1295) exaptations derive from two types of processes forming what he calls the 'exaptive pool': (1) different uses of things already in use but potentially usable in different ways; (2) uses of available things or characters not yet used. In innovation processes, examples of exaptation of the first type are the phonograph, the laser and the compact disc.[1] The phonograph was invented in 1877 by Edison as a dictating machine. However, this functionality was not recognized by potential users, and Edison's efforts to market his invention were unsuccessful. The phonograph was, instead, successfully co-opted for a different use: a tool for automatically playing popular music in the first jukebox, which became the first major use of the new technology. The laser was designed with no specific purpose. When, at the end of the 1950s, the laser technology was implemented by Theodore Maiman it was thought that it would find no commercial application in telecommunication (Rosenberg, 1996). The potential of laser technology was exapted when new functionalities were attributed to it. Through complementary innovations and already existing technologies, laser technology was co-opted in innumerable fields, giving rise to several new products not only in telecommunications but also in microsurgery, new measurement systems, identification of bar codes and cutting devices. In the case of the compact disc, the exaptation is connected with improvements of a digital-to-optical recording and playback system to reproduce sound with high quality compared to vinyl records. Later, a new functionality was attributed to this technology as a data storage tool for computers. To this end, several improvements were made that allowed the CD-ROM to be used as a storage tool for many forms of data.

The second type of exaptation derives from new functionalities attributed to existing things not yet used for a particular purpose. An example is the architecture of the agricultural tractor, in which the engine block is attached not only to the gearbox and the drive axle components, but also to the front axle, the ancillary equipment and the driver's seat. This particular architecture allows avoiding that the assembly of a heavy engine and other components on an equally heavy chassis would result in a machine too heavy to be used in agriculture (Dew et al. 2004: 79). In this case, the engine block – which, as such, has no function in the assembling the tractor's components – is used with the new functionality to serve as a chassis. In other words the engine block is exapted as a chassis.

These examples are just the tip of an iceberg. The many peaceful uses of technology originally developed for military purposes (the so-called 'dual-use technology') corroborate the idea that exaptations are a widespread phenomenon in the processes of innovation. According to Mokyr (2000: 57–58), exaptations are a ubiquitous characteristic in the history of technology.

Exaptation and Innovation

Exaptations must be considered and analysed as key elements in innovation processes (Bonifati 2010; Lane 2011). Rosenberg demonstrated that innovations arise and spread within a series of relations among firms, and among these and the final users of goods and services. The overcoming of economically relevant constraints – whether technical, social, legislative or natural – and complementarities are key aspects of the process through which innovations are generated (Rosenberg 1976). Hence, user–producer interaction networks are the appropriate context to consider when describing the dynamics of exaptation processes. For our purposes, what is relevant is that new artefacts emerge as a result of exaptations through processes nested in existing patterns of interaction between agents and artefacts.

In order to analyse these processes an appropriate ontology is required in which entities embedded within the social realm interact and generate processes of change in historical time.[2] In particular, we define artefacts in terms of three sets of interacting elements: structure, functionalities and processes of transformation. The structure of an artefact depends on its matter, transformed by human labour oriented by a project, and on the modalities through which its different parts interact. The functionalities of an artefact are determined by the properties attributed to it in relation to its usefulness for some purpose. The processes through which the functionalities are attributed and the matter is modified govern the interaction between structure and functionalities.

In the process of exaptation, the attribution of a new functionality to an existing artefact can trigger processes that change the structure of the artefact, giving rise to a new structurally different artefact. If these latter processes are not activated, the exaptation process gives rise to a new use of an artefact structurally unchanged but with a new relationship between structure and functionality. In any case, whether a structurally different artefact is generated or not, an exaptation always involves a transformation in the relationship between agents and artefacts in the production–consumption process (Bonifati 2010: 753–754).

Complex artefacts and technologies have certain characteristics that make exaptations possible. In particular the following two have attracted attention in the literature (Dew et al. 2004: 75). Firstly, a technology as complex system is characterized by the property of 'near decomposability' (Simon 1962) according to which an artefact can be divided into subparts, each of which is approximately independent of the behavior of the other subparts. Hence, each subpart can be exapted. The second characteristic of technologies is that they result in a virtually endless and unpredictable list of possibilities and consequences. These two characteristics of the artefacts are important as a necessary condition for exaptations which, however, require two more general related processes: (1) the attribution of new functionalities as a starting point for the exaptation process; and (2) the emergence of new patterns of interactions among agents and between agents and new artefacts. The analysis of these two processes by means of a theoretical framework and two simulation models represent our contribution to an exaptation-based perspective in innovation theory.

Exaptation and Uncertainty

Exaptation phenomena occur under conditions of uncertainty. In terms of the well-known distinction proposed by Knight (1921), the uncertainty associated with the process of innovation cannot be reduced to risk. Langlois and Cosgel (1993) argue that Knight's distinction between risk and uncertainty does not simply mirror the distinction between measurable and non-measurable risk. Knight, they contend, conceived uncertainty as arising 'from the impossibility of exhaustive classification of states' (Langlois and Cosgel 1993: 459). In this sense, uncertainty has a 'structural' character (Langlois 1986: 228) and is systemic in nature (Rosenberg 1996). A similar notion of uncertainty is present in organization theory, in particular in the conceptual criticism to the rational model of decision-making (March and Simon 1958; Grandori 2001), and in complexity science.[3] Lane and Maxfield (2005) argue that, in innovation processes, uncertainty arises because, at the historical moment in which agents must act, some of the very subjects, objects and criteria of value with which the consequences of their possible actions would have to be classified simply do not exist. They call this kind of uncertainty ontological uncertainty.[4] For our purposes it is important to emphasize that the existence of organized systems of relationships, from which new interactions and new artefacts emerge as the results of exaptations, provides elements – such as possible new uses of existing products and skills – that help reduce uncertainty. In fact, in the process of exaptation, novelties emerge from existing organized systems of relationships in which agents act. In such a way, agents undertake a sequence of interactions through which they orient their activities towards transforming particular zones of agent–artefact interaction networks.[5]

Exaptation and Degeneracy

One aspect of the exaptation process focuses on the notion of degeneracy. The term 'degeneracy' indicates an alteration in the structure of some element from its original structure. For a long time the term has been characterized in a negative meaning based on the implicit acceptance of the creationist idea that a degenerate form was a departure from its original perfect form (Mason 2010). We use the term 'degeneracy' in its scientific meaning according to which as a result of the processes of degeneracy structurally different elements are able to provide the same or similar and overlapping functionalities (Edelman and Gally 2001). In this sense, the concept of degeneracy is a natural complement to the concept of exaptation. In fact, when new functionalities are attributed to existing elements (whether they are natural elements, artefacts, organizational forms or cultural models), exaptation processes can generate new elements that can provide functionalities similar to those provided by existing different structural elements.

A key characteristic that distinguishes degeneracy from 'functional redundancy' – according to which identical elements perform the same function – is that, in degeneracy processes, 'different structures have similar consequences' (Edelman and Gally 2001). Redundant elements are copies of elements with a one-to-one mapping between structure and function. In other words, redundancy is characterized by isomorphic (iso-structural) and iso-functional elements. The degeneracy, instead, is characterized by polymorphic and iso-functional elements with a many-to-one mapping between structure and function. Unlike redundant elements, moreover, degenerate elements can be multi-potentials, that is, they can deliver different outputs in different contexts. This means that in different contexts, degenerate elements can provide different functionalities. In this respect, the degeneracy is characterized by polymorphic and poly-functional elements with a many-to-many mapping between structure and function (Edelman and Gally 2001; Mason 2010; Whitacre and Bender 2010).

In general, the effect of degeneracy is an increased degree of flexibility and robustness of a system in the face of environmental changes (Whitacre and Bender 2010). From this point of view, the concept of degeneracy, related to economic and social processes, has similarities with concepts such as that of equifinality – used in organizational analysis to acknowledge that there is more than one way to succeed in each type of setting (Meyer et al. 1993: 1178) – and modularity, used in the analysis of complementarities in modern manufacturing (Milgrom and Roberts 1990, 1995).

In biological systems degeneracy is present at all levels of organization, from the genetic code to the inter-animal communication (Edelman and Gally 2001). In human activity an example of degeneracy concerns the similar but non-identical linguistic structures used in human communication to convey the same meaning. Although less studied, it can be expected that degeneracy is widely present even in production and innovation systems in which many interlinked activities produce a wide variety of goods. In the context of exaptation in innovation processes, one form of degeneracy is the coexistence of many structurally different artefacts providing overlapping functionalities. Bonifati (2013), to which we refer for a fuller discussion, presents historical examples suggesting that exaptations may contribute to emerging degeneracy, which, in turn, may trigger further exaptations. In the section on 'Modelling the emergence of recurrent patterns of interactions' below we show through simulations that the basic elements of this form of degeneracy can be straightforwardly highlighted in very general and abstract situations. In particular, we examine the role of degeneracy in promoting high diversity and increasing complexity in artefact space.

EXAPTATION AT DIFFERENT LEVELS OF ORGANIZATION: AN ANALYTICAL FRAMEWORK

Artefacts are placed in a network of relationships in which interactions among agents and between agents and artefacts generate – through the organization of different patterns of interactions (Lane et al. 2009) – knowledge, capabilities, new users and producers, and new functionalities. In order to distinguish different effects of such interactions at different levels of organization we refer the exaptation process to three interrelated levels of analysis:[6] (1) the attribution of new functionalities (micro level); (2) the development of the conditions that enable new technologies and artefacts to be apt to the new functionalities (meso level); (3) the need for higher-level coordination in order to sustain and consolidate the patterns of interactions specific to the micro and meso levels (macro level).

Micro Level: The Attribution of New Functionalities

At the micro level, interactions between agents and artefacts give rise to attributions of functionalities by producers and/or users. In the process of exaptation, an attribution of a new functionality implies that a new use is attributed at the individual level (by individuals or groups of individuals) to an already existing technology or product. At this micro level the organization of interactions requires that agents come into contact with artefacts and that new information flows from users to producers (and vice versa). This condition is satisfied if users communicate to potential producers the new specifications required for the new use of an existing technology or product (and vice versa, when the producers propose new functionalities). In the section on 'Modelling exaptation' below we propose a simulation model of this process.

Meso Level: The 'Aptation' Process

In this second level of the exaptation process, new functionalities and new information activate, through interactions among agents, new knowledge, new capabilities, new users and producers. In developing new technologies and new products, the process of exaptation allows new technologies to become suited to new functionalities, some of which can co-evolve with the development of the new technologies and the new products. Complementary technologies required for new technologies or new products can be developed and the new functionalities can be better defined by users.[7] In this process of 'aptation' recurrent patterns of interactions organized around individual plans of actions in consumption and production activities emerge. In order to model this process of emergence, in the section on 'Modelling the emergence of recurrent patterns of interactions' below we use a simulation model in which many agents, producers and users of thousands of artefacts, are able to introduce innovations.

Macro Level: Coordination at a Higher Level

New artefacts and new ways of organizing interactions go together in the process of exaptation. Each level of organization of this process involves conflicts, negotiations and shared common interests and systems of beliefs. We define the macro level as that level of organization in which the interactions among these elements give rise to the emergence of organizational settings that sustain and consolidate the pattern of interactions specific to the micro and meso levels. Within the 'dense network of co-operation and affiliation by which firms are inter-related' (Richardson 1972: 883), this higher level of coordination involves the organization within the firm, the relationships between firms, and the relationships between producers and customers. For example, new artefacts may require new sales networks to sustain, and create, a new demand; or new supply agreements to implement a new supply. This can be achieved either by using existing organizational models and resources in new ways[8] or, where necessary, by creating new forms of coordination. We leave to further research the analysis of the dynamic relationships between exaptation and organizational change.[9]

THE EXAPTATION-BASED PERSPECTIVE AS AN (AT LEAST POTENTIAL) ALTERNATIVE TO THE 'ADAPTATION THROUGH SELECTION' PERSPECTIVE IN INNOVATION THEORY

Exaptation processes share the following three characteristics:

1. they require, as a necessary condition, the attribution of new functionalities to existing artefacts;
2. they exploit intrinsic but latent potentialities of existing technologies and products available for other uses;
3. in order to provide the new functionalities, new relationships between agents and artefacts must be generated and new artefacts emerge.

Combining these three characteristics it follows that an exaptation process includes an initial attribution of a new functionality and a subsequent process of 'aptation' characterized by continuous ongoing change in which existing artefacts are used in a new way, giving rise to the creation of new artefacts. This process requires, and gives rise to, new relationships between agents and artefacts.

Does this exaptation-based perspective represent an (at least potential) alternative to the 'adaptation through selection' perspective in the theory of innovation? The 'adaptation through selection' perspective in economics goes back to Alchian (1950) according to which, under uncertainty, the *ex ante* profit maximization hypothesis cannot be maintained. The market operates, rather, through a natural selection mechanism that rewards those firms that are most successful in obtaining positive *ex post* profits.[10] Penrose (1952, especially pp. 809–816) criticized Alchian, arguing that the presence of human intentionality makes the biological analogy inapplicable to firm and industry growth.[11] Thirty years later, Nelson and Winter (1982) proposed an evolutionary theory of economic change based on a mechanism of variation and selection that seeks to accommodate human intentionality in selection theory. In Nelson and Winter's theory the key element of economic change is the individual firm pursuing, in conditions of bounded rationality, the satisficing objective of obtaining a positive profit. The firm's activity is described in terms of a set of routines governing production, investment and organizational decisions.[12] The core of the theory is the mechanism that generates selection and variation. At any time, individual firms choose the levels of input and output using existing routines and existing capital stock. The profitability of each firm depends on these decisions and on market supply and demand conditions. Profitability, in turn, represents the market selection mechanism, in that the more profitable a firm, the more it grows. In such a way, the market selection mechanism generates differential growth rates of firms.

Variation arises from a change of routine within the firm. Firms follow a special class of routines to change existing routines through a search activity focused on research and development (R&D) spending. New routines are then submitted to the selection mechanism. In this type of theory, variation – that is, innovation – is the firm's response to changes in external market conditions, as signalled by an *ex post* lowering of profitability of its existing routine set. Nelson and Winter consider their theory as a theory of Lamarckian type (Nelson and Winter 1982: 11) in which the replicating instruction encoded in routines can be intentionally modified.[13]

For our purposes, what is relevant is the implication of the 'adaptation through selection' perspective as illustrated by the Nelson and Winter's theory of economic change. In such a perspective, artefacts and organizations adapt to a given functionality. Hence, this perspective overlooks that, in the same adaptation process, new functionalities can be attributed to artefacts or organizations 'selected' for other purposes, giving rise to new artefacts or new organizations. The fundamental difference between the 'adaptation through selection' and the exaptation-based perspectives in innovation theory is, then, the following. The first implies that through a selection-variation process the origin of an artefact or of an organization should be derived from its current functionality. In exaptation processes, instead, artefacts and organizations are made by using artefacts, including technologies, and organizations already available for other purposes in novel ways. It follows that in the exaptation-based perspective the origin of artefacts and organizations can not be derived from their current functionality.[14]

In the exaptation perspective there is no technology that 'adapts' to certain uses, as if those uses are waiting for a new technology to adapt. Neither can exaptation be likened to processes of speciation in which innovative entrepreneurs develop an existing technology into a new application domain in already existing market niches (Levinthal 1998). Insofar as new systems of relations among agents – old and new – emerge, exaptations lead to new market niches (Bonifati 2013).

The exaptation processes should not be confused with the notion of externalities (Dew et al. 2004: 73–74) that, as such, are unintended consequences of the actions of individual agents on a third party who is not directly involved in those actions. Exaptations, instead, result from the transformation of relations between agents triggered by an initial attribution of new functionalities. For the same reason, exaptations are not due to new combinations of existing technologies in new ways.[15] Finally, the process of exaptation can not be reduced to the accidental discovery (serendipity) or the unintended consequences of technology. The attribution of a new functionality may be intentional or accidental. However, what distinguishes the exaptation perspective is that it focuses on the organized processes by which new functionalities trigger new relationships between agents and artefacts (Bonifati 2013).

FROM THEORY TO MODELS

Several papers deal with ontologies or experimental issues relating to exaptation in a number of contexts, but only very few explicitly use modelling frameworks. These works come from the artificial life field, and mainly concern the evolution of artificial systems where the main driving forces are neutral non-adaptive changes caused by genetic drift (de Oliveira 1994; Miglino et al. 1996) or multi-objective fitness functions (Graham and Oppacher 2007; Mouret and Doncieux 2009). However, none of these refer to economic contexts, nor do they deal with artefact innovation directly.

In the next sections we shall present the main ideas and results of a series of studies that represent our distinctive contribution in modelling exaptations in innovation processes. These studies use agent-based models (ABMs), which in recent years have attracted considerable attention, as they allow accounting for agent heterogeneity, thus escaping from the constraints of the 'representative agent'. ABMs in fact are well suited to bridge the gap between hypotheses concerning the micro-behaviour of individual agents and the emergence of collective phenomena in populations composed by many interacting agents.[16]

We model exaptation in innovation processes at the micro and meso levels, leaving to further research the development of a complete model of the macro level. Following the hints provided by the theory, in order to proceed, we split and analyse the exaptation phenomenon in three stages that reflect different levels of analysis and of organization:

1. the 'initial exaptation' stage dealing with the attribution of new functionalities to an already existing artefact;
2. the 'aptation' stage concerning the consequent creation of new artefacts;
3. the 'successful exaptation' stage in which new long lasting patterns of interaction emerge.

Stage (1) is modelled as a micro-level event involving only two agents and one artefact, whereas stages (2) and (3) are processes involving many entities and therefore observable only at the meso level. Rather than using a unique complex model, we rely upon two separate agent-based models: EMIS (Exaptation Model in Innovation Studies) – specifically designed to analyse the attribution of new functionalities to artefacts (Villani et al. 2007b; Villani and Ansaloni 2010) – and I_2M (Iscom Innovation Model) that analyses the subsequent aptation and creation of new patterns of interaction between agents and artefacts (Lane et al. 2004–05; Villani et al. 2007a; Villani et al. 2008; Ansaloni et al. 2009; Serra et al. 2009).

At the micro level, EMIS is intended to address two relevant issues in promoting exaptations: the role of the quantity and quality of information exchanged among agents and the relevance of noise and learning processes. At the meso level, the simulation model I_2M deals with three crucial aspects of the emergence of recurrent pattern of interactions in innovation process: the role of 'change of suppliers', the emergence of a decentralized, but effective, coordination action and the role of degeneracy as a consequence and as a source of exaptation processes.

MODELLING EXAPTATION

The exaptation process at the microlevel is modelled by EMIS, in which two agents – a producer and a user – exchange information about the artefacts. In the model an artefact is identified by a set of characteristics representing its structural properties, including material properties and design. The agents are allowed to manipulate and use artefacts. In particular, each agent interprets and evaluates an artefact and exchanges information about it by using a set of categories. A category is defined as the set of characteristics attributed by agents to artefacts. The producer uses a category to produce an artefact. The user uses its own categories to evaluate the artefact as a whole. The evaluation of the artefact is higher, the smaller the misalignment between the category used by the producer and that used by the user. EMIS is designed to model the process of attribution of functionalities. The user continuously evaluates each artefact and returns to the producer its best evaluation (and possibly some details about the category that is returning the best evaluation). The producer tries to modify the category it is using to produce the artefact, in order to increase the user's satisfaction. During this modification process, sometimes the new artefact receives a better evaluation from what was previously a secondary category for the user, giving rise to the attribution of a new functionality and so to an exaptation occurrence (Villani et al. 2007b; Villani and Ansaloni 2010). Note that in the presence of processes of mere adaptation (for example, situations where the user owns only one category), the artefact and the related producer's category would perfectly match the user's category. In this case, the dynamics of the system would be monotonic, and no radical innovation would emerge.

EMIS therefore reproduces and defines precisely an essential characteristic of exaptation: the producer carefully designs and produces an artefact, which is interpreted, used and evaluated by another independent entity. At the microlevel exaptations appear as category changes in interpreting the artefact. The success of EMIS in reproducing this process allows us to search for the conditions that are able to increase the exaptation occurrences. Beside a measure of the artefact's evaluation, the user can communicate to the producer some of the artefact's characteristics that are giving positive (or negative) contributions to its evaluation. The perfect definition of too many details disambiguates the communication content and prevents the formation of the 'grey areas' useful for the exaptation phenomenon. Hence, while it may seem counterintuitive, we find that the higher is the quantity of transmitted characteristics, the lower are the exaptation occurrences (see Figure 10.1a). The same also holds if the user communicates (a part of) the characteristics currently not present in the artefact, but that if present can significantly contribute to a positive evaluation.

Moreover, the user can also communicate to the producer some characteristics of the artefact associated with other categories (e.g. the category generating the second-best evaluation). In this case, if both categories contribute equally to the total communication, nothing significant happens. We call this case 'symmetrical communication' (Figure 10.1b). In simulations, a partial exception occurs only for the exaptations that happen after a long while (see symmetrical communication, 50–1000 steps, Figure 10.1b). On the contrary, if the user communicates to the producer some characteristics of the better-matching category and some characteristics which, if present, could be useful for another (close) category, the exaptation occurrences considerably increase both in the initial and in the final parts of the simulations. This kind of communication is indicated as 'asymmetric communication' (Figure 10.1b).

As well as through the interaction between agents, information is conveyed through the artefacts with which agents interact. Let us consider that the producer is not a perfect maker, and it is possible that mistakes occur in building the artefact: in this case, the artefact has some characteristics that do not fit with the idealized prototype (the category the producer uses to build the artefact). This kind of noise delays the attainment of high values of functionality, but at the same time increases the frequency of exaptation occurrences. Both in symmetric and asymmetric communication, this type of noise is able to foster the attribution of new functionalities (Figure 10.1c).

Finally, we allow the user to modify its own categories (so far considered as fixed), through two different modalities:

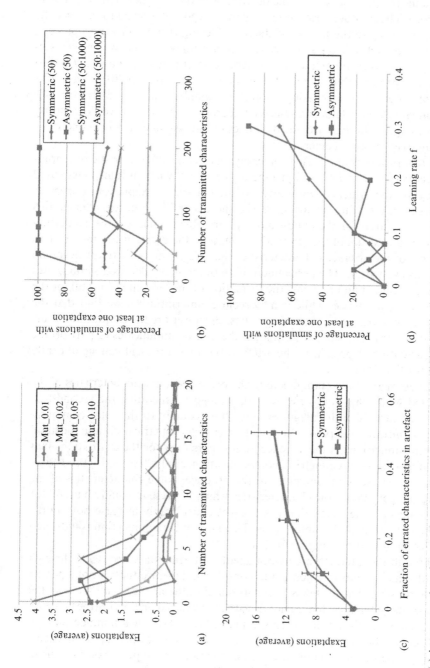

Notes: (a) Average number of exaptations (over 10 runs) vs. the number of characteristics of the best category transmitted from the user to the producer, when the producer at each step can adapt from 1% (Mut_0.01) to 10% (Mut_0.10) of the characteristics of its category. (b) The percentage of simulations (over 10 runs – case Mut_0.01) with at least one exaptation of the characteristics of the best two categories transmitted to the producer, on short (50 steps) and long runs (50–1000 steps). (c) Average number of exaptations (over 10 runs – case Mut_0.01) vs. a measure of the noise in artefacts building (the noise range belonging to the interval [0.0,1.0]). (d) The percentage of simulations (over 10 runs – case Mut_0.01) with at least one exaptation on long runs (50–1000 steps) vs. the updating rate *f*, when the users can learn from the environment.

Figure 10.1   Exaptation occurrences

1. 'Random modality': the user can randomly create a new category, and substitute one of the already existing ones (excluding the category giving the highest functionality). This represents the knowledge the user can acquire by interacting in new environments which are not explicitly modelled.
2. 'Learning modality': the user can modify a randomly selected category (all categories being involved) by introducing some information coming from the artefact.

Both modalities are characterized by the updating rate f, expressing the probability that at each time step a category of the user is selected for substitution (or for updating in the second modality). The random modality shows a small increase in the number of exaptation events: for both symmetric and asymmetric communications, higher updating rate f does not enhance this phenomenon. The learning modality shows more interesting characteristics. We find that the updating rate f significantly affects the exaptation frequency, in particular during long runs (a phenomenon previously absent; Figure 10.1d).

The modelling at the micro level corroborates therefore the importance of user–producer interactions in enhancing innovation processes, highlights that there are some elements (the categories) playing a fundamental role for the emergence of attributional shifts, and reveals that the plasticity of the categories greatly enhances the exaptation processes and that the extent and nature of communication processes, including the possibility of noise, also matter.

MODELLING THE EMERGENCE OF RECURRENT PATTERNS OF INTERACTIONS

The attribution of new functionalities at the microlevel gives rise to new patterns of relationships between agents and artefacts at the mesolevel. In this section we model the emergence of these systems of relationships using the Iscom Innovation Model (I_2M).[17] The model considers an environment where thousands of agents and artefacts maintain complex interactions, and where the creation of novelties and their integration into already existing recurrent patterns of interaction constitute an essential and uneliminable element. The meso-level model I_2M shares important characteristics with EMIS but, in order to minimize the model's complexity, in I_2M the structure of agents and artefacts is simpler, while the agents' capabilities of manipulating artefacts are more explicitly modelled. This way, we can focus our attention on the interplay among artefacts, agents' capabilities and recurrent patterns of interaction.

Artefacts

In I_2M the artefacts' material characteristics are realized by means of very simple objects, that is, integers. Artefacts are named in different ways depending on the context. In particular we refer to artefacts using the words:

*   'name' to denote a type of artefact (for example: a '12');
*   'article' defined as the artefact that a particular producer is making and selling (for example: the '12' built by agent A_5);

- 'item' to indicate a single artefact present in the stock of a producer (for example: in the stock of the '12s' built by agent A_5 there are three items).

In I_2M, articles have a unique producer, which maintains a stock containing several items of each article it is producing. Different producers could build artefacts with the same name, but they may have different material characteristics, as chairs produced by different makers are different. Therefore, artefacts having identical names could be embedded in very different patterns of interaction, with important consequences, as we will see later.

Recipes and Goals

In order to manipulate these objects the agents need tools to represent, build, store and sell them. The tools the agents use in order to produce their articles – processing the items they obtain from other agents – are called 'recipes', a recipe being an ordered sequence of articles and production operators. Recipes represent the focal points of a complex set of interactions and define the 'context' of the articles: how they are used, which other articles they are combined with, who is their owner, how many other agents know of their existence. Note that the use of the same artefact within a new recipe (dissimilar in some extent from the old ones) changes its scope, and constitutes the equivalent of an exaptation event. In I_2M therefore exaptations are frequent events. Agents can possess more than one recipe at the same time (Figure 10.2), and can increase or decrease their production level only within a pre-fixed range – because of physical constraints.[18] Agents can create new recipes: in order to achieve their goals, the agents can combine and mutate the recipes they already own until the desired outcome is reached or until the search fails (Lane et al. 2004–05; Serra et al. 2009).

Finally, the agent's goal (the name the agent wishes to produce) is set (with probability p_{inn} at each agent's turn) by two alternative strategies:

1. by randomly choosing a name with uniform probability
2. by randomly keeping a name from the set of already existing articles and occasionally mutating it.

Innovation Processes Cause the Emergence of Recurrent Patterns of Interaction

The agent and artefacts' environment is very simple, being constituted by 'raw materials' that do not need other pre-existing articles. Starting from only two raw materials, whose stocks in the simulations are assumed unlimited, and very few recipes, some tens of agents are able to develop systems where thousands of articles and hundreds of thousands of items are contemporaneously built, used, cancelled and manipulated: it is possible therefore to observe the formation and the evolution of several recurrent patterns of interactions. The recipes are the basis of these interaction patterns, because they link particular articles (the recipes' inputs) to other particular articles (the recipes' outputs). Recipes, as a consequence, link the producers to the users. Stable sequences of agents and artefacts form the recurrent patterns of interactions.

The patterns of interactions could significantly change over time for a number of

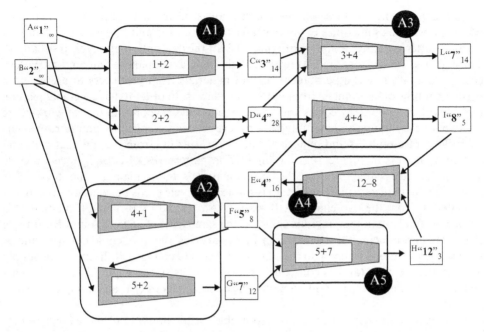

Notes: Articles 'A' and 'B' have respectively name '1' and '2' and unlimited stocks (they are raw materials, produced – in this example – in unlimited quantities). Articles {C,D,E,F,G,H,I,L} have stocks with {14,28,16,8,12,3,5,14} items respectively. The articles' names are indicated within quotes. In order to clarify the figure, the agents' goals are not shown here.

Figure 10.2   A small system, with five agents (A1–A5), eight recipes and ten articles

reasons. In particular, I_2M models the following three types of changes. Firstly, producers must decide whether to continue production or not. In this regard, we adopt the hypothesis that this decision is independent from prices. During the exaptation process the cost conditions are in progress and setting a price may require several revisions. Hence, the price may not be a sufficiently reliable reference for production decisions. For these decisions, we will attach greater importance to the quantities actually sold (say at a conventional price): in the simulation models, production will continue provided that producers sell a minimum quantity of the product during a certain period. In particular we impose that articles not used by any recipes are discarded after 15 steps. Moreover, agents without recipes are removed from the simulation. For example, in Figure 10.2 article G is functional (with article F) to produce article H; whereas article L, though having the same name as article G, is useless (not used in any recipes): in the case of 15 time steps of uninterrupted uselessness, this article will be removed from the simulation.

Secondly, the model admits that producers can change suppliers: spontaneously, or because the usual supplier is unable to provide the quantity or quality of the input demanded. Thirdly, the patterns of interactions could change as a result of innovations. In the model new articles and new names appear, produced by new recipes. Patterns of interactions change insofar as these new entities begin to interact with the already existing objects.

As a consequence of these changes, entire areas of artefact space are permanently occupied, whereas sometimes entire new areas are explored and integrated into already existing patterns of interaction (see Figure 10.3 for the description of a typical situation). Through the simulations in I_2M we highlight that a permanent interaction pattern emerges only if there is a permanent flow of materials from producers to users, and a permanent flow of 'usefulness' from users to producers. In order to have a global picture, the network composed by recipes and articles is a useful viewpoint. In this network, there are two long-lasting patterns of interactions: cycles, characterized by uninterrupted circular flows of usefulness and materials, and chains starting from the raw materials and ending on cycles. In Figure 10.2 the interaction pattern [E-A3-I-A4-E] forms a cycle and – if the cycle is able to collect the needed materials and to maintain the stocks of its articles higher than zero – this structure is stable. The cycle needs the continuous support of materials from the two chains [A,B-A2-F,G-A5-H] and [A,B-A1-D] (note that D is needed also to sustain the previous chain, at the same level of articles A and B). If these chains fail in producing the needed quantities of articles, the cycle could collapse, and as a consequence, after 15 steps also the chains will begin to collapse. If the materials supply is adequate, the cycle (and as consequence the chains) is stable. Figure 10.3a represents an already existing pattern of interactions (the existing network) as an entangled mixture of cycles.

No single agent, recipe or article is responsible for the presence of these kinds of patterns of interactions that collectively play a coordination role. For our purposes it is important to note that the main engines of this emergent action of coordination are the innovation processes themselves. In fact, recipes and agents removal cause a loss of links, but the most interesting (and constructive) events are due to the processes of 'change of supplier' and 'creation of new article', which, respectively, redirect already existing links and create new ones. The redirection allows the inclusion of new articles into long-lasting patterns of interactions.

The creation of a new article (Figure 10.3b) involves the creation of new links and of a new recipe, a process that per se cannot change the structure of the articles–recipes network insofar as it does not give rise to cycles (Figure 10.3c). Nevertheless, multiple article creations and the contemporaneous change of supplier process can produce a stable structure, which in this case embraces a new region of the artefact space. In this case, the change of supplier process has a stabilizing action, by linking (a part of) the new articles with the already existing ones (Figure 10.3d) or to each other (Figure 10.3e). As a result, both processes can contribute to the emergence of cycles composed of articles and recipes that are the basis for long lasting patterns of interaction. In Figure 10.3d by a change of supplier process an agent chooses article G, creating a stable structure. Note that articles W, E and F, without other changes on the system, will disappear. In Figure 10.3e a change of supplier links articles F and C forming a cycle that creates a new piece of network. As consequence, articles A and B also become more stable, being involved in the chains carrying materials from the original network to the new cycle. Articles G and W, without other changes on the system, will disappear. Note that the a link between this new piece of network and the original one is enough to merge them and to create in such a way a single bigger stable structure.[19]

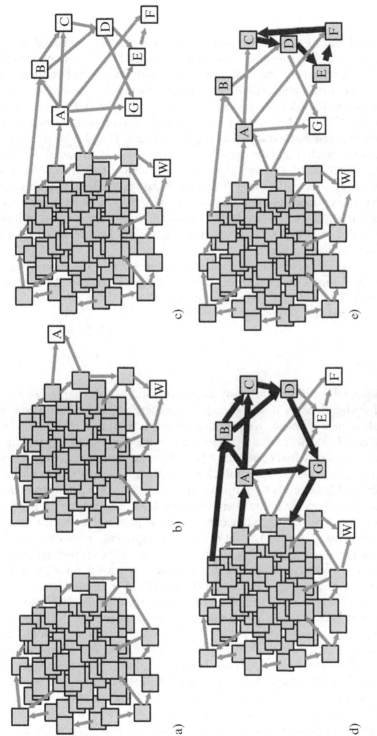

Notes: For simplicity, only articles are drawn, two articles being linked if the first is the input of a recipe whose output is the second article. Filled rectangles indicate articles participating to long-lasting structures, whereas empty rectangles indicate articles which do not.

Figure 10.3   The process of creation of a new (piece of) network

Degeneracy

As already highlighted, during this growth process similar names are embedded in very different contexts, and vice versa the same name could be realized in different parts of the system. If the artefacts having the same names have also similar functionalities (are used in similar recipes), we are witnessing a manifestation of degeneracy, a very frequent event in the I_2M system. Figure 10.2 shows a typical situation, where there are more ways to build the names '4' and '7', and where there are, for example, several paths between artefacts B and I. Moreover, despite their different origins, artefacts D and E have the same name ('4') and are both used to build the name '8' (even the recipe is the same). This last situation of degeneracy allows nevertheless asymmetries (artefact D is used also to build the name '7'). Sometimes some paths could disappear, because of lack of materials and/ or of purchases, but the presence of multiple paths ending with the same name highly facilitates the input supply. This situation is particularly useful for the support of long-lasting structures: in this way, degeneracy becomes a significant feature of the system, and strongly supports its high resilience.

Finally, the change of suppliers may significantly contribute to the emergence of degeneracy. Figure 10.3 shows that a frequent change of suppliers allows the existence of several articles with the same name, which in turn allows the existence of many other articles, a situation strongly favouring high diversity.

CONCLUSIONS

Exaptation phenomena are common in innovation processes. In this chapter we focus on the theoretical foundations of these processes proposing a theoretical framework and modelling tools to analyse them. We propose a theoretical framework founded on an ontology in which: (1) at the micro level, interactions between agents and artefacts give rise to attributions of new functionalities; (2) at the meso level, recurrent patterns of interactions emerge giving rise to new artefacts apt to provide the new functionalities; (3) at the macro level a higher level of coordination can sustain, consolidate and direct the pattern of interactions specific to the micro and mesolevel. The exaptation perspective does not allow us to derive the origin of technologies and products from their current functionality. For this reason, the analysis of exaptations represents a possible alternative to the 'adaptation through selection' paradigm in examining innovation dynamics.

By using two agent-based models, we model the process of exaptation at the micro and meso levels. At the micro level we focus on the possible conditions fostering exaptation occurrences. Among these, we examine the role of the quantity and quality of information exchanged between users and producers, and of the presence of noise and learning in the process of communication. The main results of the simulations are that exaptation occurrences decrease with the quantity of information the user communicates to the producers about the characteristics leading to a positive or negative evaluation of the artefact. This shrinkage does not take place if the information exchange concerns more than one category, while the user can increase the exaptation occurrences by asymmetrically communicating secondary (but close) categories. Noise in communication between user and producer delays the attainment of convergence among the user's and producer's categories but increases the frequency of exaptation occurrences by fostering the attribution of new functionalities. Finally, the exaptation frequency significantly increases if the user learns and actively participates in defining its own satisfaction by introducing in its categories some information coming from the interaction with artefacts.

At the meso level, we examine the emergence of recurring patterns of interaction between agents and artefacts and the role of degeneracy. The simulations strongly indicate that there is an emergent action of coordination, whose main engine is the innovation process itself. Core to the systems are particular groups of artefacts, where the circular flow – of materials from producers to the users and of 'usefulness' from users to producers – allow the presence of long-lasting and recurrent patterns of interaction. Their formation is greatly facilitated by 'change of supplier' processes, also responsible for the emergence of innovations in the agent–artefact space. These very peculiar relationships and courses of action allow the system to have high degeneracy levels and a complex internal structure.

NOTES

*   The authors would like to thank David Lane for many discussions and suggestions and Andrea Ginzburg, Anna Grandori, Federica Rossi and Margherita Russo for helpful comments on an earlier draft of this chapter. The authors gratefully acknowledge Luca Ansaloni for his help in programming. The usual disclaimers apply.
1.   These examples of exaptation are reviewed by Dew et al. (2004: 73–79).
2.   See Dopfer and Potts (2004, especially pp. 204–208), and Dopfer and Potts (2008: 3–4).
3.   The notion of epistemic uncertainty, defined as the uncertainty deriving from the lack of knowledge of quantities or processes of the system or the environment, is widely acknowledged in complexity science (Oberkampf et al. 2001).
4.   On the relationship between ontological uncertainty and Knight's notion of uncertainty see Lane and Maxfield (2005: 9–10). For a discussion of the relationship between uncertainty and exaptation see Bonifati (2013).
5.   Lane and Maxfield (1997: 194–195) define these interactions as 'generative relationships' and characterize them by the following five properties: (a) heterogeneity; (b) aligned directedness; (c) mutual directedness; (d) permissions; (e) action opportunities.
6.   On the distinction between micro, meso and macro see Dopfer et al. (2004).
7.   On the emergence of complementary innovations see Russo (2000).
8.   In a recent work on the legacy of founding institutions in US commercial banks, Marquis and Huang (2010), for example, find that capabilities originally developed for dispersed bank branch management become useful for a new purpose – bank acquisition management and integration – after an environmental shift. They consider this an exaptation. For a critical discussion of the contribution of Marquis and Huang see Bonifati (2013).
9.   In this perspective we need a deeper understanding of organizational change. For example, it is necessary to consider that, in the process of qualitative change of an organizational structure, some elements may be invariant (Grandori and Prencipe 2008).
10.   On this point see also Friedman (1953: 19–23).
11.   See also Richardson (1960: 140, n1). For a wider critical discussion of the use of biological metaphors in economics see Ginzburg (2009).
12.   Nelson and Winter follow the organization theory as developed by March and Simon (1958) and Cyert and March (1963).
13.   Recently, Knudsen (2002) and Hodgson and Knudsen (2006) argued the necessity of a generalized Darwinian theory in which the Lamarckian theory must be nested. On this subject see also Nelson (2006), Hodgson and Knudsen (2007) and Hodgson's Chapter 9 in the present volume.
14.   On the non-derivability of the historical origin from the current functionality in biological systems and in human institutions see Gould (2002: 1215–1218), and Nietzsche (1887) quoted by Gould.

15. On the innovation process in terms of recombination of existing technologies see Arthur (2009). The process of exaptation differs from the Schumpeterian vision of the innovation process as new combinations of existing factors of production (Schumpeter 1934).
16. See for example Epstein and Axtell (1996), Gilbert and Terna (2000), Cioffi-Revilla (2002), Axelrod and Tesfatsion (2006) and further references quoted therein.
17. The model refers to a corpus of theories and techniques developed during the European project ISCOM (The Information Society as a Complex System). The main results of the ISCOM project are collected in Lane et al. (2009).
18. In order to build their output, the recipes use (and decrease the stock of) the input articles. Therefore, the items distribution depends on the artefacts' availability and on the agents' aims and capabilities: as a consequence, the relative importance of the articles during the simulation is determined by the ways in which the agents use them.
19. Mathematically, these structures made of entangled circles are called 'strongly connected components' (SCCs). In I_2M only one single SCC emerges. Nevertheless, it is possible to identify in it several zones where the local density of links is particularly high, a clue indicating the existence of other levels of organization (Villani et al. 2007a).

REFERENCES

Alchian, A.A. (1950), 'Uncertainty, evolution, and economic theory', *Journal of Political Economy*, **58**(3), 211–221.

Ansaloni, Luca, M. Villani and D.A. Lane (2009), 'Distributed processes in an agent-based model of innovation', in R. Serra, M. Villani and I. Poli (eds), *Artificial Life and Evolutionary Computation: Proceedings of Wivace 2008*, World Scientific Publishing Company, pp. 201–212.

Arthur, W.B. (2009), *The Nature of Technology. What It Is and How It Evolves*, New York: Free Press.

Axelrod R. and L. Tesfatsion (2006), 'A guide for newcomers to agent-based modelling in the social sciences', in L. Kenneth, K.L. Judd and L. Tesfatsion (eds), *Handbook of Computational Economics, Vol. 2: Agent-Based Computational Economics*, Amsterdam: North-Holland, pp. 1–13.

Bonifati, G. (2010), 'More is different, exaptation and uncertainty: three foundational concepts for a complexity theory of innovation', *Economics of Innovation and New Technology*, **19**(8), 743–760.

Bonifati, G. (2013), 'Exaptation and emerging degeneracy in innovation processes', *Economics of Innovation and New Technology*, **22**(1), 1–21.

Cioffi-Revilla, C. (2002), 'Invariance and universality in social agent-based simulations', PNAS, **99**, 7314–7316.

Cyert, Richard M. and James G. March (1963), *A Behavioural Theory of the Firm*, Englewood Cliffs, NJ: Prentice-Hall.

de Oliveira P.P.B. (1994), 'Simulation of exaptive behaviour', *Lecture Notes in Computer Science*, **866**, 354–354.

Dew, N., S.D. Sarasvathy and S. Venkataraman (2004), 'The economic implications of exaptation', *Journal of Evolutionary Economics*, **14**, 69–84.

Dopfer, K. and J. Potts (2004), 'Evolutionary realism: a new ontology for economics', *Journal of Economic Methodology*, **11**(2), 195–212.

Dopfer, Kurt and Jason Potts (2008), *The General Theory of Economic Evolution*, London: Routledge.

Dopfer, K., J. Foster and J. Potts (2004), 'Micro-meso-macro', *Journal of Evolutionary Economics*, **14**, 263–279.

Edelman, G.M. and J.A. Gally (2001), 'Degeneracy and complexity in biological systems', *Proceedings of National Academy of Science USA*, **98**(24), 13763–13768.

Epstein, J.M. and R. Axtell (1996), *Growing Artificial Societies: Social Science from the Bottom Up*, Cambridge, MA: MIT Press.

Friedman, Milton (1953), 'The methodology of Positive Economics', in Milton Friedman (ed.), *Essays in Positive Economics*, Chicago, IL: University of Chicago Press, pp. 3–3.

Gilbert, N. and P. Terna (2000), 'How to build and use agent-based models in social science', *Mind and Society*, **1**, 57–72.

Ginzburg, Andrea (2009), 'Biological metaphors in economics: natural selection and competition', in David Lane, Denis Pumain, Sander E. van der Leeuw and Geoffrey West (eds), *Complexity Perspective in Innovation and Social Change*, Berlin: Springer-Verlag, pp. 117–52.

Gould, Stephen J. (2002), *The Structure of Evolutionary Theory*, Cambridge MA: Harvard University Press.

Gould, S.J. and E.S. Vrba (1982), 'Exaptation – a missing term in the science of form', *Paleobiology*, **8**(1), 4–15.

Graham L. and F. Oppacher (2007), 'A multiple-function toy model of exaptation in a genetic algorithm', IEEE *Congress on Evolutionary Computation (CEC 2007)*, pp. 4591–4598.

Grandori, A. (2001), '"Cognitive failures" and combinative governance', *Journal of Management and Governance*, **5**, 252–260.

Grandori, A. and A. Prencipe (2008), 'Organizational invariants and organizational change', *European Management Review*, **5**, 232–244.

Hodgson, G.H. and T. Knudsen (2006), 'Why we need a generalized Darwinism, and why generalized Darwinism is not enough', *Journal of Economic Behavior and Organization*, **61**, 1–19.

Hodgson, G.M. and T. Knudsen (2007), 'Evolutionary theorizing beyond Lamarckism: a reply to Richard Nelson', *Journal of Evolutionary Economics*, **17**, 353–359.

Knight, Frank H. (1921 [1971]), *Risk, Uncertainty and Profit*, Chicago, IL: University of Chicago Press.

Knudsen, T. (2002), 'Economic selection theory', *Journal of Evolutionary Economics*, **12**, 443–470.

Lane, D.A. (2011), 'Complexity and innovation dynamics', in Antonelli Cristiano (ed.), *Handbook on the Economic Complexity of Technological Change*, Cheltenham, UK and Northampton, MA, USA: Edward Elgar, pp. 63–80.

Lane, D.A. and R. Maxfield (1997), 'Foresight, complexity, and strategy', in Arthur Brian W., Steven N. Durlauf and David A. Lane (eds), *The Economy As An Evolving Complex System II*, Reading, MA: Addison-Wesley, pp. 169–198.

Lane, D.A. and R. Maxfield (2005), 'Ontological uncertainty and innovation', *Journal of Evolutionary Economics*, **15**, 3–50.

Lane, D.A., R. Maxfield, D. Read and S. van der Leeuw (2009), 'From population to organization thinking, in David A. Lane, Denis Pumain, Sander E. van der Leeuw and Geoffrey West (eds), *Complexity Perspective in Innovation and Social Change*, Berlin: Springer-Verlag, pp. 11–41.

Lane, D., D. Pumain, S.E. van der Leeuw and G. West (2009), *Complexity Perspective in Innovation and Social Change*, Berlin: Springer-Verlag.

Lane, D.A., R. Serra, M. Villani and L. Ansaloni, (2004–05), 'A theory based dynamical model of innovation processes', *Complexus*, **2**(3–4), 177–194.

Langlois, Richard N. (1986), 'Rationality, institutions, and explanation', in Richard N. Langlois (ed.), *Economics as a Process: Essays in the New Institutional Economics*, Cambridge: Cambridge University Press, pp. 225–255.

Langlois, Richard N. and M.M. Cosgel (1993), 'Frank Knight on risk, uncertainty, and the firm: a new interpretation', *Economic Inquiry*, **31**(July), 456–465.

Levinthal, D.A. (1998), 'The slow pace of rapid technological change: gradualism and punctuation in technological change', *Industrial and Corporate Change*, **7**(2), 217–247.

March, James G. and Herbert A. Simon (1958), *Organizations*, New York: John Wiley & Sons.

Marquis, C. and Z. Huang (2010), 'Acquisitions as exaptation: the legacy of founding institutions in the US commercial banking industry', *Academy Management Journal*, **53**(6), 1441–1473.

Mason, P.H. (2010), 'Degeneracy at multiple levels of complexity', *Biological Theory*, **5**(3), 277–288.

Meyer, A.D., A.S. Tsui, and C.R. Hinings (1993), 'Configurational approaches to organizational analysis', *Academy of Management Journal*, **36**(6), 175–195.

Miglino, Orazio, S. Nolfi and D. Parisi (1996), 'Discontinuity in evolution: how different levels of organization imply pre-adaptation', in R.K. Belew and M. Mitchell (eds), *Adaptive Individuals in Evolving Populations: Models and Algorithms*, Reading, MA: Addison-Wesley, pp. 399–415.

Milgrom, P. and J. Roberts (1990), 'The economics of modern manufacturing: technology, strategy, and organization', *American Economic Review*, **80**(June), 511–528.

Milgrom, P. and J. Roberts (1995), 'Complementarities and fit: strategy, structure, and organizational change in manufacturing', *Journal of Accounting and Economics*, **19**, 179–208.

Mokyr, Joel (2000), 'Evolutionary phenomena in technological change', in J. Ziman (ed), *Technological Innovation as a Evolutionary Process*, Cambridge: Cambridge University Press, pp. 52–65.

Mouret, J.-B. and S. Doncieux (2009), 'Evolving modular neural-networks through exaptation', *IEEE Congress on Evolutionary Computation* (CEC 2009).

Nelson, R. (2006), 'Evolutionary social science and universal Darwinism', *Journal of Evolutionary Economics*, **16**, 491–510.

Nelson, Richard R. and Sidney G. Winter (1982), *An Evolutionary Theory of Economic Change*, Cambridge, MA: Harvard University Press.

Nietzsche, Friedrich (1887), *On the Genealogy of Morals*, translated by W. Kaufmann, New York: Vintage 1967.

Oberkampf, W.L., J.C. Helton and K. Sentz (2001), 'Mathematical representation of uncertainty', AIAA Non-deterministic Approaches Forum, Seattle, Paper n. 2001-1645.

Penrose, E.T. (1952), 'Biological analogies in the theory of the firm', *American Economic Review*, **42**, 804–818.

Richardson, George B. (1960), *Information and Investment. A Study in the Working of the Competitive Economy*, Oxford: Oxford University Press.

Richardson, G.B. (1972), 'The organization of industry', *Economic Journal*, **82**, 883–896.

Rosenberg, N. (1976), *Perspectives on Technology*, Cambridge: Cambridge University Press.
Rosenberg, Nathan (1996), 'Uncertainty and technological change', in R. Landau, T. Taylor and G. Wright (eds), *The Mosaic of Economic Growth*, Stanford, CA: Stanford University Press, pp. 334–353.
Russo, M. (2000), 'Complementary innovations and generative relationships: an ethnographic study', *Economics of Innovation and New Technology*, **9**, 517–557.
Schumpeter, Joseph A. (1934 [1949]), *The Theory of Economic Development*, Cambridge, MA: Harvard University Press.
Serra, Roberto, M. Villani and D.A. Lane (2009), 'Modelling innovation', in David A. Lane, Denis Pumain, Sander E. van der Leeuw and Geoffrey West (eds), *Complexity Perspective in Innovation and Social Change*, Berlin: Springer-Verlag, pp. 361–388.
Simon, Herbert A. (1962), 'The architecture of complexity', *The Science of Artificial*, Cambridge, MA: MIT Press.
Villani, Marco and L. Ansaloni (2010), 'A theory-based dynamical model of exaptive innovation processes', in P. Ahrweiler (ed.), *Innovation in Complex Social Systems*, London: Routledge, pp. 250–263.
Villani, Marco, L. Ansaloni, D. Bagatti, D.A. Lane and R. Serra (2007a), 'Novelties and structural changes in a dynamical model of innovation processes', in J. Jost and D. Helbing (eds), *Proceedings of ECCS07: European Conference on Complex Systems*.
Villani, Marco, S. Bonacini, D. Ferrari, R. Serra and D.A. Lane (2007b), 'An agent-based model of exaptive processes', *European Management Review*, **4**, 141–151.
Villani, Marco, R. Serra, L. Ansaloni and D.A. Lane (2008), 'Global and local processes in a model of innovation', Umeo H. et al. (eds), *Cellular Automata. 8th International Conference on Cellular Automata for Research and Industry*, Springer Lecture Notes in Computer Science 5191, pp. 401–408.
Whitacre, J.M. and A. Bender (2010), 'Networked buffering: a basic mechanism for distributed robustness in complex adaptive systems', *Theoretical Biology and Medical Modelling*, **7**(20).

11. Interdependence and organization design
Phanish Puranam and Marlo Raveendran*

The division of labor is a defining property of organizations. This implies that inter-dependence and integration are inevitable features, as the results of partitioned efforts must somehow be integrated back. Indeed, much of the literature on organization design rests on the premise that organizational structures 'solve' the problems of cooperation and coordination that arise when integrating the efforts of interdependent actors – with varying degrees of success. In this chapter we review the diverse conceptualizations of interdependence as well as the mechanisms by which interdependence is managed, to demonstrate the unity of their underlying analytical structure. We also highlight the point that the same basic ideas can be applied at multiple levels of aggregation – that interdependence between individuals, groups, departments and firms can be conceptual-ized and analyzed using the same tools. Indeed, this 'fractal' nature of interdependence principles is a basis for optimism regarding the construction of a science of organization design. We conclude by outlining what we see as opportunities for further research into the links between interdependence and organization design.

INTRODUCTION

If organizations are multi-agent systems with goals, there must exist a mapping from organization-level goals to agent-level tasks (March & Simon 1958). Such a mapping, at least when explicitly recognized (even if not intentionally crafted) is what we think of typ-ically as division of labor. Because the results of the efforts so divided must be integrated back, the division of labor results in interdependence between the agents performing the tasks contributing to the overall goal of the organization.

Many perspectives in organization theory build on the premise that organizations 'solve' the problems of cooperation and coordination that arise when integrating the efforts of interdependent actors – albeit with varying degrees of success. This premise is common to the analysis of organizational structures using a diverse set of constructs such as information processing (e.g. Simon 1945; Thompson 1967), contingency and fit (e.g. Lawrence & Lorsch 1967), complementarities (e.g. Milgrom & Roberts 1990), epistatic interactions (e.g. Levinthal 1997), power (e.g. Pfeffer & Salancik 1978), reward interde-pendence (e.g. Kelley & Thibaut 1978) and asset specificity (e.g. Williamson 1975). Note that the solutions that an organization provides need not be consciously designed by a source of centralized authority; indeed the defining features of organization – division of labor and the integration of effort – are plainly visible in many animal and insect societies (e.g., De Waal 2001, 2005; Sendova-Franks & Franks 1999), where evolution through natural selection provides the solutions to problems of cooperation and coordination.

We have two objectives for this chapter. Firstly, we consider the conditions under which interdependence between agents gives rise to cooperation problems versus coordination problems. Coordination failures occur when interacting individuals are unable to antici-pate each other's actions and adjust their own accordingly because of conflicts of under-standing (Schelling 1960); evidence of coordination failures includes misunderstandings, delays and a lack of synchronization of activities. In contrast, cooperation failures occur when interdependent individuals lack the motivation to achieve the best collective outcome because of conflicts of interests. Shirking, free-riding and reneging on agreements are the canonical instances of cooperation failures. Cooperation and coordination failures can occur independently of each other and are therefore individually sufficient reasons for the faulty integration of efforts (Simon 1945; March & Simon 1958; Schelling 1960; Camerer 2003; Heath & Staudenmayer 2000; Grant 1996; Holmstrom & Roberts 1998).

Secondly, we consider some ways in which the cooperation and coordination prob-lems arising from interdependence can be analyzed jointly, rather than separately as traditionally has been the case; indeed it has been noted, tongue in cheek, that alien social scientists visiting our planet might be stunned by the vastly different conceptuali-zation of organizations that result from an exclusive focus on one or the other (Dosi et al. 2003). We offer some thoughts on how to bridge the gap between how interdepend-ence is treated in these two conceptualizations of organizations: as systems for obtaining cooperation as opposed to systems of coordinated action.

While much of our discussion, for expositional simplicity, will focus on an interde-pendent dyad, we emphasize the point that the same basic ideas can be applied at larger scales and multiple levels of aggregation – that interdependence between (multiple) indi-viduals, groups, departments and firms can be analyzed using the same concepts. Indeed, this 'fractal' nature of interdependence principles is a basis for optimism regarding the construction of a science of organization design (see also Grandori & Furnari 2008).

INTERDEPENDENCE AS A CONSEQUENCE OF THE DIVISION OF LABOR

The division of labor in an organization has two logically distinct components: the decomposition of the overall goal into (clusters of) tasks, and the allocation of these task clusters to individual agents (Smith 1776). We refer to these two processes as task divi-sion and task allocation.

Task Division

There are typically a variety of feasible ways to decompose a given organizational goal into a set of contributing tasks. We define a task structure as any means–end decomposi-tion (Newell & Simon 1972) of a goal into its constituent tasks and the interdependency relationships between these. A task is the fundamental, indivisible unit of a task structure and may be thought of as a production technology: it is a transformation of inputs into outputs in a finite time period. Since tasks have inputs and outputs, they have an associ-ated value (the difference between the benefits of the outputs and the cost of the inputs) as seen by the designer of the system.

Let T^R be the most fine-grained task structure visible to an omniscient organization designer; a property of objective reality. As Grandori and Soda (2006) note, this could be seen as a theoretical lower bound in terms of the units of analysis in organizations, and is determined by properties like technological separability. However, lacking omniscience, boundedly rational individuals must work with imperfect representations of T^R. As a consequence, there will typically be many different ways in which organization designers with bounded cognitive capacities can represent the same T^R (some common representations include workflow diagrams, design structure matrices, and linear programming models). These representations capture tasks and the possible interdependence relationships between tasks.

Different kinds of interdependencies between tasks can be represented analytically in terms of the different ways that each task's inputs and outputs enter a combined value function (Milgrom & Roberts 1990). Following Puranam et al. (2012) we say that two tasks are interdependent when the value generated from performing each is different when the other task is performed versus when it is not. The tasks are independent if the value of performing each task is the same whether the other task is performed or not. As a consequence the combined value created when independent tasks are performed is the same as the sum of the values created by performing each task alone. Thus interdependence is consistent with situations where the joint outputs of tasks are complements or substitutes (Milgrom & Roberts 1990). Specialization represents task decomposition into heterogeneous components, and by the definition above introduces interdependence between tasks. In contrast, non-specialized task decomposition can leave tasks independent (Leijonhufvud 1986).

Task structure matrices (Baldwin & Clark 2000; Eppinger 1991; Steward 1981) provide a compact matrix form representation of patterns of interdependence between tasks. In a task structure matrix (TSM), different tasks are mapped on both the rows and the columns of the matrix – the cells are then populated by 'x' if 'column task' is dependent on 'row task'. Each task is dependent on itself. Dependencies can be symmetric or asymmetric (see Figure 11.1). While information on the functional form of the interdependence is not given, in a TSM the overall patterns of interdependence between tasks are easy to see.

	x1	x2	x3	x4
x1	x	x		
x2	x	x		x
x3		x	x	
x4		x		x

Figure 11.1   Task structure matrix with four task elements

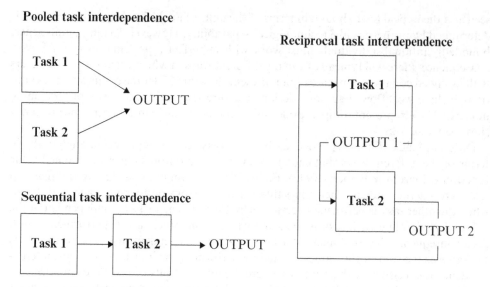

Figure 11.2   Thompson's workflow diagrams

It is possible to transform other representations of task interdependence into a task structure matrix with some loss of information. For instance, Thompson's (1967) classic discussion of interdependence is based on a workflow-based representation of tasks. Three increasingly complex levels of interdependence are discussed: pooled, sequential, and reciprocal interdependence, as shown in Figure 11.2. Pooled interdependence corresponds to no interdependence between the tasks themselves; they contribute independently to overall task performance (equivalent to resource interdependence (Pfeffer & Salancik 1978). Sequential and reciprocal interdependencies can be portrayed by asymmetric and symmetric 'x's about the diagonal, respectively. Burton and Obel (1984) represent task interdependence using a linear programming model: the task interdependence is given in the form of a series of decision variables and constraints posed on them. Interdependence exists to the extent that multiple decision variables X_i are linked to the same constraint (see Figure 11.3). If we consider each decision variable to be equivalent to a task, then to the extent that different tasks are linked to the same constraint, they are interdependent. It is possible to convert the linear program into a TSM; albeit with loss of information about the functional form of the interdependence, and on the assumption that the interdependence is always symmetric. The matrix of coefficients in the linear programming model and the corresponding TSM are shown in the lower part of Figure 11.3.

Task Allocation

There will typically be many different ways in which organization designers with bounded cognitive capacities can cluster the tasks in T^R, and these clusters of task may be allocated in different ways among the agents in the organization.

Let the matrix T^A capture the interdependencies between the clusters of tasks allocated

Maximize $\qquad$ C0X0 $\quad + \quad$ C1X1 $\quad + \quad$ C2X2 $\quad + \quad$ C3X3

X0, X1, X2, X3

Subject to: $\qquad$ A0X0 $\quad + \quad$ A1X1 $\quad + \quad$ A2X2 $\quad + \quad$ A3X3 $\quad \leq \quad$ b0

$\qquad\qquad\qquad\qquad$ B1X1 $\qquad\qquad\qquad\qquad\qquad\qquad \leq \quad$ b1

$\qquad\qquad\qquad\qquad\qquad\qquad$ B2X2 $\qquad\qquad\qquad\qquad \leq \quad$ b2

$\qquad\qquad\qquad\qquad\qquad\qquad\qquad\qquad$ B3X3 $\quad \leq \quad$ b3

	X0	X1	X2	X3
b0	A0	A1	A2	A3
b1		B1		
b2			B2	
b3				B3

	X0	X1	X2	X3
X0	1	1	1	1
X1	1	1	1	1
X2	1	1	1	1
X3	1	1	1	1

Source: Burton and Obel (1984: 24).

Figure 11.3   Burton and Obel's linear programming model

to the agents. The noteworthy difference is that whereas T^R is an $n \times n$ matrix, T^A will be an $m \times m$ matrix, where m is the number of agents in the organization. Since T^A embodies both a decomposition of the overall goal into clusters of tasks as well as an allocation of these task clusters among the agents, it is a concise abstract representation of a division of labor (Raveendran et al. 2012). Thus to consider the original example provided by Adam Smith, pin making could be divided into 'eighteen distinct operations, which, in some manufactories are all performed by distinct hands, though in others, the same man will sometimes perform two or three of them' (Smith 1776: 5). These would correspond to two different T^A of dimensions $m = 18$ and $m < 18$ respectively, for the same underlying T^R.

Given an allocation of tasks to a dyad of agents A and B, interdependence between the agents exists when the returns to A from A's actions depend on B's actions and vice versa. This conceptualization of interdependence between agents appears explicitly in the analysis of reward interdependence (Kelley & Thibaut 1978), power (Emerson 1962; Pfeffer & Salancik 1978) and in game theory in general (e.g. Von Neuman & Morgenstern 1944).

In Puranam et al. (2012) we show that interdependence between tasks is neither necessary nor sufficient for interdependence between the agents (that these tasks are allocated to) to arise. Unlike task interdependence, interdependence between agents depends entirely on a key feature of their reward structure: incentive breadth. This refers to the level of aggregation at which an agent's actions (or their results) are measured and rewarded. In the case of two agents, narrow incentives correspond to the reward of individual actions or their results in a manner that makes them independent of the other agent's actions. Broad incentives correspond to the reward of individual actions or their results in a manner that makes them at least partly dependent on the other agent's actions. For instance if A provides a critical input to B and B is measured on the final output, then the reward structure is de facto broad for B unless B's actions can be measured and rewarded independently of whether A has provided the critical input. Agents are interdependent when they face broad incentives, but are independent when they face narrow incentives.

Put differently, interdependence between tasks is assessed by examining the value function that represents the combined system of tasks, while interdependence between agents depends on the reward function of the agents. Since in general these will not be identical, there will be a corresponding divergence between task and agent interdependence. For instance, even if the tasks assigned to each agent are interdependent, the agents may be measured and rewarded narrowly for their own tasks.

Consider the pin factory example popularized by Smith (1776): as an example of independent tasks but interdependent agents, agents A and B are to produce 100 pins each (i.e. the value of A's task output does not change with B's output, and vice versa) but they are paid only if a total of 200 pins are produced. On the other hand, if this was a specialized production process, A and B could be tasked to produce a total of 300 pins, of which A produces the tails and B produces the heads. In this case, the tasks are clearly interdependent; however, if both A and B are rewarded on their individual output, respectively (i.e. A is rewarded if she produces 300 tails regardless of B's performance and vice versa), the agents are effectively independent.

Thus, the division of labor creates interdependence between tasks as well as between the agents to whom the tasks are assigned, even though these two patterns of interdependence may not be identical. Note that the same principles apply if we replace this two-task two-agent case, with the n-task m–agent case. Every dyad of agents can be rewarded with narrow or broad incentives, and their allocated tasks or clusters of tasks can be interdependent or independent with those allocated to other agents.

IMPEDIMENTS TO THE INTEGRATION OF EFFORT

The problem of the integration of effort may be stated as getting the agents to take actions that maximize the value of the system as a whole, for a given division of labor. For instance, integration in a multi-department organization has been defined as the 'quality of the state of collaboration that exists among departments that are required to achieve unity of effort by the demands of the environment' (Lawrence & Lorsch 1967: 11).

Why is it harder to achieve coordinated action around certain patterns of interdependence but not others? There are a number of reasons why the integration of effort may be problematic, but it is helpful to think of these as falling broadly into two categories, related to 'knowledge' and 'motives' of the agents, respectively (Hoopes & Postrel 1999).

Within each, we can also distinguish between situations where the agents are interdependent versus when they are independent.

Skill and Coordination Problems

Bounded rationality (Simon 1945) implies that there are limits to the agents' knowledge of how to perform their assigned task (for the moment we will assume that the right actions generate rewards large enough to cover their costs of efforts). Inadequate knowledge of the agents may act as an impediment to the integration of effort in two ways. Consider first the case where the agents are independent of each other. There may be a failure of integration if an agent does not know enough to perform the task cluster assigned to them perfectly. Even though the agents are independent of each other, the impact of this skill problem on the integration of effort in the system depends crucially on the interdependence of tasks in the system. In a system with highly interdependent tasks, skill failures at individual tasks will have different implications for system performance compared to that in a system with independent tasks.

Returning to the pin factory example, absent specialization in the case where agents produce 100 pins each, a daily output of 100 fully functional pins is possible even if B (alone) lacked the necessary skill; however, in the case where agents are specialized, the 300 faulty heads produced by B due to a lack of skill will reduce the total value of the tasks to zero, even if A produces 300 perfect pin tails.

Now consider the case where the agents are interdependent. A knowledge-related impediment to integration of effort arises if the agents' interdependence takes the form that the optimal action of each agent depends on a prediction of what the other agents will do. Puranam et al. (2012) describe this as a situation of epistemic interdependence. For two agents A and B, if the optimal action of each agent depends on a prediction of what the other agent will do, there is epistemic interdependence between them. Given epistemic interdependence, for the agents to coordinate their actions requires predictive knowledge. A's predictive knowledge about B enables A to act as if he could accurately predict B's actions.

In this view, a coordination failure is a failure to predict the actions of another in situations where such a prediction is essential for optimal action by oneself. In other words, a coordination failure occurs when there is epistemic interdependence but the agent(s) do not possess the necessary predictive knowledge. (To scale this up to the *n*-task *m*-agent case, we can examine the predictive knowledge requirements for all agents jointly.)

Informally, we often equate coordination failures with communication challenges, and the notion of epistemic interdependence helps to see why this intuition is robust, for two reasons. Firstly, a failure of communication prevents the formation of predictive knowledge; and secondly, communication itself can indeed be seen as a coordination problem, as the modern view of linguistics does: when communicating, I need to predict which among several possible meanings you chose to attach to the words you used. Talk, if it is to be understood, is seldom cheap, because communication itself is a coordination problem in the domain of meaning (Clark 1996).

Note that the presence of agent interdependence is a necessary but not sufficient condition for the occurrence of coordination problems. A second necessary (and jointly sufficient with the first) condition regards the timing of the actions – only if at least one agent (who faces broad incentives) needs to act before knowing the other agent's actions will epistemic interdependence exist. For instance, if A provides an input to B and both are rewarded on final output, both agents are interdependent with each other; but only A needs predictive knowledge about B (this is the familiar backward induction problem).

To make this concrete, consider again the pin factory with independent tasks but interdependent agents (i.e. the agents are jointly rewarded only if 200 pins are produced at the end of the day and each agent is to produce 100 pins). If A works the morning shift and B in the afternoon, and assume B can see A's total output before he starts his shift, he can decide to take the rest of the day off if A has not reached her target. However, A will have to make inferences (based, for instance on prior experience of working with B) regarding B's productivity since her final reward will be contingent on B producing his 100 pins once A has completed her part.

Skill and coordination problems have been central to classical organization theory (March & Simon 1958). Both individual competence as well as predictive knowledge can be formed through what have been broadly termed 'information processing activities': communication, mutual observation, learning and (joint) decision making by the agents (e.g. Galbraith 1973; March & Simon 1958; Tushman & Nadler 1978). While communication is the most obvious means of creating predictive knowledge (so much so that we sometimes loosely equate communication with coordination), it is not the only one. For instance, Srikanth and Puranam (2011) in their study of coordination processes in business process offshoring discuss 'tacit coordination mechanisms' that allow the formation of predictive knowledge across locations through enhancing observability of context, actions, and outcomes rather than through direct communication.

More generally, predictive knowledge need not involve shared knowledge of any order. For instance, precedents (actions used in the past that are psychologically prominent) and conventions (established principles of action that are not questioned) are forms of predictive knowledge that may arise from shared knowledge (Camerer 2003; Lewis 1969; Schelling 1960).[1] On the other hand, the mutual adaptation of agents may result in coordinated action with very little overlaps in knowledge, as each agent forms reinforced habits of action in response to the other. Interpersonal routines are quite frugal in terms of shared knowledge requirements (Cohen & Bacdayan 1994; Nelson & Winter 1982).

Even if task interdependence cannot be modified, epistemic interdependence in principle can be. The designer may understand the architecture of the system sufficiently to measure and sequence actions to reduce the need for predictive knowledge between agents. In such a system, there may be effective integration of effort even though none of the agents consciously needs to coordinate with any other. Note that a sophisticated level of architectural knowledge can help the designer choose a division of labor that makes the integration of effort easier (e.g. Baldwin & Clark 2000). In particular, by dividing the task into clusters that are mutually independent, the designer can effectively reduce interdependence between agents, while allocating the tasks to those individuals with some existing predictive knowledge of each other which will mitigate coordination problems. In general, many aspects of organization design can be seen as the interplay between the architectural knowledge of the designer and predictive knowledge among the agents (Puranam et al. 2012), though the 'designer' in some cases may of course evolve through selection.

Agency and Cooperation Problems

We now turn to a class of impediments to integration of effort that are traceable to the motivation of the agents. For the moment, we assume that there are no knowledge-related impediments to the integration of efforts: there are no skill or coordination problems. We will assume that agents are purposive (if not maximizing) and only take actions whose returns exceed their private costs. In this sense we can say that they are always 'self-interested' as long as we acknowledge that agents may derive utility from things other than cash rewards to themselves.

Thus, just as bounded rationality is the key behavioral assumption when considering impediments to integration arising from knowledge-related issues (i.e. skill and coordination problems), so the central behavioral assumption for understanding impediments to integration arising from the motives of the agents is that agents have costly actions. In general, agents do not take these costly actions unless the rewards at least cover the costs. A stronger version would assume optimization of profits (rewards minus costs).

A typical assumption also is that the agent cannot be compelled to take these costly actions (else the problem disappears); writing enforceable contracts is problematic. The problem of opportunism ('self-interest with guile'; Williamson 1975) makes contracting even more complicated because organizational contracts become harder to agree on (between agents and designers because of opportunistic bargaining with misrepresentations) and implement (because of the possibility of reneging), but the challenges of creating enforceable contracts could remain in principle even without opportunism, due to bounded rationality alone (Hodgson 2004).

As before, we will first consider the case of independent agents. In the simplest case, if the reward structure does not cover the agent's costs of efforts (and possible disutility from risk), then the agent's assigned task will not be performed adequately. For instance if the actions are not easy to contract on, and only noisy outcomes can be observed and rewarded, we get the standard principal–agent problem (for instance, see Levinthal 1988). Even though the agents are independent of each other, the impact of this agency problem on the integration of effort in the system depends crucially on the interdependence of tasks in the system. In a system with highly interdependent tasks, agency failures at individual tasks will have different implications for system performance compared to a system with independent tasks.

Returning to the pin factory example, the impact of a poorly designed reward structure for A will have more serious consequences with specialization than without. Consider the case where A produces 300 faulty heads compared to A producing 100 faulty pins. In the former case the day's production will fall to zero, while in the latter A's faulty output leaves B's output (of 100 pins) unaffected. Note that this outcome is indistinguishable from the occurrence of coordination failure, though the root cause of collaboration failure is not the same.

In the case of interdependence between agents, given that an agent will not take costly actions unless the rewards compensate these efforts sufficiently, the key question is how interdependence between agents affects their rewards and costs of efforts. In other words, interdependence between agents may cause an agent to be less likely to take an action either because their own reward is lowered because of the other's actions or because their cost of effort is raised by the other's action. Conversely, interdependence may cause an agent to be more likely to take an action if the other agent's action either raises the rewards or lowers the costs of efforts. In game-theoretic terms, interdependence between the agents may thus make their efforts strategic complements or strategic substitutes (Gibbons 1992).

Thus a key dimension of interdependence between agents that matters for the integration of efforts is whether the returns to one agent's actions increase or decrease based on the other agent's actions. We may think of this as the 'valence of interdependence': whether their actions are strategic complements (positive valence of interdependence) or strategic substitutes (negative valence). This valence describes the degree of identity of interests (Grandori 2001: 245). The magnitude of this valence depends both on the complementarity or substitution between the agents' efforts in the production function of each agent, and on the incentive breadth.[2] To see this, consider two agents A and B, each assigned a task. Assume first that A is rewarded on the performance of his own task. Let B's actions improve the returns to A's actions because their efforts are complements in A's production function. Then all else being equal, as the magnitude of this complementarity effect increases, A is more likely to invest effort in performing his task. Now consider the impact of letting B partly share in the rewards for A's task performance. Then the returns to A's actions effectively decline, and A is less likely to invest effort in his task.[3]

When the valence of interdependence between agents is such that it lowers their willingness to invest efforts and thus impedes the integration of effort, we have a cooperation problem. Consider the well-known phenomenon of free-riding: the issue is that adding agents decreases the probability of each agent taking the desirable action from the systemic perspective (see Prendergast 1999: 39–44 for a review of empirical tests of free-riding). This is because adding agents dilutes the reward function for each agent without creating complementarities in their efforts; the valence of interdependence is weakened. An extensive literature in agency theory explores various solutions to this problem, such as the use of monitoring and sanctions (Alchian & Demsetz 1972); target rate incentives (Holmstrom 1982; Petersen 1992); social norms that encourage contributions and sanction non-contribution to a public good (e.g., Ostrom 1990); the creation of 'Coasean islands' – institutions in which transaction costs are reduced sufficiently between the potential beneficiaries of a public good to be able to pool their efforts effectively (Coase 1960); the existence of privileged groups that value the public good highly enough to contribute regardless of the (non-) contributions of others (Olson 1971); and expected future interactions (Baker at al. 2002). Scholars investigating free-riding in the social psychology tradition argue that communication enables individuals to better understand the impact of their actions on individual and group outcomes through a process of discussion and learning (Dawes 1980), and that group identity induces individuals to take the group interest into account when making their own decisions (Bouas & Komorita 1996; Kollock 1998).

These diverse approaches to resolving free-riding problems broadly fall into two categories: either they modify the rewards or costs of effort to compensate for the negative valence of interdependence in a multi-agent system with shared rewards (group identity, monitoring and sanctions work in this way), or they create or highlight positive valence (communication, repeated interaction or target rate incentives work in this way).

AN 'INTEGRATED' APPROACH TO ACHIEVING THE INTEGRATION OF EFFORT

It is well known that knowledge problems (skill and coordination) and motivation problems (agency and cooperation) are independently sufficient to create integration failures (Camerer & Knez 1996, 1997; Heath & Staudenmayer 2000). For instance, consider the canonical cooperation problem: the famous prisoner's dilemma. In a standard two-agent prisoner's dilemma, the existence of both a temptation pay-off and a sucker penalty imply that the rewards from acting cooperatively for either agent are never large enough relative to the rewards from defecting. However, there is no epistemic interdependence between them because each agent has a dominant strategy: their optimal actions do not depend on a prediction of the other agent's actions. As others have noted, if there were strong synergies from cooperating such that the temptation pay-off would disappear, the game would cease to be a prisoner's dilemma (Camerer & Knez 1996, 1997). If the sucker's penalty still existed it would become a pure coordination problem – such as stag hunt – in which the valence of interdependence encourages cooperation, but a lack of predictive knowledge may still deter its achievement.

Note that with perfect predictive knowledge, it is still possible for the agents to coordinate successfully on a bad outcome from the perspective of the system designer, as in the case of two employees who collude to shirk on the job. To analytically separate coordination problems from cooperation problems, we believe it is important to define successful coordination independently of whether integration of effort is achieved; rather, successful coordination is defined in terms of mutual predictability of action. If this mutual predictability leads the agents to take actions that maximize the value of the system as a whole, then it leads to successful integration of efforts. Thus, sufficiently positive valence of interdependence and the existence of predictive knowledge are both necessary to achieve the integration of efforts.[4]

These analytical distinctions notwithstanding, it is probably true that in the real world, problems of organization design do not come neatly and separately packaged into knowledge and motivation problems. Interdependence between agents may simultaneously have a valence that discourages the agents from investing effort into their own tasks, as well as creating doubts about how to invest those efforts because of epistemic interdependence.

One obvious consequence of this is that organization designs that ignore one or the other aspect may do more harm than good. Consider the practice in many multi-unit organizations of creating 'broad' firm-level incentives to encourage inter-unit collaboration, realization of synergies and so on. However, to the extent that each sub-unit cannot influence the other unit's output as effectively as its own, total output may decline with such incentives, relative to the case where each unit is rewarded only for its own output. This is typically the case in organizations where sub-units are specialized to different tasks, and the coordination challenges between specialists implies that inter-unit collaboration effort is in general less productive than production effort. Kretschmer and Puranam (2008) show formally that ignoring the coordination challenges that arise when stimulating collaboration between specialized units through broad incentives not only impedes the achievement of synergies, but could lower organizational performance below the levels achieved when such synergies were simply ignored.

Integration with an Omniscient Designer

Even though coordination and cooperation problems are analytically distinct, their solutions may be interlinked in complex ways. Take the simplest case, in which the designer knows what the ideal actions of the agents should be but cannot communicate this to the agents, and agents pursue, if not maximize, (subjective) expected utility. Such agents, in a situation of epistemic interdependence, may be only able to estimate a probability distribution over the other agent's actions. If the probability of an agent taking the action desired by the designer increases in its expected utility to the agent, then it is trivial to show that the designer's investments in increasing the agents' predictive knowledge or in increasing the valence of interdependence between them are complements in terms of improving the overall integration of effort. (Also see Hardin and Higgins 1996 for a discussion of how improvements in predictive knowledge may effectively increase the valence of interdependence.) Yet in practice, organizational arrangements to improve predictive knowledge may simultaneously suppress motivation.

Consider the problem of post-merger integration in technology acquisitions: the acquisitions of small entrepreneurial firms by larger firms for their technological capabilities (Puranam et al. 2006). In such acquisitions, unlike mega-mergers, there are no gains from eliminating redundancies and consolidating administrative overheads. Yet acquirers often structurally integrate such acquisitions – fold them into existing organizational units – despite the organizational disruptions and weakening of incentives this creates. Structural integration results in common procedures, common goals and common authority between acquired and acquiring firms' technical employees, as they are located within common organizational units. This enhances predictive knowledge as all interacting parties adhere to the same procedures, are aware of a common goal and are directed by the same source of authority. This strong 'coordination effect' however comes at the cost of disruption and demotivation within the formerly autonomous acquired organization. These dual effects of structural integration are well documented. There is empirical evidence showing that following structural integration in technology acquisitions, the employees in the target organization may file fewer patents, though their work may be cited more often by the acquirer's employees (Puranam & Srikanth 2007); initial products based on the target's technology may have lower hazards of being launched, but conditional on the first one being launched future versions may appear more rapidly (Puranam et al. 2006). When acquirer and target have a significant pre-acquisition overlap in technical knowledge (a basis for predictive knowledge between them), then they are less likely to engage in structural integration in the first place (Puranam et al. 2009).

Thus, modifying either the valence of interdependence or the agent's predictive knowledge may be two alternative means of achieving integration of effort when the designer knows what actions the agents should take.

Integration with a Boundedly Rational Designer

Obtaining integration of effort when at least the designer knows what the agents ought to do is already challenging. This may be seen as an execution problem. The more general, and unfortunately more complicated case arises when even the designer does not know what the ideal actions for the agents are (described by Grandori & Soda 2006 as epistemic uncertainty), so that we confront a search problem. Organizational life is replete with instances of specialists from different domains searching for optimal interdependent actions. For instance, managers within a multi-business company, despite incentives to pursue synergies, may have limited knowledge of the complementarities in production or the cross-elasticities of demand across divisions. Teams of engineers developing subsystems may know that certain design choices in each subsystem could lead to dramatically enhanced performance of the system as a whole, but do not know which ones. Because the boundaries of specialization often constitute barriers to interpretation, these joint search problems are characterized by communication constraints arising from differences in perspectives, jargon, languages and technical backgrounds in addition to ignorance about how the key actors are actually interdependent (Lawrence & Lorsch 1967; Dougherty 1992; Heath & Staudenmayer 2000).

A boundedly rational designer may still be able to implement useful organizational design mechanisms in at least three ways in such situations. Firstly, some structural solutions may facilitate communication between specialists, thus improving more effective joint search (see also Foss 2007 for a review of the knowledge governance perspective on such mechanisms); for instance the delegation of decision rights to task forces or overlapping production and development teams (Clark & Fujimoto 1991).

Secondly, one may argue that merely sensitizing the agents to the fact of their interdependence (without being able to tell them how to act) may still be a major contribution that an organization designer can make towards the integration of effort. Heath and Staudenmayer (2000) present a fascinating series of examples of 'partition focus' – a tendency by individuals to place more emphasis on the task division process and less to the process of achieving the integration of efforts; as well as 'component focus' – a tendency to focus exclusively on the components tasks so created. Can a designer help in these situations? We speculate that the existence of interdependence can only be discovered as the agents perform their actions and an exogenously generated change in the value of their action is noticed. Thus, one way in which a designer may be useful is to help highlight such surprises for the agents, and rule out incorrect alternative explanations (such as bad luck) and improve the cross-visibility of the actions of one set of agents to another (Srikanth & Puranam 2011).

Thirdly, even if the designer cannot improve communication or cross-visibility of actions, the designer can provide a common (possibly faulty) prior to the agents rather than let the agents work with a mix of good and bad priors; and this can be advantageous when the agents adapt rapidly to feedback. Puranam and Swamy (2011) develop a formal model of agents engaged in joint search through a trial and error (reinforcement learning) process, in which specialists from different domains learn how to make interdependent choices. They analyze when and why faulty initial representations can be useful in such learning processes, and show that when learning is rapid but communication is restricted, faulty initial representations held by all agents can suppress superstitious learning and promote valid learning, relative to situations where no agent has a representation, or a mix of correct and incorrect representations exists among the agents. Thus, while maintaining the assumption that the designer faces the same ignorance about the nature of interdependence as the agents, their results suggest that a designer who can influence the learning rates and/or initial representations of the agents can be useful.

For instance, the use of appropriate incentives by the designer that makes agents more responsive to immediate feedback is one way in which to control learning rates.

Thus, even if a designer does not know what actions are optimal for interdependent agents, knowing they are interdependent and designing opportunities for interaction and the build-up of predictive knowledge, or ensuring common (even if inaccurate) initial beliefs may be useful.

CONCLUSION

A defining feature of organizations is the division of labor, which generates interdependence between the agents in the organization, the tasks they perform or both. We analyse the properties of interdependence that give rise to 'motivation' and 'knowledge'-related impediments to the integration of effort. Agency and cooperation problems belong in the former category; skill and coordination problems in the latter.

We argue that given interdependence between tasks, even individual skill and agency problems may generate organization-level consequences. Note that task interdependence influences the magnitude of the consequences of integration failures arising from skill and agency problems at the individual level, but cannot by itself cause integration failures. On the other hand, interdependence between agents can cause failures of integration.

Interdependence between agents gives rise to coordination problems when there is epistemic interdependence between them – when the optimal action of one depends on a prediction of the other's actions – so that the agents need predictive knowledge about each other. Interdependence between agents gives rise to cooperation problems when the valence of interdependence between agents – the extent to which the returns to one agent increase (decrease) with the actions of the other – is such as to discourage effort. The valence of interdependence and epistemic interdependence are two distinct dimensions of interdependence between agents, which is why cooperation and coordination problems can logically arise independently of each other. Thus, sufficiently positive valence of interdependence and the existence of predictive knowledge are both necessary to achieve the integration of efforts.

This gives rise to several implications for organization design. Firstly, it is obvious that ignoring either kind of impediment to the integration of effort can be counterproductive. Secondly, modifying either the valence of interdependence or the agent's predictive knowledge may be two alternative means of achieving integration of effort when the designer knows what actions the agents should take (an execution problem).

However, an organization designer can also be useful despite ignorance of what the agents ought to do (a search problem). Firstly, some structural solutions may facilitate communication between specialists, thus improving more effective joint search. Secondly, a designer may improve the cross-visibility of the actions of one set of agents to another and make them aware of their interdependence. Thirdly, even if the designer cannot improve communication or cross-visibility of actions, the designer can provide a common (possibly faulty) prior to the agents rather than let the agents work with a mix of good and bad priors; and this can be advantageous when the agents adapt rapidly to feedback.

A central idea in the study of organization design, and indeed in many perspectives in organization theory, is that organizations 'solve' the problems of cooperation and coordination that arise when integrating the efforts of interdependent actors – albeit with varying degrees of success. In this chapter we review and clarify commonly applied concepts, such as task and agent interdependence, as well as detail the sources and consequences of coordination and cooperation problems faced by interdependent agents. While we have noted a few initial steps towards developing a deeper understanding of how knowledge and motivation problems may be jointly analyzed, this remains a rich area of further inquiry into the links between interdependence and organization design.

NOTES

*   This chapter draws on joint work with several co-authors. Carliss Baldwin, Rich Burton and Dan Levinthal provided extensive feedback on the related work this chapter draws on. Donal Crilly and Niro Sivanathan offered useful suggestions on this draft. Puranam acknowledges funding from the European Research Council under Grant # 241132 for the Foundations of Organization Design project.
1.   When coordinated action arises from shared knowledge, it may also be of interest to understand exactly to how many orders knowledge must be shared for coordinated action. This is a question central to the research in epistemic game theory (e.g. Aumann & Brandenburger 1995), but one which we are agnostic about here.
2.   The magnitude of the complementarity/substitution effects in the production function can also be modeled in a reduced form as the 'gains from integration' (Kretschmer & Puranam 2008). The idea is that regardless of whether there is substitution or complementarity between actions, there is value in 'managing' this interdependence collaboratively: discovering it, modifying it, redistributing the costs and benefits, and so on. The notion of 'synergy' in corporate strategy is typically used in this reduced form sense.
3.   When the incentive structure is symmetric across A and B, then an additional trade-off arises in that broadening incentives may make B's contributions to A's task increase but at the same time may force A to share some of the rewards. See Kretschmer and Puranam (2008) for a formal analysis.
4.   However, they may not be jointly sufficient. Consider a stag hunt game in which each player correctly predicts that the other is sufficiently doubtful about the other player's intentions, leading to both agents selecting the lower equilibrium. What appears to be missing in this game is common knowledge of payoff structure – if this can be presumed, then predictive knowledge would lead to the selection of the high equilibrium.

REFERENCES

Alchian, A.A. and H. Demsetz (1972), 'Production, information costs, and economic organization', *American Economic Review*, **62**(5), 777–795.

Aumann, R. and A. Brandenburger (1995), 'Epistemic conditions for Nash equilibrium', *Econometrica*, **63**(5), 1161–1180.

Baldwin, C.Y., and K.B. Clark (2000), *Design Rules*, Cambridge, MA: MIT Press.

Baker, G., R. Gibbons and K.J. Murphy (2002), 'Relational contracts and the theory of the firm', *Quarterly Journal of Economics*, **117**(1), 39–84.

Bouas, K.S. and S.S. Komorita (1996), 'Group discussion and cooperation in social dilemmas', *Personality and Social Psychology Bulletin*, **22**, 1144–1150.

Burton, R.M. and B. Obel (1984), *Designing Efficient Organizations: Modelling and Experimentation*, Amsterdam: North-Holland.

Camerer, C. (2003), *Behavioural Game Theory: Experiments in Strategic Interaction*, Princeton, NJ: Princeton University Press.

Camerer, C. and M. Knez (1996), 'Coordination, organizational boundaries and fads in business practices', *Industrial and Corporate Change*, **5**(1), 89–112.

Clark, H. (1996), *Using Language*, Cambridge: Cambridge University Press.

Clark, Kim B. and T. Fujimoto (1991), *Product Development Performance: Strategy, Organisation and Management in the World Auto Industry*, Boston, MA: Harvard University Press.

Coase, R. (1960), 'The problem of social cost', *Journal of Law and Economics*, **3**(1), 1–44.

Cohen, M.D. and P. Bacdayan (1994), 'Organizational routines are stored as procedural memory: evidence from a laboratory study', *Organization Science*, **5**(4), 554–568.

Dawes, R.M. (1980), 'Social dilemmas', *Annual Review of Psychology*, **31**, 169–193.

Dosi, G., D.A. Levinthal and L. Marengo (2003), 'Bridging contested terrain: linking incentive-based and learning perspectives on organizational evolution', *Industrial and Corporate Change*, **12**(2), 413–436.

Dougherty, D. (1992), 'Interpretive barriers to successful product innovation in large firms', *Organization Science*, **3**(2), 179–202.

Emerson, R.M. (1962), 'Power-dependence relations', *American Sociological Review*, **27**(1), 31–41.

Eppinger, S.D. (1991), 'Model-based approaches to managing concurrent engineering', *Journal of Engineering Design*, **2**, 283–290.

Foss, N. (2007), 'The Emerging Knowledge governance approach: challenges and characteristics', *Organization*, **14**(1), 29–52.

Galbraith, J.R. (1973), *Designing Complex Organizations*, Reading, MA: Addison-Wesley.

Gibbons, R. (1992), *Game Theory for Applied Economists*, Princeton, NJ: Princeton University Press.

Grandori, A. (2001), 'The configuration of organization: a generalized model', *Organization and Economic Behavior*, London and New York: Routledge.

Grandori, A. and Furnari, S. (2008), 'A chemistry of organization: combinatory analysis and design', *Organization Studies*, **29**, 459–485.

Grandori, A. and G. Soda (2006), 'A relational approach to organization design', *Industry and Innovation*, **13**(2), 151–172.

Grant, R.M. (1996), 'Toward a knowledge based theory of the firm', *Strategic Management Journal*, **17**, 109–122.

Hardin, C.D. and E.T. Higgins (1996), 'Shared reality: how social verification makes the subjective objective', in E.T. Higgins and R.M. Sorrentino (eds), *Handbook of Motivation and Cognition: The Interpersonal Context (Vol. 3)*, New York: Guilford Press, pp. 28–84.

Heath, C. and N. Staudenmayer (2000), 'Coordination neglect: how lay theories of organizing complicate coordination in organizations', *Research in Organizational Behavior*, **22**, 53–191.

Hodgson, G.M. (2004), 'Opportunism is not the only reason why firms exist: why an explanatory emphasis on opportunism may mislead management strategy', *Industrial and Corporate Change*, **13**(2), 401–418.

Holmstrom, B. (1982), 'Moral hazard in teams', *Bell Journal of Economics*, **13**(2), 324–340.

Holmstrom, B. and J. Roberts (1998), 'The boundaries of the firm revisited', *Journal of Economic Perspectives*, **12**(4), 73.

Hoopes, D.G. and S. Postrel (1999), 'Shared knowledge, "glitches", and product development performance', *Strategic Management Journal*, **20**(9), 837–865.

Kelley, H.H. and J.W. Thibaut (1978), *Interpersonal Relations: A Theory of Interdependence*, New York: John Wiley & Son.

Kollock, P. (1998), 'Social dilemmas: the anatomy of cooperation', *Annual Review of Sociology*, **24**(1), 183.

Kretschmer, T. and P. Puranam (2008), 'Integration through incentives in differentiated organizations', *Organization Science*, **19**(6), 860–875.

Lawrence, P.R. and J.W. Lorsch (1967), *Organization and Environment: Managing Differentiation and Integration*, Boston, MA: Harvard Graduate School of Business Administration.

Leijonhufvud, A. (1986), 'Capitalism and the factory system', in R.N. Langlois (ed.), *Economics as a Process: Essays in the New Institutional Economics*, New York: Cambridge University Press, pp. 203–223.

Levinthal, D. (1988), 'A survey of agency models of organizations', *Journal of Economics Behavior and Organizations*, **9**, 153–185.

Levinthal, D.A. (1997), 'Adaptation on rugged landscapes', *Management Science*, **43**(7), 934.

Lewis, D. (1969), *Convention: A Philosophical Study*, Cambridge, MA: Harvard University Press.

March, J.G. and H.A. Simon (1958), *Organizations*, Cambridge, MA: Wiley.

Milgrom, P. and J. Roberts (1990), 'The economics of modern manufacturing: technology, strategy, and organization', *American Economic Review*, **80**(3), 511–528.

Nelson, R. and S. Winter (1982), *An Evolutionary Theory of Economic Change*, Cambridge, MA: Harvard University Press.

Newell, A. and H. Simon (1972), *Human Problem Solving*, Englewood Cliffs, NJ: Prentice Hill.

Olson, M. (1971), *The Logic of Collective Action: Public Goods and the Theory of Groups*, Cambridge, MA: Harvard University Press.

Ostrom, E. (1990), *Governing the Commons: The Evolution of Institutions for Collective Action*, Cambridge: Cambridge University Press.

Petersen, T. (1992), 'Individual, collective, and systems rationality in work groups: dilemmas and market–type solutions', *American Journal of Sociology*, **98**(3), 469–510.

Pfeffer, J. and G.R. Salancik (1978), *The External Control of Organizations: A Resource Dependence Perspective*, New York: Harper & Row.

Prendergast, C. (1999), 'The provision of incentives in firms', *Journal of Economic Literature*, **37**, 7–63.

Puranam, P. and K. Srikanth (2007), 'What they know vs. what they do: how acquirers leverage technology acquisitions', *Strategic Management Journal*, **28**(8), 805–825.

Puranam, P. and M. Swamy (2011), 'Expedition without maps: why faulty initial representations may be useful in joint discovery problems', Working Paper, London Business School, London.

Puranam, P., M. Raveendran and T. Knudsen (2012), 'Organization design: the epistemic interdependence perspective', *Academy of Management Review*, **37**(3), 419–440.

Puranam, P., H. Singh and S. Chaudhuri (2009), 'Integrating acquired capabilities: when structural integration is (un)necessary', *Organization Science*, **20**(2), 313–328.

Puranam, P., H. Singh and M. Zollo (2006), 'Organizing for innovation: managing the coordination-autonomy dilemma in technology acquisitions', *Academy of Management Journal*, **49**(2), 263–280.

Raveendran, M., P. Puranam and M. Warglien (2012), 'The emergence of the division of labor: a qualitative lab study', Working Paper, London Business School.

Schelling, T. (1960), *The Strategy of Conflict*, Cambridge, MA: Harvard University Press.

Sendova-Franks, A.B. and N.R. Franks (1999), 'Self-assembly, self-organization and division of labor', *Phil Trans R Soc Lond B*, **354**, 1395–1405.

Simon, H.A. (1945), *Administrative Behavior*, New York: Macmillan Press.

Smith, A. (1776), *An Inquiry into the Nature and Causes of the Wealth of Nations*, 8th edn, London: W. Strahan and Cadell/Penguin Classics.

Srikanth, K. and P. Puranam (2011), 'Integrating distributed work: comparing task design, communication and tacit coordination mechanisms', *Strategic Management Journal*, **32**(8), 849–874.

Steward, D.V. (1981), *Systems Analysis and Management: Structure, Strategy and Design*, New York: Petrocelli Books.

Thompson, J.D. (1967), *Organizations in Action*, New York: McGraw-Hill.

Tushman, M.L. and D.A. Nadler (1978), 'Information processing as an integrating concept in organizational design', *Academy of Management Review*, **3**(3), 613–624.

Von Neumann, J. and O. Morgenstern (1944), *Theory of Games and Economic Behavior*, Princeton, NJ: Princeton University Press.

De Waal, F. (2001), *Tree of Origin: What Primate Behavior Can Tell Us about Human Social Evolution*, Cambridge, MA: Harvard University Press.

De Waal, F. (2005), *Our Inner Ape*, New York: Riverhead Books.

Williamson, O.E. (1975), *Markets and Hierarchies: Analysis and Antitrust Implications*, New York: Free Press.

12. Dynamics of organizational structure
Nicholas Argyres and Todd R. Zenger

Large firms' organizational structures have undergone significant changes in the past 25–30 years. In this chapter, we examine key economic drivers of these changes that are external to the firm: shifts in technology, in product markets, and in capital markets. Our focus is on ways in which these shifts have led firms to adopt more centralized or more decentralized structures. However, we also highlight the motivation for, and efficiency of, structural change that occurs in the absence of shifts in external drivers. We emphasize the idea that because organizational structure choices are discrete, while the dimensionality of organizational performance is continuous and multidimensional, organization structures may endogenously oscillate between centralization and decentralization. This implies that scholars and managers must develop a more dynamic perspective on organizational design.

INTRODUCTION

Over the past 25 years, scholars and journalists alike have noted dramatic changes in the organizational structure of large firms. Two (possibly related) phenomena can be distinguished. On the one hand, evidence suggests a dramatic 'flattening' in large United States (US) firms' hierarchies (e.g., Rajan & Wulf 2006). On the other hand, accounts in the business and academic press describe a growing frequency of corporate reorganizations of various kinds (e.g., Beer et al. 1990; Capelli et al. 1997; Doppler & Lauterburg 2010). P&G (Procter & Gamble), a generally successful US consumer products firm, provides an example of this accelerating pace of corporate re-organization. From 1955 to 1987, P&G maintained essentially the same organizational structure: a product-based multidivisional form (M-form) in the US, and a country-based M-form for its European operations. From 1987 to 2005, however, the company made four major changes to its structure, successively adopting a matrix structure in the US, a product-based M-form in Europe, a global matrix structure, and finally a global product-based M-form (Piskorski & Spadini 2007).

In this chapter, we examine the primary economic drivers of these kinds of organization structure changes. We highlight three key environmental determinants of structural change: technological change, product market change, and capital market change. We specifically explore how each of these environmental forces has promoted shifts in the design of organizations. However, we also highlight the motivation for and efficiency of structural change even in the absence of any environmental shifts. Here we emphasize the idea that organizational structure choices are both rather discrete and rather clumsy, while the dimensionality of performance is both continuous and multidimensional. The discrete organizational forms available are simply unable to match the dimensionality of performance required.

ORGANIZATIONAL STRUCTURE AND TECHNOLOGICAL CHANGE

As John Roberts (2004) noted, 'In terms of its impact, not just on economic activity, but also on human life as a whole, the multidivisional organizational design must rank as one of the major innovations of the last century.' The M-form swept the corporate world during the second half of the twentieth century, and appears to maintain its dominance today (Strikwerda & Stoelhorst 2009). The M-form decomposes the firm's activities into product- or geography-based divisions rather than business functions. This allows the firm to achieve better accountability and therefore higher-powered incentives for its managers than a function-based decomposition (Williamson 1975, 1985), while also freeing corporate-level managers from resolving interfunctional conflicts so as to focus on longer-term initiatives (Chandler 1962). The M-form thereby facilitates significant decentralization of decision-making relative to function-based organization (also known as the U or unitary form).

It has long been recognized, however, that there is substantial variety amongst M-form firms, reflecting the different degrees of decomposability in various firms' activities. Moreover, there are a wide range of configurations from which to choose, with various functions either centralized or decentralized, or both. For example, many large industrial firms consist of multiple divisions that can all benefit significantly from common research and development (R&D) activities. Such firms attempt to coordinate and integrate R&D efforts that promise to benefit more than one division by forming a centralized R&D unit within the multidivisional structure, even though this weakens incentives to some degree. It appears that the most common structure among large technologically progressive US firms involves maintaining both a centralized R&D unit as well as divisional units (e.g., Argyres & Silverman 2004).

It also appears that in many industries over the past 30 years or so, firm activities have become less decomposable by product or geography (e.g., Grandori 2009). This is sometimes due to technological changes in the firms' environments that are relatively wide in scope and applicable across organization subunits. For example, advances in electronics and computer technology, and their applications in communications, robotics, sensors, and the like have affected multiple product divisions of individual M-form firms simultaneously (e.g., Doz et al. 1987). These kinds of technological changes pose a challenge for M-form firms, because pure M-forms lack the organizational mechanisms needed to facilitate common adoption and standard-setting for such new technologies. While some firms respond to such changes by adopting cross-division technology committees (e.g., Sloan 1964), the lack of authority of such committees sometimes leads firms to strengthen the coordinating role of corporate management in order to achieve the benefits of standardization, albeit again at the cost of reduced incentive intensity (e.g., Argyres 1995).

Some of the recent changes in organizational structure we observe may thus be due to the technological revolution in electronics and computer technology, as firms have moved to coordinate the deployment or infusion of technology or common technology standards within their divisions. The deployment of common information technology platforms such as ERP (enterprise resource planning) systems may also be implicated in recent efforts to centralize.

This set of explanations for centralization, however, only explains a temporary shift toward centralization. Once products or services are successfully computerized, or once common information technology (IT) systems are successfully adopted, the firm would be expected to move back toward decentralization in order to capture the benefits of greater autonomy, accountability, and corresponding incentive intensity.

Advances in information technology may also have longer-lasting effects on large firms' organizational structures, however. Yet the net direction of these effects is unclear in the literature. One the one hand, it has been argued that advanced information technology such as common databases and enterprise planning systems lead to 'permanent' decentralization, as the horizontal communication and coordination functions of middle management are substituted for by the technology (e.g., Malone et al. 1987; Zenger & Hesterly 1997; Argyres 1999; Crémer et al. 2007). Sophisticated ERP systems may provide much of this coordination. These trends have been offered as a key explanation for the 'flattening firm'.

On the other hand, it has also been argued that advanced information technology, even as it leads to flattening firms, tends on net to cause centralization of key decisions (e.g., Gurbaxani & Whang 1991). Agency-theoretic logic suggests that decision-making is most efficiently allocated to agents who possess the relevant information for the decision in question, under the assumption that communication of information vertically (i.e., up and down the hierarchy) is costly (e.g., Jensen & Meckling 1992). Because information technology reduces the cost of vertical, in addition to horizontal, information flow, it may lead to centralization of decisions (Crémer et al. 2007). Information technology may vertically elevate decision-making, because it provides top managers easy access to both local and global information about the organization and its environment.

It is also quite possible that these two trends are not mutually exclusive. Thus, the firm may enjoy at once greater autonomy through decentralization and more centralized coordination. Thus, increased information may push responsibility down to the lowest-level units of the organization, empowering these units with a dramatically expanded scope of information and enabling their performance to be more precisely measured (Zenger and Hesterly 1997). At the same time, enhanced information at the top, and an expanded capacity to coordinate, broaden the firm's ability for central control. In other words, by essentially replacing middle management with information technology, the hierarchy is flattened and both the top and bottom of the hierarchy are empowered, leading to what looks like a hierarchy that is at once both more centralized and decentralized. Wal-Mart provides an example of precisely this dynamic. Advanced IT systems facilitate a tremendous degree of centralized coordination, yet these same IT systems yield an abundance of local information, which combined with a remarkable capacity for system-wide coordination, permit local store managers to enjoy tremendous decision-making autonomy over pricing and merchandising (e.g., Bradley et al. 2002).

Clearly, a better understanding is needed of the conditions under which information technology of various kinds pushes the organization toward decentralization, or towards centralization. Or whether, alternatively, the technology has generated a trend toward both as middle managers are replaced with information technology. This kind of question regarding information technology was first raised more than 20 years ago, yet limited progress has been made due to lack of data. Firstly, it is not clear whether and which changes in organization structure we are observing are attempts to facilitate a one-time technology adoption, and which are likely longer-lasting structural shifts that take advantage of the technologies deployed. Secondly, it is not clear how information technology of various kinds is biased in its effects on organization: towards centralization or towards decentralization. However, it does appear that organizational structures are often unstable, so thinking in terms of long-lasting changes in organizational structures may miss the point. Instead, firms may move back and forth between centralization and decentralization as they are buffeted by external forces and seek to balance the trade-off between coordination for economies of scale and scope, versus accountability and incentive intensity. Such oscillation may also have its own internal dynamic, however, which we outline below.

ORGANIZATION STRUCTURE AND CHANGING PRODUCT MARKETS

Another likely source of recent change in organization structure stems from changes in product markets. One fairly clear piece of evidence that we have on this account is from Guadelupe & Wulf (2010). In a large sample study, they found that increases in product market competition faced by firms (proxied by falling trade barriers), led firms to flatten their organizational structures. One explanation is that tall structures (i.e., a bloated middle) may reflect organizational slack built up during periods of weaker product market competition. This kind of finding poses challenges for economic theories of organization, such as those mentioned above, that tend to assume more or less continuous efficiency.

Other key structural changes may be more nuanced than simply flattening, and may reflect other more nuanced changes in the environment. As mentioned above, divisions within M-form firms may experience reductions in the decomposability of their activities over time, leading them to centralize in some fashion or other. In several industry sectors, changes in the structure of demand may reduce the decomposability of activities, leading to major reorganizations. More specifically, divisions that could previously go to market quite autonomously now face a need for significant coordination in order to remain competitive. Many of these shifts in demand reflect trends toward globalization and the global homogenization of consumer preferences.

One sector in which this reduction in decomposability appears to be occurring is consumer products. P&G provides an instructive example. P&G's adoption of a matrix structure in the US was likely aimed at improving functional resource-sharing across business units in order to achieve economies of scale and scope in response to intensifying competition (Piskorski & Spadini 2007). Its adoption of a matrix structure in Europe was likely an effort to do the same in Europe, where converging consumer tastes and falling trade and regulatory barriers were making markets more homogenous continent-wide, opening up opportunities for new economies of scale and scope. P&G's eventual adoption of a global matrix likely reflected the continuing convergence of consumer tastes globally, where now the potential for economies of scale and scope existed on a global basis. The switch to a global M-form likely reflected a compromise between capturing such economies of scale and scope across broad product areas, versus achieving better accountability within product areas, especially regarding the timely roll-out of new products needed to address the intensifying competition (Piskorski & Spadini 2007). Because the product divisions in P&G today are quite broadly defined, this latest change was expected to bring net gains to the firm.

P&G's experience does not appear to be unique in the consumer products sector. Indeed, several of the major firms in that sector, including Electrolux and Unilever, have made moves away from geography-based structures to structures based on global product categories in the past 20 years or so, in an effort to globalize their brands (Kesler & Schuster 2009). The effect of these changes is in many cases to centralize authority: 'Corporate functions now demand a stronger hand in setting worldwide priorities and resources allocation . . . often sparring directly with local and global business unit demands' (Kelser & Schuster 2009: 17).

Other sectors in which changes in the structure of demand appear to be driving changes in organization structures include real estate services, information and communication technology provision, consumer electronics, and advertising. In real estate services, for example, Jones Lang LaSalle (JLL) began centralizing its structure in 2001 as its now larger and more globalized corporate customers demanded better integration of the services they were receiving from JLL's various decentralized business units. JLL began by adding a corporate-level function to its M-form organization called 'Corporate Solutions', with additional dotted line reporting relationships to this function, creating a matrix. Within a few years JLL was considering another reorganization to better integrate services on a global basis (Gulati & Marshall 2009a, 2009b).

Cisco and IBM provide examples of IT and communication companies that have experienced changes in their customers' demands that reduce the decomposability of their activities. In both cases, the firms' clients increasingly purchase multiple products and services from each firm's multiple business units, and have demanded better integration of those services. Until 2001, Cisco for example had been organized in an M-form by customer segment. With the burst of the internet bubble, the company sought cost reduction, and to do so created centralized R&D and marketing functions to take advantage of new economies of scope made available by increasing homogeneity of client demands for communication equipment. To avoid losing attention to particular client needs, Cisco later introduced numerous cross-functional committees within this structure focused on customer segments, effectively creating a matrix structure (Gulati 2007; Strikwerda & Stoelhorst 2009).

Changing market demands have impacted the ownership structure of firms, which in turn can have implications for organization structure. Von Nordenflycht (2011) argues, for example, that the emergence of the holding company in the early 1980s advertising industry was caused in part by growth in the size and scope of advertising firms' clients. As those clients (including many of the consumer products firms mentioned above) grew globally, they increasingly sought larger, more globally standardized advertising campaigns and other services to serve their increasingly homogenous customer base. Individual advertising agencies therefore became more dependent on a smaller set of clients for their revenues. Von Nordenflycht (2011) argues that one reason that the holding company emerged was to provide shareholders in advertising companies (including partners in the company) with more diversification across clients than was achievable by stand-alone advertising firms. It is likely that the introduction of the holding company has increased centralization of at least some major decisions within advertising firms, relative to the total decentralization that prevailed when agencies were fully autonomous, independently owned entities.

In summary, then, increasing competition, concentration of customer bases, and global homogenization of these customer bases have combined to push formerly decentralized M-form firms toward more centralization. In many of these cases, firms have moved from M-form toward M-forms with strong corporate functions and intervention by corporate management (sometimes called the 'CM-form' for 'centralized M-form'), in other cases the movement has been further – to matrix forms. In these cases, however, firms seem to have struggled with the loss of accountability and incentive intensity associated with CM-forms and matrix forms, and have sought to rebalance by changing again to an M-form structure, but with very large divisions that are assigned a global purview.

ORGANIZATIONAL STRUCTURE AND SHIFTING CAPITAL MARKETS

Yet another set of external influences on firms' organizational structures stems from changes in capital markets. Indeed, over the past decade capital markets appear to have had an increasingly pervasive influence on firm organizational structure through a number of distinct paths. The relationships between capital markets and organizational structure, however, have received very little attention in organizational research. Here we mention a few of the more obvious paths of influence.

Firstly, capital markets may influence organizational structure by influencing managers' choices regarding the level of firm diversification. For example, following a long period in which US capital markets appear to have rewarded unrelated diversification by large firms with elevated equity values, capital markets reversed course and began to punish diversification in the late 1970s. This led to a long period of corporate refocusing (e.g., Schleifer & Vishny 1991; Comment & Jarrell 1995; Liebeskind et al. 1996). Conglomerates using decentralized, holding company forms of organization were often broken up and replaced with more focused firms that were organized in other ways. More generally, as large firms refocused on core businesses that were more related to one another (and hence less decomposable), these firms likely increased their levels of centralization in some fashion in order to better capture the more abundant spillovers between related activities.

Other forces, however, may moderate any such capital market pressures toward centralization. For example, observers have long complained that the evolution of capital markets and the spread of rewards linked to performance in these capital markets has brought about a focus on short-term rather than long-term performance (e.g., Porter 1992). As a consequence, capital markets may discourage long-term investments such as R&D, or other large-scale centralized investments. Consistent with this, Hall (1993) found that the US stock market's valuation of R&D investment fell precipitously during the 1980s. Oriani & Sobrero's (2003) more recent meta-analysis found that R&D investments in the US are less valuable than in the past (though there may be other explanations for this result besides capital market changes). One can easily to point to several high-profile US firms that have reduced the size of their central R&D laboratories over the past 25 years or so. Any such trend would militate toward less centralization in organization structures overall, as firms reduce their efforts to innovate in the white spaces between their product divisions. However, whether short-termism has actually increased, and whether it even leads to underinvestment in R&D projects, has always been controversial (e.g., Bebchuck & Stole 1993; Abarbanell & Bernard 2000) and merits further inquiry.

The influence of capital markets on organizational structures may also vary significant by country, and specifically by the efficiency of capital markets within these countries. Thus, in developing economies where capital markets are thin, widely diversified business groups may persist in part because they provide a channel for capital allocation that substitutes for inefficient allocation by capital markets (e.g., Williamson 1975; Khanna & Yafeh 2007). Moreover, diversification may be more prevalent because capital markets are unable to provide an effective alternative path to such diversification. Hence, business groups, often family owned and structured as decentralized holding companies, are far more common in developing companies with developing capital markets. As these capital markets develop, both the level of focus and the corresponding organizational structures may shift.

Finally, the increasing importance of both institutional investors and equity analysts in the US may profoundly affect organizational structures. Institutional investors, for example, have become very important players in the US capital markets, especially since stock-market-based retirement plans began to replace traditional defined-benefit plans in the 1980s. These investment companies create a wide range of diversified investment options for their clients, which are usually large organizations offering benefits to thousands of diverse employees. In compiling these funds, fund managers appear to have strong preferences for pure play or industry-specific firms; firms though do not complicate their efforts to financially engineer either optimal diversification or industry-focused funds. These preferences in turn put pressure on firms to focus their activities, and again may push toward centralization.

Equity analysts employed by investment banks appear to have similar preferences and a similar effect on organizational structures. Analysts find it costly to learn about and assess the value of firms that are highly diversified, because of the complexity that diversification entails (Zuckerman 2000; Litov et al. 2012). Indeed, empirical evidence suggests that securities analyses are prone to pressure diversified firms to focus, in order to more neatly fit industry-focused categories (Zuckerman 2000; Litov et al. 2012). Because so many investors rely on equity analysts in making their investment decisions, these analyst preferences can be quite influential on firms' decisions regarding their levels of diversification. This analyst pressure toward focus may again result in greater centralization.

STRUCTURAL OSCILLATION

While the largely exogenous market factors discussed above may explain significant patterns of structural change, patterns of structural change may also stem from endogenous forces. More precisely, the structure of last period's organizational design may quite powerfully predict the structure of next period's design. The source of this endogeneity in design choice is a fundamental tension between the structure of performance drivers (i.e., those factors that are central to organizational performance) and the general lumpiness of effective organizational design choices (Nickerson & Zenger 2002; Boumgarden et al. 2011). For instance, scholars have widely discussed an organization's need to both explore (discover new products and services) and exploit (generate them with efficiency and quality) (Burns & Salker 1961; Cyert & March 1963; Lawrence & Lorsch 1967). As Levinthal and March (1993: 105) suggest: 'the basic problem confronting an organization is to engage in sufficient exploitation to ensure its current viability and, at the same time, devote enough energy to exploration to ensure future viability'. The underlying logic here is that exploration and exploitation operate as functional complements in delivering organizational performance (Boumgarden et al. 2011). Thus, increases in exploration are more valuable in the presence of a greater capacity for exploitation, and increases in exploitation are more valuable in the presence of a greater capacity for exploration. Hence, the firm maximizes performance by generating simultaneously high levels of both performance drivers. Such complementary performance drivers, often more precisely specified as quality, efficiency, invention, product quality, or service quality, pervade all organizations. Performance may, for instance, require an organization that is both globally efficient and locally responsive, or one that is both responsive to customers, but efficient in manufacturing.

The task of the manager is therefore to design an organization that simultaneously delivers on critical complementary performance dimensions. The guiding principle of organizational design is therefore the concept of fit, in which structures are chosen to fit the necessary organizational objectives, to deliver on the desired performance drivers, and fit the chosen strategy. Implicitly, the design literature views the manager as an organizational architect with a vast array of tools to rather finely craft the delivery of the desired outcomes. However, decades of design research also suggest that design choices are rather lumpy, governed by their own fundamental complementarities among design elements. For instance, designing an organization that generates both exploration and exploitation is considered by many to be quite impossible (Abernathy 1978; Duncan 1972; Cyert & March 1963). As a consequence, managers face an array of rather discrete choices, or at least fundamental design trade-offs.

What makes organizational design particularly challenging is that one complementary bundle of design elements promotes one performance dimension, while a distinctly different set of complementary design elements promotes the other. Thus, one design may promote exploration, while another promotes exploitation (Nickerson & Zenger 2002). Even more problematic is that frequently the design elements that promote one performance dimension generate externalities for design elements that promote another. In this manner, efforts to compile design elements that generate both (or multiple) dimensions may damage rather than enhance performance. Thus, while the distinct performance dimensions are complements in generating performance, the design elements that generate each of these performance dimensions are often non-complementary, or more precisely they demonstrate properties of negative externalities. One set of design elements undermines or precludes the effectiveness of another.

The key managerial question then is how to resolve this fundamental paradox in design. Many advocate that clever design adaptations can generate balance in performance dimensions such as exploration and exploitation (O'Reilly & Tushman 2004, 2008) and thereby largely avoid these negative externalities. The increasingly extensive organizational ambidexterity literature advocates this resolution (see Raisch et al. 2009). In this literature, the organizational architect is assumed to have a capacity to design, with some precision, mechanisms that generate multiple performance drivers.

Other scholars suggest that simply identifying and then measuring or perhaps even rewarding the competing desired performance drivers will resolve these design dilemmas. For instance, the 'balanced scorecard' literature developed and widely popularized by Kaplan and Norton (1992) essentially advocates this approach. Implicitly, this work builds on the extensive mechanism design literature in economics that views organizational design as a process of optimally configuring incentives. Thus, firms can achieve high performance by simply holding individuals accountable for the diverse array of performance dimensions that generate high performance. Here the senior manager is not an organizational architect, but rather a designer of measures and rewards. The design premise is that by placing on each contributor's desk a recurring stream of information about performance along key dimensions – those dimensions critical to overall organizational performance – the organization will generate high and appropriate levels of each. The key design question here is whether simply articulating measures for the key drivers of performance, many of which are likely behaviorally antithetical, can actually optimize performance. More specifically, does articulating performance measures generate the balanced attention to performance dimensions that is desired? Or as other economists articulate, does such an exercise create an unresolvable multi-tasking problem (Hölmstrom & Milgrom 1991, 1994)?

The alternative design approach – one that also helps explain the abundance of organizational change which we have noted – is that organizational design is not about static engineering or crafting an organizational edifice that delivers on all key performance drivers. Rather, the organizational architect seeks to dynamically engineer an organization's performance using rather discrete bundles of complementary design choices. The manager's task is to monitor and observe performance trajectories, recognizing that effective designs are rather discrete and promote one desired outcome, while undermining another. Somewhat paradoxically, the benefits of this dynamic approach to design are fundamentally enabled by the inherent inertia within organizations. Thus, the routines, communication patterns, and design choices that generate high levels along a particular performance driver have inert properties. As an organization shifts its design from one choice to another, in order to address a different performance driver, there are distinct legacy effects that dissipate only with time (Nickerson & Zenger 2002; Gulati & Puranam 2009). Thus, in a shift from centralization to decentralization, the relationships and patterns of communication built up with one organizational design do not instantly disappear as the shift is made to another. Thus, valuable relationships or communication patterns that facilitated coordination and efficiency under centralization do not disappear when a shift is made to decentralize. It is the presence of this inertia that enables benefits from oscillation or cycling in structure.

This dynamic approach to organizational design recognizes that static balance in performance along key performance drivers, the ostensible target of both the ambidexterity approach and the balanced scorecard approach, is not really an accurate articulation of how performance is maximized among a bundle of complementary performance drivers. After all, balance among performance drivers can exist at rather low levels of each.

Exploiting complementarity instead requires high levels of each performance driver, albeit with some semblance of balance. Whether a static or a dynamic approach to design yields higher performance is therefore an empirical question.

As we noted above, causal observation suggests tremendous dynamics in patterns of organizational design. Moreover, oscillation between or cycling among structures appears rather common. For instance, Mintzberg (1979), Cummings (1995), and Eccles and Nohria (1992) have all commented on a pervasive undulating pattern in organizations between centralization and decentralization. Over a 25-year period during which HP evolved into the world's largest IT firm, the company switched from centralization to decentralization or from decentralization back to centralization about every four years (Nickerson & Zenger 2002; Boumgarden et al. 2011). Moreover, the pattern over these 25 years was remarkably consistent. A decision to centralize would facilitate coordination across disparate divisions, reduce redundancy, and provide coordinated solution selling to customers and initially increase performance. However, eventually innovation would flag and performance would decline. HP would then decentralize. Innovation would accelerate and performance would improve. However, eventually issues of incompatibility, redundancies, and confused customers would arise and performance would decline. HP would then reverse course.

Such oscillating patterns of structural change are also observed in regard to global geographic structures. For instance, up until 1994 Ford was highly decentralized on a global basis with independent manufacturing, product design, and procurement in various regions of the world. The result was locally tailored designs that generally sold well, but globally inefficient manufacturing and design. Product platforms and parts were incompatible across regions, and design efforts were redundant around the globe. In 1994, Ford implemented a major global reorganization that centralized engineering, manufacturing, and purchasing. The result was a significant improvement in efficiency as common product platforms were developed and common parts and global procurement were adopted. However, automobile designs became less tailored to local tastes and sales eventually slipped. As a consequence, Ford again decentralized in 2000 with a resulting improvement in responsiveness to local tastes. At same time, however, not all of the benefits generated during the episode of centralization disappeared instantaneously upon reversing course. Rather, global social connections were been reshaped, common standards and platforms were adopted, and important centralized procurement opportunities were maintained.

Another pattern observed in many organizations is oscillation between integration and outsourcing for a particular activity. A common candidate for this pattern is the IT function. Thus, a firm outsourcing a particular IT activity becomes frustrated with slow response or a lack of firm-specific investment by an external provider, and chooses to integrate. Performance initially improves, but insulated from market demands and market pressures the internal provider's skills atrophy and costs balloon. As a consequence, the firm again outsources the activity and costs decline. But again, with time, frustration with slow response and the lack of firm-specific investments returns.

Our contention, then, is that organization design is not really about static fit, but rather about dynamic design. The effort is about dynamically crafting the organization to optimize performance outcomes inter-temporally. It requires remaining cognizant of negative externalities in design elements, attentive to complementarities in performance drivers, and acutely aware of the costs of any organizational change. The result is that even if the external environment encompassing technology, products, and capital markets were to suddenly stabilize, we are still likely to see dramatic changes in organization for any given firm.

While we have emphasized the efficiency-enhancing role of oscillation in the chapter, the process of achieving dynamic fit may also involve organizational innovations. These innovations might include new combinations of organizational elements that better fit the environment (e.g., Grandori & Furnari 2008). One can see such innovations as breaking down the 'lumpiness' of organizational designs to some degree. Indeed, in some cases one might observe oscillation together with recombination.

CONCLUSION

The study of organizational design has traditionally been static in nature. Various designs are compared with one another in terms of their capacity for efficiently and effectively handling various kinds of contingencies. Rapid changes in organizational structures over the last 25 years or so, however, have focused scholarly attention on the dynamics of organizational structures. For example, organizations have responded in different ways to different kinds of changes in their external environments. Even if the static approach to organizational design provides insights into these changes, we still lack a good understanding of basic relationships, such as between IT adoption and organizational structure change. Better understandings will first and foremost require better and broader data, something that has been sorely lacking in studies of organization structure. Hopefully, researchers will find the resources necessary to gather much more systematic data about the dynamics of organizational structures.

In addition to respond to external changes, many organizations appear to follow an internal dynamic of oscillation. This dynamic is driven on the one hand by the inherent discreteness of organizational structures, and on the other by inertia in communication patterns and routines, even as organizational structures change. A better understanding of this dynamic, such as the determinants of the frequency of modulation, the circumstances in which it does and does not occur, and the interactions between externally and internally driven structure changes, is a high priority for future research. This kind of research will be longitudinal in nature, focusing on the dynamics or organizational structures over relatively long periods of time. This is necessary in order to move from a static to a dynamic approach to the study of organization structure.

REFERENCES

Abarbanell, J. and V. Bernard (2000), 'Is the stock market myopic?' *Journal of Accounting Research*, **38**, 221–242.
Abernathy, R. (1978), *The Productivity Dilemma: Roadblocks to Innovation in the Automobile Industry*, Baltimore, MD: Johns Hopkins University Press.
Argyres, N. (1995), 'Technology strategy, governance structure and interdivisional coordination', *Journal of Economic Behavior and Organization*, **28**, 337–358.

Argyres, N. (1999), 'The impact of information technology on coordination: evidence from the B-2 "Stealth" bomber', *Organization Science*, **10**, 162–180.

Argyres, N.S. and B.S. Silverman (2004), 'R&D, organization structure and the development of corporate technological knowledge', *Strategic Management Journal*, **25**, 929–958.

Bebchuck, L. and L. Stole (1993), 'Do short-term managerial objectives lead to under- or overinvestment in long-term projects?' *Journal of Finance*, **48**, 719–729.

Beer, M., R. Eisenstadt and B. Spector (1990), *The Critical Path to Corporate Renewal*, Cambridge, MA: Harvard Business School Press.

Boumgarden, P., J. Nickerson and T. Zenger (2011), 'Sailing into the wind: exploring the relationships between ambidexterity, vacillation and organizational performance', *Strategic Management Journal*, **33**(6), 587–610.

Bradley, S., P. Ghemawat and S. Foley (2002), 'Wal-Mart Stores', Harvard Business School case #794024.

Burns, T. and G. Salker (1961), *The Management of Innovation*, New York: Oxford University Press.

Capelli, P., L. Bassi, H. Katz, D. Knoke, P. Osterman and M. Useem (1997), *Change at Work*, New York: Oxford University Press.

Chandler, A. (1962), *Strategy and Structure: Chapters in the History of the Multidivisional Enterprise*, Cambridge, MA: MIT Press.

Comment, R. and G. Jarrell (1995), 'Corporate focus and stock market returns', *Journal of Financial Economics*, **37**, 67–87.

Crémer, J., L. Garicano and A. Prat (2007), 'Language and a theory of the firm', *Quarterly Journal of Economics*, 373–407.

Cummings, L.L. (1995), 'Centralization and decentralization: the never-ending story of separation and betrayal', *Scandinavian Journal of Management*, **11**(2), 103–117.

Cyert, R. and J. March (1963), *Behavioral Theory of the Firm*, New York: Wiley-Blackwell.

Doppler, K. and Lauterburg, C. (2010), *Managing Corporate Change*, New York: Springer.

Doz, Y., R. Angelmar and C.K. Prahalad (1987), 'Technological innovation and interdependence: a challenge for the large complex firm', in Mel Horwitch (ed.), *Technology and the Modern Firm*, New York: Pergamon Press, pp. 14–34.

Duncan, R. (1972), 'Characteristics of organizational environments and perceived environmental uncertainty', *Administrative Science Quarterly*, **17**, 313–327.

Eccles, R. and N. Nohria (1992), *Beyond the Hype: Rediscovering the Essence of Management*, Cambridge, MA: Harvard Business School Press.

Grandori, A. (2009), 'Poliarchic governance and the growth of knowledge', in N. Foss and S. Michailova (eds), *Knowledge Governance: Processes and Perspectives*, New York: Oxford University Press, pp. 88–107.

Grandori, A. and S. Furnari (2008), 'A chemistry of organization: combinatory analysis and design', *Organization Studies*, **29**, 459–485.

Guadelupe, M. and J. Wulf (2010), 'The flattening firm and product market competition: the effect of trade liberalization on corporate hierarchies', *American Economic Journal: Applied Economics*, **2**, 105–127.

Gulati, R. (2007), 'Cisco Systems 2001: building and sustaining a customer-centric culture', Harvard Business School case #409061.

Gulati, R. and Lucia Marshall (2009a), 'Jones Lang Lasalle: reorganizing around the customer', Harvard Business School case #410007.

Gulati, R. and Lucia Marshall (2009b), 'Corporate solutions at Jones Lang Lasalle', Harvard Business School case #4091111.

Gulati, R. and P. Puranam (2009), 'Renewal through reorganization: the value of inconsistencies between formal and informal organization', *Organization Science*, **20**, 422–440.

Gurbaxani, V. and S. Whang (1991), 'The impact of information systems on firms and markets', *Communications of the ACM*, **34**, 59–73.

Hall, B. (1993), 'The stock market's valuation of research and development investment in the 1980s', *American Economic Review*, **83**, 259–264.

Holmström, B. and P. Milgrom (1991), 'Multitask principal–agent analyses: incentive contracts, asset ownership and job design', *Journal of Law, Economics and Organization*, **7**, 24–52.

Holmström, B. and P. Milgrom (1994), 'The firm as an incentive system', *American Economic Review*, **84**, 972–991.

Jensen, M. and W. Meckling (1992), 'Specific and general knowledge and organization structure', in L. Werin and H. Wijkander (eds), *Contract Economics*, Oxford: Blackwell, pp. 251–291.

Kaplan, R. and D. Norton (1992), 'The balanced scorecard: measures that drive performance', *Harvard Business Review* (January–February), 71–79.

Kesler, G. and M. Schuster (2009), 'Design your governance model to make the matrix work', *People and Strategy*, **32**, 17–25.

Khanna, T. and Y. Yafeh (2007), 'Business groups in emerging markets: paragons or parasites?' *Journal of Economic Literature*, **45**, 331–372.

Lawrence, P. and J. Lorsch (1967), *Organization and Environment: Managing Differentiation and Integration in Complex Organizations*, Cambridge, MA: Harvard University Press.

Levinthal, D. and J. March (1993), 'The myopia of learning', *Strategic Management Journal*, 14, 95–112.

Liebeskind, J., T. Opler and D. Hatfield (1996), 'Corporate restructuring and the consolidation of US industry', *Journal of Industrial Economics*, 44, 53–68.

Litov, L., P. Moreton and T. Zenger (2012), 'Corporate strategy, analyst coverage, and the uniqueness discount', *Management Science*, 58, 1797–1815.

Malone, T., J. Yates and R. Benjamin (1987), 'Electronic markets and electronic hierarchies', *Communications of the ACM*, 30, 484–497.

Mintzberg, H. (1979), *The Structuring of Organizations: A Synthesis of the Research*, Englewood Cliffs, NJ: Prentice Hall.

Nickerson, J. and T. Zenger (2002), 'Being efficiently fickle: a dynamic theory of organizational choice', *Organization Science*, 13, 547–566.

O'Reilly, C. and M. Tushman (2004), 'The ambidextrous organization', *Harvard Business Review*, April, 74–81.

O'Reilly, C. and M. Tushman (2008), 'Ambidexterity and a dynamic capability: resolving the innovator's dilemma', *Research in Organizational Behavior*, 28, 185–206.

Oriani, R. and M. Sobrero (2003), 'A meta-analytic study of the relationships between R&D investments and corporate value', in M. Calderini, P. Garrone and M. Sobrer (eds), *Corporate Governance, Market Structure and Innovation*, Cheltenham, UK and Northampton, MA, USA: Edward Elgar, pp. 177–199.

Piskorski, M. and A. Spadini (2007), 'Procter & Gamble 2005', Harvard Business School case #707519.

Porter, M. (1992), 'Capital disadvantage: America's failing capital investment system', *Harvard Business Review*, 70, 65–82.

Raisch, S., J. Birkinshaw, G. Probst and M. Tushman (2009), 'Organizational ambidexterity: balancing exploration and exploitation for organizational performance', *Organization Science*, 20, 685–695.

Rajan, R. and J. Wulf (2006), 'The flattening firm: evidence from panel data on the changing nature of corporate hierarchies', *Review of Economics and Statistics*, 88, 759–773.

Roberts, John (2004), *The Modern Firm*, New York: Oxford University Press.

Schleifer, A. and R. Vishny (1991), 'Takeovers in the 60s and the 80s: evidence and implications', *Strategic Management Journal*, 12, 51–59.

Sloan, A. (1964), *My Years with General Motors*, New York: Doubleday.

Strikwerda, J. and J.W. Stoelhorst (2009), 'The emergence and evolution of the multidimensional organization', *California Management Review*, 51, 11–31.

von Nordenflycht, A. (2011), 'Firm size and industry structure under human capital intensity: insights from the evolution of the global advertising industry', *Organization Science*, 22, 141–157.

Williamson, O.E. (1975), *Market and Hierarchies*, New York: Free Press.

Williamson, O.E. (1985), *The Economic Institutions of Capitalism*, New York: Free Press.

Zenger, T. and W. Hesterly (1997), 'The disaggregation of corporations: selective intervention, high-powered incentives, and modular units', *Organization Science*, 8, 209–222.

Zuckerman, E. (2000), 'Focusing the corporate product: securities analysts and de-diversification', *Administrative Science Quarterly*, 45, 591–619.

13. Design rules for dynamic organization design: the contribution of computational modeling
Richard M. Burton and Børge Obel

Organizational design rules are contingent 'if-then' statements about what a good design should be for a given situation. Today's challenge is to look forward to devise organization design rules for a different future with greater uncertainty and greater interdependency – all with dynamic performance demands. These new demands call for new design rules for coordination, incentives and leadership, among others. Our existing rules are mostly based upon past experience and empirical studies of what is. 'What might be' – going beyond what we have observed and explained of yesterday and today to help design for a future new situation – is a disciplined response to examine the new contingencies of organizational design and their design consequences. Computational laboratories permit us to go beyond what is to develop and examine new design possibilities and boundaries to explore a future world of what might be. We need to revise existing rules and perhaps devise totally new design rules for managing uncertainty and interdependency to design efficient, effective and sustainable organizations. In this chapter, we explore the development and evaluation of organizational design rules for the future.[1]

INTRODUCTION

Organization design is a systematic approach to configuring and aligning structures, processes, leadership, culture, people practices, and metrics to enable organizations to achieve their mission and strategy. Academics and practitioners alike are calling for a greater focus on organizational design to meet the new challenges in business for better performance (Miller et al. 2009). Organizational design must relate to the business conditions of tomorrow, and in particular changing business conditions. Cisco on 5 May 2011 announced that it had reorganized the basic structure and dramatically changed the decision-making process in its council structure. Further, the overall structure was adjusted:

> Our five company priorities are for a reason – they are the five drivers of the future of the network, and they define what our customers know Cisco is uniquely able to provide for their business success. The new operating model will enable Cisco to execute on the significant market opportunities of the network and empower our sales, service and engineering organizations. (Gary Moore, COO, Cisco, http://newsroom.cisco.com/press-release-content?type=web content&articleId=752727)

This change was made to meet new competition as well as allow for a capability to adapt to the fast-changing technology base within Cisco's domain. Cisco's problem was compounded as this change did not yield the performance results anticipated (Rosoff 2011).

Today, Cisco has dismantled the council structure. From a design view, could it have anticipated that the council structure might be problematic and risky?

Similarly Aarhus University on 1 January 2011 completely changed its organization from a nine-faculty organization to a complex matrix structure with a strong interdisciplinary focus to meet the challenges of tomorrow. The grand research and teaching challenges of tomorrow cannot be addressed individually by a single discipline. A multi-scholastic approach is required. For a university this is a new structure to meet a new demand. Little knowledge exists to establish whether this particular structure will work in this context. Will this multi-scholastic design yield the desired outcomes?

Romme (2003: 558), building upon Simon (1996), argues that the 'idea of a design involves inquiry into systems that do not yet exist – either complete new systems or new states of existing systems'. Organizational design has to be forward-looking and provide insights and recommendations for practice, based upon rigorous science and methodology. 'What might be' – going beyond what we have observed and explained of yesterday and today – is a disciplined response to examine the new contingencies of organizational design. Traditional empirical research exploring the past is not sufficient. Computational modeling is a laboratory to explore what might be and develop design rules which can help us in thinking about the future challenges and opportunities (Burton 2003; Davis et al. 2007).

The concept of organizational design is both a noun and a verb. 'Organizational design' as a noun refers to a set of state variables about the organization; that is, a statement of a choice in the design space, for example the structure, coordination and communications networks, and the incentives, among others. The verb 'organizational design' refers to the process of how the design state variables are created or designed and implemented, but not how the organization will operate in fact, as this is the resulting outcome of the organization design.

The need for and importance of organization design is much greater in changing and volatile environments than in simple and stable environments (Håkonsson et al. 2012). Fiss (2011) more generally points to the fact of asymmetry in the relationship between variables in the organization design space as an important issue in understanding the relationship between performance and organization design. Such asymmetry has to be incorporated into our design rules.

Grandori (1997: 44) concludes her in-depth challenge for organizational design, 'to design new organizational arrangements not as mere choices among given organizational models but in the strong sense of devising or finding new possible organizational configurations resulting from the allocation of property rights and from the choice of a coordination mechanisms mix'.

The premise of the 'if-then' is not a static set and may require the development of a revised set of organizational design rules. Our goal here is to develop further the 'what might be' logic for organizational design. We focus on the coordination mechanisms using an information-processing argument to devise new organizational design rules.

DESIGN RULES

What is a design rule? Design rules are what should be statements. They incorporate both feasibility of 'what might be', and desirability for the organization. They can be based upon 'what is', using the logic that what has been successful in the past is likely to work for the future in somewhat similar conditions – sometimes even applied in circumstances going beyond what has been observed.

Theories of organizational design have been addressed by studying configurations (Miles & Snow 1978), contingency theory (Donaldson 2001) and multi-contingency theory utilizing complex sets of design rules (Burton & Obel 2004). The development of such design rules has originally focused on simple design rules focusing on one or a limited set of contingencies, such as Lawrence and Lorsch (1967) on the relationship between environment and organizational design, or Woodward (1965) on technology and organizational design.

Here, we focus on a few design rules which are rationalized from an information-processing view of organization of who talks to whom about what, and who makes which decision based upon what information (Marshack & Radner 1972; Cyert & March 1963). We will start with two classic design contingencies: uncertainty and interdependency. Uncertainty has been defined as an incomplete description of the world (Arrow 1974), unpredictability, or perhaps more precisely as Knightian uncertainty where the probability distribution is not well defined; and further uncertainty has included complexity or the number of variables in the environmental space (Burton & Obel 2004). Interdependency can be defined as the correlation among the variables in the environmental space or task space. Simon (1996) examined interdependencies as the degree of decomposability using a matrix representation of the connections: the more connected or dense the matrix, the more interdependent the tasks; and the sparser the matrix entries, the less connected and the more decomposable the tasks.

Uncertainty is a primary contingency for organizational design. In Galbraith's (1974) seminal article on the information-processing view of organization, he argued that:

If the task uncertainty is high, then a decentralized structure is superior to a centralized structure.

Decentralization means that significant decisions should be made at lower levels in the organization – delegation of decision making putting the decision close to operations or sales to maintain a balance between the need for information and the capacity to process information for decision making and control.

Galbraith (1973, 1974) presented the organizational design problem as an information-processing problem: 'the greater the uncertainty of the task, the greater the amount of information that has to be processed between decision makers' (Galbraith 1974: 10). The task uncertainty can arise from the technology and environment (Thompson 1967) as well as other sources. Organizations can either reduce their need for information processing or increase their capacity to process information (Galbraith 1974). The need for information processing can be reduced by increasing slack resources. However; reducing information needs must be balanced with the returns to coordinating the activities. In a simulation experiment, Kim and Burton (2002) confirmed the Galbraith rule, but also added a nuanced understanding for different performance measures where they found that for high task uncertainty a decentralized organization performs better in terms of cost and time, but a centralized organization does better for organizational quality or less errors. For low uncertainty, decentralized and centralized organizations perform the same in terms of cost and time, but again the centralized organization does better for quality. There is an asymmetry: for high uncertainty, decentralization makes a difference; but for low uncertainty, there is little performance difference. In terms of information processing, when the uncertainty is low both the decentralized and the centralized organization meet the demands for information. Multiple goals create a new challenge which we discuss in more detail below.

Another contingency is the interdependency among the tasks. One design rule indicates that the multidivisional form should be adopted if the interdependency – which can be represented as the decomposability (Simon 1996) of the matrix of task relations among the organizational tasks – is low. Burton and Obel (2004) state the design rule as:

If the task is nearly decomposable, then divisional forms are superior to unitary forms.

This hypothesis has been supported in numerous studies applying different approaches. Chandler (1962), a historian, chronicled the creation and the wide adoption of the divisional organization in the early twentieth century. Later, Williamson (1975: 150), an economist, formalized the proposition as the M-form hypothesis using a tight economic rationale: 'The organization and operation of the large enterprise along the lines of the M-form favors goal pursuit and least-cost behavior more nearly associated with the neoclassical profit maximization hypothesis than does the U-form organization alternative.'

Williamson emphasized the size of the organization as the driver. Armour and Teece (1978) supported the M-form hypothesis in an empirical examination of the oil industry where they found a continuing adoption of the M-form among the major companies. Burton and Obel (1980, 1984) supported the M-form hypothesis, utilizing a simulation approach where they found the M-form performed better for greater decomposability or less dependency among the tasks, keeping the organizational size constant. Later, in a laboratory experiment, they found that the M-form was less vulnerable to opportunism or cheating. Taken all together, there is strong support for the M-form hypothesis when there is a reasonable level of decomposability or low interdependency among the organizational tasks. The design rules may be simple 'if-then' statements. But there may be a relationship among several statements. A conditional requirement for proposing an M-form design is that the organization has the requisite size to allow for economies of scale within each division (Burton & Obel 2004). This will change the design rule to:

If the task is nearly decomposable and the size of the organization is large, then the divisional M-form is superior to a unitary form.

Information processing is a way to view organizations and their designs. The basic theoretical perspective behind design rules is the information processing perspective where the primary work of the organization is observation and generation of data; the exchange of these data among the organizational actors; and application of these data to analyze, make decisions and control the implementation of those decisions. The organization processes information in order to coordinate and control its interdependent activities in the face of uncertainty (Arrow 1974: 34). Information processing may reduce uncertainty by observing what is happening, analyzing and making choices about what to do, and communicating among its members. Information 'channels can be created or abandoned. Their capacities and the types of signals to be transmitted over them are subject to choice, a choice based on a comparison of benefits and costs' (Arrow 1974). Both information systems and individuals possess a capacity to process information, but 'this capacity is not, however, unlimited and the scarcity of information-handling ability is an essential feature for the understanding of both individual and organizational behavior' (Arrow 1974). Organizational work involves information processing: individuals are information and knowledge workers. They talk, read, write, calculate, analyze, store and exchange knowledge. They exchange information using face-to-face communication, information and communication technology (ICT) systems, social networks, and so on. The basic design problem is to create an organizational design that matches the demand for information processing with the information-processing capacity. The demand comes from information requirements from customers, suppliers and regulatory bodies, among other stakeholders.

Uncertainty and interdependency are important, but an incomplete set of variables for organization design. Incomplete in two ways: firstly, the elements of organizational design also include goals, strategy, form, leadership, climate coordination, and control and incentives (Burton et al. 2011); and secondly and extremely importantly, the design rules must fit together in a consistent and comprehensive manner.

Burton and Obel (2004) presented an interrelated set of design rules based on the information-processing paradigm. The design rules express in a simple way when there is a balance between the information-processing capacity and the information-processing demand. An organizational design is said to be in fit when the design does not violate any design rule. Further, the basic hypothesis is that when fit is obtained the performance of the organization is higher than when it is not in fit. There exists a whole literature on fit (Tushman & Nadler 1978; Donaldson 1987; Gresov 1989; Miller 1992; Nissen & Burton 2011).

In the development of their design rules, Burton and Obel (2004) extracted knowledge on organization design and composed it into 'if-then' rules for design. This knowledge came from the literature, theoretical and empirical, and executive experience. The design rules represent an accumulated knowledge of more than 40 years of research on organizational design from March and Simon (1958), including Huber (2003). Further, these rules were implemented into an experts system – OrgCon.[2] In construction of the knowledge base for diagnosis and design of the organization the structure of 'if-then' rules was chosen and composed to enhance the effectiveness and/or the efficiency goals of the organization. The validity of the OrgCon (Baligh et al. 1996) follows a two-step approach: (1) develop the design rule from the literature, supported on a theoretical and empirical foundation; and (2) check the results of the recommended designs with executives to validate the design rules. This approach works well with 'what is' designs but less well with 'what might be' designs which have not been tested for feasibility and desirability.

Are 'what might be' designs very different from 'what is' designs (Zacharias et al. 2008)? Fenton and Pettigrew (2000: 6) state that 'a closer inspection of the literature reveals that many of the new forms are not entirely new but are reminiscent of earlier typologies, such as Burns and Stalker's (1961) organic and mechanistic forms and Galbraith's preoccupation with lateral relations'. Thus fundamental concepts and principles of organizational design remain very important for the modern organization of today and tomorrow. Why do we still see mostly functional, M-form divisional, and matrix organizations (Grandori 1997)? The answer may be the lack of approaches to develop new designs.

'What might be' studies are needed to release us from the mimetic isomorphism logics of doing what we have done (DiMaggio & Powell 1991). Not to be able to design the right organization creates a lost opportunity of significant magnitude (Burton et al. 2002 [2003]; Bryan & Joyce 2007). The logic of contingency theory suggests that adaptation and change generate great variation in designs. Yet, the challenge to generate these new possibilities is an underdeveloped challenge. The change in risk, sustainability and new technologies might demand very new designs. How can we investigate designs that have not been tried before? How can we create new designs by not engaging in expensive and very risky real-world trial and error 'experiments'?

'What might be' computational modeling can help generate new possible designs and also be an experimental laboratory to test these new possibilities. The challenge is to create new forms which are science based, upon experimentation and logic. Knowledge has to be conveyed to practice in a way that makes it applicable. Design rules are a particular way to handle that issue. But we need to do more elaborating and find new rules.

Grandori (1997: 29) was critical of lack of variety in the choice of organizational designs. The approach of examining only configurations such as M-form, U- (or unitary) form and matrix are overly limiting. The OrgCon has more than 500 design rules and their composition is one response to the challenge. In short, the OrgCon is a complex system made up of a large number of relatively simple design rules. Its validity depends upon both the rules and the composition of the rules to yield organizational design recommendations and insights.

One major challenge is the new and evolving IT for an organization and the information-processing view of organizational design. Today's design rules are based upon descriptive studies from the past, implicitly incorporating that observation, communications, analysis and control are relatively slow to reflect what is possible today and for the future. Uncertainty as a description of the world can be greatly reduced. Yet, the inherent uncertainty in the world remains high, perhaps higher for organizations than ever. Thus, 'what might be' studies are needed to complement what we think we know from the past, where what happened is a small part of what might have happened. The information-processing perspective may have one form of rules in a 'what is' scenario and a very different form in a 'what might be' scenario. There is ample opportunity to create design rules with other elements such as growth or retraction, emotional rules, new rules on cultural differences, diversity, new types of regulation, and user-driven innovations.

'WHAT MIGHT BE' RULES AND DYNAMIC ORGANIZATION DESIGN

What is it about the future that makes it different from the past? For the future we suggest that the space of what might occur is much larger, perhaps quite different from what has occurred in the past. 'What might be' is the large space of what the future might be; the development and exploration of possibilities, many of which we have experienced before; an examination of variations and boundaries beyond what we have observed;

the development of new feasibilities, stretching what is possible; the creation of alternative futures (Burton 2003). So the future of organizational design has two challenges: to create new designs and then to find a way to evaluate what will work well.

Dynamic Contingencies

The dynamics and changes in the environment are increasingly important for organizational design. The contingencies of environmental uncertainty and interdependency implicitly highlight the dynamics; the explicit consideration of dynamics requires that we take time seriously beyond comparative statics.

Here, we return to the two contingencies which we discussed above, and now we want to introduce time explicitly, as the change in time perspective is a new challenge:

If the environment is uncertain, then decentralize.

If the task interdependency is low, then decentralize.

Both high environmental uncertainty and low task interdependency suggest that the organization should be decentralized. Implicitly, both statements suggest a time aspect, but are in fact comparative static rules. Is that good enough for the future with a focus on significant changes?

Siggelkow and Levinthal (2003) conducted a computational model experiment where time and change are explicit; that is, when the model is time dependent they find that:

If the competitive landscape shifts, then decentralize temporarily.

The design rule itself is time-dependent 'temporarily', which suggests that a contingency is not only the environment but also the transition between the two static states – before and after. Their design rule says that when a change happens we may not know much about the new situation, and exploration is required. Thus we need a temporary decentralization that will make the exploration of the new situation more efficient. Once we understand the new landscape we may have to change again – thus 'temporary' decentralization. We might be misled to think that the transition would create uncertainty and thus centralization is a good idea. But the explicit introduction of time and change reverses the recommendation. This is a different way to look at the punctuated equilibrium perspective, where the design equilibrium is punctuated and requires a new design (Tushman & Romanelli 1985). The implicit assumption is that you analyze the situation and then make the appropriate redesign. Sastry (1997) in her simulation experiment showed that a temporary period with no performance appraisal is needed after a change. Siggelkow and Levinthal (2003) suggest that a temporary design is needed to explore the situation before returning to the permanent design. In both situations new design rules were devised.

More generally, the dynamics of organizational design is an opportunity for greater understanding and modification of our design rules. Here, Siggelkow and Levinthal examine how the organization can return to a good performance state under an environmental shift; that is, back to a fit situation. Nissen and Burton (2011) call this adaptation 'dynamic fit'. A higher level of dynamic fit is maneuverability where the organization must change to a new level of performance as discussed in Burton et al. (2011, Ch. 11).

The Siggelkow and Levinthal study is a 'what might be' study introducing a new variable – the time of change – in an explicit way. In their study they also consider the opportunity of creating a modular design if the level of interconnectedness is low, thus allowing for a high degree of decomposability. This is a confirmation of the multicontingency model which suggests that a simultaneous consideration of the contingencies and the design elements require an integrated set of design rules – not separate consideration of a single contingency. The competitive landscape may change on many dimensions. The regulatory terms have shifted. So has the economic situation. Prices on real estate have gone down while prices on food and raw materials have gone up. Changes in labor force demand and availability are emerging. At the same time major changes in ICT introduce new relations with customers. Taking these issues one by one will create uncoordinated responses which are non-optimal and perhaps dangerous. A temporary decentralization may be needed to cope with such changes.

Dynamic Fit and Maneuverability

For organizational design, fit is a matching of the organizational design to the environment (and other contingencies) to yield good performance (Donaldson 1987). Despite the fact that most environments are dynamic, the emphasis has been on static fit. The new contingencies as we discussed above include environmental shifts which call for dynamic fit and maneuverability.

As a metaphor, aerodynamics provides key concepts and insights: dynamic fit and maneuverability for organizational design (Nissen & Burton 2011). An airplane is not an organization, but it can be viewed as a goal-directed complex system. A cargo airplane does well on static stability, but less so on dynamic stability and not well on maneuverability. The cargo airplane uses its adaptability to maintain its course with as little turbulence as possible. In contrast, a fighter airplane is much the opposite, with superior performance on maneuverability. A fighter airplane has to be able to change its course swiftly for viability. Each of the two types of airplanes is designed for different goals or performance criteria indicating that there are design alternatives and trade-offs for different purposes and different types of turbulence.

The static stability, dynamic stability and maneuverability concepts also relate to an organization. Some organizations need to be able to absorb turbulence for the purpose of providing a stable service that does not change dramatically over time. Many public organizations and hospitals fall in this category. Other organizations may be designed to make big changes quickly. In the financial industry we now see many banks that are forced to make dramatic changes quickly to survive – a situation that would have been unthinkable just a few years ago. We want to use dynamic fit and maneuverability ideas as a guide for new organizational designs.

More formally: static stability is the resistance of the organization (system) to a performance goal after a deviation due to an external shock; dynamic stability is the quickness or timeliness of an organization's return to the same desired performance after a shock; and maneuverability is the capacity and quickness of an organization to move to a new desired performance, that is, from one performance level to another goal level. Static stability does not consider time; dynamic stability introduces time – the time to adjust; and maneuverability also includes the time to change to a new performance. With time included, the notion of opportunity loss is defined as the loss in performance over the time the organization is not realizing its goals: the greater the performance deviation, the greater the opportunity loss; the longer the time duration, the greater the opportunity loss. For example for financial institutions, the inability to create a design that will meet the new regulation will result in a risk evaluation downgrade, with the effect that the cost of funding will increase significantly or funding will not be possible at all.

Returning to our consideration of decentralization in organization, we posit that:

If the organizational performance goal is static fit, then the centralization may be a good fit.

If the organizational performance goal is dynamic fit, then the decentralization may be a good fit.

If the organizational performance goal is maneuverability, then a mix of decentralization and centralization may be a good fit.

Are these design rules good ones? Let us use the information-processing argument to support the statements. We suggest that when not much is changing, then centralization works well. The information-processing demand is stable and much can be planned for. There is no need for local adaptations as little is changing. Thus a centralized decision making ensures coordination at the lowest cost. But when there is change, it is more complex; a local adaption may be required. Decentralization permits quick reaction and adjustment to the new situation without a transmittal of all information. If the goal is dynamic fit, a decentralized decision making may be the better response. If the goal is maneuverability, then the organization has to get back on track after a change. Here a local response and understanding of the change is required, but also some centralized decision making to make sure that the local decisions do not let the organization drift away from its stated purpose.

These design rules may be adjusted and complemented by incorporating many other of the contingencies mentioned above. The set of 'what might be' possibilities is very large. So, how do we guide our search to a much smaller plausible set? The dynamic fit concepts of dynamic stability and maneuverability focus the search on a meaningful subset of possibilities. The space of statically stable airplane designs which can move heavy loads is a small subset of the possible airplanes. Similarly, the subset of highly maneuverability airplanes is also small, but quite different than airplanes which are statically stable. To design an organization which is dynamically stable under shock, the space of 'what might be' goes beyond only decentralization or centralization, and includes temporary decentralization (Siggelkow & Levinthal 2003). Dynamic-fit criteria give us criteria to focus our search of possible futures.

Organizations which we redesigned for static stability will incur large opportunity losses under environmental shocks which are occurring more frequently – calling for a dynamic fit. If we want an organization which is maneuverable and minimizes opportunity losses to obtain a different performance level, it may be quite a different design. Further, the maneuverable organization which can adjust quickly may be inherently unstable. That is, the space of designs which meets the criteria of dynamic stability and maneuverability is extremely small, perhaps null for some environments.

The dynamic fit guidance for creating 'what might be' possibilities includes:

- There will be more environmental shocks which require a maneuverable organization to limit opportunity losses, but at the same time, not all organizations need to be maneuverable.
- An organization cannot perform well on static fit and maneuverability simultaneously, so trade-offs and choices of priorities are necessary.
- Those choices need not be limited to past organizational designs for future possibilities.
- Applying dynamic-fit criteria can yield a relatively small number of novel designs for the future.

The concept of temporary decentralization discussed above brings together organization design as a noun and a verb. The temporary decentralization used to explore the new landscape is a part of the design process and design implementation.

Multiple Goals

Above, we examined design rules for good organizational designs. The desired organizational performance has usually been assumed to be one-dimensional, for example profits; and time-invariant or stable, for example it did not change over time. There seems to be a demand for broadening our performance concepts to be multidimensional, for example profits, sustainability; and time-dependent, for example what performance do we need to satisfy the stock market in the next quarter's result and what do we need in the long term? Organizational design performance however cannot be time-invariant and one-dimensional.

Organizations do have multiple goals: profit, which is short term like ROA (return on assets), while capital value in principle is long term as the discounted future cash flow; an organization can perform well in the short run at the expense of the longer run. Thus even within economic measures alone, time itself can create multiple goals. Sustainability is a different dimension, it includes social goals and environmental goals as well as economic goals. Here too, there may be a trade-off as high short-run profits may have detrimental effects on the environment. But not always, as inefficient utilization of energy is both costly to the firm and polluting to the environment (air and water). But it may require long-term investment in new technology to increase sustainability goals. Putting both together, we could have several goals. In a different way, companies talk about the 'triple bottom line': people, planet and profits. Moving from a one-dimensional goal to two or more goals is challenging and has to be taken into account in design rules for the design of the organization for the future.

More generally, multiple goals can be complementary: more efficient use of energy can be less costly and also good for the environment; multiple goals can be substitutes, for example reducing chemical waste is costly and can reduce profits. Complementary goals are easier. Substitutes involve trade-offs which are frequently incompatible. How do we trade off lower corporate profits with social benefits such as water quality? For organizational design, we have not rationalized design rules for multiple goals where there are trade-offs between (among) the goals. Since one of the important organizational design parameters is the incentive scheme, an explicit focus on the goals is very important.

At best we can project into the future, that is, multiple organizational goals which include sustainability and other social goals will become even more important (Carroll & Shabana 2010). The challenge is clear: our design rules need to be re-examined to assess how well they meet multiple and new types of goals. The number of goals an organization decides to pursue is a design question. It is quite likely that our existing design rules should be modified as well as new design rules created. Consistent with Ashby's 'law of requisite of variety' (Ashby 1956) a more complex goal structure will require a more complex design rule structure. 'What might be' modeling is one approach which can help us understand a new world that we have not yet experienced, but will design and create.

From the computational laboratory, can we get any advice with respect to the design of the organizational goals? Ethiraj and Levinthal's (2009) 'Hoping for A to Z while rewarding only A: complex organizations and multiple goals' found using simulation studies that incomplete guides to action prove more effective at directing and coordinating behavior than more complete representations.

Fewer goals provide clarity and focus for boundedly rational actors. Even if the organization from a complete perspective would like to pursue many goals, a better total goal fulfillment will be obtained by only pursue a limited number of goals. In a very concrete way the organizational design experiments using SIMVISION takes three goals into account: cost, time to finish a project, and the quality. Here we often see one design that favors one goal relative to other goals (Kim & Burton 2002). Usually, time to finish and cost are complementary, but both are substitutes with quality, that is, there are trade-offs.

The number of goals is part of the design and a basis for designing the incentive system. Thus to design the organization for the future we need tools and approaches that can help us devise and evaluate new design rules. We have given a few examples of new contingencies that have to be taken into account in the process of evaluating our current state of the art of organizational design rules.

THE CONTRIBUTION OF COMPUTATIONAL MODELING

We have argued that 'what might be' questions will be an increasing focus of our science, and computational modeling should play a central role here. In our fast-changing world, we want to go beyond 'what is' and 'what has been' to understand better the possibilities of 'what might be' in order to address questions and issues of 'what should be'. We anticipate that computational modeling will be increasingly utilized, not as a stand-alone approach, but together with other approaches to give a deeper and better understanding of 'what might be' or the possibilities for tomorrow's world (Burton & Obel 2011). Burton and Obel (2011) argue for a triangulation using several different approaches. For 'what might be' a triangulation using different computational models can be used to both develop and evaluate new possible designs. Thus computational modeling will help us in developing and investigating new theories of organizational design as well as providing relevant insights for helping to design the organizations of tomorrow.

Computational modeling is a laboratory where we can extend our experimentation and reach beyond describing and explaining 'what is' to exploring 'what might be'. Burton (2003: 91) defined a computational laboratory as 'a "place" where we can: ask a question about an organization and its processes, build a computational experiment, design and conduct an experiment, and answer or comment on the question'. The most apparent aspect of a computational model is computation, that is, the model is a specification of relations, equations, variables, parameters, rules, procedures, or, more generally, algorithms which are computed. It is then utilized as a laboratory where one does an experiment – a formally stated model which can be manipulated to answer a question – a 'computational model of system behavior coupled with an experimental design' (Harrison et al., 2007: 1234). The validity of the computational laboratory is whether the model and the experiment address the purpose or question in an informative manner (Burton & Obel, 1995).

Earlier, Simon (1996) posited that the artificial world is central to our science. Computational modeling is a laboratory where we can extend our experimentation and reach beyond describing and explaining to exploring 'what might be' into the realm of possibility and imagination for the future. Many different computational modeling or simulation approaches have been used. In organizational design, various agent-based models have been applied:

- mathematical programming decomposition;
- virtual design team;
- NK modeling;
- system dynamics.

Mathematical Programming Decomposition

Structure, goals, uncertainty, interdependency, decision processes, resource allocation, opportunism (Burton & Obel 1980, 1988).

In a decomposition approach the organization is modeled as an input–output matrix representing activities, processes and resources. The goals of the organization are represented as an objective function. The total system is a mathematical programming model. The mathematical programming model can be decomposed to represent the structure of the organization to be studied. The simulation study carries out a number of iterations where information is passed between (among) the various units to find the optimal solution for the mathematical programming model with as few iterations as possible. These iterations can be interpreted as planning phases for a resource allocation procedure.

Using a decomposition approach Burton and Obel (1980) as described above compared the U-form and the M-form of organization under various under a fixed level of environmental uncertainty. They used the following model:

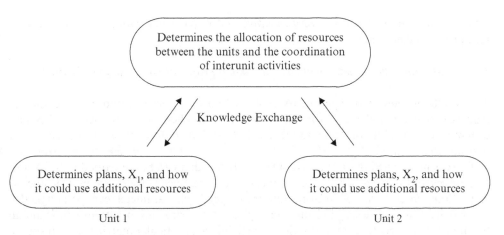

Figure 13.1   Iterative information flows in resource allocation system

$$\text{Max } \Sigma c_i x_i$$
$$\text{with respect to } x_1, \ldots \ldots \ldots x_m$$
$$\text{St. } \Sigma A_i x_i \leqslant b_0$$
$$B_j X_j \leqslant b_j \, J = 1, \ldots \ldots m$$

The x_j, represents activities in subunit j. The $\Sigma A_i x_i \leqslant b_0$ represents resource constraints that go across the m units. The $B_j X_j \leqslant b_j$ represents resource constraints for the individual unit j. The model represents an organization with activities and resources. The model can be solved using a variety of algorithms that represent the information flow in a planning context. In their study Burton and Obel created two versions of the model for a particular organization: one version representing the U-form and one version representing the M-form. Either form of organization can be represented in such a model. The model is then solved in an iterative fashion with information flowing between sub-models for each unit, see Figure 13.1. The exchange of information is done to obtain coordination of activities in the organization. Burton and Obel (1980) used an iterative transfer price scheme emulating an internal market procedure for coordination. Further they ran a comparison for two types of technology represented by different sizes and forms of the matrices. The conclusion of the simulation supports Williamson's (1975) M form hypothesis that for highly diversified organizations the M-form performs better than the U-form. When the organization is less diversified the conclusion is less strong. In particular the conclusion holds true for large organizations that require a decentralized decision making. Thus:

If the task is nearly decomposable and the size of the organization is large, then the divisional M form is superior to a unitary form.

In Burton and Obel (1988) a similar study was done, but with a human decision maker replacing one of the organizational units. Further, this study also introduced and compared various incentive schemes to assess the degree of opportunism taken by the decision maker. The result was that the M-form was less sensitive to the choice of incentive scheme, while the U-form was very sensitive and in particular worked less well with a unit profit scheme. Thus:

If the organization has a functional structure a unit profit scheme should not be used.

The results in these two experiments explained and supported a number of empirical studies that compared the U-form and the M-form where some of these studies had different results. Thus Burton and Obel's (1980, 1988) studies provided important and relevant triangulation.

There is no restriction on the structure and forms that can be embedded in the A and B matrices and more generally, the model can be non-linear. There are in principle no restrictions on the type of information exchange. Each parameter can be assigned a probability function describing uncertainty. Thus the simulation system can evaluate 'what might be' structures and situations which include particular matrix forms, resource relations, activities, connections to the market, incentive systems, and information exchange and decision making.

Tools: can be programmed in any system that has optimization module for mathematical programming. No dedicated tools required.

NK Modeling

Structure, goals, uncertainty, complexity, decision processes (Siggelkow & Levinthal 2003).

NK modeling is an agent-based, computational model where the N represents the number of variables or decisions in the model and the K represents the connections among those variables. The agents use rules to search this space to find a good solution. The 'ruggedness' of the NK landscape is related to K: a low K yields a smooth surface to search for a solution; and a higher K is more rugged and then more difficult to search for overall optimality. With myopic search algorithms, local peaks can be sticking points. A frequent specification is where the N decision variables are binary and the K represents the connection relations among those variables or decisions. For example, the size of organization can be either large (0) or small (1) – one of the N decision variables. Thus, the total number of organizational types is 2^N. An N-digit string of zeroes and ones summarizes all the decisions a firm makes that affect its performance: a 'choice configuration' $\mathbf{d} = d_1 d_2 \ldots d_N$ with each d_i either 0 or 1. The contribution of decision i makes a contribution C_i to overall firm performance is dependent on the configuration of itself and the other N related decisions. An $N \times N$ 'influence matrix' records the relationships among decisions. The contribution from each activity is determined by a random draw from a U[0,1] uniform distribution. $F(\mathbf{d})$, the overall performance of the one type of organization – configuration $\mathbf{d}$ – is the average contribution over the N decisions in the configuration $1/N \sum_1^N C_i$. Therefore, the contextuality implies that the contribution of each activity is dependent on how K related activities are configured. The central aspect of modeling is to find the optimal configuration of N activities whose performance is the greatest. The type of interactions between the two activities cannot be expressed in the NK model because the value of contributions is assigned randomly.

As discussed above, Siggelkow and Levinthal (2003) utilized an NK specification where K represents the interaction structure; low K is decomposable into divisions and higher K is less decomposable or more interdependent. The K is then determined by the structure incident matrix I. $K = 1$ means that the incident matrix is block angular. $K = N$ means a complete incident matrix. A non-decomposable configuration is where K is greater than 1 but lower than N. They then partition the decisions into two divisions where each chooses or controls some subset of the total variables. They find that in a decomposable environment the decentralized firm performs better than the centralized firm. For the non-decomposable situation where K is low at 2, the decentralized firm does better. For increased K, there is an increased probability that search will be stuck on a local peak; thus, the value of reintegration becomes important. However, the reintegration need not be accomplished immediately; that is, temporary decentralization performs well. Thus:

If the competitive landscape shifts, then decentralize temporarily

Here, time is explicit; the design rule captures the transition and does not rely upon stable conditions. This illustrates well the implication of Nissen and Burton (2011) that dynamic fit cannot be inferred from what we know about time independent comparisons.

NK models are particularly well suited to investigate 'what might be' possibilities in a laboratory setting. Further, NK models and the rugged landscape properties with many connections or large K move us beyond the limitations of smooth or low K landscape as evident in models with well-behaved first- and second-order conditions that permit optimal myopic search techniques.

Tools: NK models can be adapted and programmed on regular PCs.

Virtual Design Team

Project structure, goals, uncertainty, decision processes, work allocation, time management, multiple performance measures (Jensen et al. 2010; Levitt 2012).

The virtual design team (VDT) simulation system is an agent-based, computational, discrete-event simulation model of information flow and multi-agent decision making in project organizations. Particularly, VDT has been applied to simulate and evaluate project organizations. A VDT model comprises of tasks, resources and actors and their relationship and organization. VDT includes non-numerical attributes such as individual team members' skills and experience, task attributes of work volume, complexity and uncertainty, and ordinal organizational variables such as the level of centralization and formalization. VDT simulates stochastically using Monte Carlo sampling methods. The SimVision (commercial version of VDT) tutorial model is shown in Figure 13.2. Activities (rectangular boxes in Figure 13.2) are organized along paths of precedence relationships (tasks are semi-ordered) and describe the work to be accomplished to reach specified project milestones. Coordination requirements among activities are modeled through failure-dependency and information-exchange links. The actors are organized in a hierarchy defined by the formal exception handling structures and are assigned formal roles such as project manager, sub-team leader and subordinate. Each actor has project experience, a certain skill level, and so on (these parameters do not appear in Figure 13.2). Task responsibility links connect actors to tasks for which they are responsible,

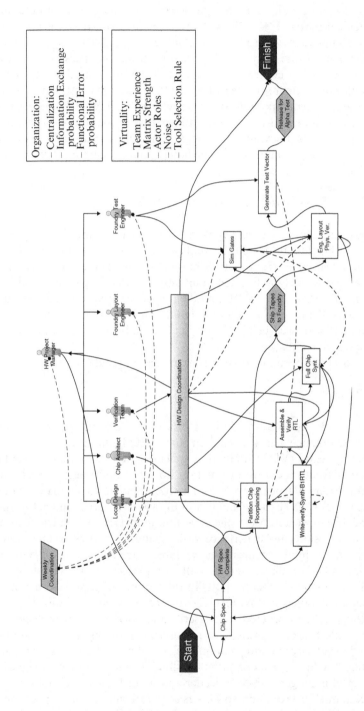

Figure 13.2   SimVision tutorial model used in Jensen et al. (2010)

238

and task interdependencies are reassigned to information-processing requirements among the actors. VDT was originally and still is used to evaluate large projects and it has been developed to include new issues such as internal and external climate and culture (Levitt 2012). However, the VDT has also been used as a laboratory to simulate and evaluate organizational design questions. The actor's behavior is based on a behavioral matrix and other parameters. These can be changed, and extended to create new organizational project designs and to evaluate existing project designs. Jensen et al. (2010) used SimVision to simulate the relationship between decision-making authority and virtualization. The specification of the parameters in their study is shown in Figure 13.2. Jensen et al. found that in a project organization a high degree of vitalization requires a high degree of centralization – contrary to the normal design rule that that a high degree of virtualization requires a high degree of decentralization. Here the performance was measured on cost, quality and time to complete the project.

Tools: SimVision.

System Dynamics

Policy analysis, design, interdependency, goals, uncertainty, feedback processes, time dependency (Schwaningera & Ríos 2008).

System dynamics is a computer-aided approach to policy analysis and design. It applies to dynamic problems arising in complex social, managerial, economic or ecological systems – literally any dynamic systems characterized by interdependence, mutual interaction, information feedback and circular causality (Schwaningera & Ríos 2008).

Mathematically, it is a system of coupled, non-linear, first-order differential (or integral) equations:

$$\frac{d}{dt}x(t) = f(x,p)$$

where x is a vector of levels (stocks or state variables), p is a set of parameters, and f is a non-linear vector-valued function.

System dynamics focuses on understanding the dynamics of complex systems for the purpose of policy analysis and design. The model includes feedback thinking, stocks and flows, the concept of feedback loop dominance, and an endogenous point of view – important to the complex system understanding. Diagrams of loops of information feedback and circular causality are tools for conceptualizing the structure of a complex system and for communicating model-based insights. Intuitively, a feedback loop exists when information resulting from some action travels through a system and eventually returns in some form to its point of origin, potentially influencing future action. Here the system dynamics has a lot in common with the VDT system. The loop concept underlying feedback and circular causality by itself is not enough, however. The explanatory power and insightfulness of feedback understandings also rest on the notions of active structure and loop dominance. Complex systems change over time. In a system of equations, the ability to shift loop dominance is important. Non-linear models can endogenously alter their active or dominant structure and shift loop dominance. The concept of endogenous change is fundamental to the system dynamics approach. It is the basis of the model formulation.

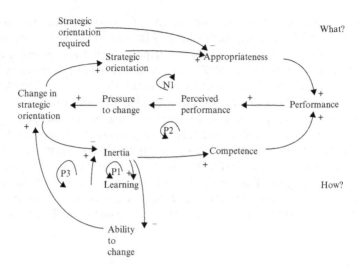

Figure 13.3   Sastry (1997) model of punctuated organizational change

Sastry (1997) re-evaluated the theory of punctuated equilibrium (Tushman & Romanelli 1985) using a system dynamics model. The central proposition of punctuated equilibrium refers to a long period of relatively unchanged form which is punctuated by a radical change over a short period.

One of the key punctuations noted is a major environmental change caused by technological innovation (Romanelli & Tushman 1994) where a technological discontinuity triggers a period of instability, before it settles at a new equilibrium. Sastry developed a system dynamic model to explain why some organizations fail to adjust and reorient to adjust to an external shock. Her model is shown graphically in Figure 13.3.

Figure 13.3 shows the relationships in the systems dynamics model of punctuated change theory. The performance of an organization depends on what it does with respect to strategic orientation and how well it accomplishes the adjustment. The organization needs competence and appropriate strategic orientation to perform. Competence comes from inertia – which is built up over time. Inertia reduces the firm's ability to change. Experience with change enhances ability to change. Strategic orientation is changed by senior management under perceived performance pressures. From her model she concluded 'while external events may set the pace of organizational change in some environments, under turbulent conditions successful change requires internal pacing, which suspends performance evaluation for the period following a reorientation'. Sastry's model is an example of maneuverability to new performance requirements.

Sastry's work puts more detail into a design rule related to change and added time, as in the study by Siggelkow and Levinthal (2003). This work was further extended by Håkonsson et al. (2009) to include continuous change. They find that in continuous changing environments organizations which adapt on an ongoing basis have a lower variance on performance than those that remain stable over longer period of time. This again adds precision on a design rule related to the design process.

Tools: VENSIM, MyStrategy, STELLA, iThink, PowerSim and AnyLogic.

COMPUTATIONAL MODELING AS A VALID LABORATORY FOR 'WHAT MIGHT BE' DESIGN RULES

'What might be' computational laboratories can address many of the challenges for a better understanding of organizational design – and in particular the development of design rules. Perhaps the greatest challenge is to incorporate time explicitly into our understanding. The decomposition models with iterative planning algorithms treat time, adjustment and coordination for the multi-agent planning problem. The NK model analyzes the 'temporary' gains of decentralization, but in the longer term coordination becomes important. In the VDT project team models, the precedence relations introduce time as tasks that must be done in a semi-ordered fashion. System dynamics with its emphasis on feedback and adjustment is again time dependent. Time dependency is fundamental to our understanding of organizational design.

Dynamic fit and maneuverability are fundamentally time concepts: how quickly the organization can return to its performance level or move to a new level of performance. The time it takes for planning is important, and shorter time improves performance. Temporary decentralization is a means to adjust back to a performance with low opportunity loss. System dynamics is a model of continuing adjustment to achieve a good fit.

Multiple goals are evident in the M-form experiments to analyze the efficiency of the planning processes, but also opportunism and the incentives to cheat: the M-form did well on both. The NK decentralization experiment analyzed short-term and long-term goals, and the balance between the two. The VDT simulation measures cost, time and project quality for a project, illustrating that there can be a trade-off in the choice of a good organizational design.

These illustrate the future challenges for organizational design. The fundamental aspects of organizational design are based in how an organization can make good decisions (and implement them) in a coordinated fashion with the information that it has or can obtain. Burton et al. (2011) present a step-by-step approach to organizational design using design rules where there must be a fit among goals, strategy, structure, tasks, people, leadership, climate, coordination and control systems including IT, and the incentives. These computational approaches provide an array of possibilities to develop and refine design rules and can be important in a triangulation perspective to evaluate new design rules (Burton & Obel 2011).

SUMMARY AND CONCLUSION

We began with organizational design issues for Cisco and Aarhus University. Their high levels of uncertainty and task interdependency call for new designs and design changes. How do they realize the needed coordination among a large number of organizational units to achieve their goals? How do they create innovation to meet the demands of their environment? In information-processing terms – who talks with whom about what, and who makes what decisions – we find there are a large set of design elements which must be designed in concert: organizational form, information systems, control mechanisms, incentives and leadership style, among others, to achieve the required coordination. As both Cisco and Aarhus University know, it is not an easy task. To design a multi-location project organization, NASA (Carroll et al. 2006) utilized computational modeling – OrgCon and SimVision – to examine 'what might be' alternative designs. They demonstrated that experienced administrators proposed a design which was infeasible and would not work; that is, experience alone can be misleading. They avoided a costly mistake. Avoiding future mistakes through 'what might be' modeling is very important, as well as devising totally new exploratory design possibilities.

Throughout we have focused on 'what might be' design rules. These are 'if-then' statements about 'what should be' a good design property for an effective and efficient organization. We focused on two classic and continuingly important 'if' contingencies: uncertainty and interdependency. Recommended organizational properties are the 'then' part of the statements, here the level of centralization. Each design rule should stand on its own as a reasonable and valid recommendation. Perhaps more importantly, the composition of the rules must be reasonable and valid as an ensemble of consistent and reasonably comprehensive design rules for the whole of the organization. Much of our research has been focused on examining what has occurred in the past and then making sense of it – largely to examine single or a small number of rules; that is, one or two 'if-then' statements of hypotheses. There are a very large number of single design rules. The OrgCon has more than 500 design rules which are a composition of singular rules into a consistent and comprehensive rule-based organizational design program. With 68 'if' questions in OrgCon, each with five possible answers, there are 340 possible premises for the 'if' part with simple rules alone. With composite rules this results in a very large number of possible design recommendations when the more than 500 design rules are applied. The recommended design is not necessarily unique and the most important recommendations are statements about what will not work and inconsistencies in design possibilities. The OrgCon 'if-then' statements are based upon the best research – largely empirical studies of what was or what is. For the future, we need to explore and expand the set of 'if-then' rules to incorporate 'what might be'.

What is the future and how can we utilize 'what might be' logic to help us avoid costly mistakes and implement good organizational designs in situations which we have not experienced before? We reviewed a few computational or simulation studies: Siggelkow and Levinthal's temporary decentralization for environmental shifts; Wickstrøm Jensen et al.'s study of virtuality in organization; and Carroll et al.'s (2006) NASA study which utilized the OrgCon and SimVision to develop a multi-location project organization – avoiding an infeasible design based upon experience. We argued that the future also requires new concepts. Multiple goals are to be expected as short-run profits must be balanced with long-run sustainability of the firm and the environment. However, using a computational model, Ethiraj and Levinthal (2009) demonstrated that an organization can deal with only a small handfull of goals. A laundry list of goals will not work. Nissen and Burton (2011) took up another challenge – time – to examine what we mean by dynamic fit and maneuverability. With an environment shock, the time required to adjust and recover is very important and our 'if-then' design rules are lacking in this domain as most are based on a static comparative logic where a 'what might be' logic is needed.

NOTES

1. Our thanks to George P. Huber, Carl R. Jones and Andrew Van de Ven for comments on an earlier version of this chapter. Anna Grandori, our editor, has been most supportive and helpful through numerous iterations of this chapter.
2. www.ecomerc.com

REFERENCES

Armour, H.O. and D.J. Teece (1978), 'Organization structure and economic performance: a test of the multi-divisional hypothesis', *Bell Journal of Economics*, 9, 106–122.

Arrow, K.J. (1974), *The Limits of Organization*, New York: Norton.

Ashby, W.R. (1956), *Introduction to Cybernetics*, London: Methuen.

Baligh, H.H., R.M. Burton and B. Obel (1996), 'Organizational consultant: creating a useable theory for organizational design', *Management Science*, 42(12), 1648–1662.

Bryan, L.L. and C.I. Joyce (2007), 'Better strategy through organizational design', *McKinsey Quarterly*, May, 2.

Burns, T. and G.M. Stalker (1961), *The Management of Innovation*, New York: Oxford University Press.

Burton, R.M. (2003), 'Computational laboratories for organization science: questions, validity and docking', *Computational and Mathematical Organization Theory*, 9(1), 91–108.

Burton, R.M. and B. Obel (1980), 'A computer simulation test of the M-form hypothesis', *Administrative Science Quarterly*, 25(3), 457–466.

Burton, R.M. and B. Obel (1984), *Designing Efficient Organizations: Modelling and Experimentation*, Amsterdam: North-Holland.

Burton, R.M. and B. Obel (1988), 'Opportunism, incentives, and the M-form hypothesis: a laboratory study', *Journal of Economic Behavior and Organization*, 10, 99–119.

Burton, R.M. and B. Obel (1995), 'The validity of computational models in organization science: from model realism to purpose of the model', *Computational and Mathematical Organization Theory*, 1(1), 57–71.

Burton, R.M. and B. Obel (2004), *Strategic Organizational Diagnosis and Design: The Dynamics of Fit*, 3rd edn, Boston, MA: Kluwer Academic Publishers.

Burton, R.M. and B. Obel (2011), 'Computational modeling of what-is, what-might-be and what-should-be studies – and triangulation', *Organization Science*, 22(5), 1195–1202.

Burton, R.M., G. DeSanctis and B. Obel (2011), *Organizational Design: A Step By Step Approach*, 2nd edn, Cambridge: Cambridge University Press.

Burton, Richard M., Jørgen Lauridsen and Børge Obel (2002 [2003]), 'Return on assets lost from situational and contingency misfits', *Management Science*, 48, 1461–85; (2003) Erratum, *Management Science*, 49, 1119.

Carroll, A.B. and K.M. Shabana (2010), 'The business case for corporate social responsibility: a review of concepts, research and practice', *International Journal of Management Review*, 12(1), 85–106.

Carroll, T.N., Thomas J. Gormley, Vincent J. Bilardo and Richard M. Burton (2006), 'Designing a new organization at NASA: an organization design process using simulation', *Organization Science*, 17(2), Special Issue on Organizational Design, 200–214.

Chandler, A.D., Jr. (1962), *Strategy and Structure: Chapters in the History of Industrial Enterprise*, Cambridge, MA: MIT Press.

Cyert, R.M. and J.G. March (1963), *A Behavioral Theory of the Firm*, Englewood Cliffs, NJ: Prentice-Hall.

Davis, J.P., K.M. Eisenhardt and C.B. Bingham (2007), 'Developing theory through simulation methods', *Academy of Management Review*, 32(2), 480–499.

DiMaggio, P.J. and W.W. Powell (1991), *The New Institutionalism and Organizational Analysis*, 2nd edn, Chicago, IL: University of Chicago Press.

Donaldson, L. (1987), 'Strategy and structural adjustment to regain fit and performance: in defence of contingency theory', *Journal of Management Studies*, 24(1), 1–24.

Donaldson, L. (2001), *The Contingency Theory of Organizations*, Thousand Oaks, CA: Sage.

Ethiraj, S.K. and D. Levinthal (2009), 'Hoping for A to Z while rewarding only A: complex organizations and multiple goals', *Organization Science*, 20(1), 4–21.

Fenton, A.M. and E.M. Pettigrew (2000), *The Innovating Organization*, London: SAGE Publications.

Fiss, P.C. (2011), 'Building better casual theories: a fuzzy set approach to typologies in organizational research', *Academy of Management Journal*, 54(2), 393–420.

Galbraith, J.R. (1973), *Designing Complex Organizations*, Reading, MA: Addison-Wesley.
Galbraith, J.R. (1974), 'Organizational design: an information processing view', *Interfaces*, **4**, 28–36.
Grandori, A. (1997), 'Governance structures, coordination mechanisms and cognitive models', *Journal of Management and Governance*, **1**, 29–47.
Gresov, C. (1989), 'Exploring fit and misfit with multiple contingencies', *Administrative Science Quarterly*, **34**(3), 431–453.
Håkonsson, D.D., P. Klaas and T.N. Carroll (2009), 'Organizational adaptation, continuous change, and the positive role of inertia', *Academy of Management Annual Meeting Proceedings*, 1–6.
Håkonsson, D.D., R.M. Burton, B. Obel and J.T. Lauridsen (2012), 'Strategy implementation requires the right executive style: evidence from Danish SMEs', *Long Range Planning*, **45**, 182–208.
Harrison, J.R., L. Zhiang, R.G. Carroll and K.M. Carley (2007), 'Simulation modeling in organizational and management research', *Academy of Management Review*, **32**(4), 1229–1245.
Huber, G. (2003) *The Necessary Nature of Future Firms. Attributes of Survivors in a Changing World*, London: SAGE.
Jensen, K.W., D.D. Håkonsson, R.M. Burton and B. Obel (2010), 'The effect of virtuality on the functioning of centralized versus decentralized structures – an information processing perspective', *Computational and Mathematical Organization Theory*, **16**(2), 144–170.
Kim, J. and R.M. Burton (2002), 'The effect of task uncertainty and decentralization on project team performance', *Computational and Mathematical Organization Theory*, **8**, 365–384.
Lawrence, P.R. and J.W. Lorsch (1967), 'Differentiation and integration in complex organizations', *Administrative Science Quarterly*, **12**(1), 1–47.
Levitt, R.E. (2004), 'Computational modeling of organizations comes of age', *Computational and Mathematical Organization Theory*, **10**(2), 127–145.
Levitt, R.E. (2012), 'The virtual design team (VDT): designing project organizations as engineers design bridges', *Journal of Organization Design*, **1**(1), 14–41.
March, J.G. and H.A. Simon (1958), *Organizations*, New York: John Wiley.
Marschak, J. and R. Radner (1972), *Economic Theory of Teams*, New Haven, CT: Yale University Press.
Miles, R.E. and C.C. Snow (1978), 'Organizational strategy, structure, and process', New York: McGraw-Hill.
Miller, D. (1992), 'Environmental fit versus internal fit', *Organization Science*, **3**(2), 159–178.
Miller, D., R. Greenwood, R. Prakash (2009), 'What happened to organization theory?' *Journal of Management Inquiry*, **18**(4), 273–279.
Nissen, M.E. and R.M. Burton (2011), 'Designing organizations for dynamic fit: system stability, maneuverability, and opportunity loss', *IEEE Transactions on Systems, Man, and Cybernetics, Part A: Systems and Humans*, **41**(3), 418–433.
Romanelli, E. and M.L. Tushman (1994), 'Organizational transformation as punctuated equilibrium: an empirical test', *Academy of Management Journal*, **37**(5), 1141–1166.
Romme, A.G.L. (2003), 'Making a difference: organization by design', *Organization Science*, **14**(5), 558–573.
Rosoff, M. (2011), 'Cisco's crazy management structure wasn't working, so chambers is changing it', *Business Insider*, 5 May.
Sastry, A. (1997), 'Problems and paradoxes in a model of punctuated organizational change', *Administrative Science Quarterly*, **42**(2), 237–275.
Schwaningera, M. and J.P. Ríos (2008), 'System dynamics and cybernetics: a synergetic pair', *System Dynamics Review*, **4**(2).
Siggelkow, N. and D.A. Levinthal (2003), 'Temporarily divide to conquer: centralized, decentralized, and reintegrated organizational approaches to exploration and adaptation', *Organization Science*, **14**(6), 650–669.
Simon, H.A. (1996), *The Sciences of the Artificial*, 3rd edn, Cambridge, MA: MIT Press.
Tushman, M.L. and D.A. Nadler (1978), 'Information processing as an integrating concept in organizational design', *Academy of Management Review*, **3**(3), 613–624.
Tushman, M.L. and E. Romanelli (1985), 'Organizational evolution: a metamorphosis model of convergence and reorientation', in L.L. Cunnings and B.M. Stacer (eds), *Research in Organizational Behavior*, San Francisco, CA: JAI Press, pp. 171–222.
Williamson, O.E. (1975), *Markets and Hierarchies: Analysis and Antitrust Implications*, New York: Free Press.
Woodward, J. (1965), *Industrial Organization, Theory and Practice*, Oxford: Oxford University Press.
Zacharias, G.L., J. MacMillan and S.B. Van Hemel (2008), *Behavioral Model and Simulation: From Individual to Societies*, Washington, DC: National Academies Press.

14. Organizational formation and change: lessons from economic laboratory experiments*

Peter H. Kriss and Roberto Weber

This chapter reviews research in which economic laboratory experiments shed light on the processes that influence organizational formation and change. An organization, in these experiments, is represented by an abstract collective production activity that takes place in a controlled laboratory setting with incentivized human subjects. The studies typically attempt to identify factors that enhance efficient production. Our review focuses on experiments that explore features of how organizations originate, grow, and implement change, and the roles of communication and leadership in managing these processes. Our survey concludes that laboratory experiments of this type present a useful way to identify important factors that influence the relationship between individual behaviors and organizational performance at critical stages, which might otherwise be difficult to isolate outside the laboratory.

INTRODUCTION

Understanding the factors that affect organizational performance is an important area of scientific and applied inquiry, as reflected in many other chapters in this volume. This chapter similarly explores conditions that allow some organizations to function 'better' than others. In particular, we are interested in research that employs, in our mind, an underutilized tool for the study of organizational processes – the structured, largely abstract, and incentivized laboratory experiment regularly employed in economics. The research we review studies the behavior and decisions of small groups of individuals who are placed in a context carefully designed to mimic important aspects of production in organizations, including well-specified incentives, high levels of interdependence and social considerations. By considering the relationship between individual behavior and collective outcomes such as firm output and profitability, the experiments present a way to bridge micro- and macro-level organizational research. The research also bridges economic and organizational research, by using the incentive-based, highly structured approach of the former to study issues centered in the latter, such as the roles of culture and leadership in organizational performance.

It is important to note that our review is not of the broad field of experimental economics. While laboratory experiments have grown in prominence and utilization within economics over the past several decades, their application has traditionally been focused in areas such as markets and auctions (Smith 1962; Kagel et al. 1987), testing departures from traditional normative decision- and game-theoretic models (Ochs & Roth 1989; Harless & Camerer 1994), and explorations of the motivations underlying other-regarding behavior (Hoffman et al. 1994; Fehr & Gächter 2000). Where experimental economists devote attention to the behavior of firms, it is often in the context of experiments on industrial organization, where the 'firm' consists of a single subject unilaterally making pricing or production decisions, as tests of the relevant theoretical predictions.[1]

The kind of experiment on which we focus here considers the firm – a collection of interdependent individuals jointly engaged in production (cf. Marschak & Radner 1972) – as the unit of analysis, and is less common.[2] But as we will show, this type of experiment is particularly well suited to the study of how 'successful' firms start out, how they deal with change, and how important organizational factors, such as leadership, influence success.

In most of the research we review, an 'organization' is a collection of a small number of individuals, grouped together either by the experimenter or some endogenous process (e.g., as when subjects decide, within the experiment, whether to join a firm), and a production technology that combines the actions of the group members into some collective output. Capturing a key feature of many organizations, the impact of individuals' actions on collective production is often interdependent (March & Simon 1958), meaning that the product of one employee's effort depends on that of another.

Given their complexity and scope, most modern organizations may seem to have little in common with small groups of individuals (often college students) in sterile laboratory environments, making decisions for relatively small stakes. But the value of the economic laboratory experiment lies precisely in its simplicity. By stripping away all but the most essential aspects of a social or economic interaction – either to test the precise point predictions of a formal economic model or to otherwise obtain an improved understanding of how different factors affect outcomes – the researcher is able to obtain unparalleled control in understanding causality and isolating the key factors of importance.[3]

For example, many organizational contexts involve high degrees of complementarity and interdependence, where the product of one person's work depends on that of others within the organization. Such production with very high complementarities can be modeled using simple coordination games, such as the one in Table 14.1.[4] This 'minimum-effort' coordination game, which we return to throughout our chapter, models production in firms where quality or output is very sensitive to the lowest effort of any employee. This applies, for example, on an assembly line where production can proceed only as fast as the slowest worker (Brandts & Cooper 2006), in a service estab-

Table 14.1   Minimum-effort coordination game

		Minimum effort chosen in firm (e^{min})					
		7	6	5	4	3	2	1
Employee's effort choice (e_i)	7	130	110	90	70	50	30	10
	6		120	100	80	60	40	20
	5			110	90	70	50	30
	4				100	80	60	40
	3					90	70	50
	2						80	60
	1							70

Source: Van Huyck et al. (1990).

lishment where customers are highly sensitive to the lowest quality of service received (Camerer & Knez 1997), or in a network where security can only be maintained if several interdependent units do their part (Kunreuther & Heal 2003).

In the game, N employees, where N typically ranges from 2 to 16, each independently select effort levels (rows) and output is determined by the lowest effort level exerted in the firm (columns). Employees face costs for higher effort, but benefit when output is higher. Thus, if everyone exerts the highest possible effort, 7, then the highest pay-off obtains for all employees (130). Unlike production with incentives to free-ride (modeled by social dilemmas and public-good games), employees here have no incentive to shirk when others exert high effort: if a worker believes that all others will exert high effort, then the worker wants to do so as well. For this reason, all employees giving high effort is a Nash equilibrium. The problem in the minimum-effort coordination game arises because players might be unsure of how much effort others will expend. When someone in the organization exerts low effort, then all other employees have an incentive to do so as well. Thus, all employees providing effort of 1 is also an equilibrium, yielding a pay-off of 70 for all workers. Of course, workers would prefer the high-effort equilibrium, but strategic uncertainty may undermine their ability to get there.

A group of experimental subjects playing this game repeatedly can serve as a simple test bed for studying factors that make coordination easier or more difficult in organizational settings. For example, early experiments in which this game was repeated with fixed groups showed that groups of size five or more often end up at the worst equilibrium, with the lowest possible effort (Van Huyck et al. 1990). Starting from this simple version of an organization facing coordination problems, the laboratory researcher can create multiple replications of such 'firms', while varying features of interest to study the effect they have on coordination and firm profitability.[5]

Thus, simple economic laboratory experiments of this kind provide a valuable method for learning about how organizational characteristics affect outcomes. The main benefit of this approach is that it yields the researcher unparalleled control – to create multiple, identical replica organizations and to vary only intended organizational characteristics. It thus provides the ability to more carefully identify causality than is typically possible in the field, where multiple factors are likely to vary simultaneously, often in a correlated manner.

Of course, laboratory experiments are but one methodological tool for learning about organizations, and serve as a complement to other, equally valuable methodologies (Weick 1969). While one can rarely exert the necessary control over naturally occurring environments to test theories in the manner afforded by laboratory experiments, one must ultimately look to the field to confirm whether insights and theories developed in the laboratory actually account for what occurs in real organizations.

ORGANIZATIONAL FORMATION

An important question for understanding organizations is how they should start off. As we discuss later in this chapter, there are important path-dependencies in how effectively an organization's members are likely to deal with coordination problems that arise from the interdependence of their actions. Therefore, having an organization that begins well – that is, efficiently solves coordination problems – is critical for having one that subsequently performs well. In this section, we review aspects of how an organization might be established by its founders, and the impact of these design choices on organizational success.

Because our review is narrow in scope, we do not attempt a broad survey of the experimental literature that studies productivity under alternative incentive mechanisms, including incentives based on social considerations such as reciprocity.[6] This research is important, as it shows that the kind of incentives a founder employs in establishing an organization can critically affect the resulting effort and productivity. For the interested reader, this research is reviewed in Camerer and Weber (2012).

Organizational Composition

One critical issue in organizational formation is who should make up an organization. Standard theories of organizational economics generally assume homogeneously self-interested agents, who may differ in terms of skill and expertise. However, this approach ignores potentially important heterogeneity in people's socially oriented motivations and how these may impact what they do within an organization (Benabou & Tirole 2006; Akerlof & Kranton 2005; Camerer & Malmendier 2007). As we note above, recent behavioral research in organizational economics considers how to get the incentives 'right' in the presence of such motives.

Related to the question of how to properly motivate the employees in an organization, however, is how to attract and identify the organizational members that are most likely to benefit the firm. Laboratory experiments present a valuable context in which to directly compare, while holding all else constant, the behavior and productivity of groups comprised of different kinds of individuals. From these simple laboratory experiments, one can begin to understand what kind of people are the most desirable to attract into an organization – particularly in the early stages at which an organization's culture and norms are being established – and how best to attract such people.

The organizational composition experiments discussed in this section consider two different potential sources of inefficiency. One source is the free-rider problem. That is, individual-level incentives may be in direct conflict with firm-level profit maximizing, leading to the question of how to maintain high levels of cooperation when doing so involves a net sacrifice by each employee. The second source of inefficiency is strategic uncertainty and its potential to undermine coordination, as in the minimum-effort coordination game introduced earlier.

When free-riding may undermine efficiency
Consider an organization in which employees' individual efforts yield some collective output and the profits from this output are at least partly shared among workers (i.e., as in 'revenue sharing' compensation schemes; see Nalbantian & Schotter 1997). If each individual employee's share of the return from higher output is less than the cost of the individual's effort to produce that output, but the collective return to all employees from an individual's effort is higher than the cost of that effort, then the production process mimics the provision of a public good under voluntary cooperation. If the firm observes only the collective output or cannot otherwise contract with employees on their individ-

ual input of effort, then each employee faces moral hazard, in that the employee has an incentive to shirk and free-ride from others' provision of effort. This results in a unique low-effort equilibrium in which it is not worthwhile for an individual employee to work harder, even though it would benefit the firm and employees, collectively, by more than it costs the employee.[7]

An experiment by Page et al. (2005) shows how allowing individuals to decide with whom to associate can mitigate the free-rider problem in these kinds of situations. In their experiment, groups of subjects engaged in the above type of production repeatedly, by selecting numerical strategies that can be interpreted as effort directed towards collective production. In a baseline treatment, subjects were randomly matched, while in another treatment subjects could form new groups every three periods, by indicating with whom they wanted to be grouped. At the time they indicated these preferences, subjects could observe how much others had contributed to the collective production. Subjects were then matched according to these preferences by an algorithm that grouped together those who mutually viewed each other as most desirable. This simple form of grouping increased production from 38 percent of the possible maximum to 70 percent. Thus, letting people decide with whom they want to work yields more productive units. These results suggest, for example, that in a small start-up, in which the founders voluntarily decide to join together to work on a venture, the kind of motivation problems that otherwise may arise from collective production may be less important than, say, among a project team in a large firm where employees are assigned to work together.

However, related research reveals that giving people the opportunity to voluntarily associate is not sufficient to overcome such motivation problems. It is also necessary that those willing to work hard are able to exclude shirkers. Ehrhart and Keser (1999) conducted an (earlier) experiment similar to Page et al., in which subjects also could decide with whom to be grouped prior to making production decisions. However, in their experiment, subjects could unilaterally join a group, meaning that those forming a group had no ability to exclude others attempting to join. As in Page et al.'s experiment, they find that subjects are attracted to form groups with those who contribute high effort to production. However, unlike in Page et al.'s experiment, where those high contributors could exclude shirkers from joining their group, the absence of this exclusion ability from Ehrhart and Kesser's experiment results in everyone attempting to join the groups with high production. Mean per-employee production therefore falls as more shirkers enter such desirable groups. This, in turn, leads hard workers to leave the group, and the efficiency gains in Page et al.'s experiment are not realized.

These results are important for understanding basic properties of organizations. Organizations will do better when formed by the mutual interest of high-effort 'types' in working together, but they should also critically possess a screening mechanism that allows the exclusion of those who are less cooperatively oriented. While this point is obtained implicitly by comparing the experiments of Ehrhart and Kesser and Page et al., it is demonstrated more directly in later studies that vary, by treatment, whether those wishing to form a group with others are required to get their approval (Ahn et al. 2008, 2009). In such 'restricted entry' conditions, contributions are higher than when no entry restrictions exist.

Other experimental research similarly identifies how to attract the 'best' types into an organization. For example, an experimental study by Dohmen and Falk (2011) considers what kinds of employees are attracted to different firms that vary in their compensation schemes. Their experiment first measured individual productivity in a simple experimental task involving effort. They then gave subjects the option of performing this task, for pay, under two different compensation schemes: a flat wage or variable pay, with the latter varying between a piece-rate payment for each completed problem, a relative-performance mechanism in which subjects' pay depended on whether they outperformed another subject, and a revenue-sharing payment scheme that mimicked the public-goods production function described above. More productive employees are attracted to organizations with variable pay and this sorting is partly accounted for by heterogeneity in individual preferences such as risk attitudes.[8]

Other research suggests that attracting employees primarily through higher financial incentives may have detrimental effects. Lazear et al. (2012) study how the decision to enter an environment with opportunities for behaving pro-socially, as when one helps another worker or does something to benefit the organization, is affected by the incentives present for doing so. Using a higher payment to attract people into the sharing environment has the perverse effect of attracting primarily those who are least willing to help others. Extending this to organizational formation, an organization that relies on voluntary effort and cooperativeness from its workers should be wary that paying a higher wage may most attract those who are least intrinsically motivated to work cooperatively.

When strategic uncertainty may undermine efficiency

How groups are formed can also matter for efficiency under other kinds of production, such as when inputs are highly interdependent and there are both efficient and inefficient equilibria. Recall that, in such situations, the critical problem is that employees may be unsure of whether others will exert high effort, and if they lack such confidence in others they are unwilling to do so themselves. In games that model this kind of problem, such as the minimum-effort coordination game discussed above, several experiments show that how a group is formed affects the degree of efficiency and effort subsequently obtained.

For example, Riedl et al. (2011) study a version of the game in Table 14.1, using a design in which individuals can decide with whom they want to play the game, and in which there is an incentive for playing in larger groups. They find that this ability of individuals to voluntarily associate, and exclude others with whom they do not want to associate, allows for very large, efficiently coordinated groups.

Voluntary association may also interact with incentives to create an organization in which workers have high mutual confidence in others also selecting high effort. For example, Van Huyck et al. (1993) and Cachon and Camerer (1996) use experiments with coordination games similar to the one in Table 14.1 to show that when employees have to voluntarily sacrifice in order to join a firm, they tend to coordinate on higher-effort equilibria. To see one reason why, consider a firm made up of people who each had to sacrifice an outside pay-off of 100 to join and play the production game in Table 14.1. When employees sacrifice to join the firm, and they know that others who joined chose to do so as well, then they are likely to possess the mutual confidence that others would not have joined if they did not intend to pursue the high-effort equilibria.[9] In fact, this is the result. Firms formed by employees having to sacrifice for the right to belong coordinate more efficiently.

By reviewing the above experiments, we observe an important property of efficient organization. From the moment a group of independent actors begins interacting jointly in production – that is, they form an 'organization' – how they were brought together matters greatly for how well the organization functions. The above experiments show that bringing together a group of individuals in the right way can significantly alleviate problems that arise from free riding or shirking (cooperation problems) and from individuals' uncertainty about the actions others will take (coordination problems).

Delegation

Another fundamental question in organizational formation is how much the organization's founders and leaders should delegate to other members of the organization. Within economics, theoretical research explores the influence of delegation and hierarchy on profit maximization (Grossman & Hart 1986; Baker et al. 1999). In these models, as in most economic theories, complex concepts such as authority and delegation are highly simplified and stylized. For example, 'authority' is often modeled as a decision right that an individual in a hierarchy either keeps or delegates to a subordinate (Aghion & Tirole 1997). Economic laboratory experiments that study delegation and hierarchy – often primarily intended to test whether delegation works and is used as predicted by the theory – similarly employ very simple designs.

For example, Huck et al. (2004) use a laboratory experiment to explore whether a firm 'owner' in the context of a Cournot duopoly delegates to a 'manager' by providing either the same incentives as those facing the owner – to maximize firm profits – or with an additional incentive to act aggressively in setting the quantity produced by the firm – by providing an additional sales bonus. Prior theory (Fershtman & Judd 1987; Sklivas 1987) predicts that by creating the ability to commit to the high-sales contract, the ability to choose between such contracts should confer an advantage to the firm that does so. Thus, according to theory, the sophisticated owner incentivizes his manager to act more aggressively than the owner would otherwise act himself. When both owners can offer such contracts, they do so and the managers compete more aggressively than if the owners made their own quantity decisions. This yields an outcome with lower payoffs than under the Cournot equilibrium that results when owners decide for themselves (or offer managers contracts without a sales bonus).

The results of Huck et al.'s experiment provide little support for this prediction of strategic advantage from delegation. Incentivized managers do not act as aggressively as theory predicts and, conversely, those managers who are not provided with the sales-bonus contract, but face a manager who is, act more aggressively than predicted by theory. The end result is that strategic delegation is less effective than predicted – partly because of the managers' preferences for fairness or equality – and owners therefore offer the more timid contract without a sales bonus.

Further evidence that the actual use of strategic delegation departs from theoretical predictions comes from recent laboratory experiments by Fehr et al. (2011) and by Lai and Lim (2012). These studies explore situations in which one member of an organization may delegate a decision right to a subordinate – a simple form of 'authority' – but in this case the context involves a manager and employee jointly implementing one from a set of many possible projects (Holmstrom 1984). Both papers explore the manager's decision to delegate, based on the degree of alignment between the manager's and subordinate's preferences and information, and compare the degree of delegation with the optimal benchmark proposed by theory.

For example, in the paper by Fehr et al., both the manager and subordinate are initially uncertain about the value of the different projects, and their preferences over projects do not coincide. In the experiment, the manager must decide whether to retain the power to unilaterally implement a project, in which case the employee has little incentive to engage in costly information acquisition regarding the value of different projects, or to delegate the decision right to the employee, in which case the employee has greater incentives to engage in search but may also implement a different project than the one preferred by the manager. When the divergence in interests between the manager and employee is small, managers should be willing to delegate to an employee. Instead, the experiment reveals that managers hold on to the decision power too often, resulting in lower pay-offs than if they delegated the decision to the employee. A similar observation obtains in the experiment by Lai and Lim (2012). These results suggest that authority itself is intrinsically valued, meaning that founders, owners, and managers in organizational contexts are likely to under-delegate and do too much themselves. Herz et al. also demonstrate that such authority has a motivating effect that goes beyond the incentives accounted for in traditional theories (Aghion & Tirole 1997) – those with decision rights work harder and those without them work less hard than what is predicted by the theory.

Fershtman and Gneezy (2001) provide further evidence for the discrepancy between theoretically predicted and observed outcomes under delegation. They study delegation in an ultimatum bargaining context, in which a proposer makes a take-it-or-leave-it offer to a responder. They compare offers made directly by proposers with offers made by agents on behalf of proposers, where the agents receive payment contingent on the amount that they obtain for the proposer. They find that delegation provides an advantage to proposers who delegate rather than make their own offers, even when theory predicts no such advantage. The advantage to the proposers results from the fact that the responders are more likely to accept low offers made by agents.

The above results are important as they demonstrate discrepancies between theoretical predictions about when delegation is likely to benefit a manager and when it actually does. Indeed, the complex social preferences of organizational members seem to neutralize some advantages of delegation while simultaneously creating other advantages overlooked by theory.

An experiment by Hamman et al. (2010) further studies the powerful effects of delegation in contexts involving fairness. Their experiment compares a standard dictator game, in which a decision maker allocates $10 between themself and a passive recipient, with a delegation treatment in which the dictator hires an agent to make the decision on the dictator's behalf. The agent receives a fixed payment for being hired, and is free to share any amount with the recipient. The main incentive for an agent is to get rehired by the principal, to obtain the fixed payment again. The experiment therefore explores how generously or ethically people behave, either when they act directly or when acting through an intermediary. In organizational contexts, this corresponds to the extent to which members of a firm act – either directly or through subordinates – in a fair or socially responsible manner towards external third parties.

Figure 14.1 presents the results from Experiment 2 by Hamman et al. (2010). The baseline condition, in which dictators made allocation decisions personally, shows high

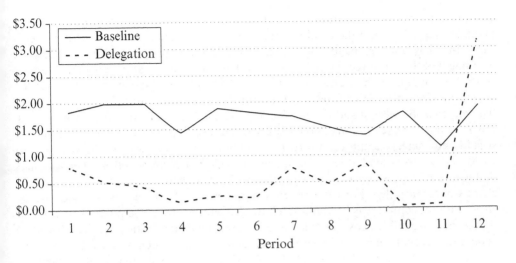

Source: Hamman et al. (2010, Experiment 2).

Figure 14.1 *Average generosity in baseline and delegation conditions*

degrees of sharing consistent with prior experimental evidence (cf. Camerer 2003, Ch. 2). However, the agent conditions, in which dictators instead selected someone to make the decisions for them, reveal that delegation dramatically reduces how much is shared. This occurred primarily through subjects seeking the agent who was willing to act most selfishly on their behalf. In other conditions, in which subjects could make delegation decisions themselves, or choose instead to hire an agent, sharing similarly declined to near zero. Thus, aside from delegation yielding strategic advantages, these findings suggest that it also allows people to feel better about taking unethical or immoral actions, a form of 'moral outsourcing'. Indeed, when asked how responsible they felt for the fate of the recipient, subjects reported significantly less responsibility under delegation. Thus, the degree of vertical delegation can be an important factor in determining the extent to which an organization ultimately acts ethically towards outsiders.[10]

A similar point is made by Ellman and Pezanis-Christou (2010). Their paper considers different kinds of organizational hierarchies and the degree to which they yield ethical outcomes that do not impose a negative externality on a third party. They find that flat, horizontal structures yield more ethical behavior than vertical ones in which responsibility for the unethical conduct is diffused by vertical specialization. They also find that communication plays an important role in the level of ethical conduct observed. For example, in vertical structures, increased communication yields more ethical behavior, as subordinates have greater ability to voice objections to proposed unethical conduct.

Finally, two recent experimental papers by Falk and Kosfeld (2006) and Charness et al. (2012), show that delegation may also be beneficial because of the goodwill it creates among subordinates. Falk and Kosfeld demonstrate that giving an employee greater control can induce positive reciprocal behavior. Conversely, controlling a subordinate's behavior is likely to incur 'hidden costs' in that the employee will react negatively to the control. In their experiment, an employee has discretion over how much costly effort,

e, between 0 and 120, to exert in working for a manager. For any effort expended, the manager receives $2e$ and the employee incurs a cost of e, making effort costly but efficient. In a baseline treatment, the manager does not control the employee's decision, meaning that the employee can choose any level of effort. In a treatment with managerial control, the manager chooses whether to limit the employee's possible effort choices by setting a lower limit, $c > 0$. Thus, control eliminates some low-effort actions available to the employee, between 0 and c, while leaving the employee with full discretion over all other actions. The key finding in their study is that exerting control, which theoretically should only increase employee effort (i.e., by forcing those employees who would exert effort below c to expend at least this much effort), often decreases effort. The reason is that many employees exerting effort greater than c when there is no control decrease their effort when controlled. For example, in a treatment in which c equaled 5, the average effort without control was 25.1, but it fell to 12.2 with control. The point of their paper is that there are hidden costs of control, or of exerting formal authority, that should be taken into account when deciding how much of it to exert over employees' actions.

Charness et al. (2012) demonstrate the flip-side of this result, that is, that there are 'hidden benefits to delegation'. They conduct an experiment in which a decision regarding how high a wage to pay to an employee is delegated to the employee. They find that employees given the ability to set their own wages exert higher effort and, as a result, firms that delegate the wage-setting decision to the employees often produce higher profits for both employees and for the firm.

As the papers above show, the degree of delegation can have profound implications for how an organization functions. Perhaps most importantly, delegation decisions can be driven by individual preferences that are distinct from those present in traditional models in organizational economics. People may under-delegate because they intrinsically value possessing authority; they may delegate to circumvent ethical considerations or personal responsibility; and subordinates may reciprocate delegation with kindness. Such findings have important implications for how much delegation and hierarchy is observed in organizations, and for the resulting behavior of organizational actors.

Communication

Another important consideration in organizational formation is what communication structures should be in place to allow information to be pooled and transferred. In this section, we review laboratory experiments that shed light on when and how well communication solves one particular kind of production problem.[11] In particular, we focus on production problems with high complementarities, of the kind in Table 14.1. Recall that, in these minimum-effort coordination games, which have been widely applied to organizational contexts, everyone does better when all employees exert high effort, so the problem is not one of motivation.[12] Rather, the difficulty in obtaining efficient coordination stems from the fact that employees may be unsure about what others will do. Indeed, such strategic uncertainty is sufficient to yield the result that groups of size five or larger almost universally coordinate on the inefficient equilibrium in which everyone exerts the lowest possible effort (Van Huyck et al. 1990).

Because the main problem underlying production inefficiencies in this kind of context is uncertainty about the actions that will be taken by others, communication, even when

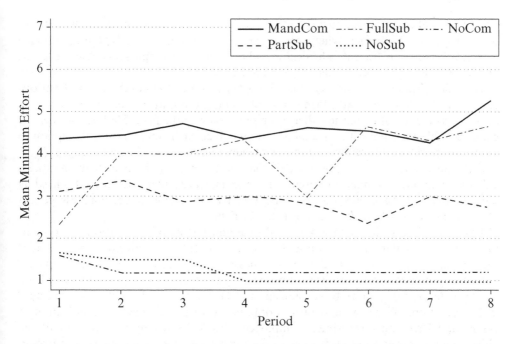

Sources: combined data from Blume and Ortmann (2007) and Kriss et al. (2011) in No Communication and Mandatory Communication treatments. Data from remaining treatments are from Kriss et al. (2011).

Figure 14.2 Mean minimum effort by treatment under alternative communication policies

it consists of non-binding ('cheap talk') pre-play messages between players, might serve a powerful role in assisting efficient coordination. This is explored in an experiment by Blume and Ortmann (2007), who use the game in Table 14.1 with nine players. In a baseline, no-communication condition they find that all firms converge to the inefficient equilibrium of 1 in repeated play when communication is not possible. In an alternative condition, with mandatory communication, Blume and Ortmann require each player to send a costless and non-binding message ('1', '2', '3', '4', '5', '6' or '7') to all others in the firm, indicating an intended choice of effort in the subsequent play of the game. This introduction of mandatory pre-play communication leads to substantial improvements in efficiency relative to the baseline (NoCom) treatment (see Figure 14.2). Similar results have also been found in simpler two-player coordination games: pre-play communication allows pairs of players to coordinate efficiently (Cooper et al. 1992; Charness 2000).

These studies demonstrate that although coordination failure can be very common in the absence of communication, communication structures can be implemented to mitigate such failure. Though this result is encouraging for organizations struggling with coordination failure, we should not overlook just how idealized the communication structures considered in these experiments really are. Communication in real organizations is often voluntary, not mandatory, and it usually entails some costs, such as installation of technology or the opportunity costs of time. Given these costs, and that people in organizations often have discretion regarding whether to communicate, the effectiveness of communication mechanisms needs to be evaluated under conditions with these properties. Moreover, when sending pre-play messages is costly, the use of such messages becomes inefficient – the firm would be better off if employees could use fewer, or even no, messages to coordinate their actions.

To address these concerns, Kriss et al. (2011) consider the effectiveness of various communication policies that a firm can implement, given that the sending of messages incurs costs that must be borne either by employees or by the firm. That is, consider the game in Table 14.1, but with a pre-play stage in which each employee has the option to send a message to the other employees, and where the cost of sending a message is k.

Different communication policies that may be enacted by the firm make messages either mandatory, voluntary, or absent. Messages may be fully or partially subsidized by the firm; that is, for a level of subsidy, s, between 0 and 1, employees bear a message cost of $(1 - s)k$, with a cost of sk being borne by the firm.

Two possible policies correspond to Blume and Ortmann's conditions – no communication and mandatory communication that is fully subsidized ($s = 1$). Under the assumption that the cost of sending a message is $k = 5$, Kriss et al. also consider voluntary communication that is unsubsidized by the firm ($s = 0$), partially subsidized by the firm ($s = 0.8$) or fully subsidized ($s = 1$). Given the dramatic improvement in coordination, efficiency, and profits obtained with mandatory communication in Blume and Ortmann's experiment, employees should be willing to incur any of the above costs in order to send messages, since it always increases their profits by significantly more (in expectation) than when communication is impossible.[13] Indeed, in Kriss et al.'s experiment, fully subsidized and voluntary communication is used 94 percent of the time and yields high minimum effort levels (FullSub condition in Figure 14.2). However, small message costs significantly deter message use: when messages are either unsubsidized or partially subsidized, only about 20 to 25 percent of employees send messages, and this frequency declines with repetition. As Figure 14.2 reveals, the decrease in communication when message costs are unsubsidized (NoSub) is sufficient to eliminate all the benefit from communication: average minimum effort when senders bear the full cost of sending messages is indistinguishable from when communication is not possible.[14]

However, as Figure 14.2 shows, efficiency does not suffer as greatly under partial communication subsidies, even though message use is almost as infrequent under the partial subsidy as under no subsidy. Because of the substantial cost savings created by the infrequency of message use, Kriss et al. show that, depending on how much the firm earns from increases in the minimum employee effort, the policy of partial communication subsidies, where the firm makes communication available but requires employees to bear a small portion of the costs of sending messages, may be optimal. Thus, in contrast with Blume and Ortmann's results, which highlight the value of universal mandatory communication, but ignore the potential importance of message costs, Kriss et al. show that organizations with communication structures that employ moderate amounts of communication – by partially subsidizing communication and letting employees decide whether or not to communicate – can be quite effective.

Broadly, the above results suggest that people in organizations may do well at solving coordination problems when they can trade off the benefit of communication versus low costs of using it.[15] However, as the communication costs faced by individual employees rise, they risk deterring communication use to the point where its value is eliminated completely. This research highlights the value of simple laboratory experiments for understanding how organizations can overcome coordination difficulties to yield efficient production among interdependent employees.[16]

ORGANIZATIONAL CHANGE

Aside from the critical events that take place when organizations are formed, the process through which they undergo change is also of fundamental importance. For example, when growing, either by adding new employees or through acquisitions of other organizations, or when attempting to induce a change in strategy or implement new efficient practices, it is important to understand the factors that will help an organization manage these transitions effectively. Again, as a complement to the extensive empirical and theoretical literatures that exist on these topics, laboratory experiments prove a valuable resource for obtaining improved understanding of organizational phenomena.

Organizational Growth

Once successfully established, most organizations go through periods of growth. A critical question in obtaining successful growth is how best to manage the entrance of new employees, while maintaining efficient practices and organizational culture.

Weber (2006) uses a laboratory experiment to study the role that managed growth plays in the ability of a firm to maintain efficient coordination on a high-effort equilibrium in the production game in Table 14.1. The paper begins by noting that prior laboratory evidence on such coordination games reveals efficient large-group coordination – that is, on minimum effort levels closer to 7 than to 1 – to be virtually impossible. But, if this is the case, then how might an organization undergo growth while coordinating efficiently? The experiment explores whether successful growth can be obtained by, first, ensuring efficient coordination early on, when the group is small; and, second, by managing the growth process so that the introduction of new employees does not overwhelm this efficient coordination.

More precisely, in a managed growth condition, firms start off with two employees, who almost always coordinate on the efficient effort level of 7. Thus, starting small allows firms to begin with early success in coordinating interdependent activity. Then, firms begin to grow slowly, by adding one employee at a time and allowing several periods between growth episodes. Entrants are provided with the complete history (of successful coordination) of the firm they are entering, and this is known to everyone in the firm. Under these conditions, Weber (2006) shows that firms that start off small, grow slowly, and expose entrants to the firm's history are able to grow into efficiently coordinated firms consisting of 12 employees. In contrast, control firms that simply start off with 12 employees find it impossible to sustain efficient coordination.

A crucial element of such successful growth appears to be the information provided to entrants about the firm's history. In a condition in which entrants are not provided with this information, growth is never successful. Thus, in growing an organization while maintaining efficient coordination, it is crucial not only to grow slowly,[17] but also to make sure that policies are in place to expose and train entrants in the firm's history, culture, and practices.

Building on this research, a more recent paper uses a similar experiment to explore different policies for managing the entry of employees (Salmon & Weber 2011). Unlike in Weber (2006), where the entrants had no history of playing the coordination game, this experiment attempts to introduce entrants from groups historically coordinated on low-effort equilibria, and thus presents a stronger test of whether managed growth can work. The experiment considers the effectiveness of three different policies for managing growth: slow growth (as in Weber 2006), an entry quiz through which entrants have to demonstrate understanding of the production game and the firm's history, and the combination of these two policies. The results reveal that any of these policies works, and that they all work equally well. Thus, as long as some effort is made to manage growth by either limiting entry or ensuring that employees are properly 'trained', efficient coordination and growth can be simultaneously accomplished.

Despite the need for carefully managing growth so that entry does not overwhelm the efficient coordination of activity, organizational decision makers may not be aware of the need for such care. For example, in a companion paper to the first one above, Weber (2005) demonstrates that subjects placed in the role of 'managers' who must decide how rapidly to grow firms engage in too-rapid growth, leading to coordination failure. Further evidence of the pitfalls associated with growth can be seen in experiments involving mergers between laboratory firms. Real-world firms regularly grow by acquiring other firms, and it is important to understand how well the integration of two firms with different practices and cultures is likely to proceed.

Knez and Camerer (1994) explore what happens when two three-person firms engaged in minimum-effort production are merged into a larger six-person firm. The result is disappointing: minimum effort in the large firm almost always collapses to a level equal or below that of the lowest-performing firm prior to the merger. Thus, rather than mergers bringing up the low-performing firm to the level of performance of the successful one, as is often argued prior to a merger will occur, the result seems to be the opposite. Fehr (2011) conducts a similar experiment except that he introduces the possibility that the employees may communicate prior to merging. Such communication is beneficial when it is used, but employees opt to use it infrequently and therefore fail to realize its benefits.

Weber and Camerer (2003) study cultural conflict in merging firms and provide a striking example of how coordination problems can produce coordination failure. Their experiment develops a novel paradigm to study organizational culture. In the experiment, a firm consists of employees who have to develop a language or code to jointly identify a set of pictures. Thus, much as organizational members develop idiosyncratic practices, perspectives or internal codes for facilitating coordination, the experiment allows firms to develop something very similar. Indeed, firms develop codes through repeated experience, and these codes allow them to perform the experimental production task (jointly identifying pictures) quickly. The left part of Figure 14.3 presents the amount of time that it took, on average, for two firms to complete the laboratory task prior to a merger. The improvement is driven entirely by the employees in a firm developing the shared code.

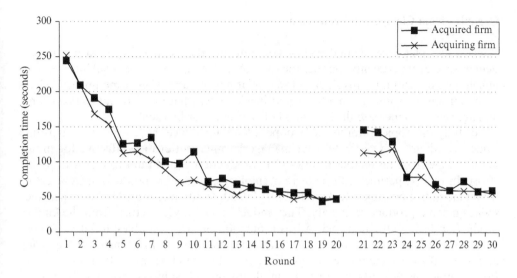

Source: Weber and Camerer (2003). Reprinted by permission, Weber, R.A., C.F. Camerer. Cultural conflict and merger failure: an experimental approach. *Management Science*, 49(4), 2003, 400–415. Copyright 2003, the Institute for Operations Research and the Management Sciences, 7240 Parkway Drive, Suite 300, Hanover, MD 21076 USA.

Figure 14.3   Firm performance, measured by task completion time, pre- and post-merger

The experiment then exogenously imposed a merger after period 10. At this point, the employees of two independent firms were brought together into a single, larger firm and had to communicate with employees from the other pre-merger firm in order to perform the task quickly. Highlighting the pitfalls in integrating organizations with distinct cultures, the task proved very difficult after the merger. Not only did the merger lead to slower completion times for 'acquired' employees, who had to learn the new firm's code, but it also slowed down the employees in the acquiring firm, who now had to wait while managerial resources were directed towards integrating the new employees. As the right side of Figure 14.3 reveals, this decrease in performance took a while to overcome.

The experiment also asked subjects, pre-merger, to forecast how difficult the integration process would be, by providing estimates of the post-merger completion times. These estimates were far too optimistic, reflecting the fact that subjects underestimated how hard it would be to reconcile the two codes, and mirroring the frequent surprise following real-world organizational mergers at the difficulty in integrating two distinct organizational cultures. Moreover, following the merger, employees of the two pre-merger firms blamed each other for the slow production and decreased earnings.

Overall, the above experiments are valuable because they highlight the difficulty in managing organizational growth and expansion. The experiments reveal both that adding new people or acquiring another firm can have disastrous consequences for efficient coordination, and that people are regularly unaware of and surprised by the difficulty in integration. These are both important points in understanding why organizations often fail because they attempt to grow or expand too quickly.

Organizational Change and Leadership

We next consider experimental evidence on inducing change in an organization. In particular, several experiments consider the roles of leadership and managerial interventions in helping turn around firms stuck in low-performance traps. These experiments address an important question: given a history of inefficiency, what institutional changes can a manager enact to increase the likelihood of efficient coordination?

To study this topic, Brandts and Cooper (2006) introduce the 'corporate turnaround game' paradigm to investigate what managerial interventions are effective for inducing a change from an inefficient low-effort production equilibrium to one with higher effort. In their experiment, firms of four employees engage in production by selecting from among five possible effort levels (0, 10, 20, 30, or 40), interpreted as hours per week spent on some productive activity. They model an employee's return from the kind of production technology in Table 14.1 as a function of three variables: a flat wage (W), a cost of effort (C), and a bonus (B) paid for each additional increment in the group minimum effort. An employee's pay-off in a period is therefore: $\pi_i^E = W + Be^{min} - Ce_i$. For example, the pay-offs in Table 14.1 implicitly provide subjects with $W = 60$, $C = 10$ and $B = 20$.

In the first stage of the experiment – to induce coordination failure and low effort – firms engage in production with pay-offs that make coordination quite difficult, $W = 200$, $C = 5$, $B = 6$. This reliably makes the four person firms converge to the equilibrium with the lowest possible effort, which, in their experiments, is zero. Brandts and Cooper then examine the efficacy of interventions intended to overcome the history of low performance.

In the initial use of this paradigm, Brandts and Cooper (2006) demonstrate that a sudden increase in the monetary incentives for coordination leads to increased effort and efficiency. More precisely, after groups establish a history of coordination failure, the experiment introduces a turnaround stage, in which the bonus is increased to 8, 10, or 14. As Figure 14.4 shows, this causes the average minimum effort to rise considerably. Thus, even though zero effort remains an equilibrium under the higher bonus, the increase in the bonus is sufficient to create a turnaround in many firms.

But beyond this primary result, there are two especially noteworthy details from Brandts and Cooper's experiment. Firstly, large increases in incentives do not have a greater impact than small increases in incentives, suggesting that the effectiveness of this intervention is due not to incentives per se, but to the provision of a focal point that the players recognize as a coordinating opportunity. Secondly, subsequently decreasing the incentives for coordination (in rounds 21 to 30 of their experiment the bonus returned to 6) does not cause behavior to revert to pre-increase levels. That is, a one-time increase in incentives for efficient coordination can provide a path out of low-performance traps, even if the increased incentives are not maintained.

A similar result is by obtained by Hamman et al. (2007) who consider other kinds of temporary bonus increases or wage decreases as a way to induce a change from a low-effort equilibrium. In their experiment, the change in bonus comes in the form of a flat payment to employees for obtaining desired levels of minimum effort or a penalty for ending up at undesirable low efforts. These temporary incentive changes also work, though slightly less effectively than those considered by Brandts and Cooper (2006).

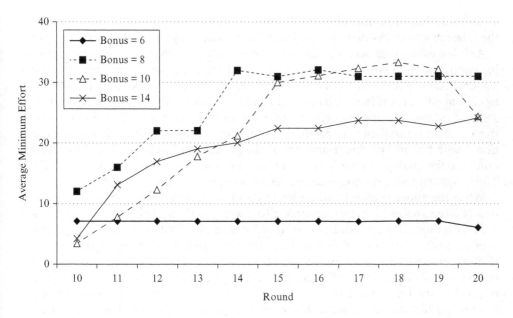

Note: Round 10 corresponds to the final round in which all firms faced a bonus of 6.

Source: Brandts and Cooper (2006, Figure 14.1).

Figure 14.4 *Mean minimum effort in turnaround stage by treatment*

In another experiment, Brandts and Cooper (2007) consider a case where a manager has two tools for inducing a turnaround: increasing incentives and communication to employees. In these experiments, a fifth subject assumes the role of the firm manager and attempts to induce a change to a higher-effort equilibrium. The manager receives more money for higher minimum effort in the firm, but also has to pay for higher bonuses, which the manager can set. In a one-way communication treatment, the manager can send a free form message to the four employees. In a two-way communication treatment, each employee can also send a message back to the manager. Consistent with Brandts and Cooper (2006), changes in incentives lead to increases in efficiency. Additionally, both communication structures improve efficiency, with two-way communication being more effective than one-way. But the most surprising finding is that communication has a greater positive impact on efficiency than increases in incentives.[18] This suggests again that though incentives can be powerful, they may not operate directly through pay-offs, but indirectly through changing expectations of the actions of others. In some environments, communication from a manager may be a more effective method of changing such expectations than incentives alone (see Foss 2001).

Other research demonstrates that a manager's characteristics can matter for obtaining successful turnarounds. For example, Cooper (2007) shows that subjects in the role of manager, who have managerial experience in the real world, are more effective than student subjects randomly assigned to the role. Brandts et al. (2012) show that leaders are more effective at inducing positive change when those they lead have elected them.

Thus, aside from demonstrating that having a leader in place can facilitate turnarounds, the research also shows that who the leader is, and how they were appointed, can matter.

Another experiment serves a cautionary note, however, that some situations involving coordination failure cannot be overcome by communication from a leader and that leaders in those situations may be blamed for their inefficacy. Weber et al. (2001) use the minimum-effort coordination game and include a leader with the opportunity to make a statement encouraging high effort. However, in ten-person groups, a simple message from a leader is insufficient to produce a turnaround. Moreover, even though coordination failure was in fact due to the size of the group, employees attributed the group's failure to the quality of their leader, and were even willing to pay to replace the leader. Thus, unmanageable situations can affect perceptions of a leader's ability.

While the above studies focus on leadership that operates either through manipulation of incentives or by statements urging followers to take a particular course of action, another tool available to leaders is to lead by example. That is, by taking a particular action a leader may induce followers to do the same. Indeed, in the Brandts and Cooper (2006) experiment described above, the data reveal that a major reason why the temporary increase in incentives is effective for inducing a turnaround is that some employees respond to the incentive change by acting as informal 'leaders' who raise their effort in response to the change and wait for other employees to follow. The fact that other employees do indeed subsequently improve their behavior speaks to the effectiveness of such strategies. This type of leadership by example in the contexts of coordination of efforts is studied more directly by Brandts et al. (2007) and in Gillet et al. (2009).

Leadership by example can also be effective in production environments that require cooperation. When employees face an incentive to shirk and free-ride on others' efforts, a leader who sets an example of working hard might induce similarly high effort on the part of subordinates, thus overcoming the inherent problem of motivation. Along these lines, Güth et al. (2007) study the effect of leading by example in obtaining voluntary contributions from followers, using a production game in which employees face incentives to free-ride, as in a public-good game. In particular, a team of four subjects must each decide how much to contribute to a collective activity, where contributing effort costs the employee more than it returns to that employee, but yields a benefit for the other employees that makes contributing effort collectively beneficial. Their experiment also manipulates whether the leader has the power to exclude specific players from the game, which they call a 'strong leader'. Figure 14.5 presents the average-effort contributions across the three main treatments in their experiment. The presence of a leader increases contributions and this effect is greater for leaders with exclusion power. Other experimental studies similarly demonstrate increased cooperation with leadership by example (Moxnes & van der Heijden 2003; Gächter et al. 2010).[19]

Güth et al. also introduce a phase in which the presence of a leader in a firm is endogenous. They find that players are reluctant to take on the leadership role if they do not wield exclusion power and players are reluctant to grant a leader exclusion power. Thus, many groups fail to elect a leader even though doing so would be beneficial. This failure of groups to appoint leaders in the Güth et al. study has similarities to the tendency to underutilize communication or to under-delegate in experiments that we reviewed earlier. That is, all of this research shows that even when there are mechanisms through which members of an organization can improve their collective performance, they are

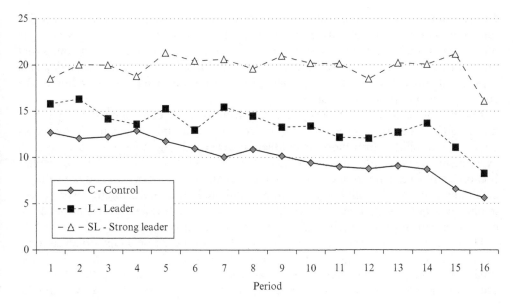

Source: Güth et al. (2007).

Figure 14.5   *Mean effort (contributions) by treatment*

often unwilling to bear the relatively small sacrifices required to implement these beneficial mechanisms.

CONCLUSIONS

Our review focuses on experiments in which interdependent agents engage in some form of production, and in which the laboratory setting allows researchers to manipulate key variables in pursuit of understanding what makes some organizations work better than others. To conclude, we summarize some main findings and present suggestions for potentially valuable avenues for future research.

On organizational formation, laboratory experiments demonstrate the importance of the process through which people are brought together to form an organization. In particular, voluntary association by individuals who wish to work together along with the ability to exclude those with whom they do not wish to work, a central feature of organization, mitigates problems associated with cooperation (free-riding) and coordination (strategic uncertainty). Moreover, different kinds of compensation schemes attract different kinds of people and affect organizational composition and the resulting ability to resolve these kinds of problems.

Laboratory experiments also demonstrate that the delegation of decision rights in a hierarchy matters in ways very different than predicted by economic theory. For example, in domains where theory shows delegation to have strategic advantages, it is often not used and these advantages are not realized, while in other situations, where theory predicts delegation to have no benefit, it provides advantages to those that use it.

Delegation can also be an instrument for creating goodwill among subordinates, which ultimately benefits the delegating manager. Each of these studies illustrates how the interaction of social motivations with organizational structure can lead to outcomes that are difficult to anticipate. Given the failure of traditional theory in this domain, such experiments provide an especially valuable tool for an improved understanding of the consequences and functions of delegation.

Another factor that has efficiency implications for firms is communication. By reducing strategic uncertainty, even very simple forms of communication can improve coordination and make a firm more profitable. However, adding realistic features to such experiments demonstrates impediments to efficient communication use. In particular, because employees tend to underestimate the difficulty of coordination and the value of communication, very small costs can dramatically reduce its use and effectiveness. An implication for firms is, therefore, that the costs borne by employees for using communication can critically affect their ability to solve coordination problems.

The experiments we review also provide insights into how to manage organizational change. Several studies demonstrate the importance of carefully managing growth and expansion, and show the value of the laboratory for isolating factors that determine successful growth. For example, where coordination is important, slow growth and the acculturation of entrants can be critical for maintaining efficient practices. However, managers may not always pay heed to the importance of carefully managed growth. Leadership is also important for managing change and, particularly, for leading an organization through a 'turnaround' from inefficient to efficient practices. Moreover, the effectiveness of different kinds of leadership can vary in ways that are easily studied in the laboratory.

While having already generated important results, the research approach we review also presents additional opportunities to explore critical questions for organizations. Simple experiments at the intersection of economics and organizational behavior can further our understanding of the factors that determine the effectiveness of complex organizational processes.

One area we view as promising is the further study of growth and integration. The experiments we review demonstrate the importance of carefully managing transitions that bring new people into an organization. These experiments demonstrate that things often go poorly when new people are brought in. However, these experiments may understate the degree of such integration problems, due to the low degrees of complexity in organizational tasks and low heterogeneity of individual employees. Thus, if integration problems arise even when homogenous subjects perform only one task repeatedly, integration problems may be exacerbated when heterogeneous individuals – with different professional and cultural backgrounds, for example – interact in varied ways that are complex and fluid. Therefore, we view the studies on integration that we report here as a starting point for understanding much more complex issues of organizational integration and growth. Moreover, as experiments studying integration become more complex and add realism, we believe that the necessary interventions likely to aid efficient integration will similarly become richer and more generalizable to contexts outside the laboratory.

Future studies might also build on the research on leadership that we review to learn more about when and what kinds of leadership improve worker motivation and satisfaction. Such research could introduce more realistic kinds of leadership and tasks performed by workers than are typically studied in economic experiments. These experiments could also make the leader's task more complex, by having them simultaneously and separately manage diverse sets of employees performing multiple tasks. Such additional complexity and realism in experiments – whether applied to studying leadership or other organizational phenomena – would not only create results more generalizable to real organizational settings, but would also begin to establish closer connections to related research in organizational behavior.

Finally, another potentially valuable research line deals with the many 'mistakes' that we observe organizational actors committing. In particular, individuals in simple laboratory organizations often fail to properly utilize mechanisms – such as communication, delegation, or leadership – that might help them function efficiently. These mistakes are likely to extend beyond the laboratory. Therefore, future research should identify interventions that help people in organizations make better use of the mechanisms available to them. As with the other work described above, economic experiments on simple laboratory organizations can generate knowledge and practical insights that help analogous real-world entities function more efficiently.

NOTES

*   We gratefully acknowledge support from the research priority program at the University of Zurich, Foundations of Human Social Behavior, and from the National Science Foundation (SES-1021659) for funding research related to this chapter.
1. Exceptions include the team-play experiments of Cooper and Kagel (2005). Excellent overviews of research in experimental economics are provided by Kagel and Roth (1995, forthcoming) and Plott and Smith (2008).
2. There exists a fairly large body of laboratory experiments, relevant to our chapter, in the general area of 'organizational economics'. This work studies the behavior of individual agents within an organizational context, such as effort expenditure by employees under alternative incentive mechanisms (Nalbantian & Schotter 1997), simultaneous learning by interdependent organizational members (Blume et al. 2009), or the decision by a principal (manager) of whether to delegate agency to an employee (Fehr et al. 2011). Our focus in this chapter is slightly different and centers on collective outcomes among highly interdependent individuals. For a review of experiments on organizational economics, more broadly, see Camerer and Weber (2012).
3. Indeed, the laboratory experiment in economics, motivated by the 'induced value' approach pioneered by Vernon Smith (1976), has yielded valuable insights into the functioning of many other complex and important economic and organizational contexts (see Roth 1995; Camerer 2003; Falk & Heckman 2009).
4. Bryant (1983) introduced this kind of game to model investment in macroeconomic contexts. However, the application to understanding organizational production under complementarities is widespread.
5. These economic experiments often share features with laboratory experiments conducted by management psychologists over the past several decades (Leavitt 1951; Cohen & Bacdayan 1994). One key departure, from the viewpoint of economics, is that the economic approach relies on carefully specified incentives as the primary motivating influence for laboratory participants, intended to mirror the kinds of incentives faced in real-world firms and economic models.
6. This work spans from early laboratory experiments exploring productivity under varying extrinsic and social incentives (Bull et al. 1987; Nalbantian & Schotter 1997; Fehr et al. 1998) to more recent related field experiments (Carpenter et al. 2010; Kube et al. 2012)
7. Public goods have been widely studied in economics experiments (for reviews, see Ledyard 1995; Andreoni & Vesterlund forthcoming). While the connection to production in organizations is often not made explicitly in this work, understanding the factors that increase contributions to a public good are relevant for understanding how to motivate employees with an incentive to free-ride off others' effort.
8. Highlighting the value of comparing outcomes observed in the lab to those in the field, Dohmen and Falk corroborate their main findings using survey data from a large representative sample of German households.

9.   This kind of reasoning is similar to the notion of 'forward induction', which can select some equilibria over others in coordination games, based on players' inferences about the rationality and intentions of others (see Blume et al. 2012). Cachon and Camerer (1996) also demonstrate that loss avoidance provides another interpretation for such effects.

10. Related research demonstrates that individuals are less likely to be punished for unethical conduct when decisions are delegated, as in a hierarchy (Bartling & Fischbacher 2012; Coffman 2011).

11. Theoretical literature in organizational economics considers the optimal degree of communication within organizations (Dessien 2002; Dewatripont & Tirole 2005). For more general theoretical analyses of communication in economic contexts, see Crawford and Sobel (1982) and Townsend (1987).

12. Laboratory experiments also study how communication affects contributions under revenue sharing (public goods) production incentives, where communication often helps overcome incentives to shirk or free-ride (Dawes et al. 1977; Ostrom et al. 1992).

13. To see why, consider that the pay-off for the inefficient equilibrium (in which effort equals 1) is 70, while the average minimum effort in the mandatory communication conditions is always greater than 4, which yields an equilibrium pay-off greater than 100. Thus, in equilibrium, players benefit on average by 30 from the improved coordination due to universal message use.

14. This result is consistent with prior evidence of 'coordination neglect', or the tendency to underestimate the difficulty of coordination and view as unnecessary mechanisms to help facilitate efficient coordination (Heath & Staudenmayer 2000).

15. Blume et al. (2012) make the related point that employees in small groups may be able to properly judge when to employ costly communication and even provide others with reassurance by forgoing communication use altogether. Thus, firms can again save on communication costs by giving employees the discretion to communicate.

16. For other examples of papers that study communication and production in simple laboratory coordination games, see Chaudhuri et al. (2009), Dugar (2010) and Cason et al. (2012). Related empirical work in the organizational literature similarly studies how communication can solve coordination problems (e.g., Argote 1982).

17. More recent work similarly demonstrates that slow growth can help maintain efficient voluntary cooperation and overcome incentives to free-ride (Ranehill et al. 2012). A loosely related set of papers demonstrates that 'starting small' – that is, with versions of problems that are easier to solve, either because the interdependence is weaker or because the incentives to free-ride are smaller – can yield better outcomes subsequently (Andreoni & Samuelson 2006; Ye et al. 2011). Thus, in an organization, beginning with tasks in which cooperation and coordination problems are likely to be resolved successfully can subsequently produce success in more challenging settings.

18. In particular, the most effective messages from managers are those that request high effort from employees, point out the mutual benefits of high effort, and imply that current incentives are fair.

19. Leading by example may also be effective in situations where leaders have private information about the profitability of investing effort in a particular task (Hermalin 1998). Potters et al. (2007) demonstrate that, indeed, leaders who are privately aware of payoff-relevant information are followed by those who make contributions later, though they find no effect of leading by example when there is no asymmetry in information.

REFERENCES

Aghion, P. and J. Tirole (1997), 'Formal and real authority in organizations', *Journal of Political Economy*, **105**(1), 1–29.

Ahn, T., R. Isaac and T. Salmon (2008), 'Endogenous group formation', *Journal of Public Economic Theory*, **10**(2), 171–194.

Ahn, T., R. Isaac and T. Salmon (2009), 'Coming and going: experiments on endogenous group sizes for excludable public goods', *Journal of Public Economics*, **93**(1–2), 336–351.

Akerlof, G. and R. Kranton (2005), 'Identity and the economics of organizations', *Journal of Economic Perspectives*, **19**(1), 9–32.

Andreoni, J. and L. Samuelson (2006), 'Building rational cooperation', *Journal of Economic Theory*, **127**(1), 17–154.

Andreoni, J. and L. Vesterlund (forthcoming), 'Voluntary giving to public goods', in John Kagel and Alvin Roth (eds), *Handbook of Experimental Economics*, Vol. 2, Princeton University Press.

Argote, L. (1982), Input uncertainty and organizational coordination in hospital emergency units', *Administrative Science Quarterly*, **27**(3), 420–434.

Baker, G., R. Gibbons and K.J. Murphy (1999), Informal authority in organizations', *Journal of Law, Economics, and Organization*, **15**(1), 56.

Bartling, B. and U. Fischbacher (2012), 'Shifting the blame: on delegation and responsibility', *Review of Economic Studies*, **79**(1), 67–87.

Benabou, R. and J. Tirole (2006), 'Incentives and prosocial behavior', *American Economic Review*, **95**(6), 1652–1678.

Blume, A. and A. Ortmann (2007), 'The effects of costless pre-play communication: experimental evidence from games with Pareto-ranked equilibria', *Journal of Economic Theory*, **132**(1), 274–290.

Blume, A., J. Duffy and A. Franco (2009), 'Decentralized organizational learning: an experimental investigation', *American Economic Review*, **99**(4), 1178–1205.

Blume, A., P. Kriss and R. Weber (2012), 'Pre-play communication with forgone costly messages: experimental evidence on forward induction', *Working Paper*.

Brandts, J. and D. Cooper (2006), 'A change would do you good . . . an experimental study on how to overcome coordination failure in organizations', *American Economic Review*, **96**(3), 669–693.

Brandts, J. and D. Cooper (2007), 'It's what you say, not what you pay: an experimental study of manager–employee relationships in overcoming coordination failure', *Journal of the European Economic Association*, **5**(6), 1223–1268.

Brandts, J., D. Cooper and E. Fatas (2007), 'Leadership and overcoming coordination failure with asymmetric costs', *Experimental Economics*, **10**(3), 269–284.

Brandts, J., D. Cooper and R. Weber (2012), 'Legitimacy, social distance and leadership in the turnaround game', Working Paper.

Bryant, J. (1983), 'A simple rational expectations Keynes-type model', *Quarterly Journal of Economics*, **98**(3), 525–528.

Bull, C., A. Schotter and K. Weigelt (1987), 'Tournaments and piece rates: An experimental study', *Journal of Political Economy*, **95**(1), 1–33.

Cachon, G. and C. Camerer (1996), 'Loss-avoidance and forward induction in experimental coordination games', *Quarterly Journal of Economics*, **111**(1), 165.

Camerer, C. (2003), *Behavioral Game Theory: Experiments in Strategic Interaction*, Princeton, NJ: Princeton University Press.

Camerer, C. and M. Knez (1997), 'Coordination in organizations: a game-theoretic perspective', in Z. Shapira (ed.), *Organizational Decision Making*, Cambridge: Cambridge University Press, pp. 158–188.

Camerer, C. and U. Malmendier (2007), 'Behavioral economics of organizations', in P. Diamond and H. Vartiainen (eds), *Behavioral Economics and Its Applications*, Princeton, NJ: Princeton University Press.

Camerer, C. and R. Weber (2012), 'Experimental organizational economics', *Handbook of Organizational Economics*, Princeton: Princeton University Press.

Carpenter, J., P. Matthews and J. Schirm (2010), 'Tournaments and office politics: evidence from a real effort experiment', *American Economic Review*, **100**(1), 504–517.

Cason, T., R. Sheremeta and J. Zhang (2012), 'Communication and efficiency in competitive coordination games', *Games and Economic Behavior*, **76**(1), 26–43.

Charness, G. (2000), 'Self-serving cheap talk: a test of Aumann's conjecture', *Games and Economic Behavior*, **33**(2), 177–194.

Charness, G., R. Cobo-Reyes, N. Jimenez, J. Lacomba and F. Lagos (2012), 'The hidden advantage of delegation: Pareto-improvements in a gift-exchange game', *American Economic Review*, **102**(5), 2358–2379.

Chaudhuri, A., A. Schotter and B. Sopher (2009), 'Talking ourselves to efficiency: coordination in intergenerational minimum effort games with private, almost common and common knowledge of advice', *Economic Journal*, **119**(534), 91–122.

Coffman, L. (2011), 'Intermediation reduces punishment (and reward)', *American Economic Journal: Microeconomics*, **3**(4), 77–106.

Cohen, M. and P. Bacdayan (1994), 'Organizational routines are stored as procedural memory: evidence from a laboratory study', *Organization Science*, **5**(4), 554–568.

Cooper, D. (2007), 'Are experienced managers experts at overcoming coordination failure?' *Berkeley Electronic Journal: Advances in Economic Analysis and Policy*, **6**(2), 1–50.

Cooper, D. and J. Kagel (2005), 'Are two heads better than one? Team versus individual play in signaling games', *American Economic Review*, **95**(3), 477–509.

Cooper, R., D. DeJong, R. Forsythe and T. Ross (1992), 'Communication in coordination games', *Quarterly Journal of Economics*, **107**(2), 739–771.

Crawford, V. and J. Sobel (1982), 'Strategic information transmission', *Econometrica*, **50**(6), 1431–1451.

Dawes, R., J. McTavish and H. Shaklee (1977), 'Behavior, communication, and assumptions about other peoples' behavior in a commons dilemma situation', *Journal of Personality and Social Psychology*, **35**(1), 1–11.

Dessein, W. (2002), 'Authority and communication in organizations', *Review of Economic Studies*, **69**(4), 811–838.

Dewatripont, M. and J. Tirole (2005), 'Modes of communication', *Journal of Political Economy*, **113**(6), 1217–1238.

Dohmen, T. and A. Falk (2011), 'Performance pay and multi-dimensional sorting: productivity, preferences and gender', *American Economic Review*, **101**(2), 556–590.

Dugar, S. (2010), 'Nonmonetary sanctions and rewards in an experimental coordination game', *Journal of Economic Behavior and Organization*, **73**(3), 377–386.

Ehrhart, K.-M. and C. Keser (1999), 'Mobility and cooperation: on the run', CIRANO Working Paper 99s-24.

Ellman, M. and P. Pezanis-Christou (2010), 'Organizational structure, communication, and group ethics', *American Economic Review*, **100**(December), 2478–2491.

Falk, A. and J. Heckman (2009), 'Lab experiments are a major source of knowledge in the social sciences', *Science*, **326**(5952), 535.

Falk, A. and M. Kosfeld (2006), 'The hidden costs of control', *American Economic Review*, **96**(5), 1611–1630.

Fehr, D. (2011), 'The need for integration: a coordination experiment', Working Paper.

Fehr, E. and S. Gachter (2000), 'Fairness and retaliation: the economics of reciprocity', *Journal of Economic Perspectives*, **14**(2), 159–181.

Fehr, E., H. Herz and T. Wilkening (2011), 'The lure of authority: motivation and incentive effects of power', unpublished manuscript.

Fehr, E., E. Kirchler, A. Weichbold and S. Gächter (1998), 'When social norms overpower competition: Gift exchange in experimental labor markets', *Journal of Labor Economics*, **16**(2), 324–351.

Fershtman, C. and U. Gneezy (2001), 'Strategic delegation: an experiment', *Rand Journal of Economics*, **32**(2), 352–368.

Fershtman, C. and K. Judd (1987), 'Equilibrium incentives in oligopoly', *American Economic Review*, **77**(5), 927–940.

Foss, N. (2001), 'Leadership, beliefs and coordination: an explorative discussion', *Industrial and Corporate Change*, **10**(2), 357.

Gächter, S., D. Nosenzo, E. Renner and M. Sefton (2010), 'Sequential vs. simultaneous contributions to public goods: experimental evidence', *Journal of Public Economics*, **94**(7), 515–522.

Gillet, J., E. Cartwright and M. Van Vugt (2009), 'Leadership in a weak-link game', *Studies in Economics*, Department of Economics, University of Kent.

Grossman, S. and O. Hart (1986), 'The costs and benefits of ownership: a theory of vertical and lateral integration', *Journal of Political Economy*, **94**(4), 691–719.

Güth, W., M.V. Levati, M. Sutter and E. van der Heijden (2007), 'Leading by example with and without exclusion power in voluntary contribution experiments', *Journal of Public Economics*, **91**(5–6), 1023–1042.

Hamman, J., G. Loewenstein and R. Weber (2010), 'Self-interest through delegation: an additional rationale for the principal–agent relationship', *American Economic Review*, **100**(4), 1826–1846.

Hamman, J., S. Rick and R. Weber (2007), 'Solving coordination failure with 'all-or-none' group-level incentives', *Experimental Economics*, **10**(3), 285–303.

Harless, D. and C. Camerer (1994), 'The predictive utility of generalized expected utility theories', *Econometrica*, **62**(6), 1251–1289.

Heath, C. and N. Staudenmayer (2000), 'Coordination neglect: how lay theories of organizing complicate coordination in organizations', *Research in Organizational Behavior*, **22**, 153–192.

Hermalin, B. (1998), 'Toward an economic theory of leadership: leading by example', *American Economic Review*, **88**(5), 1188–1206.

Hoffman, E., K. McCabe, K. Shachat and V. Smith (1994), 'Preferences, property rights, and anonymity in bargaining games', *Games and Economic Behavior*, **7**(3), 346–380.

Holmstrom, B. (1984), 'On the theory of delegation', in M. Boyer and R. Kihlstrom (eds), *Bayesian Models in Economic Theory*, New York: North-Holland, pp.115–141.

Huck, S., W. Muller and H.T. Normann (2004), 'Strategic delegation in experimental markets', *International Journal of Industrial Organization*, **22**(4), 561–574.

Kagel, J. and A. Roth (eds), (1995), *The Handbook of Experimental Economics*, Princeton, NJ: Princeton University Press.

Kagel, J. and A. Roth (eds) (forthcoming), *The Handbook of Experimental Economics, Volume 2*, Princeton, NJ: Princeton University Press.

Kagel, J., R. Harstad and D. Levin (1987), 'Information impact and allocation rules in auctions with affiliated private values: a laboratory study', *Econometrica*, **55**(6), 1275–1304.

Knez, M. and C. Camerer (1994), 'Creating expectational assets in the laboratory: coordination in "weakest-link" games', *Strategic Management Journal*, **15**(S1), 101–119.

Kriss, P., A. Blume and R. Weber (2011), 'Organizational coordination with decentralized costly communication', Working Paper.

Kube, S., M.A. Maréchal and C. Puppe (2012), 'The currency of reciprocity: gift-exchange in the workplace', *American Economic Review*, **102**(4), 1644–1662.

Kunreuther, H. and G. Heal (2003), 'Interdependent security', *Journal of Risk and Uncertainty*, **26**(2), 231–249.

Lai, E. and W. Lim (2012), 'Authority and communication in the laboratory', *Games and Economic Behavior*, **74**(2), 541–560.

Lazear, E., U. Malmendier and R. Weber (2012), 'Sorting in experiments with application to social preferences', *American Economic Journal: Applied Economics*, **4**(1), 136–163.

Leavitt, H. (1951), 'Some effects of certain communication patterns on group performance', *Journal of Abnormal Psychology*, **46**(1), 38–50.

Ledyard, J. (1995), 'Public goods experiments', in A. Roth and J.H. Kagel (eds), *Handbook of Experimental Economics*, Princeton, NJ: Princeton University Press, pp. 111–194.

March, J. and H. Simon (1958), *Organizations*, New York: Wiley.

Marschak, J. and R. Radner (1972), *Economic Theory of Teams*, New Haven, CT: Yale University Press.

Moxnes, E. and E. van der Heijden (2003), 'The effect of leadership in a public bad experiment', *Journal of Conflict Resolution*, **47**(6), 773–795.

Nalbantian, H. and A. Schotter (1997), 'Productivity under group incentives: an experimental study', *American Economic Review*, **87**(3), 314–341.

Ochs, J. and A. Roth (1989), 'An experimental study of sequential bargaining', *American Economic Review*, **79**(3), 355–384.

Ostrom, E., J. Walker and R. Gardner (1992), 'Covenants with and without a sword: self-governance is possible', *American Political Science Review*, **86**(2), 404–417.

Page, T., L. Putterman and B. Unel (2005), 'Voluntary association in public goods experiments: reciprocity, mimicry and efficiency', *Economic Journal*, **115**(506), 1032–1053.

Plott, C. and V. Smith (eds) (2008), *Handbook of Experimental Economic Results, Vol. 1*. Amsterdam: North-Holland.

Potters, J., M. Sefton and L. Vesterlund (2007), 'Leading-by-example and signaling in voluntary contribution games: an experimental study', *Economic Theory*, **33**(1), 169–182.

Ranehill, E., R. Schneider and R. Weber (2012), 'Growing groups, cooperation, and the rate of entry', Working Paper.

Riedl, A., I. Rohde and M. Strobel (2011), 'Efficient coordination in weakest-link games', Working Paper.

Roth, A. (1995), 'Introduction to experimental economics', in A. Roth and J.H. Kagel (eds), *Handbook of Experimental Economics*, Princeton, NJ: Princeton University Press, pp. 3–109.

Salmon, T. and R. Weber (2011), 'Maintaining efficiency while integrating entrants from lower-performing environments: an experimental study', Working Paper.

Sklivas, S. (1987), 'The strategic choice of managerial incentives', *Rand Journal of Economics*, **18**(3), 452–458.

Smith, V. (1962), 'An experimental study of competitive market behavior', *Journal of Political Economy*, **70**(2), 111.

Smith, V. (1976), 'Experimental economics: induced value theory', *American Economic Review*, **66**(2), 274–279.

Townsend, R. (1987), 'Economic organization with limited communication', *American Economic Review*, **77**(5), 954–971.

Van Huyck, J., R. Battalio and R. Beil (1990), 'Tacit coordination games, strategic uncertainty, and coordination failure', *American Economic Review*, **80**(1), 234–248.

Van Huyck, J., R. Battalio and R. Beil (1993), 'Asset markets as an equilibrium selection mechanism: coordination failure, game form auctions, and tacit communication', *Games and Economic Behavior*, **5**(3), 485–504.

Weber, R. (2005), 'Managing growth to achieve efficient coordination in large groups: theory and experimental evidence', Working paper.

Weber, R. (2006), 'Managing growth to achieve efficient coordination in large groups', *American Economic Review*, **96**(1), 114–126.

Weber, R. and C. Camerer (2003), 'Cultural conflict and merger failure: an experimental approach', *Management Science*, **49**(4), 400–415.

Weber, R., C. Camerer, Y. Rottenstreich and M. Knez (2001), 'The illusion of leadership: misattribution of cause in coordination games', *Organization Science*, **12**(5), 582–598.

Weick, K. (1969), 'Laboratory organizations and unnoticed causes', *Administrative Science Quarterly*, **14**(2), 294–303.

Ye, M., S. Asher, L. Casaburi and P. Nikolov (2011), 'One step at a time: does gradualism build coordination?' Unpublished manuscript.

PART IV

HUMAN RESOURCES AND ECONOMIC ORGANIZATION BETWEEN ASSETS AND ACTORS

15. Human capital and property rights*
Anna Grandori

The chapter reviews of some key classics in economics and some main relevant modern organizational perspectives, on the relationship between human capital (HC) and property rights (PR). The review leads to a typology linking the features of HC used or invested and the rights they should give origin to. The review also leads to identifying some types of HC investments that are neglected in the former literature, in which therefore the rights to be assigned to HC providers are generally under-recognized. This neglect has implications for economic theory as it is rooted in the long-lasting assumption of the inseparability of people from their human capital and of HC 'inalienability'. An innovative point of the chapter is to endogenize this assumption and to transform it into a variable.

Some pertinent qualitative and quantitative evidence, both already published and original – on firm founding contract negotiations, on the internal organization of new economy firms, and on inter-firm knowledge-intensive collaboration contracts – supporting the typology is provided.

INTRODUCTION

The issue of PR assignments to human resource holders has been a core concern in early economic science, especially in Marx's and Marshall's thought. Recently, the theme has been resurrected, in part in response to the often stressed and increased 'criticality' of human assets in economic activity. Perspectives in organizational economics, such as the HC perspective, property right theory (PRT), transaction cost economics (TCE), and law and economics (L&E), have put center stage the role of human assets and of investments into them, especially if specific to firms, developing implications for labor contract length, the nature and level of rewards, the intensity of protective provisions and the identity of firm owners. In spite of all these developments, some puzzles stand out, and a conspicuous 'hole' in theory is detectable. This chapter, firstly, revisits classic views and more recent developments on the issue, and identifies open questions; secondly, it provides a typology of HC and the PR that should be attached to it that introduce some new possibilities that would fill the 'hole'.

RECEIVED THEORIES: CORE ASSUMPTIONS, ENSUING PROPOSITIONS AND KEY PROBLEMS

Labor Services, Human Resources and Human Capital

Marx was the first economist to stress, and to use as a core assumption, the observation that there are two very different components in labor: 'labor force' and 'labor services'.

Labor services can be sold as a commodity, while 'labor force' is a resource that remains (in the absence of slavery) in the possession of workers. The dependence of labor service providers on the providers of technical assets for selling their services, and their higher substitutability, has been seen as the source of an asymmetric bargaining power, lying at the heart of the capitalistic organization of production.

Three key assumptions were introduced in the economics of capitalism by Marx: (1) labor services are saleable, as a commodity, while human resources are not; (2) labor inputs providers are generally more substitutable than financial and technical inputs providers; and (3) labor providers are inseparable from their labor force. Those assumptions were realistic in the industrial production of the nineteenth century but, I shall argue, they should be reinterpreted as a particular case in modern economies, especially as the knowledge components of human resources have been gaining prominence. The risk, otherwise, is that those assumptions, paradoxically, help in perpetuating the type of 'capitalistic' order they were intended to criticize.

Later perspectives have gradually modified some of those assumptions, envisaging more varied conditions: work services are saleable, but not really as a 'commodity', due to barriers to mobility that 'considerably hinder the adjustment of the supply and demand' (Marshall 1898: VI.IV.19); workers may not be highly substitutable due to the acquisition of firm-specific competences of the individual and collective kind (Marshall 1898; Doeringer and Piore 1971; Williamson 1975); and there are circumstances under which human resources are more critical than financial resources (Hart and Moore 1990; Aoki 2010). Hence, it can be observed that later perspectives have endogeneized assumptions (1) and (2) into variables. However, it should also be remarked that assumption (3) – the impossibility of people selling their 'labor force' – remained unchallenged. It was restated by Marshall as follows:

> The first point to which we have to direct our attention is the fact that human agents of production are not bought and sold as machinery and other material agents of production are. The worker sells his work, but he himself remains his own property: those who bear the expenses of rearing and educating him receive but very little of the price that is paid for his services in later years. (Marshall 1898: VI.IV.4)

In this statement, an additional concern appears, central in later developments on HC: the problem of who bears the costs, and reaps the benefits, of the investments in HC. Hence, Marshall's contribution links Marx to modern HC and PR theories (even though he also provides some cues for going beyond all of them, as shown in the next section).

HC 'Inalienability' and PR

The assumption of the 'inalienability of human capital' is in fact not only present, but absolutely central in modern PRT. In search of what the 'glue' keeping a firm together is, Grossman and Hart (1986) and Hart and Moore (1990) stated that the control of physical assets is the core mechanism allowing the party owing them to 'selectively fire the workers of the firm if he dislikes their performance' (p. 1120). The firm is therefore defined as a 'collection of physical assets' because otherwise the 'glue' keeping the firm together would be difficult to understand (out of the 'very particular' conditions of workers' quasi-indifference on tasks making authority relation a Pareto-optimal agreement). Out of those conditions, plain bargaining power, rather than authority, is seen as distinguishing firm-like organization from market contracting.

This analysis is quite close to Marx's (the basic difference lying in the assessment of whether that 'power-based' arrangement is defensible in terms of efficiency, and whether 'power' is a defensible source of 'right'). Some of the objections, relevant for the HC and PR issue, can therefore be similar to those moved to Marxian analysis. In fact, it has been observed that the early PRT model applies only to the particular case in which technical assets are critical and are separable and separated from complementary HC (Aoki 2004). In fact, Hart and Moore's (1990) recognized that their initial model was too restrictive and then offered a more contingent model of owners identity, resting on three principles: property rights on transaction-specific assets should go to the party whose investments are relatively more important, whose contribution is indispensable for using the assets or for whom the assets are essential, and who owns other strictly complementary assets. These propositions, together with the assumption that people are inseparable from HC, imply that if HC happens to be critical, the economic activity deriving from the employment of those resources should be owned by people (e.g. through a worker' co-operative) (Hart and Moore 1990; Hart 1995; Hansmann 1996).

The assumption of inalienability of HC (together with some additional assumptions on the decision process costs of owners' heterogeneity) then led to an 'either/or' view, according to which the identity of PR holders is homogeneous and mutually exclusive: PR are assigned all together either to technical and financial resource providers, or to human and social resource providers.

This view, however, gives an account of a still too particular range of cases: in particular it rules out PR sharing among different types of actors, which is by contrast very common, especially in HC-intensive situations, both in intra-firm and inter-firm contracts of collaboration (Kaplan and Stromberg 2003; Lerner and Merges 1998; Aoki 2010).

Human Asset 'Specificity', 'Team Production' and 'Relational Contracting'

TCE has stressed the dimension of asset specificity as a predictor of PR 'unification'. The assumption of HC inalienability plays a role also in TCE, although it has been made less explicit. In fact, while the unification of PR over technical assets can be a solution of transactional problems between formerly separated firms, the assumption that human assets cannot be conferred into and owned by firms ruled out a PR solution to the problem of human assets specificity. The consequences of transaction-specific human assets are therefore confined to be regulated by contract, more or less incomplete, complex and integrated by decision procedures that are seen as extra-contractual, as authority. As in PRT, only in very particular cases, like activities based predominantly on human assets linked by team production, may PR be efficiently assigned to the team members themselves in a 'collective' enterprise (Williamson, 1980). The just mentioned, and seldom used, article by Williamson, however includes a classification of forms of enterprise according to PR assignments, and a comparative assessment exercise under a series of 'assumptions' that may help in specifying a much wider range of contingency conditions, beyond HR specificity. In 'capitalistic firms' PR are assigned to one homogeneous group of actors who provide financial resources to buy technical assets, labor is hired and entitled to no PR; in 'entrepreneurial firms', there is one party – the entrepreneur or entrepreneurial team – who owns technical assets and provides complementary know-how through labor services, hence the key providers of labor services are also entitled to PR over technical assets; in 'collective firms' the holders of human assets and labor providers own collectively all the firm's assets and 'hire' all other inputs. The conditions under which the capitalistic organization of production can be ranked as superior to entrepreneurial and collective organization are specified as follows: technical resources are specialized, production stages are separable and there are economies of specialization in the different stages; market transactions across stages are very costly and there are economies from common location; workers' preferences are randomly distributed over organizational solutions (whereby they do not count); there is no innovation. If this is so, it seems that the classic 'capitalistic firm', defined by unilateral PR assignments to financial assets' investors, qualifies as an efficient arrangement only under quite particular conditions. Team production and unseparabilities, uncertainty and innovation, and firm-specific HC are all factors to be expected to move efficient governance and organizational arrangements away from the classical architecture of a capitalistic firm. As said though, in TCE contributions so far, those modifications are sought mostly on the terrain of a range of contractual protections of the employment relation and of voice rights, configuring a 'relational governance' regime (Williamson 1981, 2009) rather than on the terrain of PR proper. In addition, 'relational governance' is conceived in that literature in a narrower sense than it could (Grandori 2006): it is reduced to self-enforcing informal agreements, eventually accompanied by formal and informal norms of reciprocity (Williamson & Ouchi 1981); while it could also refer to a mode of governance based on an ongoing, enduring association, guaranteed by open-ended contracts, rich in joint decision-making procedures (Goldberg 1976), and including representation of workers' interests (Williamson 2009).

Components of HC and HR Packages

Becker' s foundational work institutionalized the use of the notion of 'human capital' (rather than of 'labor force') highlighting that human assets do possess the two main features indicated by Marshall as characterizing capital proper (rather than just 'resources'): capital is a resource with the features of 'prospectiveness' and 'productiveness' (Marshall 1898), a stock of things that can be accumulated and put to productive use, generating value. Human resources are considered a form of capital because they can be accumulated and dedicated to economically valuable uses (Becker 1964). According to Becker, who in turn revisits and makes use of earlier classic economists, human capital is distinguished by the particular type of resources compounding it. The argument is that, while the traditional focus in economics has been on material assets, such as machinery and natural resources, the growth prospects of modern economies derive to a large extent from the growth in human assets. These assets have various components: personal attributes (including physical energy and health); competence and abilities; and knowledge (Becker 2002).

Becker's foundations nurtured empirical research both in economics and in organization and management. Although all studies contributed to operationalizing the construct of HC, economic and organizational studies differ in object, purpose and connection with the theme of PR. Studies in economics focused on the incentives to invest in HC and the consequences on a variety of macroeconomic variables, such as occupation and income prospects; hence they lie outside the scope of this review. Studies in organizational economics, and organization and management theory, instead have come closer to the problem of the rights to govern organizations as linked to HC holding and contribution.

Operationalizations of the concept of HC have refined the analysis of HC components, in a way that is conducive to study their link with various rights. It has been highlighted that personal attributes and capabilities include not only physical energy and health, but also cognitive and relational skills and 'intellectual capital' (Stuart 1997; Youndt et al. 2004). It has been pointed out that knowledge includes both explicit knowledge – notions, ideas, methods and know-how that can be communicated to others – as well as 'tacit knowledge' – what one knows beyond what can be communicated (Nahapiet and Ghoshal 1998). Competences have been seen as including formal education, measurable as the qualifications achieved; as well as 'expertise', the body of competences acquired in the field through learning by doing, and through observation of other actors' experiences (Petty and Guthrie 2000; Colombo and Grilli 2005). In addition, 'relationships' and 'social capital' are acknowledged as a form of human capital of growing importance in economic ventures (Burt 2002).

This disaggregated analysis of HC components has facilitated an analysis of the rights that are to be associated to them. The arrays of effective HR systems are in fact found to be configured differently according to HC intensity, task complexity and human resource specificity (Lepack et al. 2002): the higher the value of those independent variables, the more 'inclusive' and 'partnership-like' the effective employment contract and HR systems packages are.

These studies have contributed to refine the notion of HC and to develop contingency propositions linking types of HC with organizational configurations, including some PR elements (e.g. residual reward and decision rights). A limitation of those analyses is a persisting lack of distinction between persons and the resources they possess. As long as people 'are' resources, they are things to be managed, rather than actors entitled to negotiate about human resources use. In addition, if people 'are' resources, human resources cannot be invested into firms, whereby residual claims over firm assets are implicitly reduced.

HC Holders as Stakeholders

An approach going beyond a view of people-as-resources, admitting and actually building on the assumption that governance arrangements should be reconstructed in a 'multiple actors', 'multiple interests' frame, has been developed in 'stakeholder' approaches (Aoki 1984, 2010; Blair 1996, 1999; Blair & Stout 2006; Sacconi et al. 2010).

These works are coming closer to formulating and responding to the question of 'who should be entitled to what right' and why. They make use of the important lessons coming from TCE and PRT, but also draw directly from Marshall's notion that the continued association of resources in production typically imply team production and generate quasi-rents over which all resource providers have a claim. Then, they explicitly acknowledge the possible different interests of actors investing in different types of production inputs. The result of those analyses has been to stress that economic organization, most often than not, requires people to make transaction-specific investments in their HC. This situation would be similar to that of any supplier investing in resources that are specific to a user (Klein et al. 1978); and the investor would be similarly exposed to quasi-rent expropriation. Then, fair bargaining over the surplus generated should be in order, as well as long-term association, pension and security provisions, union-based or representative decision right sharing (Blair 1999; Blair and Stout 2006; Aoki 1984).

The substantive proposition that specific investments in HC should be associated to rights to long-term, protected employment relations, rich in voice rights and in limitations to exit rights of the counterpart, is therefore currently well established and accepted in all approaches in economic organization.

There are some questions, though, on what has not been considered in those analyses, even in the wider stakeholder approaches. Have they told the entire story? Are specific investments in HC and bargaining power due to unsubstitutability the only reason why human resource providers may gain the status of residual claimants on firm rents? Does the absence of specific investments in HC lead directly to having no claim on property rights? Are there any types of HC investments that may give title to other classes of property rights, such as ownership of assets or outputs?

The next section sets out an enlarged, more general analysis of the types of property rights to which human capital holders should be entitled, according to the different characteristics that HC itself may have, as well as to the different modes in which it may be constituted and used.

AN EXTENDED TYPOLOGY OF HC AND PR

A few contributions have provided analyses and typologies in which the types of rights that human assets providers should be entitled to are made 'contingent' to the state of some independent variables. Early on, in the debate in Germany about the theoretical justifications of *Mitbestimmung*, Vanberg took some steps in the direction of specifying why different groups of 'members' of an organization may be efficiently assigned different mixes of rights, ranging from 'residual claim and co-determination rights' to 'contractual income and no co-determination rights', adding that further combinations can be found (Vanberg 1982). More recently, typologies specifying which those 'various combinations' might be and under what conditions they might be Pareto-efficient have been elaborated (Grandori 2001; Aoki 2010). Interestingly, those conditions pertain to the two different domains analyzed in economic and organizational approaches, respectively. One type of conditions pertains to the relative 'criticality' of human assets with respect to other inputs, and comes from the PRT tradition. A second type of conditions pertains to the nature of activities – as interdependence and task complexity and uncertainty – and comes from the OT tradition.

In Grandori's (2001) typology, a contingency model of firm ownership and work organization was elaborated, building on earlier contributions in PRT, TCE and OT such as Hart and Moore (1990), Williamson (1980) and Thompson (1967). It used two dimensions: the relative criticality of technical versus human assets – driving the formation of capitalistic, entrepreneurial and collective ownership structures; and the relative criticality of task uncertainty-related variables versus economies of scale and specialization variable – driving the formation of different organizational arrangements under each ownership structure: enriched versus Taylorized; inside contracting versus putting out; and peer group versus federative.

In Aoki's (2010) typology the dimension of the relative 'criticality' or 'essentiality' of human assets with respect to other assets, drawn from PRT, is split according to the type of actor providing human assets (in particular knowledge-based 'cognitive' assets): managers (as investors' agents) and workers. The result is a typology of governance and organizational forms in which the classic shareholder governance cum hierarchical organization is contingent to high essentiality of management knowledge assets and low essentiality of workers' knowledge assets. In other combinations, the more 'essential' workers' assets are, the more the rights assigned to them should expand, through rent-sharing procedures, representation in boards and other participatory devices, protections from other parties' exit, and horizontal rather than vertical organization (that should be highest in the combination of high essentiality of both management and workers' assets). The type of interdependence and the presence of economies of specialization also appear in the argument, accounting for more or less separation of units (called 'encapsulation') versus knowledge sharing.

These typologies are convergent in: (1) reconstructing the classic capitalistic authority-based firm as a particular case; (2) co-designing ownership and organizational structures so that ownership and control rights are allocated to actors according to the criticality of their contributions and the locus of knowledge; and (3) exploiting the possibility of property right sharing among actors to fit the various contingencies better (rather than assigning all rights to one class of actor).

In the reminder of this chapter, an extension of this approach is proposed, admitting a further possibility, typically overlooked in all prior perspectives. At least one distinction has in fact never been made in the above contributions (or never made in a way to make it visible and analyzed in terms of governance consequences). It is the distinction between human resources and the persons – physical and/or juridical – owing them, *de jure* or *de facto*. This distinction is missing because human resources are assumed to be inseparable from people, whereby the distinction becomes irrelevant. But the times are ripe to question that assumption. The key question to be posed is: are all the components of human capital equally 'inalienable' and equally 'inseparable' from the person? The answer, once the question is asked in that way, seems to be obvious: they are not so. Which components are more or less separable? Physical energy, personal skills and tacit know-how are not separable from the person; but ideas, explicit knowledge and know-how, contacts and information are to a large extent separable (Grandori 2010). Actually, they are so separable as to be often exposed to expropriation risks and to create intellectual property rights protection issues, on which a wide literature in fact exists. Hence, let us start with the following modified assumption: some components of human capital – especially knowledge, intellectual and relational assets – are separable from the person; hence they may be 'alienable' to another person or their ownership can be transferred to a juridical person. The consequence is that *HC, either specific to a use or of general value, can be invested into firms.*

In order to show that the assumption has an empirical basis, consider the following qualitative and quantitative data on agreements granting PR vis-à-vis investments 'of'

HC into entities regulating economic ongoing cooperations, in which those PR assignments are particularly explicit and visible, actually contractually stated.

Some Relevant Evidence

In both internal contracts constitutive of firms and in external contracts regulating cooperation between independent entities, in HC-intensive situations, a share of PR is allocated to HC providers for that provision. In particular the types of HC investments compensated through PR over assets or output, residual reward rights and decision and control rights, are intellectual capital (knowledge and ideas) and social capital (contacts and relationships) investments. Entrepreneur–venture capitalist contracts are a case in point. In the words of Silicon Valley entrepreneurs: 'It's a highly negotiated relation and contract. The main issue is how much is the human capital versus the financial capital worth' (Grandori and Gaillard 2011). And in the words of VC investors:

> The entrepreneurial team provides mainly technical competence and business ideas. The negotiation of the contract between the two involves an estimate of the value of the firm before the financial investment: this is the value of the entrepreneurial investment. Thus, according to how much we invest, we arrive at the division of shares. In our case, we entered with 33 percent in preferred shares. We were more interested in liquidation preferences than in board control: our board turned out to be composed of two entrepreneurial representatives, two VC representatives and two independents. (Grandori and Gaillard 2011)

Clearly, these interviews support the view that: (1) PR can be unbundled and assigned in various types and amounts to different actors-investors; (2) HC is partitioned from the person of the entrepreneur, invested into the firm of which it becomes an asset; (3) the entrepreneur gains a right of ownership over firm assets vis-à-vis their investment, that can be recovered in the form of money when they cash in on their shares.

As to inter-organizational associations, Table 15.1 offers an elaboration on a database of 540 records, each corresponding to an inter-organizational project in knowledge-intensive sectors (high tech, creative industries, and construction and engineering), that was successfully completed and produced valuable outputs in the former three years, gathered in an international research project in 2006–07.[1] One of the questionnaire items asked about the relative incidence of the investments of different types of capital – financial, technical, and human and social – into the projects by the three most important partners and the relative incidence of PR assigned to each of these three key partners.

Table 15.1   Incidence of capital invested by type and property rights assignments in inter-organizational projects

Average %	Tech & fin investments	Human & social capital investments	Property rights assignments
Partner 1	47.7	55	56.1
Partner 2	31.5	27.3	26.8
Partner 3	20.7	17.5	13.3
Total	99.9	99.8	96.2

Those projects are entities set up by partnership contracts of various kinds, which may or may not have juridical personality, but always apportion PR to the constituent parties.

The response pattern cannot be explained unless we admit that human and social capital investments command PR assignments, beyond any technical and financial capital investment. In fact, the interesting pattern emerging is that PR assignments, while being generally proportional to the invested assets reflect in a particularly close way the proportion of human and social capital invested.

Propositions on the Relations between HC and PR, with Special Reference to the Firm

If we accept the revised assumption that (some components of) HC can be invested into economic and legal entities, the road is open to endogeneize also the 'third' Marxian assumption (the 'inalienability' of 'labor force' or HC) as a variable: a 'degree of inalienability' or 'separability' of HC from persons, as much as a degree of specificity, and a degree of criticality can be defined. This endogeneization of the assumption of 'inalienability' is important as it allows us to talk about different types of investment (or the lack thereof) of HC into entities as a source of various types of legitimate claims or rights the investors have on the economic entity. If not acknowledged, those HC investments would simply go unrecognized and uncompensated. As we have seen, in inter-firm cooperative relations, where common ongoing activities are in order, participating entities do in fact demand PR in case they invest any form of capital – financial, technical, or human and social – no matter whether specific or not. In case of the participation of individuals to the common ongoing activities of a firm, the situation is not different: if investments are made, PR should be demanded.

If we add this new variable to those already considered in the literature reviewed in the first part, we can specify the typology of HC&PR depicted in Table 15.2.

Table 15.2   A model of HC and contingent PR holding

HC investments or uses	Claims on different types of rights
Investments OF HC in an entity	Full PR
Investments IN entity-specific HC	Open-ended contracts, long-term human asset shielding
Provision of relevant knowledge assets	Residual and non residual decision rights, contractually guaranteed against over-ruling
Team production & Performance Uncertainty	Residual reward rights
HC depletion	Representation/voice rights over use of HC, indemnities for HC consumption

Investible HC and full PR   The intellectual and knowledge component of HC is typically the more investible. The difference with financial capital is that typically it cannot be disinvested in the same form in which it has been invested: it should give the right to a return on investment in other forms (residual rewards, royalties on patents or brands, sale of stock). As for any investor, it should also give the right to a voice on how the investments are used (Hart and Moore 1990), or the incentives to invest will be low (Osterloh and Frey 2006). These investments are more pervasive than usually recognized: they include products and process innovations, contacts and personal relations used for the firm. Management techniques such as the mapping and codification of best practices, in order to 'transfer' and diffuse them to the entire organization, amount to an (often unreckoned) investment made by those people into the organization.

In the case of new firms, PR assignments to HC providers are highly visible and openly negotiated, as already illustrated above, and documented in many studies on new firm governance (e.g. Kaplan and Stromberg 2003). However, 'islands of HC investors' property' can be and often are constituted also within established corporations that, as a whole, are owned by a different set of investors. For example, at 3M, an internal patenting system grants property rights and royalties to internal inventors and infuses transparency in the evaluation of 'ideas' submitted by applicants for patent protection and exploitation; or the 'own business program' grants property rights to those who have provided the relevant knowledge on the business lines emerging from their human capital investments (Turati 1998). Miles et al. (1997) describe how some firms such as TCG (Technical and Computer Graphics) or Acer are federations of smaller, self-managed entrepreneurial firms, with different specializations giving rise to the overall structure through the formation of joint ventures (among them and with external partners) on projects, according to formalized procedures.

Hence, there is a mutual interest stemming from the complementarity of assets (Rajan and Zingales 2000) but the association of assets is guaranteed in a formal and enforceable way by proprietary alliances and contracts, specifying the allocation of property and exit rights to the various internal parties (Grandori 2010).

Investments in HC, 'human asset shielding' and return on investments

> A person's total income is found by deducting from his gross income the outgoings that belongs to its production; and this gross income includes many things which do not appear in the form of money payments and are in danger of being overlooked. First, we do not here reckon the expenses of education, general and special, involved in the preparation for any trade (Marshall 1898, VI.III.18)

In other words, investments of both a 'general and specific kind' may be made in any component of HC: formal education and training, learning on the job and expertise, skills and abilities, contacts and relationships. Whoever bears the costs of those investments is entitled to get a return on the investment. The case of specific investments in HC is that typically analyzed in OE, as giving the right to significant protection of the occupational investment, to a substantial share of firm quasi-rent, and to decision rights in firm governance (Blair and Stout 2006; Rajan and Zingales 2000; Sacconi et al. 2010). It has also been observed that, even where human assets cannot be 'partitioned' from the owner, they can however to some extent be 'shielded', from withdrawal as well as from dismissal, through other means (Hansmann et al. 2006). These means include property rights subject to a 'vesting period' (e.g. vesting of options in start-ups) (Kaplan and Stromberg 2003) and employee stock ownership, whether individual or associated through union and pension funds (Barney 1990).

These analyses imply that where investments in human assets are not firm-specific, and can be moved from firm to firm, the 'shielding' and the length of the relationship may be reduced in the interests of all parties. What has been less stressed, however, is that due to other factors there are limits to the effective reduction in the shielding and length of employment relations, even when investments in HC are not specific.

As Marshall noticed, there would be little incentive for a person to invest in their own formation and HC if they cannot get access to returns on those investments in the series of employment contracts they will over time obtain. Those returns on investments can only consist in some economic and positional rent, that is, in some property rights sharing. Studies on the PR consequences of investments in non-specific HC do not abound, given that the most common theoretical framework focuses on specific ones. A study on the profile of employment contracts that workers holding high-value or critical but not highly firm-specific HC (e.g. managers with postgraduate education) would be most likely to accept, and that firms (representatives) would like to offer, provides some pertinent data (Grandori and Soda 2004) on how some PR sharing can be efficient even in 'short-lived' employment relationships with high but not specific investments in HC. The study was conducted on a sample of 'human capital-intensive' workers constituted by 201 managers working in 190 large companies distributed in a wide variety of industries, and on a sample of 60 board directors or presidents of the largest 200 firms in Italy. The questionnaire asked for the preferred level – on percentage scales or absolute levels – of the following relevant items: incidence of residual rewards contingent to individual or group and firm performance; managerial representation on boards; managerial shareholding and ownership; autonomy in decision-making (percentage of work time and matters self-managed); relative investment by individuals and by firms in HC development; length of stay in each firm (in years). The results indicated that the holders of this type of high but not highly specific human capital on average prefer short periods of attachment to any single firm (four years, even shorter than the seven years the firm would prefer); would accept risk transfers in the form of compensation contingent to firm performance (a residual reward item) at approximately the same level that firms would like to offer (around 30 percent); but would like to have them accompanied by residual decision rights in the form of board representation (at higher levels, approximately 40 percent, than firms would prefer to see – approximately 30 percent); and property rights in the form of employee shareholding (also around 35–40 percent, with a maximum gap with firm representatives' preferences of around 10 percent). The study then provides some evidence that Pareto-efficient contracts for non-specific but critical HC holders should include various types of property rights.

Knowledge assets and decision rights   Even if not invested or not investible, and even if not specific, knowledge assets should give title to decision rights, for effectiveness reasons. The co-location of relevant knowledge with decision rights has been a core principle in organization theory ever since. Those knowledge considerations should temper the PRT principle that the more decision rights one party can obtain, the better off they are. In fact, in many cases one party is better off by giving out decision rights – even of a residual kind – to a more competent party or partner. In the case of employment relations, if the property of firm assets remains with the investors of financial and technical capital, which 'delegate' decision rights, those transfers of decision rights should be accompanied by credible commitments of not over-ruling (Foss et al. 2006).

But in many other cases the diffused allocation of decision rights does not stem out of 'delegation' from investors. Rather, the case is that the knowledge-intensive worker – for example, a professional or professor – would not enter into an authority relation, as he is not quasi-indifferent and is more knowledgeable about tasks than the employer. Then, a Pareto-efficient contract would be one in which decision rights on task selection (which may extend up to the whole organization activities) are 'retained' by the 'worker' rather than passed on to an authority (Simon 1951). In fact, employment contracts and organizational practices in professional and knowledge-based firms often include guarantees of professional autonomy and rights of being represented in policy decisions.

Risk and human resource consumption   Are people holding unskilled, unspecific 'labor force' entitled to any property right? And of what kind? The only type of right, and reason for it, envisaged in (some) received organizational economics contributions is a right to collective bargaining; due to the cost of negotiating and enforcing employment contracts, which typically make collective bargaining more efficient than individual bargaining (Freeman and Medoff 1984). This argument does not do justice, however, to the reasons why an internal employment contract is there in the first place for this type of unskilled, unspecific workers. An explanation of the employment relation independent from asset specificity was however available in the classic works by Marshall and Simon, revealing that relations, including the transfer to or sharing of option rights on workers' actions with an employer-coordinator, can be justified by uncertainty alone, irrespectively of asset specificity: workers get protection from wage risk while the firm gets decision rights over action. That contract was argued to be Pareto-optimal precisely under the conditions that may be defined as 'low HC intensity': the firm (representatives) know more about, and are more interested in, the best allocation of workers' efforts, than the workers themselves. Goldberg (1980) added a control and coordination capacity argument: the observation that, if the employment relation were not 'relational', 'long term' and 'protected', the (un-specific) worker would face little cost of exit and any coordinator would have little bargaining power basis for coordinating anything.

Reasoning on human capital, in addition to labor services, would help in seeing a further reason for the internal, long-term or otherwise 'protected' organization of the employment relation in those 'simple labor' situations, even including a reason for some PR assignments: the fact that, especially in those 'simple labor' situations, while releasing labor services, human resources are often exposed to consumption and depletion and to natural risks (health damages, work accidents). Parts of human capital – in this case especially the traditional 'physical' rather than intellectual components of human capital – are like 'natural resources' and 'physical assets': as such they are subject to 'consumption' and 'depletion' when used to produce services. Marshall's insights again help in recalling and taking into account these rather neglected 'investments' of human capital 'into' firms. The phrase quoted above from paragraph VI.III.18 of the *Principles* – 'we do not here reckon the expenses of education, general and special, involved in the preparation for any trade' – goes on by saying: 'nor do we take into account of the exhaustion of a person's health and strength in his work'.

For some labor services, this risk is absent or low: for example, professional work, legal or administrative data analysis, typewriting and secretarial services. The state of affairs is however different for activities involving physical safety issues and a depletion of physic and psychic capability (rather than a growth of it, as in many knowledge-intensive activities) due to the provision of work; a consumption of the natural resource of the human body. This may be seen as a different reason for the association of workers to firms, and for human asset shielding, with respect to both asset specificity and uncertainty reasons, as well as with respect to bargaining power arguments. Therefore human capital depletion may help in explaining the wide empirical anomaly with respect to specificity-based and even to knowledge-based theories of both the internal employment relation and of PR holding by HC providers: how it is that in many parts of the world the contracts regulating the provision of unskilled and unspecific work are open-ended and long-lasting; and workers' interests are represented – through trade unions and negotiation, or through other voice and representation rights – in firm governance. The argument developed here should help to show that these arrangements do have a Pareto-efficiency justification; hence, that there are efficiency-based reasons for the assignment of some categories of PR – in particular, representation or voice rights, and indemnities for HC consumption – also where HC is neither specific nor knowledge intensive.

CONCLUSIONS

This chapter has offered a review of studies relevant for answering the question of which categories of property rights, and in what proportion, should be assigned to the providers of HC in economic activities. The conclusions innovate with respect to received theories, which maintain that it is never efficient to unbundle different kinds of decision rights and to share them among different actors; that HC is 'inalienable' and human assets not investible into economic entities; and that only firm-specific HC holders are entitled to shielded long-term employment contracts. Leveraging on OT and on empirical studies on governance and organization, as well as on a development of PRT, the analysis conducted here has highlighted that: (1) the PR can be unbundled and shared among different input providers; (2) the actors having a title are investors of any type of capital, including HC; and (3) HC can be partitioned from people and invested into economic entities involving a 'continued association of dedicated assets'. Those 'associations' (of which firms are an important subset) typically generate a 'rent' and a fair rent division problem among resource providers. Hence, the very nature of those continued associations of dedicated assets (of both general and specific kinds) should typically imply negotiated governance, as highlighted especially by Marshall and Aoki. The contingent rightholder analysis performed here also provided propositions on the type and amount of rights: (1) the higher the investments of HC into the association, the higher the share of PR (in their full range – property of assets and/or outputs as well as residual rewards and decision rights) assigned to those investors; (2) the higher the knowledge component of HC possessed by a participant (investible or not investible) relevant for effective action selection, the wider should be the decision rights assigned to him/her in non-renegeable ways; (3) the higher the investments made in association-specific HC, the stronger human asset shielding provisions should be in the governance of the association; and (4) the higher the investments of non-recoverable human resources (also of a non-specific and non-knowledge-intensive kind) into the association, the more a corresponding economic right representing the value of investment and a voice right on the use of the infused human capital should be present.

If human capital is central to economic growth, as Becker stressed and many recognize, it is important that there are incentives and conditions not only favoring significant investments 'in' HC, but also favoring significant investments 'of' HC into the various entities in which economic activity is organized, in particular into firms. Hence acknowledging the possibility of those investments in the first place is the first step to be taken. In the course of reviewing the literature on HC and PR in economic organization, this chapter has offered and extended a typology for the design of PR assignments and other organizational rights that recognizes those investments and should therefore also extend, if applied, human capital-driven economic growth.

NOTES

*   Earlier versions and sections of this chapter were presented at the 16th International Economic Association World Congress, Beijing in July 2011, and at seminars (Cass Business School Seminar Series; CROMA Think-Tank on Democracy and Performance) in September 2011. I thank all the colleagues who have provided feedback in those discussions, in particular Masahiko Aoki, Igor Filatotchev, Bruce Kaufman, Lorenzo Sacconi and Lynn Stout.
1.   KGP (Knowledge, Governance and Projects) is an international research project conducted by the Bocconi Center of Research on Business Organization in partnership with the following universities and investigators: Anna Grandori, Crora Bocconi, principal investigator; Peter Maskell, Copenhagen Business School; Mark Ebers, Universities of Augsburg and Cologne; Gernot Grabher, University of Bonn; Patrick Cohendet, University of Strasbourg; Andrea Prencipe, SPRU, University of Sussex and University of Pescara – and co-financed by MIUR (Italian Ministry of University and Research) and by the partner universities. The analysis presented here is original and developed specifically for this chapter.

REFERENCES

Aoki, M. (1984), *The Cooperative Game Theory of the Firm*, Oxford: Oxford University Press.
Aoki, M. (2004), 'Comparative institutional analysis of corporate governance', in A. Grandori (ed.), *Corporate Governance and Firm Organization*, Oxford: Oxford University Press, pp. 31–44.
Aoki, M. (2010), *Corporations in Evolving Diversity*, Oxford: Oxford University Press.
Barney, J.B. (1990), 'Employee stock ownership and the cost of equity in Japanese electronic firms', *Organization Studies*, 11(3), 353–372.
Becker, G.S. (1964), *Human Capital. A Theoretical and Empirical Analysis, with Special Reference to Education*, New York: Columbia University Press.
Becker, G.S. (2002), 'Human capital theory', *The Concise Encyclopedia of Economics*, New York: Columbia University Press.
Blair, M. (1996), *Wealth Creation and Wealth Sharing: A Colloquium on Corporate Governance and Investments in Human Capital*, Washington, DC: Brookings Institute.
Blair, M.M. (1999), 'Firm-specific human capital and theories of the firm', in Margaret M. Blair and Mark J. Roe (eds), *Employees and Corporate Governance*, Washington, DC: Brookings Institution Press, pp. 58–90.
Blair, M.M. and L.A. Stout (2006), 'Specific investment and corporate law'. *European Business Organization Law Review*, 7(2), 473–500.
Burt, R.S. (2002), *Brokerage and Closure. An Introduction to Social Capital*, Oxford: Oxford University Press.
Colombo, M.G. and L. Grilli (2005), 'Founders' human capital and the growth of new technology-based firms: a competence-based view', *Research Policy*, 34(6), 795–816.
Doeringer, P.B. and M.J. Piore (1971), *Internal Labor Markets and Manpower Analysis*, Lexington, KY: Heath.

Foss, K., N. Foss and X.A. Vàzquez (2006), 'Tying the manager's hands: constraining opportunistic managerial intervention', *Cambridge Journal of Economics*, **30**, 797–818.

Freeman, R.B. and J.L. Medoff (1984), *What Do Unions Do*, New York: Basic Books.

Goldberg, V.P. (1976), 'Regulation and administered contracts', *Bell Journal of Economics*, **7**, 426–448.

Goldberg, V.P. (1980), 'Bridges over contested terrain: exploring the radical account of the employment relationship', *Journal of Economic Behavior Organization*, **1**, 249–274.

Grandori, A. (2001), *Organization and Economic Behavior*, London: Routledge.

Grandori A. (2006), 'Uncertainty, innovation and relational governance: a typology', *Industry and Innovation*, **13**(2), 127–133.

Grandori, A. (2010), 'Asset commitment, constitutional governance and the nature of the firm', *Journal of Institutional Economics*, **6**(3), 351–375.

Grandori, A. and Giordani L. Gaillard (2011), *Organizing Entrepreneurship*, London: Routledge.

Grandori, A. and G. Soda (2004), 'Governing with multiple principals: an empirically-based analysis of capital providers' preferences and superior governance structures', in A. Grandori (ed.), *Corporate Governance and Firm Organization*, Oxford: Oxford University Press, pp. 67–88.

Grossman, S. and O. Hart (1986), 'The costs and benefits of ownership: a theory of vertical and lateral integration', *Journal of Political Economy*, **94**, 691–719.

Hansmann, H., (1996), *The Ownership of the Enterprise*, Cambridge: Belknap Press.

Hansmann, H., R. Kraakman and R. Squire (2006), 'Law and the rise of the firm', *Harvard Law Review*, **119**(5), 1333–1403.

Hart, O. (1995), *Firm, Contracts, and Financial Structure*, Oxford: Clarendon Press.

Hart, O. and J. Moore (1994), 'A theory of debt based on the inalienability of human capital', *Quarterly Journal of Economics*, **109**(4), 841–879.

Kaplan, S.N. and P. Strömberg (2003), 'Financial contracting theory meets the real world: an empirical analysis of venture capital contracts', *Review of Economic Studies*, **70**(2), 281–315.

Klein, B., R. Crawford and A. Alchian (1978), 'Vertical integration, appropriable rents and the competitive contracting process', *Journal of Law and Economics*, **21**(2), 297–326.

Lepak, D.P, A. Scott and S.A. Snell (2002), 'Examining the human resource architecture: the relationships among human capital, employment, and human resource configurations', *Journal of Management*, **28**, 517–543.

Lerner, J. and R.P. Merges (1998), 'The control of technology alliances: an empirical analysis of the biotechnology industry', *Journal of Industrial Economics*, **46**, 125–156.

Marshall, A. (1898), *Principles of Economics*, 4th edn, London: Macmillan.

Miles, R.E., C.S. Snow, J.A. Mathews, G. Miles and H.J. Coleman, Jr. (1997), 'Organizing in the knowledge age: anticipating the cellular form', *Academy of Management Executive*, **11**(4), 7–21.

Nahapiet, J. and S. Ghoshal (1998), 'Social capital, intellectual capital, and the organizational advantage', *Academy of Management Review*, **23**(2), 242–266.

Osterloh, M. and B. Frey (2006), 'Shareholders should welcome knowledge workers as directors', *Journal of Management and Governance*, **10**(3), 325–345.

Petty, R. and J. Guthrie (2000), 'Intellectual capital: literature review', *Journal of Intellectual Capital*, **1**(2), 155–176.

Rajan, R.G. and L. Zingales (2000), 'The governance of the new enterprise', in X. Vives (ed.), *Corporate Governance*, Cambridge: Cambridge University Press, pp. 201–232.

Sacconi, L., M. Blair, E. Freeman and A. Vercelli (eds) (2010), *Corporate Social Responsibility and Corporate Governance*, London: Palgrave Macmillan.

Simon, H.A. (1951), 'A formal theory of the employment relationship', *Econometrica*, **19**(3), 293–305.

Stuart, T.A. (1997), *Intellectual Capital*, New York: Doubleday.

Thompson, J.D. (1967), *Organization in Action*, New York: McGraw-Hill.

Turati C. (1998), 'Minnesota Mining and Manufacturing', Case Study, SDA Bocconi.

Vanberg, V. (1982), 'Das Unternehmen als Sozialverband. Zur Sozialtheorie der Unternehmung und zur juristischen Diskussion um ein neues Unternehmensrecht' [The firm as a social organization. The social theory of the firm and the legal discussion on a new law of business corporations], Jahrbuch für Neue Politische Ökonomie, Vol. I, Tübingen, pp. 276–307.

Youndt, M.A., M. Subramaniam and S.A. Snell (2004), 'Intellectual capital profiles: an examination of investments and returns', *Journal of Management Studies*, **41**(2), 335–361.

Williamson, O.E. (1975), *Markets and Hierarchies: Analysis and Antitrust Implications*, New York: Free Press.

Williamson, O.E. (1980), 'The organization of work: a comparative institutional assessment', *Journal of Economics Behavior and Organization*, **1**, 5–38.

Williamson, O.E. (1981), 'The economics of organization: the transaction cost approach', *American Journal of Sociology*, **87**, 548–577.

Williamson, O.E. (2009), 'Organization matters', Paper presented at the 13th ISNIE Conference, Berkeley.
Williamson, O.E. and W.G. Ouchi (1981), 'The markets and hierarchies program of research: origins, implication, prospects', in A.H. Van de Ven and W.F. Joyce (eds), *Perspectives on Organization Design and Behavior*, New York: Wiley, pp. 347–370.

16. The economic organization of employment: systems in human resource management and industrial relations

Bruce E. Kaufman

This chapter examines the economic organization of employment relationships. Topics examined include the concept of employment systems; the foundation of the employment relationship in coordination cost and the division of labor; reasons for internalization versus externalization of employment relationships; alternative organizational configurations of employment systems; and theoretical explanation of the structure and performance of different employment systems. The chapter draws on literatures and explanations spanning the economics–organization interface but with particular reference to the complementary fields of human resource management and industrial relations (hereafter industrial and employment relations).

INTRODUCTION

Organization theory has long roots into the nineteenth century but only became a recognized field of study shortly after World War II (Starbuck 2003). Although economists such as Herbert Simon played an important role in creating the field, soon economics and organization theory began to diverge and by the 1970s were more like the proverbial two ships passing in the night with relatively little research interaction or integration. In the last two decades, however, the situation has noticeably reversed, a fruitful joint research conversation has developed, and new subfields have emerged (e.g., organizational economics, new institutionalism, economic sociology). A particularly fruitful point of contact has been in the area of labor and employment, given that the central topic of investigation, the employment relationship, spans the market–organization interface.

An employment relationship commences when one person offering labor services is taken on by another person or business entity and is paid a wage for performing various directed tasks and activities. As emphasized by Simon (1951), the employment contract is distinctive because it creates not only a buyer–seller relationship but also an authority relationship between a boss (employer) and worker (employee). The starting point for this chapter is the observation that while the employment relationship is a central feature of all modern economies it nonetheless exhibits numerous institutional configurations and modes of operation across firms, industries and nations. A major subject area of research, therefore, has been identifying discrete patterns in employment relationships and the important factors that create them. Often these patterns are conceptualized as employment systems (Marsden 1999).

Embedded within employment systems (ESs) are numerous component parts typically associated with the activities of personnel and human resource management (PHR) and industrial and employment relations (IER). In North America and Britain, industrial and employment relations is frequently defined to include all aspects of the employment relationship, including personnel and human resource management (Kaufman 2008a); in continental Europe and other regions, however, IER is defined more narrowly to include only collective aspects of employment relations (Hall & Soskice 2001a). Which definition is used is largely immaterial for this chapter so, for expositional simplicity, European practice is followed and PHR is identified with management activities and practices used to acquire, place, motivate, train, reward and discipline employees; while the provenance of IER is workforce governance, joint employer–employee relations, negotiation and administration of collective labour agreements, and administration of government employment laws and regulations.

Although the recent literature on employment systems features greater economic–organization integration, this particular research program continues to have considerable diversity of theories and models across contributing disciplines and subfields. Also, somewhat autonomous literatures exist for the micro (firm) level and macro (nation state) level. To keep the chapter well focused and compact, the micro component is emphasized here. The chapter aims in part to promote a tighter integration and synthesis of diverse ES models and theories and, in equal measure, to advance the literature with some relatively new and independent ideas and perspectives.

EMPLOYMENT SYSTEMS: CONCEPT AND FOUNDATION

An organization has a demand for labor because labor services are embedded in human beings and production cannot move forward without human beings coordinating and performing certain essential tasks that cannot be done by inanimate capital and natural resources. Human labor in production is thus generic to an economic system.

Coase (1937) and Simon (1951) also note, however, that organizations may acquire labor services through alternative institutional methods. Simon, for example, distinguishes between obtaining labor services through a sales contract and an employment contract. The generic nature of labor in production, along with the sales versus employment contract dichotomy, can be helpfully illustrated using a neoclassical production function $Q = f(K, L, N)$. It states that an organization's level of output is a function of the level of technology and the amount of the capital, labor, and natural resource inputs. Without human beings providing positive labor services ($L > 0$), the production function yields no output ($Q = 0$). However, organizations can acquire labor services through product or labor markets. The first is equivalent to a sales contract; that is, entering into a commercial contract with an independent contractor who for a price P agrees to perform a work task, like driving his truck from point A to point B to deliver the company's freight. The second is equivalent to an employment contract; that is, hiring the same person but in a labor market to serve as an employee who for a wage W agrees to follow orders and drives the company's truck from point A to point Z and delivers the freight.

Reasons why the employee mode is often selected are discussed later. Suffice it to note at this point that if the employment mode is adopted then organizations necessarily take on a range of activities and responsibilities associated with employees. In particular, every organization with employees – subject to laws, social norms and possible union negotiation – has to develop an employment system that coordinates and governs the part of the production function involving the labor input variable L. In particular, the ES is the matrix of organizational structures, rules, processes and tools used to acquire, assign, motivate, develop, utilize, compensate, govern and dispose of the labor input of employees. These employment-related activities, particularly as researched and taught in business schools, form the core subjects of the applied and overlapping fields of PHR and IER. The ES concept can therefore be seen as a research program that seeks to open up the black box of the production function and flesh out the institutional fabric that embeds and enables the $L \rightarrow Q$ transformation in cases where firms hire employees and use PHR and IER activities to coordinate and control the process.

The various distinctions described to this point can be strengthened and sharpened by considering in more detail an economy's division of labor. Outside an economy of autarky, production takes place through a division of labor in which many people specialize in certain tasks. The division of labor (DoL) can itself be differentiated into two components, a technical division (emphasized by economists) that creates a differentiation of tasks, jobs and functions among people based on features of the production technology and skill sets of workers; and a social division (emphasized by sociologists) that creates a similar differentiation by job assignment, authority level and status position based on personal characteristics (gender, race, etc.) and group affiliations (class, union membership, etc.). The two together create a social system of production (Hollingsworth & Boyer 1997; Amable 2003). The challenge for a human-run economy is to organize and coordinate the DoL in an efficient manner. This becomes a large challenge, in part because the technical division features many millions of different jobs, people and products in a modern nation (Marsden 1999) and also because the social dimension makes efficiency contingent on equity, morale and other social-psychological factors (Foss 2005; Rubery 2010; Jessop 2002).

An economy's DoL is illustrated in Figure 16.1. Tasks, denoted by the ten vertical hash marks, are arrayed from left to right according to their place in the various stages of production. For expositional simplicity the DoL is assumed to have a total of ten tasks. The left end-point (Task 1) represents the first stage while the right end-point (Task 10) represents the final stage. A concrete case cited by Adam Smith in the *Wealth of Nations* (1776 [1937]) is pin production. Smith distinguished separate tasks, such as smelting the wire, drawing out the wire, sharpening the point and forming the head. The chain

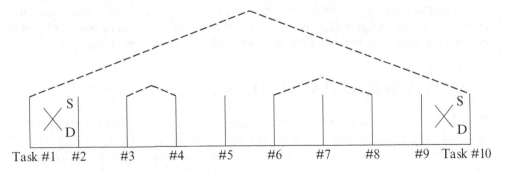

Figure 16.1 Division of labor and make vs. buy

of production, however, actually extends much farther in both leftward and rightward directions in Figure 16.1; examples relevant to pin production are, in the former case, the mining of the iron ore and coal that goes into smelting the wire and, in the latter, producing the paper boxes that contain the finished pins.

These tasks must be coordinated (Becker & Murphy 1992; Hollingsworth & Boyer 1997; Ferguson & Ferguson 2000). One approach is to have markets, prices and competition do it. In a completely marketized economy, each worker is an independent contractor or similar owner-operator, performs a particular task in the DoL, and then passes the product on to the next person through a sales contract coordinated by price and forces of demand and supply (DS). Thus, the person who puts the point on the pin goes into a market, buys the wire at a price, performs the sharpening task, and then sells the sharpened pin to the next person in the DoL. This is represented in Figure 16.1 by the small DS diagrams between Tasks #1/#2 and #9/#10 (others not shown). If there are too many wire drawers and not enough pin sharpeners or if one of the tasks is not done to customer specification, demand and supply curves shift and prices change until an equilibrium supply of workers for each task and specified product for each customer is re-established.

A second approach is to have some person in authority, typically called an employer or manager, perform the coordination function (Holmström 1999). Thus, tasks #3/#4 and #6/#7/#8 in Figure 16.1 are taken out of the market and put inside multi-person and often hierarchically structured organizations, denoted by the area under the two smaller 'roofs' and within the pentagon-type shapes. The pentagon-type shape is meant to convey that at the relatively broad base two or more contiguous tasks in the DoL are performed under one organizational roof while at the narrow apex an authority figure, such as a manager or employer, directs the performance of tasks through command and administration. If there is not the right mix of workers in the pin factory or supply of different types of pins for customers, the employer or factory manager issues orders to correct the situation. When the intermediate product is worked up the organization sells it through the market to the next person or organization in the DoL. Complete organization of the DoL, such as with central planning, is illustrated by the overarching roof.

Figure 16.1 typifies a mixed economy in the sense that some parts of the production process are organized within firms and other parts are organized within markets (Simon 1990). The dividing line is known as the 'boundary issue'; that is, the determination of the line in the DoL that separates organizational and market coordination (Holmström & Roberts 1998; Zenger et al. 2011; Kaufman 2003; Yang 2001). More attention is given to this matter later; at this point, however, it is useful to examine in greater detail the internal structure and coordination of labor within organizations. The place to begin is with the concepts of internal and external labor markets (Lazear & Oyer 2004).

EMPLOYMENT SYSTEMS: INTERNAL AND EXTERNAL

The existence of labor markets presupposes that at least a portion of an economy's labor input is acquired and governed by employment contracts. The structure and nature of employment contracting, and therefore associated employment systems, differs markedly, however, across firms and industries. A fundamental dichotomy for explaining this variation in ESs is between the internal and external labor market.

The internal labor market (ILM) is the area within each pentagon where the DoL is coordinated by management, subject to negotiation with workers' collective representatives (where they exist) and the constraints of law, social norms and ethics. The external labor market (ELM) is an area outside the pentagons (but separate from the contractors in product markets) where wage-earning labor suppliers search for satisfactory link-ups with employers, as coordinated by market forces of demand and supply – albeit constrained and influenced by institutional forces such as workers' organizations and legal infrastructure. This distinction is apparent in the definition of an ILM by Doeringer and Piore (1971: 1–2, slightly paraphrased): 'an administrative unit within an organization where the pricing and allocation of labor is governed by a set of rules and procedures'. Piore (2002) has recently emphasized that the idea of 'rules and procedures' needs to be framed broadly to include both formal and informal rules and those constructed not only in organizations but also by social conventions and cultural norms.

Thus, firms – defined broadly to include plants, stores, government agencies, and so on – hire new labor input from the ELM, typically at the bottom of the pentagon through 'ports of entry'; allocate and coordinate their workforce through management-created structures, rules and processes within the ILM; and then discharge surplus labor back into the ELM. In effect, the ILM is where the firm manages its rented stock of human capital and the ELM is where flows in and out take place through hiring and firing. The ILM introduces structure and long-term contracting into the employer–employee relation, orders the DOL along both horizontal and vertical dimensions in the organization, and arises from both technical and social factors. The ELM and ILM are ideal archetypes; in real life they overlap and meld together in varying degrees (Camuffo 2002).

The ILM can be considered a regime of workforce governance and mode of regulation of the production system; different ILM configurations, in turn, imply different regulation regimes in the workplace (Edwards 2003). ILMs perform a variety of functions typically identified with PHR and IER. They include: job analysis and design; recruiting, selection and staffing; training and development; compensation; benefits; performance management; individual and collective employee relations; discipline, discharge and dispute resolution; government mandates; and organizational culture and change. These activities are unilaterally organized and administered in firms without worker representation; with collective representation the process becomes bilateral and negotiated.

It is important to note that ELMs also take care of these PHR and IER activities, but differently. For example, wage differentials established by demand and supply regulate flows in and out of employment; workers finance their own skill acquisition (e.g., go to school or take a low-paid apprenticeship); the threat of immediate termination and unemployment motivates work effort and good citizenship behavior; workers who feel unfairly treated do not form unions or need labor laws but 'vote with their feet' by quitting for a better job elsewhere; and workers self-select into firms that offer the desired package of benefits. Employment relationships in an ELM are much more short-term, anonymous, informal and fluid, so some issues such as organizational culture are moot. In effect, labor is coordinated by the 'visible hand' of management in ILMs through commands, procedures and rules; while in ELMs the 'invisible hand' does the same through price signals, competition and turnover. This distinction approximates the one made in the macro-level variety of capitalism's literature between 'liberal market economies' and 'coordinated market economies' (Hall & Soskice 2001b; Streeck & Yamamura 2001; Wailes et al. 2008; Hamann & Kelly 2008).

Some economists claim that, *ceteris paribus*, ELMs are the more efficient way to coordinate production. In this perspective, firms and ILMs arise from market failure, such as positive transaction costs from imperfect information and asset specificity. Boeri and van Ours (2008), for example, portray ILMs and other labor market institutions as 'distortionary wedges' in an otherwise efficient competitive price system. Similarly, Williamson (1985) advances a 'market favoring' premise. It states (p. 87): 'only as market-mediated contract breaks down [due to market failure] are the transactions in question removed from markets and organized internally'. In this view, ILMs are an efficient coordination device but only in a second-best way. Alternative theories of the firm, such as the resource or capabilities view popular in management and organization theory (e.g., Foss & Knudsen 1996), conversely indicate that ILMs create efficiency gains relative to an externalized employment system and can (*ceteris paribus*) be a first-best choice. Here the emphasis is on organizational success rather than market failure.

Economic logic suggests that organizations choose the optimal degree of externalization versus internalization of labor based on a comparison of relative benefits and costs (the boundary issue). These benefits and costs can be divided into, respectively, production and contracting/coordination (transaction) components (Demsetz 1991; Furubotn & Richter 2005). If markets have lower contracting/coordination cost relative to management, economic rationality leads firms to externalize most of the relevant DoL. In this case Henry Ford decides to buy tires (a sales contract) from an outside supplier rather than hire employees to produce them in-house. Ford, therefore, chooses to keep the company as a smaller organization (as measured by employment) and focus on its core competency of auto assembly. If the reverse is the case, Ford chooses to vertically integrate these parts of the DoL into the company. The DoL in Figure 16.1 begins to agglomerate and ILMs grow in breadth and depth while intermediate product markets and ELMs shrink. Likewise, if internalization creates productivity-enhancing and hard-to-acquire employee skills or large synergies from teamwork and cooperation, ILMs are again favored and the DoL agglomerates into larger-sized firms.

An insight of this model is that the size and structure of labor and other input markets is endogenously determined by the owners of firms as they weigh the benefits and costs of centralization versus decentralization (Rosen 1991; Kaufman 2010a). Managers are from this perspective just as much 'labor market makers' as they are pin makers or auto makers (Anderson & Gatignon 2005). Also revealed is that economic models that start with the proposition 'assume a competitive labor market' are based on empirically problematic assumptions of, respectively, zero (or close-to-zero) external market transaction costs and equally negligible gains in labor productivity from internalization.

Balancing benefits and costs of ELMs versus ILMs is a logically sound but empirically empty decision rule for explaining employment systems. Also required is a theory that identifies specific variables that determine benefits and costs and the nature of the causal relationship. Among alternatives (see Grandori & Furnari 2008), transaction cost theory provides a foundation which can then be expanded with ideas from other theoretical perspectives.

Transaction cost theory demonstrates that a necessary condition for positive market coordination cost is imperfect information and bounded rationality (Kaufman 2007).

Given these, the variable most extensively cited in this literature as a determinant of market coordination cost is some form of asset specificity. Asset specificity occurs when the value of a resource has greater value in one use or situation than another. Williamson (1985: 95–96), for example, distinguishes four kinds of specificity: site specificity, physical asset specificity, human asset specificity and buyer-dedicated specificity.

Human asset specificity is the most important type for employment systems, particularly with regard to skills, knowledge and training (SKT). Following Becker (1964), skills, knowledge and training can be distinguished as general or firm specific. General SKTs are portable across firms and retain their value regardless of company; firm-specific types, however, are more productive at a particular company and lose value if transferred elsewhere. General SKTs, therefore, are consistent with an ELM-type employment system while those that are firm specific complement an ILM-type system. In particular, with the firm-specific type both employer and employee have an incentive to maintain their relationship since their joint investment in human capital loses economic value if the match is broken (Williamson 1985). Hence, human capital asset specificity encourages agglomeration of tasks in the DoL, management coordination of production and the size of firms (pentagons in Figure 16.1).

The internalization process creates forces that both reinforce and retard the shift toward ILMs. According to resource and capability theories of the firm, pooling employees and managers in an organization creates productivity gains through various interdependencies in knowledge creation, skill development and task performance (Langlois & Robertson 1995; Foss 2005). In a market, for example, information and knowledge are scarce goods and one person shares them with another only at a price; in a firm, on the other hand, sharing of information and knowledge is encouraged by teamwork in a common enterprise. Likewise, many skills useful in the production process are best developed by working with other people, say to acquire tacit knowledge about a work process or gain instruction from an experienced employee. Internalization may also boost productivity through interdependencies in utility functions of employees and managers. For example, both groups may develop strong feelings of team spirit and company loyalty that translates into more effective cooperation, greater work effort and willingness to sacrifice for a common goal (Pfeffer 1998; Hecksher & Adler 2006; Baron & Kreps forthcoming). In team-oriented companies with a mutual gain culture, these dispositions create a socio-psychological form of high-powered incentives that are possibly more effective than the contrasting motives of self-interest and pecuniary gain in market exchange. However, in poorly managed or strife-prone companies with an adversarial 'we against them' culture, these utility function interdependencies may work in the opposite direction and create anti-employer and anti-capitalist solidarity among the workers. The strategy and implementation of PHR and IER, therefore, has a direct influence on the success and longevity of an internal ES.

Internalization of employment also creates forces that act as a drag or limit on the size of ILMs (Rosen 1991). For example, bounded rationality and positive transaction cost create incomplete employment contracts. With such contracts, risks open up related to agency, opportunism, moral hazard and asymmetric information; similarly, both sides to the employment relationship have greater space and incentive to take advantage of these contracting imperfections when the other party's outside alternatives are constrained by costs of turnover and hiring and firing (Williamson 1985; Marsden 1999; Malcolmson

1999; Lazear & Oyer forthcoming). Thus, at the time of hiring, workers may exaggerate their skills and experience or once on the job work at only half-speed if not closely supervised; likewise, employers may exaggerate to job applicants the chances of promotion, or renege on their promise of job security for good performance. These kinds of contracting problems, akin to the defection choice in a Prisoner's Dilemma game (Miller 1991), undercut incentives to internalize production and at some point put a limit to ILM expansion. In this context, PHR and IER function as control, monitoring and sanction devices.

PHR and IER may, however, also be used to solve these problems in a more strategic and positive manner. Defection in a Prisoner's Dilemma game, for example, can be substantially reduced by policies that encourage ongoing communication, trust and long-term mutual gains (Grundei 2006). Thus, PHR and IER can increase the surplus from cooperation and internal contracting by creating gain-sharing compensation plans, job security provisions, integrative employee involvement programs and egalitarian corporate cultures (Rebitzer & Taylor 2011). Cooperation and trust are also enhanced by power balancing; thus collective representation and joint governance may make ILM structures more stable and long-lasting (Freeman & Lazear 1995).

THE STRUCTURE OF EMPLOYMENT SYSTEMS: COMPLEMENTARITY, FIT AND DEMAND

The external versus internal dimension of labor markets is the foundation for theorizing about employment systems; in this section the theory is extended to explain additional ES features and categories. To do so, new concepts are introduced, such as complementarities, strategic fit and a demand function for PHR and IER inputs. The first two concepts are well developed in the literature while the latter is relatively new.

A useful place to start is again with the production function. Economic models of production usually assume substitutability between factor inputs, such as capital and labor and different types of labor. The same assumption seems reasonable regarding the formal types of PHR and IER activities firms use to help effectuate the $L \rightarrow Q$ transformation in the labor process. One could specify, therefore, $Q = f(K, L, N, HRM_{i,k})$ where for notational simplicity HRM is used as an abbreviated label for the totality of PHR and IER, i indexes the formal PHR and IER activities listed earlier, and k indexes alternative ways to accomplish these activities. HRM_1 and HRM_2 might represent, respectively, job design and employee recruitment and $HRM_{2,k}$ might represent k different ways of recruiting new hires (e.g., 1 = walk-ins, 2 = job postings on a company website, 3 = a jobs fair, etc.).

Assuming the organization's goal is maximum profit, the individual $HRM_{i,k}$ have different marginal products, and the $HRM_{i,k}$ also have different positive prices and costs, then one can write out the standard profit maximization equation for the firm, solve for the first-order conditions, and determine the efficient level and mix of the $HRM_{i,k}$ (Kaufman & Miller 2011). The level and mix of the $HRM_{i,k}$, however, is simply another name for the object of interest – an employment system.

To develop and flesh out the ES concept, the first-order condition can be used to graphically derive a firm's HRM demand curve. An example is depicted in panel (a) in Figure 16.2.

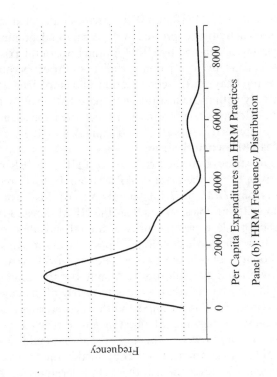

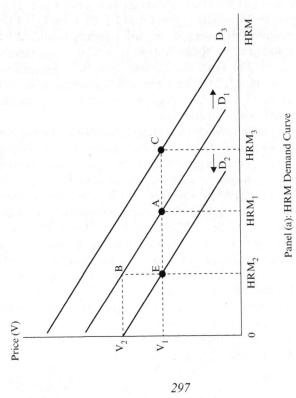

Panel (b): HRM Frequency Distribution

Panel (a): HRM Demand Curve

Figure 16.2   HRM Frequency and Demand Curve

297

The price (per unit cost) of formal PHR and IER activities is denoted by V on the vertical axis, the quantity of such activities (expressed in the common denominator of dollars, as done with physical capital) is denoted by HRM on the horizontal axis. This framework is managerialist, but realistically so for non-socialist countries, because it assumes the firm's managers have final say on the construction and implementation of PHR and IER activities, albeit only within the institutional space left open by government laws, collective bargaining contracts, social norms and other such constraints. For simplicity at this point, $HRM_{i,k}$ is summed across all i,k and expressed on the horizontal axis as the aggregate amount of HRM used in the firm.

The demand curve illustrates that the firm's use of PHR and IER inputs follows the law of demand; that is, a rise in the price of HRM from V_1 to V_2 reduces quantity of HRM used in the firm from HRM_1 to HRM_2 (points A to B). Just as other input demand functions also contain shift variables, so too does the HRM demand function. A representative list includes: output level, relative price of capital and labor, breadth and depth of labor laws, type of production technology, types of worker skills and knowledge, presence of a union, boom or bust in the macroeconomy, workforce demographic characteristics, and employee relations philosophy. A shift variable representing the firm's business strategy might also be included, as it is in nearly all management and many organizational studies (Boxall & Purcell 2008), but the theoretical grounding is problematic. The reason is because strategy (i.e., the best means to reach a given end) arguably lacks independent explanatory power to the degree that it is endogenously determined by the same revenue and cost variables already contained in the firm's constrained profit maximization calculation. Whatever the list, these shift variables are similar to contingencies in organization theory models (Donaldson 2006; Grandori & Furnari 2008).

Illustratively, in Figure 16.2 the HRM demand shifts left from D_1 to D_2 for (say) a smaller-sized firm, an economy in recession, or with a lightly regulated labor market, indicating that at the same price V_1 these firms have a relatively smaller demand for HRM (from point A to E). For large-sized firms, firms in a full-employment labor market, or firms subject to numerous government employment mandates, the demand curve shifts rightward from D_1 to D_3 and demand for HRM practices and programs commensurately increases (from point A to C).

Trade unionism, collective bargaining and other forms of collective representation (e.g., works councils) may shift the demand curve in either direction. For example, unions frequently negotiate contract provisions that require firms to formalize and expand their PHR and IER programs. Examples include additional staff for contract negotiation and day-to-day consultation with employee representatives, greater investment in training and workplace health and safety, and bilateral procedures for grievance resolution. Similarly, non-union firms may expand PHR, either as a form of union substitution (e.g., paying wages higher than the union level) or union repression (e.g., covert use of job performance evaluations to discriminate against union activists), in order to diminish workers' desire for collective representation. On the other hand, the firm's HRM demand curve may shift leftward if unions provide certain PHR or IER activities that employers would otherwise have to provide. As examples, firms may reduce employee recruitment and selection expenditures if unions perform these activities through hiring halls; likewise, firms may cut back on expensive performance evaluation procedures if unions mandate promotion by seniority.

Given these qualifications and contingencies, the position of the HRM demand curve determines for each firm the extent of expenditure on formal PHR and IER practices and therefore sets the broad outline for the breadth, depth and structure of its employment system. A firm with a demand curve to the left of D_2, for example, spends relatively little on PHR and IER and therefore operates with a more informal and externalized ES; on the other hand, a firm with a demand curve to the right of D_3 most likely has a well-developed internal type of ES.

Panel (b) of Figure 16.2 helps put this idea into concrete form. It shows the distribution of PHR and IER expenditures per employee ('per capita') for a sample of several hundred American firms for the years 2004–05 (Kaufman & Miller 2011). It traces out a bell-shaped curve with a skewed right-hand tail. A roughly similar bell-shaped frequency distribution (with a less skewed right-hand tail) has been found for Britain (Bryson et al. 2005). Analytically, the HRM frequency distribution in panel (b) can be conceptualized as a plot of the equilibrium HRM quantities from panel (a), implying that the distribution of HRM demand curves (for a given level of V) maps into a similar distribution of observed PHR and IER outcomes across firms.

At an aggregate level, the frequency distribution in Figure 16.2 plots for a particular moment in time the cross-section of firms by breadth and depth of their employment systems. An application of this concept comes from the varieties of capitalism literature (Hall & Soskice 2001b). It hypothesizes that different countries and regions of the world have distinct HRM frequency distributions and, therefore, employment systems. Amable (2003), for example, distinguishes five systems: Anglo-Saxon market, continental European, Asian capitalism, social democratic and Mediterranean. These ES models differ, in part, because they are embedded in different social systems (Jessop 2002).

An alternative approach is to look at changes in ES systems over time. For example, a century ago even the largest American and European firms used almost zero formal PHR and IER practices (Jacoby 1985; Gospel 1992; Kaufman 2008b, 2010b). Indeed, before 1910, no American firm had a formal PHR or IER department and only a handful had a hiring office or written statement of employment policies. Rather, the widespread practice was for each department supervisor or gang boss to go to the plant gate in the morning and fill out that day's crew with new hires, fire the ones that did not quickly prove satisfactory, and personally determine each person's pay rate and job assignment. Hence, in the context of panel (a) most HRM demand curves in this period were located either on or very close to the vertical axis, indicating the near-exclusive reliance on an informal and market-driven ELM-type employment system.

Over time, the HRM demand curves for firms in America and other industrializing countries shifted rightward due to changes in various shift variables, such as more complex and interdependent production technologies, a more highly educated workforce, expanded labor and employment laws, the positive HRM effect of trade unions, and a greater sense of human rights and ethical duties toward employees.

Although the use of formal PHR and IER increased in practically all organizations over the twentieth century, the transformation from 'buy' (ELM) to 'make' (ILM) was neither uniform nor unidirectional. Some HRM demand curves shifted rightward considerably more than others, indicating that over the century some companies maintained a relatively open and unstructured ELM-oriented employment system (e.g., 'HRM-light' production systems, such as in fast-food restaurants and small to medium-sized construction) while others moved toward a much more structured, extensive and relatively bureaucratized ILM-type system ('HRM-intensive' production systems, such as at large hi-tech firms and banks). This process gradually shifted the HRM frequency distribution to the right over the twentieth century and increased both its mean and variance.

Quite possibly, however, this process came to a halt in the last two decades, particularly in market and neoliberal-oriented countries such as the United States of America (USA). Since the early 1990s, many companies have downsized their workforces, opened up once sheltered ILMs, and moved toward more flexible and market-sensitive employment, compensation and benefit policies (Cappelli et al. 1997; Baumol et al. 2003). In this situation, HRM demand curves either remained stable or shifted leftward and became more compact as firms on balance shifted their employment systems toward greater externalization.

In Europe, contrasting effects seem present – that is, the decline in union density in most countries has led to diminished IER and either more or less PHR (as noted above, the union effect on PHR can be positive or negative); on the other hand, the expansion of European Union employment directives has increased the demand for PHR and IER (Brewster 2007; Scholz & Müller 2010). Demand for PHR and IER has also, on balance, increased over the last two decades in Eastern Europe, Russia and China as these countries convert to market economies and a capitalist-style employment relationship. Whatever the particular case, this model implies that variation in the shift variables in the HRM demand function over time and across industries and firms gives rise to a similar variation in HRM frequency distributions and type of ESs.

In the context of this model, going toward the left-hand tail of the HRM frequency distribution is a movement toward a more ELM type of employment system while going toward the right-hand tail is a movement toward a more ILM system. The model can be further enriched to predict additional structure and features. In particular, with the help of the production function concept and the idea of complementarity – including related characteristics such as non-separability, indivisibility, modularity and asset specificity (Alchian and Demsetz 1972; Langlois 2002; Boyer 2006) – it is possible to say more about why firms choose a more ELM- or ILM-oriented employment system and what specific types of PHR and IER practices they choose to include in an ES.

Two inputs may be independent in production or, alternatively, may be related as complements or substitutes. Capital K and labor L or two individual HRM practices HRM_1 and HRM_2 are complements if an increase in the usage of one input raises the marginal profit return to the other (Milgrom & Roberts 1992: 108). Alternatively, inputs may be substitutes in that greater usage of one reduces the marginal profit return to the other. A third possibility is that the inputs are completely separable and non-connected.

Complementarities create what are often called 'synergies', with the idea that a combination of two (or more) HRM practices yields more profit when used together as a package (MacDuffie 1995; Laursen & Foss 2003). This idea has been generalized to include not only input complementarities in the production system but also institutional complementarities (Boyer 2006; Crouch 2010). From these come a corollary idea, 'fit' (Grandori & Furnari 2008). Fit is the degree to which individual HRM inputs and institutions are well matched to the enterprise's production system and business strategy. Thus, in the management literature it is common to distinguish two types of fit: vertical and horizontal (Becker & Huselid 2006; Boxall & Purcell 2008). The former (also called external fit) is achieved when the firm adopts the particular HRM bundle (ES) that most closely aligns with and supports accomplishment of its business strategy and performance objectives; the latter (also called internal fit) is achieved when the firm creates an ES where the individual HRM components yield maximum synergy. Both conditions in a simple economic model are ensured as part of the first-order conditions for maximum profit. As a concrete example, consider two employment systems, one relatively externalized and the other relatively internalized.

The hallmark of an ELM system is reliance on market forces to coordinate the labor input. Given this, one can readily deduce the kind of HRM practices that would (and would not) maximize vertical and horizontal fit. The first principle, in accord with vertical fit, is to invest relatively little in any kind of formalized HRM. The more 'perfect' the labor market, the less HRM expenditure is required, since walk-ins arrive daily, work knowledge and skills are portable and homogeneous, a labor shortage is solved by increasing the wage rate, poor work performance is dealt with by quickly terminating the employee, and as indicated earlier workers can easily quit and find another job if they are dissatisfied. The second principle, in accord with horizontal fit, is to use individual HRM practices that are consistently matched for an ELM-type system. Thus, with a high turnover rate a firm would waste money to invest in formal selection tests, company-financed training programs, or a dispute resolution forum. Even one misaligned HRM practice in this group may throw off the performance of the entire bundle.

Much the opposite implications hold for an ILM-type system. Because the employment relationship is more likely to be long term, the entire ES is restructured with this in mind. Employees are no longer disposable hired hands but valuable human capital assets and, accordingly, the emphasis shifts from an ELM that supports a product market strategy of competitive advantage through low-cost standardized (no-frills) output to an ILM that supports market advantage through higher-margin quality, product differentiation and long-term service.

In this situation, it pays firms to invest in more active recruiting and careful screening of job candidates, perhaps even to the extent of having a specialized staffing department with trained psychologists and professional interviewers. The training and development function in firms with ILMs also broadens and deepens since beyond the entry level (where skills can be acquired from the market) new skills and abilities have to be created in-house, in part by a promotion and seniority process where workers learn the new skills and abilities through experience in higher-level jobs, and partly through formal workshops, conferences and multi-week training classes. Other shifts in PHR and IER practice include a change in compensation to pay programs geared to longer-term and company-related performance, a greater proportion of benefits in the compensation mix (since benefits are more valuable to and also help retain longer-term employees), formal programs for employee voice and participation (since exit is expensive), and creation of an organizational culture that gives more stress to company identification, team spirit and loyalty.

The foundational building blocks for understanding and explaining employment systems have now been presented. The next step is to generalize and apply these concepts to additional ES typologies.

EMPLOYMENT SYSTEMS: TRADITIONAL AND INNOVATIVE

The ES typology that has drawn the most attention in the recent economics–organization literature is 'traditional' versus 'innovative' (Waldman forthcoming). Another frequently encountered label for 'innovative' is high-performance work system (HPWS) (Appelbaum et al. 2000; Frost 2008).

As the 'traditional' label suggests, this ES is the ILM model long in existence among medium-sized and large firms, particularly after World War II. It is built on top-down command-and-control forms of management; internal coordination through bureaucratic structures and standardized rules and procedures; a Taylorist or Fordist production system of finely divided jobs with narrow skills and minimal discretion; pay and reward systems geared to labor input (hours worked, years of seniority) rather than labor output; and an organizational culture featuring sharp status distinctions and often antagonistic atmospherics between the white-collar (management) and blue-collar (line employees) parts of the organization. Many traditional ILMs have unions and collective bargaining. The traditional model achieves competitive advantage through economies of scale, a fine division of labor, stable and standardized work routines, labor-saving technological change, and workforce SKTs that are widely available and low priced.

The traditional model was challenged by a new high-involvement employment system that formed in the 1970s and spread into the 1990s (Beer & Spector 1984; Piore & Sabel 1984; Kochan et al. 1986). This model has diverse roots, as described in detail in Leoni's Chapter 17 in this volume. It seeks competitive advantage by 'doing more with less' through flatter organizational hierarchy, a team-oriented production system, performance-related pay, expanded cross-training, smaller-scale and more flexible plants, and egalitarian culture (Black & Lynch 2001; Boxall & Macky 2009).

Empirical evidence indicates that the high-performance ES spread from the 1970s into the 1990s in the USA and then post-2000 plateaued or even receded. Surveys in the 1990s of American firms (e.g., Osterman 2000) found that various high-performance practices, such as teams and performance-based pay, had diffused to a substantial segment (30–40 percent) of medium-sized and large firms, creating considerable expectation that an HPWS-type employment system was rapidly gaining ground. More recent reviews (e.g., Blasi and Kruse 2006), however, have come to the far more sober conclusion that the diffusion of HPWS practices has stalled amidst widespread corporate downsizing and cost-cutting and that the full HPWS package is found at only a very tiny share of firms (they estimate 1 percent). Survey evidence also finds very small take-up of the entire HPWS package in European firms (Dell'Aringa et al. 2003). Some researchers argue that this is in part because the HPWS is an American-centric phenomenon and is not well suited to different economic and cultural contexts (Brewster 2007; Boxall & Macky 2009).

In addition to surveys of adoption rates, empirical studies have proliferated that use regression analysis to test for a cross-section of establishments and firms whether innovative work practices are indeed associated with higher productivity and profitability (Huselid 1995; Ichniowski et al. 1997; Cappelli & Neumark 2001). The standard approach has some measure of organizational performance (e.g., rate of return on capital) as the left-hand variable and on the right-hand side a large number of control variables (e.g., type of industry, workforce demographics) and one or more variables that represent the presence or extent of high-performance PHR and IER practices.

Sometimes the individual innovative practices are aggregated into a composite measure.

This empirical literature is reviewed and critiqued in Leoni's Chapter 17 in this volume so I highlight only the most salient points as it relates to employment systems. Despite some heterogeneity in findings, a relatively recent meta-analysis of over 90 empirical studies (Combs et al. 2006) concludes, 'The use of HPWPs [high-performance work practices] is positively related to organizational performance' (p. 504), and 'our results lay to rest any doubt about the existence of a [positive] relationship' (p. 524). Likewise, Becker and Huselid (2006) estimate that a one standard deviation increase on high-performance practices increases a firm's return on assets by 10–20 percent. Evidence on the existence of input complementarities among PHR and IR practices, however, is surprisingly weak and mixed (Becker & Huselid 2006; Subramony 2009).

Evidence of this kind has led many researchers to look at the traditional employment systems model as akin to an early twentieth century organizational dinosaur that is increasingly being selected out by competitive forces and replaced by some twenty-first-century version of the innovative high-performance employment system. Extra caution is warranted, however, before making this inferential leap (Kaufman and Miller 2011; Kaufman 2012). Most studies report, for example, cross-section associations but these are easily confounded by co-variation with other unobserved or omitted determinants of productivity and profit. Also problematic are issues of selection bias, simultaneity and causality (Gerhart 2007; Ichniowski and Shaw forthcoming), along with publication bias as researchers consciously or unconsciously emphasize positive findings. Equally worrisome problems arise on the theory front. For example, the central hypothesis guiding these studies (more HPWS → higher profitability) is not consistent with competitive equilibrium reasoning. That is, if any factor of production has a positive marginal profit effect then economic rationality drives firms to increase its usage until the marginal return is driven to zero. This is simply a restatement of the first-order condition described above for the HRM demand function. Hence, while it is consistent with microeconomic theory for innovative employment practices to create higher firm-level productivity, it is not consistent for these practices to also create long-lasting rents (above normal profit returns) – unless one appeals to some kind of barrier to entry or other non-competitive element that blocks equalization of factor returns (Chadwick & Dabu 2009).

EMPLOYMENT SYSTEMS: HIGHER CONFIGURATIONAL DIMENSIONALITY

So far only two-dimensional employment systems have been discussed (e.g., external versus internal; traditional versus innovative). A portion of the literature, particularly associated with industrial and employment relations and human resource management, goes further and distinguishes in both theory and empirical work between three-, four- and five-dimensional ESs (Rubery & Grimshaw 2003).

For historical context it is useful to point out that the employment system concept can be considered an adaptation of John Dunlop's 'industrial relations system' idea developed a half-century ago (Dunlop 1958; Kaufman 2004). His IR colleague and co-author Clark Kerr (1954) advanced a model of 'structured' and 'unstructured' labor systems that is also a forerunner of modern theory. The unstructured market is Kerr's version of an ELM, while he divides the structured market into two different ILM types: a 'private property' internal system (emphasizing vertical structure and mobility based on seniority) and a 'communal ownership' system (emphasizing horizontal structure and mobility based on occupation or craft). Going back further in time, the American IR field's founder John Commons put forth in his book *Industrial Goodwill* (1919) five models of labor, including 'commodity' (ELM coordinated by DS), 'machine' (Frederick Taylor's version of scientific management) and 'goodwill' (positive-sum or high-involvement ILM).

An important early work in the modern PHR and IER literature is Osterman (1987). He identifies four dominant ES types: salaried, industrial, craft and secondary. The latter three are essentially taken from Kerr. What distinguishes Osterman's paper is that he links different ES models to different configurations of four HRM practice areas – job classification, deployment (staffing), security and wage rules – and identifies five factors as the chief determinants of ES selection – goals of the firm (cost minimization, flexibility, predictability), production technology, social technology, labor force characteristics and government policies.

Another pioneering IR work on models of employment systems is *Strategic Employment Policy* by James Begin (1991). Begin builds his ES model from the complementary organization theory of Henry Mintzberg (1983). Begin's principle hypothesis is that the breadth, depth and composition of employment practices in an ES need to align with the organizational structure of the firm (also see Short et al. 2008). Given four basic kinds of organizational structure, Begin derives four accompanying ES types – simple, machine, professional and adhocracy – and matches the complementary configuration of nine HRM/IER practices to each ES. In a follow-up study, Verburg et al. (2007) give Begin's four models more transparent labels: market, bureaucratic, professional and flexible.

A third example drawn for the industrial and employment relations literature is Arthur (1992). His article is noteworthy because it integrates the IER system idea; the role that strategy plays in shaping ESs; and the high-performance model of work organization. He looks at steel mini-mills, differentiates between cost minimization and product differentiation business strategies, and then examines whether they map into a command-and-control or 'high-commitment' employment system. Cluster analysis reveals that the ESs in the mini-mills sort into distinct types in line with the two strategies. Arthur's use of cluster analysis has been followed in many subsequent ES studies.

More recent research on typologies of employment systems has shifted from the IER field to others (but see Hendry 2003; Orlitzky & Frenkel 2005), such as HRM and organizational sociology (OS). In HRM, an early study is by Delery and Doty (1996). They contrast two polar opposite employment systems that correspond closely to those found in industrial and employment relations; that is, a 'market-type' and 'internal' ES. Their study deserves mention because it shifts the discourse on ESs from an IER/economics framework to one from strategic management and organizational behavior (OB). They give considerable attention to linking specific HRM practices to the two different kinds of systems via the fit concept. Thus, they deduce that the market ES adopts primarily market-based pay, features hire-and-fire staffing methods, and provides little formal employee voice; the internal system, on the other hand, provides forms of organizational gain-sharing, employment security and formal voice mechanisms.

Lepak and Snell (1999) develop a model of employment systems called 'HRM archi-tectures'. They identify two central attributes that distinguish human capital across firms – value and uniqueness – and based on transaction cost and the RBV (resource-based view) theory of the firm (Barney 1991) derive a fourfold typology of ESs: commitment, market-based, compliance and collaborative. The first three ES types correspond to versions already encountered; that is, commitment = HPWS; compliance = technical/bureaucratic; market-based = simple/external labor market. The collaborative model is a hybrid ES discussed more fully below.

A third example from the management literature is the recent typology developed by Toh et al. (2008; also see Sheppeck and Militello 2000; Youndt and Snell 2004). They identify five ES's: cost minimizers, contingent motivators, competitive motivators, resource makers and commitment maximizers. They then seek to match each of these ES types to a particular configuration of employment practices based on four key PHR functions: staffing, development, reward and evaluation. Consistent with much of the literature, these authors identify the goals and strategy of the firm as a key determinant of ES choice. For example, firms that seek competitive advantage through a low cost strategy are led to adopt a minimalist ELM-type system while those pursuing a high-quality or high-service strategy adopt a PHR-intensive ILM system. Labor cost minimiz-ers (ELM) and commitment maximizers (ILM), therefore, anchor the opposite ends of the ES spectrum. The other three ES models fall in-between these end points: contingent motivators, for example, use considerable incentive types of pay; competitive motivators purchase human capital from the labor market and use pay to elicit work effort; and resource makers invest more in training, development and empowerment.

Moving on to the OS field, Baron et al. (1999) develop a fourfold typology of employ-ment systems based on field research with founders of 100 high-tech start-ups in Silicon Valley. They asked each founder to describe the organizational blueprint used in forming the structure of the company, and the various HRM/IER programs and practices that fleshed it out. The data revealed that ESs form around three core parts of the employ-ment process and, in turn, there are three alternative modes of implementation for each core part. The three core parts (and alternative implementation modes) are: basis of attachment (love, work, money), basis of control and coordination (peer, professional, formal) and employee selection criterion (task, potential, values). These core parts and alternative modes yield 27 ES permutations. Examination of the data revealed that most of the start-ups sort into one of four distinct ESs. These are: 'star' (work, profes-sional, potential) 'engineering' (work, peer, task), 'commitment' (love, peer, values) and 'factory' (money, formal, and task). The small number of actual ESs (four) relative to the possible domain (27) suggests the existence of significant complementarities in employ-ment practices and selection pressures in the environment.

Next introduced is a subfield of the ES literature that is less often mentioned in the mainstream journals, widely known as labor process (LP). The term 'labor process' comes from Marx (1867 [1906]) and denotes the idea that firms buy units of labor time from the market (e.g., eight hours of an employee's time per day) but must then trans-form this labor time into effective labor power (or 'work') in order to produce goods and make a profit. Marx is making early use here of the idea that labor contracts are incomplete. Building on this insight, modern LP writers such as Braverman (1974) and Friedman (1977) argue that managerial control of labor is therefore key to the labor time to labor power conversion process and, accordingly, firms form distinct regimes of control (employment systems). A basic two-way typology is between Fordist and post-Fordist production systems, the former being associated with mass production and the latter with flexible specialization (Piore & Sabel 1984). A more differentiated fourfold ES typology is developed by Edwards (1979). He distinguishes 'simple,' 'technical', 'craft' and 'bureaucratic' models, formed around the most efficacious method of labor control. Later writers have added an additional form of control: affective commitment.

A final ES typology that has gained growing attention in recent years is the 'hybrid'. As the name implies, this employment system melds features from two traditionally distinct and perhaps even polar opposite models into a new synthetic ES (Grandori & Furnari 2008). Hybrid models take different forms. For example, one permutation is a dual core–periphery model where the enterprise's ES is separated into two distinct parts (Ko 2003; Gamble & Huang 2009). One part is a version of a high-performance or bureaucratic ILM for the high-value core employees with considerable training, compensation rewards and the prospect of a long-term relation; while the second part is a more open and contingent ELM-type system for non-core employees featuring greater turnover, standardized and routine jobs, shorter job ladders and less prospects for pay growth. This bifurcation partly forms as an efficiency response to separable parts of the production process; for example, an internalized ES forms around the enterprise's core source of competitive advantage where jobs involve specific skills, tacit knowledge and team complementarities; while for the non-core part an externalized ES is used for jobs where skills are general and tasks are relatively independent and easily monitored (Kato & Owan 2011). The externalized part of the dual ES also provides a short-run demand-shock buffer so that firms can stabilize and protect core employment by expanding and contracting the non-core workforce through lay-offs and new hires. Another motivation, particularly salient in Europe where strong job guarantees and high welfare state taxes and benefits are mandated for permanent employees (Bosch 2004), is to lower labor cost and preserve flexibility by using contract, temporary and short-service employees in non-core jobs (Ko 2003; Cappelli & Neumark 2004).

A second hybrid ES configuration is an 'alliance' or 'collaborative' model (Lepak & Snell 1999). Here the ES forms across firms that are formally independent in terms of ownership but are nonetheless linked together in some kind of longer-term alliance or collaborative arrangement; say in a vertical supply chain, Italian-style industrial district, or joint research and development (R&D) program (Piore & Sabel 1984). In terms of the division of labor illustrated in Figure 16.1, the alliance model is a hybrid or 'half-way house' in the sense of preserving some aspects of firm autonomy and market coordination (i.e., smaller-sized production units, or 'pentagons' in the diagram) while in other respects it fosters greater agglomeration and administrative coordination (larger-sized units). The reasons for this type of hybrid configuration are various; for example, to internalize firm-level externalities in general workforce training and R&D; reap the benefits of larger scale but without the bureaucracy and inflexibility that go with agglomeration into one larger organization; and exploit complementarities in design, production and distribution. Regarding PHR and IER practices, the prediction is that the ES in each firm becomes an amalgam of two models: the ES that would exist if the firm was completely unconnected to the others in the network, and the ES that would exist if all firms were merged into one large company (Boxall & Purcell 2008). Formalization of employment practices, for example, may be at an intermediate level (more than an independent small firm, less than one giant large firm), provision of general training may be greater (since firms are less worried about competitors pirating newly trained workers), and individual firms may be able to provide more employee insurance benefits by pooling risks and realizing economies of scale. The effect on unionism again seems mixed: smaller-sized firms are less likely to be organized but, on the other hand, a union can take labor costs out of competition among smaller firms and allow each to pursue a more collaborative and trust-building culture with its employees.

CONCLUSION

Research on employment systems is a particularly fruitful interface for people in economics, management, sociology and organizational science. Each field brings important concepts, ideas and methods to the subject. Economics provides a basic analytical framework, as illustrated here by the HRM demand curve model and empirical HRM frequency distribution. Within this framework a variety of factors can be embedded that influence the breadth, depth, configuration and change in employment systems. Examples include production and institutional complementarities, managerial control strategies, transaction cost, horizontal and vertical fit, organizational structure, general and specific human capital, workforce resources and capabilities, and social interdependencies and norms. Different permutations of these variables yield distinct configurations of employment systems; these in turn are then further modified and shaped by nation state traditions, trade union representation and legal mandates. Evidently employment systems are complex and interdependent coordination mechanisms; the challenge moving forward is to achieve better theoretical integration without losing sight of diverse and interdisciplinary contingencies.

REFERENCES

Alchian, Armen and Harold Demsetz (1972), 'Production, information costs, and economic organization', *American Economic Review*, **72**, 777–795.

Amable, Bruno (2003), *The Diversity of Modern Capitalism*, Oxford: Oxford University Press.

Anderson, Erin and Hubert Gatignon (2005), 'Firms and the creation of markets', in Claude Menard and Marsh Shirley (eds), *Handbook of New Institutional Economics*, Berlin: Springer, pp. 401–431.

Appelbaum, Eileen, Thomas Bailey, Peter Berg and Arne Kalleberg (2000), *Manufacturing Advantage: Why High-Performance Work Systems Pay Off*, Ithaca, NY: Cornell University Press.

Arthur, Jeffrey (1992), 'The link between business strategy and industrial relations systems in American steel minimills', *Industrial and Labor Relations Review*, **45**, 488–506.

Barney, Jay (1991), 'Firm resources and sustained competitive advantage', *Journal of Management*, **17**, 99–120.

Baron, James, Diane Burton and Michael Hannan (1999), 'The road not taken: origins of employment systems in emerging companies', in G. Carroll and D. Teece (eds), *Firms, Markets, and Hierarchies*, New York: Oxford University Press, pp. 428–464.

Baron, James and David Kreps (forthcoming), 'Employment as an economic and social relationship', in R. Gibbons and J. Roberts (eds), *Handbook of Organizational Economics*, Princeton, NJ: Princeton University Press.

Baumol, William, Alan Blinder and Edward Wolff (2003), *Downsizing in America*, New York: Sage.

Becker, Brian and Mark Huselid (2006), 'Strategic human resource management: where do we go from here?' *Journal of Management*, **32**, 898–925.

Becker, Gary (1964), *Human Capital*, New York: NBER.

Becker, Gary and Kevin Murphy (1992), 'The division of labor, coordination costs, and knowledge', *Quarterly Journal of Economics*, **107**, 1137–1160.

Beer, Michael and Burt Spector (1984), 'Human resources management: the integration of industrial relations and organizational behavior', *Research in Personnel and Human Resource Management*, Vol. 2, Stamford, CT: JAI Press, pp. 261–297.

Begin, James. (1991), *Strategic Employment Policy: An Organizational Systems Perspective*, Englewood Cliffs, NJ: Prentice-Hall.

Black, Lisa and Sarah Lynch (2001), 'How to compete: the impact of workplace practices and information technology on productivity', *Review of Economics and Statistics*, **83**, 434–445.

Blasie, Joseph and Douglas Kruse (2006), 'US high performance work practices at century's end', *Industrial Relations*, **45**, 457–478.

Boeri, Tito and Jan van Ours (2008), *The Economics of Imperfect Competition*, Princeton, NJ: Princeton University Press.

Bosch, Gerhard (2004), 'Towards a new standard employment relationship in Western Europe', *British Journal of Industrial Relations*, **42**, 617–636.

Boxall, Peter and Keith Macky (2009), 'Research and theory on high-performance work systems: progressing the high-involvement stream', *Human Resource Management Journal*, **19**, 3–23.

Boxall, Peter and John Purcell (2008), *Strategy and Human Resource Management*, 2nd edn, New York: Palgrave Macmillan.

Boyer, Robert (2006), 'How do institutions cohere and change? The institutional complementarity hypothesis and extension', in Geoffrey Wood and Phil James (eds), *Institutions, Production, and Working Life*, Oxford: Oxford University Press, pp. 13–61.

Braverman, Harry (1974), *Labor and Monopoly Capital: The Degradation of Work in the Twentieth Century*, New York: Monthly Review Press.

Brewster, Chris (2007), 'A European perspective on HRM', *European Journal of International Management*, **1**, 239–259.

Bryson, Alex, Raphael Gomez and Tobias Kretchmer (2005), 'Catching a wave: the adoption of voice and high-commitment workplace practices in Britain, 1984–1998', CEP Discussion Paper No. 676, London Centre for Economic Performance, London School of Economics.

Camuffo, Arnaldo (2002), 'The changing nature of internal labor markets', *Journal of Management and Governance*, **6**, 281–294.

Cappelli, Peter and David Neumark (2001), 'Do "high-performance" work practices improve establishment-level outcomes?' *Industrial and Labor Relations Review*, **54**, 737–775.

Cappelli, Peter and David Neumark (2004), 'External churning and internal flexibility: evidence on the functional flexibility and core–periphery hypothesis', *Industrial Relations*, **43**, 148–182.

Cappelli, Peter, L. Bassie, H. Katz, D. Knoke, P. Osterman and M. Unwin (1997), *Change at Work*, New York: Oxford University Press.

Chadwick, Clint and Adina Dabu (2009), 'Human resources, human resources management, and the competitive advantage of firms: toward a more comprehensive model of causal linkages', *Organization Science*, **20**, 253–272.

Coase, Ronald (1937), 'The nature of the firm', *Economica*, **4**, 386–405.

Combs, James, Yongmei Liu, Angela Hall and David Ketchen (2006), 'How much do high-performance work practices matter? A meta-analysis of their effects on organizational performance', *Personnel Psychology*, **59**, 501–528.

Commons, John (1919), *Industrial Goodwill*, New York: McGraw Hill.

Crouch, Colin (2010), 'Complementarity', in Glenn Morgan, J. Campbell, C. Crouch, O. Pedersen and R. Whitley (eds), *Oxford Handbook of Comparative Institutional Analysis*, Oxford: Oxford University Press, pp. 117–138.

Dell'Aringa, Carlo, Paolo Ghinetti and Claudio Lucifora (2003), 'High performance works systems, industrial relations, and pay setting in Europe', Working Paper, Milan: Catholic University.

Delery, John and D. Harold Doty (1996), 'Modes of theorizing in strategic human resource management: tests of universalistic, contingency, and configurational performance predictions', *Academy of Management Journal*, **39**, 802–835.

Demsetz, Harold (1991), 'The theory of the firm revisited', in O. Williamson and S. Winter (eds), *The Nature of the Firm*, New York: Oxford University Press, pp. 159–178.

Doeringer, Peter and M. Piore (1971), *Internal Labor Markets and Manpower Analysis*, Lexington, MA: Lexington Books.

Donaldson, Lex (2006), 'The contingency theory of organizational design: challenges and opportunities', in R. Burton, B. Eriksen, D Håkonsson and C. Snow (eds), *Organizational Design: The Evolving State-of-the-Art*, New York: Springer, pp. 18–40.

Dunlop, John (1958), *Industrial Relations Systems*, New York: Holt.

Edwards, Paul (2003), 'The employment relationship and the field of industrial relations', in P. Edwards (ed.), *Industrial Relations: Theory and Practice*, 2nd edn, London: Blackwell, pp. 1–36.

Edwards, Richard (1979), *Contested Terrain: The Transformation of the Workplace in the Twentieth Century*, New York: Basic Books.

Ferguson, Paul and Glenys Ferguson (2000), *Organizations: A Strategic Approach*, New York: St Martin's.

Foss, Nicholai (2005), *Strategy, Economic Organization, and the Knowledge Economy*, Oxford: Oxford University Press.

Foss, Nicholai and Christian Knudsen (1996), *Towards a Competence Theory of the Firm*, London: Routledge.

Freeman, Richard and Edward Lazear (1995), 'An economics analysis of works councils', in Joel Rodgers and Wolfgang Streeck (eds), *Works Councils: Consultation, Representation and Cooperation in Industrial Relations*, Chicago, IL: University of Chicago Press, pp. 27–52.

Friedman, Andrew (1977), *Industry and Labor: Class Struggle and Monopoly Capitalism*, London: Macmillan.

Frost, Ann (2008), 'The high performance work systems literature in industrial relations', in N. Bacon, P. Blyton, E. Heery and J. Fiorito (eds), *Sage Handbook of Industrial Relations*, London: Sage, pp. 420–433.

Furubotn, Erik, and Rudolf Richter (2005), *Institutions and Economic Theory: The Contribution of the New Institutional Economics*, 2nd edn, Ann Arbor, MI: University of Michigan Press.

Gamble, Jos and Qihai Huang (2009), 'One store, two employment systems: core, periphery and flexibility in China's retail sector', *British Journal of Industrial Relations*, **47**, 1–26.

Gerhart, Barry (2007), 'Modeling HRM and performance linkages', in P. Boxall, J. Purcell and P. Wright (eds), *Oxford International Handbook of Human Resource Management*, New York: Oxford University Press, pp. 552–580.

Gospel, Howard (1992), *Markets, Firms, and the Management of Labor in Modern Britain*, Cambridge: Cambridge University Press.

Grandori, Anna and Santi Furnari (2008), 'A chemistry or organization: combinatory analysis and design', *Organization Studies*, **29**, 459–485.

Grundei, Jens (2006), 'Examining the relationship between trust and control in organizational design', in R. Burton, B. Eriksen, D. Håkonsson and C. Snow (eds), *Organizational Design: The Evolving State-of-the-Art*, New York: Springer, pp. 43–66.

Hall, Peter and David Soskice (2001a), 'An introduction to varieties of capitalism', in P. Hall and D. Soskice (eds), *Varieties of Capitalism: The Institutional Foundations of Competitive Advantage*, Oxford: Oxford University Press, pp. 1–68.

Hall, Peter and David Soskice (2001b), *Varieties of Capitalism: The Institutional Foundations of Comparative Advantage*, Oxford: Oxford University Press.

Hamann, K. and J. Kelly (2008), 'Varieties of capitalism and industrial relations', in P. Blyton, N. Bacon, J. Fiorito and E. Heery (eds), *The Sage Handbook of Industrial Relations*, New York: Sage, pp. 129–48.

Hecksher, Charles and Paul Adler (2006), *The Firm as a Collaborative Community: Reconstructing Trust in the Knowledge Community*, Oxford: Oxford University Press.

Hendry, C. (2003), 'Applying employment systems theory to the analysis of national models of HRM', *International Journal of Human Resource Management*, **14**, 1430–1442.

Hollingsworth, J. and R. Boyer (1997), *Contemporary Capitalism: The Embeddedness of Institutions*, Cambridge: Cambridge University Press.

Holmström, Bengt (1999), 'The firm as a subeconomy', *Journal of Law, Economics and Organization*, **15**, 74–102.

Holmström, Bengt and John Roberts (1998), 'The boundaries of the firm revisited', *Journal of Economic Perspectives*, **12**, 73–94.

Huselid, Mark (1995), 'The impact of human resource management practices on turnover, productivity, and corporate financial performance', *Academy of Management Journal*, **38**, 635–672.

Ichniowski, Casey and Kathryn Shaw (forthcoming), 'Insider econometrics', in R. Gibbons and J. Roberts (eds), *Handbook of Organizational Economics*, Princeton, NJ: Princeton University Press.

Ichniowski, Casey, Katherine Shaw and Giovanna Prennushi (1997), 'The effects of human resource management practices on productivity: a study of steel finishing lines', *American Economic Review*, **87**, 291–313.

Jacoby, Sanford (1985), *Employing Bureaucracy: Managers, Unions, and the Transformation of Work in American Industry: 1900–1945*, New York: Columbia University Press.

Jessop, B. (2002), 'The social embeddedness of the economy and its implications for economic governance', in F. Adaman and P. Devine (eds), *Economy and Society: Money, Capitalism and Transition*, New York: Black Rose Books, pp. 192–224.

Kato, Takao and Hideo Owan (2011), 'Market characteristics, intra-firm coordination, and the choice of human resource management systems: theory and evidence', *Journal of Economic Behavior and Organization*, **80**, 375–396.

Kaufman, Bruce (2003), 'The organization of economic activity: insights from the institutional economics of John R. Commons', *Journal of Economic Behavior and Organization*, **52**, 71–96.

Kaufman, Bruce (2004), 'Employment relations and the employment relations system: a guide to theorizing', in B. Kaufman (ed.), *Theoretical Perspectives on Work and the Employment Relationship*, Champaign, IL: Industrial Relations Research Association, pp. 41–75.

Kaufman, Bruce (2007), 'The impossibility of a perfectly competitive labor market', *Cambridge Journal of Economics*, **31**, 775–87.

Kaufman, Bruce (2008a), 'Paradigms in industrial relations: original, modern, and versions in-between', *British Journal of Industrial Relations*, **46**, 314–39.

Kaufman, Bruce (2008b), *Managing the Human Factor: The Early Years of Human Resource Management in American Industry*, Ithaca, NY: Cornell University Press.

Kaufman, Bruce (2010a), 'The theoretical foundation of industrial relations and its implications for labor economics and human resource management', *Industrial and Labor Relations Review*, **64**, 74–108.

Kaufman, Bruce (2010b), *Hired Hands or Human Resources: Case Studies of HRM Programs and Policies in Early American Industry*, Ithaca: Cornell University Press.

Kaufman, Bruce (2012), 'Strategic human resource management research in the United States: a failing grade after 30 years?', *Academy of Management Perspectives*, **26**, 12–36.

Kaufman, Bruce and Ben Miller (2011), 'The firm's choice of HRM practices: economics meets strategic human resource management', *Industrial and Labor Relations Review*, **64**, 526–557.

Kerr, Clark (1954), 'The Balkanization of labor markets', in E. Bakke (ed.), *Labor Mobility and Economic Opportunity*, Cambridge, MA: MIT Press, pp. 92–110.

Ko, Jyh-Jer (2003), 'Contingent and internal employment systems: substitutes or complements?' *Journal of Labor Research*, **24**, 473–490.

Kochan, Thomas, Harry Katz and Robert McKersie (1986), *The Transformation of American Industrial Relations*, New York: Basic Books.

Langlois, Richard (2002), 'Modularity in technology and organization', *Journal of Economic Behavior and Organization*, **49**, 19–37.

Langlois, Richard and Paul Robertson (1995), *Firms, Markets and Economic Change*, London: Routledge.

Laursen, Keld and Nicholai Foss (2003), 'New human resource management practices, complementarities, and the impact on innovative performance', *Cambridge Journal of Economics*, **27**, 243–263.

Lazear, Edward and Paul Oyer (2004), 'External and internal labor markets: a personnel economics approach', *Labour Economics*, **11**, 527–554.

Lazear, Edward and Paul Oyer (forthcoming), 'Personnel economics', in R. Gibbons and J. Roberts (eds), *Handbook of Organizational Economics*, Princeton, NJ: Princeton University Press.

Lepak, David and Scott Snell (1999), 'The human resource architecture: toward a theory of human capital allocation and development', *Academy of Management Review*, **24**, 31–48.

MacDuffie, J. Paul (1995), 'Human resource bundles and manufacturing performance: organizational logic and flexible production systems in the world auto system', *Industrial and Labor Relations Review*, **48**, 197–221.

Malcolmson, James (1999), 'Individual employment contracts', in O. Ashenfelter and D. Card (eds), *Handbook of Labor Economics*, Vol. 3B, New York: Elsevier, pp. 2292–2372.

Marsden, David (1999), *A Theory of Employment Systems: Micro Foundations of Societal Diversity*, Oxford: Oxford University Press.

Marx, Karl (1867 [1906]), *Capital: A Critique of Political Economy*, Vol. 1, 4th edn, New York: Random House.

Milgrom, Paul and John Roberts (1992), *Economics, Organization, and Management*, Englewood-Cliffs, NJ: Prentice-Hall.

Miller, Gary (1991), *Managerial Dilemmas*, New York: Cambridge University Press.

Mintzberg, Henry (1983), *Structure in Fives: Designing Effective Organizations*, Englewood Cliffs: Prentice-Hall.

Orlitzky, Michael and Stephen Frenkel (2005), 'Alternative pathways to high performance workplaces', *International Journal of Human Resource Management*, **16**, 1325–1348.

Osterman, Paul (1987), 'Choice of employment systems in internal labor markets', *Industrial Relations*, **26**, 46–67.

Osterman, Paul (2000), 'Work reorganization in an era of restructuring: trends in diffusion and effects on employee welfare', *Industrial and Labor Relations Review*, **53**, 179–196.

Pfeffer, Jeffrey (1998), *The Human Equation*, Boston, MA: Harvard University Business School Press.

Piore, Michael (2002), 'Thirty years later: internal labor markets, flexibility and the new economy', *Journal of Management and Governance*, **6**, 271–279.

Piore, Michael and Charles Sabel (1984), *The Second Industrial Divide: Possibilities for Prosperity*, New York: Basic Books.

Rebitzer, James and Lowell Taylor (2011), 'Extrinsic rewards and intrinsic motives: standard and behavioral approaches to agency and labor markets', in D. Card and O. Ashenfelter (eds), *Handbook of Labor Economics*, Vol. 4, New York: North-Holland, pp. 701–772.

Rosen, Sherwin (1991), 'Transaction costs and internal labor markets', in Oliver Williamson and Sidney Winter (eds), *The Nature of the Firm*, New York: Oxford University Press, pp. 75–89.

Rubery, Jill (2010), 'Institutionalizing the employment relationship', in Glenn Morgan, J. Campbell, C. Crouch, O. Pedersen and R. Whitley (eds), *Oxford Handbook of Comparative Institutional Analysis*, Oxford: Oxford University Press, pp. 497–526.

Rubery, Jill and Damian Grimshaw (2003), *The Organization of Employment: An International Perspective*, London: Palgrave Macmillan.

Scholz, Christian and Stefanie Müller (2010), 'Human resource management in Europe: looking again at the issue of convergence', Working Paper No. 98, Saarbrucken: University of Saarlandes.

Sheppeck, Michael and Jack Militello (2000), 'Strategic HR, configurations, and organizational performance', *Human Resource Management*, **39**, 5–16.

Short, Jeremy, G. Tyge Payne and David Ketchen (2008), 'Research on organizational configurations: past accomplishments and future challenges', *Journal of Management*, **34**, 1053–1079.

Simon, H. (1951), 'A formal theory of the employment relationship', *Econometrica*, **19**, 293–305.

Simon, Herbert (1990), 'Organizations and markets', *Journal of Economic Perspectives*, **5**, 25–44.

Smith, Adam (1776 [1937]), *An Inquiry into the Nature and Causes of the Wealth of Nations*, New York: Modern Library.

Starbuck, William (2003), 'The origins of organization theory', in H. Tsoukas and C. Knudsen (eds), *The Oxford Handbook of Organization Theory*, Oxford: Oxford University Press, pp. 143–182.

Streeck, Wolfgang and Kozo Yamamura (2001), *The Origins of Nonliberal Capitalism: Germany and Japan in Comparison*, Ithaca, NY: Cornell University Press.

Subramony, Mahesh (2009), 'A meta-analytic investigation of the relationship between HRM bundles and firm performance', *Human Resource Management*, **48**, 745–768.

Toh, Soo, Frederick Morgeson and Michael Campion (2008), 'Human resource configurations: investigating fit with the organizational context', *Journal of Applied Psychology*, **93**, 64–82.

Verburg, Robert, Deanne Hartog and Paul Koopman (2007), 'Configurations of human resource management practices: a model and test of internal fit', *International Journal of Human Resource Management*, **18**, 184–208.

Wailes, Nick, Jim Kitay and Russell Lansbury (2008), 'Varieties of capitalism, corporate governance, and employment relations under globalization', in S. Marshall, R. Mitchell and I. Ramsey (eds), *Varieties of Capitalism, Corporate Governance and Employees*, Melbourne: Melbourne University press, pp. 19–38.

Waldman, M. (forthcoming), 'Theory and evidence in internal labor markets', in R. Gibbons and J. Roberts (eds), *Handbook of Organizational Economics*, Princeton, NJ: Princeton University Press.

Williamson, Oliver (1985), *The Economic Institutions of Capitalism*, New York: Free Press.

Yang, Xiaokai (2001), *Economics: New Classical Versus Neoclassical*, London: Blackwell.

Youndt, Mark and Scott Snell (2004), 'Human resource configurations, intellectual capital, and organizational performance', *Journal of Managerial Issues*, **16**, 337–360.

Zenger, Todd, Tepo Felin and Lyda Bigelow (2011)), 'Theories of the firm–market boundary', *Academy of Management Annals*, **5**, 89–133.

17. Organization of work practices and productivity: an assessment of research on world-class manufacturing

*Riccardo Leoni**

The chapter presents a review of research on an increasingly diffused set of work organization practices, known under various acronyms – as 'world-class manufacturing' (WCM), 'high-performance work systems' (HPWS), and others – which is supposed to sustain productivity and to constitute a new form of organizing industrial work. The analysis is primarily developed with reference to the world of manufacturing firms, focusing particularly on practices such as processes organization, high-involvement work practices, positive industrial relations and information and communication (ICT) technologies, also considering their complementarities. The review conducted here indicates that the new organizational configuration emerging as effective is composed by innovative bundles of different 'ingredients', that can be applied with different weights and in a variety of possible combinations. While the superior performance of this new form of work organization is acclaimed by a number of econometric studies, this chapter also highlights that some methodological questions remain open and gives some indications for future research oriented to solving them.

INTRODUCTION

Empirical research has widely documented, virtually without exception, enormous and persistent measured productivity differences across firms or establishments, even within narrowly defined industries. Syverson (2004), for example, demonstrates that within four-digit SIC industries in the United States (US) manufacturing sector, the ratio of total factor productivity among plants at the 90th percentile of productivity distribution is in the order of 2:1 with respect to the 10th percentile; namely, twice the amount. However, this accounting refers to the average 90–10 range: taking into account the range's standard deviation, a plant at the 90th percentile of productivity distribution is over four times as productive as a plant at the 10th percentile in the same four-digit sector.

Mainstream economic theory attributes different productivity levels, as well as different changes, to a set of factors such as: (1) capital accumulation per employee or per hour worked (capital deepening); (2) new investments as a mechanism to transmit new ideas (technological progress embodied in capital goods); (3) exogenous (or disembodied) technical progress flowing mainly from one or more sources of learning such as learning-by-doing, learning-by-using, learning-by-interacting and learning-by-searching; (4) returns to scale; (5) research and development (R&D) activity; and (6) externalities (infrastructures, intra-market competition, regulations, schooling system, public administration, etc.). However, the cornerstone of this theoretical approach has always been allocative efficiency (see a discussion of this idea in Banerjee and Duflo 2005), in spite of Leibenstein's effort to draw the attention of scholars to the fact that 'the data suggests that in a great many instances the amount to be gained by increasing allocative efficiency is trivial while the amount to be gained by increasing X-efficiency is frequently significant' (Leibenstein 1966: 413). Unfortunately, Leibenstein's warning has been largely neglected, with the consequence that work organization, such as job and workplace design, and human resource management, has also been largely neglected – from both a theoretical and a modelling perspective – as a potentially powerful source of productivity.

Only quite recently has empirical evidence begun to appear on the scope of different forms of work organization and human resource management practices, as well as on their effects on firm productivity, based on econometric estimates using different types of data (firm or establishment level, panel or cross-section datasets). I devote the next section to a detailed survey of this literature, but can already disclose that the key results converge in sustaining a positive association between firm productivity and new work organization – including just-in-time, team working, job rotation within and across teams, participation in problem-solving groups, suggestion systems, job design and delayering, the existence of multiple incentives to boost motivation such as performance-related pay, and participation in decision making.

However, the empirical results are not without problems, to the point that at times they have given rise to diverse interpretations and extremely critical evaluations (Godard 2004). For example, as concerns new work practices, a distinction is not always made between the extension of their adoption amongst the population of firms, which can be represented by a simple dummy variable, and the intensity of adoptions of each work practice, which instead requires a scalar variable. At the same time, a given work practice can have several dimensions, which in turn need to be treated with a vector variable. In addition to these problems, the extension and intensity of new work practices that a researcher measures need to be clearly understood as both their size and their effects could depend on a set of factors such as: (1) firm starting conditions; (2) time spent from the beginning of the re-engineering process; and (3) the internal resistance that Schumpeterian employers and/or managers face during the re-engineering process. The risk is dealing with variables that capture, at the time of a given empirical survey, an incomplete implementation either of a new work practice, or of a bundle of these, thus fostering potentially divergent effects and interpretations.

An aspect of the relationship between workplace characteristics and firm productivity that should be pointed out is the existence of complementarity among work practices, which would imply that implementing (more of) any one of these should increase the returns to implementing (more of) the others (Milgrom & Roberts 1995: 181). Complexity increases when complementarity encompasses other features of the firm, such as new technology and industrial relations 'regimes'. The questions of how a bundle forms, which elements form part of the bundle, what intensity of each element fits better, and whether a 'best and wider bundle' exists, are still far from fully answered; I will address these questions below.

A relevant question to confront is whether these bundles are consistent with the contingency approach or they are of a universalistic nature, regardless of the structural shape of the organizational form of the firm. In the first case, different bundles implemented in different firms could be interpreted as a result of the degree of freedom in combinations contingently selected by managers according to some relevant 'state of the world' or simply to their *weltanschauung*. An alternative way of looking at the question is whether these bundles are a set of building blocks used to re-engineer the organizational form, passing from a traditional model based on functions, towards an innovative model based on processes. In the latter case, it would be useful to recall that each bundle implemented in a given firm (and as such, observed by the researcher with his empirical investigations at a given point in time) should more likely be considered as part of a long process, where the sequence of building blocks to be implemented could have a unique path. If this were the case, the violation of this path could be responsible for the inefficacy of some bundles of new work practices simply because the preceding part of the process may have been omitted.

When jointly implemented, new organizational work design, new work practices, positive industrial relations and ICT represent a clear departure from existing traditional practices; they give rise to a different configuration of the firm and new lifeblood, raising the question of whether the new firm configuration should be considered as the point of reference for a 'new one best way'. To our understanding, an interpretation and explanation of the dynamic nature of the new firm configuration requires going beyond Nelson and Winter's (1982) evolutionary approach, passing through the J-firm (Aoki 1990), and arriving at Nooteboom's (2009) cognitive theory of the firm: in fact it does not appear to be a matter of selecting the most efficient routines, but rather of seeing how – in a context where hierarchical monitoring and control is substituted by alignment of goals, values and motives through loyalty and intrinsic motivation, enhanced and, at least in part, enforced by high involvement and material incentives – competence building, learning and innovation simultaneously and interactively take place since they are among the most powerful contenders to explain the survival and development of the firm.

A new key view that could emerge from the literature I am going to critically survey seems to have been clearly anticipated by Grandori (2005) when asserting that organization design has to be at the root and the core of organization science. At the same time, empirical investigations on organizational design in this period seem capable of enlightening and enriching not only the reasons for structural productivity dispersion among firms but also internal factors that may contribute to determining the heterogeneous dynamics of productivity. This is the case especially if taking into consideration that bundles of new work practices and new organizational features of firms, in addition to ICT, are to a certain extent responsible on one side for both knowledge creation and diffusion, which lead to product and process innovations (see Santangelo & Pini 2011; Gritti & Leoni 2011 and references therein), and on the other, the informal development of key competences (see Leoni 2012 and references therein).

The determinants of productivity are manifold, and the aim of the chapter is to survey and evaluate recent empirical studies concerning the contribution of alternative ways of work organization on manufacturing firm productivity, irrespective – given my aim – of any other sources. The chapter is structured as follows: it first examines the new form of organization; precisely, the origin of the new approach, the pillars of new work organization and their complementarities, and the role of ICT. It then looks at the critical aspects of the diffusion of new work organization, while the following section considers some relevant and still-open questions. Some final remarks are then offered.

THE NEW FORM OF WORK ORGANIZATION: ORIGIN, EVOLUTION, MAIN CHARACTERISTICS AND PERFORMANCE

Various acronyms have been coined to represent the new features of work organization in summary form, such as HPWO (high performance work organization), HPWS (high performance work system), HPWP (high performance work practices), TQM (total quality management), as well as several new terms, such as Toyotism and lean production. While largely evoking the same elements, each new term tends to attract attention to some of these elements, considering them from time to time as having more distinct value. Throughout this chapter I will refer to the acronym WCM (world-class manufacturing), which is the internationalized and institutionalized point of reference of the lean production model indicating a full range of organizational elements of production that characterize firms competing in the world market, but also embodies the concept of a dynamic organization in continuous and rapid movement.

The Origin of the New Approach

Academic research usually attributes the growth of Western economies in the 1945 to 1970 period to cumulative productivity gains brought about by the interrelationship of a number of factors including: dedicated technology; a Taylorist factory and labour organization system; some revenue sharing between workers and firms; consumption linked to the growth of real wages; and finally, investment dynamics based on the accelerator principle, together with the notion that improvements in technology would be incorporated in the last vintage of capital (Appelbaum and Batt 1994: 14).

Subsequently, however, the system broke down as a result of the ability of some new emerging countries (see Japan) to compete on price in the product market. The outstanding performance of Japanese companies, especially Toyota and Ohno's lean production model, led an MIT Commission (Dertouzos at al. 1989) to investigate the productivity differential in US and Japanese firms, paying particular attention to organizational factors. The fear of foreign domination of the American market (Womack et al. 1991: 274) generated in the course of the 1980s prompted managers of the largest corporations to first seek public barriers against Japan's competitiveness, and then to understand and imitate the way of organizing the enterprise. The most striking example is the joint venture between General Motors and Toyota, which gave rise to the extraordinary success of NUMMI (Womack et al. 1991: 278), based on American technology but with Japanese organizational management.[1] This example set a fashion, getting rid of the weak attempts to keep the old production system alive with margin adjustment operations, prompted on one side by psychological organizational behaviour theories, by motivation, job enlargement and job enrichment; and on the other by the idea of cutting costs through reducing the workforce employed for an indefinite period, the extensive use of programmable machine tools, outsourcing and the use of atypical workers.

The remarkable productivity results, product quality and satisfaction of workers attained inspired not only the organizational efforts of two other pilot schemes – GM's Saturn project, also in the USA, and Volvo's factory in Uddevalla (Sweden) – but also the proliferation of articles in the most prestigious management journals, which de facto accredited the greater universality and portability of this organizational model in other countries and thus facilitated its spread in many American and European firms. The main characteristics of the new corporate production model are summarized by a stream of studies known as lean production (or world-class manufacturing). Lean is not only a set of tools that assist in the identification and steady elimination of waste, followed by quality improvements, and production time and cost reductions. Lean also means a flow or smoothness of work, thereby steadily eliminating unevenness throughout the system instead of waste reduction per se. In addition, on the management side, lean also means abandoning three of the most important traditional management techniques; respectively standard costing in favour of activity-based costing, management-by-objectives in favour of activity-based management, and finally traditional planning and control in favour of activity-based budgeting, all relatively well-known concepts and tools that here require no further articulation. It seems important instead, for the purposes of this chapter, to dwell on two aspects: organization based on processes, and multi-valence or multi-competencies.

The former is a profound reversal of the way of understanding the organization of activities, passing from functions to processes. This is defined by Hammer and Champy (1993) as the sequence of all activities (from planning to production and marketing) that absorb resources (one or more inputs) and create output value for the customer. Compared to pyramidal organization, where the individual 'functional' units are structured as real silos with their own hierarchies on top, organization 'by processes' recomposes into units the various activities that cross over the functional units, putting them in the hands of a manager (the process owner) who relates on the one hand as a real supplier with the customer, and on the other as a real customer with internal suppliers (constituted by support activities). Indeed, for Coriat (1991), organization is actually *'pensée à l'envers'* in that it begins from the customer, while the sequence of activities designed to please the customer are recomposed in reverse. The most important partner of this approach is modern ERP technology (Enterprise Resource Planning), a software system that supports not individual functional areas but the entire business process.

The second aspect concerns the multi-competencies of employees; effective towards their construction are mentoring, job rotation (within and among production islands and teams), on-the-job training (directing classroom training to respond to 'know-why' criterion), and finally, short-term economic incentives (designed to recognize and encourage learning rather than to achieve immediate results: thus, input-oriented rather than output-oriented incentives). The objective is to build the roles and competencies that are closest to those required, which include – in this new context – not only the execution of certain actions, but also the maintenance of the technology of the postings (both white and blue collar), ensuring that the role holder acquires mastery of the structure, functions, the operating mechanisms of the artefact and the production process, as well as quality control exercises at each manufacturing stage of processing, identifying the defects and their causes from when they first form (Koike 1994). All this involves dismantling the traditional quality control system carried out for statistical sampling at the end of the product's construction in favour of ongoing control. Work competencies thus constructed are no longer ascribable to only those pertaining to implementation, the identification of defects and causes, and troubleshooting, but also include those related to changes (fluctuations in production volumes, new products, new production methods) and the problems that arise from these.

The Pillars of New Work Organization: Organizational Design, Work Practices, Industrial Relations and their Complementarities

Lean production is a multi-dimensional approach that encompasses a wide variety of work practices and organizational designs, which differ markedly from the Taylor–Ford tradition. Lean production can be described from two perspectives: the first is a philosophical perspective relating to guiding principles (Womack & Jones 1996); the second is a practical perspective of a set of organizational design and work practices that are linked to better performance and can be directly observed. However, since lean production focuses on setting a goal not only for a specific level of leanness, but also for a continuous improvement process, it would be inappropriate, in our understanding, to set a definition of the lean production model starting from the instruments or superficial characteristics of the organizational structures – such as Kanban, 'andon cords' or similar instruments, which so many outsiders have emphasized – in that they represent a temporary response to specific problems.

Much of the literature, however, provides an interpretation of the new work organization that very much leans on the side of human resources and work practices, emphasizing the high-involvement dimension underlying the new work practices. The core set of practices commonly identified as composing the high-involvement model and generating higher productivity includes online teams, participation in problem-solving groups, multiple incentives to boost motivation such as performance-related pay and participation in decision making, suggestion systems, selection based on psychometric tools to single out transversal and technical competencies, and extension training on relational, managerial and cognitive competencies: see, for example, Ichniowski et al. (1997), Black and Lynch (2001, 2004) and Boning et al. (2007) for the US; Patterson et al. (1997) and Guest et al. (2003) for the UK; Bauer (2003) and Zwick (2004) for Germany; Greenan and Guellec (1998), Janod and Saint-Martin (2004) on French data, Caroli and Van Reenen (2001) on both French and UK data; Cristini et al. (2003), Piva et al. (2005) and Mazzanti et al. (2006) for Italy; and Bloom and Van Reenen (2010) for several industrialized and non-industrialized countries; and Rizov and Croucher (2009) for European firms.

In order to control for whether returns from investments in high-involvement work practices exceed their costs (of labour and others), by lower employee turnover and greater productivity, with a consequent enhancing of financial performance, some researchers focused alternatively on Tobin's q, and gross rate of return to capital (Huselid 1995) or returns on investment (ROI) (Colombo et al. 2007), as a dependent variable, finding positive results. Other studies focused on the distribution of productivity gains between firms and workers, finding mixed results: for example, Black and Lynch (2004) and Osterman (2006) find higher performance and higher wages; while Freeman and Kleiner (2000) and Freeman et al. (2000) find weak effects on productivity but strong and positive effects on workers' well-being.

Several studies have already endeavoured to synthesize the literature with a narrative review (see Ichnioswki & Shaw 2009; Bloom & Van Reenen 2010). Methodological issues are at the core of well-known critical aspects, to which I will return selectively below. Here it is worthwhile recalling a couple of new and fascinating critical issues dealt with in the last two surveys. In the first, the authors place strong emphasis on the fact that all empirical studies are non-experimental, and as such lack random assignment, undermining with this the causality link. Their argument is that researchers normally control for selection bias – for example using Heckman's two-step procedure or another adoption equation – between respondents and non-respondents, controlling for endogeneity and thereafter testing the treatment effects between those firms adopting and not adopting new management practices; but these are the traditional problems in using non-experimental data, that is, survey data. Ichniowski et al. (1996: 7) observe that unfortunately 'we can't know the unobserved counterfactuals about what would have happened if non-adopting firms adopted some new management practice or if adopting firms had not adopted'. In the second survey, the novel experiment by Bloom et al. (2010), as providers of free management consulting to a random set of Indian textile firms, effectively test the 'genuine' treatment effect of lean manufacturing practices randomly assigned across different plants. They found a strong and positive productivity effect in the treatment group compared to the set of control firms that were not recipients of the intervention. This is surely a very positive step towards controlling for selection bias, but a further step would be to also randomly select both managers of different production units and individual workers (or groups of workers) within the same unit. This objective, however, runs the risk of being ineffectual if managers do not adopt new practices randomly, or if they do not adopt single practices but multiple practices that complement each other, or if the performance of the individuals or groups of workers 'treated' are not isolable.

The transversality of the adoption of practices typical of lean production and the positive results arising therefrom, measured in firms belonging to different industries and countries (industrialized and developing), argue against a contingency view of the organizational and managerial practices, which instead illustrates that every firm adopts its own best practices given the circumstances in which it finds itself.

The great majority of the above-mentioned studies tend to concentrate on work practices (supply side) or on management practices (demand side) with respect to employees. Scant attention is paid to organizational design in the strict sense such as, for example, internal organization (by process versus function), just-in-time, hierarchical levels versus job autonomy, job design (extended versus reduced job demarcations), and teamwork versus individual work in relation to both productivity and other outcomes (job satisfaction, illness and injuries, firm propensity to innovation, etc.). However, a few studies include, among the covariates, variables reflecting organizational factors that mirror the new form of work organization. Amongst others, Bresnahan et al. (2002), Zwick (2004), Cristini et al. (2003), Bauer (2003), Bertschek and Kaiser (2004) and Rajan and Wulf (2006) find that teamwork and flattening the firm's hierarchy have a positive effect on productivity. Despite its crucial and characterizing role in lean production models, no studies (to our knowledge) have tested the discriminant value of organization based on processes rather than on functions. On the contrary, in several of these studies, complementarity between innovative human resource management systems and some traits of new organizational design – namely, the joint effect on productivity – has been proven.

As regards industrial relations – more precisely, the 'collective involvement' of human resources – a distinction needs to be made: involvement may imply a direct relation between manager and employee, and an indirect relation between manager and workers' representative (unions, works councils, etc.). While the former is a management instrument, and as such is usually included among human resource management techniques emphasizing high-commitment employment practices, the latter refers to the workplace activities of worker delegates or shop stewards as an autonomous and collective voice.

Within traditional organizational regimes, in the 1980s and 1990s, unions decreased both in prevalence and in power, at least in Europe and in the so-called liberal market economies (the USA, Canada, Australia, New Zealand and the United Kingdom) (Visser 2003). With significant changes induced by business process re-engineering, the union was presented with an opportunity to recoup its role, collecting information on the preferences of all workers and aggregating them to determine the social demand for shared and new working conditions. It is likely that without a collective-type 'voice', workers have too little incentive to reveal their preferences when the outcome of such significant changes is due to several choices and the behaviours of a wide variety of agents. However, Freeman and Medoff (1984: 65) assert that the 'voice' cannot succeed without an appropriate response from management (and vice versa: from unions in response to any changes proposed by management). At the same time, they predict that 'some managers will adjust to the union and turn unionism into a positive force at the workplace; others will not . . . [admonishing that] . . . over the long run, those that respond positively will prosper while those that do not will suffer in the market place' (ibid.).

The argument is extendable to include transaction costs, according to which unions can reduce these when employers and managers are facing big changes: (1) by lowering resistance to organizational changes, paving the way for the introduction and development of productivity-enhancing practices in exchange for some benefit (pecuniary and non-pecuniary); (2) by improving organizational coordination through improving information flows to decision makers; (3) by reducing the cost of motivation of employers and managers towards workers; and (4) by lessening the moral hazard of supervisors (Willman et al. 2006). Paraphrasing Greenberg (1987) on organizational justice theories, I maintain that unions not only pursue distributive justice (by reacting to unfair distribution of both rewards and income, between profit and wage), but are also interested in procedural fairness (that is, fairness of procedures pursued to make organizational decisions and to implement those decisions, postulating that unions and workers would be more satisfied if they had process control with respect to when they do not) as well as in relational fairness (which concerns the nature of the relationship between the parties involved in organizational change, and the consequences of organizational changes on the social harmony of group members).

These dimensions of the exchange between workers and employers and managers constitute the prerequisites of an employment relation characterized by mutual trust and respect, similar to a form of Akerlof's 'gift exchange', which may induce unions to legitimize the ensuing organizational changes (Bryson et al. 2005) when not assisting the counterparty in their management functions (Kochan and Osterman 1994; Willman et al. 2006). In these contexts, collective bargaining at firm level may take the form of information exchange, consultation or negotiation around changes. Unfortunately, empirical research is not always instructive on the distinctive forms of these issues, leaving the question open of which of these actions is most efficient – providing that there is only one, and not various actions – based on the different industrial relations previously accumulated in managerial and organizational change projects and closely linked to the formal and informal exercising of power.

Studies that identify direct evidence on the combined impact of new organizational design, new work practices and the proactive role of unions on productivity are: Black and Lynch (2004), Metcalf (2003), Cristini et al. (2003), Zwick (2004), Bryson et al. (2005) and Mazzanti et al. (2006), even if it should be recognized that at times elements of the first two categories are mixed and not precisely the same.

Before concluding, it seems appropriate to point out the risk of WCM coming adrift, above all in Europe, motherland of 'social dialogue' between labour and capital social parties, often working in concert with government to choose social and economic policies. The risk relates to a possible attempt to forcibly break this tradition, which – paradoxically – constitutes precisely the most fertile ground for the full deployment of the virtuous effects of WCM itself. Originating in the Japanese economy, more aligned to the European Union (EU) institution-affected system than the more market-driven US (Freeman 2007: 221), the WCM model rests on two major assumptions. On the one hand, organizational principles such as just-in-time, autonomation and systematic monitoring of the economic-production parameters of the production process, driven by the calculability and predictability of production factors aimed at the full and efficient use of resources. On the other, organizational behaviours, such as the continuous improvement and management of variances (events that go beyond the range of proceduralized treatments), which require quick decisions, and in close proximity to the locations where they arise, but for which greater independence is required. The activation of this autonomy requires, in turn, incentives but also active involvement and cooperation. The recognition of the new content of work positions that no longer consist of only implementation skills but also problem-solving skills (for variances and improvements), as well as employee involvement, shift systems and overtime management, require the legitimacy and collective consensus that trade unions can offer – in the traditional social dialogue channel – on condition that a role is recognized to them. An underestimation of this dimension is likely to undermine the rationalization potential of WMC, directing it towards the afore-mentioned drift.

ICT as a New Pillar of Complementarities

It is widely recognized that the traditional work organization, based on extensive hierarchy, low levels of delegation and narrow skills, is inadequate to fully exploit the potential of general-purpose computer-based technology (ICT). The diffusion of the latter – spurred by sharp declines in real prices – is expected to have a pervasive impact on the firm's life, causing both technical and organizational changes, which in turn affect work practices and industrial relations. Higher computation speed on the one hand allows processing a large quantity of data, and on the other enables new work techniques based on sophisticated and flexible machines and equipment (such as CNCs, flexible manufacturing systems, robotics, group technologies and automated stores). As concerns the first dimension (computational speed), to exploit the increased amount of computer-processed information, more employees are empowered and given some decisional control (Brynjolfsson et al. 2002; Bresnahan et al. 2002), communication is facilitated, information sharing among employees and between employees and managers is encouraged and this enhances employee involvement, autonomy and discretion.

As concerns the second dimension (new work techniques), positive effects on productivity are generated since ICT: (1) allows more customized manufacturing products and services; (2) improves the efficiency of all stages of the production process by reducing set-up times, run times and inspection times (making it less costly to switch production from one product to another and consequently supporting the customization of products to meet individual requirements); and (3) increases the competency requirements of machine operators (technical and problem-solving competencies), inducing the adoption of new work practices that implicitly and informally develop these competencies. Overall, these events are expected to trigger major reorganization processes within the firm: middle and line managers become crowded out, flattening the hierarchical structure; new workplace practices entailing employee involvement are adopted; competencies in technical, relational and cognitive skills are upgraded by training and job rotation; and trust is mutually exchanged.

However, the decreasing cost of information technologies is not enough to produce a net productivity gain if not accompanied by new workplace design, new human resource practices and proactive industrial relations. Only simultaneous changes in the four components are expected to raise the productivity and quality of factors, enabling cost reduction, endorsing knowledge creation and eventually spurring innovation and firm growth. If the net gain to the firm's pay-off is positive, investments in the four components are said to be complements.

This broad-brush progression of events is rather well observed and documented by the empirical literature, even if numerous studies exist that analyse the impact on productivity of a single component (for example, ICT: Athey & Stern 2002; Brynjolfsson & Hitt 2003; Hubbard 2003) or two components (e.g. ICT and competencies: Caroli & van Reenen 2001; Autor et al. 2003; or ICT and new work practices: Black & Lynch 2001; Bresnahan et al. 2002; Cristini et al. 2008). More difficult to find simultaneously are all four components: usually one or two of the four are inferred in the sense that they are assumed coherent with the variable in question; or the three non-technological components are merged into a single factorial variable, clearly due to the primary interest of exhaustively treating the technological variable; or finally, due to the implicit difficulty involved in dealing with very complex causal models, controlling for resulting endogeneity, heterogeneity and self-selection in the adoption of work practices.

It is worthwhile recalling that most of the quoted literature recognizes that firm specificities render each redesign process particular; a fully standardized reorganization scheme is difficult to conceive for various reasons: firm characteristics such as size, age and the technical aspects of production may determine complementarity gains to a different extent. Due to the given firm characteristics, the reorganization process still involves some discretionary actions by managers, particularly if different strategies are possible; some complementary changes may be of a sequential rather than a simultaneous nature. Consequently, complementarity between the introduction of ICT and firm reconfiguration is ultimately idiosyncratic and the complementarity-induced gains are firm specific.

The distinctiveness of each firm renovation process explains why the empirical analysis is essentially of the micro type, based on either case studies or firm-level data. In this regard, the latter type of data, if available for representative samples, allows more general conclusions than those obtained from case studies, but usually provides less detail on qualitative and non-accountable information. This is particularly limiting for the analysis in object since the reorganization of the workplace entails complex interactions of practices that concern various aspects of firm life.

There is also a time dimension, however, which is very important. Any workplace redesign, associated with investments in ICT, can be viewed as a process that evolves over time and takes some time to be completed. The lagged and time-phased effects of investments in the four components may give origin to results that do not always converge and are even negative in cases (see, for example, Cappelli & Nuemark 2001) where the estimates are made when the process of adjustment has not yet been completed, and the likely adjustment costs outweigh the gains. I shall return to this issue below.

One of the most controversial issues concerning complementary between organizational innovation and ICT investments is the underlying relationship between ICT and skills, on which at least three distinctive schools of thought contend against another. The first (recalled above) views the WCM organizational design as per se empowering the role and the skill of each worker (core as well as rank-and-file workers), with ICT legitimizing the empowerment process. The second school of thought is the neoclassical human capital theory in its most recent and sophisticated variant, intervening in the deskilling–upskilling debate on the nature of technological progress, precisely skill-biased technical change. The consequence is an increasing demand for higher skills and qualifications, which in turn drives up wages, and reduced demand for intermediate and low skills, with a consequential reduction in real wages. However, job polarization and consequent wage inequality (Michaels et al. 2010) obtained different explanations according to factors that are not related to technical change. For example, Goos et al. (2010) argue that the offshoring of routine middle-skill jobs associated with the growing importation of labour-intensive goods from low-wage countries may have reinforced the inequality between high- and low-skill workers, while Lafer (2002) points out that in all developed economies a range of institutional factors and structural changes interceded, such as for instance a large reduction in union density, to which Card and DiNardo (2002) add minimum wage trends. Last but not least, the generalized presence of the overqualification phenomenum in industrialized countries, with the potential waste associated with overeducation (Leuven & Oosterbeek 2011), is an enigma in human capital theory and does not fit well with skill-biased technical change. The third school of thought contending the previous explanations is that of the neo-institutionalists, who stress that the acquisition of high and intermediate skill levels by a large proportion of the workforce depends on a set of interlocking institutional arrangements governing not only training but also industrial relations, industry policy, education and welfare (Crouch et al. 1999).

THE DIFFUSION OF NEW WORK ORGANIZATION AND THE MODERN FIRM BETWEEN HYBRIDIZATION, MANAGERIAL FASHIONS AND RESISTANCE TO CHANGE

The positive results accredited by the literature at times elicit scepticism and incertitude due to the fact that the new work organization is not as diffused in Western as it is in Far Eastern economic systems, and in Europe as it is in the USA. Moreover, even in its variegated diffusion, implementation has not occurred linearly and swiftly, and with the intensity that might have been expected following the initially promising performance. Different explanatory reasons can be found in the literature, related to some extent to aspects that may lay some foundations for contingencies, which will be briefly described below.

According to the first, new work organization had to confront itself in Europe with some models that had already partly evolved – with respect to Taylor–Fordist tradition – independently of Japanese benchmarking. I here refer to the Swedish socio-technical model, the German co-determination and diversified quality models, and the Italian models of flexible specialization and industrial districts, which de facto incorporated some of the characteristics of the Japanese model: team production in the Swedish case, the involvement of participative trade unions in the German case, and relational capital within district firms in the Italian case. This prevented grasp of the full scope of the lean model, and its revolutionary reversal of the traditional model. To this are added the captivating traits of the TQM movement, accrediting the gradualism of changes, rendering the cost of change more manageable since it can be diluted over time, compared to the radical but indispensable changes through BPR (business process re-engineering) to achieve the real implementation of the new form of organization. Both BPR and TQM place focus on the process and on the customer, but rather than substituting one another, as often occurred, they should have been seen as complementary: in fact, BPR is a means of converting functions into processes while TQM is nothing but an organized Kaizen, namely, continuous improvement activities carried out by quality circles and by the suggestion system from the bottom, improvements that must be continuously pursued, in Japanese tradition, even after transforming the company into a lean organization. Moreover, the Western applicative nuances have rendered TQM a little different from the Japanese declination: more limited and more oriented to products in the former, compared to the broader and more people-oriented (customers and employees) of the latter, thus reducing the impact of TQM.

The second reason is the enthusiasm surrounding the first positive findings, which soon transformed the re-engineering process into a managerial fashion and into a panacea of corporate performance problems, giving rise to at least three negative consequences: (1) any action to reduce inefficiencies and optimization along the internal phases within individual organizational units has become 're-engineering', distorting the concept and scope of the BPR – a prelude to many failures; (2) a BPR is mostly interpreted as a stand-alone practice, neglecting both incipient conflicts and complementarities with other governance practices; (3) the BPR proposal was also weakened by the misbelief that organization based on processes was only feasible in medium-sized to large industrial enterprises, which relegated industrial small and medium-sized enterprises (SMEs), service firms and public organizations to the storeroom, despite the fact that re-engineering is nothing more than rethinking the way to organize internal activities, and as such is applicable to all organizational sizes. The same proponents of BPR (Hammer & Champy 1993, Ch. 13) were fully aware of these problems.

The third reason does not concern diffusion as such, but rather the difficulty of measuring and interpreting elsewhere the diffusion of the lean model. It cannot be seen as a cloning of the original model since it developed in a cultural, legal and institutional context differing from that of the economic-productive systems and countries that have adopted it. Thus, it should not be surprising that there are different degrees of hybridization in the applications (from the production to the administration sphere, from that of relationships with suppliers to industrial relations, and so forth), as documented by the literature on lean production case studies in the US and Europe (see, e.g., Koike 1998). The diffusion took place with greater progression first in the US and then later in Europe, albeit with different levels of completeness: as noted by Ichniowski et al. (1996), analyses should distinguish between the adoption of single innovative practices and the incidence (or extension) of the practice itself, namely, the degree of its application to the various organizational units or the workforce employed, since if adoption by the firm is via a single practice and not a group of complementary practices (bundles), and if extension is not on a significant level, the expected effect on firm performance is practically zero. The metric used in empirical surveys is not always the same, and this prevents a stringent comparison of the degree of real diffusion of new work practices among different firms operating in different economic systems (sectors and countries); see for example, Coriat (2001).

The fourth reason corresponds to obstacles and resistance. Despite the positive results generated by organizational innovation, in terms of reduced costs and improved quality of products and services as well as motivation, commitment and competency development of workers, the reasons for the limited and variegated diffusion of the promising model were rightly questioned through both specific questionnaires (European Commission 2002) and critical theoretical analyses. From the former, four major issues emerged. The first is linked to the differing intensity of competitive pressure to which firms are exposed, which affects the willingness of top management to implement a BPR process. The second issue relates to the fact that not all firms have the financial resources and expertise to address the significant costs of the changes in question. The third relates to the fact that knowledge in this area (BPR and lean organization) is poorly codified and disseminated, and firms can only access it by using consultants or turning to specific organizations. The fourth issue is that this type of change involves the system's hierarchical structure and the firm's governance, and thus the entire social structure as such is variously involved in the perception of risk of loss of status and professional power in a BPR operation: from managers to foremen and finally to line workers.

Rapid innovation as well as the replacement of products on one side, and the internationalization of business on the other, increase uncertainty and render formal governance, especially governance by contracts, difficult to specify; performance difficult to judge; and conduct more difficult to understand. This increases the importance – according to Nooteboom (2002) – of collaborations based on trust, although trust does have its limits and as such should not be, and indeed seldom is, blind or unconditional.

From a theoretical point of view, given that the centralization of decisions becomes relatively ineffective, the re-engineering of a pyramidal organization into a flat and lean one with increased delegation of authority to – or an empowerment process of – subordinates, has been strongly legitimized by the economics of (internal) transaction costs. In spite of several favourable arguments, the phenomenon of inertia must be taken into account: factors that slow down change (for example, crystallization of knowledge in routine, Nelson & Winter 1982; the 'hold-up' problem, Menezes-Filho & Van Reenen 2003; internal resistance against changes, Zwick 2002) could also apply to new work organization.

The quality of these and other theoretical arguments (consider those linked to agency theory, to transaction cost economies, to property rights theory) are not often taken into account either in designing questionnaires (which should include specific questions) or in explanations of why new organizational configurations are diffusing so slowly, in spite of their promising outcomes, thus preventing reliable policy prescriptions. Conversely, we must recognize that for some theorizations it is very difficult to turn concepts into empirical measures.

The awareness of the positive results of WCM on the dynamics of productivity, but also of resistance, costs and barriers that meet their implementation, has prompted several European governments, mainly in the Centre-North, to pursue industrial policies to encourage organizational innovations across the board, simultaneously supporting a policy of industrial relations based on partnerships between firms and unions. Aloisini (2009) provides a comparative analysis of strategies aimed at promoting workplace innovation in nine national and regional European contexts in the last few years, raising crucial issues for promoting learning across national borders in workplace development.

SOME CRITICAL QUESTIONS

To fully answer the question on whether lean organization is really more efficient and more profitable than Taylor–Fordist organization, with more robust and incontrovertible estimates, researchers have to compete with the set of ambiguities, aporias and methodological doubts that still exist in the empirical literature. As mentioned above, some studies have already attempted to synthesize the literature through a narrative review, highlighting several critical aspects that are fairly diffused in literature, such as: omitted-variable bias, heterogeneity bias, response bias, subjective versus objective measures, the role of responders (top-level managers versus multiple responders at different levels and in different roles within the organizations), identifying bundles, longitudinal versus cross-sectional datasets, unit of analysis (firm, establishment or workplace) and endogeneity.

Rather than replicating a similar exercise, in the following I draw attention to three issues which are rather neglected or poorly understood in the literature, and as such risk perpetuating an unsatisfactory way of completing further empirical researches.

Ways of Combining Single Practices to Represent the Multidimensional Nature of WCM: The Identifying Bundles

A crucial aspect of the research process concerns the effort of turning concepts into workable, valid and reliable survey questions. It is not uncommon in numerous surveys to see single respondents from each organizational unit being asked to provide a single numerical rating that describes each practice on a unit-wide basis. Broad and profound concepts cannot be reliably measured with a single question (or single item) asking whether or not a given practice is implemented, or a given management tool is used: a series of specific questions are required on the various dimensions of a given practice. Naturally, the end user of a survey is constrained by the survey designer's choices upstream of the process.

There are mainly two ways to combine individual practices to represent a multidimensional phenomenon. However, before proceeding in this direction, an important preliminary step (largely neglected) consists in checking the 'internal consistency' – by estimating, for example, Cronbach's α coefficient – between the items forming a single practice or a bundle of practices.

From items to single practices

To deal with a multidimensional phenomenon, the most frequently used method (see, for example, Osterman 1994; MacDuffie 1995) is the 'additive' index, which summarizes several items, generally expressed in terms of dichotomy dummies, forming a scalar variable that depicts a given single practice for each single organizational unit. Perplexingly, a more powerful tool such as factor analysis is less used at this level of data elaboration.

From a single practice to a bundle of practices

Exploratory or confirmatory factor analyses are instead much more frequently used to form orthogonal and unidimensional factors, starting from several single practices. A factor (called 'bundle' in our context) refers to a systematic interrelationship (namely, mutually reinforcing the effects of multiple elements) among the variables under investigation. It is worthwhile emphasizing that bundles in themselves are thus already conceptualized as complementary among the elements that compose them.

The nature of bundles

A final word must be reserved for the nature of bundles, in the sense that in the estimated models bundles that differ in nature should be contrasted (for example, innovative versus non-innovative), or – despite operating with a single bundle, operationalized with a continuous variable (for example, with a factorial variable) – clarifying which part of the distribution of the variable in question captures the innovative and the non-innovative dimensions (for example, high values of the distribution of the variable may be linked to the high intensity of innovative elements, and vice versa).

Similar arguments have to be extended to industrial relations (for example, participative versus adversarial) and ICT (new versus more traditional technologies), to the extent that they are dealt with in terms of bundles, and the interest is in searching for the complementarity of the new organizational configuration of the firm, the renowned WCM.

Adoption of Changes: Simultaneously Altogether or a Sequence of Adoptions?

The bundling of practices finds empirical and theoretical support from the review developed above. However, whether practices that form a bundle, identified at the time of a survey, reflect the adoption of practices simultaneously implemented or whether they are simply steps along a 'unique' sequential process of adoption is still an open and relevant question. On the one hand, the different initial conditions, different constraints or different worldviews of managers could induce each firm to start the process of change by adopting different practices from other firms, so that the bundles identified at a point in time (precisely, at the time of the survey) differ *ceteris paribus* between firms or groups of firms. On the other hand, one might imagine that the path along which adoption starts and is completed is unique, but each firm, for a number of reasons (for instance, due to the crises favouring significant non-simultaneous changes) starts the adoption process at different times. The cross-sectional picture that emerges would be observationally equivalent to the previous picture but would in fact reflect a different adoption process. Unfortunately, the temporal dimension of studies on workplace practices typically suffer from poor data since no information on the time of adoption of each practice is usually available. Freeman et al. (2000) are an exception, since they know the number of years a practice has been in use. They find that the most diffused practices are those that have been in use for a longer period, suggesting that a sequential ordering of the practices may exist so that some practices form the basis for other subsequent (and probably more advanced) practices.

Using cross-section data, some information on the sequential ordering of practices may be obtained by recording the intercorrelation among practices. Let *a*, *b* and *c* be three practices in decreasing order of frequency, then counting, among firms that have adopted practice *a*, those that have adopted practice *b* and those have adopted practice *c*; by repeating the count for all practices a matrix of data is obtained (Freeman et al. 2000). If the order of frequency reflects the (unobserved) order of adoption, and this is unique, then we expect that all firms that have adopted practice *b* have already adopted practice *a*, where a lesser percentage has already adopted practice *c*; if this happens exactly, all numbers above the diagonal should be 100 and those below should be less than 100 and decreasing. All this complicates the framework of analysis.

The Temporal and Staggered Lags of Effects

We expect that investments in general-purpose ICT are a relatively low-cost and easy change to make, whereas other changes, specifically those relating to organizational changes and new work practices, are both costlier and slower to activate. Another argument holds that some time needs to elapse for new workplace systems to show their entire effect on productivity: employees need to acquire the necessary competencies, become familiar with the new work methods, get used to the new roles, responsibilities and decision-making before performing in the new organizational environment. Thus, it is possible that complementarity between contemporaneous ICT and organizational changes does not emerge or may even be negative in some cases, signalling for example that the process of adjustment has not yet be completed or that the adjustment costs outweigh the gains. Usually, where investigations can rely on panel data, a considerable time lag between adoption and productivity results is observed. The Danish Ministry of Business and Industry (1996) documents that the implementation of both ICT investments and organizational changes induces a positive and rising impact on productivity from the fourth year after adoption; Brynjolfsson et al. (2002) find that the performance effect of the interacted ICT–reorganization term rises appreciably in the third year. With regard to bundles of workplace practices, the time lag appears to be even longer: Kato and Morishima (2002) find that complementary participatory human resource management practices lead to a significant increase in productivity only seven years after their introduction; similarly, Bauer (2003) and Basu et al. (2004) demonstrate that the productivity effect of implementing high-performance workplace practices rises over time and has a positive impact on labour efficiency only in the long run (from three to five years).

Moreover, adjustment costs may depend on the extent of reorganization: a situation where the workplace is undergoing extensive renovation (many dimensions are being changed) differs considerably from a situation where only a few changes have to be introduced, although the sign of the difference is not clear. For example, one expects that where many changes are being undertaken, potential complementarity gains are higher although employees, in this case, may need more time to learn and adapt to the new environment or may even resist the change, thereby reducing the benefits of restructuring.

It follows that the comparison of two firms (or sectors) at a given point in time may reveal that – for the same investment in ICT – one firm shows an acceleration of its TFP and the other a deceleration for the simple fact that the former could have made investments in complementary organizational capital in some previous period,[2] or because the latter has violated the sequential adoption of new practices.

FINAL REMARKS

Porter's (1985) distinction between two generic firm strategies – cost minimization, and innovative and quality strategies – attributing the former to a Taylorist system and the latter to lean production, appears to be obsolete and inadequate in understanding market processes and the thwarting forces that operate in market economies. The former strategy, which in the first instance points to a reduction of monetary labour costs through outsourcing, currency devaluation or atypical contracts, gives rise to effects that are initially positive, but after a certain point quickly diminish over time: this is a short-run and transient strategy, not able to procure a sustainable competitive advantage for the firm in the medium to long run.

Even the simple contraposition of the characteristic features of mass production models and those of modern manufacturing (e.g. Milgrom & Roberts 1995) does not per se seem greatly significant since it confines itself to singling out monolithic dimensions on which the two patterns differ, supplemented by a possible explanation of the frequency with which they occur together in successful manufacturing organizations and the timing of their adoption. The same mathematics of complementarity, which enables following sequential responses among an assumed set of interconnected variables, only affords conclusions of a static nature.

Finally, nor is the dispute very useful between those who think the non-Taylorist organization is a best-practice model – regardless of how it is constituted – and those who view its relevance as dependent on the organization's strategy and context. The main limitation in this dispute is that neither view fully acknowledges the different combinative possibilities (Grandori & Furnari 2008). In fact, a new organizational performance practice or a new performance bundle of practices is the result not only of different ingredients but also of the different weights of each ingredient. Hence, the employer and/or manager has two levers – ingredients and their intensity of application – in potentially innumerable combinations to pursue efficiency and performance. For example, if one considers the impact effect on performance of a bundle composed of three work practices, measured by respective coefficients (three main effects and four interactive effects), in the presence of continuous variables, the marginal return depends on the value of each work practice, namely, the intensity of the adoption, which is firm specific. It follows that one obtains different results when reducing or increasing the mean value of one or more practices, or else when enlarging (to four practices) or restricting (to two practices) the bundle.

In other words, the latter dispute does not take account of the fact that the new organizational performance configuration has to be built on performance stemming from the 'internal chemistry of the firm' (Grandori & Furnari 2008), and from factors of a dynamic nature such as 'social capabilities' (Abramowitz 1989), which primarily include learning and knowledge creation. These are internal primary sources of innovation that are not easily transferable and require (to become powerful) appropriate workplace design, specific new work practices and organizational well-being (namely, good and trusting industrial relations), which empirical research has recently identified and documented as improving firm performance, competences of employees and innovations.

Recognizing as a stylized fact that lean production performs better than the traditional form does not mean that we are facing a new 'one best way' (which is a nonsense category): the persistent heterogeneity across firms, and even more across countries, in their abilities to develop, imitate and adopt organizational and technological innovations is an equally robust stylized fact, which leads to predictions of – irrespective of old or new forms of organizing – interfirm heterogeneity in innovative patterns, asymmetries in innovative performance across firms, possible path-dependency and lock-in phenomena.

From an analytical perspective, the fact that international research has not yet endorsed well-established complementarities among organizational design, new work practices, industrial relations and new technologies across firms seems to keep the idea of 'contingencies' alive: namely, there is not 'one best way' to organize a flexible firm. This chapter has documented that the incomplete and imperfect implementation of the new performance configuration may be due to several reasons, quite different when compared to those used by contingentists. If so, then several contingent elements may be viewed as transient, or as changeable elements belonging to different layers of organization building.

All this appears to be in perfect harmony with the thought of Grandori (2005), who strongly supports the emerging movement to restitute to organization design the central position it deserves, at the same time renewing the approach to it. Lingering on a contingency approach has prevented organization theory not only from readily grasping the structural capacity of the new lean production organizational form with respect to the Taylor–Fordist, but also from contributing to developing design tools in a creative, generative, problem-solving, architectural sense (Grandori 2005: 52), and the emerging new theory of 'organizational combinations', which recognizes the existence of some 'basic elements' (governance, coordination mechanisms) that – as in chemistry – can give rise to different (exterior) forms mainly due to different combinative possibilities (Grandori 2005: 58).

The world-class manufacturing model clearly involves fundamental shifts with respect to traditional firm organization: the turning point may be glimpsed in leveraging the participatory circuits of knowledge development, through which tacit knowledge becomes explicit and codified, and thereafter incorporated into new products, new services and new ways of working (Nonaka & Takeuchi 1995; Nooteboom 2000). Yet, these developments cannot happen in any undifferentiated work environment: Kenney and Florida (1993) highlight that WCM (even in its numerous 'chemistry' versions) has precisely the characteristic of mobilizing the intelligence of a larger number of workers involved in the enterprise, creating a new and qualitatively better synthesis between manual work and mental work, compared to the traditional model. Intelligence is all the more necessary, precisely because it is required of both individuals and production organizations in a context of constant change, high volatility and substantial uncertainty (Cainarca & Zollo 2001). Lester and Piore (2004) note in this regard how 'analytical processes' are at work when the alternative outcomes are well understood and can be clearly defined and distinguished from each other, while the 'interpretative processes' are activated when possible outcomes are not known, that is, when the task is precisely to create the results and determine their properties. The two processes are somehow opposed to each other, but the distinctive competence is in the integration of the two processes, namely, thinking of them independently but managing them simultaneously. The work organization structure that best stimulates and assists in this integration of the two processes is a flexible form of world-class manufacturing, provided that intelligence in production engineering and in productive methodologies is complemented with intelligence in workshop social governance (i.e., individual and collective involvement, and participative industrial relations). A potential deficit of the second type of intelligence implies an authoritarian torsion to WCM – incongruent with the model itself – which can also give rise to an increase in performance in the short run, but is very unlikely do so in the medium to long run.

The two types of intelligences working together is a precondition to achieving a learning organization, where individuals, but also individual production units within the organization, relate to each other in a more complex but also more fruitful and sustainable way than is possible through the classical mechanism of hierarchy or the market-price mechanism.

NOTES

*   Financial support from the University of Bergamo (Italy) is gratefully acknowledged. I also thank Anna Grandori for her valuable comments on a previous version of this chapter and Annalisa Cristini, colleague and co-author of several papers, for her remarkable idea expounded in the section on 'Adoption of Changes: Simultaneously Altogether or a Sequence of Adoptions?'
1.   According to Adler et al. (1998), Toyota's decision to enter into partnership with GM in the NUMMI project can be viewed as the attempt by Japanese management (followed by other Japanese companies) to overcome the trade dispute with the US and build factories in America. From here begins the story of the Japanese transplants, first in the US and then in Europe, that have tended to privilege greenfield rather than brownfield investments.
2.   This is precisely the situation that emerges in the comparison between the US and United Kingdom (UK) in the work of Basu et al. (2004), who ask themselves whether ICTs are able to explain why the US has accelerated in its TFP while the UK – which has the same rate of investment in ICT as the US – has decelerated. The answer lies in the different rate of investments in organizational change in the US and the UK, and the time lag. This is because the US had already begun to invest in ICT and organizational changes in the 1980s, while the UK only joined the rhythm of investment in ICT in the

1990s. Moreover, in this latter period, the data rightly show the divergent TFP dynamics of the two countries.

REFERENCES

Abramovitz, M. (1989), *Thinking About Growth*, Cambridge: Cambridge University Press.
Adler, P.S., B. Goldoftas and D.I. Levine (1998), 'Stability and change at NUMMI', in R. Boyer, E. Charron, U. Jurgens and S. Tolliday (eds), *Between Imitation and Innovation: The Transfer and Hybridization of Productive Models in the International Automobile Industry*, Oxford: Oxford University Press, pp. 128–160.
Aloisini, T. (2009), 'Strategies to promote workplace innovation: a comparative analysis of nine national and regional approaches', *Economic and Industrial Democracy*, 30(4), 614–642.
Aoki, M. (1990), 'Toward an economic model of the Japanese firm', *Journal of Economic Literature*, 28, 1–27.
Appelbaum, E. and R. Batt (1994), *The New American Workplace*, Ithaca, NY: IRL Press.
Athey, S. and S. Stern (2002), 'The impact of information technology and job design on emergency health care outcome', *RAND Journal of Economics*, 33(3), 399–432.
Autor, D., F. Levy and R. Murnane (2003), 'The skill content of recent technological change: an empirical exploration', *Quarterly Journal of Economics*, 118(4), 1279–1333.
Banerjee, A. and E. Duflo (2005), 'Growth theory through the lens of development economics', in P. Aghion and S. Durlauf (eds), *Handbook of Economic Growth*, Amsterdam: Elsevier, pp. 473–552.
Bartel, A., C. Ichniowski and K. Shaw (2007), 'How does information technology really affect productivity? Plant-level comparisons of product innovation, process improvement and worker skills', *Quarterly Journal of Economics*, 122(4), 1721–1758.
Basu, S., J.G. Fernald, N. Oulton and S. Srinivasan (2004), 'The case of the missing productivity growth, or does information technology explain why productivity accelerated in the United States but not in the United Kingdom?' *NBER Macroeconomics. Annual 2003*, Cambridge, MA: MIT Press.
Bauer, T.K. (2003), 'Flexible workplace practices and labor productivity', Bonn: IZA Discussion paper, n.700.
Bertschek, I. and U. Kaiser (2004), 'Productivity effects of organizational change: microeconometric evidence', *Management Science*, 50(3), 394–404.
Black, S. and L. Lynch (2001), 'How to compete: the impact of workplace practices and information technology on productivity', *Review of Economics and Statistics*, 83(3), 434–445.
Black, S. and L. Lynch (2004), 'What's driving the new economy: the benefits of workplace innovation', *Economic Journal*, 114(493), 97–116.
Bloom, N. and J. Van Reenen (2010), 'Why do management practices differ across firms and countries?' *Journal of Economic Perspectives*, 24(1), 203–224.
Bloom, N., R. Sadun and J. Van Reenen (2010), 'Americans do IT better: American multinationals and the productivity miracle', LSE/Stanford mimeo (revision of NBER Working Paper 13085/2007).
Boning, B., C. Ichniowski and K. Shaw (2007), 'Opportunity counts: teams and the effectiveness of production incentives', *Journal of Labor Economics*, 25(4), 613–650.
Bresnahan, T., E. Brynjolfsson and L.M. Hitt (2002), 'Information technology, workplace organization, and the demand for skilled labor: firm-level evidence', *Quarterly Journal of Economics*, 117(1), 339–376.
Brynjolfsson E. and L.M. Hitt (2003), 'Computing productivity: firm-level evidence', *Review of Economics and Statistics*, 85(4), 793–808.
Brynjolfsson, E., L.M. Hitt and S. Yang (2002), 'Intangible assets: computers and organizational capital', *Brooking Papers on Economic Activity*, 1, 137–181.
Bryson, A., J. Forth and S. Kirby (2005), 'High-involvement management practices, trade union representation and workplace performance in Britain', *Scottish Journal of Political Economy*, 52(3), 451–491.
Cainarca, G. and G. Zollo (2001), 'The management of human resources under uncertainty and ambiguity', in Gil-Aluja J. (ed.), *Handbook of Management under Uncertainty*, Dordrecht: Kluwer Academic Publishers, pp. 537–612.
Cappelli, P. and D. Neumark (2001), 'Do "high-performance" work practices improve establishment level outcomes?' *Industrial and Labor Relations Review*, 5(4), 737–776.
Card, D. and J. DiNardo (2002), 'Skill-biased technological change and rising wage inequality: some problems and puzzles', *Journal of Labor Economics*, 20(4), 733–783.
Caroli, E. and J. Van Reenen (2001), 'Skill biased organizational change? Evidence from a panel of British and French establishments', *Quarterly Journal of Economics*, 116(4), 1449–1492.

Colombo, G.M., M. Delmastro and L. Rabbiosi (2007), '"High performance" work practices, decentraliza-tion, and profitability: evidence from panel data', *Industrial and Corporate Change*, 16(6), 1037–1067.
Coriat, B. (1991), *Penser à l'envers. Travail et organisation dans la firm japonaise*, Paris: C. Bourgois.
Coriat, B. (2001), 'Organizational innovation in Europe firms: a critical overview of the survey evidence', in D. Archibugi and B.A. Lundvall (eds), *The Globalizing Learning Economy*, Oxford: Oxford University Press, pp. 195–215.
Cristini, A., A. Gaj and R. Leoni (2008), 'Direct and indirect complementarity between workplace reorganiza-tion and new technology', *Rivista di Politica Economica*, 48(3–4), 87–117.
Cristini, A., A. Gaj, S. Labory and R. Leoni (2003), 'Flat hierarchical structure, bundles of new work practices and firm performance', *Rivista Italiana degli Economisti*, 8(2), 137–165.
Crouch, C., D. Finegold and M. Sako (1999), *Are Skills the Answer? The Political Economy of Skill Creation in Advanced Industrial Countries*, Oxford: Oxford University Press.
Danish Ministry of Business and Industry (1996), 'Technological and organisational change: implications for labour demand', *Enterprise Performance and Industrial Policy*, Copenhagen.
Dertouzos, M.L., R.K. Lester and R.M. Solow (1989), *Made in America*, Cambridge, MA: MIT Press.
European Commission (2002), 'New forms of work organization: the obstacles to wider diffusion, dg employ-ment and social affairs', report prepared by Business Decisions Limited, October.
Freeman, R. (2007), 'Searching for the EU social dialogue model', in N. Acocella and R. Leoni (eds), *Social Pacts, Employment and Growth*, Heidelberg: Physica-Verlag.
Freeman, R. and M. Kleiner (2000), 'Who benefits most from employee involvement: firms or workers', *American Economic Review*, 90(2), 219–223.
Freeman, R. and J. Medoff (1984), *What Do Unions Do?* New York: Basic Books.
Freeman, R., M. Kleiner and C. Ostroff (2000), 'The anatomy of employee involvement and its effects of firms and workers', NBER Working Paper no. 8050.
Godard, J. (2004), A critical assessment of the high-performance paradigm, *British Journal of Industrial Relations*, 42(2), 349–378.
Goos, M., A. Manning and A. Salomons (2010), 'Explaining job polarization in Europe: the roles of technol-ogy, globalization and institutions', London: CEP/LSE Discussion Paper No 1026.
Grandori, A. (2005), 'The changing core of organization theory: from contingency to combinative', in R. Leoni and G. Usai (eds), *Organizations Today*, New York: Palgrave Macmillan, pp. 47–60.
Grandori, A. and S. Furnari (2008), 'A chemistry of organization: combinatory analysis and design', *Organization Studies*, 29(3), 459–485.
Greenan, N. and D. Guellec (1998), 'Firm organisations, technology and performance: an empirical study', *Economics of Innovation and New Technology*, 6(4), 313–347.
Greenberg, J. (1987), 'A taxonomy of organizational justice theories', *Academy of Management Review*, 12(1), 9–22.
Gritti P. and R. Leoni (2012), 'High performance work practices, industrial relations and firm propensity for innovation', in A. Bryson (ed.), *Advances in the Economic Analysis of Participatory and Labor-Managed Firms*, Vol. 13, Bingley: Emerald Group Publishing, pp. 267–309.
Guest, D., J. Michies, M. Sheehan and N. Conway (2003), 'Human resource management and corporate performance in the UK', *British Journal of Industrial Relations*, 41(2), 291–314.
Hammer, M. and J. Champy (1993), *Reengineering the Corporation. A Manifesto for Business Revolution*, New York: Harper Business.
Hubbard, T.N. (2003), 'Information, decisions and productivity: on-board computers and capacity utilization in trucking', *American Economic Review*, 93(4), 1328–1353.
Huselid, M. (1995), 'The impact of human resource management practices on turnover, productivity and cor-porate financial performance', *Academy of Management Journal*, 38(3), 635–672.
Ichniowski, C. and K. Shaw (2009), 'Insider econometrics: empirical studies of how management matters', NBER working paper 15618.
Ichniowski, C., K. Shaw and G. Prennushi (1997), 'The effects of HRM systems on productivity: a study of steel finishing lines', *American Economic Review*, 87(3), 291–313.
Ichniowski, C., T.A. Kochan, D. Levine, C. Olson and G. Strauss (1996), 'What works at work: overview and assessment', *Industrial Relations*, 35(2), 299–333.
Janod, V. and A. Saint-Martin (2004), 'Measuring the impact of work reorganization on firm performance: evidence from French manufacturing, 1995–1999', *Labour Economics*, 11(4), 785–798.
Kato, T. and M. Morishima (2002), 'The productivity effects of participatory employment practices: evidence from new japanese panel data', *Industrial Relations*, 41(4), 487–452.
Kenney, M. and R. Florida (1993), *Beyond Mass Production: The Japanese System and its Transfer to the US*, Oxford: Oxford University Press.
Kochan, T. and P. Osterman (1994), *The Mutual Gains Enterprise: Forging a Winning Partnership among Labor, Management and Government*, Boston, MA: Harvard Business School Press.

Koike, K. (1994), 'Learning and incentive systems in Japanese industry', in M. Aoki and R.P. Dore (eds), *The Japanese Firm*, Oxford: Oxford University Press, pp. 41–65.

Koike, K. (1998), 'NUMMI and its prototype plant in Japan: a comparative study of human resource development at the workshop level', *Journal of the Japanese and International Economies*, **12**(1), 49–74.

Lafer, G. (2002), *The Jobs Training Charade*, Ithaca, NY, USA and London, UK: Cornell University Press.

Leibenstein, H. (1966), 'Allocative efficiency versus X-Efficiency', *American Economic Review*, **56**(3), 392–415.

Leoni, R. (2012), 'Workplace design, complementarities among work practices and the formation of key competencies: evidence from Italian employees', *Industrial and Labor Relation Review*, **65**(2), 316–349.

Lester, R.K. and M.J. Piore (2004), *Innovation: The Missing Dimension*, Cambridge, MA: Harvard University Press.

Leuven, L. and H. Oosterbeek (2011), 'Overeducation and mismatch in the labor market', in E. Hanushek, S. Machin and L. Woessman (eds), *Handbook of Economics of Education*, Vol. 4, Amsterdam: Elsevier, pp. 283–326.

MacDuffie, J.P. (1995), 'Human resources bundles and manufacturing performance: organisational logic and flexible production systems in the world automobile industry', *Industrial and Labour Relations Review*, **48**(2), 197–221.

Mazzanti, M., P. Pini and E. Tortia (2006), 'Organizational innovations, human resources and firm performance: the emilia-romagna food sector', *Journal of Socio-Economics*, **35**(1), 123–141.

Menezes-Filho, N. and J. Van Reenen (2003), 'Unions and innovation: a survey of the theory and empirical evidence', in J.Y. Addison and C. Schnabel (eds), *International Handbook of Trade Unions*, Cheltenham, UK and Northampton, MA, USA: Edward Elgar, pp. 293–334.

Metcalf, D. (2003), 'Trade unions', in R. Dickens, P. Gregg and J. Wadsworth (eds), *The Labour Market under New Labour. The State of Working Britain 2003*, Basingstoke: Palgrave Macmillan, pp. 170–190.

Michaels, G., A. Natraj and J. Van Reenen (2010), 'Has ICT polarized skill demand? Evidence from eleven countries over 25 years', NBER Working Paper 16138.

Milgrom, P. and J. Roberts (1995), 'Complementarities and firms: strategy, structure and organisational change in manufacturing', *Journal of Accounting and Economics*, **19**(2–3), 179–208.

Nelson, R.R. and S.G. Winter (1982), *An Evolutionary Theory of Economic Change*, Cambridge, MA: Belknap Press of Harvard University Press.

Nonaka, I. and H. Takeuchi (1995), *The Knowledge Creating Enterprise*, Oxford: Oxford University Press.

Nooteboom, B. (2000), *Learning and Innovation in Organisations and Economies*, Oxford: Oxford University Press.

Nooteboom, B. (2002), *Trust: Forms, Foundation, Functions, Failures and Figures*, Cheltenham, UK and Northampton, MA, USA: Edward Elgar.

Nooteboom, B. (2009), *A Cognitive Theory of the Firm. Learning Governance and Dynamic Capabilities*, Cheltenham, UK and Northampton, MA, USA: Edward Elgar.

Osterman, P. (1994), 'How common is workplace transformation and who adopts it?' *Industrial and Labor Relations Review*, **47**(2), 173–188.

Osterman, P. (2006), 'The wage effects of high performance work organisation in manufacturing', *Industrial and Labor Relations Review*, **59**(2), 187–204.

Patterson, M., M.A. West, R. Lawthom and S. Nickell (1997), *The Impact of People Management Practices on Business Performance*, London: Institute of Personnel and Development (*Issues in People Management*, 22).

Piva, M., E. Santarelli and M. Vivarelli (2005), 'The skill bias effect of technological and organisational change: evidence and policy implications', *Research Policy*, **34**(2), 141–157.

Porter, M.E. (1985), *Competitive Advantage*, New York: Free Press.

Rajan, R. and J. Wulf (2006), 'The flattening firm: evidence from panel data on the changing nature of corporate hierarchies', *Review of Economics and Statistics*, **88**, 759–773.

Rizov, M. and R. Croucher (2009), 'Human resource management and performance in European firms', *Cambridge Journal of Economics*, **33**(2), 253–272.

Santangelo, G.D. and P. Pini (2011), 'New HRM practices and exploitative innovation: a shopfloor level analysis', *Industry and Innovation*, **18**(6), 611–630.

Syverson, C. (2004), 'Product substitutability and productivity dispersion', *Review of Economics and Statistics*, **86**(2), 534–550.

Visser, J. (2003), 'Unions and unionism around the world', in J. Addison and C. Schnabel (eds), *International Handbook of Trade Unions*, Cheltenham, UK and Northampton, MA, USA: Edward Elgar, pp. 366–413.

Willman, P., A. Bryson and R. Gomez (2006), 'The sound of silence: which employers choose no employee voice and why?' *Socio-Economic Review*, **4**(2), 283–299.

Womack, J.P. and D.T. Jones (1996), *Lean Thinking: Banish Waste and Create Wealth in Your Corporation*, New York: Simon & Schuster.

Womack, J.P., D.T. Jones and D. Roos (1991), *The Machine That Changed the World*, New York: Harper Perennial.

Zwick, T. (2002), 'Employee resistance against innovations', *International Journal of Manpower*, **23**(6), 542–552.

Zwick, T. (2004), 'Employee participation and productivity', *Labour Economics*, **11**(6), 715–740.

PART V

TECHNICAL ASSETS AND ECONOMIC ORGANIZATION BETWEEN DETERMINANTS AND OPPORTUNITIES

18. Technical assets and property rights
Ugo Pagano

This chapter reviews the role of technical assets in economic organization by integrating two directions of causation present in the literature. While in standard neoclassical theory the nature of the technical assets employed in production does not influence (nor is influenced by) the shape of organization, in new institutional economics the specificity of technical assets do affect the efficient allocation of property rights. By contrast, radical economics have emphasized that the opposite direction of causation is also plausible: holding property rights on them affects the nature of technical assets. By integrating these two directions of causation in a single concept of organizational equilibrium, it is possible to better explain some recent global trends, such as the increasing reification of intellectual capital and the growing financialization of the world economy.[1]

INTRODUCTION

Standard neoclassical theory is characterized by a 'double neutrality': the nature of the technical assets employed in production does not influence property rights and, vice versa, the property right structure does not influence technology. However, technological innovations and changes in the composition of productive sectors have an important role in the evolution of the property rights structure of an economy and, vice versa, the nature of the owners influences the features of the technical assets[2] employed in production.

New institutional economics has offered a powerful rationale for the first direction of causation: in a world of positive transaction costs, property rights will tend to be acquired by the owners of the most specific and difficult-to-monitor technical assets because they can save most on agency costs when they control the organization. However, some radical economists have emphasized that the opposite direction of causation is also highly plausible: when some agents have rights on a firm, the specificity and monitoring costs of their assets tend to be dramatically reduced. Thus, if it is true that actors which are relatively difficult to monitor and specific tend to acquire the rights on organizations, it is also true that the actors controlling them tend to become relatively more specific and difficult to monitor. Other relations, such as that between the degree of modularity of technical assets and intellectual property rights (IPR), can be analyzed in a similar manner.[3] All these relations are likely to generate self-reinforcing interactions between property rights and technical assets, and a multiplicity of possible organizational equilibria. This multiplicity can explain the different paths that characterize the history of real-life systems and can offer analytical tools for comparative institutional analysis.

The next section considers the grounds and limitations of the neoclassical neutrality between property rights and technical assets. The chapter then focuses on the challenge raised by the new-institutional and the new property rights literature to the 'property-rights neutrality' of technical assets and on the mechanisms by which technology can influence the rights on and governance of economic enterprises. It goes on to show that the 'technical-assets neutrality' of property rights can also be challenged because the opposite direction of causation, from property rights to technical assets, can be grounded on precise economic mechanisms. The next section introduces the concept of 'organizational equilibria' which integrates the two directions of causation. The complexity and multiplicity of these equilibria entails that organizations follow a path-dependent evolutionary dynamic characterized by periods of stasis and punctuated by sudden changes. This framework is used to explain, respectively, the post-war varieties of capitalism and the recent emergence of intellectual monopoly capitalism.

THE DOUBLE NEUTRALITY OF TECHNOLOGY AND RIGHTS: THE NEOCLASSICAL APPROACH

A definition of a production organization has two basic ingredients. The first consists of the technological characteristics of the resources used in production, that is, the organization's technical assets; while the second refers to the legal and/or customary rights existing on those resources. The relationship between these two factors has always been a controversial issue in the social sciences: if causation exists, it can go both ways. On the one hand, property rights can shape the nature of technical assets; on the other, the technical assets employed in production can influence the system of property rights.

This two-way relationship is at the very root of the Marxian approach. In Marx's theory of history the level of development of productive forces is considered to be the cause of a certain set of production relations or property rights. At the same time, the production relations may not only foster or hamper the development of productive forces but also determine their qualities.[4]

While the relationship between property rights and technical assets created many interesting problems and contradictions (as well as many wrong 'predictions') in the Marxian approach, it became a non-issue in neoclassical theory. In a market economy, workers' or capitalists' ownership had no effect on the characteristics of the resources (or of the productive forces) employed by the firm. At the same time, the characteristics of the resources employed in the firm had no implications whatever in regard to the form of ownership which would characterize the firm.

This point of view was well expressed by Samuelson when he argued that: 'In a perfectly competitive economy it doesn't really matter who hires whom' (1957: 894). Samuelson's statement can be understood as a double neutrality that makes sense within the framework of standard neoclassical theory. On the one hand, the nature and the combinations of the factors employed in the firm do not have any bearing on the ownership attributes of the organization (technical assets are property-neutral). All possible owners would efficiently maximize the firm's value independently of the particular combination of assets employed in it. On the other hand, the different property rights arrangements bias neither the combinations of the factors employed nor their nature (i.e. property rights are technology-neutral) because all possible owners would choose those technical assets that maximized the value of the firm.

The double neutrality characterizing the neoclassical relationship between technical assets and property rights had an evident influence on the training of economists. History lost relevance for economists, in a double sense. On the one hand, the history of technology became irrelevant to explaining the evolution of ownership and governance systems. On the other hand, alternative arrangements of property rights and economic organization could not contribute to the understanding of the different paths of technological development characterizing different countries and different enterprises. In other words, taken from the title of a book by Geoff Hodgson (2001), this double neutrality provides one route to understanding *How Economics Forgot History*.

NON-NEUTRAL TECHNICAL ASSETS: THE NEW-INSTITUTIONAL APPROACH

The rejection of the hypothesis of nil transaction costs destabilizes the foundations of the neoclassical edifice. The double neutrality of property rights and technical assets of rights is bound to collapse. The mechanisms identified by new-institutional economists have shown that technologies are not neutral in regard to the nature of property rights and of corporate governance, and the radical economists, who will be examined in the next section, have challenged the neutrality of property rights and of other institutional arrangements relatively to the nature of technical assets.

According to Williamson (1985),[5] when it is impossible to write complete contracts, the characteristics of the productive forces influence the attribution of control rights. In the presence of contractual incompleteness,[6] those in possession of relatively specific resources (i.e. resources which cannot be put to other uses without losing some of their value) may fall victim to the opportunism of the counterpart. By contrast, in the neoclassical world of zero transaction costs and complete contracts, resource specificity is not a problem. In this case it is always possible to protect oneself against the opportunism of the counterparties with a complete contract.

If it is not possible to obtain adequate safeguards by the means of a sufficiently complete contract, those controlling the firm have stronger guarantees than the other individuals. In these circumstances, those who invest in specific resources are made vulnerable by the absence of alternative uses for their resources, and they will seek to obtain property rights on the organization or other safeguards. Samuelson's proposition no longer holds, because in this situation 'who hires whom' becomes important. When different technologies are employed, the specific assets used in production also change, and so do the kinds of property and control rights that best fit the technical assets. This is the case even if also in the new-institutional approach, as in the Marxian tradition, productive forces influence production relations and property rights via different mechanisms and outcomes.

A similar reasoning applies to information asymmetries. By virtue of the latter, some agents may possess hidden private information which makes complete contracts impossible to stipulate. If some agents possess concealed information, their monitoring becomes difficult, or even impossible.

In this situation, the technologies employed influence the distribution of information among agents, and certain attributions of property rights tend to prevail because they fit the technical assets better (Alchian and Demsetz 1972). Given these assets, the rights attribution that allocates the rights deriving from ownership to agents difficult to control (and/or controllable at very high costs) will be more efficient because the latter possess a greater amount of concealed private information. Also this argument implies a rejection of the property-neutrality of technology that characterizes the neoclassical model.

Using the new-institutional approach, it is possible to explain the changes in the structure of property rights that accompany the development of the economy. For instance, development is usually characterized by employment shifts from agriculture to industry (and, later, from industry to services), and the monitoring and the specificity characteristics of the labor input are different in these three sectors. Agriculture activity requires that workers be dispersed on the land and implies that their effort cannot be easily inferred from their output because of the influence of the weather. These two circumstances do not characterize the industrial sector, and they make agricultural workers more difficult and costly to monitor by outside observers than industrial work. At the same time, a considerable amount of human capital-specificity characterizes agricultural work. Land and weather conditions differ from place to place. Knowledge about them (often in the form of 'tacit' skills) can influence productivity. The same holds less generally true for industrial production. In many respects, the service sector shares many of the characteristics of agriculture. Work is necessarily dispersed. Services must be specific to particular customers and hence require specific skills.

The development of an economy may therefore require that many workers have rights in relatively small organizations in the 'early' agricultural and 'late' service stage of an economy. Larger organizations in which workers have few rights may prevail in the intermediate industrial stage. This example may be excessively schematic, but it nevertheless shows that, unlike in neoclassical economics, and similarly to the Marxian theory, new-institutional economics can aid understanding of how changes in productive forces influence property relations. In the new-institutional approach, history once again matters, decreasing the gap between theory and reality. However, it matters in a rather mechanical and linear manner (Hodgson 1996). One-way causation from technical assets to property rights cannot explain the multiplicity and the complexity of the organizational paths that characterize the real-life dynamics of economic systems.

Consider the case of the Taylorist organization of production in which workers perform repetitive tasks that are very easy to monitor and require no specific skills, while machinery is highly specific to the production process and its proper use is difficult to monitor for agents not involved with it. New-institutional economists correctly point out that the employment of these technical assets is not property-neutral. Under these conditions, the insurance costs for the use of specific assets and the overall monitoring cost can be saved by assigning the rights on the organization to the most difficult-to-monitor and specific actors. Thus, the institutions of capitalism evolve according to the efficiency requirements of the technical assets embodied in human beings. Moreover, when a large amount of difficult-to-monitor and co-specific pieces of capital have to be employed in production, there should be individuals who are wealthy enough to own substantial amounts of this equipment.

However, the new-institutional view does not tell us where these technical assets come from and whether they are independent of the distribution of property rights. The fact that other forms of organizations, involving different rights and technical assets, have co-existed with Taylorism also challenges the assumption of the technological neutrality of property rights.

PROPERTY BIASING TECHNICAL ASSETS: THE RADICAL CRITIQUE

The technological neutrality of property rights was criticized by Braverman in his book *Labour and Monopoly Capitalism* and by many other radical economists.[7] Braverman (1974) argued that the characteristics of the assets employed under classical capitalism were outcomes of its property rights. Braverman saw the essence of classical capitalism in Taylor's 'scientific management' that extended and translated into a 'science' the principles of the division of labor stated by Babbage (1832). Braverman summarized Taylor's approach in three fundamental principles:

1. Dissociation of the labor process from the skills of the workers.[8]
2. Separation of conception from execution.[9]
3. Use of this monopoly over knowledge to control each step of the labor process and its mode of execution.[10]

In traditional agency theory, the distribution of information is exogenously given. The problem is how endogenously to determine the incentive structure or the distribution of assets that can best solve the agency problem. In scientific management, by contrast, the distribution of assets is exogenously given, and the problem of Taylorism is to determine endogenously the distribution of information which is best for a given distribution of assets. When, under a certain ownership system, because of asymmetric information, the use of a technology is particularly costly, attempts will be made to devise technologies that imply a distribution of information that fits that system better.

In Braverman's analysis, there is a tendency under capitalist ownership relations to devise technologies that, by transforming (and often inverting) pre-existing information asymmetries, make labor an easy-to-monitor factor. A similar process occurs for the specificity of assets. The three principles of Taylorism imply that much of the specific knowledge used by the workers is made redundant by introducing a technology under which the workers are ordered to perform homogeneous tasks requiring only generic skills.

Observe that both the difficult-to-monitor character of resources and their specificity attributes define high-agency-cost resources in the sense that they involve high agency costs[11] when other individuals employ them in situations of goal incongruence. In general, any property rights system tends to use technologies that minimize high-agency-cost resources owned by individuals with goals different from (or even conflicting with) those of the owners of the firm. Thus, under 'classical capitalism' workers tend to become low-agency-cost resources.

By contrast, under 'classical capitalism', similar inhibitions do not hold for the owners of resources who have rights on the organization or who can be, somehow, motivated to share its goals. Thus, under 'classical capitalism' employers and managers tend to become high-agency-cost resources. The owners of machines and other non-human inputs control the production process. Machinery can be difficult to monitor in the sense that its user-induced depreciation may not be easy to estimate by observing the state of machinery before and after use. However, this is not a problem for its owners if they are also the owners of the firm and control the production. The choice of a technology such that work is easy to monitor cheapens the use of difficult-to-monitor capital: the user-induced depreciation of machines can be easily checked by observing the actions of the workers. At the same time, employers and capitalists can be certain of the fact that they will organize the production process in such a way as to take account of the user-induced depreciation of their own difficult-to-monitor machinery. The overall result is that the technology is biased towards the intensive use of difficult-to-monitor non-human capital. A similar argument holds for the specificity of the non-human assets: the owners of machinery, in that they control the organization, can be sure that the specific nature of their machinery will be taken into account in the firm's future decisions, and that they will be safeguarded against the possible opportunism of the other agents. Capitalist property rights tend to make machines specific and to transform labor into an asset *à la* Taylor deprived of specific skills (Pagano 1991).

The joint implication of the monitoring and specificity arguments is that, unlike workers, machines and employers tend to become high-agency-cost factors. An unequal distribution of wealth is not a technical necessity and may instead induce the use of technical assets favoring the control of concentrated capital ownership. Technical assets employed in production are not property-neutral and cannot offer an unbiased ground on which to judge the property rights shaping their nature.

TECHNOLOGY-RIGHTS COMPLEMENTARITIES AND ORGANIZATIONAL EQUILIBRIA

Joining together the neo-institutionalist and the radical arguments implies that neither are technical assets property-neutral nor are property rights technologically-neutral as is implicitly assumed in the neoclassical world. We thus have to deal with technological-rights complementarities where technical assets and property rights influence each other. This outcome is shown in Figure 18.1.

According to the direction of causation considered by the new institutionalists (NI), causation runs from the agency (specificity and monitoring) characteristics of the resources to property rights and organizational form. The owners of high-agency-cost factors can save the most when they control the organization. According to radical economists (RE), the relation runs in the opposite direction: owning actors have a greater tendency to become specific and/or difficult factors or, in other words, high-agency-cost factors. This is due to the fact that an owning actor has no 'inhibition' to becoming firm-specific nor to developing situations of asymmetric information under which it becomes a difficult-to-monitor factor. The NI and the RE directions of causation are far from being incompatible, and their integration can enable the definition of multiple organizational equilibria satisfying the complementarities between technical assets and property rights.[12]

The RE direction of causation can be better understood by considering that changes in property rights have an effect similar to changes in relative prices. They increase the

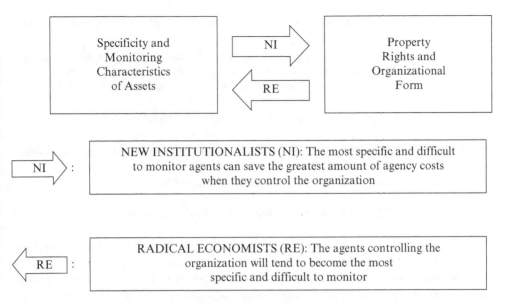

Figure 18.1   New institutionalists versus radical economists

agency costs of using the non-owning factors relatively to those of the owning factors. Thus, similarly to changes in relative prices, changes in property rights have a substitution effect: the high-agency-cost resources of the non-owning actors tend to be substituted away; for this reason, non-owning actors tend to become low-agency-cost factors. Or, in other words, they tend to become less firm-specific and less difficult to monitor than owning factors.

Thus, the changes in the technological characteristics of the resources can be explained by a mechanism familiar in standard economic theory. A change in property rights induces a process of technological substitution that tends to make non-owning agents low-agency-cost resources.

The core of the RE approach can be captured by the assumption that different agents face different costs when they own and run the organization and are therefore able to choose different technologies. This assumption can be formalized in a simple way that clarifies why changes in property rights induce a process of technological substitution.

In order to simplify the analysis, we may assume that there are only two types of agents – capitalists and workers – that can own the organization and four types of factors: low-agency-cost and high-agency-cost capital and labor. We assume the existence of a standard production function $Q(k, K, l, L)$ such that the output Q can be produced with different combinations of low-agency-cost capital and labour (k, l) and high-agency-cost capital and labor (K, L).

We assume that when workers own the organization they pay an additional agency cost Z in order to employ a unit of difficult-to-monitor or specific capital K – a cost that is saved when K is employed under capitalist ownership.[13] By contrast, when the capitalists own the organization, they pay an additional agency cost H when they employ a unit of difficult-to-monitor or specific labor L – a cost that is saved when L is employed under labor ownership. No such additional costs are paid for easy-to-monitor and general-purpose labor and capital k and l when they are employed by either capitalists or workers.[14]

We denote with r and w the prices of respectively easy-to-monitor and/or general capital and labor, and with R and L the prices (net of agency costs) of respectively difficult-to-monitor and/or specific capital and labor. We also set the price of output equal to 1.

Under capitalist ownership, the surplus S^c of the firm is equal to:

$$S^c = Q\,(k, K, l, L) - [rk + RK + wl + (H + W)L] \qquad (18.1)$$

Under labor ownership, the surplus S^L of the firm is equal to:

$$S^L = Q\,(k, K, l, L) - [rk + (Z + R)K + wl + WL \qquad (18.2)$$

We may thus formulate the RE direction of causation by simply assuming that the firm maximizes S^c under capitalist ownership and S^L under labor ownership. Property rights influence technology because they involve changes in the relative costs of using factors. The relative prices of the high-agency-cost capital and labor are (H + W)/R under capitalist ownership and W/(Z + R) under workers' ownership. Thus, under standard assumptions, the intensity of high-agency-cost capital K relatively to the intensity of high-agency-cost labor L is higher under capitalist ownership than under labor ownership; or in other words, the technology T has an intensity K/L when the property rights P are characterized by capitalist ownership. In this framework, the value of the elasticity of substitution among factors becomes a measure of the 'strength' of the effects of changes of property rights on the nature of the technology.

We have seen that the NI approach considers a causation mechanism running in the opposite direction. For given technical assets, the firm is supposed to be owned by that factor able to earn the highest ownership rent. This rent is equal to the difference between the cost of employing the factor in a firm that is the property of the owners of the factor and the cost of employing it in a firm that is the property of other owners. We can therefore restate the NI direction of causation as follows:

For any given combination of factors employed in the firm, ownership of the firm will be acquired by the factor which can get the highest ownership rent. Therefore, capitalist property rights can prevail if, given the factors currently employed, $S^c \geqslant S^L$ or, alternatively:

$$ZK - HL \geqslant 0 \qquad (18.3)$$

Workers' property rights can prevail if, given the factors currently employed, $S^L \geqslant S^c$, or alternatively:

$$HL - ZK \geqslant 0 \qquad (18.4)$$

Technologies T characterized by a higher K/L ratios bias property rights P, making it relatively more appealing (or less disadvantageous) to have property rights P characterized by capitalist (instead of labor) ownership.

Thus the radical approach focuses on the choice of the firm's technical assets for given (capitalist or workers') ownership arrangements. By contrast, the new-institutionalist approach analyses the property rights arrangements of the firm for any given combination of factors employed in the firm. We say that we have an 'organizational equilibrium' when both the RE and NI directions of causation are simultaneously taken into account. For instance, in an organizational equilibrium, the behavior of the firm under particular ownership conditions must bring about technologies characterized by factor intensities that do not upset the initial ownership conditions.

The following definition of organizational equilibrium can therefore be given: an institution of production is in organizational equilibrium when it is defined by a system of property rights P and technical assets T such that T are the optimal technology under the property rights P, and P is the property rights system that maximizes ownership surplus when the technical assets T are employed in production.

Let:

$$(k^c, K^c, l^c, L^c) = \text{argmax } S^c\,(k, K, l, L) \tag{18.5}$$

$$(k^L, K^L, l^L, L^L) = \text{argmax } S^L\,(k, K, l, L) \tag{18.6}$$

Then a firm will be in a capitalist organizational equilibrium (COE) if:

$$ZK^c - HL^c \geqslant 0 \tag{18.7}$$

and in a labor organizational equilibrium (LOE) if:

$$HL^L - ZK^L \geqslant 0 \tag{18.8}$$

Condition (18.7) has an immediate intuitive meaning. Suppose that a firm is under capitalist ownership and that the production technique is such to maximize profits. Condition (18.7) implies that, with these technical assets, the ownership rent accruing to capitalists is at least as great as the rent which workers could obtain if they owned the firm. Hence, with this production technique, the workers would have no incentive to buy out the capitalists. This is what is meant by a capitalist organizational equilibrium. Condition (18.8) has an analogous intuitive meaning.

If we rearrange conditions (18.7) and (18.8) in the following ways:

$$K^c/L^c \geqslant H/Z \tag{18.7'}$$

$$K^L/L^L \leqslant H/Z \tag{18.8'}$$

we can see that both conditions are simultaneously satisfied if:

$$K^c/L^c \geqslant H/Z \geqslant K^L/L^L \tag{18.9}$$

Since the relative prices of the high-agency-cost capital and labor are $(H + W)/R$ under capitalist ownership and $W/(Z + R)$ under workers' ownership, we have that:

$$K^c/L^c \geqslant K^L/L^L \qquad\qquad (18.10)$$

(18.7') and (18.8') can be simultaneously satisfied, and we can have multiple organizational equilibria when (18.9) is satisfied.

Even if the four-factors model is a radical oversimplification of reality, it helps one to grasp the basic mechanisms by which property rights and technical assets, influencing each other, can generate multiple organizational equilibria.[15] If, for instance, capitalist property rights prevail, some of the capitalists' agency costs are saved and a higher proportion of high-agency-cost capital is employed, making capitalist rights more convenient. However, if workers' property rights had prevailed, some of labor's agency costs would have been saved and a higher proportion of high-agency-cost labor would have been employed, making workers' property rights more convenient. These interactions between property rights and technical assets are obviously much more complex when many factors interact within the same organization. However, a multiplicity of organizational equilibria seems to be an even more likely outcome in this more realistic setting.

VARIETIES OF CAPITALISM AS ORGANIZATIONAL EQUILIBRIA

The interactions between property rights and technical assets have the capacity to generate a variety of arrangements. Even if analysis is limited to capitalist economies, the varieties of capitalism which have characterized the world economy since the World War II provide a good example of the multiple ways in which rights and technologies can interact to generate multiple organizational arrangements.

In the post-World War II period, until the mid-1990s, different models of capitalism prevailed in the US, (West) Germany and Japan. In each of these economies there was a plurality of organizational arrangements. However, the stereotypes with which each model was characterized contained some truth in the sense that, in each system, network externalities in property rights and technologies involved the prevalence of some self-reinforcing organizational arrangements.

In comparison to Germany and Japan, the US was marked by a prevalence of firms based on Taylorism and Fordism, which were both developed and applied in the US. In this variety of capitalism, shareholders and management have strong liberties, including the freedom to fire workers easily. Workers are vulnerable to this freedom and have no right to a well-defined occupation or some generic job within a certain firm. The firm can be traded as a commodity, and a new management, on taking over the organization, can easily break the implicit contracts with the workers. This set of property rights is associated with technical assets characterized by the centralization of knowledge in the hands of management and by top-down coordination and innovations such that workers at the bottom of the hierarchy perform very detailed jobs and are simply required to execute very narrow and rigid instructions. Thus, following this highly imperfect stereotype, the 'American' variety of capitalism can be seen as an organizational equilibrium in which, *inter alia*, relatively weak property rights induce a low investment in workers' high-agency-cost skills and, vice versa, this configuration of technical assets entails that workers have scant incentives to acquire assets in firms. Specific machinery and centralized skilled scientific management are the necessary counterparts of this organizational model.

The post-war Japanese and German varieties of capitalism departed from the classical Taylorist–Fordist stereotype in two different ways. Both models relied on some decentralization of knowledge and bottom-up innovation. Japan relied very much on a company workers' capitalism mainly based on organizational rights. Whilst Japan was not the only country with firms offering lifelong employment, this organizational form was so prevalent in Japan that most people identify company workers' capitalism with that country. The German model was characterized not so much by strong rights at firm level as by strong centralized unions and widespread occupational rights.[16] Germany shared the existence of strong unions with many European countries, but its variety of capitalism was seen as an efficient blend between centralized workers' rights and their skills. As a consequence, the skills and the technology of the firms prevailing in the Japanese and German varieties of capitalism were biased in two different directions.

The Japanese model was also based on two complementary rights and technologies. This variety of capitalism emerged as a consequence of the political shocks which hit Japan after the end of World War II. At that time, the crackdown first on the traditional *zaibatsu* capitalist families and then on the centralized unions produced the *keiretsu* system. In this system, the workers had relatively strong rights but only within the organization – a circumstance that favored the development of organizational skills but backfired on organizational rights, reinforcing their institutional stability. More precisely, the post-war Japanese model was based on a distribution of rights which restricted the freedom to fire of shareholders and management, while complementary institutions, such as main banking and cross-shareholding, isolated the firm from the stock exchange and protected the workers' implicit contracts from takeovers. The Japanese variety of capitalism has also been based on complementary technical assets defining a consistent organizational equilibrium. The decentralization of a great deal of knowledge, bottom-up coordination and innovation, and rotation among different jobs led to the acquisition of remarkable team-specific skills difficult for outsiders to monitor. In turn, this configuration of technical assets implied that the long-term commitment to the firm and the job rights within it were valuable for both the organization and the workers.

The German model is also rooted in the political circumstances that have characterized the history of that country. In this case, centralized employers' and employees' associations have run the economy together with a centralized banking system. Consensus on the nature of the 'social market' characterized both the Christian Democratic and the Social Democratic Party, and it allowed the (West) German state to run the economy in cooperation with these two centralized associations.[17] The existence of these political actors granted economy-wide rights to workers.

While Japanese workers were safeguarded against the specificity of their skills by rights at firm level, German workers were (also) directly safeguarded against the firm-specificity of their skills.[18] Job specifications were set and standardized by the employers' associations and the unions, with the help of the state, which also organized an excellent system of vocational education consistent with the agreed job requirements. These types of arrangement allowed the development of skills that were 'occupation specific' but at the same time 'general purpose' in the sense that they could be applied in a large number of firms. Again, a self-reinforcing interaction characterized the relation between technological assets and property rights. A system of occupational rights made it convenient to develop a technology based on general-purpose skills. At the same time, the very existence of this technology was a strong incentive for the development of institutions providing the rights and safeguards for the numerous general-purpose skills employed under this technology. Thus, the German variety of capitalism is also likely to have emerged from a complex interaction between property rights and technical assets that generated a different kind of organizational equilibrium.

The high intensity of trade which characterized the post-World War II period did not involve a convergence of these varieties of capitalism towards a single economic model. By contrast, if we consider them as different organizational equilibria, we see how the high intensity of international trade may have favored a process of international differentiation.

From the organizational equilibria perspective, different varieties of capitalism rely on different rights that change the agency costs of using different technical assets. Thus, the different rights existing in the three major capitalist economies implied different factor prices, with the consequence that each of them had a different institutional comparative advantage and a different intensity in the use of the high-agency-cost technical assets. Thus, following the predictions of standard economic theory on international trade, they specialized in those sectors where they held a comparative advantage. In each variety of capitalism, the growing intensity of international trade expanded the sectors where property rights had the effect of abating agency costs and increasing the employment of certain technical assets. Inter-country institutional diversity was thus increased by expanding only those sectors where each national system of rights entailed a comparative institutional advantage in the use of the associated technical assets. At the same time, intra-country institutional diversity could be decreased by the fact that each country tended to abandon comparatively disadvantaged institutions. As international trade intensified, the varieties of capitalism were not bound to be reduced. Different types of organizational equilibria were still feasible and could contribute to its biodiversity.

GLOBAL RIGHTS AND INTELLECTUAL MONOPOLY CAPITALISM

While the increasing intensity of international trade may even stimulate institutional diversity, the global rules underlying financial integration and the regime of intellectual property rights have acted in the reverse direction. Unbounded capital mobility and the global enforcement of intellectual property rights came about in the 1990s after the fall of the socialist regimes, and they were formalized with the 1994 institution of the World Trade Organization (WTO) and the annexed TRIPS (Trade-Related Aspects of Intellectual Property Rights) agreement. Financial globalization has not only had the effect of introducing uniform, and often minimum standards, in the realm of finance; it has also applied a great deal of pressure on countries to reduce various forms of social protection (Rodrik 2011). It has greatly contributed to reducing the possible set of capitalist varieties, increasingly restricting their features to those compatible with the evaluations of international capital markets. The global regime of intellectual property rights has played an equally important, even if not similarly evident, role in the reduction of the biodiversity of the organizational equilibria underlying the different varieties of capitalism.

We saw above how Braverman maintained that the monopoly over knowledge to control each step of the labor process and its mode of execution is a characteristic feature of capitalism. However, not even Braverman mentioned the most extreme and significant step in this monopolization process: the privatization of knowledge and its direct transformation into the most valuable proprietary asset of the firm. This process, which has characterized the last two decades, motivates the addition of the word 'intellectual' to the term 'monopoly capitalism' used by Harry Braverman (Pagano 2012b).

The main characteristic of intellectual monopoly capitalism is that monopoly is not only due to the concentration of knowledge in the hands of capital and management advocated by Taylor. It becomes also a legal global monopoly on some pieces of technological knowledge. While patents and other forms of intellectual monopoly existed before the industrial revolution, they were considered as a necessary evil to encourage innovation. Their enforcement was weak, and it was limited by the fact that nation-states could enforce them only within the boundaries of their jurisdictions. With the institution of the 1994 TRIPS agreement intellectual monopoly was promoted to the rank of standard private property, and its enforcement became global. The privatization of property entails that no other individual can use a piece of knowledge even if it is by its nature non-rival and all individuals could use it without depleting its availability. Unlike traditional forms of private property that interfere with the liberty of the individual in a limited physical space, intellectual private property involves a global limitation of the liberties of the other individuals. Thus the enforcement of intellectual property became really effective only when it became global.

The reinforcement and the extension of intellectual property have been compared to the enclosure of common land that preceded the industrial revolution.[19] Also in this case, some commons were turned into exclusive private property. There is, however, a fundamental difference. In the case of land, the object of privatization was a local common that involved the legal positions of few individuals. By contrast, the privatization of intellectual property changes the legal positions of many individuals and has major implications for the international standing of different countries. Whilst privatizing land has only local implications, the holders of property rights on knowledge end up with global rights equivalent to the imperial powers of the past. They can decide whether a certain production process can be undertaken in particular country and they limit the future technological opportunities of other firms.

The existence of global rights in some important spheres of the economy implies that, in some cases, the choice of technical assets is limited to the set of them which is compatible with these rights and the related constraints on others' liberties. In some extreme cases, only one organizational equilibrium is possible and the number of possible varieties of capitalism may be seriously limited.

Indeed, the global privatization of much new knowledge has involved some sort of revenge by the Taylorist model on the German and Japanese organizational forms (or their stereotypes that were enviously studied by American firms in the late 1980s). Until the 1980s, one could have easily gained the impression that a Taylorist system of top-down coordination and innovation was bound to be outcompeted by a system which relied also on continuous bottom-up inputs. The precise instructions and routines issued by the former could be easily imitated by the latter, which was based on tacit knowledge and uncodified routines that made imitation by the former difficult. The privatization of intellectual property reversed the situation. The private appropriation of knowledge was easier when it was formalized and centralized in Taylorist–Fordist organizations. At the same time, the increased protection of private knowledge made it difficult to exploit the advantages of marginal bottom-up improvements, which were often constrained by patents and licenses.

With the massive use of private intellectual property rights, the separation between conception and execution has become much wider. Intellectual property rights have made conception the source of non-human technical assets that are often the most valuable part of the firms' capital. Execution is then driven by privatized intellectual capital to an extent that even Taylor, with his idea of well-defined tasks, would have found difficult to predict. Execution can be decentralized to cheap labor countries, while a distant ideation process increases the firm's capital in the form of proprietary knowledge. While there is still a remarkable variety of capitalist economies, one cannot exclude the possibility that a new form of 'global Taylorism' may prevail as the unique form of organizational equilibrium of the future world economy. The unbounded mobility of financial capital and the massive privatization of knowledge are very likely to apply pressure in that direction.

Privatized knowledge must now be included among the most important technical assets available to a firm, and the skills of an organization's members are likely to become highly co-specific to those assets. The extent of the knowledge owned by the firm sets limits on its possible future technological development, including the skills which are worth developing within the organization. Firms may find themselves in a virtuous circle where the ownership of intellectual assets stimulates the acquisition of the co-specific skills and, vice versa, the availability of these skills makes it possible to acquire new intellectual property rights. However, if a firm is to enjoy this virtuous circle, it must have monopoly on certain technical assets. This monopoly implies that some other firms will find themselves in a vicious circle: because of the lack of intellectual property rights, they do not find it convenient to enhance their skills, and because of the lack of the relevant skills, they are unable to acquire intellectual property. These virtuous and vicious circles can be seen as different organizational equilibria generated by different configurations of property rights and technical assets. The polarization of organizations between these different organizational equilibria may be another undesirable consequence of intellectual monopoly capitalism.

Globalization may involve a tendency to simplify the varieties of capitalism into two equilibria: a virtuous high-skills, high-IPR equilibrium for a few firms and a vicious low-skills, low-IPR equilibrium for many others (Pagano & Rossi 2004). The two main novelties of globalization – the integration of financial markets and the privatization of knowledge – push in the same direction. Grandori (Chapter 14 in this volume) observes that, whilst not all human capital can be disembodied from the minds of agents, the degree of inalienability of human capital from the agents producing it should be considered (at least partially) endogenous. Indeed, the post-WTO process of knowledge privatization has greatly increased the degree of alienability of human capital; and at the same time it has increased the reliability of financial control by firms. Privatized knowledge, like machines and buildings, can now be included among the firm's assets. Unlike the knowledge embodied in humans (who can always quit the firm), privatized knowledge is a secure asset contributing with increasing intensity to the financial value of the firm.

Financial markets have expanded because, thanks to TRIPS, much knowledge has been made alienable. Notwithstanding the much-publicized 'de-materialization' of production, an increased amount of assets has become the object of secure property rights to be exchanged on financial markets. At the same time, the globalization of finance has opened unprecedented options for financial capital, and it has induced each firm to compete, in all possible ways, to attract finance. This has greatly increased the pressure on each firm to increase the intensity of its capital disembodied from human beings and on which secure property rights can be defined.[20] Thus, financial global integration and the global privatization of knowledge are two mutually self-reinforcing processes which are likely to push all varieties of capitalism towards a single model characterized by the greatly increased alienability and reification of human capital.[21] Whilst a variety of organizational arrangements is unlikely to disappear, the coupling of these two processes may severely reduce the biodiversity of capitalism.

NOTES

1. I am very grateful to Anna Grandori for her comments and suggestions.
2. Technical assets include the human and non-human resources as well as the blueprints that allow their combinations for productive uses. The production function, defining these combinations, is not independent of human capabilities. The feasible technological combinations must be discovered by the agents and define the opportunities that are open to the economy (Arthur 2009). A differential development of combination capabilities can be stimulated by different factor prices (Allen 2011) and it is more likely to occur in neighboring characteristics of the product space (Hidalgo & Hausman 2009). Also property rights influence factor prices (see below in this chapter) and, therefore, the available technical assets.
3. Landini (2012) shows that the software industry division between open-source and proprietary software can be interpreted as a co-existence of multiple organizational equilibria.
4. There is a tension between these two direction of causation within the Marxian approach. The latter oscillates between technological determinism (stressing the primacy of technical assets) and property rights romanticism (new property rights shape individual incentives and technical assets). Cohen (1978) and Brenner (1986) are examples tending, respectively, towards the former and the latter approach. According to Pagano (2007b), this tension is rooted in the work of Marx and it is still relevant to evaluating the relevance of his contributions after the revival of institutional and radical economics.
5. See also Alchian (1984).
6. Contractual incompleteness plays an important role also in the 'new property rights' approach (Hart 1995). However, in the latter, the verification cost is either zero (total contractual completeness for some transactions) or infinitely high (total contractual incompleteness for some other transactions). In this setting the strictly positive investments in *ex post* verification capabilities by actors of private orderings (managers) or of public orderings (judges) cannot make sense. A theory of the firm is not really possible in this framework. By contrast, the contributions of Williamson (1985) and Calabresi and Melamed (1972) focus on *ex post* governance and can provide a useful starting point for developing Coase's (1937) analysis of the firm and of other institutions (Pagano 2010, 2012a).
7. See for instance Marglin (1974), Rowthorn (1974), Pagano (1985) and Bowles (1985, 1989).
8. According to Braverman, this is implicit in the following quotation from Taylor 'The managers assume . . . the burden of gathering together all the traditional knowledge which in the past has been possessed by the workmen and then classifying, tabulating, and reducing this knowledge to rules, laws, and formulae' (F. Taylor, quoted in Braverman 1974: 112)
9. Braverman refers to the following statement by Taylor: 'All possible brain work should be removed from the shop and centered in the planning or laying-out department' (F. Taylor, quoted in Braverman 1974: 113)
10. Braverman maintains that this is clearly pointed out by Taylor when he states that, unlike under traditional types of management, under scientific management the managers should give the workers

detailed instructions about each task to be performed. 'The most prominent single element in modern scientific management', Taylor writes, 'is the task idea. The work of every workman is fully planned in advance, and each man receives in most cases complete written instructions, describing in detail the task which he is to accomplish, as well as the means to be used in doing the work . . . This task specifies not only what is to be done, but how it is to be done and the exact time allowed for doing it . . . Scientific management consists very largely in preparing and carrying out these tasks' (Taylor, quoted in Braverman 1974: 118).

11. On the notion of agency costs see Jensen and Meckling (1976).
12. On the notion of organizational equilibria see Pagano (1992, 1993, 2011) and Pagano and Rowthorn (1994). According to Aoki (2001: 396), Pagano (1993) and Pagano and Rowthorn (1994) are two of the earliest analytical contributions to institutional complementarities. Pagano (2007a) distinguishes between weak and strong analytical complementarities. Aoki (2010) offers an innovative analysis of the complementarities that characterize the acquisition of cognition by the different types of corporations.
13. These additional agency costs will be paid not only when the workers rent high-agency-cost capital but also under alternative contractual arrangements where the workers borrow monetary capital and use high-agency-cost capital as collateral. On this point refer to note 9.
14. I concentrate on a model with only two types of capital and labor. Likewise, I consider only the extreme cases of 'pure capitalist' and 'pure labor' ownership. This is for analytical simplicity. Observe that the symbols could stand for different factors: this allows alternative interpretations of the model that could be used to study the outsider–insider problem in the labor market or the relation between financial and industrial capital.
15. The set of agency costs (Z,K) for which there are multiple equilibria increases with the elasticity of substitution among production factors (Pagano & Rowthorn 1994). The more malleable the technology, the greater the effect of the causation flow running from property rights to technology. In the limiting case of no substitutability among factors, there is only one couple of agency costs (Z,K) for which multiple organizational equilibria exist. Earle et al. (2006) show that the causation running from property rights to technology is stronger than the relation flowing in the opposite direction.
16. In Japan, workers had organizational rights, mainly in terms of job tenure and work organization, within a certain company. By contrast, in Germany the workers had (also) occupational rights on a certain activity intended to fulfill the same standards and the same job definition across all companies – a tradition rooted in never dismantled system of craft guilds (Epstein 2008). Japan approximated a 'company workers' variety of capitalism' while Germany was close to a 'unionized variety of capitalism' as defined in Pagano (1991).
17. Fioretos (2001) shows how the consensus on the nature of the German economy has shaped the approach to the European Community shared by both of the two major German parties, distinguishing them from the similar common approach of the Labour and Conservative parties in Britain. This continuity and these national differences can only be explained by considering the different characteristics of these two economies. For their analysis see also Wood (2001).
18. Estevez-Abe et al. (2001) observe that Germany is characterized by both high unemployment protection and high employment protection. Thus, there is some inducement to acquire both industry-specific and firm-specific skills. They observe (p. 152) that 'high unemployment protection is also important in so far as it allows workers to turn down job offers outside their previous industry or occupation. If compelled to accept a job offer outside the worker's core competencies, either because of low benefits or a strict requirement to accept almost any job offer, this undermines the worker's incentives to invest in industry-specific skills.' Thus, according to Estevez-Abe et al., it lies somewhere in between a model of 'company workers' capitalism' characterized by a system of organizational rights and a model of 'unionized capitalism' characterized by occupational rights. The characteristics of these 'ideal-types' of capitalism are outlined in Pagano (1991) and, with a different terminology, in Hall and Soskice (2001).
19. For instance, see Shiva (2001: 44–48) and Boyle (2003). On the industrial revolution see Vespasiani (2010). Whilst the private appropriation of knowledge is supposed to stimulate growth and innovation, there is growing evidence that, beyond a certain level, private appropriability hampers economic development (Hardin 1968; Heller & Eisemberg 1998; Dosi et al. 2006; Boldrin & Levine 2008; Pagano & Rossi 2004; David 2011) and, according to Pagano and Rossi (2009), it is one of the causes of the present depression.
20. By contrast, labor cooperatives flourish in regions where local banks have the relevant information on their clients (Gagliardi 2009).
21. Since knowledge is a fugitive resource on which it is increasingly difficult to define private property rights (Arrow 1996), Bowles (2004) predicts that, in the long run, its private appropriation is not sustainable.

REFERENCES

Alchian, A. (1984), 'Specificity, specialization and coalition', *Journal of Economic Theory and Institutions*, **140**, 34–39.

Alchian, A. and H. Demsetz (1972), 'Production, information costs and economic organisation', *American Economic Review*, 62, 777–795.

Allen, R.C. (2011), *Global Economic History: A Very Short Introduction*, Oxford: Oxford University Press.

Aoki, M. (2001), *Towards a Comparative Institutional Analysis*, Cambridge, MA: MIT Press.

Aoki, M. (2010), *Corporations in Evolving Diversity. Cognition, Governance and Institutions*, Oxford: Oxford University Press.

Arrow, K.J. (1996), 'Technical information and industrial structure', *Industrial and Corporate Change*, **5**(5), 645–652.

Arthur, W.B. (2009), *The Nature of Technology. What It Is and How It Evolves*, New York: Free Press.

Babbage, C. (1832), *On the Economics of Machines and Manufactures*, London: Charles Knight.

Boldrin, M. and D.K. Levine (2008), *Against Intellectual Monopoly*, Cambridge: Cambridge University Press.

Bowles, S. (1985), 'The production process in a competitive economy: Walrasian, Neo-Hobbesian, and Marxian models', *American Economic Review*, **75**, 16–36.

Bowles, S. (1989), 'Social institutions and technical change', in M. Di Matteo, R.M. Goodwin and A. Vercelli (eds), *Technological and Social Factors in Long Term Fluctuations*, New York: Springer-Verlag, pp. 66–87.

Bowles, S. (2004), *Microeconomics. Behaviour, Institutions and Evolution*, Princeton, NJ: Princeton University Press.

Boyle, J. (2003), 'The second enclosure movement and the construction of the public domain', *Law and Contemporary Problems*, **5**(66), 33–74.

Braverman, H. (1974), *Labour and Monopoly Capital*, New York: Monthly Review Press.

Brenner, R. (1986), 'The social basis of economic development', in J. Roemer (ed.), *Analytical Marxism*, Cambridge: Cambridge University Press, pp. 23–53.

Calabresi, G. and A. Douglas Melamed (1972), 'Property rules, liability rules, and inalienability: one view of the cathedral', *Harvard Law Review*, **85**(6), 1089–1128.

Cohen, G.A. (1978), *Karl Marx's Theory of History: A Defence*, Oxford: Oxford University Press.

Coase, R.H. (1937), 'The nature of the firm', *Economica*, pp. 386–405; reprinted in R.H. Coase (1988), *The Firm, the Market and the Law*, Chicago, IL: University of Chicago Press.

David, P.A. (2011), 'Mitigating "anti-commons" harms to science and technology research', SIEPR Discussion Paper. University of Stanford, CA.

Dosi, G., L. Marengo and C. Pasquali (2006), 'How much should society fuel the greed of innovators? On the relations between appropriability, opportunities and rates of innovation', *Research Policy*, **35**, 1110–1121.

Earle, J., U. Pagano and M. Lesi (2006), 'Information technology, organizational form and transition to the market', *Journal of Economic Behavior and Organization*, **60**, 471–489.

Epstein, S.R. (2008), 'Craft guilds in the pre-modern economy', *Economic History Review*, **61**, 155–174.

Estevez-Abe, M., T. Iversen and D. Soskice (2001), 'Social protection and the formation of skills: a reinterpretation of the welfare state', in P.A. Hall and D. Soskice (eds), *Varieties of Capitalism. The Institutional Advantages of Comparative Advantage*, Oxford: Oxford University Press, pp. 145–183.

Fioretos, O. (2001), 'The domestic sources of multilateral preferences: varieties of capitalism in the European Community', in P.A. Hall and D. Soskice (eds), *Varieties of Capitalism. The Institutional Advantages of Comparative Advantage*, Oxford: Oxford University Press, pp. 213–246.

Gagliardi, F. (2009), 'Financial development and the growth of cooperative firms', *Small Business Economics*, **32**(4), 439–464.

Hall, P.A. and D. Soskice (2001), 'An introduction to varieties of capitalism', in P.A. Hall and D. Soskice (eds), *Varieties of Capitalism. The Institutional Advantages of Comparative Advantage*, Oxford: Oxford University Press.

Hardin, G. (1968), 'The Tragedy of the Commons', *Science*, **5**(162), 1243–1248.

Hart, O. (1995), *Firms, Contracts and Financial Structure*, Oxford: Oxford University Press.

Heller, M.A. and R. Eisemberg (1998), 'Can patents deter innovation? The anticommons in biomedical research', *Science*, **280**, 698–701.

Hidalgo, C. and R. Hausman (2009), 'The building blocks of economic complexity', *Proceedings of the National Academy of Sciences*, **106**(26), 10570–10575.

Hodgson, G. (1996), 'Organisational form and economic evolution: a critique of the Williamsonian hypothesis', in U. Pagano and R. Rowthorn (eds), *Democracy and Efficiency in the Economic Enterprise*, London, UK and New York, USA: Routledge.

Hodgson, G. (2001), *How Economics Forgot History: The Problem of Historical Specificity in Social Sciences*, London, UK and New York, USA: Routledge, pp. 98–115.

Jensen, M.C. and W.H. Meckling (1976), 'Theory of the firm: managerial behaviour, agency costs and ownership structure', *Journal of Financial Economics*, **3**(4), 305–360.

Landini, F. (2012), 'Technology, property rights and organizational diversity in the software industry', *Structural Change and Economic Dynamics*, **23**(2), 137–150.

Marglin, S. (1974), 'What do bosses do?' *Review of Radical Political Economy*, **6**, 60–112.

Pagano, U. (1985), *Work and Welfare in Economic Theory*, Oxford: Basil Blackwell.

Pagano, U. (1991), 'Property rights, asset specificity, and the division of labour under alternative capitalist relations', *Cambridge Journal of Economics*, **15**(3), 315–342; reprinted in G. Hodgson (ed.), *The Economics of Institutions*, The International Library of Critical Writings in Economics, Cheltenham, UK and Northampton, MA, USA: Edward Elgar.

Pagano, U. (1992), 'Organisational equilibria and production efficiency', *Metroeconomica*, **43**(1–2), 227–246.

Pagano, U. (1993), 'Organizational equilibria and institutional stability', in S. Bowles, H. Gintis and B. Gustafson (eds), *Markets and Democracy*, Cambridge: Cambridge University Press, pp. 86–115.

Pagano, U. (2007a), 'Legal positions and institutional complementarities', in F. Cafaggi, A. Nicita and U. Pagano (eds), *Legal Orderings and Economic Institutions*, London, UK and New York, USA: Routledge, pp. 54–83.

Pagano, U. (2007b), 'Karl Marx after new institutionalism', *Evolutionary and Institutional Economic Review*, **4**(1), 27–55.

Pagano, U. (2010), 'Marrying in the cathedral: a framework for the analysis of corporate governance', in A.M. Pacces (ed.), *The Law and Economics of Corporate Governance*. Cheltenham, UK and Northampton, MA, USA: Edward Elgar, pp. 264–289.

Pagano, U. (2011), 'Interlocking complementarities and institutional change', *Journal of Institutional Economics*, **7**(3), 373–392.

Pagano, U. (2012a), 'No institution is a free lunch: a reconstruction of Ronald Coase', *International Review of Economics*, **59**(2), 27–55.

Pagano, U. (2012b), 'The crisis of intellectual monopoly capitalism', *Quaderni del Dipartimento di Economia Politica*. *Università di Siena*. WP N. 634 http://www.econ-pol.unisi.it/dipartimento/it/node/1630.

Pagano, U. and M.A. Rossi (2004), 'Incomplete contracts, intellectual property and institutional complementarities', *European Journal of Law and Economics*, **18**(1), 55–76.

Pagano, U. and M.A. Rossi (2009), 'The crash of the knowledge economy', *Cambridge Journal of Economics*, **33**(4), 665–683.

Pagano, U. and R. Rowthorn (1994), 'Ownership, technology and institutional stability', *Structural Change and Economic Dynamics*, **5**(2), 221–243.

Rodrik, D. (2011), *The Globalization Paradox. Democracy and the Future of the World Economy*, New York: W.W. Norton & Co.

Rowthorn, R. (1974), 'Neo-classicism, Neo-Ricardianism and Marxism', *New Left Review*, **86**, 63–82.

Samuelson, P. (1957), 'Wage and interest: a modern dissection of Marxian economic models', *American Economic Review*, **47**, 884–912.

Shiva, V. (2001), *Protect or Plunder? Understanding Intellectual Property Rights*, London, UK and New York, USA: Zed Books

Vespasiani, D. (2010), 'La rivoluzione industriale inglese nell'ottica degli equilibri organizzativi', Studi e Note di Economia, Anno XV, n. 2, pp. 227–60.

Williamson, O.E. (1985), *The Economic Institutions of Capitalism*, New York: Free Press.

Wood, S. (2001), 'Business, government, and patterns of labor market policy in Britain and the Federal Republic of Germany', in P.A. Hall and D. Soskice (eds), *Varieties of Capitalism. The Institutional Advantages of Comparative Advantage*, Oxford: Oxford University Press, pp. 247–374.

19. Open innovation and organizational boundaries: task decomposition, knowledge distribution and the locus of innovation

Karim R. Lakhani, Hila Lifshitz-Assaf and Michael L. Tushman

This chapter contrasts traditional, organization-centered models of innovation with more recent work on open innovation. These fundamentally different and inconsistent innovation logics are associated with contrasting organizational boundaries and organizational designs. We suggest that when critical tasks can be modularized and when problem-solving knowledge is widely distributed and available, open innovation complements traditional innovation logics. We induce these ideas from the literature and with extended examples from Apple, the National Aeronautics and Astronomical Agency (NASA) and LEGO. We suggest that task decomposition and problem-solving knowledge distribution are not deterministic but are strategic choices. If dynamic capabilities are associated with innovation streams, and if different innovation types are rooted in contrasting innovation logics, there are important implications for firm boundaries, design and identity.[1]

INTRODUCTION

Abernathy's (1978) seminal empirical work on the automotive industry examined the relations between a productive unit's boundary (all manufacturing plants), its organizational design (fluid versus specific), and its ability to execute product and/or process innovation. Abernathy's work and his associated ideas of dominant designs and the locus of innovation have been central to scholars of innovation, research and development (R&D) and strategy. Similarly, building on March and Simon's (1958) ideas of organizations as decision-making systems, Woodward (1965), Burns and Stalker (1966), Lawrence and Lorsch (1967 [1986]) and Thompson (1967) explored the relations between organization boundaries (business units), organization design (differentiation and integration), and innovation in a set of industries that varied by uncertainty. This early empirical work led to a wide range of scholarship investigating the relations between a firm's boundaries, its organizational design and its ability to innovate.

In organizational economics, the notion of organizational boundaries has been rooted in transaction cost logic. Economists favor an explanation based on minimizing transaction costs (Coase 1937). Many activities related to innovation and the design and production of goods and services are difficult to contract on the open market. These transaction costs make it efficient for the emergence of firms and associated boundaries that reduce these costs by integrating these activities inside the firm (Williamson 1975, 1981). This transaction cost tradition has clarified the relations between innovation and the logic of differentiation between the firm and its surrounding environment (or market). This literature has focused on understanding which set of activities should be inside or outside the firm's boundaries (e.g. Pfeffer & Salancik 1978 [2003]; Grandori 2001; Santos & Eisenhardt 2005; Jacobides & Billinger 2006; Lavie et al. 2011). The primary approaches employed by these traditions have been rooted in cost–benefit, knowledge access or resource dependence analyses (e.g. Scott & Davis 2007).

Organization theory and strategy scholars have noted that core to value creation is the production of complex goods and services requiring ongoing knowledge development and transfer amongst diverse settings (March & Simon 1958; Chandler 1977; Grandori 2001; Nickerson & Zenger 2004). The burden of continuous knowledge creation imposes high coordination costs that are best minimized through a managerial hierarchy as opposed to a distributed approach in open markets (Thompson 1967; Tushman & Nadler 1978; Kogut & Zander 1992; Nonaka & Takeuchi 1995). For anything but the simplest problems, the visible hand of an organization's management is required to define and select problems that firms solve for value creation (Chandler 1990; Nickerson and Zenger 2004). Finally, a significant body of research in organization theory is rooted in setting a firm's boundaries in a way that protects it from dependencies in its task environment and puts boundaries around critical tasks, power and competence contingencies (e.g. Thompson 1967; Pfeffer & Salancik 1978 [2003]; Aldrich 1979; Santos & Eisenhardt 2005).

However, users outside the firm are also an important source of functionally novel innovations (von Hippel 1988, 2005). These users constitute self-organizing communities that freely share knowledge (Baldwin & von Hippel 2011; Franke & Shah 2003; Faraj & Johnson 2011, O'Mahony & Lakhani 2011). The open source software movement crystallized an alternative innovation ecosystem where external-to-the-firm user communities design, develop, distribute and support complex products on their own or in alliance with (or in some cases opposition to) incumbent firms (Lakhani & von Hippel 2003; von Hippel 2005; Boudreau & Lakhani 2009; Lerner & Schankerman 2010; O'Mahony & Lakhani 2011). The rise and prevalence of community or peer innovation, with its contrasting loci of innovation and non-hierarchical bases of organizing, pose a challenge to the received theory of innovation, the firm and the firm's boundaries.

In this chapter, we attempt to reconcile these divergent scholarly perspectives on the relationship between firm boundaries and the locus of innovation. We argue that the innovation and organizational design literatures must move beyond debates between open versus closed boundaries and instead embrace the notion of complex organizational boundaries where firms simultaneously pursue a range of boundary options that include 'closed' vertical integration (e.g. Lawrence & Lorsch 1967 [1986]; Nadler & Tushman 1997; Knott 2001), strategic alliances with key partners (e.g. Lavie & Rosenkopf 2006; Rothaermel & Alexandre 2009), and 'open'[2] boundaries and open innovation (e.g. von Hippel 2005; Chesbrough 2006). This simultaneous pursuit of multiple types of organizational boundaries results in building organizations that can attend to these complex, often internally inconsistent, innovation logics and associated organization design requirements (O'Reilly & Tushman 2008; Boumgarden et al. 2012; Gulati & Puranam 2009).

We suggest that two contingencies drive the degree to which a firm chooses along this closed-to-open boundary continuum; the degree to which critical tasks can be decomposed and the extent to which problem-solving knowledge for these tasks is distributed. These task and knowledge contingencies are not deterministic; they involve strategic choice by the firm and shift as the product life cycle evolves (Child 1972; Grandori 2001; Foss et al. 2010; Foss, Chapter 4 in this volume). Choices about task decomposition and knowledge distribution inform the choice of firm boundaries. The ability to understand the nature of these critical task characteristics and, in turn, link these choices to the firm's boundaries may be an important dynamic managerial capability (Helfat and Peteraf 2003). Further, because firms have several critical tasks that differ along these decomposition/knowledge dimensions, the firm is likely to have multiple boundary types.

We also suggest that open innovation may increasingly crowd out more traditional intra-firm innovation. Such a shift in the locus of innovation has profound implications for the design, boundaries, and identity of incumbent firms. Two secular trends in the economy drive the increasing importance of open innovation. The first is the increasing prevalence and importance of 'digitization' (Greenstein 2010), wherein information and physical products are represented in the binary language of computers. While initially confined to pure information products and software production, digitization is a trend that now envelopes large parts of the economy. Importantly, material objects are undergoing transformations so that their 'information shadow' (Baldwin & Clark 2006), that is, the information component of any material object, is now being represented as a digital good. Thus material and physical objects can now be created, represented, modified and transformed with the same relative ease as software goods. An implication of this digitization is the opportunity to apply the principles of task decomposition widely used in the computer hardware and software industries (Baldwin & Clark 2000) to many more parts of the economy.

The second and related trend is the increasing number of actors that can participate in knowledge production at very low costs. Over the past three decades, the internet and other advanced information and network technologies have democratized the tools of knowledge creation. This trend has significantly eased the cost of knowledge dissemination, reduced communication and coordination costs, and made it easier to find and access distributed knowledge from almost anywhere in the world (Benkler 2006; Castells 2000; Shirky 2008).

Key to our understanding of the relations between organizational design, firm boundaries and innovation is the ability of a firm and its leaders to engage in strategic decomposition of underlying innovation tasks and understand the associated locus of knowledge required to effectively deliver products. The strategic decomposition and locus of knowledge perspective argues that the architecture of products is not fixed either in the firm or in industries. Instead, executives (managers and technologists) choose to partition and repartition the problem space such that they have the option to access distributed knowledge above and beyond the traditional emphasis on intra-firm technological development.

Strategic task decomposition enables organizations to access the distributed knowledge of external individuals or communities without resorting to traditional means of backwards or forwards integration. Task decomposition in the context of low-cost communication has catalyzed the emergence of self-organizing communities that are as effective as firms in innovation and knowledge production (O'Mahony & Lakhani 2011). Thus previously firm-based innovation activities may now be done on the outside in market or community settings (Boudreau & Lakhani 2009).[3] At the same time, firms may decide to exit relationships with external or open sources of innovation for a perceived propriety advantage associated with more integrated task choices. We argue that a firm's ability to 'refactor', or dynamically compose or decompose critical tasks, is an important determinant of the firm's boundaries and, in turn, its ability to innovate.

Hand in hand with strategic decomposition is the recognition that the appropriate knowledge required to solve innovation problems is both widely distributed (Hayek 1945) and sticky (von Hippel 1988). The widespread and general phenomenon of user-based innovation is rooted in users having unique needs and solution information (von Hippel 1988). Users exploit this knowledge to create novel innovations (Riggs & von Hippel 1994). Thus the locus of innovation shifts to where knowledge may be the stickiest to transfer, often with users that are widely distributed in the economy. Users may also form self-organizing collectives and communities where need and solution information are rapidly discovered and transferred under a common free-revealing paradigm (Fjeldstad et al. 2012; Franke & Shah 2003; Lakhani & von Hippel 2003; Baldwin & von Hippel 2011).

With the democratization of the tools of both knowledge production and dissemination, a range of actors outside traditional firm boundaries have access to unique solution knowledge that may be applicable to innovation tasks within firms (Fjeldstad et al. 2012; Jeppesen & Lakhani 2010; Boudreau et al. 2011). Such task decomposition and the fact that widely distributed actors have access to differentiated knowledge push the locus of innovation outside traditional firm boundaries. We suggest that task decomposition and knowledge distribution provide a framework for the choice of firm boundaries. These strategic contingencies lead to a different set of design and boundary choices than the traditional contingencies of asset specificity, information processing or strategic 'coreness' (see also Grandori 2001; Nickerson & Zenger 2004). Finally, we suggest that firm-centered innovation logic is fundamentally different and inconsistent from open innovation logic, and that open innovation logic is increasingly gaining momentum. If so, our theories of innovation, organizational design and organizational change must capture the tensions between these contrasting innovation modes.

Our chapter is organized as follows. First we analyze Apple and its ability to alter (open and close) its boundaries across a range of activities, to build an empirical grounding for our theoretical reconciliation. The next section outlines the extant literature on firm boundaries and the locus of innovation. We then present drivers of complex boundaries by illustrating the joint impact of strategic task decomposition and distributed knowledge for incumbent firms as diverse as LEGO and NASA. The following section induces a model of innovation and complex organizational boundaries. We suggest several core contingencies associated with the firm's boundaries and discuss implications of organizing when firms must attend to multiple and inconsistent innovation logics. Finally, we suggest implications of complex organizational boundaries for the organization theory, strategy and innovation literatures.

COMPLEX AND DYNAMIC BOUNDARIES AT APPLE

All computer manufacturers, such as Apple, Hewlett Packard (HP), Lenovo, and Dell, address the following five distinct technical domains in order to produce and sell a computer system: (1) hardware; (2) operating system; (3) standards (the main specifications that allow for interoperability); (4) user experience (the user interface); and (5) applications. Figure 19.1 lays out how these domains have been addressed by PC manufacturers by locating them in a matrix comprised of task decomposability and the degree of knowledge distribution. For simplicity purposes we present a binary choice for both axes, between high and low task decomposition; that is, modular and integrated tasks (see also Nickerson & Zenger 2004) in the rows, and narrow and broad knowledge distribution for the columns. This results in a range of boundary choices for firms, from internal development, to complex intra-firm structures (e.g. ambidextrous designs), to working with partners and/or consortia, to working with markets or communities.

In Figure 19.1, the lower-left quadrant shows the traditional, internally driven organizational model for innovation. Managers of the firm determine that the relative task decomposition opportunities are low and requisite problem-solving knowledge is all within the firm, resulting in internally developed innovation. The upper-left quadrant indicates that the firm managers have decomposed innovation tasks in a way that enables external parties to contribute, however the knowledge required to accomplish such tasks lies within a strategic partner. The lower-right quadrant indicates that while task decomposition is low, the benefits of having several actors participating in the creation of innovations, via a consortium, are high enough that the incumbent firm absorbs the added cost of integration. Finally, the upper-right quadrant indicates that the firm has enabled task decomposition in a way that allows a range of actors to join in by market or community-based approaches. The distinction between using a market or a

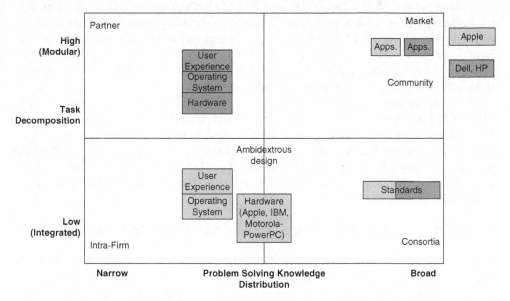

Figure 19.1   Apple and the computer industry

community approach to innovation is grounded on the relative degree of social relations and interdependence a firm has with the external parties. Markets rely mostly on formal contracts and arm's-length relationships with suppliers, while communities require the firm to have employees actively participate in the innovation process (see for example Rosenkopf et al. 2001; West & O'Mahony 2008).

An ambidextrous design (ie. intra-firm structural heterogeneity with structural link-ages) is an appropriate design choice when there is strategic interdependence after tasks have been decomposed and where there is knowledge heterogeneity either within the firm or with the firm and external actors (O'Reilly & Tushman 2008; Rothaermel & Alexandre 2009; Lavie et al. 2011). Ambidextrous designs build in boundary and structural hetero-geneity such that the firm can operate simultaneously in distinct innovation modes.

Figure 19.1 shows that a typical personal computer (PC) firm in the 1990s chose a strategy of problem decomposability across all technical domains. Most vendors had chosen Intel and/or AMD as suppliers of the hardware microprocessor and had relied on Microsoft Windows for the operating system and the user experience. These partner-ships allowed PC manufacturers to work as integrators of the dominant technologies developed by Intel and Microsoft. The supply of applications was left to an unregulated market where any actor could create software and sell directly to users (see Morris & Ferguson 1993). Standards for interoperability were developed through various insti-tutes for electrical and electronic engineers (IEEE), internet engineering task force (IETF) committees and other ad hoc organizations (for example the WiFi standard, the TCP/IP standard and the USB standard).

In contrast, driven by Steve Jobs's strategic point of view, Apple followed an inte-grated and internal strategy for most of its PC stack (Isaacson 2011). In the late 1990s the hardware used by Apple was built in close consortium between IBM and Motorola and created a software operating system and user interface that was unique and different from the Windows–Intel industry standard. No one had the rights to either use or modify the integrated combination of Apple's hardware, operating system and user interface stack. Similar to the rest of the PC industry, applications were developed in an unregu-lated market of developers. Figure 19.1 illustrates the contrast between Apple's primarily integrated internal development strategy and the practice of working on decomposable tasks with partners in the rest of the computer industry.

However, by the late 1990s, Apple was in financial and technical trouble. The Microsoft–Intel-based platform was significantly outperforming Apple systems in technical and cost performance. Apple failed to update its operating system to modern requirements and the financial press speculated that the firm was in its last throes. Apple was on the losing side of a dominant design that comprised Intel-architecture hardware and Microsoft-originated operating system, user interface and compatible applications (Cusumano and Selby 1995).

Strategic Decomposition of the Operating System and Working with Communities

In the early to mid-1990s Apple began three independent attempts to update and mod-ernize its computer operating systems. All three attempts failed due to lack of appropri-ate programming talent and poor execution of the various projects. In 1996, Apple's executives decided that they did not have the internal capability to completely invent a

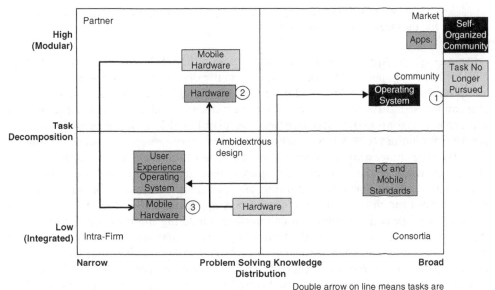

Figure 19.2   Dynamic boundaries at Apple

new operating system and recommended that the next version of the operating system be obtained through an acquisition of NeXT Software (the company Steve Jobs founded after he was ousted from Apple in 1985). Apple released the open source components of its operating system as a separate software distribution called 'Darwin' in 2000.

The NeXT operating system itself was based on the Mach kernel, developed at Carnegie Mellon University as a research project to further advance knowledge of operating systems, and on two open source software projects, FreeBSD and NetBSD, that have had thousands of contributors participate in them. Apple thus took the fruits of the open source community and leveraged it for its own next-generation operating system, released in 1999: OS X. Figure 19.2(1) illustrates the integration of the open source community in Apple's proprietary process. The OS X operating system now powers all Apple products including personal computers and mobile devices. Note that Apple did not abandon its own operating system development efforts. Rather, some of the modules of the software were now developed in concert with the community, and some internally.

Apple acknowledges the importance of open source communities in this core aspect of its product:

As the first major computer company to make Open Source development a key part of its ongoing software strategy, Apple remains committed to the Open Source development model. Major components of Mac OS X, including the UNIX core, are made available under Apple's Open Source license, allowing developers and students to view source code, learn from it and submit suggestions and modifications. In addition, Apple uses software created by the Open Source community, such as the HTML rendering engine for Safari, and returns its enhancements to the community.

Apple believes that using Open Source methodology makes Mac OS X a more robust, secure operating system, as its core components have been subjected to the crucible of peer review for decades. Any problems found with this software can be immediately identified and fixed by Apple and the Open Source community.[4]

An analysis of Apple's use of open source within the OS X system reveals that over 500 distinct components of the operating system use open source components from over 180 projects. Thus while the popular perception of Apple is as the paragon of proprietary and closed software development, its involvement in and use of open source reveals a more nuanced approach that leverages the distributed knowledge of external open source communities to its strategic advantage.

At the same time, while open source works within the core of the operating system, the key elements of the user interface and the user interaction model are proprietary and remain under Apple's strict purview and oversight. Indeed the Darwin operating system cannot run most of the Macintosh OS X applications as it does not have access to Apple's proprietary graphical user interface, rendering libraries, or engine. Thus, Apple has been able to separate the technical problems that are core to its success (but invisible to its users) and has pursued an open boundary approach in that area. In sharp contrast, in areas that require direct consumer interaction that differentiates Apple from Microsoft, Apple made proprietary and closed investments in technologies and designs that it does not make available to anyone else.

Apple's decomposition of the operating system enables it to simultaneously use open and closed boundaries for its strategic tasks. This attention to strategic boundary management has enabled Apple to release a new version of the operating system every one to two years. The use of open boundaries has a significant cost advantage, as a large portion of Apple's operating system software is developed externally to the firm by others.

Simultaneous Decomposition and Reintegration

Apple's actions around the computer processor for its various products indicate a sophisticated understanding of managing firm boundaries to meet strategic objectives. Up to 2005, Apple had relied on the PowerPC chip architecture for microprocessors within its computer line. The PowerPC alliance was a joint technology venture between IBM, Apple and Motorola to create chips that would compete against Intel processors for a range of computer applications. In effect Apple and its partners were in the custom chip design business against a competitor that had orders of magnitude more volume.

In the early 2000s, Apple discovered that its PowerPC partnership was not keeping up with the technological requirements needed to stay competitive. This prompted the firm to exit the PowerPC consortium and enter into a special partnership with Intel to incorporate its standard chip design into Apple's computing platform. In this case Apple devolved the advantages of vertical integration for the benefits of working within the framework of Intel's dominant design. Apple customers were not purchasing its products for its microprocessor, but instead wanted access to the proprietary Apple operating system and user interface. As long as the chips by Intel kept up with the standards in computing there was no strategic reason for Apple to be engaged in activities in chip design and manufacturing. Hence Apple decomposed the innovation tasks related to hardware to an external partner (Figure 19.2(2)).[5]

In contrast, in mobile devices, Apple decided to reject the prevalent dominant chip design of the mobile-ARM architecture and instead invested in acquiring several firms that enabled Apple to design its own custom chips. In this case the logic of following the dominant design via decomposition is reversed. In Apple's assessment, the technical performance criteria for mobile chips are strategically core. As such, there was a strategic logic to have a proprietary approach that minimizes power consumption and maximizes speed and responsiveness customized to its own device. Apple's assessment of the technological frontier in mobile chips was that adopting the dominant design would not provide strategic benefits to the firm. Adopting this standard would instead allow its competitors to achieve similar performance outputs and claim parity in performance in mobile devices. All of the recent Apple mobile computing devices now have this custom chip technology (Figure 19.2(3)).

The simultaneous acceptance of dominant design in microprocessors for computers and the rejection of the dominant design for mobile applications illustrate the linkages between choices of task decomposition and the firm's boundary. These examples also illustrate that adoption of a dominant design is contingent on a firm's strategy and the shifting basis of competition. Apple's ability to alter its boundaries at these critical junctures illustrates that the locus of innovation shifts are based not just on a cost minimization logic, but also on access to knowledge that provides competitive advantage.

Figure 19.2 provides a full accounting of Apple's current stage of boundaries in the various aspects of its business. The figure shows that Apple has been able to continuously shift boundaries to suit strategic, technical and competitive needs. These innovation patterns have the quality of shifting firm boundaries from integrated, intra-firm boundaries to ever more complex intra- and extra-firm boundaries. These set of firm boundaries include intra-firm differentiation, external partners and consortia, as well as leveraging open innovation. These boundary choices are associated with strategic decisions as to whether the product is decomposable or is inherently integrated (at a point in time) as well as the locus of solution knowledge. Apple keeps integrated components within its control and hierarchy, while it has explored more complex boundary relations for components that can be decomposed and whose solution knowledge is widely distributed.

Note that Apple employed these complex and dynamic boundaries in the context of performance crises associated with its prior more simple approach to boundary management. These organizational shifts were, in turn, associated with the transformation of Apple as a firm. Such complex sets of boundary types and boundary relations triggered significant identity, governance, intellectual property (IP) and associated leadership issues within Apple (Isaacson 2011). In particular, Apple's organizational design evolved such that it could simultaneously attend to the complex challenge of holding some innovation within the firm's control while other innovation was executed with communities of actors outside Apple and, in the extreme, with anonymous contributors.

INNOVATION AND FIRM BOUNDARIES: THE CONTROL OF CRITICAL CONTINGENCIES

Since Schumpeter (1947), Barnard (1938 [1968]), Chandler (1962) and Myers and Marquis (1969), scholars have emphasized innovation as a source of a firm's competitive advantage. Much of the early innovation work was rooted in R&D investments, the building of internal R&D capabilities, and the associated specialized assets associated with the invention, patenting and execution of portfolios of innovations (e.g. Allen 1977; Cohen & Levinthal 1990; Clark & Fujimoto 1991; Dougherty & Heller 1994; Fleming 2001; Dougherty & Dunne 2011).

There is extensive literature on designing organizations to create streams of innovations (e.g. O'Reilly & Tushman 2008). In a world of uncertainty and asset-specific investments, transaction costs logic argues that firms with tight boundaries outperform markets in the production of innovative outcomes (e.g. Williamson 1975, 1981; Knott 2001). Similarly, the knowledge-based view of the firm suggests that when products or services are complex and non-decomposable, the firm outperforms market mechanisms (e.g. Kogut & Zander 1996; Grandori 2001; Nickerson & Zenger 2004). In such 'M'- or 'U'-form firms, authority is vested with senior leaders who create structures, processes, capabilities, cultures and information processing capabilities such that firms gain the benefits of specialization as well as integration (e.g. Tushman & Nadler 1978; Nonaka & Takeuchi 1995).

In a similar spirit, the resource dependency literature is rooted in a logic where the boundaries of the firm are established to maximize the control of critical contingencies. For those contingencies that are not internalized, the firm acts to minimize dependence on, gain control of, co-opt or negotiate with critical external actors (Pfeffer & Salancik 1978 [2003]; Davis & Greve 1997; Aldrich 2008). This design literature with its firm focus and efficiency logic is associated with specifying the firm's formal boundaries as well as its power, competencies and identity boundaries (Santos & Eisenhardt 2005).

Strategic contingencies shift over time. Research on the sociology of innovation and technical change suggests that new markets open with a burst of technical variants competing for dominance. This era of technical ferment ends with the closing of industry standards or dominant designs (e.g. Abernathy & Utterback 1978; Tushman & Rosenkopf 1992; Rao 1994) For example the automobile engine (Abernathy 1978; Rao 1994), power system (Hughes 1983), watch (Landes 1983), chemical and dye (Murmann 2003), disk drive (Christensen 1997) and flight simulator (Rosenkopf et al. 2001) industries were initiated by periods of technological variability. During these eras of ferment, integrated products compete for both technical and market dominance (Anderson & Tushman 1990). Such periods of uncertainty are closed as dominant designs emerge by either competitive selection, coalition or law (see Suarez 2004; Murmann & Frenken 2006).

Once a dominant design emerges, the nature of innovation shifts to the product's components, process innovation becomes more intense and innovation becomes more incremental (see Rao 1994; Rosenkopf & Tushman 1998; Murmann 2003). Eras of incremental change are associated with a shake-out in the product class and increases in the size and scale of those firms associated with the industry standard (e.g. Jenkins & Chandler 1975; Wise 1985; Anderson & Tushman 2001). These eras of incremental change, in turn, are disrupted by subsequent technological discontinuities which trigger a subsequent technological cycle (Tushman & Anderson 1986; Tushman & Murmann 1998). There are profound task, organizational, and boundary implications to these technology cycles. During eras of ferment, integrated firms with organic structures are better at exploration; while during eras of incremental change, more mechanistic structures are better at exploiting a given technical trajectory (e.g. Abernathy 1978; Lawrence & Lorsch 1967 [1986]; March 1991).

At these transitions, when firms shift from integrated innovation to modular or decomposed innovation, firms also shift to more intense process innovation and grow in scale. These punctuated changes are associated with higher levels of both boundary differentiation as well as more extensive structural and cultural integration (e.g. Van de Ven et al. 1989; Schoohoven et al. 1990; Romanelli & Tushman 1994). Finally, for incumbents that survive these dynamics, the next wave of variation, selection and retention is executed through a range of boundary-expanding mechanisms including ambidextrous structures, alliances or joint ventures (e.g. Gulati 1995; Lavie & Rosenkopf 2006; Tushman et al. 2010).

The literature on managing innovation streams has a focal firm as its unit of analysis (or in some cases the product class) and has built an extensive literature on the architectures, structures, cultures, linking mechanisms, alliances and governance modes associated with firms that can exploit as well as explore within the firm as well as with selected partners (e.g. Lavie & Rosenkopf 2006; Helfat et al. 2007; O'Reilly & Tushman 2008; Boumgarden et al. 2012; Agarwal & Helfat 2009). Such complicated designs to execute innovation streams are also associated with distinctive identities that permit contradictory architectures and their associated complex boundaries to coexist (Gioa et al. 2000).

This innovation and organization design literature has a logic where the focal firm internalizes those innovation components that are core to its strategy even as it builds complex boundaries and internally contradictory architectures to explore and exploit. For example, Ciba Vision extended its innovation beyond incremental innovation in conventional lenses (within Ciba Vision's extant organization) to include daily-disposable and extended-wear lenses (via an ambidextrous design), as well as developing an age-related macular degeneration product (executed in collaboration with an Australian partner). These set of complex structures and associated boundaries were managed by the senior team anchored with Ciba Vision's identity as a firm dedicated to 'healthy eyes for life' (Tushman et al. 2010). The driving impulse in this literature on innovation and organization boundaries and design has been the control or buffering of the firm's context through complex boundary selection and management.

Innovation and Open Boundaries: The Firm in the Context of Distributed Innovation

In contexts where computational costs are low and widely available and where distributed communication is inexpensive, open or peer innovation communities displace organization-based innovation (Baldwin & von Hippel 2011). In these contexts, communities of peers spontaneously emerge to freely share information on innovation production as well as problem solving. Such radically decentralized, cooperative, self-organizing modes of problem solving and production are in sharp contrast to organizationally centered innovation (Lakhani and von Hippel 2003; von Hippel 2005; von Hippel and von Krogh 2003; Murray and O'Mahony 2007)

Open innovation is most clearly seen in open source software development. Open source software development depends on many individuals contributing their time, for free, to a common project. Legally, participants retain copyrights for their contributions but then license them to anyone at no cost (see Benkler 2006; Lerner & Schankerman

2010 for more detail). These self-organized communities develop their own emergent social structure (e.g. O'Mahony and Ferraro 2007; Fleming and Waguespack 2007). Such communities of developers rely on the availability of easy communication, the modularity of the project and intrinsic motivation. This open software innovation regime creates robust products and is equivalent to private market software development methods in features, functionality and quality (Raymond 1999; Benkler 2006; Lerner & Schankerman 2010).

Community-based innovation is not limited to software development. Peer modes of innovation, where actors freely share and co-create innovation, have been documented in a range of product domains. For example, von Hippel and his colleagues have documented user and peer innovation in heart–lung machines, gas chromatography, mountain bikes and in many other products (Franke & Shah 2003; von Hippel 2005). In each of these examples, user communities spontaneously emerge to create new markets. Once the product is developed, only then do incumbents enter and shift the nature of innovation to cost and scale.

While communities are associated with the creation of new markets and the adjudication of uncertainty during the associated eras of ferment, autonomous problem solving also occurs through prize and contest-based mechanisms that allow for free entry but emphasize competition amongst peers. Perhaps the most famous early example of innovation contests is the British government's contest to find a way to accurately gauge longitude at sea (Sobel 1995). While contests are associated with prizes, the prizes are often relatively small and most problem solvers do not win. Yet analyses of these tournament settings reveal large-scale entry into tournaments, far above predictions from an economics perspective (Che & Gale 2003; Boudreau et al. 2011). This extensive external participation indicates the presence of complex intrinsic and extrinsic motivations (Boudreau and Lakhani 2009; Jeppesen and Lakhani 2010; Boudreau et al. 2011).

Both community- and contest-based problem solvers are motivated by a heterogeneous blend of intrinsic and extrinsic motivations and the emergent social properties of interactions in online settings (Lakhani & Wolf 2005; Fleming & Waguespack 2007; Gulley & Lakhani 2010; Boudreau et al. 2011). When the problems are modular in nature, these communities have had dramatic impact on problem solving outcomes (see Kogut & Metiu 2001; Lakhani & von Hippel 2003). These anonymous communities are self-motivated, self-selected and self-governed (von Krogh et al. 2003; Boudreau et al. 2011; Dahlander & Gann 2010). In these anonymous contexts, self-selection drives both participation and effort (von Krogh et al. 2003; Boudreau & Lakhani 2009).

The availability of inexpensive computation power and ease of communication permits a fundamentally different form of innovation; a mode of innovation that is rooted in sharing and openness free of formal boundaries and formal hierarchy. If so, these non-market, peer innovation methods promise to complement, and under some conditions displace, firm-centered innovation models (e.g. Wikipedia's substitution for Microsoft Encarta and the *Encyclopedia Britannica*). For incumbent firms, community-based innovation modes stand in sharp contrast to their historically anchored organizationally based innovation mode.

To the extent that market and non-market innovation modes are complements, firms build multiple and contrasting innovation regimes in service of innovation streams (O'Reilly & Tushman 2008; Boumgarden et al. 2012; von Hippel & von Krogh 2003).

Such paradoxical, internally inconsistent innovation modes require, in turn, organizational designs, complex boundaries and senior team attention to such contrasting requirements (Smith & Lewis 2011; Andriopoulos & Lewis 2009). In contrast, if these distributed communities dominate incumbents at new-product creation and are effective in modular problem solving, these communities will displace the traditional firm in key domains of the innovation system.

Solution Generation and Selection Knowledge and Locus of Innovation

Under what conditions do these various innovation modes dominate? King & Lakhani (2012) develop a framework to reconcile the coexistence of various modes of organizing innovation from internal development to markets using voting, approval contests, prizes and tournaments, and to communities. Building on Campbell's (1969) evolutionary concepts, they argue that the central tasks in organizing for innovation are two knowledge-based activities: (1) generating a range of solutions to an innovation problem; and (2) selecting the appropriate solution(s) from the myriad of alternatives available (Terwiesch & Ulrich 2009).

Based on this variation and selection approach to innovation (see also Vincenti 1994; Murmann & Frenken 2006), King & Lakhani (2011) develop a knowledge-based approach to the locus of innovation (see also Nickerson & Zenger 2004; Grandori 2001). If the knowledge needed to accomplish either knowledge generation or selection is narrowly held in the firm, the associated innovation boundaries will be fundamentally different than when knowledge is more widely distributed amongst multiple external actors and disciplines. The more either solution generation or selection knowledge is broadly held, the greater use of open boundaries. In contrast, to the extent that either solution or selection knowledge is narrowly concentrated in the firm, the more internal boundaries dominate (see Figure 19.3).[6]

As tasks become more modular (or decomposable) and as solution and use knowledge is more widely distributed, the locus of innovation shifts to open communities. If so, the nature of the incumbent's identity, its structures, associated boundaries, culture and incentives cannot be rooted in theory and research anchored on cost, control and extrinsic incentive premises. An innovation model based on traditional firm and more open assumptions requires a theory of when and under what conditions different types of boundaries are associated with innovative outcomes. Further, if dynamic capabilities are rooted in multiple types of innovation executed simultaneously, we must build a theory of the firm that can handle complex boundaries, organizational designs and associated complex identities (see also Pratt & Foreman 2000; Santos & Eisenhardt 2005; Murray & O'Mahony 2007).

DRIVERS OF DYNAMIC BOUNDARIES IN INCUMBENT FIRMS

Core to our perspective on the locus of innovation and complex organizational boundaries is the ability of senior executives to engage in strategic task decomposition (or reintegration) based on their firm's shifting competitive context. The Apple example provided

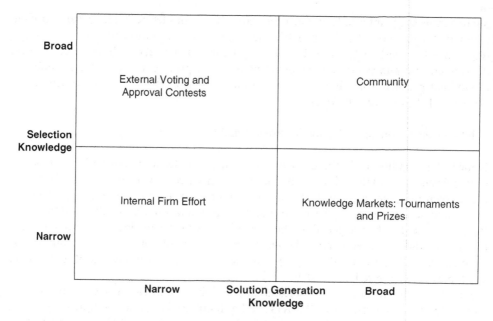

Figure 19.3   Generation and selection knowledge and locus of innovation

an illustration of a firm taking advantage of the advances in task modularity in its industry and, in turn, accessing distributed knowledge by opening (and closing) its boundaries
to external actors. Building on our Apple example, we examine the response of LEGO
to community toy development and NASA's space life sciences laboratory to open innovation. We use these examples to induce a contingent model of complex organizational
boundaries, locus of innovation and innovation outcomes.

LEGO

LEGO Group's experience with complex boundaries illustrates how an organization
stumbled into the advantages of decomposition and distributed knowledge and then
learned to effectively use this capability for subsequent innovation efforts. Founded in
1932 to make toys for children, the firm's main product line since 1949 has been plastic
'bricks' that enable creative play and ignite imagination amongst children around the
world. The bricks business at LEGO has been traditionally organized with the firm
having core competence in both the manufacturing process (extremely high-tolerance
plastic injection moldings) and the creation of various themes and scenes that are sold as
pre-packaged playsets.

As extensively documented by Antorini (2007), LEGO, initially unbeknownst to the
company and outside of its control, attracted legions of adult fans, the so-called Adult
Fans of LEGO (AFOL). These engaged users self-organized into various online communities and shared knowledge on creative designs and use of bricks for a set of complicated
projects. These communities of passionate fans not only wrapped their personal identity
around AFOL, but also innovated in the classic user innovation sense by modifying and

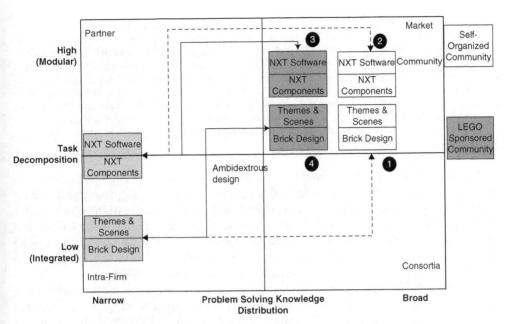

Figure 19.4   Dynamic boundaries at LEGO

extending the original bricks, inventing new bricks and developing new designs (e.g. von Hippel 1988). The community went as far as creating an online software tool kit where both designs for new bricks as well as new LEGO inspired creations were modeled and shared. Built just like an open source community, the AFOL members openly shared designs, tools and techniques to collectively enhance their experience with LEGO bricks (see Figure 19.4(1)). LEGO executives initially considered these user communities a minor 'shadow market' and did not engage with them in a meaningful manner (Hatch & Schultz 2010).

In 1998 Lego released a brick-based robotics kit called LEGO Mindstorms aimed primarily at children. The kit, with its 727 parts, enabled children to create and program robots that could perform various tasks. However, within weeks of the release of the Mindstorms kit, adult enthusiasts discovered that these kits also served their intellectual curiosity about robots. One of them, a Stanford University graduate student, Kekoa Proudfoot, within months of the release, reverse engineered the kit and released to the internet all his detailed findings including the underlying software for the robot's operations.

The software release led to a burgeoning online community that created their own Mindstorm programming kits. These kits included the creation of custom and more user-friendly software language and an open source operating system to operate the Mindstorms bricks (LegOS). Soon there were more engineers and software developers working on Mindstorm development outside the firm than within it.

Within LEGO there were divergent opinions about how to deal with external communities innovating, without permission, on their products. As described by Koerner (2006):

Lego's Danish brain trust soon realized that their proprietary code was loose on the Internet and debated how best to handle the hackers. 'We have a pretty eager legal team, and protecting our IP is very high on its agenda,' Nipper says. Some Lego executives worried that the hackers might cannibalize the market for future Mindstorms accessories or confuse potential customers looking for authorized Lego products. After a few months of wait-and-see, Lego concluded that limiting creativity was contrary to its mission of encouraging exploration and ingenuity. Besides, the hackers were providing a valuable service. 'We came to understand that this is a great way to make the product more exciting,' Nipper says. 'It's a totally different business paradigm – although they don't get paid for it, they enhance the experience you can have with the basic Mindstorms set.

LEGO's decision to allow community innovation to flourish resulted in the establishment of dozens of websites devoted to sharing third-party robotics programs that built systems such as soda machines and blackjack dealers, and the creation of new sensor and capabilities that were well beyond the original kit. Over 40 guidebooks were written to help users extend the capability of the Mindstorms kits. Just like the AFOL, LEGO executives followed a benign neglect strategy with these communities, allowing them to exist but not impacting their own internal direction (see Figure 19.4(2)).

In 2004, LEGO realized that its external community had done more to add value to LEGO than its own internal efforts and decided to formally integrate key external contributors for the release of Mindstorms NXT (Koerner 2006). Initially limited to four community members with expertise in sensors and software, the Mindstorms User Panel (MUP) closely collaborated with LEGO R&D to improve the next release of the product. The MUP members provided rapid feedback on a range of technical and market issues and further suggested new features and configuration that would make the user experience standout:

> Once the MUPers signed on, they sent numerous suggestions to Lund (the LEGO Manager responsible for NXT) and his team. The executives responded with appeals for feedback on planned improvements. 'We would ask them about a planned feature,' Lund says, 'and within half an hour, there would be a four-page email on it.' The Lego team was eager to piggyback on the work MUP members had already done.

LEGO then decided to further increase the number of MUP members to over 100 participants and credits their involvement with the successful launch of the NXT program (Hatch and Schultz 2010), see Figure 19.4(3).

While LEGO was pushed into supporting community-based innovation with the Mindstorms experience, the firm has now embraced this open innovation mode throughout its customer-facing operations. LEGO has established an ambassadors program that selects 75 individuals from its user communities to work hand in hand with LEGO staff on a range of innovation and product development issues. LEGO is also experimenting with having users showcase their custom designs and then create an ability to sell them to other interested users (see Figure 19.4(4)). More generally, LEGO has integrated communities inside its major product lines so that users can showcase their talents and creations. These activities are now part of LEGO's new business unit, Community, Education and Direct (CED), which contributes 15 percent of revenues and is growing twice as fast as the larger LEGO Group (Hatch and Schulz 2010).

This shift to these more complex boundaries at LEGO, managing innovation through internal as well as open mechanisms, was not easy to execute. These shifts in managing innovation were only executed under crisis conditions and under a new, externally recruited leadership team. This new senior team transformed LEGO by broadening its innovation mechanisms to include complex intra-firm structures as well as open innovation. This use of complex organizational boundaries in service of innovation streams was coupled, in turn, with transformational organization changes in LEGO's vision, identity, culture, structures and competencies (Hatch & Schultz 2010).

NASA – Space Life Sciences

On the surface, space sciences represent the ultimate in completely vertically integrated programs where all elements are done internally. NASA has had the monopoly on civilian United States (US) space travel for the past more than 50 years. Historically the space agency has worked in close connection with select and elite aerospace and defense contractors for the joint development of space vehicles and programs. NASA contractors are closely integrated into its innovation and decision-making activities.

Since 2008, NASA's Space Life Science Directorate (SLSD) has launched a series of pilot projects to examine whether community and contest-based models of innovation development might feasibly be applied to a variety of technical challenges that have traditionally been managed internally or with traditional suppliers. Central to this approach has been significant effort by SLSD innovation management to determine which tasks are amenable for broadcast search and possible solution generation by external providers. SLSD staff decomposed previously integrated problems into challenges that could be put out to the rest of the world for solving.

During 2009–10, SLSD initiated three pilot projects with leading open innovation platforms (InnoCentive, TopCoder, Yet2.com) to connect NASA problems with worldwide problem-solving communities. Worldwide engagement in solving NASA's problems was extremely high. The seven problems posted on InnoCentive engaged over 2900 problem solvers from 80 countries and yielded solutions from 347 individuals. On average each problem had 49 independent solution submissions. Previously intractable innovation issues such as forecasting of solar events, improved food barrier layers, and compact aerobic resistive device designs were rapidly resolved in communities.

NASA's experience with the forecasting of the solar events indicates how open innovation can substitute for traditionally firm-based innovation approaches. Unexpected solar flares wreak havoc on space equipment and are dangerous to the health of astronauts in orbit. Since the start of the space program, NASA has invested significant financial and intellectual resources towards the development of better flare forecasts. After years of investment, the best algorithms achieved a 55 percent prediction accuracy, slightly better than tossing a coin. NASA decided that this challenge would be suitable for contest-based problem solving. Working with InnoCentive, NASA engineers developed a problem statement that sufficiently described the required innovation in a way that transformed the problem from one of helio-physics to a general computational development. The challenge was posted on InnoCentive and had a reward amount of $30 000. In a three-month time period over 500 individuals expressed interest in trying to solve the problem by downloading the problem statement and signing the solver agreement. At the close of the contest 11 individuals submitted solutions. The winning solution

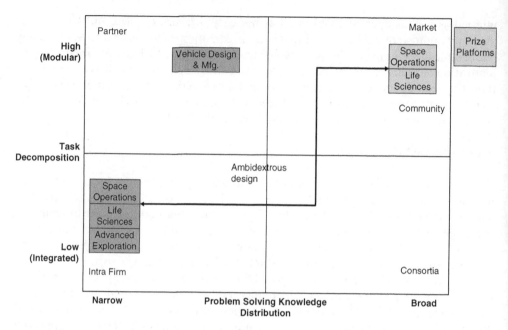

Figure 19.5   Dynamic boundaries at NASA

came from a retired telecommunications engineer. Using only ground-based equipment instead of the traditional use of orbiting spacecraft, this algorithm improved forecasting accuracy to 85 percent.

The extraordinary results of the pilot program prompted NASA to build out a generalized capability of decomposing tasks from various parts of space operations and to consider using external innovation communities as a routine part of its research and development efforts. In this case, contrary to Apple and LEGO, NASA did not build out its own community of external solvers. Instead NASA chose to leverage the investment of existing commercial platforms that have amassed via the internet hundreds of thousands of individuals who have an interest in solving scientific and technical problems (see Figure 19.5). However, similarly to Apple and LEGO, NASA's shift to more dynamic innovation boundaries was initiated under performance pressures and was accompanied by changes in NASA's culture, capabilities, structure and identity as it attempted to manage internal and open innovation modes simultaneously.

OPEN INNOVATION AND COMPLEX ORGANIZATIONAL BOUNDARIES

In settings where a product's core tasks can be modularized and where the costs of communication are low, traditional modes of organizing for innovation may not be comparatively effective or efficient. Under these ubiquitous conditions, open innovation, as exemplified by communities and contests, transforms the economics and social organization of innovation activities. Traditional organizing models based on cost minimization,

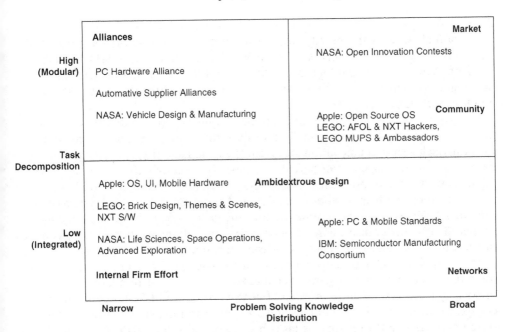

Figure 19.6   Task Decomposition, Problem Solving Knowledge Distribution, and Locus of Innovation

power, control of contingencies and extrinsic motivation, and where the locus of innovation is either within the firm or with the firm and trusted partners, must be supplemented with organizing models rooted in logics of openness, sharing, intrinsic motivation, and communities.

What are the contingent variables that push innovation from more traditional closed and hierarchical modes to more open and distributed modes? We suggest that the fundamental contingent variables in selecting innovation modes and associated boundaries are the extent to which the product is integrated in nature and the extent to which problem-solving knowledge is distributed (see Figure 19.6). When core tasks are integrated in nature (e.g. Apple's consumer experience, NASA's advanced exploration or LEGO's plastic brick toys) and problem-solving knowledge is concentrated, traditional intra-firm innovation logic applies (see also Nickerson & Zenger 2004). Under these conditions, firms internalize R&D and build an innovative culture, capabilities, absorptive capacities and processes that locate solution search and evaluation within the firm. These intra-firm boundaries vary from simple functional boundaries to more complex ambidextrous designs.

However, if problem-solving knowledge for an integrated product or service is broadly available and distributed, firms may choose to participate in networks where co-creation with external partners becomes a feasible alternative. The development of technology standards is a canonical example; however, firms also employ consortia and other forms of networks to drive innovation (IBM's semiconductor manufacturing consortium provides a vivid illustration; King et al. 2011). Similarly, increasing modularity via task decomposition, without the requisite expansion of knowledge distribution, leads firms to develop alliances with limited other organizations that can fulfill specialized tasks. PC hardware alliances between system integrators and Intel and AMD are the most common examples. A similar logic drove Apple's embrace of Intel. More generally, firm-driven alliances emerge when task decomposition increases (the automobile industry is another example).

In sharp contrast, when the product can be decomposed (or modularized) and when problem-solving knowledge is broadly dispersed, the locus of innovation shifts outside the firm. Such a shift in innovation locus requires incumbent firms to engage with external communities in open, transparent, collaborative relations (for example, NASA's relations with external problem solvers; LEGO's relations with its involved users; and Apple's relations with applications suppliers and anonymous operating system collaborators). When costs of collaboration are low, the greater the task's modularity and the greater the knowledge dispersion, the more open innovation and its associated complex organizational boundaries displace intra-firm innovation.

These shifts from closed to open innovation are associated with organizational transformations as they involve integrated changes in the firm's structure, boundaries, competencies, culture and identity. As seen at NASA, Apple and LEGO, these punctuated changes occur under crisis conditions and are typically initiated by top teams. Further, these boundaries shift over time as tasks become more or less strategic. At Apple, for example, its shift in mobile processors from open to closed innovation reflected its judgment about the strategic value of integrated mobile chips. Finally, firms are made up of portfolios of innovation types. For example, LEGO makes traditional plastic blocks even as it makes Mindstorm robots; NASA innovates internally on advanced exploration projects even as it employs open innovation on a range of modular tasks; and Apple innovates internally on customer experience even as it innovates with communities in applications and its operating system. The more complex the firm's innovation streams, the more complex its set of innovation logics, the more complicated and internally inconsistent its organizational architecture and associated set of boundaries.

The organization design issues associated with the combination of open and closed innovation modes are substantial because these innovation modes are themselves rooted in fundamentally inconsistent organizing logics and because they go against the inertia of the incumbent's history. As seen at LEGO, NASA and Apple, such complex innovation streams involve complex and heterogeneous identities, complex boundaries and boundary-spanning capabilities, and complex governance modes (e.g. see also Fleming & Waguespack 2007; O'Mahony & Bechky 2008). Firms must build on the capacity to attend to paradox and contradiction as open and closed innovation logics are based on contrasting organizing assumptions. The more complex the set of boundaries spanned, the greater the importance of a firm's absorptive capacity (Cohen & Levinthal 1990). But where absorptive capacity has been traditionally related to R&D spending and its associated enhanced combinative capabilities (e.g. Kogut & Zander 1992; Rothaermel & Alexandre 2009), in an open innovation context, absorptive capacity includes both combinative as well as collaborative capabilities (e.g. Rosenkopf et al. 2001; King & Lakhani 2011).

Finally, if open and closed innovation modes are complementary yet internally inconsistent, the firm's senior team must attend to and deal with both innovation logics.

Agency associated with innovation streams and the associated complex organizational boundaries is rooted in strategic choices of task integration (or decomposition) as well as the leaders' diagnosis of knowledge distribution (Nickerson and Zenger 2004; Jeppesen and Lakhani 2010; King and Lakhani 2012). Thus our Apple example illustrates strategic choice in both task decomposition in operating systems as well as task integration for mobile hardware and user interface. Once complex innovation modes are chosen, the associated organizational architectures and boundaries are executed in settings that can handle the identity and innovation logic conflicts and punctuated changes associated with operating in open and closed innovation modes simultaneously (e.g. Gioia et al. 2000; Smith & Tushman 2005; Kaplan & Tripsas 2008).

While open and closed innovation modes may be complementary, when might they be substitutes? As products and services become more modularized and as communication costs drop such that dispersed knowledge is widely available, open innovation communities emerge that increasingly displace closed innovation (Benkler 2006; Baldwin & von Hippel 2011; O'Mahony & Lakhani 2011). Under these increasingly common conditions, open innovation does not complement firm-based innovation, but rather is a substitute (e.g. EMI's inability to deal with new forms of music generation, funding, production and distribution). If so, incumbents may be pushed out of generating anything but incremental and/or process innovation (von Hippel 2005). It may be that new entrants dominate incumbents in new product creation by relying on community innovation for all substantive innovation except for innovation in customer experience and/or product integration. For example, new entrants LuLuLemon and Threadless innovate in women's yoga apparel and fashion T-shirts, respectively, by relying on community innovation in product generation and selection. If community innovation does substitute for firm innovation, the incumbent may switch its innovation strategy to focus on incremental innovation and scale and partner with (or acquire) open-oriented new entrants for new products.

IMPLICATIONS AND CONCLUSIONS

Open innovation, enabled by low-cost communication and the decreased costs of memory and computation, has transformed markets and social relations (Benkler 2006). In contrast to firm-centered innovation, open innovation is radically decentralized, peer based, and includes intrinsic and pro-social motives (Benkler 2006; von Hippel 2005). While the community nature of peer innovation is developing its own literature, and we understand the nature and social structure of these communities (e.g. O'Mahony & Lakhani 2011; O'Mahony & Ferraro 2007; Rosenkopf et al. 2001), the impact of this innovation mode on the firm is not well understood. We do not yet have a theory of the firm, either for incumbents or new entrants, which takes into account community innovation. Thus far, the impact of open innovation on the organization and strategy literatures has been minimal (e.g. see Argote 2011).

The literature in organizational theory and innovation is firmly rooted in the focal firm managing its transaction costs, minimizing its dependence on its context, and building absorptive capacity based on R&D and combinative relations with selected partners. Open innovation, with its fundamentally different organizing assumptions, is at least a complement, if not a substitute, for firm-based innovation. If so, our theory of innovation, organizational design and leadership for innovation must be informed by these contrasting innovation modes. The literature on the management of innovation has been built on a base of industrial product-oriented research in a world where communication costs across boundaries were substantial. Exploration now increasingly resides outside the boundaries of the traditional firm. It is inconceivable that today's models of organizations and innovation reflect the reality of innovation in a world that is ever more open and modularized. Our organizational, innovation and leadership literatures need to reflect and reconcile the implications of open innovation models.

As open and firm-based innovation are based on contrasting assumptions of agency, control, motivation and locus of innovation, our emerging theories of organizing for innovation must reflect these paradoxical and internally inconsistent innovation modes. Our innovation research must move to the institutional level as we explore how communities inform and shape the firm, and how the firm shapes and leverages its communities in service of its innovation streams (e.g. Rosenkopf et al. 2001; O'Mahony & Lakhani 2011; Jacobides & Winter forthcoming). Similarly, if open and market-based innovation are complements and the firm's boundaries are contingent on the product's degree of modularity and knowledge distribution, multiple types of boundaries will be employed to manage innovation. These boundaries will range from traditional intra-firm interfaces to complex inter-firm relations (e.g. ambidextrous designs), to webs of interdependence with partners, to interdependence with potentially anonymous communities. Just how are the mechanisms associated with leading complex intra-firm boundaries (e.g. O'Reilly & Tushman 2008) and relations with partners (e.g. Rothaermel & Alexandre 2009) different from shaping relations in open communities (e.g. Fjeldstad et al. 2012; O'Mahony & Ferraro 2007)?

The theory of innovation and complex organizational boundaries can build on extant literature on paradox (e.g. Andriopoulos & Lewis 2009) and extend this work to contradictory innovation modes. These paradoxical innovation modes require theory and research on governance, incentives, intellectual property, professional and organizational identity, and organizational cultures to attend to these heterogeneous innovation requirements (e.g. Gioia et al. 2000; Baldwin & von Hippel 2011; Murray & O'Mahony 2007). As so much of this work on dynamic boundaries involves senior leaders making choices involving contrasting innovation modes in the context of the firm's history, it is also important to understand how managers think about innovation and organizational design in a way that admits these contradictions (e.g. Smith & Tushman 2005; Kaplan & Tripsas 2008; Smith & Lewis 2011).

Finally, we have focused here on the challenges faced by incumbent firms having to respond to increasingly open innovation requirements. Much work needs to be done on the characteristics of new entrants that are born in contexts already rooted in open innovation. It may be that the founding of firms anchored in open innovation is fundamentally different than that of traditional entrepreneurial start-ups. It may also be that firms like LuLuLemon or Threadless build their initial business models based on open innovation logic and only deal with more traditional innovation and organizational dynamics when they go to scale (Lakhani & Kanji 2009).

While the theoretical and research implications of contrasting innovation modes and associated complex boundaries are substantial, so too are the implications for managerial choice and agency. If open and firm-based innovation are complements, firms must chose which tasks will be executed in each innovation mode. We suggest that these choices are contingent on the extent to which critical tasks can be decomposed and the extent to which the tasks' knowledge requirements are concentrated. These strategic choices need then to be executed with the systems, structures, incentives, cultures and boundaries tailored to open and firm-based innovation modes. Further, if the firm is ever more dependent on open communities, how do leaders act to influence these external communities? Finally, senior teams must build their own personal capabilities to deal with contradictions as well as their firm's ability to deal with contradictions (Smith & Lewis 2011). While building internally contradictory organizational architectures is difficult (see O'Reilly & Tushman 2011; O'Reilly et al. 2009), building these architectures to attend to contrasting innovation modes will be more challenging.

In sum, in contexts of increasing modularity and decreased communication costs, open innovation will at least complement, if not increasingly substitute, for more traditional innovation modes. We have suggested a set of contingent variables associated with building organizational boundaries that attend to task and associated knowledge requirements. As these task requirements are not stable, these organizational boundaries are inherently complex and dynamic. Further, open innovation is rooted in the ability of external actors to directly influence the rate and direction of innovation activity, and is associated with a fundamentally different set of organizing assumptions than traditional firm-based innovation. This set of contrasting innovation modes, where traditional firm-based innovation logic is ever more replaced by open innovation and its associated boundary complexities and organizational tensions, represents an important opportunity for scholars of strategy, innovation and organizations. These challenges also represent a great opportunity for those leaders and senior teams that can take advantage of these contrasting innovation modes, paradoxical organizational requirements and associated dynamic boundaries.

NOTES

1. We sincerely thank Paul Adler, Carliss Baldwin, Anna Grandori, Eric von Hippel and Charles O'Reilly for their critique and suggestions for improvements for this chapter. All mistakes and omissions are our own. The authors acknowledge the support of Harvard Business School's Division of Research and Faculty Development. The Harvard–NASA Tournament Lab also supported Karim Lakhani's work.
2. By 'open' we mean that problem-solving needs and knowledge flow both inside and outside the firm via interaction with multitudes of external actors who could be embedded in communities or participating in innovation platforms.
3. Markets feature many distributed actors that are working independently, in parallel and often in competition to solve innovation problems. Communities, in contrast, feature actors that are highly socialized and are working collectively on interdependent tasks to create solutions to innovation problems.
4. http://www.apple.com/opensource/.
5. Gilson et al. (2009) provide an interesting perspective on Apple's journey in manufacturing outsourcing by focusing on its decision to sell its logic board manufacturing plant to SCI along with a parts purchase contract and a collaborative innovation agreement.
6. Note that in contrast to Figure 19.2, King and Lakhani (2012) do not explicitly concern themselves with task decomposition: instead they focus on the distribution of knowledge for both the generation and selection of innovations.

REFERENCES

Abernathy, W.J. (1978), *The Productivity Dilemma: Roadblock to Innovation in the Automobile Industry*, Baltimore, MD: Johns Hopkins University Press.

Abernathy, W. and J.M. Utterback (1978), 'Patterns of industrial innovation', *Technology Review*, **80**, 40–47.

Agarwal, R. and C.E. Helfat (2009), 'Strategic renewal of organizations', *Organization Science*, **20**(2), 281–293.

Aldrich, H. (1979), *Organizations and Environments*, Englewood Cliffs, NJ: Prentice-Hall.

Aldrich, H. (2008), *Organizations and Environments*, Stanford, CA: Stanford Business Books.

Allen, T.J. (1977), *Managing the Flow of Technology: Technology Transfer and the Dissemination of Technological Information within the R&D Organization*, Cambridge, MA: MIT Press.

Anderson, P. and M. Tushman (1990), 'Technological discontinuities and dominant designs: a cyclical model of technological change', *Administrative Science Quarterly*, **35**(1), 604–633.

Anderson, P. and M. Tushman (2001), 'Organizational environments and industry exit: the effects of uncertainty, munificence and complexity', *Industrial and Corporate Change*, **10**(3), 675–711.

Andriopoulos, C. and M.W. Lewis (2009), 'Exploitation-exploration tensions and organizational ambidexterity: managing paradoxes of innovation', *Organization Science*, **20**(4), 696–717.

Antorini, Y.M. (2007), *Brand Community Innovation: An Intrinsic Case Study of the Adult Fans of LEGO Community (Doctoral Dissertation)*, Copenhagen Business School: Copenhagen, Denmark.

Argote, L. (2011), 'Introduction to the Special Issue', *Organization Science*, **22**(5), 1121–1122.

Baldwin, C.Y. and K.B. Clark (2000), *Design Rules: The Power of Modularity*, Cambridge, MA: MIT Press, pp. 299–328.

Baldwin, C. and E. von Hippel (2011), 'Modeling a paradigm shift: from producer innovation to user and open collaborative innovation', *Organization Science*, **22**(6), 1399–1417.

Baldwin, Carliss Y. and Kim B. Clark (2006), 'Between "knowledge" and "the economy": notes on the scientific study of designs', in B. Kahin and D. Foray (eds), *Advancing Knowledge and the Knowledge Economy*, Cambridge, MA: MIT Press.

Barnard, C.I. (1938 [1968]), *The Functions of the Executive*, 30th Anniversary edn, Cambridge, MA: Harvard University Press.

Benkler, Y. (2006), *The Wealth of Networks: How Social Production Transforms Markets and Freedom*, New Haven, CT: Yale University Press.

Boudreau, K.J. and K.R. Lakhani (2009), 'How to manage outside innovation', *MIT Sloan Management Review*, **50**(4), 69–76.

Boudreau, K.J., N. Lacetera and K.R. Lakhani (2011), 'Incentives and problem uncertainty in innovation contests: an empirical analysis', *Management Science*, **57**(5), 843–863.

Boumgarden, P., J. Nickerson and T.R. Zenger (2012), 'Sailing into the wind: exploring the relationships among ambidexterity, vacillation, and organizational performance', *Strategic Management Journal*, **33**(6), 587–610.

Burns, T. and G.M. Stalker (1966), *The Management of Innovation*, London: Tavistock Publications.

Campbell, D.C. (1969), 'Variation and selective retention in socio-cultural evolution', *General Systems: Yearbook of the Society for General Systems Research*, **16**, 69–85.

Castells, M. (2000), *The Rise of the Network Society*, 2nd edn, Oxford, UK and Malden, MA: Blackwell Publishers.

Chandler, A.D. (1962), *Strategy and Structure: Chapters in the History of the Industrial Enterprise*, Cambridge, MA: MIT Press.

Chandler, A.D., Jr. (1977), *The Visible Hand: The Managerial Revolution in American Business*, Cambridge, MA: Harvard University Press.

Chandler, A.D. (1990), *Scale and scope*, Cambridge, MA: Harvard University Press.

Che, Y.-K. and I. Gale (2003), 'Optimal design of research contests', *American Economic Review*, **93**(3), 646–671.

Chesbrough, H.W. (2006), *Open Business Models: How to Thrive in the New Innovation Landscape*, Boston, MA: Harvard Business School Press.

Child, J. (1972), 'Organizational structure, environment and performance: the role of strategic choice', *Sociology*, **6**, 2–21.

Christensen, C.M. (1997), *The Innovator's Dilemma: When New Technologies Cause Great Firms to Fail*, Boston, MA: Harvard Business School Press.

Clark, K.B. and T. Fujimoto (1991), *Product Development Performance: Strategy, Organization, and Management in the World Auto Industry*, Boston, MA: Harvard Business School Press.

Coase, R.H. (1937), 'The nature of the firm', *Economica*, **4**(16), 386–405.

Cohen, W.M. and D.A. Levinthal (1990), 'Absorptive capacity: a new perspective on learning and innovation', *Administrative Science Quarterly*, **35**(1), 128–152.

Cusumano, M.A. and R.W. Selby (1995), *Microsoft Secrets: How the World's most Powerful Software Company Creates Technology, Shapes Markets, and Manages People*, New York: Free Press.

Dahlander, L. and D.M. Gann (2010), 'How open is innovation?' *Research Policy*, **39**(6), 699–709.

Davis, G.F. and H.R. Greve (1997), 'Corporate elite networks and governance changes in the 1980s', *American Journal of Sociology*, **103**(1), 1–37.

Dougherty, D. and D.D. Dunne (2011), 'Organizing ecologies of complex innovation', *Organization Science*, **22**(5), 1214–1223.

Dougherty, D. and T. Heller (1994), 'The illegitimacy of successful product innovation in established firms', *Organization Science*, **5**(2), 200–218.

Faraj, S. and S.L. Johnson (2011), 'Network exchange patterns in online communities', *Organization Science*, **22**(6), 1464–1480.

Fjeldstad, Ø.D., C.C. Snow, R.E. Miles and C. Letti (2012), 'The architecture of collaboration', *Strategic Management Journal*, **33**(6), 734–750.

Fleming, L. (2001), 'Recombinant uncertainty in technological search', *Management Science*, **47**(1), 117–132.

Fleming, L. and D.M. Waguespack (2007), 'Brokerage, boundary spanning, and leadership in open innovation communities', *Organization Science*, **18**(2), 165–180.

Foss, N.J., K. Husted and S. Michailova (2010), 'Governing knowledge sharing in organizations: levels of analysis, governance mechanisms, and research directions', *Journal of Management Studies*, **47**(3), 455–482.

Franke, N. and S. Shah (2003), 'How communities support innovative activities: an exploration of assistance and sharing among end-users', *Research Policy*, **32**(1), 157–178.

Gilson, R.J., C.F. Sabel and R.E. Scott (2009), 'Contracting for innovation: vertical disintegration and inter-firm collaboration', *Columbia Law Review*, **109**(3), 431–502.

Gioia, D.A., M. Schultz and K.G. Corley (2000), 'Organizational identity, image, and adaptive instability', *Academy of Management Review*, **25**(1), 63–81.

Grandori, A. (2001), 'Neither hierarchy nor identity: knowledge governance mechanisms and the theory of the firm', *Journal of Management and Governance*, **5**, 381–399.

Greenstein, S. (2010), 'The economics of digitization, an agenda (remarks to the Sloan Foundation August 2010 meeting): The compilation of many ideas from participants in the April 6, 2010 meeting at the Sloan Foundation'.

Gulati, R. (1995), 'Social structure and alliance formation patterns: a longitudinal analysis', *Administrative Science Quarterly*, **40**(4), 619–652.

Gulati, R. and P. Puranam (2009), 'Renewal through reorganization: the value of inconsistencies between formal and informal organization', *Organization Science*, **20**(2), 422–440.

Gulley, N. and K.R. Lakhani (2010), 'The determinants of individual performance and collective value in private-collective software innovation', *Harvard Business School Working Paper Series*, No. 10-065.

Hatch, M.J. and M. Schultz (2010), 'Toward a theory of brand co-creation with implications for brand governance', *Journal of Brand Management*, **17**(8), 590–604.

Hayek, F.A. v. (1945), *The Use of Knowledge in Society*, Menlo Park, CA: Institute for Humane Studies.

Helfat, C.E. and M.A. Peteraf (2003), 'The dynamic resource-based view: capability lifecycles', *Strategic Management Journal*, **24**(10), 997–1010.

Helfat, C.E., S. Finkelstein, W. Mitchell, M. Peteraf, D. Teece and S. Winter (2007), *Dynamic Capabilities: Understanding Strategic Change in Organizations*, Malden, MA: Blackwell.

von Hippel, E. (1988), *The Sources of Innovation*, New York: Oxford University Press.

von Hippel, E. (2005), *Democratizing Innovation*, Cambridge, MA: MIT Press.

von Hippel, E. and G. von Krogh (2003), 'Open source software and the "private-collective" innovation model: issues for organization science', *Organization Science*, **14**(2), 209–223.

Hughes, T.P. (1983), *Networks of Power: Electrification in Western Society, 1880–1930*, Baltimore, MD: Johns Hopkins University Press.

Isaacson, W. (2011), *Steve Jobs*, New York: Simon & Schuster.

Jacobides, M.G. and S. Billinger (2006), 'Designing the boundaries of the firm: from "make, buy, or ally" to the dynamic benefits of vertical architecture', *Organization Science*, **17**(2), 249–261.

Jacobides, M.G. and S. Winter (forthcoming), 'Capabilities, structure, and evolution', *Organization Science*.

Jenkins, R. and A.D. Chandler (1975), *Images and Enterprise: Technology and the American Photographic Industry, 1839 to 1925*, Baltimore, MD: Johns Hopkins University Press.

Jeppesen, L.B. and K.R. Lakhani (2010), 'Marginality and problem-solving effectiveness in broadcast search', *Organization Science*, **21**(5), 1016–1033.

Kaplan, S. and M. Tripsas (2008), 'Thinking about technology: applying a cognitive lens to technical change', *Research Policy*, **37**(5), 790–805.

King, A.A. and K.R. Lakhani (2011), 'The contingent effect of absorptive capacity: an open innovation analysis', Harvard Business School Working Paper Series, No. 11-102.

King, A.A. and K.R. Lakhani (2012), 'Accessing the ideas cloud for innovation', Harvard Business School Working Paper.

Knott, A.M. (2001), 'The dynamic value of hierarchy', *Management Science*, **47**(3), 430–448.

Koerner, B.I. (2006), February, Geeks in Toyland, *Wired Magazine*, http://www.wired.com/wired/archive/14.02/lego_pr.html.

Kogut, B. and A. Metiu (2001), 'Open-source software development and distributed innovation', *Oxford Review of Economic Policy*, **17**(2), 248–264.

Kogut, B. and U. Zander (1992), 'Knowledge of the firm, combinative capabilities, and the replication of technology', *Organization Science*, **3**(3, Focused Issue: Management of Technology), 383–397.

Kogut, B. and U. Zander (1996), 'What firms do? Coordination, identity, and learning', *Organization Science*, **7**(5), 502–518.

von Krogh, G., S. Spaeth and K.R. Lakhani (2003), 'Community, joining, and specialization in open source software innovation: a case study', *Research Policy*, **32**(7), 1217–1241.

Lakhani, K.R. and E. von Hippel (2003), 'How open source software works: "free" user-to-user assistance', *Research Policy*, **32**(6), 923–943.

Lakhani, K.R. and Z. Kanji (2009), 'Threadless: the business of community (TN)', *Harvard Business School Teaching Note 608-169,* Boston, MA: Harvard Business School Publishing.

Lakhani, K.R. and R. Wolf (2005), 'Why hackers do what they do: understanding motivation and effort in free/open source software projects', in J. Feller, B. Fitzgerald, S. Hissam, and K. Lakhani (eds), *Perspectives on Free and Open Source Software*, Cambridge, MA: MIT Press, pp. 3–21.

Landes, D.S. (1983), *Revolution in Time: Clocks and the Making of the Modern World*, Cambridge, MA: Belknap Press of Harvard University Press.

Lavie, D. and L. Rosenkopf (2006), 'Balancing exploration and exploitation in alliance formation', *Academy of Management Journal*, **49**(4), 797–818.

Lavie, D., J. Kang and L. Rosenkopf (2011), 'Balance within and across domains: the performance implications of exploration and exploitation in alliances', *Organization Science*, **22**(6), 1517–1538.

Lawrence, P.R. and J.W. Lorsch (1967 [1986]), *Organization and Environment: Managing Differentiation and Integration*, rev. edn, Boston, MA: Harvard Business School Press.

Lerner, J. and M. Schankerman (2010), *The Comingled Code: Open Source and Economic Development*, Cambridge, MA: MIT Press.

March, J.G. (1991), 'Exploration and exploitation in organizational learning', *Organization Science*, **2**(1), 71–87.

March, J.G. and H.A. Simon (1958), *Organizations*, New York: Wiley.

Morris, C.R. and C.H. Ferguson (1993), 'How architecture wins technology wars', *Harvard Business Review*, March–April, 86–95.

Murmann, J.P. (2003), *Knowledge and Competitive Advantage: The Coevolution of Firms, Technology, and National Institutions*, Cambridge: Cambridge University Press.

Murmann, J.P. and K. Frenken (2006), 'Toward a systematic framework for research on dominant designs, technological innovations, and industrial change', *Research Policy*, **35**(7), 925–952.

Murray, F. and S. O'Mahony (2007), 'Exploring the foundations of cumulative innovation: implications for organization science', *Organization Science*, **18**(6), 1006–1021.

Myers, S. and D.C. Marquis. (1969), *Successful Industrial Innovations*, Washington, DC: National Science Foundation, NSF 69-17.

Nadler, D.A. and M.L. Tushman (1997), *Competing by Design: The Power of Organizational Architecture*, New York: Oxford University Press.

Nickerson, J.A. and T.R. Zenger (2004), 'A knowledge-based theory of the firm – the problem-solving perspective', *Organization Science*, **15**(6), 617–632.

Nohria, N. and R.G. Eccles (eds) (1992), *Networks and Organizations: Structure, Form, and Action*, Boston, MA: Harvard Business School Press.

Nonaka, I. and H. Takeuchi (1995), *The Knowledge-Creating Company: How Japanese Companies Create the Dynamics of Innovation*, New York: Oxford University Press.

O'Mahony, S. and B.A. Bechky (2008), 'Boundary organizations: enabling collaboration among unexpected allies', *Administrative Science Quarterly*, **53**(3), 422–459.

O'Mahony, S. and F. Ferraro (2007), 'The emergence of governance in an open source community', *Academy of Management Journal*, **50**(5), 1079–1106.

O'Mahony, S. and K.R. Lakhani (2011), 'Organizations in the shadow of communities, in communities and organizations', in C. Marquis, M. Lounsbury and R. Greenwood (eds), *Research in the Sociology of Organizations*, Vol. 33, Bingley: Emerald Group Publishing, pp. 3–35.

O'Reilly, C. and M. Tushman (2008), 'Ambidexterity as a dynamic capability: resolving the innovator's dilemma', *Research in Organizational Behavior*, **28**, 185–206.

O'Reilly III, C.A. and M.L. Tushman (2011), 'Organizational ambidexterity in action: how managers explore and exploit', *California Management Review*, **53**(4), 5–21.

O'Reilly III, C.A., J.B. Harreld and M.L. Tushman (2009), 'Organizational ambidexterity: IBM and emerging business opportunities', *California Management Review*, **51**(4), 75–99.

Pfeffer, J. and G.R. Salancik (1978/2003), *The External Control of Organizations: A Resource Dependence Perspective*, Stanford, CA: Stanford Business Classics.

Pratt, M. and P. Foreman (2000), 'Classifying managerial responses to multiple organizational identities', *Academy of Management Review*, **28**(1), 18–42.

Rao, H. (1994), 'The social construction of reputation: certification contests, legitimation, and the survival of organizations in the American automobile industry: 1895–1912', *Strategic Management Journal*, **15**(Special Issue: Competitive Organizational Behavior), 29–44.

Raymond, E.S. (1999), *The Cathedral and the Bazaar: Musings on Linux and Open Source by an Accidental Revolutionary*, 1st edn, Cambridge, MA: O'Reilly Media.

Riggs, W. and E. von Hippel (1994), 'Incentives to innovate and the sources of innovation: the case of scientific instruments', *Research Policy*, **23**(4), 459–469.

Romanelli, E. and M.L. Tushman (1994), 'Organizational transformation as punctuated equilibrium: An empirical test', *Academy of Management Journal*, **37**(5), 1141–1666.

Rosenkopf, L. and M.L. Tushman (1998), 'The coevolution of community networks and technology: lessons from the flight simulation industry', *Industrial and Corporate Change*, **7**(2), 311–346.

Rosenkopf, L., A. Metiu and V.P. George (2001), 'From the bottom up? Technical committee activity and alliance formation', *Administrative Science Quarterly*, **46**(4), 748–772.

Rothaermel, F.T. and M.T. Alexandre (2009), 'Ambidexterity in technology sourcing: the moderating role of absorptive capacity', *Organization Science*, **20**(4), 759–780.

Santos, F.M. and K.M. Eisenhardt (2005), 'Organizational boundaries and theories of organization', *Organization Science*, **16**(5), 491–508.

Schoonhoven, C.B., K.M. Eisenhardt and K. Lyman (1990), 'Speeding products to market: waiting time to first product introduction in new firms', *Administrative Science Quarterly*, **35**(1), 177–207.

Schumpeter, J.A. (1947), *Capitalism, Socialism, and Democracy*, 2nd edn, New York: Harper & Brothers.

Scott, W.R. and G.F. Davis (2007), *Organizations and Organizing: Rational, Natural, and Open Systems Perspectives*, 1st edn, Upper Saddle River, NJ: Pearson Prentice Hall.

Shirky, C. (2008), *Here Comes Everybody: The Power of Organizing without Organizations*, New York: Penguin Press.

Smith, W.K. and M.W. Lewis (2011), 'Toward a theory of paradox: a dynamic equilibrium model of organizing', *Academy of Management Review*, **36**(2), 381–403.

Smith, W.K. and M.L. Tushman (2005), 'Managing strategic contradictions: a top management model for managing innovation streams', *Organization Science*, **16**(5), 522–536.

Sobel, D. (1995), *Longitude: The True Story of a Lone Genius Who Solved the Greatest Scientific Problem of His Time*, New York: Walker.

Suarez, F.F. (2004), 'Battles for technological dominance: an integrative framework', *Research Policy*, **33**(2), 271–286.

Terwiesch, C. and K.T. Ulrich (2009), *Innovation Tournaments: Creating and Selecting Exceptional Opportunities*, Boston, MA: Harvard Business Press.

Thompson, J.D. (1967), *Organizations in Action*, New York: McGraw Hill.

Tushman, M.L. and P. Anderson (1986), 'Technological discontinuities and organizational environments', *Administrative Science Quarterly*, **31**(3), 439–465.

Tushman, M.L. and J.P. Murmann (1998), 'Dominant designs, technology cycles, and organizational outcomes', in B.M. Staw and L.L. Cummings (eds), *Research in Organizational Behavior*, Vol. 20, Greenwich, CT: JAI Press, pp. 231–266.

Tushman, M.L. and D.A. Nadler (1978), 'Information-processing as an integrating concept in organizational design', *Academy of Management Review*, **3**(3), 613–624.

Tushman, M.L. and L. Rosenkopf (1992), 'Organizational determinants of technological change: toward a sociology of technological evolution', in L.L. Cummings and B.M. Staw (eds), *Research in Organizational Behavior*, Vol. 14, Greenwich, CT: JAI Press, pp. 311–347.

Tushman, M., W.K. Smith, R.C. Wood, G. Westerman and C. O'Reilly (2010), 'Organizational designs and innovation streams', *Industrial and Corporate Change*, **19**(5), 1331–1366.

Van de Ven, A.H., H.L. Angle and M.S. Poole (1989), *Research on the Management of Innovation: The Minnesota Studies*, Cambridge, MA: Ballinger Pub.

Vincenti, W.G. (1994), 'Retractable airplane landing gear and the Northrop "anomoly": variation-selection and the shaping of technology', *Technology and Culture*, **35**(1), 1–33.

West, J. and S. O'Mahony. (2008), 'The role of participationg architecture in growing sponsored open source communities', *Industry and Innovation*, **15**, 145–168.

Williamson, O.E. (1975), *Markets and Hierarchies, Analysis and Antitrust Implications: A Study in the Economics of Internal Organization*, New York: Free Press.

Williamson, O.E. (1981), 'The economics of organization: the transaction cost approach', *American Journal of Sociology*, **87**(3), 548–577.

Wise, G. (1985), *Willis R. Whitney, General Electric, and the Origins of US Industrial Research*, New York: Columbia University Press.

Woodward, J. (1965), *Industrial Organization: Theory and Practice*, New York: Oxford University Press.

20. Modularity and economic organization: concepts, theory, observations, and predictions
Ron Sanchez and Joseph T. Mahoney

This chapter addresses modularity as a basis for organizing economic activity. We first define the key concepts of architecture and of modularity as a special form of architecture. We then suggest how modular systems of all types may exhibit several properties of fundamental importance to the organization of economic activities, including greater adaptability and evolvability than systems that lack modular properties. We draw extensively on our original 1996 paper on modularity and subsequent research to suggest broad theoretical implications of modularity for: (1) firms' product strategies and the nature of product market competition; (2) the organization designs firms may adopt and the industry structures that can result when significant numbers of firms adopt modular product architectures; and (3) learning processes and knowledge structures at the firm and industry levels in modular product markets. We also discuss an evolutionary perspective on modularity as an emergent phenomenon in firms and industries. We explain how modularity as a relatively new field of strategy and economic research may provide a new theoretical perspective on economic organizing that has significant potential for achieving important integrations of microeconomic and macroeconomic theory. We suggest some areas for further research that may be especially fruitful in this regard.[1]

INTRODUCTION

At the most general level, this chapter addresses modularity as a fundamental approach to organizing complex systems of all kinds – technical, social, and economic. A complex system is one made up of a large number of parts that may have many different kinds of interactions. Modularity is a way of hierarchically[2] ordering complex systems into quasi-separable subsystems. This ordering may be applied recursively to subsystems until the lowest level of elementary components is reached. Within this hierarchical ordering, modular systems have the property of 'near decomposability' in which intra-component linkages within subsystems are stronger than inter-component linkages among subsystems (Simon 1962). As a result of this characteristic, modular systems of all types exhibit several properties of fundamental importance to the organization of economic activities, including greater adaptability and evolvability than systems that lack modular properties.[3]

In the following discussion, we draw extensively on our original paper on modularity (Sanchez and Mahoney 1996) as well as on a growing body of modularity research to outline the major implications for economic organization of the use of modularity in product, process, and organization designs.

We begin our discussion with formal definitions of modularity and several related concepts that are important in our exposition of the implications of modularity for economic organization. We then draw on our original paper and related research to suggest three broad theoretical implications of modularity for the ways in which the economic activities of creating, producing, and supporting products and services can be – and increasingly are – organized. We consider in turn the predicted impacts of modularity on: (1) firms' product strategies and the nature of product market competition; (2) firm organization and industry structures; and (3) learning processes and knowledge structures at the firm and industry levels. We also provide some observations to support these predictions. We then discuss a relatively new perspective introduced by Boisot and Sanchez (2010) on modularity as an emergent phenomenon in firms and industries.[4]

Finally, we conclude by suggesting the further potential of the modularity concept – and more generally, of an architectural perspective on economic organization – to provide an integrated theoretical view of the dynamic interdependencies that link firms and industries. We suggest that further development of the modularity and architectural perspectives may provide a new conceptual basis for integrating micro- and macro-level theories of economic organization that can deepen our understanding of both the micro-processes and resulting macro-outcomes of economic organizing – that is, of both the formative processes and emergent forms of economic systems of all kinds – that are as yet not clearly articulated in strategy or economics theories.

DEFINITIONS

Modularity is a special form of architecture, and thus to define modularity we must first clarify the meaning of an architecture. An architecture is a way of describing or defining the design of a system – whether the design is an intended system design for a product, process, or organization (Sanchez & Mahoney 1996), or an emergent system design for an organization, industry, or economy (Boisot & Sanchez 2010). An architecture is a two-part concept. First, an architecture defines the way in which the overall functions that a design is intended to perform have been decomposed into specific functional components – that is, the functional 'building blocks' of the design (Sanchez & Collins 2001; Tu et al. 2004). Second, an architecture also defines the ways in which the functional components that make up the design will interact when the components function together as a system – what are most commonly known as the interface specifications that define how components will connect or otherwise interact together (Sanchez 1995; Sanchez & Mahoney 1996). Figure 20.1 provides an illustration of product and process architectures meeting this definition.

Describing an architecture requires identifying (1) the type of function each component will or does perform, and (2) the kinds of interfaces through which the functional components will or do interact with each other and/or with their surrounding environment. *Defining* a specific architecture requires: (1) specifying the functional and behavioral properties of each component to a degree sufficient to determine the exact nature of the interactions that will take place between each component and all other components and between each component and its surrounding environment; and (2) specifying the exact component interfaces that will enable the functional components to function together as a system in a defined context and/or across some identified range of conditions. Sanchez

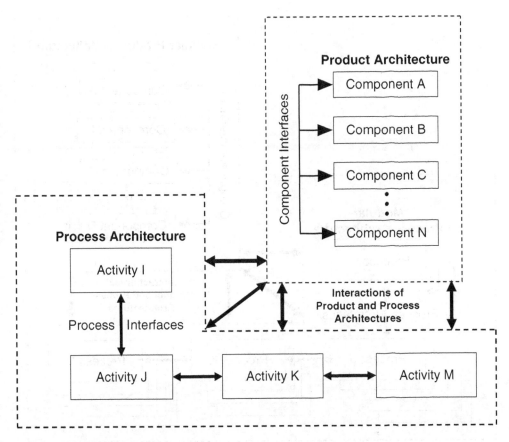

Source: Sanchez (1999).

Figure 20.1   Product and process architectures

(1999) has defined six major types of interfaces that exist in product architectures; related types of interfaces exist in process and organization architectures (Sanchez 2012 and forthcoming).

The concept of architecture defined above may be used to describe or define the design of a product, a process, an organization, an industry, or any other system that performs some kind or kinds of definable functions. In this discussion, we apply the architecture concept as defined above in characterizing not just product architectures, but also process architectures, organization architectures, and industry architectures. Thus all of these terms refer to a specific way of representing a system design – a representation that defines: (1) the functional component structure of the design; and (2) the interfaces between components that determine how the functional components interact in their particular instance of a system design.

Architectures may be modular or non-modular. A modular architecture is one in which the interfaces have been specified (either as the result of a strategic intent or as an emergent outcome) so that a range of component variations can be introduced into the system design without having to make changes in either other functional components or

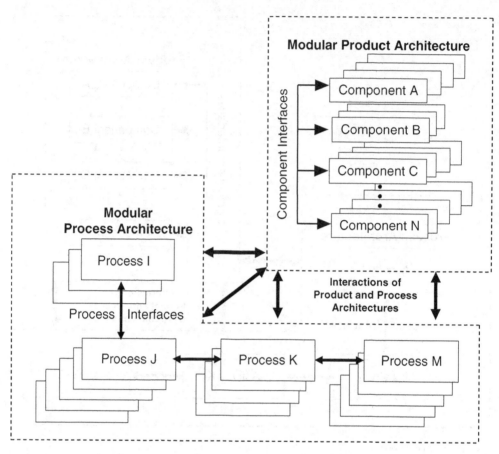

Source: Sanchez (1999).

Figure 20.2   Modular product and process architectures

in any interface specifications, as suggested for both product and process architectures in Figure 20.2.[5] In effect, a modular architecture is one in which some range of functional components – whether product components or process activities – can readily 'plug and play' in a system design.

The ability to introduce component variations into a modular architecture enables a given modular architecture to configure potentially large numbers of specific design variations by 'mixing and matching' component variations.[6] Thus, when modularity is intentionally 'designed into' an architecture, or when modularity emerges in a natural system through an evolutionary process, it confers a range of configurability on the system that endows the system with a resulting capacity to adapt or be adapted to changing environmental demands or opportunities, thereby enabling the system to serve a range of purposes across a range of conditions.

A non-modular architecture is a system design in which the introduction of a new component variation would require redesigning the architecture to some extent by making changes in the types or variations of functional components used in the architecture, and/or by creating new interface specifications to manage the interactions between the new component variation and other components. Such system designs may sometimes be created to serve a single intended purpose under well-defined and stable environmental conditions, but they cannot be adapted to new purposes or new conditions without a significant re-architecting of the system design.

In fundamental respects, creating any kind of system design is an exercise in optimization, a process in which designers have one of two tasks: either maximize some performance attribute(s) subject to cost or other resource constraints; or minimize cost or some other resource considerations subject to some performance constraint(s).[7] Thus, a fundamentally important design difference between modular and non-modular architectures is that modular architectures are system designs that are *dynamically optimized* to adapt to some range of changing purposes or conditions (either by overt design or through processes of emergence), while non-modular architectures are typically *statically optimized* to meet a single purpose under constant conditions (Sanchez 1994).

Finally, modular architectures may have one of two types of modularity properties (Sanchez 2008). What Sanchez (2009) refers to as 'technical modularity' exists in any architecture when at least some interfaces between two or more components happen to allow the introduction of some range of component variations into the architecture. Technical modularity is often used in 'back office' engineering activities to simplify or 'rationalize' designs through reuse of pre-existing interface specifications (Sanchez forthcoming).

'Strategic modularity', on the other hand, is created through a strategically motivated design process in which designers consider the various ways in which the overall functions of the design could be decomposed to create the most strategically desirable range of configurability in the architecture – a process that Sanchez (2000a, 2008) refers to as 'strategic partitioning' of the architecture. The basic intent of strategic partitioning is twofold: first, to technically isolate components that do not need to change during the intended lifetime of the design from those that it would be desirable to be able to change; and second, to achieve a 'one-to-one mapping' of each strategically important function to be delivered by the architecture into a single functional component (or single subsystem in larger architectures). Appropriate strategic partitioning of a modular architecture enables a range of strategically (or evolutionarily) important design variations to be configured through simple, direct introductions of component variations into the architecture.

THEORETICAL IMPLICATIONS AND OBSERVATIONS

Research into the influence of product architectures on organizations and their development processes began with the pioneering work of Miller and Sawyers (1968) and Gardiner (1986). Drawing on this early research, Henderson and Clark (1990) suggested that the influence of a firm's product architecture on its internal communication flows during product development may have significant competitive and strategic consequences. They suggested that when a firm's communication flows in product development processes become structured around a firm's current product architecture, the firm may have difficulty recognizing possibilities for innovating new architectures, which may lead to a 'failure of established firms' to innovate architecturally and thereby maintain market leadership (however, see note 8).[8]

Subsequently, Garud and Kumaraswamy (1995) examined Sun Microsystems' strategy in the workstation market and suggested that firms may be able to pursue new kinds of product strategies based on open-system product architectures that give their customers the ability to use industry standard components in configuring their systems. Concurrently, Sanchez (1995) identified modular product architectures as a potentially significant source of strategic flexibility to quickly configure new product variations and to rapidly upgrade products technologically in dynamic product markets. These two papers helped to stimulate a growing awareness in the strategy field of the important roles that open-system and/or modular product architectures can play in enabling new kinds of product strategies that had not previously been recognized in the field.

The Sanchez and Mahoney (1996) paper published in *Strategic Management Journal* is generally recognized as the first to suggest that modularity as a form of system design has important implications not just for competitive strategies, but more broadly for economic organization. The arguments made in the paper about modularity's impacts on product market competition, on the design of organizations and the organization of industries, and on processes for generating, structuring, and managing knowledge in firms and industries all put forward a number of propositions that have spawned new streams of theory development and research in strategy, organization theory, knowledge management, and economic organization.

We next consider the three strategic aspects of modular architectures identified by Sanchez and Mahoney (1996) from which they and later researchers derive propositions with significant theoretical implications for economic organization. We subsequently consider a fourth perspective on modularity suggested by Boisot and Sanchez (2010) that introduces an evolutionary theoretical perspective on modularity as an emergent phenomenon in economic organizing.

Modularity's Impact on Product Strategies and Product Competition

Extending the argument originally introduced by Sanchez (1995), Sanchez and Mahoney (1996) suggest that the ability to design rapid, low-cost configurability into modular product architectures endows firms with the strategic flexibility to offer more product variations and more rapid technological upgrading of products than can be accomplished through traditional (i.e., statically optimized) product designs, *ceteris paribus*. A strategically important consequence of the configurability of modular product architectures is that firms that learn how to design modular product architectures may start to offer more product variations and more frequent technological upgrades in their products, resulting in more dynamic and more finely segmented product markets and enabling the possible mass-customization of products (Sanchez 1999).

The use of modular product architectures to generate more product variety targeted at more finely grained market preferences is likely to establish new patterns and levels of competition in which modular design becomes an essential firm competence (Sanchez & Collins 2001; Sanchez 2004a). In product markets in which product variety, rapid technological upgrading to improve performance, and/or speed to market are important in achieving competitive advantage, modularity is likely to become a new 'dominant logic' (Prahalad & Bettis 1986). Both casual observation and empirical research in a growing number of product markets have broadly confirmed these predictions (e.g., Langlois & Robertson 1992; Schilling & Steensma 2001; Worren et al. 2002).

Modularity's Impacts on Organization Designs and Industry Structures

Sanchez and Mahoney (1996) advanced a broad proposition suggesting a fundamentally important relationship between the product architectures a firm uses and its own organization architecture:

> We suggest that although organizations ostensibly design products, it can also be argued that *products design organizations*, because the coordination tasks implicit in specific product designs largely determine the feasible organization designs for developing and producing those products. (1996: 64)

In effect, Sanchez and Mahoney (1996) suggest that the product architecture a firm uses will significantly influence – and thus will tend to be reflected in – the firm's choices of organization architecture for developing and producing the products to be derived from its architecture. In the current research literature, this proposition is usually referred to as the *mirroring hypothesis*.[9] For example, if a firm develops a non-modular architecture – which was ostensibly the type of architecture used by the photolithography firms studied by Henderson and Clark (1990) – then the decomposition of the overall product development task into specific component development tasks will reflect the component structure in the product architecture, and communication channels in the development process may become tightly structured around key interfaces between components, as suggested by Henderson and Clark (1990) as well as by Miller and Sawyers (1968) and Gardiner (1986) before them.

Sanchez and Mahoney (1996) went on to suggest, however, that the standardized interfaces in modular product architectures can provide essential embedded coordination of loosely coupled development processes (and production processes as well) and may therefore enable new kinds of modular organization designs and 'self-organizing' industry structures. The potential impact of modular architectures and their standardized interfaces on organization designs suggested by Sanchez and Mahoney (1996) works like this: if a firm adopts a modular architecture development process in which it first focuses on defining and then standardizing (i.e., freezing) the interfaces between the functional components in a modular architecture, and then constrains the development of all components to conform to the standardized interface specifications for the modular architecture, then the tasks of developing individual components become 'loosely coupled' and can then be undertaken simultaneously by distributed development processes (see p. 71, Figure 2).[10]

If development of a new product architecture is undertaken in this way by a firm, then functional component development activities performed by different teams within or external to a firm can 'plug and play' in a modular development process and will not require intensive communication flows or significant managerial intervention to achieve coordination.[11] In effect, adopting this 'modular process architecture' for developing a modular product architecture enables a modular development process to be undertaken through a modular organization design (Brusoni & Prencipe 2001; Sanchez 2000a, 2004b; Sanchez & Collins 2001; Sturgeon 2002).[12]

Note, however, that Sanchez and Mahoney (1996) do not assert that a firm's use of modular product architectures will *necessarily* lead to its adoption of a modular organization design – only that modular product architectures *enable* the use of modular organization designs. Managerial, organizational, and industry strategic factors may also affect a firm's choice of organizational form. Managerial and organizational factors, for example, center around issues such as: (1) Do managers realize that there would be important speed and flexibility advantages in adopting a modular development process and modular organization design? (2) Are managers willing and able to undertake the strategic organizational change required to implement modular development processes and organization designs? (3) Will technical development staff have the discipline to adhere to the principles of the modular development processes – especially the discipline required to constrain development of new components to conform to the standardized interface specifications of the modular architecture under development? (See Sanchez 2000a, 2008, and forthcoming for further discussion of these key issues.)

Some research (usually based on cross-sectional industry data) that has sought to test the 'mirroring hypothesis' has found mixed results (e.g., Hoetker 2006; Parmigiani & Mitchell 2009; Sosa et al. 2004). Moreover, some interpretations of the mixed empirical results have inferred (incorrectly, we believe) that modular product architectures offer only weak incentives to adopt modular organization architectures. By contrast, longitudinal research into firms that have managed to implement modular product, process, and organization architectures has confirmed that adopting modular development processes and organizational structures has conferred considerable strategic benefits in the form of increased speed and flexibility in development and more effective knowledge capture and retrieval, among other benefits (Sanchez and Collins 2001; Sanchez 2000a, 2000b, 2004b, 2008). We suggest therefore that the predictive power of the mirroring hypothesis is more likely to be confirmed if greater empirical attention is given to the moderating effects of managerial and organizational factors – especially those relating to managerial cognitive limitations and risk-averse behaviors (Sanchez and Heene 2004).

As Sanchez and Mahoney (1996) also noted, widespread adoption of modular product architectures in an industry can also profoundly influence industry structures:

> We observe, for example, that modularity in product designs can facilitate modularity in manufacturing processes as well as in development processes. In industries whose products are typically most modularized (e.g., personal computers), production, assembly, and servicing of components are commonly carried out by globally dispersed, loosely coupled organizations. (1996: 74, n.8)

In effect, Sanchez and Mahoney (1996) suggest that an industry's adoption of modular product architectures may (eventually) lead to the emergence of a modular industry architecture in which 'globally dispersed, loosely coupled organizations' can freely plug and play in developing, producing, assembling, and servicing the components used in the industry's modular product and process architectures.

The industry-level implications of modular product architectures are further explored by Sanchez (2008, forthcoming) and Sanchez et al. (2012), who suggest that industry structures and dynamics are fundamentally determined by the open versus closed system and modular versus non-modular nature of the product and process architectures used by firms in the industry. In particular, Sanchez (2008) contrasts the industry structures and dynamics of two polar architectural cases. At one end of the architectural spectrum, industries based on use of closed-system (i.e., firm-specific) and non-modular product and process architectures are likely to be characterized by high levels of vertical integration by firms within the industry, and by almost exclusively competitive interactions between firms at all stages of the industry value chain. Such competitive behaviors tend to be driven by the significant risks inherent in creating and competing with stand-alone, firm-specific product architectures.

At the other end of the architectural spectrum, however, industries based on open-system, modular product and process architectures are likely to be characterized by significant use of outsourcing and partnering relationships to develop and produce components and products, as well as by high levels of upstream firm cooperation to set standards and agree on 'industry standard architectures' based on product architectures with standard types of components interconnected by standardized interfaces (Sanchez 2008; Sanchez et al. 2012). Sanchez (2002) provides an in-depth analysis of the incentives for technological and architectural cooperation in adopting standard open-system, modular product architectures in an industry.

Relatively recent research into industry architectures suggests that there is now growing awareness of the implications for strategy and economic organization of Sanchez and Mahoney's (1996) observations about industry structures. However, the concept of 'industry architecture' invoked in this research is often rather vaguely defined or is defined at a very high level of description (such as 'a set of products, processes, and players' or the like). We suggest that the definition of an architecture suggested in the 'Definitions' section of this chapter would provide a more precise conceptual basis for characterizing industry architectures – and for examining interrelationships between product architectures, process architectures, organization architectures, and industry architectures in a conceptually consistent way.

Modularity's Impact on Learning Processes and Knowledge Structures at Firm and Industry Levels

Sanchez and Mahoney (1996) also put forward a number of both specific and broad propositions about the impacts of modular product and process architectures on organizational learning and knowledge management at both firm and industry levels.

At the firm level, non-modular development processes typically focus on developing components and then trying to manage the evolution of interfaces between the components as component-focused development processes move forward. As Sanchez and Mahoney (1996) and Sanchez (2000b, 2001) point out, however, this approach to technical learning while developing a product or process architecture inherently 'tightly couples' many ongoing processes for developing new technical solutions for specific components in the architecture, thereby making it very difficult to isolate, analyze, and manage specific cause-and-effect relationships between specific pairs of components. Thus, non-modular development processes are unlikely to be conducive to high levels of architectural learning during development projects (Sanchez 2001). Moreover, the idiosyncratic and unstructured nature of non-modular development processes often makes collaborating with other firms in developing products and processes highly problematic.

As Sanchez and Mahoney (1996) note, however, when a firm implements a modular architecture development process in which the interfaces between components have to be fully specified before beginning development of individual components, modularity can have a major beneficial impact on a firm's learning processes and on the way a firm structures and develops its technical knowledge. First developing interface specifications that assure that a contemplated set of component types will interact reliably in an architecture primarily involves architectural and technological learning – a form of learning that can largely be decoupled from more focused technical design learning subsequently undertaken during individual component development processes. Intentionally decoupling these two forms of organizational learning can significantly improve the effectiveness and efficiency of both kinds of learning (Sanchez 1994, 2000a, forthcoming).

If a firm's managers assume that developing the architectural knowledge needed to specify component interfaces before undertaking component development processes is too risky to attempt – or if they simply lack the sophistication to understand the potential for decoupling the two forms of learning processes – then their firms will be unlikely to adopt modular development processes and to pursue the more systematic approach to architectural and technological learning that is possible in modular development processes.

Yet firms do exist in many, if not all, industries that do have the managerial vision and organizational discipline needed to implement modular development processes and to derive the benefits of the more systematic processes for architectural and technological learning that are possible in modular development processes (Sanchez 2001; Sanchez & Collins 2001). These firms have often developed explicit, strategically focused, and systematically managed architectural learning processes that help them deepen their understanding of the system behaviors of various component designs that they use or could use in their architectures. By using the principle of strategic partitioning (discussed under 'Definitions') to achieve a 'one-to-one mapping' of specific functions into components whose interfaces have been specified so as to isolate them technically from other components in the architecture, learning about component-level design variables can proceed in a relatively straightforward manner in largely decoupled component development processes (Sanchez 2001).

Thus, the way knowledge becomes structured in modular development firms is likely to directly reflect the product and process architectures that the firm designs and uses. Moreover, as Sanchez (2000b, 2001) suggests, when a firm discovers that it lacks adequate knowledge of the system behaviors of one or more components in its modular architecture, it can then target its organizational learning processes on the aspect of the component's system behavior that it does not currently understand adequately. In effect, clearly identifying what one does not know is an important first step in designing a focused and effective architectural learning process (Sanchez 2000b, 2001).

When firms in an industry use or develop a common modular product architecture – that is, an industry standard product architecture (Sanchez 2008; Sanchez et al. 2012) – they can then cooperate in collaborative learning processes by dividing up the task of architectural learning. Because firms will be researching component behaviors and interactions within the same technical structure of functional components, architectural knowledge developed in one firm about a component's system behaviors can directly 'plug and play' into other firms' knowledge structures and development processes. Thus, as Sanchez (2000b, 2001) has noted, it is no coincidence that industries with high levels of adoption of industry standard product architectures (personal computers, telecoms products, and many others) are also likely to have high sustained rates of architectural learning (usually driven by collaborative learning processes), leading to high rates of product performance improvements and overall technological progress.

Modularity as Emergent Firm and Industry Phenomena

Boisot and Sanchez (2010) suggest that both specific and generic forms of economic organization can be understood as instances of 'nexus of rules and routines' that emerge from the recurrent interactions of economic decision makers. Boisot and Sanchez further suggest that compared to the rules and routines that obtain in non-modular development processes, modular architectures and development processes can be understood as instances of 'independent rules with high combinatorial potential' (2010: 385, n.8) that can offer both significant economies (reduced development cost and time) and market benefits (greater product variety and more rapid technological upgrading) when modularity is adopted as a basis for economic organizing.

Boisot and Sanchez (2010) submit that trial-and-error learning by firms in experimenting with different approaches to creating and offering products to markets may drive an evolutionary process that leads to the emergence of modularity in an industry's product, process, and organization architectures. If managers begin to judge that modularity's rules and routines for ordering the creation and realization of a firm's products appear to offer a Pareto-preferable way of organizing the firm's economic activities, and if individual firms in the industry then begin to adopt modularity rules and routines for ordering the creation and realization of their products, then modularity will emerge as an industry-level phenomenon. This prediction provides an evolutionary theoretical explanation for the observation that in product markets in which effective use of modularity can bring competitive advantages, once one firm in an industry 'goes modular', other firms are either likely to follow or will be 'selected out' of the industry, and modularity will eventually become the dominant logic for participating in the new 'modular industry' (Sanchez and Collins 2001; Sanchez 2008).

This prediction also leads to a further theoretical implication that Sanchez at al. (2012) have termed the 'reverse mirroring hypothesis'. This hypothesis suggests that the alternative organization architectures that managers believe are possible for their firm to adopt will influence their choice of product and process architectures. In effect, before deciding on a specific approach to organizing product creation and realization, managers will try to identify all the *strategic options* (Sanchez 1995) for organizing product creation and realization that are available to them – or that could be available as a result of their future efforts to engage other firms in collaborative action. Managers will then jointly choose the product, process, and organization architectures that appear to offer the best (Pareto-preferable) basis for organizing their firm's economic activities.

Thus, in terms of the broad evolutionary view of the emergence of organization forms suggested by Boisot and Sanchez (2010), modular product, process, and organization architectures may emerge in an industry as the result of firm-level managerial choices made among the alternative organization forms that are perceived by managers to be feasible for their firms. Once one firm adopts modularity, more managers may begin to perceive that significant economies and benefits may actually be available through modularity, including the benefits that may be created through collaborative action with other modular firms. As more firms contemplate and adopt modularity strategies – creating increasing positive externalities for other firms interested in modularity as a basis for collaboration – the incentives for other firms to adopt modularity increase. Eventually a virtuous circle of increasing positive gains available through modularity may lead to a widespread managerial judgment that modularity offers the best possibility for economic organizing in their industry. In this way, in product markets in which effective use of modularity can bring competitive advantages, modularity may emerge as the 'dominant logic' for economic organizing in an industry (Prahalad and Bettis 1986).

CONCLUSION

Our reprise of the main implications of modularity for economic organization developed since the publication of our 1996 SMJ paper leads us now to suggest that there are still fundamentally important implications of modularity for economic theory that have yet to be elaborated and thus form a fruitful domain for further theory development and empirical research. In particular, we suggest that modularity as a field of strategy and economic research provides a new theoretical perspective on economic organizing with significant potential for achieving a useful integration of microeconomic and macroeconomic theory.

As a special form of architecture, modularity has inspired research in management that is now leading to new understanding of not only the interrelationships of firm-level strategies, structures, and processes, but also of how those factors and their interrelationships shape – and thus are reflected in – industry-level structures, processes, and competitive and cooperative dynamics. At a fundamental systems view of economic organizing (Sanchez & Heene 1996, 2004), the architecture concept defined in this discussion enables a well-defined concept of industry architectures that can bring new and deeper meaning to the sometimes amorphous notion of industry structures that has long been a theme in industrial organization economics (Porter 1979, 1980). The rigorous and consistent application of both architecture and modularity concepts at the industry level would enable a more fundamental, comprehensive, and integrated view of the structures, processes, and dynamics of economic organizing at the industry level. We further suggest that ongoing research on architectures and modularity may eventually – and perhaps sooner rather than later – lead to much sharper understanding of the fundamental systemic interrelationships between managerial decision-making about economic organizing made at the firm level (as studied by Sanchez & Mahoney 1996) and the evolutionary trajectories of structures, processes, and dynamics at the industry level that result from the aggregated economic organizing decisions of entrepreneurs and managers (as suggested by Boisot & Sanchez 2010).

In effect, the adoption of modular architectures in product designs makes it possible to reflect ('mirror') the modular architecture in an organization design and indeed in an industry structure. However, the mixed empirical results in tests to date of the 'mirroring hypothesis' suggest that there are significant cognitive, managerial, and organizational challenges to be overcome in reshaping organizations and industries to mirror any modular product architectures they may use. How individual firms and collectivities of firms make the decision to adopt modular architectures, how they then (perhaps) decide to reorganize to reflect their modular architectures in their organization designs, and how they then go about implementing such decisions organizationally at firm and industry levels – these fundamental cognitive processes in creating modular firms and modular markets are as yet poorly understood and little researched.

Nevertheless, it is clear that both firms and industries with modular architectures reflective of their product architectures do exist and continue to emerge. Indeed, modular products and modular organizations appear to be an increasingly common phenomenon and an increasingly dominant strategy for participating in many kinds of product markets (Sanchez & Collins 2001; Worren et al. 2002). Further elaboration of the 'reverse mirroring hypothesis' recently proposed by Sanchez et al. (2012) is now needed to identify the technical, competitive, and other strategic conditions that are likely to broadly induce firms to adopt modular product and organization architectures.

Combined with the mirroring hypothesis, a more fully elaborated reverse mirroring hypothesis may provide the essential conceptual link now necessary to 'close the loop' between firms and industries in developing an integrated theoretical representation of the organizational structures, processes, and dynamics that inextricably link firms in an industry in a dynamically evolving feedback system (Forrester 1960; Sanchez & Heene 1996, 2004).

If so, perhaps it may eventually come to pass that a dynamic architectural perspective on economic organizing – within which achieving a close alignment of modular product, process, and organizational architectures at firm and industry levels often appears to be an optimal case – will provide the conceptual lens that enables a new synthesis of micro- and macro-levels of organizational economics theory.

NOTES

1. We thank Peter Galvin and Norbert Bach for helpful discussions on industry architectures, and Anna Grandori and Chiu Liu for their insightful comments on earlier drafts of the chapter. The usual disclaimers apply.
2. The current chapter uses a more general conception of 'hierarchy' than is usually invoked in organizational economics (e.g., Williamson 1975), where hierarchy typically denotes subordination to an authority relationship. Our interest here, however, is in understanding hierarchical systems for creating new products in which there is little or no overt exercise of managerial authority (Sanchez & Mahoney 1996). Thus, 'hierarchy' in our discussion refers to a structural decomposition of a complex system into an ordering of successive sets of subsystems in the manner suggested by Simon (1962); that is, a partitioning of a system into subsystem relationships that collectively define the parts of any whole.
3. Advanced technological knowledge about component interactions can be used to fully specify and standardize the component interfaces that make up a modular product architecture, creating a system of nearly independent, loosely coupled components (Sanchez & Mahoney 1996). The interface specifications in a modular product architecture can in turn provide an essential form of embedded coordination that makes possible the concurrent and autonomous development of components through loosely coupled organization structures (Orton & Weick 1990; Williamson 1975). The architectural concepts of functional decomposition and interface specification have strong parallels in classic organization theory's concepts of specialization and differentiation among and integration of organizational subunits (Lawrence & Lorsch 1967; March & Simon 1958). Thus, as Sanchez and Mahoney (1996) suggest, both product designs

and organization designs are governed by fundamental principles of decomposition and may be designed to achieve the property of 'near decomposability' (Simon 1962).

4. What happens by design at the firm level generates an emergent phenomenon at the industry level – thus modularity as an emergent outcome at the industry level is a logically dependent result of *outcomes by design* at the firm level of analysis.

5. When the designs of a modular product architecture and a modular process architecture (e.g., a flexible production process) are coordinated so that the configurability of both architectures can be used to support a well-defined strategic objective – such as providing a defined range of product variations and/or a plan for upgrading product performance – the combination of the two architectures constitutes a *modular platform* for accomplishing the strategic objective (Sanchez 2004b).

6. This 'power of modularity' is easy to illustrate: imagine a system design consisting of ten different types of components whose interfaces have been specified to allow the 'mixing and matching' of ten different variations of each type of component. The number of specific design variations that be configured within this simple modular architecture is $10^{10} = 10\,000\,000\,000$ design variations. Of course, as a practical matter the range of variations in components that can be introduced into a modular architecture is both enabled and limited technically by the interface specifications in the architecture for each type of component. Interfaces may be specified to be 'flexible' in the sense that they allow a broad range of component variations to be introduced into an architecture (e.g., a USB or Firewire interface), or they may be specified to be 'inflexible' (either as a strategy or by simple default) in the sense that they allow only one or perhaps a narrow range of component variations to 'plug and play' in an architecture (e.g., Sony's proprietary 'Memory Stick' interface). Contrary to popular perceptions, the standardized interfaces in modular architectures may in fact be designed to be quite flexible in their ability to support the mixing and matching of existing and new component variations over an extended period of technological evolution (again, consider the ubiquitous and long-lived USB interface or the standardized 128-field magnetic strip on the back of bank cards around the world.)

7. We note that optimization in the design world usually consists of choosing among alternative imagined designs in a discrete choice context. Discrete system designs are typically selected (at the firm level) and retained (at the industry level) on the basis of their ability to deliver an adequate level of performance given some resource constraint(s) (a relative effectiveness criterion) or their ability to minimize resource requirements while meeting some minimum performance constraint (a relative efficiency criterion).

8. Henderson and Clark's (1990) broad proposition that the structuring of internal communication patterns around a firm's current architecture may lead to 'the failure of established firms' to innovate architecturally is supported in their paper by reports of interviews with managers involved in product development in a few firms in the photolithography industry in the 1970s and 1980s, and by data they present on the changing positions of major firms in the photolithography industry during the same period (see p. 24, Table 2, in their paper). However, Sanchez (forthcoming) suggests that the data presented in their paper appear to be based on an inadequate sample of firms that may have resulted in an incomplete and thus possibly misleading view of firm strategies, entries, incumbencies, and market shares in the industry during the period studied. If so, there may be little actual empirical support in Henderson and Clark's (1990) study for their well-known proposition that a firm's efforts to extend and exploit its current product architecture may significantly contribute to 'the failure of established firms'.

9. One of the earliest uses of the term 'mirroring hypothesis' can be found in Colfer (2007), which was updated in Colfer and Baldwin (2010). This research reviewed 102 empirical studies spanning three levels of organization: within a single firm, across firms, and in open-community-based development projects. Colfer (2007) credits Sanchez and Mahoney (1996) for being one of the first to articulate explicitly the mirroring hypothesis, although it was also noted that the use of the term 'mirror' can be found in Henderson and Clark (1990). The mirroring hypothesis was supported in 69 percent of the cases. Support for the hypothesis was strongest in the within-firm sample (77 percent), slightly less strong in the across-firm sample (74 percent), and relatively weak in the open collaborative sample (39 percent). Notable studies providing support in the within-firm sample include: Amrit and Hillegersberg (2008), Herbsleb and Grinter (1999), King (1999), Ovaska et al. (2003) and Sosa et al. (2004). Notable studies providing support in the across-firm sample include: Cacciatori and Jacobides (2005); Consoli (2005); Fixson and Park (2008), Gulati et al. (2005), Jacobides (2005); Monteverde (1995), Novak and Eppinger (2001), Parmigiani (2007), Sahaym et al. (2007), Shibata et al. (2005) and Tiwana (2008a, 2008b). Notable studies that did not support the mirroring hypothesis include: Appleyard et al. (2008), Argyres (1999), Barlow (2000), Bonaccorsi and Lipparini (1994), Helper et al. (2000), Mikkola (2003), Miller et al. (1995), Sako (2004), Scott (2000), Staudenmayer et al. (2005) and Takeisha (2001).

10. The modular development process described here is generally referred to as 'object-oriented development' in the software industry.

11. Sanchez (2000a, 2001, forthcoming) suggests that adoption of standardized component interfaces before beginning development of individual components for a modular product architecture may therefore

help to avoid the problems of narrowly focused communication flows that Henderson and Clark (1990) suggest may afflict firms in development processes and (putatively) lead to alleged 'failure of established firms'.

12. The current chapter focuses on the specific influence of modularity on organization, rather than on the broader topic of technology's influence on economic organization. In this broader topic, an important question arises concerning the degrees of freedom of organization with respect to technology (and the degrees of freedom of technology with respect to organization). This question is beyond the scope of the current chapter, but warrants consideration in future research. We thank the editor, Anna Grandori, for highlighting this research question.

REFERENCES

Amrit, C. and J. van Hillegersberg (2008), 'Detecting coordination problems in collaborative software development environments', *Information Systems Management*, **25**(1), 57–70.

Appleyard, M., C.Y. Wang, J.A. Liddle and J. Carruthers (2008), 'The innovator's non-dilemma: the case of next-generation lithography', *Managerial and Decision Economics*, **29**(5), 407–423.

Argyres, N.S. (1999), 'The impact of information technology on coordination: evidence from the B-2 "Stealth" bomber', *Organization Science*, **10**(2) 162–180.

Barlow, J. (2000), 'Innovation and learning in complex offshore construction projects', *Research Policy*, **29**(7), 973–989.

Boisot, M. and R. Sanchez (2010), 'Organization as a nexus of rules: emergence in the evolution of systems and exchange', *Management Revue: The International Review of Management Studies*, **21**(4), 378–405.

Bonaccorsi, A. and A. Lipparini (1994), 'Strategic partnerships in new product development: an Italian case study', *Journal of Product and Innovation Management*, **11**(2), 134–145.

Brusoni, S. and A. Prencipe (2001), 'Unpacking the black box of modularity: technologies, products and organizations', *Industrial and Corporate Change*, **10**(1), 179–205.

Cacciatori, E. and M.G. Jacobides (2005), 'The dynamic limits of specialization: vertical integration reconsidered', *Organization Studies*, **26**(12) 1851–1883.

Colfer, L. (2007), 'The mirroring hypothesis: theory and evidence on the correspondence between the structure of products and organizations', Working Paper, Harvard Business School.

Colfer, L. and C.Y. Baldwin (2010), 'The mirroring hypothesis: theory, evidence and exceptions', Harvard Business School Finance Working Paper No. 10-058. Available at http://ssrn.com/abstract=1539592

Consoli, D. (2005), 'The dynamics of technological change in UK retail banking services: an evolutionary perspective', *Research Policy*, **34**(4), 461–480.

Fixson, S.K. and J. Park (2008), 'The power of integrality: linkages between product architecture, innovation, and industry structure', *Research Policy*, **37**(8), 1296–1316.

Forrester, J. (1960), *Industrial Dynamics*, Cambridge, MA: MIT Press.

Gardiner, J.P. (1986), 'Design trajectories for airplanes and automobiles during the past fifty years', in C. Freeman (ed.), *Design, Innovation, and Long Cycles in Economic Development*, London: Francis Printer, pp. 121–141.

Garud, R. and A. Kumaraswamy (1995), 'Technological and organizational designs for realizing economies of substitution', *Strategic Management Journal*, **16**(Summer), 93–109.

Gulati, R., P.R. Lawrence and P. Puranam (2005), 'Adaptation in vertical relationships: beyond incentive conflict', *Strategic Management Journal*, **26**(5), 415–440.

Helper, S., J.P. MacDuffie and C. Sabel. (2000), 'Pragmatic collaborations: advancing knowledge while controlling opportunism', *Industrial and Corporate Change*, **9**(3), 443–488.

Henderson, R.M. and K.B. Clark (1990), 'Architectural innovation: the reconfiguration of existing product technologies and the failure of established firms', *Administrative Science Quarterly*, **35**(1), 9–30.

Herbsleb, J. and R. Grinter (1999), 'Architectures, coordination, and distance: Conway's Law and beyond', *IEEE Software*, **16**(5) 63–70.

Hoetker, G. (2006), 'Do modular products lead to modular organizations?' *Strategic Management Journal*, **27**(6), 501–518.

Jacobides, M.G (2005), 'Industry change through vertical disintegration: how and why markets emerged in mortgage banking', *Academy of Management Journal*, **48**(3), 465–498.

King, A. (1999), 'Retrieving and transferring embodied data: implications for the management of interdependence within organizations', *Management Science*, **45**(7), 918–935.

Langlois, R.N. and P.L. Robertson (1992), 'Network and innovation in a modular system: lessons from the microcomputer and stereo component industries', *Research Policy*, **21**(4), 297–313.

Lawrence, P.R. and J.W. Lorsch (1967), *Organization and Environment: Managing Differentiation and Integration*, Boston, MA: Harvard University Press.

March, J.G. and H.A. Simon (1958), *Organizations*, New York: John Wiley & Sons.

Mikkola, J.H. (2003), 'Modularity, component outsourcing, and inter-firm learning', *R&D Management*, **33**(4), 439–454.

Miller, R. and D. Sawyers (1968), *The Technical Development of Modern Aviation*, New York: Praeger.

Miller, R., M. Hobday, T. Leroux-Demers and X. Olleros (1995), 'Innovation in complex systems industries: the case of flight simulation', *Industrial and Corporate Change*, **4**(2), 363–400.

Monteverde, K. (1995), 'Technical dialog as an incentive for vertical integration in the semi-conductor industry', *Management Science*, **41**(10), 1624–1638.

Novak, S. and S.D. Eppinger (2001), 'Sourcing by design: product complexity and the supply chain', *Management Science*, **47**(1), 189–204.

Orton, J.D. and K.E. Weick (1990), 'Loosely coupled systems a reconceptualization', *Academy of Management Review*, **15**(2), 203–223.

Ovaska, P., M. Rossi, and P. Marttiin (2003), 'Architecture as a coordination tool in multi-site software development', *Software Process: Improvement and Practice*, **8**(4) 233–247.

Parmigiani, A. (2007), 'Why do firms both make and buy? An investigation of concurrent sourcing', *Strategic Management Journal*, **28**(3) 285–311.

Parmigiani, A. and W. Mitchell (2009), 'Complementarity, capabilities, and the boundaries of the firm: the impact of within-firm and interfirm expertise on concurrent sourcing of complementary components', *Strategic Management Journal*, **30**(10), 1065–1091.

Porter, M. (1979), 'How competitive forces shape strategy', *Harvard Business Review*, **57**(2), 137–146.

Porter, M. (1980), *Competitive Strategy: Techniques for Analyzing Industries and Competitors*, New York: Free Press.

Prahalad, C.K. and R.A. Bettis (1986), 'The dominant logic: a new linkage between diversity and performance', *Strategic Management Journal*, **7**(6), 485–501.

Sahaym, A.H., K. Steensma and M.A. Schilling (2007), 'The influence of information technology on the use of loosely coupled organizational forms: an industry-level analysis', *Organization Science*, **18**(5), 865–880.

Sako, M. (2004), 'Supplier development at Honda, Nissan and Toyota: comparative case studies of organizational capability development', *Industrial and Corporate Change*, **13**(2) 281–308.

Sanchez, R. (1994), 'Towards a science of strategic product design: system design, component modularity, and product-leveraging strategies', *Proceedings of the 2nd International Product Development Management Conference, Goteborg, Sweden, 30–31 May*, Brussels: European Institute for Advanced Studies in Management (EIASM).

Sanchez, R. (1995), 'Strategic flexibility in product competition', *Strategic Management Journal*, **16**(Summer), 135–159.

Sanchez, R. (1999), 'Modular architectures in the marketing process', *Journal of Marketing*, **63**(Special Issue), 92–111.

Sanchez, R. (2000a), 'Modular architectures, knowledge assets and organizational learning: new management processes for product creation', *International Journal of Technology Management*, **19**(6), 610–629.

Sanchez, R. (2000b), 'Product, process, and knowledge architectures in the management of knowledge resources', in P. Robertson and N. Foss (eds), *Resources, Technology, and Strategy*, London: Routledge.

Sanchez, R. (2001), 'Product, process, and knowledge architectures in organizational competence', in R. Sanchez (ed.), *Knowledge Management and Organizational Competence*, Oxford: Oxford University Press, pp. 227–250.

Sanchez, R. (2002), 'Industry standards, modular architectures, and common components: strategic incentives for technological cooperation', in F. Contractor and P. Lorange (eds), *Cooperative Strategies and Alliances*, Oxford: Elsevier Science, pp. 659–687.

Sanchez, R. (2004a), 'Understanding competence-based management: identifying and managing five modes of competence', *Journal of Business Research*, **57**(5), 518–532.

Sanchez, R. (2004b), 'Creating modular platforms for strategic flexibility', *Design Management Review*, **15**(1), 58–67.

Sanchez, R. (2008), 'Modularity in the mediation of market and technology change', *International Journal of Technology Management*, **42**(4), 331–364.

Sanchez, R. (2012), 'Architecting organizations: a dynamic strategic contingency perspective', *Research in Competence-based Management*, **6**, 7–48.

Sanchez, R. (forthcoming), *Modularity: Strategy, Organization, and Knowledge Management*, Oxford: Oxford University Press.

Sanchez, R. and R.P. Collins (2001), 'Competing – and learning – in modular markets', *Long Range Planning*, **34**(6), 645–667.

Sanchez, R. and A. Heene (1996), 'A systems view of the firm in competence-based competition', in R. Sanchez, A. Heene and H. Thomas (eds), *Dynamics of Competence-Based Competition*, Oxford: Pergamon, pp. 39–64.

Sanchez, R. and A. Heene (2004), *The New Strategic Management: Organization, Competition, and Competence*, New York: John Wiley & Sons.

Sanchez, R. and J.T. Mahoney (1996), 'Modularity, flexibility, and knowledge management in product and organization design', *Strategic Management Journal*, **17**(Winter), 63–76.

Sanchez, R., P. Galvin and N. Bach (2012), '"Closing the loop" in the architectural perspective on economic organizing: towards a reverse mirroring hypothesis', Working Paper INO-2012-1, Copenhagen Business School.

Schilling, M.A. and H.K. Steensma (2001), 'The use of modular organizational forms: an industry-level analysis', *Academy of Management Journal*, **44**(6), 1149–1168.

Scott, J.E. (2000), 'Facilitating interorganizational learning with information technology', *Journal of Management Information Systems*, **17**(2) 81–113.

Shibata, T., M. Yano and F. Kodama (2005), 'Empirical analysis of evolution of product architecture: Fanuc numerical controllers from 1962 to 1997', *Research Policy*, **34**(1), 13–31.

Simon, H.A. (1962), 'The architecture of complexity', *Proceedings of the American Philosophical Society*, **106**(December), 467–482.

Sosa, M., S. Eppinger and C. Rowles (2004), 'The misalignment of product architecture and organizational structure in complex product development', *Management Science*, **50**(12), 1674–1689.

Staudenmayer, N., M. Tripsas and C.L. Tucci (2005), 'Interfirm modularity and its implications for product development', *Journal of Product Innovation Management*, **22**(4), 303–321.

Sturgeon, T.J. (2002), 'Modular product networks: a new American model of industrial organization', *Industrial and Corporate Change*, **11**(3), 451–496.

Takeishi, A. (2001), 'Bridging inter- and intra-firm boundaries: management of supplier involvement in automobile product development', *Strategic Management Journal*, **22**(5), 403–433.

Tiwana, A. (2008a), 'Does interfirm modularity complement ignorance? A field study of software outsourcing alliances', *Strategic Management Journal*, **29**(11), 1241–1252.

Tiwana, A. (2008b), 'Does technological modularity substitute for control? A study of alliance performance in software outsourcing', *Strategic Management Journal*, **29**(7), 769–780.

Tu, Q., M.A. Vonderembse, T.S. Ragu-Nathan and B. Ragu-Nathan (2004), 'Measuring modularity-based manufacturing practices and their impact on mass customization capability: a customer-driven perspective', *Decision Sciences*, **35**(2), 147–168.

Williamson, O.E. (1975), *Markets and Hierarchies*, New York: Free Press.

Worren, N., K. Moore and P. Cardona (2002), 'Modularity, strategic flexibility and firm performance: a study of the home appliance industry', *Strategic Management Journal*, **23**(12), 1123–1140.

21. The organizational design of high-tech start-ups: state of the art and directions for future research

Massimo G. Colombo and Cristina Rossi-Lamastra

The aim of this chapter is to review the literature on the organizational design of start-ups operating in high-tech industries. For this purpose, we highlight 'stylized facts' and articulate some novel research directions which deserve further exploration. Specifically, we focus attention on two prominent elements of high-tech start-ups' organizational design, which are highly interrelated: organizational structure and decision system. We consider the influence exerted on these elements by the high human capital intensity of these firms and the high velocity environment in which they operate. The chapter finally indicates, as a promising avenue for future research, further investigation of the consequences of technical intensity of human capital and appropriability regime on the heterogeneity of high-tech start-ups.

INTRODUCTION

Literature on organizational design has mainly focused attention on established firms, whilst less research effort has been devoted to start-ups. Scholars recognize that choices on organizational design, as defined by firm's structure and decision system, are fundamental for nascent firms (David & Han 2003). However, with few exceptions (e.g. Grandori & Gaillard Giordani 2011), these choices have generally been regarded as idiosyncratic processes (Sine et al. 2006: 130) where general wisdom on organizational design takes a back seat to the exigencies of the moment (Aldrich 1999).

Start-ups differ from established firms in many respects. They have usually limited financial resources (Carpenter & Petersen 2002), simple governance mechanisms (Ambos & Birkinshaw 2010), fluid identity and scanty legitimacy (Stinchcombe 1965). Consequently, knowledge on organizational design of established firms cannot be generalized to start-ups. The study of the organizational design of start-ups requires the development of new interpretative models and research designs. This is simultaneously an attractive and daunting research avenue.

The newness (and the consequent typical smallness) of start-ups facilitates theory building in the domain of organizational design. In established firms, the core elements of organizational design are confounded by less relevant elements, which have been added over time. Conversely, start-ups are still in a nascent state: the core elements of their organizational design are brightly evident and easy to isolate from the background. Likewise, the relationship between organizational design elements, strategic behaviors and performance is surrounded by less causal ambiguity. The micro level of the individuals can be easily linked with the meso level of the organizational design elements and the macro level of the firm as a whole. Specifically, in the early days of a start-up, individuals (i.e. founders, owner-managers and employees) are less constrained by both internal and external forces. Thus, they can exert a significant impact on the organizational design elements and on the firm as a whole (Daily & Dalton 1992).

Nonetheless, setting up a proper empirical methodology to study the organizational design of start-ups poses major challenges. Data collection in this realm is both time- and resource-consuming. New ventures are hardly recorded in public databases and rarely mentioned in press releases. Moreover, their organizational design elements are poorly codified. Scholars must resort to sophisticated data collection techniques: triangulation among several information sources, extensive face-to-face interviews with key informants, and inspection of start-ups' internal documents. Serious methodological problems arise as regards to the measurement of the variables of interest. For instance, how to account for the founders' psychological attachment to their venture which has proven to crucially influence organizational design elements (e.g., reducing the probability of founder–chief executive officer (CEO) succession, Wasserman 2003)? Likewise, the choice of the appropriate econometric modeling technique is far from simple (e.g., how to solve reverse causality problems in presence of a short company history? Hambrick 2007).

The aim of this chapter is to review the literature on start-ups' organizational design by focusing on start-ups operating in high-tech industries (henceforth: high-tech start-ups). The organizational design of high-tech start-ups is of great practical and academic relevance. These firms account for large portions of the wealth generated yearly in the economic system and are an important source of new technologies and employment growth (Audretsch 1995). Since the organizational design of high-tech start-ups affects their strategies and performances, practitioners and policy-makers can greatly benefit from learning more about it. Moreover, since the seminal contributions of the Stanford Project on Emerging Companies (henceforth: SPEC; see Baron & Hannan 2002 for a summary of its main findings) in the late 1990s, there has been a surge of interest on high-tech start-ups' organizational design (Eisenhardt 2010). Nonetheless, scholarly work on this theme is highly fragmented, while theoretical developments are still lagging behind. The research stream largely consists of empirical contributions, which are grounded on a plethora of different and sometime incoherent theoretical approaches. Theoretical lens range from the lifecycle theory (e.g. Boeker & Karichalil 2002), imprinting perspective (e.g. Simons & Roberts 2008), resource dependence view (e.g. Pollock et al. 2009), stewardship and agency theory (e.g. Wasserman 2006) and theories on legitimacy and identity of new organizations (e.g. Delmar & Shane 2004), among others. The lack of a consistent theoretical background threatens the coherence of the field and often leads to controversial empirical findings.

In this chapter, we selectively review studies on high-tech start-ups' organizational design with the aim of highlighting 'stylized facts' and articulating some novel research directions which in our view deserve further exploration. For sake of synthesis, we focus on two prominent constituent elements of start-ups' organizational design, which turn out to be highly interrelated: organizational structure and decision system.

The structure of an organization is typically defined as 'the sum total of the ways in which it divides its labor into distinct tasks and then achieves coordination among them' (Mintzberg 1979: 2). In general, new ventures, and high-tech start-ups alike, have a simple structure (Stinchcombe 1965). Their corporate hierarchy is usually flat and the vertical depth (i.e. the number of layers between the top and the bottom of the hierarchy) is small. At foundation, high-tech start-ups typically adopt a two-layer hierarchy composed by the top management team (henceforth: TMT) and non-executive employees (Baron & Burton 1999). Accordingly, the TMT is the structural element of high-tech start-ups that has attracted most scholarly attention (Boeker & Karichalil 2002).

Decision system (DS) is defined in terms of the set of: (1) the decisions which a firm has to make in order to run its business; (2) the organization members who are responsible for these decisions; and (3) the modes in which these decisions are made (see e.g. Keidel 1995).

In reviewing the literature on the aforementioned constituent elements of high-tech start-ups' organizational design, we move from two widely acknowledged peculiarities of these firms. Firstly, high-tech start-ups operate in high-velocity environments characterized by rapid and unpredictable changes (Bourgeois & Eisenhardt 1988). Secondly, the human capital of key individuals – notably, their top managers – is a primary source of value creation (Unger et al. 2011). Extant literature has shown that high-velocity environments demand a peculiar design of high-tech start-ups' structure and decision system (Davis et al. 2009). Moreover, the prominence of human capital makes it fundamental to organize for leveraging the human capital of its members and using their personal knowledge in decision making (Jensen and Meckling 1992).

The chapter is organized as follows. It first addresses the challenges posed to the organizational design of high-tech start-ups by the high-velocity environments in which these firms operate. The next section reviews contributions on high-tech start-ups' TMTs in the light of the aforementioned centrality of human capital. The chapter concludes by discussing some promising avenues for future research.

THE ORGANIZATIONAL DESIGN CHALLENGES OF HIGH-VELOCITY ENVIRONMENTS: HIGH-TECH START-UPS' STRUCTURE AND DECISION SYSTEM

Contingency theory acknowledges that firms' organizational design is strongly shaped by external contingencies (Drazin and Van de Ven 1985). The industry in which a firm operates is probably the most relevant of these contingencies. High-tech start-ups operate in high-velocity environments characterized by rapid and discontinuous changes in demand, competitors, technology and regulation (Bourgeois and Eisenhardt 1988: 816). In a high-velocity environment, true uncertainty (in the sense of Knight 1921) renders it impossible to specify all the future states of nature (Eisenhardt and Martin 2000: 1111), while rapid and discontinuous changes make the information on markets, technologies, and competitive and regulatory settings quickly obsolete. Firms operating in high-velocity environments must be at the same time flexible and efficient (Davis et al. 2009). Flexibility is fundamental to capture new and unexpected opportunities by quickly adapting to unpredicted environmental changes (Weick 1993). Likewise, efficiency is needed to rapidly exploit these opportunities (Adler et al. 1999). However, the well-known trade-off between these two aspects (see again Davis et al. 2009) makes the design of a start-up's organization for achieving both flexibility and efficiency a paradoxical problem (Smith & Lewis 2011).[1]

In a string of influential contributions, Eisenhardt and co-authors (Bourgeois & Eisenhardt 1988; Eisenhardt 1989; Eisenhardt & Tabrizzi 1995; Eisenhardt et al. 2010) have fuelled a lively debate on how high-tech start-ups should design their structure and decision system to properly balance flexibility and efficiency. These contributions move from the premise that flexibility and efficiency result from having both decision speed and comprehensiveness.[2] While the former is mandatory to cope with rapid changes, the latter is crucial to effectively exploit new opportunities.[3] High-tech start-ups can achieve both decision speed and comprehensiveness through formalization of roles and specialization of tasks within their TMTs,[4] combined with selective decentralization of decisions (see also Sine et al. 2006). Role formalization avoids ambiguity and confusion about who is supposed to do what, and clearly delineates what members of the TMT can and cannot decide, thus reducing the need for decision-making by consensus and the associated coordination costs. Task specialization allows TMT members to focus on a narrow decision domain in which they have specific knowledge. As to the decision system, the CEO should be powerful, but should also selectively delegate decisions to other top executives (Bourgeois & Eisenhardt 1988). Specifically, the CEO should retain decision authority on high-level strategic decisions (i.e. decisions that are made infrequently, but critically affect firms' health and survival; Eisenhardt & Zbaracki 1992: 17).[5] Decision comprehensiveness does not hamper decision speed provided that it is confined to a few decisions on which the CEO is betting the destiny of the firm and, when deciding, the CEO makes use of real-time information obtained by other executives who are highly experienced in the considered decision domain (Bourgeois & Eisenhardt 1988; Eisenhardt 1989). Then, the implementation of high-level decisions and operating decisions must be delegated to other members of the TMT to whom specific roles and tasks are assigned on the basis of their functional competences. Such an organizational design results in a more timely and accurate decision making (Sine et al. 2006), which reconciles efficiency and flexibility.

Quite surprisingly, extant literature has neglected the impact of the high velocity of the environment on high-tech start-ups' vertical depth. In accordance with the above reasoning, the creation of a middle-management layer and the consequent delegation to middle managers of operating decisions foster flexible and efficient adaptation to rapidly changing environmental conditions. As far as we know, Colombo and Grilli (forthcoming) is the only study that has extensively investigated the creation of a middle-management level in two-layered high-tech entrepreneurial ventures. Their econometric estimates – based on a large sample of Italian owner-managed high-tech start-ups that are observed from their foundation – support the view that the likelihood of recruiting a middle manager, and thus switching to a three-layer corporate hierarchy, is considerably higher for firms operating in a highly competitive and uncertain business environment.

The arguments proposed by the studies reviewed in the present section echo general principles of the economic literature on organizational design. Firstly, the information-processing stream has argued that when decision authority is centralized, there are organizational failures due to leaks (Keren & Levhari 1979, 1983, 1989) and delays (Radner 1993; Van Zandt 1999) in transmitting information upwards and downwards through the corporate hierarchy. This is especially worrisome when decision speed and comprehensiveness is crucial, as in high-velocity environments. Delegation reduces leaks and delays because it allows tasks to be performed concurrently and independently (see also Sah and Stiglitz 1986). Secondly, selective delegation of decision-making frees the CEO's time so that they can focus attention and efforts on the high-level strategic decisions (Harris & Raviv 2002. See also the work by Garicano and colleagues on 'knowledge hierarchies', e.g. Garicano 2000). Thirdly, formalization of roles and specialization of tasks assign decision authority to the TMT members who have the best information set on a given decision domain. Consequently, 'specific knowledge' (Jensen & Meckling 1992) possessed by the various members of the TMT is efficiently used in decision making, in accordance with the predications of delegation theory (Dessein 2002; Alonso & Matouschek 2008).

THE ORGANIZATIONAL DESIGN CHALLENGES OF HUMAN CAPITAL CENTRALITY: TMTs IN HIGH-TECH START-UPS

Although the bulk of the academic research on TMTs has been traditionally framed in the context of established firms (Bournois et al. 2011), scholars have increasingly devoted attention to high-tech start-ups' early TMTs, formed by founders and early-hired top executives (Beckman & Burton 2008). Scholarly interest on the topic stems from the prominent role that early TMTs play within the organization of high-tech start-ups. Whilst in many industries entrepreneurs have generalist skills and can thus act as 'Jacks-of-all-trades' (Lazear 2005), entrepreneurs in high-tech industries possess highly specialized human capital (Colombo & Grilli 2005), which mainly consists of technological knowledge. Such knowledge is largely tacit, has an innovative content and an untested nature. Consequently, it has an uncertain economic value and can hardly be exploited either through licensing (Lowe 2001) or arm's-length arrangements with other companies (e.g., offering consultancy or scientific advice). Then, in accordance with the cephalization principle proposed by Knight (1921), the best way for commercially exploiting technological knowledge by individuals possessing it consists in founding a new venture, which epitomizes their skills and capabilities (He 2008; Gimeno et al. 1997).

Moving in a long-lasting tradition in technology entrepreneurship and in line with Hambrick and Mason's (1984) 'upper echelon theory',[6] the bulk of the research effort on high-tech start-ups' early TMTs has been applied to the analysis of the demographic characteristics of their members (e.g., age, gender, education, work experience). Organizational design speculations have been comparatively rarer (Hambrick 2007). These speculations have mainly revolved around two themes: (1) imprinting effects of early TMTs on the subsequent organizational design of new ventures; and (2) founder–CEO succession and founders' turnover.

Imprinting Effects of Early TMTs

Rooting on the influential contributions of the SPEC project, several studies have adhered to the idea that high-tech start-ups' early TMTs exert a strong imprinting effect on the organizational design of their firms (see Schreyögg & Sydow 2011 for a recent review on imprinting). It has been documented that founders and early top executives tend to lock in the adoption of particular structures and decision systems (Baron et al. 1999). Beckman and Burton (2008) found that the structure of early TMTs in terms of top executives' roles and task specialization predicts its subsequent structure. Initial strengths and fallacies in the structure of early TMTs turn out to be highly path-dependent and persist over time. Notably, it is difficult for early TMTs which have a limited array of functional positions and are composed by narrowly experienced individuals to add the functional competences which are not embodied in the team from the inception, even though the addition of these competences would clearly be beneficial for the firm.

One may wonder about the sources of the difficulties that early TMTs formed by top executives with a narrow range of functional competences have in attracting new members with diverse expertise. The SPEC project emphasizes the role of the blueprints of early TMTs' members in shaping future evolution of a TMT composition (Baron & Hannan 2002). An alternative explanation lies in the imperfections of the market for top executives. Firstly, TMTs' incumbent members bear high transaction costs (Williamson 1985) in scouting for new candidate top executives who can bring novel functional competences to the team. Indeed, these candidates can hardly be reached through the social network of the incumbent executives, which is likely to include individuals experienced in the same functional domains. Secondly, there are asymmetric information problems (Akerlof 1970) between candidate top executives and early TMTs' members. Once a potential candidate has been identified, incumbent TMT members have to evaluate their competences. Given the difference in expertise domains, such an assessment is far from simple. Moreover, incumbent TMT members have to convince the candidate of the quality of the firm and the strength of its future prospects. Premium compensation may be required in order to induce a candidate to join a TMT formed by executives who have competences which are distant from her own expertise.

Founder–CEO Succession and Founders' Turnover in the TMTs of High-Tech Start-Ups

As mentioned above, a newly created high-tech start-up is largely dependent on its founder(s) who had the entrepreneurial idea leading to firm inception. Accordingly, in the early days of most high-tech start-ups, the CEO's role is held by one of the founders. Literature has extensively discussed the advantages for a start-up of having a founder-CEO (Wasserman 2008). A founder-CEO is usually intrinsically motivated (Wasserman 2006). They tend to view their venture as an extension of themselves and usually work hard towards its success (Pierce et al. 2001). Such a strong commitment reduces the need for high-powered incentives to foster the profusion of managerial effort (Wasserman 2006) and favorably impacts on the evaluations that external stakeholders form about a new venture (Dobrev and Barnett 2005).[7] Moreover, being the firm's originator, the founder-CEO is likely to have more firm-specific knowledge, which may prove to be crucial for firm's success (Acharya et al. 2011). Such knowledge usually encompasses the mastering of firms' production processes and technologies (i.e. firm-specific human capital; Becker 1994). In addition, the founder-CEO normally has an in-depth acquaintance of the people in various ways linked to the start-up (e.g. other members of the TMT, employees, members of the board of directors, lead costumers and external investors) and of the relationships among them (firm-specific social capital; Offstein et al. 2005). All this fosters problem solving, effective decision-making, and coordination with the firm's members and stakeholders. However, having a founder as CEO has its own drawbacks. The most important of them is related to the lack of the required managerial competences (e.g., Jayaraman et al. 2000). As a start-ups evolves towards an established business, it quickly outgrows the managerial capabilities of its founders. Moreover, scholars have observed that the presence of a founder-CEO is detrimental for a new venture's legitimacy in that such a structural arrangement does not mimic the typical organization of established firms (Delmar & Shane 2004). Other studies have shown the dark side of founders' psychological attachment that may result, for instance, in insane reactions to a new venture's unfavorable performance. Therefore, the addition to the TMT of professional managers and the replacement of the founder-CEO are mandatory to evolve into a successful business (Audia & Rider 2005; Hofer & Charan 1984).

Several studies have analyzed the antecedents of the founder-CEO succession in high-tech start-ups relying on quantitative research designs. These studies have documented that a founder-CEO's succession is related to their personal characteristics (Wasserman 2003). Specifically, Jain and Tabak (2008) have documented a negative relationship between the founder's age and the probability that a start-up goes public with the founder-CEO at the helm. Likewise, it has been shown that more experienced founder-CEOs normally have a longer tenure in their new ventures (e.g. Boeker and Fleming 2010). A longer tenure is also associated with the possession of a higher share of equity ownership (DeTienne 2010) by the founder-CEO and with the founder-CEO's stronger influence on the board of directors (Gao & Jain 2012).[8] Moreover, the succession of the founder-CEO has been related to milestone company events, like the granting of the first patent or the receipt of venture capital (VC) (see below). Specifically, whether or not to retain the founder-CEO is a key decision for a VC investor (Pollock et al. 2009: 200). Evidence exists that, when first looking at a high-tech start-up, VC investors move from the default assumption that the founder-CEO cannot lead the company (Wasserman 2003: 167). Replacing the founder-CEO is a concrete action that VC investors often undertake to provide an important signal of good and active governance to other stake-holders. Such an action is also intended as a crucial passage to move the organization in new strategic directions (Finkelstein et al. 2009; Wiesenfeld et al. 2008).

Scholars agree that, whatever its antecedents, the founder-CEO succession usually engenders substantial consequences on the future of a high-tech start-up. Firstly, it triggers the reorganization of the TMT (Baron et al. 1999; Beckman & Burton 2008). High-tech start-ups with founder-CEOs are expected to maintain over time a founder-centric structure (Nelson 2003) with poorly formalized roles and an autocratic decision system (i.e. most of decisions are centralized to the CEO). Conversely, high-tech start-ups headed by professional CEOs are likely to have TMTs with more formalized roles, specialized tasks and more decentralized decision systems (Talaulicar et al. 2005). Additionally, extant literature has shown that founder-CEO succession positively impacts on new ventures' ability to attract key employees (Baron et al. 2001) and acquire financial resources (Boeker & Karichalil 2002; Certo et al. 2001; Nelson 2003). Conversely, the available evidence on the performance consequences of the founder-CEO's succession is rather inconclusive. Some studies find that replacing a founder-CEO enhances performance (e.g. Beckman et al. 2007), while other works document no impact of CEO succession on performance (e.g. Daily & Dalton 1992), and yet others find that firms benefit from founder-CEO retention (Fischer & Pollock 2004; Forbes et al. 2010).

As high-tech start-ups age and grow, TMT professionalization may involve not only the succession of the founder-CEO, but also the replacement of other founders who serve as top executives. The evolution of TMT in terms of founders' turnover has been comparatively less explored. As noted by Hambrick (2007), the literature on TMT has not only mainly focused on established companies, but it has also largely concentrated on the CEO role. Studies by Boeker and co-authors are notable exceptions. Boeker and Karichalil (2002) have examined the factors that determine founders' departure from early TMTs, showing that the size and the growth rate of high-tech start-ups positively predict founders' turnover. Conversely, due to the high-tech nature of the business, founders' background in research and development (R&D) reduces their turnover as founders' technical competences are required to run the business. Boeker and Wiltbank (2005) have brought further support to these results by documenting that the need to change the composition of the early TMT is tempered by both founders' greater industry experience and functional diversity. Another result of Boeker and Wiltbank's study mimics a finding which is common in works on founder-CEO succession. Specifically: founders' ownership of equity capital and their good relationships with the board of directors negatively affect founders' turnover.

Finally, an issue that has remained almost unexplored in the literature is the relationship between the TMT and the other components of high-tech start-ups' managerial hierarchy. In fact, besides the substitution of top executive founders or the addition of functional positions to the TMT, the professionalization of high-tech start-ups may encompass the increase of the firm's vertical depth. In this respect, the creation of a middle-management level is an important milestone (Charan et al. 1980). As it is highlighted by the aforementioned study by Colombo and Grilli (forthcoming), the recruitment of one or more middle managers to which authority over specific (mainly operating) decisions can be delegated by the TMT has two (potential) advantages. Firstly, in accordance with the insights of the knowledge hierarchy literature (Garicano 2000), it alleviates information overload problems and protects the time of TMT members who can concentrate on strategic decisions. Secondly, it helps to use in decision making the specific knowledge possessed by individuals who are elevated to the managerial ranks (Aghion & Tirole 1997), thus improving the firm's decision system. Results of econometric estimations support the former argument. They show that the higher the human capital of the TMT's members, as measured by their education (especially in management and economics) and work experience, the greater the likelihood of the appointment of a middle manager. Conversely, there is no evidence that the lack of functional competences within the TMT, as reflected by the homogeneity of the work experience of TMT's members, favors the creation of a middle-management position. Moreover, the work of Colombo and Grilli (forthcoming) highlights that high-tech start-ups often face severe imperfections in the labor market for middle managers, which echo those of the market for top executives (see infra). These imperfections make it difficult for high-tech start-ups to deepen their corporate hierarchy, but can be alleviated by credible signals of firm quality. Accordingly, Colombo and Grilli (forthcoming) show that backing by a VC investor (and to a less extent receipt of competitive R&D grants) leads to an increase in the likelihood of creating a middle-management position, while uncertainty as regards a firm's value and business prospects has an opposite effect.

PROMISING AVENUES FOR FUTURE RESEARCH

The aim of the present section is to highlight gaps in the extant literature on the organizational design of high-tech start-ups and indicate promising avenues for future research. We move from the acknowledgement of the heterogeneity of high-tech start-ups, which differ along several dimensions. The organizational design literature has not adequately dwelled on this heterogeneity. Further inquiry is thus needed to understand how it influences the organizational design of high-tech start-ups and moderates the link between organizational design and firm performance. This is a wide and challenging research project. For sake of synthesis, we focus here on two crucial dimensions along which high-tech start-ups allegedly differ: (1) the technological nature of the competences of their founders, that is, the technical intensity of their human capital; and (2) the appropriability regime under which these firms operate.

Technical Intensity of Human Capital: Consequences for High-Tech Start Ups' Organizational Design

A telling example of high-tech start-ups characterized by a high technical intensity of their founders' human capital is offered by start-ups created by academic personnel (i.e. academic start-ups, ASUs) (Colombo & Piva 2008; see Rothaermel et al. 2007 for a comprehensive review on ASUs). ASUs' founders are typically highly skilled in scientific and technological fields. However, they generally lack industry-specific experience (both technical and commercial), and managerial and entrepreneurial experience (Ensley & Hmieleski 2005). Indeed, academic founders seldom hold managerial positions in other companies or have been involved in self-employment episodes before the foundation of their focal venture (Siegel et al. 2007). Colombo and Piva (2012) have documented that the high-technical intensity of ASUs' human capital shapes the strategies that these firms adopt to enlarge their initial competence endowment. These strategies differ considerably from those of other high-tech start-ups. Specifically, ASUs are more oriented to invest in R&D, hire qualified technical personnel and establish technological collaborations with public research organizations. To the best of our knowledge, no study has yet investigated in a systematic way whether and how ASUs' peculiar human capital characteristics and associated competence-enlarging strategies impact on their organizational design. We consider this as a promising avenue for future research.

Firstly, we expect that the human capital characteristics of ASUs' founders, and notably, the homogeneity of their human capital, hamper task specialization and role formalization within ASUs' TMTs. Secondly, ASUs' founders generally lack social contacts outside academic circles (Stuart & Ding 2006), whilst the science-based nature of ASUs' businesses makes information asymmetries between firm insiders (i.e. the ASUs' academic founders) and outsiders especially severe. As a consequence, ASUs face major challenges in enlarging the functional competences of their initial TMT, even though this move would be highly beneficial for them. A similar reasoning applies to ASUs' vertical depth. In accordance with this argument, Colombo and Piva (2012) have shown that ASUs find it difficult to create a middle-manager position, thereby increasing the vertical depth of their organization (i.e. switching from a two- to a three-layer structure).

The human capital characteristics of ASUs are likely to affect their decision systems alike, although their net effect on this element of firm organizational design is undetermined as opposite forces are at work. On the one hand, we mentioned above that ASUs concentrate their investments in the R&D function. Hence, they generally have a simple value chain consisting in few well-defined technological tasks. The number of information items to be processed and communicated is smaller and the set of relevant strategic decisions is narrower than for the other start-ups. The pressure to adopt a decentralized decision system to protect top executives' time is more limited. On the other hand, the success of ASUs largely depends on their ability to leverage the knowledge possessed by talented scientists and engineers, with opposite implications for the decentralization of decision authority.

As high-tech start-ups created by individuals with outstanding technical skills (e.g. star scientists and engineers) age and grow, they are likely to catch the attention of VC investors, who may be attracted by the high technical intensity of the human capital of these firms. The receipt of VC is a crucial milestone along the lifecycle of this type of high-tech start-ups. Bringing novel skills and external relations, the advent of a VC investor challenges the central role of founders' technical competences. A growing stream of literature has explored the modifications that VC investors engender on high-tech start-ups' TMTs, focusing in particular on founder-CEO succession (Pollock et al. 2009). Other studies (e.g., Flynn 1991) have analyzed how VC backing shapes high-tech start-ups' decision systems. However, these contributions failed to recognize that the effects of VC backing on high-tech start-ups' organizational structures and decision systems are likely to depend on the type of the VC investors, who are heterogeneous in their nature and goals. Independent venture capitalists (IVCs) are interested in scaling up firms' technical offering before exiting the investment (Gompers & Lerner 2004). Evidence exists that IVCs usually add new functional competences to the TMTs of the ventures they back, specialize roles within their TMTs, hire salaried managers and establish more decentralized decision systems (Bottazzi et al. 2008; Colombo & Grilli 2010; Hellmann & Puri 2002).

Conversely, corporate venture capital (CVC) is generally used by incumbent firms to gain a window onto valuable technologies possessed by high-tech start-ups (e.g., Dushnitsky & Lenox 2005). To the extent that CVC-backed high-tech start-ups are induced to concentrate effort on technology development, and leave responsibility for management of complementary assets to the parent company of their CVC investors, the effects on firms' organizational design are likely to be opposite to those engendered by IVC backing. Specifically, we expect that CVC-backed high-tech start-ups centralize decisions in the CEO's hands, have a small and poorly specialized TMT and a flat corporate hierarchy.

Lastly, empirical evidence documents that governmental VC (GVC) is less effective than other VC investors in providing coaching and other support services (see, e.g., Cumming & MacIntosh 2006). Accordingly, one can expect that GVC backing has a limited impact on high-tech start-ups' organizational design as it does not have ability for (and the interest in) shaping the structure and decision systems of its investee firms.

Differences in Appropriability Regimes: Consequences for High-Tech Start-Ups' Organizational Design

Differences in appropriability regime play a major role in determining high-tech start-ups' heterogeneity (Gans & Stern 2003). If the appropriability regime is 'tight', high-tech start-ups may choose to focus on the market for ideas (Arora & Gambardella 2010). It is reasonable to expect that the organizational design challenges of high-tech start-ups operating in the market for ideas differ substantially from those of their peers that are active in the market for products. As a matter of fact, high-tech start-ups in the market for ideas act as R&D labs. Firstly, like ASUs, they have a narrower set of decisions in comparison with firms operating in the market for products and, accordingly, less information items to be processed and transmitted. Specifically, TMT members must make few crucial decisions about technology development and licensing strategies, and they are less likely to suffer from information overload. Consequently, one expects that high-tech start-ups in the market for ideas centralize these few crucial decisions in the CEO's hands and are less compelled both to enlarge the initial TMT by adding new roles and to increase the vertical depth of their corporate hierarchy. Secondly, for high-tech start-ups in the market for ideas it is crucial to protect technological knowledge from imitation. In this respect, the award of the first patent is a crucial milestone that changes the technology protection strategy from one relying on secrecy to one based on formal projection of intellectual property rights (IPRs). We expect a firm's organizational design to change accordingly.[9] In the pre-patenting phase secrecy is the best, if not the only, protection mechanism for high-tech start-ups, which must thus cope with significant appropriability hazards. The need to minimize these hazards may exert a significant impact on the firm's organizational design. We argue that high-tech start-ups which rely mainly on secrecy prefer to avoid adding new functional competences to their TMT or hiring middle managers, so as to reduce the risks of technological leakages. If the need for new competences becomes particularly compelling, it is reasonable to expect that high-tech start-ups would prefer to enlarge the TMT by taking another owner-manager on board instead of appointing a salaried top executive. Indeed, the financial investment that the new owner-manager makes in the high-tech start up acts as an hostage, making their commitment not to disclose corporate secrets more credible (Williamson 1983). Such a hostage is lacking in the case of the appointment of a salaried manager, who provides only labor services from their human capital without investing resources. In this latter case, opportunistic behaviors may arise, paving the way to detrimental technological leakages as the salaried executive may be hired by a competitor or found their own start-up. In a similar vein, we posit that in their pre-patenting phase, high-tech start-ups would prefer to adopt more centralized decision systems, so as to reduce unintended technological linkages that may arise if firm's staff is highly involved in decision making.

Conversely, when high-tech start-ups operate under a weak appropriability regime, complementary assets do play a crucial role for successfully developing the business (Teece 1986; Gans & Stern 2003). High-tech start-ups do not normally have the resources and competences needed to develop these complementary assets internally. Thus, collaborations with external parties possessing these assets are of crucial importance. Accordingly, to compete successfully on the market, high-tech start-ups must adopt an organizational design suitable to leverage these external collaborations (Colombo et al. 2012). Indeed, with a centralized decision system and a flat hierarchy, a firm's numerous collaborative links with third parties may cause information overload of the CEO and TMT members (Simsek 2009). In addition, relevant knowledge needed to effectively manage external collaborations may be dispersed across multiple individuals within and outside the TMT. Adding new functional competences to the TMT, specializing tasks within the TMT or increasing the vertical depth of the organization by appointing middle managers and delegating to them responsibility for specific tasks, may help in coping with information overload and dispersion of relevant knowledge. For instance, high-tech start-ups operating under a weak appropriability regime might find it useful to appoint an alliance manager and to delegate their (strategic or operating) decisions regarding external collaborations with other firms.

NOTES

1. The design of the organizational structure that optimally copes with environmental contingencies by balancing efficiency and flexibility has been a long-debated issue in the organizational design field. Contingency theorists (e.g. Lawrence & Lorsch 1967) have championed the idea that firms should be less structured under conditions of high uncertainty and change. In an early study, Burns and Stalker (1961) found that organizations characterized by decentralized decision making, broader and more fluid roles and wider span of control perform well in dynamic markets because they have higher flexibility which gives executives more degrees of freedom to operate. In contrast, other authors (Mintzberg 1979; Vroom & Yetton 1973) proposed an autocratic approach according to which a centralized structure is more suitable to changing environments. For instance, a powerful CEO is more able to resolutely and authoritatively head their company in troubled waters.
2. The construct of decision speed points to the rapidity of decision-making processes. A comprehensive decision-making process is one that is exhaustive in the generation and evaluation of the alternatives (Fredrickson & Mitchell 1984: 402).
3. On the need to balance decision speed and comprehensiveness when designing the structure of high-tech start-ups, see also Talaulicar et al. (2005).
4. Role formalization in start-ups' TMTs captures 'what one is asked to do'. Specialization of tasks refers to the concentration of the tasks assigned to each member of the TMT, with greater specialization involving less concentration of tasks (Sine et al. 2006).
5. Bourgeois and Eisenhardt's (1988: 823–824) case studies on high-tech start-ups located in Silicon Valley document that CEOs usually made an initial, decisive choice and then laid out subsequent decisions to be triggered by a schedule, a milestone or a specific event. In the case of high-tech start-ups high-level strategic decisions typically encompass the choice of concentrating a firm's scarce resources on radical innovation projects in nascent technological domains, entering a foreign market, acquiring a competitor, or establishing an alliance with a lead customer.
6. According to the 'upper echelon theory' firms' strategic behavior and performance are shaped by the actions of their top executives who form the TMT. In turn, TMT members' actions are determined by their cognitions and personal interpretations of the situations they face. Cognitions and personal interpretations can be proxied by top executives' demographic characteristics (i.e. age, gender, functional experience, prior affiliations and educational background; Hambrick 2007: 334).
7. As to this latter aspect, the literature has documented that the presence of a founder-CEO positively affects the valuation and returns to first-day investors on the occasion of a new venture's initial public offering (Certo et al. 2001; Certo et al. 2003).
8. The relationship between founder-CEO succession and the founder-CEO's influence on the board

of directors has been extensively investigated by the literature on CEO duality (i.e. the CEO being also the chair of the board of directors). See Dalton and Dalton (2011) for a recent survey of this literature.

9. Note, however, that high-tech start ups may not have the financial resources to commit to an aggressive patent protection strategy (Acs & Audretsch 1990; Aroundel 2001). Hence, the introduction of changes in firm organizational design crucially depends on the availability of financial resources.

REFERENCES

Acharya, V.V., S.C. Myers and R.G. Rajan (2011), 'The internal governance of firms', *Journal of Finance*, **66**(3), 689–720.

Acs, Z.J. and D.B. Audretsch (1990), *Innovation and Small Firms*, Cambridge, MA: MIT Press.

Adler, P.S., B. Goldoftas and D.I. Levine (1999), 'Flexibility versus efficiency? A case study of model change-overs in the Toyota production system', *Organization Science*, **10**, 43–68.

Aghion, P. and J. Tirole (1997), 'Formal and real authority in organizations', *Journal of Political Economy*, **105**, 1–29.

Akerlof, G.A. (1970), 'The market for "lemons": quality uncertainty and the market mechanism', *Quarterly Journal of Economics*, **84**, 488–500.

Aldrich, H.E. (1999), *Organizations Evolving*, Newbury Park, CA: Sage.

Alonso R. and N. Matouschek (2008), 'Optimal delegation', *Review of Economic Studies*, **75**, 259–293.

Ambos, T.C. and J. Birkinshaw (2010), 'How do new ventures evolve? An inductive study of archetype changes in science-based ventures', *Organization Science*, **21**(6), 1125–1140.

Arora, A. and A. Gambardella (2010), 'Ideas for rent: an overview of markets for technology', *Industrial and Corporate Change*, **19**(3), 775–803.

Aroundel, A. (2001), 'The relative effectiveness of patents and secrecy for appropriation', *Research Policy*, **30**, 611–624.

Audia, P.G. and C.I. Rider (2005), 'A garage and an idea: what more does an entrepreneur need?' *California Management Review*, **48**, 6–28.

Audretsch, D.B. (1995), *Innovation and Industry Evolution*, Cambridge, MA: MIT Press.

Baron, J.N. and M.D. Burton (1999), 'Engineering bureaucracy: the genesis of formal policies, positions, and structures in high-technology firms', *Journal of Law, Economics, and Organization*, **15**(1), 1–41.

Baron, J.N. and M.T. Hannan (2002), 'Organizational blueprints for success in high-tech start-ups', *California Management Review*, **44**(3), 8–36.

Baron, J.N., M.T. Hannan and M.D. Burton (1999), 'Building the iron cage: determinants of managerial intensity in the early years of organizations', *American Sociological Review*, **64**, 527–547.

Baron, J.N., M.T. Hannan and M.D. Burton (2001), 'Labor pains: change in organizational models and employee turnover in young, high-tech firms', *American Journal of Sociology*, **106**(4), 960–1012

Becker, G. (1994), *Human Capital: A Theoretical and Empirical Analysis with Special Reference to Education*, Chicago, IL: University of Chicago Press.

Beckman, C.M. and M.D. Burton (2008), 'Founding the future: path dependence in the evolution of top management teams from founding to IPO', *Organization Science*, **19**(1), 3–24.

Beckman, C., M. Burton and C. O'Reilly (2007), 'Early teams: the impact of team demography on VC financing and going public', *Journal of Business Venturing*, **22**(2), 147–173.

Boeker W. and B. Fleming (2010), 'Parent firm effects on founder turnover: parent success, founder legitimacy, and founder tenure', *Strategic Entrepreneurship Journal*, **4**, 252–267.

Boeker, W. and R. Karichalil (2002), 'Entrepreneurial transitions: factors influencing founder departure', *Academy of Management Journal*, **45**, 818–826.

Boeker, W. and R. Wiltbank (2005), 'New venture evolution and managerial capabilities', *Organization Science*, **16**(2), 123–133.

Bottazzi, L., M. Da Rin and T. Hellmann (2008), 'Who are the active investors? Evidence from venture capital', *Journal of Financial Economics*, **89**, 488–512.

Bourgeois, L.J. and K.M. Eisenhardt (1988), 'Strategic decision processes in high velocity environments: four cases in the microcomputer industry', *Management Science*, **34**(7), 816–835.

Bournois, F., J. Duval-Hamel, S. Rossiglione and J.L. Scaringella (2011), *Handbook of Top Management Teams*, London: Palgrave Macmillan.

Burns, T. and G.M. Stalker (1961), *The Management of Innovation*, London: Tavistock Publications.

Carpenter, R.E. and B.C. Petersen (2002), 'Is the growth of small firms constrained by internal finance?' *Review of Economics and Statistics*, **84**, 298–309.

Certo, S.T, J.G. Covin, C.M. Daily and D.R. Dalton (2001), 'Wealth and the effects of founder management among IPO-stage new ventures', *Strategic Management Journal*, **22**(6–7), 641–658.

Certo, S.T., C.M. Daily, A.A. Cannella, Jr. and D.R. Dalton (2003), 'Giving money to get money: how CEO stock options and CEO equity enhance IPO valuations', *Academy of Management Journal*, **46**(5), 643–653.

Charan, R., C.W. Hofer and J.F. Mahon (1980), 'From entrepreneurial to professional management; a set of guidelines', *Journal of Small Business Management*, **19**, 110–119.

Colombo, M.G. and L. Grilli (2005), 'Founders' human capital and the growth of new technology-based firms: a competence-based view', *Research Policy*, **34**(6), 795–816.

Colombo, M.G. and L. Grilli (2010), 'On growth drivers of high-tech start-ups: exploring the role of founders' human capital and venture capital', *Journal of Business Venturing*, **25**(6), 610–626.

Colombo, M.G. and Piva, E. (2008), 'Strengths and weaknesses of academic startups: a conceptual model', *IEEE Transactions on Engineering Management*, **55**(1), 37–49.

Colombo, M.G. and E. Piva (2012), 'Firms' genetic characteristics and competence-enlarging strategies: a comparison between academic and non-academic high-tech start-ups', *Research Policy*, **41**(1), 79–92.

Colombo, M.G., N.J. Foss and C. Rossi-Lamastra (2012), 'Organizational design for absorptive capacity linking individual and organizational levels', CBS Working Paper.

Cumming, D.J. and J.G. MacIntosh (2006), 'Crowding out private equity: Canadian evidence', *Journal of Business Venturing*, **21**(5), 569–609.

Daily, C.M. and D.A.N.R. Dalton (1992), 'The relationship between governance structure and corporate performance in entrepreneurial firms', *Journal of Business Venturing*, **7**(5), 375–386.

Dalton, D.A.N.R. and C.M. Dalton (2011), 'Integration of micro and macro studies in governance research: CEO duality, board composition, and financial performance', *Journal of Management*, **37**(2), 404–411.

David, R. and S. Han (2003), 'A systematic assessment of the empirical support for transaction cost economics', *Strategic Management Journal*, **25**, 39–58.

Davis, J.P., K.M. Eisenhardt and C.B. Bingham (2009), 'Optimal structure, market dynamism, and the strategy of simple rules', *Administrative Science Quarterly*, **54**(3), 413–452.

Delmar, F. and S. Shane (2004, 'Legitimating first: organizing activities and the survival of new ventures', *Journal of Business Venturing*, **19**(3), 385–410.

Dessein, W. (2002), 'Authority and communication in organizations', *Review of Economic Studies*, **69**, 811–838.

DeTienne, D.R. (2010), 'Entrepreneurial exit as a critical component of the entrepreneurial process: theoretical development', *Journal of Business Venturing*, **25**, 203–215.

Dobrev, S. and Barnett, W. (2005), 'Organizational roles and transition to entrepreneurship', *Academy of Management Journal*, **48**, 433–449.

Drazin, R. and A.H. Van de Ven (1985), 'Alternative forms of fit in contingency theory', *Administrative Science Quarterly*, **30**(4), 514–539.

Dushnitsky, G. and M.J. Lenox (2005), 'When do incumbents learn from entrepreneurial ventures?' *Research Policy*, **34**(5), 615–639.

Eisenhardt, K.M. (1989), 'Making fast decision in high-velocity environments', *Academy of Management Journal*, **32**(3), 543–576.

Eisenhardt, K.M. (2010), 'Silicon Valley, theories of organization, and the Stanford legacy', in C.B. Schoonhoven and F. Dobbin (eds), *Stanford's Organization Theory Renaissance, 1970–2000*, Research in the Sociology of Organizations, Vol. 28, Brighton: Emerald, pp. 191–205.

Eisenhardt, K.M. and Martin J.A. (2000), 'Dynamic capabilities: what are they?' *Strategic Management Journal*, **21**(10–11), 1105–1121.

Eisenhardt, K.M. and B.N. Tabrizzi (1995), 'Accelerating adaptive processes: product innovation in the global computer industry', *Administrative Science Quarterly*, **40**, 84–110.

Eisenhardt, K. and Mark J. Zbaracki (1992), 'Strategic decision making', *Strategic Management Journal*, **13**, 17–37.

Eisenhardt, K.M., N.R. Furr and C.B. Bingham (2010), 'Microfoundations of performance: balancing efficiency and flexibility in dynamic environments', *Organization Science*, **21**(6), 1263–1273.

Ensley, M.D. and K.M. Hmieleski (2005), 'A comparative study of new venture top management team composition, dynamics and performance between university-based and independent start-ups', *Research Policy*, **34**(7), 1091–1105.

Finkelstein, S., D.C. Hambrick and A.A. Cannella, Jr. (2009), *Strategic Leadership: Theory and Research on Executives, Top Management Teams, and Boards*, New York: Oxford University Press.

Fischer, H.M. and T.G. Pollock (2004), 'Effects of social capital and power on surviving transformational change: the case of initial public offerings', *Academy of Management Journal*, **47**(4), 463–481.

Flynn, D.M. (1991), 'The critical relationship between venture capitalists and entrepreneurs: planning, decision-making, and control', *Small Business Economics*, **3**(3), 185–196.

Forbes, D.P., M.A. Korsgaard and H.J. Sapienza (2010), 'Financing decisions as a source of conflict in venture boards', *Journal of Business Venturing*, **25**(6), 579–592.

Fredrickson, J.W. and T.R. Mitchell (1984), 'Strategic decision processes: comprehensiveness and performance in an industry with an unstable environment', *Academy of Management Journal*, **27**(2), 399–423.

Gans, J.S. and S. Stern (2003), 'The product market and the market for ideas: commercialization strategies for technology entrepreneurs', *Research Policy*, **32**(2), 333–350.

Gao, N. and B.A. Jain (2012), 'Founder management and the market for corporate control for IPO firms: the moderating effect of the power structure of the firm', *Journal of Business Venturing*, **27**(1), 112–126.

Garicano, L. (2000), 'Hierarchies and the organization of knowledge in production', *Journal of Political Economy*, **108**, 874–904.

Gimeno, J., T. Folta, A. Cooper and C. Woo (1997), 'Survival of the fittest? Entrepreneurial human capital and the persistence of underperforming firms', *Administrative Science Quarterly*, **42**, 750–783.

Gompers, P.A. and J. Lerner (2004), *The Venture Capital Cycle*, Cambridge, MA: MIT Press.

Grandori, A. and L. Gaillard Giordani (2011), *Organizing Entrepreneurship*, Abingdon, UK and New York: Routledge.

Hambrick, D.C. (2007), 'Editor's forum upper echelons theory: an update', *Academy of Management Review*, **32**(2), 334–343.

Hambrick, D.C. and P.A. Mason (1984), 'Upper echelons: the organization as a reflection of its top managers', *Academy of Management Review*, **9**, 193–206.

Harris, M. and A. Raviv (2002), 'Organization design', *Management Science*, **48**(7), 852–865.

He, L. (2008), 'Do founders matter? A study of executive compensation, governance structure and firm performance', *Journal of Business Venturing*, **23**(3), 257–279.

Hellmann, T. and M. Puri (2002), 'Venture capital and the professionalization of start-up firms', *Journal of Finance*, **57**(1), 169–198.

Hofer, C.W. and R. Charan (1984), 'The transition to professional management: Mission Impossible?' *American Journal of Small Business*, **9**(1), 1–11.

Jain, B. and F. Tabak (2008), 'Factors influencing the choice between founder versus non-founder CEOs for IPO firms', *Journal of Business Venturing*, **23**(1), 21–45.

Jayaraman, N., A. Khorana, E. Nelling and J. Covin (2000), 'CEO-founder status and firm financial performance', *Strategic Management Journal*, **21**(12), 1215–1224.

Jensen, M. and C. Meckling (1992), 'Specific and general knowledge, and organizational structure', in L. Werin and H. Wijkander (eds), *Contract Economics*, Cambridge, MA: Blackwell, pp. 251–274.

Keidel, R.W. (1995), *Seeing Organizational Patterns: A New Theory and Language of Organizational Design*, San Francisco, CA: Berrett-Koelher Publisher.

Keren, Michael and David Levhari (1979), 'The optimum span of control in a pure hierarchy', *Management Science*, **25**(11), 1162–1172.

Keren, Michael and David Levhari (1983), 'The internal organization of the firm and the shape of average costs', *Bell Journal of Economics*, **14**(2), 474–486.

Keren, Michael and David Levhari (1989), 'Decentralization, aggregation, control loss and costs in a hierarchical model of the firm', *Journal of Economic Behavior and Organization*, **11**(2), 213–236.

Knight, F. (1921), *Risk, Uncertainty, and Profit*, Boston: Houghton Mifflin.

Lawrence, P. and J. Lorsch (1967), 'Differentiation and integration in complex organizations', *Administrative Science Quarterly*, **12**, 1–30.

Lazear, E.P. (2005), 'Entrepreneurship', *Journal of Labor Economics*, **23**(4), 649–680.

Lowe, R.A. (2001), 'The role and experience of inventors and start-ups in commercializing university research: case studies at the University of California', in G.D. Libecap (ed.), *Entrepreneurial Inputs and Outcomes: New Studies of Entrepreneurship in the United States*, Advances in the Study of Entrepreneurship, Innovation and Economic Growth, Vol. 13, Brighton: Emerald Group Publishing, pp. 189–222.

Mintzberg, H. (1979), *The Structuring of Organizations: A Synthesis of the Research*, Englewood Cliffs, NJ: Prentice-Hall.

Nelson, T. (2003), 'The persistence of founder influence: management, ownership, and performance effects at initial public offering', *Strategic Management Journal*, **24**(8), 707–724.

Offstein, E.H., D.R. Gnyawali and A.T. Cobb (2005), 'Strategic human resource perspective of firm competitive behavior', *Human Resource Management Review*, **15**, 305–318.

Pierce, J.L., T. Kostova and K.T. Dirks (2001), 'Toward a theory of psychological ownership in organizations', *Academy of Management Review*, **26**(2), 298–310.

Pollock, T.G., B.R. Fund and T. Baker (2009), 'Dance with the one that brought you? Venture capital firms and the retention of founder-CEOs', *Strategic Entrepreneurship Journal*, **3**, 199–217.

Radner, R. (1993), 'The organization in decentralized information processing', *Econometrica*, **61**, 1109–1146.

Rothaermel, F.T., D.A. Shanti and L. Jiang (2007), 'University entrepreneurship: a taxonomy of the literature', *Industrial and Corporate Changes*, **16**(4), 691–791.

Sah, R.K. and J.E. Stiglitz (1986), 'The architecture of economic systems: hierarchies and polyarchies', *American Economic Review*, **76**, 716–727.

Siegel, D.S., M. Wright and A. Lockett (2007), 'The rise of entrepreneurial activity at universities: organizational and societal implications', *Industry and Corporate Changes*, **16**(4), 489–504.

Simons, T. and P.W. Roberts (2008), 'New organizational form penetration: the case of the Israeli wine industry', *Administrative Science Quarterly*, **53**, 235–265.

Simsek, Z. (2009), 'Organizational ambidexterity: towards a multilevel understanding', *Journal of Management Studies*, **46**, 597–624.

Sine, W.D., H. Mitsuhashi and D.A. Kirsch (2006), 'Revisiting Burns and Stalker: formal structure and new venture performance in emerging economic sectors', *Academy of Management Journal*, **49**(1), 121–132.

Smith, W.K and M.W. Lewis (2011), 'Toward a theory of paradox: a dynamic equilibrium model of organizing', *Academy of Management Review*, **36**(2), 381–403.

Stinchcombe, A.L. (1965), 'Social structure and organizations', in James G. March (ed.), *Handbook of Organizations*, New York: Rand McNally, pp. 142–193.

Stuart, T.E. and W.W. Ding (2006), 'When do scientists become entrepreneurs? The social structural antecedents of commercial activities in the academic life science', *American Journal of Sociology*, **112**(1), 97–114.

Talaulicar, T., J. Grundei and A. Werder (2005), 'Strategic decision making in start-ups: the effect of top management team organization and processes on speed and comprehensiveness', *Journal of Business Venturing*, **20**(4), 519–541.

Teece, D.J. (1986), 'Profiting from technological innovation: implications for integration, collaboration, licensing, and public policy', *Research Policy*, **15**(6), 285–305.

Unger, J.M., A. Rauch, M. Frese and N. Rosenbusch (2011), 'Human capital and entrepreneurial success: a meta-analytical review', *Journal of Business Venturing*, **26**(3), 341–358.

Van Zandt, T. (1999), 'Real-time decentralized information processing as a model of organizations with boundedly rational agents', *Review of Economic Studies*, **66**, 633–658.

Vroom, V.H., Yetton H.P. (1973), *Leadership and Decision-Making*, Pittsburgh, PA: University of Pittsburgh Press.

Wasserman, N. (2003), 'Founder-CEO succession and the paradox of entrepreneurial success', *Organization Science*, **14**(2), 149–172.

Wasserman, N. (2006), 'Stewards, agents, and the founder discount: executive compensation in new ventures', *Academy of Management Journal*, **49**(5), 960–976.

Wasserman, N. (2008), 'The founder's dilemma', *Harvard Business Review*, **86**(2), 102–109.

Weick, K.E. (1993), 'The collapse of sense-making in organizations: the Mann Gulch disaster'. *Administrative Science Quarterly*, **38**(4), 628–652.

Wiesenfeld, B.A., K.A. Wurthmann and D.C. Hambrick (2008), 'The stigmatization and devaluation of elites associated with corporate failures: a process model', *Academy of Management Review*, **33**(1), 231–251.

Williamson, O.E. (1983), 'Credible commitments: using hostages to support exchange', *American Economic Review*, **73**(4), 519–540.

Williamson, O.E. (1985), *The Economic Institutions of Capitalism*, New York: Free Press.

PART VI

FORMS OF ECONOMIC ORGANIZATION BETWEEN DISCRETE ALTERNATIVES AND COMBINATIVE CONFIGURATIONS

22. Entrepreneurship, entrepreneurial governance and economic organization
Nicolai J. Foss and Peter G. Klein

We propose an integration of the theory of entrepreneurship and the economics of organization. We start with the concept of entrepreneurship as judgment associated with Knight (1921) and some Austrian school economists, which aligns naturally with the theory of the firm. Judgment is embodied in resource ownership and, while resources can be traded in markets, judgment itself cannot. Hence the entrepreneur needs a firm – a set of alienable assets he controls – to carry out his resource-allocation function. We show how the notion of judgment illuminates key themes in the modern theory of the firm (existence, boundaries and internal organization). In our approach, uses of resources are not data, but are created as entrepreneurs envision and try out new ways of using assets to produce final goods. The entrepreneur's problem is aggravated by the fact that capital assets are heterogeneous. Asset ownership allows the entrepreneur to experiment with novel combinations of heterogeneous assets. The boundaries of the firm, as well as aspects of internal organization, may also be understood as responses to entrepreneurial processes of experimentation. In particular, we offer the notion of 'proxy entrepreneurship', the delegation to employees of the right to act in an entrepreneurial manner. In effect, we build a theory of entrepreneurial governance.[1]

INTRODUCTION: ENTREPRENEURSHIP IN THE CONTEXT OF GOVERNANCE

Firms are created by entrepreneurs, and entrepreneurship is manifest in firms. Indeed, large parts of the entrepreneurship literature ask questions about firms: Why do certain people start firms, while others prefer to be employed? Is this choice explained by incentives, personality differences, cognitive biases, work experience, family background, or something else? Given this emphasis, one might expect a healthy literature on the entrepreneurial nature of firms and the organizational and governance aspects of entrepreneurship – a literature informed by the economics of the firm as well as relevant organizational theory, for example, organizational design theory. Specifically, such a literature would explore issues both of the governance of entrepreneurship (e.g., where in the firm does entrepreneurial activity mainly take place? How does the organization of the firm influence entrepreneurial actions?) and of entrepreneurial governance (e.g., how is entrepreneurship manifest in the design of new organizational forms? Is there such a thing as an 'entrepreneurial firm', distinct from other firms?).

However, the governance of entrepreneurship and (if less so) entrepreneurial governance have relatively little attention in the research literature (see also Grandori & Giordani 2011). The main interest has been the antecedents of entrepreneurship, defined as the formation of 'entrepreneurial' firms, and the characteristics of the founder: experience, cognitive biases, self-efficacy, confidence, and so on (e.g., Shane 2000, 2003). Hence the entrepreneurship literature has shown little interest in entrepreneurial behaviors or attributes within established firms (for example, the Global Entrepreneurship Monitor, one of the most important entrepreneurship databases, generally defines entrepreneurship as new firm formation).

Recently, the emerging strategic entrepreneurship literature (Hitt et al. 2002; Baker & Pollock 2007) has made strides in the conceptualization of entrepreneurship at the level of established firms (i.e., non-start-ups), and some contributions seek to model organizational antecedents of firm-level opportunity recognition and exploitation (e.g., Ireland et al. 2009). While this literature has linked, for example, notions of 'entrepreneurial orientation' to established firms and considered it and its organizational embodiments as relevant antecedents of firm-level entrepreneurship, it is fair to say that relatively little progress has been made on issues of the governance of entrepreneurship and entrepreneurial governance. However, this literature does not yet amount to a coherent conceptualization of entrepreneurial firms. In particular, it adds little to conventional explanations of firm existence, boundaries and internal organization. In short, the firm per se remains a shadowy character in entrepreneurship studies, a passive instrument in the entrepreneur's hands.

As a result, there is no serious entrepreneurial theory of the firm to guide decision-making for the kind of problems that intimately involve both entrepreneurship and organizing; and hence, no theory of the governance modes that are appropriate for governing the entrepreneurial resource allocation process either. To be sure, there are theories of start-up firms in economics and in management and large literatures on product, process and organizational innovation. But mature firms, as well as new firms, act entrepreneurially – witness the emphasis on 'corporate renewal' and 'entrepreneurialism' among practitioners – and entrepreneurship reveals itself in many activities besides innovation. However, when the entrepreneur and the firm are considered together it is usually to explain why established firms fail to be entrepreneurial (Foss 2011). Clayton Christensen's *Innovator's Dilemma* (1997), one of the most influential business books of the last few years, deals with the difficulties facing established firms that try to innovate.

In other work we have given detailed historical accounts of how economics and entrepreneurship research developed in such a way that they become separate (Foss & Klein 2005, 2012). In this chapter we focus less on the historical details and more on a positive strategy for linking entrepreneurship and the theory of the firm. In particular, we show that an entrepreneurial approach to the firm helps link 'resource-based' and 'knowledge-based' approaches to economic organization. In fact, our analysis of the difficulties of trading entrepreneurial judgment may be seen as supplying a theory of the existence and boundaries of the firm that complements these latter approaches.

JUDGMENT: A FOUNDATION FOR ENTREPRENEURSHIP

Our approach begins with a key construct that links entrepreneurship and the theory of the firm: 'entrepreneurial judgment'. Knight (1921) defined judgment as decision-making under uncertainty that cannot be captured in a set of formal decision rules and cannot be hired on the market. Entrepreneurship is judgment about the deployment of productive resources in pursuit of profit, the residual remaining after the factors of production have been paid their rental prices.

Judgment is a meaningful notion of decision making that is intermediate between decision-making via formalizable rules, and pure luck or random behavior (see Casson 1982). It is the kind of decision-making that concerns unique business investments for which it is difficult, or even impossible, to assign meaningful probabilities to outcomes, or even to specify the set of possible outcomes (Shackle 1972; Zeckhauser 2006). When confronted with such a situation, individuals will reach different decisions, even if they share the same objectives and the data are presented to them in exactly the same manner, because they have access to different information and interpret the data in different ways (Lachmann 1977; Casson & Wadeson 2007). In Bayesian terms, priors are diffuse and updating rules may differ.

Judgment and Uncertainty

Economists have usually discussed judgment in a specific epistemic context, namely that of 'uncertainty', sometimes called 'Knightian uncertainty' as homage to the first economist to discuss it systematically (Knight 1921). Uncertainty is one of the most fascinating and perplexing concepts in economics, one that has also recently been picked up by management scholars in the entrepreneurship field (e.g., McMullen & Shepherd 2006). Following Knight we link judgment to uncertainty, treating judgment as the exercise of a particular skill, namely that of dealing successfully with resource allocation decisions under uncertainty.

Certain entrepreneurs and investors seem to have a persistent, successful track record in making such decisions. One explanation for repeated entrepreneurial success, suggested by Alchian (1950) and Taleb (2007) (drawing on a famous thought experiment about coin-flipping by Emile Borél), is that this reflects persistent luck. This hypothesis is rooted in the idea that Knightian uncertainty is fundamentally debilitating, epistemologically, and hence might as well be randomness. Many economists hold this view (e.g., Schultz 1980: 437–438). Knight (1921: 298), however, clearly thought that some people systematically deal with uncertainty better than others: 'Like a large portion of the practical problems of business life, as of all life, this one of selecting human capacities for dealing with unforeseeable situations involves paradox and apparent theoretical impossibility of solution. But like a host of impossible things in life, it is constantly being done.'

Opening the Black Box of Judgment

The question, then, is how 'it is constantly being done'. We can try to open up the black box of judgment, noting that individuals employ a number of decision heuristics to deal with uncertainty. Grandori (2010) draws on the philosophy of science, noting that scientists inherently confront uncertain decision situations, even if they are working within the bounds of normal science (see also Felin & Zenger 2009). Indeed, many heuristics and procedures of established science are fundamentally procedures for dealing with uncertainty. Grandori convincingly argues that those heuristics are not particular to the scientific community, but are the same or close to the heuristics employed by entrepreneurs (see also Loasby 1986; Harper 1996).

In our interpretation, judgment is rooted in skills for handling uncertainty, an idea that was key to Knight's thought. Thus, while the exercise of judgment is a function (or, rather, a set of complementary functions), it is based on perceptions, skills and heuristics (Casson 1982: 25). The link between those characteristics and the judgment they inform is not deterministic, of course; if it were, we would not be talking about judgment, but decision-making according to formal rules. As Phelps (2006: 5) puts it, citing Hayek, 'actors in the world have to make judgments that are not fully implied by their formal models'.

Formulating a decision problem requires specifying potential strategies for dealing with the problem, requiring imaginative skills (Gartner 2007); deriving decision rules (even if, in the spirit of Knight, highly personal and idiosyncratic ones) requires analytical skills; and collecting data requires skills at searching. Certain firms or types of firms may be particularly good at fostering these stills among their employees (Klepper 2002; Braguinsky et al. 2009; Elfenbein et al. 2010). While such skills may be necessary to realizing entrepreneurial ventures, they do not necessarily underlie judgment, even if they are complementary to judgment. Judgment is exactly that extra ingredient added to the above more mundane skills which makes an entrepreneurial venture 'tick'. Because of this 'intuitive' component, judgment involves a high level of tacit knowledge and can perhaps never be made fully explicit.

Skills and knowledge, such as knowledge of specific markets, customer problems, marketing tools, and so on, play a role in entrepreneurial judgment (Shane 2000; Ardichvili et al. 2003), but how? Sarasvathy and colleagues suggest (Sarasvathy 2008; Dew et al. 2009; Read et al. 2009) that such knowledge could in principle be fed into existing analytical frameworks (i.e., frameworks for industry and analysis, procedures for setting up business plans, etc.) to be used in a predictive and analytical way. However, they also argue (e.g., Dew et al. 2009) argue that this is exactly the approach of the 'novice' (fresh, presumably, from the MBA), and that experienced and successful entrepreneurs follow an altogether different logic, namely that of 'effectuation'. Effectuation is an incremental and flexible approach, in which goals are often adjusted under the impact of learning about what can be done with available resources and feedback from the nascent entrepreneur's network.

Judgment also is related to creativity. Influential research (Csikszentmihalyi 1996) posits that creativity can be understood in five stages: preparation, incubation, insight, evaluation and elaboration. Lumpkin et al. (2004) argue that prior experiential knowledge underlies the preparation and incubation stages, in a non-deterministic manner. During the insight phase the entrepreneur has his 'Aha!' moment (Corbett 2005: 478). The two last stages refer to market testing and actual opportunity exploitation. In essence, entrepreneurial creativity is about exploring, defining and redefining the problem space in the pursuit of new opportunities, as memorably captured by Schumpeter's (1911 [1934]) notion of 'new combinations'.

Finally, a key characteristic of entrepreneurship is often taken to be an above-normal willingness to accept gambles with unclear odds (Bhidè 2000). This is not the same as having below-normal risk aversion (as in Kihlstrom & Laffont (1979)), but is rather a matter of ambiguity. The once-influential notion that entrepreneurs are less risk averse than the population at large seems now to have been discarded (Caliendo et al. 2009), and many entrepreneurship scholars argue instead that entrepreneurs tend to come from the ranks of people who are particularly confident when they confront ambiguous decisions (Bhidè 2000; Rigotti et al. 2009) – even irrationally confident (Busenitz & Barney 1997; Bernardo & Welch 2001; Forbes 2005; Koellinger et al. 2007). Coase (1937: 249) argued similarly in his summary of Knight's ideas that 'good judgment is generally associated with confidence in one's judgment'.

ENTREPRENEURIAL JUDGMENT AND THE FIRM

How is judgment manifested, not only in the creation of new firms, but also in the ownership and management of existing firms? In general, agents may realize returns from their human capital through three means: (1) selling labor services on market conditions; (2) entering into employment contracts; or (3) starting a firm. Barzel (1987) argues that moral hazard implies that options (1) and (2) are often inefficient means of realizing these returns. In other words, entrepreneurs know themselves to be good risks but are unable to communicate this to the market. For this reason, firms may emerge because the person whose services are the most difficult to measure (and therefore are most susceptible to moral hazard and adverse selection) becomes an entrepreneur, employing and supervising other agents, and committing capital of his own to the venture, thus contributing a bond.

The judgment-based explanation is somewhat different. Bewley (1989) interprets Knight as providing an explanation of why markets are incomplete that is not quite the same as, while complementary to, explanations based on moral hazard, adverse selection and transaction costs (see also Foss 1993; Langlois & Cosgel 1993). A key point in Knight (1921) is that entrepreneurs are those individuals 'who undertake investments with unevaluatable risks' (Bewley 1989: 32). These risks are therefore uninsurable. Casson (1982: 14) takes a more Schumpeterian position, arguing that, 'The entrepreneur believes he is right, while everyone else is wrong. Thus the essence of entrepreneurship is being different because one has a different perception of the situation' (see also Casson 1997). In these cases, non-contractibility arises because, 'The decisive factors . . . are so largely on the inside of the person making the decision that the "instances" are not amenable to objective description and external control' (Knight 1921: 251). A nascent entrepreneur may be unable to communicate his 'vision' of a commercial experiment – a specific way of combining heterogeneous capital assets to serve future consumer wants – in such a way that other agents can assess its economic implications. In such a case, this nascent entrepreneur cannot be an employee, but will instead start his own firm. The existence of the firm can thus be explained by a specific category of transaction costs, namely, those that close the market for entrepreneurial judgment.

Markets for Judgment?

The argument that markets for judgment are incomplete may seem to be contradicted by the existence of markets for advice-giving. Isn't a strategy consultant essentially in the business of offering judgment to the market regarding resource allocation decisions that are highly uncertain? (Hence, the frequent resort to non-probabilistic scenario analysis.) Aren't businesspeople frequently hired for company boards exactly because their judgment is valued, and aren't they often paid handsomely for this?

Coase (1937) criticized Knight's argument that the attempt to capture the returns to judgment is the fundamental feature of the firm. Thus, Coase (1937: 249) argues that Knight does not, in modern parlance, sufficiently cast the problem in terms of comparative contracting:

> the fact that certain people have better judgment or better knowledge does not mean that they can only get an income from it by themselves taking part in production. They can sell advice or knowledge. Every business buys the advice of a host of advisers. We can imagine a system where all advice or knowledge was bought as required. Again, it possible to get a reward from better knowledge or judgment not by actively taking part in production but by making contracts with people who are producing.

Foss (1996) argues that Coase missed the crucial point of Knight, namely that while much can be 'imagined', the 'system where all advice or knowledge was bought as required' cannot include entrepreneurial judgment; in particular, the entrepreneur's judgment about whether to accept or reject the teachings of his 'host of advisers'. Coase therefore did not recognize that Knight's theory of why the price mechanism is 'superseded' is simply different from his own. Costs of moral hazard or of trying to communicate entrepreneurial judgments close markets for judgments, for the same reasons that judgment is uninsurable. As a result, the entrepreneur has to start a firm to capture the returns to his judgment. Such a firm consists as a minimum of the entrepreneur and the assets he owns. It may, or may not, include employees.

Moreover, keep in mind that our approach associates judgment with ownership and the residual control rights that accrue to ownership under Knightian uncertainty and incomplete contracting. It is true that owners of complementary resources may join an entrepreneurial project, by 'betting on the jockey' (the human resources) rather than 'betting on the horse' (the project itself) (Kaplan et al. 2009). But doing so does not make them entrepreneurs, in the Knightian sense, unless they take equity stakes in the project. If they do not join the entrepreneur in exercising such residual rights, they are like other resource providers who contract with the entrepreneur, but do not themselves exercise the entrepreneurial function.

Judgment and Mundane Activities

In our approach, judgment is required not only for 'novel' activities, in 'dynamic' settings, or within younger organizations. Rather, judgment is exercised whenever productive assets are used in production under conditions of Knightian uncertainty. Even in mature industries, in markets for 'traditional' products in which the technical aspects of production are familiar, market conditions relatively stable, and so on, judgment is required – even if only to make decisions about maintaining the status quo. It is easy to see that innovation requires judgment, but the decision not to invest in research and development (R&D), or to experiment with new combinations or new organizational arrangements, also incorporates entrepreneurial judgment. This is because judgment is part and parcel of residual control rights; it cannot be separated from asset ownership.

By analogy, consider the conventional distinction made by strategists between 'operational' and 'dynamic' capabilities: the former describing a firm's ability to generate profit in the present, the latter denoting its ability to change its current practices and procedures (Winter 2003; Helfat et al. 2007). As Helfat & Winter (2011: 1245) point out, this distinction is hardly iron-clad, as: '(1) change is always occurring to at least some extent; (2) we cannot distinguish dynamic from operational capabilities based on whether they support what is perceived as radical versus non-radical change, or new versus existing businesses; and (3) some capabilities can be used for both operational and dynamic purposes.' Likewise, when productive assets are deployed under Knightian uncertainty, judgment is always occurring, we cannot limit judgment to situations involving radical change, and judgment is necessary for both ongoing and novel activities.

Judgment and the Multi-Asset, Multi-Person Firm

The idea of incomplete markets for judgment helps us understand the one-person firm. However, similar ideas may also be useful for understanding the multi-person firm. As discussed by Foss et al. (2007), when capital is homogenous it is easy to conceive, coordinate and implement plans for producing, marketing and selling goods and services. In the real world of heterogeneous capital assets, by contrast, production plans are much more difficult to conceive, coordinate and implement. It is not necessarily obvious to which activities capital goods are most profitably applied and account has to be taken of complex relations between capital goods. As Lachmann (1956 [1978]: 16) notes:

> the entrepreneur's function ... is to *specify* and make decisions on the concrete form the capital resources shall have. He specifies and modifies the layout of his plant ... As long as we disregard the heterogeneity of capital, the true function of the entrepreneur must also remain hidden. In a homogenous world there is no scope for the activity of specifying.

Judgment and its embodiment in business plans and their execution typically pertain over multiple decision domains, because the services of several heterogenous assets (including multiple skills and capabilities) need coordination. Capital assets nearly always possess undiscovered attributes, for example, new ways in which they may be combined with other assets (cf. Schumpeter 1911 [1934]; Denrell et al. 2003). The entrepreneurial process of combining and recombining heterogeneous resources plays out continually, through time, as new attributes are created or discovered (and as consumer preferences and technological capabilities change). The entrepreneurial act is not restricted to new venture formation; entrepreneurial judgment is necessarily exercised on an ongoing basis.[2]

As Kirzner (1966) emphasized, these attributes are not objective, given, explicit properties of resources, but are always defined in terms of the entrepreneur's subjective business plan. Indeed, the very notion of a 'resource' in this approach is subjective, endogenous and tacitly perceived. Much of the literature on the firm, particularly in management research, often distinguishes between 'resource-based' and those approaches that stress distinct, knowledge-based assets (rather than all resources), such as the 'dynamic capabilities' or 'knowledge-based' views (e.g., Grant (1996). However, combining the Knightian idea of entrepreneurial judgment with the Austrian approach to capital heterogeneity illustrates that resource-based theories of economic organization are essentially knowledge-based, and that, moreover, they implicitly rest on an entrepreneurial founda-tion: 'Resource-bundles' do not simply arrive ready-made, but with different efficiencies (as in Barney 1991). Neither are they generated by a stochastic process (as in Lippman & Rumelt 1982). Rather, resource bundles are assembled by entrepreneurs.

Matching heterogenous assets as a process of experimentation

Given that the optimal relationships among assets is often shrouded in uncertainty *ex ante*, and often so complex that entrepreneurs cannot resort to analytical methods (Galloway 1996), some kind of experimental process is typically required. 'Experiments' should be understood in a wide sense, ranging all the way from setting up and fine-tuning an assembly line to designing and implementing organizational architectures, to invent-ing and commercializing a new product. In other words, experimental activity in this sense covers much of 'the main activity of a firm, running a business' (Coase 1988: 37).[3]

Because many of the valued dimensions of assets only become apparent from experi-menting with the uses of assets and discovering the best uses of those assets, it may be difficult for the entrepreneur to specify all valued dimensions of assets before specializa-tion. Given the interdependence that typically exists in a complex production system spanning several stages of production and involving myriads of inputs and numerous tasks, the best time and place to use an asset depend on the specification of the uses of all other assets that are needed in production (Hayek 1941). This creates costs of specializa-tion due to coordination problems. In firms, such coordination problems emerge as, for example, problems of bottlenecks (Foss 2001). These are problems where complexity and interdependent activities make it difficult to specify how best to sequence various activities, or where the introduction of more specialized tools and equipment creates capacity utilization problems due to technical indivisibilities, or where innovations in individual activities result in an uneven development of tools, equipment and compo-nents. Basically these problems arise when those who deliver parts or carry out activities are not aware of the need for mutual adjustment, or do not have the incentive to make their activities mesh with those of others. Reducing them through the specification of means of coordination (planning, standard operation procedures, liaison mechanisms, and so on) is, of course, paramount. However, designing such means of coordination already presupposes considerable knowledge about the process of production; and it is just this knowledge that is lacking.

In the context of optimizing a production system (e.g., Galloway 1996), and absent templates that can be copied exactly (Winter and Szulanski 2001), an experimental approach may proceed in the following manner. Firstly, one must isolate the system boundaries, that is, where the relevant relationships among assets are most likely to be. Secondly, the process of adjusting assets to each other must be organized like a controlled experiment (or a sequence of such experiments) to isolate the system from outside disturbances. Thirdly, there must be some sort of guidance for the experiment (Foss 2001). This may take many forms, ranging from centrally provided instructions to negotiated agreements to shared understandings of where to begin experimenting, how to avoid overlapping experiments, how to revise the experiment in light of past results, and so on. While the analogy is inexact, problem-solving activities in firms have many of the features of experimental activity. For example, iteration between the problem-solving efforts of distributed, but highly interdependent teams often characterizes major development efforts, such as the Boeing 777 development effort and Microsoft Windows (Cusumano 1997). In the Boeing project, the team working on a 20-piece wing flap found 251 interferences where parts occupied the same coordinates in space, which gave rise to constant iteration between design efforts in different sub-problems (Sabbagh 1995).[4] The following quotation from a software developer is illustrative:

> A lot of time people don't realize that they are dependent on something. It's just not obvious. For example, you don't realize that you have a dependency because you are not familiar with that part of the code. Or a dependency just sort of materializes out of thin air because of a need and is tracked informally. Or instances where the solution to one dependency creates problems for a third party. The real problems with the hidden interdependencies – the ones that no one thought about pop up at the last minute. (quoted by Staudenmayer and Cusumano 1998: 18–19)

The developer goes on to stress the need for carefully managing the process of iteration. Such management often mimics a controlled experiment in which all connected developments efforts, except for a few whose exact links need to be further investigated, are temporarily halted.

Organizing the experimental process
How is a problem-solving, experimental process best organized? Does the need for experimentation help explain the existence of the firm, or can such experimentation be organized efficiently through markets? Nickerson and Zenger (2004) address this using a problem-solving perspective derived from Simon (1962) and Kauffman (1995). In their approach, 'problems' come well defined. However, solutions to problems (which may relate to virtually any business activity, such as a problem of setting up a greenfield investment, reducing production costs with a certain percentage, marketing new products, and so on) do not exist in ready-made form and need identification and exploration. Nickerson and Zenger argue that firms search and that such search depends on the characteristics of the problem (its degree of decomposability; Simon (1962) as well as the search heuristics employed by the firm. Search for problems that are highly decomposable may take place in the market; however, less decomposable problems are best solved within the hierarchy. This is partly because the latter involves deep knowledge sharing, which thrives best inside hierarchy. But it is also a matter of coordinating heterogeneous assets.

In a world of heterogeneous assets with attributes that are costly to measure and foresee, complete contracts cannot be drafted. The resulting set of incomplete contracts may constitute a firm, a process of coordination managed by the entrepreneur's central direction. If relationship-specific assets are involved, and contractual relations must be frequently renegotiated, then the hold-up problem becomes a serious concern, as clarified in transaction cost economics (Williamson 1996: 102–103). Transaction cost theorists may not use the metaphor of the laboratory experiment, but the idea is similar: namely that 'coordinated adaptation' may be necessary in complex, interdependent systems surrounded by with Knightian uncertainty.[5] Because the 'experiment' in a dynamc world is repeated (i.e., opportunities come and go), the entrepreneur's central direction is continually needed, though it may differ in intensity.

A Clarification: Firms versus Entrepreneurial Firms?

We pause here to offer a clarification. The foregoing analysis offers an entrepreneurial theory of the firm. It is not intended as a theory of the 'entrepreneurial firm', as opposed to a theory of other types of firms. Indeed, our approach generally rejects this distinction. Entrepreneurial judgment is manifest at all stages of the firm's life cycle, within small and large firms, in high-growth, newly established industries and in mature industries, and so on. As noted above, judgment applies to mundane activities as well as innovative or dynamic ones.

By contrast, other authors attempt to link the theory of entrepreneurship to the theory of the firm by focusing on particular types of firms. As Langlois (2007:1118–1119) eloquently puts it:

> The pipe-smoking, thin-lapelled executive of a 1950s Chandlerian firm was still – I claim – a Knightian entrepreneur. He (probably not she) exercised judgment in an uncertain world and coped with problems of coordination by directly designing and directing the effort (including the judgment) of others. This is technically true. At a fundamental philosophical level, the nature of even a Chandlerian firm in the black-and-white era is entrepreneurial. But let's get real. This is not what most people have in mind by an entrepreneurial firm.

We agree. Indeed, while our approach has implications for innovation and firm growth, particularly from a Penrosian (1959) perspective, these issues are not at the heart of our theory. We do think the judgment-based approach helps illuminate the nature and development of the top-management team's 'subjective opportunity set', which has implications for diversification and growth (Foss et al. 2008). Langlois (2007) takes a different approach, noting that if 'entrepreneurial' implies novelty, then existing firms, structured to exploit accumulated, tacit capabilities (Penrose 1959; Richardson (1972; Nelson & Winter 1982), cannot be entrepreneurial. 'The upshot of this is not that firms are doomed to inertia and cannot cope with, let alone generate, novelty; rather, the implication is that what novelty firms can generate will be limited by the capabilities they already possess' (Langlois 2007: 1119). Hence, Langlois (2007: 1119) argues, 'an entrepreneurial firm must be either a new firm or a firm somehow willing and able creatively to destroy its own memory', suggesting that the latter is more likely under particular industry and technological conditions (e.g., modularity).

THE BOUNDARIES OF THE FIRM

In mainstream economic theories of the firm, the boundaries of the firm are explained in comparative-static terms. For Coase (1937), optimum boundaries exist where the transaction costs of organizing a transaction internally are exactly equal to costs of the relevant contractual alternative, on the margin. When this marginal equality is established for all transactions that the firm is involved in, the firm's optimum boundaries are defined. Later theories (e.g., Hart 1995; Williamson (1991) cast the analysis in more discrete, rather than marginal terms, but in these analyses boundaries still result from well-specified optimization problems. Although Williamson (1985, 1996) explicitly allows for process considerations, uncertainty and unexpected events, the governance ramifications of these can be anticipated at the time of contracting and folded into the choice and design of efficient governance structures. New property rights theory (Grossman & Hart 1986; Hart & Moore 1990) explicitly assumes that parties to a relation can anticipate (probabilistically) the distribution of pay-offs associated with various ownership structures (essentially, they have rational expectations). Given this, they choose the efficient structure of ownership (because the pay-offs are common knowledge; that is, uncertainty is ruled out). However, in spite of these features we can make use of new property rights theory to illuminate the boundaries of the firm from an entrepreneurial perspective.

Firm Boundaries in an Entrepreneurial Perspective

Consider a version of Hart's incomplete-contracting approach with an entrepreneurial twist. Assume there are two aspiring entrepreneurs, Bill and Mary, whose activities are vertically related.[6] Bill is active upstream from Mary, producing an intermediate product with the help of a resource A. Mary produces and sells the final product, using the resource B. Both could invest into searching for a business idea, that is, forming judgment, that makes production on the respective stage of production more efficient or enhances its quality. We assume that the business ideas lead to a higher quality of the final product in the following. Both Bill and Mary are interested in making the final product more competitive through quality benefits, thereby allowing a higher price than competitors. That is, the vertical structure and the existing resources A and B provide guidance in the entrepreneurial search. The implementation of a business idea requires access to both assets A and B. The investments into a business idea are therefore relationship-specific.

For the sake of simplicity, assume that the relationship only exists for two periods. In t_0, Bill and Mary separately decide on investments into searching and developing business ideas that increase the price of the final product. However, in t_0, there is uncertainty about the exact specification of the intermediate product to be delivered to Mary, so the two contracting parties are unable to write a complete contract. Uncertainty about the specification of the intermediate product is resolved in t_1, when the final product is produced and sold. Under those conditions, both contracting parties may be reluctant to make substantial investments into a business idea, because they anticipate a possible hold-up by the other contracting party. For example, after Bill makes substantial investments into a quality-improving idea, Mary might demand a much higher quality for the agreed-upon price. Because Bill's business idea requires access to both resources A and B, Bill grudgingly has to accept a much lower share of profit to cover his initial investment costs.

Who, then, should own the assets? The new property rights approach argues that ownership of resources influences the incentives to make specific investments. Ownership of a resource is defined in terms of having the residual control rights over a resource, especially the right to exclude others from a resource. The allocation of ownership rights thereby shapes the bargaining positions of contracting parties. If Mary owns resources A and B, she can exclude Bill from accessing the resources and implementing his business idea. Due to her ownership position, she can hold Bill up and appropriate most of the value created by Bill's business idea.

The benefits of vertical integration and placing both resources under common ownership are therefore the increase in bargaining power by the owner and the strengthening of the owner's incentive to invest money into the search for a business idea. It also implies that there are costs to vertical integration, the weaker incentives to engage in entrepreneurial search by non-owners. If Mary owns both resources, Bill does not have a high-powered incentive to search for business ideas for these, because Mary can appropriate much of the value created simply by threatening Bill with exclusion from the needed resources. Ownership over resources thus influences the ability to appropriate entrepreneurial rents, and thereby shape the incentives to engage in forming entrepreneurial judgment in the first place. It also implies that the identity of the entrepreneur matters. From a new property rights perspective, who develops and implements judgment and acquires ownership rights to assets critically depends on the respective potential for value creation. Mary acquires ownership rights over A and B if she expects that the added value outweighs the surplus created by Bill. Under those conditions, Mary is ready to offer a higher price for acquiring the resources and placing them under common ownership. In sum, the argument that judgment and asset ownership are complementary also makes sense from the perspective of hold-up and underinvestment.

Overall, the new property rights approach adds important insight into entrepreneurship by highlighting the importance of the *ex post* bargaining position for the *ex ante* incentives to forming and refining judgment (conceived here as entrepreneurial search). The primary way to secure prospective entrepreneurial rewards, according to the new property rights approach, is to acquire ownership rights of complementary resources. Ownership rights contain residual rights of control over a resource and especially the right to exclude others from accessing a resource. They increase the bargaining position of the owner *vis-à-vis* other resource owners. In addition, the resources currently under common ownership guide entrepreneurial search in the vast space of possible resource combinations. However, the new property rights approach at best allows for a stark, somewhat limited picture of entrepreneurship; only owners engage in entrepreneurial search and make substantial investments into relationship-specific resources. It is unclear how non-owners may be motivated to engage in entrepreneurial search. As we clarify below, one way to do this is to give employees 'access' (Rajan & Zingales 1998) to the entrepreneur's idea and to become what we call 'proxy entrepreneurs'. Before we consider this, we first go beyond the static perspective of the new property rights economics and address the dynamics of firm boundaries.

The Dynamics of Firm Boundaries

The judgment-based approach may also cast light over the existence and boundaries of the multi-person firm. Entrepreneurs also form cognitive representations (Nickerson & Zenger 2004; Gavetti 2005; Gavetti & Rivkin 2007) about which assets they need to secure the services from, the major contractual hazards associated with such procurement, and the most effective ways of protecting against such hazards.[7] This suggests that the same transaction might be governed very differently, as human agents may hold heterogeneous cognitive representations (see Argyres & Liebeskind 1999; Furubotn 2002; Mayer & Argyres 2004). Cognitive representations and the viability of resulting business models get tested in the marketplace, and they get updated and revised by feedback (Stieglitz & Heine 2007).

Explicitly accounting for the heterogeneity of the mental models of management teams (Foss et al. 2008) and entrepreneurs introduces an evolutionary twist that so far has been absent from transaction cost economics. In the context of different governance modes existing for managing similar transactions, Williamson (1985) refers to 'mistaken integration'. However, in an entrepreneurial setting with fundamental uncertainty and heterogeneity, it is not necessarily obvious what is and what is not 'mistaken' economic organization (Furubotn 2002). In particular, because managers and entrepreneurs hold different mental models, they will value resources differently (Barney 1986; Denrell et al. 2003). Firm boundaries, and boundary changes, may be understood in this light.[8]

Consider also boundary changes through mergers, acquisitions, divestitures and other reorganizations. The academic literature clearly suggests that corporate restructurings do, on average, create value (Jarrell et al. 1988; Andrade et al. 2001). A recurring puzzle, however, is why so many mergers are later 'reversed' in a divestiture, spin-off or carve-out. From a static, equilibrium perspective, reversals indicate error, mendacity or both, and cast doubt on the efficiency of the market for corporate control (Ravenscraft & Scherer 1987). In this view, entrenched managers make acquisitions primarily to increase their own power, prestige or control, producing negligible efficiency gains, and those acquisitions by manager-controlled firms are likely to be divested *ex post*. A process-oriented, entrepreneurial view recognized instead that unprofitable acquisitions may be 'mistakes' *ex post*, but argues that poor long-term performance does not indicate *ex ante* inefficiency (Klein & Klein 2001). In this perspective, a divestiture of previously acquired assets may mean simply that profit-seeking entrepreneurs have updated their forecasts of future conditions or otherwise learned from experience. They are adjusting the structure of heterogeneous capital assets specific to their firms.

ENTREPRENEURIAL GOVERNANCE

Competition in product, factor and capital markets thus provides one set of constraints upon entrepreneurial judgment. What about experimentation and creativity within the organization? Much recent literature on organizational design, particularly in the context of the 'knowledge economy', emphasizes delegation, teams, self-evaluation, and other forms of 'flattening' the corporate hierarchy to achieve competitive advantage in highly dynamic environments (Hodgson 1998; Rousseau & Shperling 2003; Brafman & Beckstrom 2006; Tapscott & Williams 2008). Indeed, employees often play a key role in developing and pursuing business opportunities through 'intrapreneurship', 'autonomous strategic initiatives' and 'corporate venturing' at all levels of the organization (e.g., Day & Wendler 1998; Yonekura & Lynskey 2002; Bhardwaj et al. 2006; De Clercq et al. 2007; Covin & Miles 2007).

And yet, as Baumol (1990) emphasized, entrepreneurial activities do not always create value. Rent-seeking, influence activities, shirking and other manifestations of principal–agent conflicts can generate returns to the agent, while destroying value for the organization or society at large. How, then, can organizations encourage 'productive' entrepreneurial behavior among employees, while discouraging 'destructive' forms of innovation and creativity?

To suggest the rudiment of a theory of intra-firm judgment, we distinguish the pure form of Knightian entrepreneurship – what we term 'original judgment' – from a secondary form we call 'derived judgment'. Original judgment, as described above, is inseparable from resource ownership, and is exercised by owners even if they delegate most day-to-day decisions to subordinates. In our framework, employees holding decision authority act as 'proxy entrepreneurs', exercising delegated or derived judgment on behalf of their employers. Such employees are asked not to carry out routine instructions in a mechanical, passive way, but to apply their own judgment to new circumstances or situations that may be unknown to the employer. Such discretion is ultimately limited, because owners retain the rights to hire and fire employees and to acquire or dispose of complementary capital goods.

The precise manner in which employees' discretion is limited is given by the firm's organizational structure: its formal and informal systems of rewards and punishments, rules for settling disputes and renegotiating agreements, means of evaluating performance, and so on. Under some organizational structures, the employment relation is highly constrained, giving employees few opportunities to engage in proxy-entrepreneurship; exercising a form of judgment derived from the primary, or original, judgment of the entrepreneur-owner. In other firms the employment relation may be much more open. Granting such latitude to employees brings benefits and costs. As agents become less constrained, they are likely to engage in both 'productive' proxy-entrepreneurship – activities that increase firm value – and 'destructive' proxy-entrepreneurship, meaning activities that reduce firm value. One important function of contracts and organizational design is to balance productive against destructive proxy-entrepreneurship by selecting and enforcing the proper contractual constraints. The optimal organizational structure encourages employees to use derived judgment in ways that increase firm value, while discouraging unproductive rent-seeking, influence activities and other forms of proxy-entrepreneurship that destroy value.

This can be done by regulating carefully the 'access' of proxy entrepreneurs (Rajan & Zingales 1998), by limiting the aspects of assets they are allowed to influence. On the one hand, this gives proxy entrepreneurs additional bargaining power which serves to incentivize them (Rajan & Zingales 1998). On the other hand, the entrepreneur can control the amount of destructive entrepreneurship by regulating access. The allocation of ownership rights and the characteristics of the employment relation thus matter for the efficient exercise of judgment.

Many firms operate on the presumption that beneficial effects can be produced by giving employees more rights to work with company assets, monitoring them less, and trusting them more. We will call this 'reducing constraints on employees' in various dimensions. For example, firms such as 3M give research employees free time to pursue their own experimental projects, in the hope of encouraging serendipitous discoveries (and as a perquisite that can attract and retain high-quality researchers). Many consulting firms have adopted similar practices. Industrial firms have long known that employees with many decision rights (senior industrial researchers, for example) can be monitored and constrained more loosely than employees charged only with routine tasks. More broadly, the increasing emphasis on 'empowerment' during recent decades reflects a recognition that employees derive a benefit from controlling aspects of their job situation (Osterloh & Frey 2000; Gagné & Deci 2005). The total quality movement emphasizes that delegating various rights to employees motivates them to find new ways to increase the mean and reduce the variance of quality (Wruck & Jensen 1994). Foss et al. (2009) find that highly autonomous job designs (i.e., strong delegation, allowing employees to control significant parts of a work process) increase creativity and encourage knowledge sharing. To the extent that such activities create value, they represent productive entrepreneurship.[9]

Stimulating the productive creation and discovery of new asset attributes by reducing constraints on employees and tying pay to performance results in principal–agent relationships that are open-ended, as agents have opportunities to exercise their own judgment in expanding the set of potential actions beyond those envisioned by the principal. While this open-endedness could bring the principal unanticipated benefits, reducing the constraints that agents face introduces potentially destructive proxy entrepreneurship. Managing the trade-off between productive and destructive proxy entrepreneurship thus becomes a critical management task.

We are agnostic here about the precise form the compensation for productive proxy-entrepreneurship should take. It could be bonuses tied to specific outcomes (profit, market value, patents or other innovation measures, introduction of new products, etc.), direct equity stakes, stock options, or something else. However proxy entrepreneurship is compensated, firms will seek to reduce the chance that derived judgment will be used in ways harmful to the firm. How, though, can destructive proxy entrepreneurship be minimized? Firms may delimit employees' use of assets, such as telephone and internet, by specifying use rights over the relevant assets, instructing employees to act in a proper manner towards customers, to exercise care when operating the firm's equipment, and the like. However, firms are unlikely to succeed entirely in their attempt to curb value-destroying activities in this way, given the open-endedness described above. Not only is it costly to monitor employees (including costs of reducing intrinsic motivation; see Gagnè and Deci 2005), but employees may creatively circumvent constraints, for example by finding ways to hide their behavior, or inventing behaviors that are not formally prohibited (employment law in many countries stipulates that firms must explicitly define banned behaviors before more drastic sanctions, such as termination, can be imposed on employees).

Although firms may know that such destructive entrepreneurship takes place, they may prefer not to try to constrain it further; the various constraints that firms impose on employees (or, more generally, that contracting partners impose on each other) to curb destructive entrepreneurship may have the unwanted side-effect that productive entrepreneurship is also stifled (see Kirzner 1985). More generally, imposing (too many) constraints on employees may reduce their propensity to create or discover new attributes of productive assets within the limits set by the business plan.

In this context, the employment relation and asset ownership are important because they give owner-entrepreneurs the rights and the ability to define formal and informal contractual constraints; that is, to choose their own preferred trade-offs. Ownership by conferring authority allows the employer-entrepreneur to establish their preferred organizational structure – and therefore a certain combination of productive and destructive entrepreneurship – at lowest cost. This function of ownership is particularly important in a dynamic world (Schumpeter 1911 [1934]; Kirzner 1973; Littlechild 1986; D'Aveni 1994), where the trade-offs between productive and destructive entrepreneurship inside the firm are likely to change as the entrepreneur-owner revises his judgment.

CONCLUSION

A fundamental claim, which we first expressed in Foss and Klein (2005), is that the historic isolation of entrepreneurship studies and the theory of the firm has created substantial unexploited gains from trade. Entrepreneurship should not be treated as a separate domain, focusing on specialized outcomes such as self-employment, business formation, new product introduction, and the like, or as a way of thinking or acting that applies only to a few individuals acting in unique situations. In the most general sense, all human behavior is entrepreneurial, as we live in a world of Knightian uncertainty, not the artificial world of neoclassical economic models. We argue, therefore, for a closer integration between the theory of entrepreneurship and the economic theory of the firm, building upon the Knightian notion of entrepreneurship as judgment.

Our arguments are developed more fully in Foss and Klein (2012). While Kirzner's (1973, 1985, 2000) and Schumpeter's (1911 [1934], 1942) work on entrepreneurship is fairly well known among scholars of organization and strategy, Knight's (1921) and Mises's (1949) contributions remain obscure. Our long-term objective is to rehabilitate the concept of entrepreneurship as judgmental decision-making about the deployment of resources under 'true' uncertainty, a perspective we think fits well with modern work on organization and strategy. Entrepreneurs establish and operate firms to realize their judgments, and firms are organized to take advantage of productive proxy-entrepreneurship by employees while discouraging the destructive kinds. Firms also change their boundaries, strategies and organizational structures as entrepreneurs and proxy-entrepreneurs experiment with different ways of combining and managing productive resources.

NOTES

1. Parts of this chapter draw on our book *Organizing Entrepreneurial Judgment: A New Approach to the Firm* (Foss & Klein 2012). We are grateful to Anna Grandori for comments on a previous version of this chapter.
2. An important implication is that the effectual logic described by Sarasvathy (2008) does not apply only in the process of forming a venture, but also describes the operations of ongoing ventures, large and small, old and new.
3. The need for firm-wide (and smaller-scale) experimentation of this kind is generally recognized in the change management literature, but not in the theory of the firm more broadly.
4. The need for iteration between sub-problems and succeeding design changes follows from the impossibility of getting the decomposition of the problem right initially (see Simon 1973: 191).
5. Asset specificity may itself be an outcome of an experimental process. To be sure, Williamson (e.g. 1985, 1996) clearly allows for intertemporal considerations relating to what he calls the 'fundamental transformation' (i.e., the transformation of large-numbers to small-numbers situations, and therefore the emergence of asset specificity). In our approach, as experimental activity provides information about how to organize the 'system', assets will be increasingly specific in time and location. Temporal and site specificity will tend to increase as assets become more efficiently coordinated. This provides a further rationale for organizing the experiments inside firms.
6. This follows Stieglitz and Foss (2009).

7. In contrast, Denrell et al. (2003) take a more Kirznerian stance, arguing that entrepreneurs stumble upon resource combinations by serendipity. Entrepreneurial search or discovery is guided by prior access to idiosyncratic resources, but not by entrepreneurial cognition: 'What is the role of strategizing and intentionality in this story? According to the argument it is unlikely that the firm acquired most of the components based on some vision of the value of the eventual combination. In this sense, the process of opportunity recognition is serendipitous' (Denrell et al. 2003: 986).
8. Entrepreneurship can also be invoked as way of endogenizing transaction costs (Jacobides & Winter 2007).
9. Our notion of 'more constrained' and 'less constrained' employment relations includes, but is broader than, the notion of contractual completeness in the transaction cost literature (e.g., Crocker & Masten 1991; Crocker & Reynolds 1993; Saussier 2000). Crocker and Reynolds (1993) define completeness as the probability that a contingency not covered by prior contractual agreement arises. Under Knightian uncertainty, all contracts are incomplete, meaning that it is impossible to specify all contingencies *ex ante*. The firm's organizational structure, governing the employment relation more broadly, can constrain employee opportunism even when formal contracts are highly incomplete in the Crocker and Reynolds sense.

REFERENCES

Alchian, Armen A. (1950), 'Uncertainty, evolution, and economic theory', *Journal of Political Economy*, **63**, 211–221.

Andrade, Gregor, Mark Mitchell and Erik Stafford (2001), 'New evidence and perspectives on mergers', *Journal of Economic Perspectives*, **15**, 103–120.

Ardichvili, Alexander, Richard Cardozo and Sourav Ray (2003), 'A theory of entrepreneurial opportunity identification and development', *Journal of Business Venturing*, **18**(1), 105–123.

Argyres, Nicholas S. and Julia Porter Liebeskind (1999), 'Contractual commitments, bargaining power, and governance inseparability: incorporating history into transaction cost theory', *Academy of Management Review*, **24**(1), 49–63.

Baker, T. and T.G. Pollock (2007), 'Making the marriage work: the benefits of strategy's takeover of entrepreneurship for strategic organization', *Strategic Organization*, **5**, 297–312.

Barney, Jay B. (1986), 'Organizational culture: can it be a source of sustained competitive advantage?' *Academy of Management Review*, **11**(3), 656–665.

Barney, J.B. (1991), 'Firm resources and sustained competitive advantage', *Journal of Management*, **17**, 99–120.

Barzel, Yoram (1987), 'The entrepreneur's reward for self-policing', *Economic Inquiry*, **25**, 103–16.

Baumol, William J. (1990), 'Entrepreneurship: productive, unproductive, and destructive', *Journal of Political Economy*, **98**(5), 893–921.

Bernardo, Antonio E. and Ivo Welch (2001), 'On the evolution of overconfidence and entrepreneurs', *Journal of Economics and Management Strategy*, **10**(3), 301–330.

Bewley, T.F. (1989), 'Market innovation and entrepreneurship: a Knightian view', Cowles Foundation Discussion Paper No. 905.

Bhardwaj, Gaurab, John C. Camillus and David Hounshell (2006), 'Continual corporate entrepreneurial search for long-term growth', *Management Science*, **52**(2), 248–261.

Bhidè, Amar V. (2000), *The Origin and Evolution of New Businesses*, Oxford: Oxford University Press.

Brafman, Ori, and Rod A. Beckstrom (2006), *The Starfish and the Spider: The Unstoppable Power of Leaderless Organizations*, London: Penguin.

Braguinsky, Serguey, Steven Klepper and Atsushi Ohyama (2009), 'Schumpeterian entrepreneurship', working paper, Carnegie-Mellon University, Department of Social and Decision Sciences.

Busenitz, Lowell W. and Jay B. Barney (1997), 'Differences between entrepreneurs and managers in large organizations: biases and heuristics in strategic decision-making', *Journal of Business Venturing*, **12**(1), 9–30.

Caliendo, Marco, Frank M. Fossen and Alexander S. Kritikos (2009), 'Risk attitudes of nascent entrepreneurs: new evidence from an experimentally validated survey', *Small Business Economics*, **32**(2), 153–167.

Casson, Mark C. (1982), *The Entrepreneur: An Economic Theory*, 2nd edn, Aldershot, UK and Brookfield, VT, USA: Edward Elgar.

Casson, Mark C. (1997), *Information and Organization*, Oxford: Oxford University Press.

Casson, Mark C. and Nigel Wadeson (2007), 'The discovery of opportunities: extending the economic theory of the entrepreneur', *Small Business Economics*, **28**(4), 285–300.

Christensen, Clayton M. (1997), The *Innovator's Dilemma: When New Technologies Cause Great Firms to Fail*, Cambridge, MA: Harvard Business School Press.

Coase, Ronald H. (1937), 'The nature of the firm', *Economica*, **4**, 386–405.

Coase, Ronald H. (1988), 'The nature of the firm: influence', *Journal of Law, Economics, and Organization*, **4**(1), 33–47.

Corbett, Andrew C. (2005), 'Experiential learning within the process of opportunity identification and exploitation', *Entrepreneurship Theory and Practice*, **29**(4), 473–491.

Covin, Jeffrey G. and Morgan P. Miles (2007), 'Strategic use of corporate venturing', *Entrepreneurship Theory and Practice*, **31**(2), 183–207.

Crocker, Keith J. and Scott E. Masten (1991), 'Pretia ex machina? Prices and process in long-term contracts', *Journal of Law and Economics*, **34**, 69–99.

Crocker, Keith J. and Kenneth J. Reynolds (1993), 'The efficiency of incomplete contracts: an empirical analysis of air force engine procurement', *Rand Journal of Economics*, **36**, 126–146.

Csikszentmihalyi, Mihaly (1996), *Creativity: Flow and the Psychology of Discovery and Invention*, New York: HarperCollins.

Cusumano, Michael A. (1997), 'How Microsoft makes large teams work like small teams', *Sloan Management Review*, **39**, 9–20.

D'Aveni, Richard A. (1994), *Hypercompetition*, New York: Free Press.

Day, Jonathan D. and James C. Wendler (1998), 'The new economics of organization', *McKinsey Quarterly*, **1**, 4–17.

De Clercq, Dirk, Xavier Castañer and Imanol Belausteguigoitia (2007), 'The secrets of intrapreneurship', *European Business Forum*, **31**, 40–45.

Denrell, Jerker, C. Fang and Sidney G. Winter (2003), 'The economics of strategic opportunity', *Strategic Management Journal*, **24**(10), 977–990.

Dew, Nicholas, Stuart Read, Saras D. Sarasvathy and Robert Wiltbank (2009), 'Effectual versus predictive logics in entrepreneurial decision-making: differences between experts and novices', *Journal of Business Venturing*, **24**(4), 287–309.

Elfenbein, Daniel W., Barton H. Hamilton and Todd R. Zenger (2010), 'The small firm effect and the entrepreneurial spawning of scientists and engineers', *Management Science*, **56**, 1–23.

Felin, Teppo and Todd R. Zenger (2009), 'Entrepreneurs as theorists: on the origins of collective beliefs and novel strategies', *Strategic Entrepreneurship Journal*, **3**(2), 127–146.

Forbes, Daniel P. (2005), 'Are some entrepreneurs more overconfident than others?' *Journal of Business Venturing*, **20**(5), 623–40.

Foss, Kirsten (2001), 'Organizing technological interdependencies: a coordination perspective on the firm', *Industrial and Corporate Change*, **10**(1), 151–178.

Foss, Kirsten, Nicolai J. Foss, Peter G. Klein and Sandra Klein (2007), 'The entrepreneurial organization of heterogeneous capital', *Journal of Management Studies*, **44**(7), 1165–1186.

Foss, Nicolai J. (1993), 'More on Knight and the theory of the firm', *Managerial and Decision Economics*, **14**, 269–276.

Foss, Nicolai J. (1996), 'The "alternative" theories of Knight and Coase, and the modern theory of the firm', *Journal of the History of Economic Thought*, **18**, 76–95.

Foss, Nicolai J. (2011), 'Do we have an entrepreneurial theory of the firm?' in *Crafoord Lecture Series, 2010*, Lund, Sweden: University of Lund, pp. 41–77.

Foss, Nicolai J. and Peter G. Klein (2005), 'Entrepreneurship and the economic theory of the firm: any gains from trade?' in Rajshree Agarwal, Sharon A. Alvarez and Olav Sorenson (eds), *Handbook of Entrepreneurship Research: Disciplinary Perspectives*, Dordrecht: Springer, pp. 55–80.

Foss, Nicolai J. and Peter G. Klein (2012), *Organizing Entrepreneurial Judgment: A New Approach to the Firm*, Cambridge: Cambridge University Press.

Foss, Nicolai J., Peter G. Klein, Yasemin Y. Kor and Joseph T. Mahoney (2008), 'Entrepreneurship, subjectivism, and the resource-based view: towards a new synthesis', *Strategic Entrepreneurship Journal*, **2**(1), 73–94.

Foss, Nicolai J., Dana Minbaeva, Mia Reinholt and Torben Pedersen (2009), 'Stimulating knowledge sharing among employees: the contribution of job design', *Human Resource Management*, **48**, 871–893.

Furubotn, Eirik G. (2002), 'Entrepreneurship, transaction-cost economics, and the design of contracts', in É. Brousseau and J.-M. Glachant (eds), *The Economics of Contracts: Theories and Applications*, Cambridge: Cambridge University Press, pp. 72–97.

Gagné, Marylène and Edward L. Deci (2005), 'Self determination theory and work motivation', *Journal of Organizational Behavior*, **26**(4), 331–362.

Galloway, Les (1996), *Operation Management: The Basics*, London: International Thomson Business Press.

Gartner, William B. (2007), 'Entrepreneurial narrative and a science of the imagination', *Journal of Business Venturing*, **22**, 613–627.

Gavetti, Giovanni (2005), 'Cognition and hierarchy: rethinking the microfoundations of capabilities development', *Organization Science*, **16**(6), 599–617.

Gavetti, Giovanni and Jan W. Rivkin (2007), 'On the origin of strategy: action and cognition over time', *Organization Science*, **18**, 420–439.

Grandori, Anna (2010), 'A rational heuristic model of economic decision making', *Rationality and Society*, **22**, 477–504.

Grandori, Anna and Laura Gaillard Giordani (2011), *Organizing Entrepreneurship*, Cheltenham, UK and Northampton, MA, USA: Edward Elgar.

Grant, R.M. (1996), 'Prospering in dynamically-competitive environments: organizational capability as knowledge integration', *Organization Science*, **7**, 375–387.

Grossman, Sanford J. and Oliver D. Hart (1986), 'The costs and benefits of ownership: a theory of vertical and lateral integration', *Journal of Political Economy*, **94**, 691–719.

Harper, David (1996), *Entrepreneurship and the Market Process: An Enquiry into the Growth of Knowledge*, London: Routledge.

Hart, Oliver D. (1995), *Firms, Contracts, and Financial Structure*, Oxford: Clarendon Press.

Hart, Oliver D. and John Moore (1990), 'Property rights and the nature of the firm', *Journal of Political Economy*, **98**(6), 1119–1158.

Hayek, F.A. (1941), *The Pure Theory of Capital*, Chicago, IL: University of Chicago Press.

Helfat, Constance E. and Sidney G. Winter (2011), 'Untangling dynamic and operational capabilities: strategy for the (n)ever-changing world', *Strategic Management Journal*, **32**, 1243–1250.

Helfat, Constance E., Sidney Finkelstein, William Mitchell, Margaret A. Peteraf, Harbir Singh, David J. Teece and Sidney G. Winter (2007), *Dynamic Capabilities: Understanding Strategic Change in Organizations*, Malden, MA: Blackwell.

Hitt, M.A., R.D. Ireland, S.M. Camp and D.L. Sexton (2002), *Strategic Entrepreneurship: Creating a New Mindset*. Oxford and Malden, MA: Blackwell.

Hodgson, Geoffrey (1998), *Economics and Utopia*, London: Routledge.

Ireland, R.D., J.G. Covin and D. Kuratko (2009), 'Conceptualizing corporate entrepreneurship strategy', *Entrepreneurship Theory and Practice*, **33**, 19–46.

Jacobides, M.G. and S.G. Winter (2007), 'Entrepreneurship and firm boundaries: the theory of a firm', *Journal of Management Studies*, **44**, 1213–1241.

Jarrell, Gregg A., James A. Brickley and Jeffry M. Netter (1988), 'The market for corporate control: the empirical evidence since 1980', *Journal of Economic Perspectives*, **2**, 49–68.

Kaplan, Steven N., Berk A. Sensoy and Per Strömberg (2009), 'Should investors bet on the jockey or the horse? Evidence from the evolution of firms from early business plans to public companies', *Journal of Finance*, **64**, (1), 75–115.

Kauffman, Stuart (1995), *At Home in the Universe: The Search for Laws of Self-Organization and Complexity*, New York: Oxford University Press.

Kihlstrom, Richard E. and Jean-Jacques Laffont (1979), 'A general equilibrium entrepreneurial theory of firm formation based on risk aversion', *Journal of Political Economy*, **87**(4), 719–748.

Kirzner, Israel M. (1966), *An Essay on Capital*, New York: Augustus M. Kelley.

Kirzner, Israel M. (1973), *Competition and Entrepreneurship*, Chicago, IL: University of Chicago Press.

Kirzner, Israel M. (1985), *Discovery and the Capitalist Process*, Chicago, IL: University of Chicago Press.

Kirzner, Israel M. (2000), *The Driving Force of the Market Economy: Essays in Austrian Economics*, London: Routledge.

Klein, Peter G. and Sandra K. Klein (2001), 'Do entrepreneurs make predictable mistakes? Evidence from corporate divestitures', *Quarterly Journal of Austrian Economics*, **4**(2), 3–25.

Klepper, Steven (2002), 'The capabilities of new firms and the evolution of the US automobile industry', *Industrial and Corporate Change*, **11**(4), 645–666.

Knight, Frank H. (1921), *Risk, Uncertainty, and Profit*, New York: August M. Kelley.

Koellinger, Philipp.D., Maria Minniti and C. Schade (2007), 'I think I can, I think I can: overconfidence and entrepreneurial behavior', *Journal of Economic Psychology*, **28**, 502–527.

Lachmann, Ludwig M. (1956), *Capital and Its Structure*, Kansas City: Sheed Andrews & McMeel.

Lachmann, Ludwig M. (1977), *Capital, Expectations, and the Market Process*, Kansas City: Sheed Andrews & McMeel.

Langlois, Richard N. (2007), 'The entrepreneurial theory of the firm and the theory of the entrepreneurial firm', *Journal of Management Studies*, **44**(7), 1107–1124.

Langlois, Richard N. and Metin Cosgel (1993), 'Frank Knight on risk, uncertainty, and the firm: a new interpretation', *Economic Inquiry*, **31**, 456–465.

Littlechild, Steven C. (1986), 'Three types of market process', in Richard N. Langlois (ed.), *Economics as a Process: Essays in the New Institutional Economics*, Cambridge: Cambridge University Press, pp. 27–40.

Loasby, Brian J. (1986), 'Competition and imperfect knowledge: the contribution of G.B. Richardson', *Scottish Journal of Political Economy*, **33**(2), 145–158.

Lumpkin, G.T., G.E. Hills and R.C. Shrader (2004), 'Opportunity recognition', in Harold L. Welsch (ed.), *Entrepreneurship: The Road Ahead*, London: Routledge, pp. 73–90.

Mayer, Kyle J. and Nicholas S. Argyres (2004), 'Learning to contract: evidence from the personal computer industry', *Organization Science*, 15(4), 394–410.

McMullen, Jeffrey and Dean A. Shepherd (2006), 'Entrepreneurial action and the role of uncertainty in the theory of the entrepreneur', *Academy of Management Review*, 31(1), 132–152.

Mises, Ludwig von (1949), *Human Action: A Treatise on Economics*, New Haven, CT: Yale University Press.

Nelson, Richard R. and Sidney G. Winter (1982), *An Evolutionary Theory of Economic Change*, Cambridge, MA: Harvard University Press.

Nickerson, Jackson and Todd R. Zenger (2004), 'A knowledge-based theory of the firm: the problem-solving perspective', *Organization Science*, 15(6), 617–632.

Osterloh, Margit and Bruno S. Frey (2000), 'Motivation, knowledge transfer, and organizational forms', *Organization Science*, 11(5), 538–550.

Penrose, E.T. (1959), *The Theory of the Growth of the Firm*, New York: John Wiley.

Phelps, Edmund P. (2006), 'Further steps to a theory of innovation and growth – on the path begun by Knight, Hayek, and Polanyí', paper for the 2006 ASSA meetings.

Rajan, R. and L. Zingales (1998), 'Power in a theory of the firm', *Quarterly Journal of Economics*, 113, 387–432.

Ravenscraft, David J. and F.M. Scherer (1987), *Mergers, Sell-offs, and Economic Efficiency*, Washington, DC: Brookings Institution.

Read, S., N. Dew, S.D. Sarasvathy and R. Wiltbank (2009), 'Marketing under uncertainty: the logic of an effectual approach', *Journal of Marketing*, 73, 1–18.

Richardson, George B. (1972), 'The organisation of industry', *Economic Journal*, 82, 883–896.

Rigotti, Luca, Matthew Ryan and Rhema Vaithianathan (2001), 'Ambiguity aversion, entrepreneurship and innovation', mimeo, Duke University, USA.

Rousseau, Denise M. and Zipi Shperling (2003), 'Pieces of the action: ownership and the changing employment relationship', *Academy of Management Review*, 28(4), 553–570.

Sabbagh, Karl. (1995), *21st Century Jet: The Making of the Boeing 777*, New York: Scribner.

Sarasvathy, Saras (2008), *Effectuation: Elements of Entrepreneurial Expertise*, Cheltenham, UK and Northampton, MA, USA: Edward Elgar.

Saussier, Stéphane (2000), 'Transaction costs and contractual incompleteness: the case of Electricitie de France', *Journal of Economic Behavior and Organization*, 42, 189–206.

Schultz, Theodore W. (1980), 'Investment in entrepreneurial ability', *Scandinavian Journal of Economics*, 82(4), 437–448.

Schumpeter, Joseph A. (1911 [1934]), *The Theory of Economic Development*, Cambridge, MA: Harvard University Press.

Schumpeter, Joseph A. (1942), *Capitalism, Socialism, and Democracy*, New York: Harper & Row.

Shackle, George L.S. (1972), *Epistemics and Economics*, Cambridge: Cambridge University Press.

Shane, Scott (2000), 'Prior knowledge and the discovery of entrepreneurial opportunities', *Organization Science*, 11, 448–469.

Shane, Scott (2003), *A General Theory of Entrepreneurship*, Cheltenham, UK and Northampton, MA, USA: Edward Elgar.

Simon, Herbert A. (1962), 'The architecture of complexity', *Proceedings of the American Philosophical Society*, 106, 467–482.

Simon, Herbert A. (1973), 'The structure of ill structured problems 1', *Artificial Intelligence*, 4(3–4), 181–201.

Staudenmayer, Nancy and Michael A. Cusumano (1998), 'Alternative designs for product component integration', Working Paper, MIT.

Stieglitz, Nils and Nicolai J. Foss (2009), 'Opportunities and new business models: transaction cost and property rights perspectives on entrepreneurship', in Jackson A. Nickerson and Brian S. Silverman (eds), *Economic Institutions of Strategy*, New York: Emerald, pp.67–96.

Stieglitz, Nils and Klaus Heine (2007), 'Innovations and the role of complementarities in a strategic theory of the firm', *Strategic Management Journal*, 28(1), 1–15.

Taleb, Nicholas N. (2007), *The Black Swan: The Impact of the Highly Improbable*, New York: Random House.

Tapscott, Don and Anthony D. Williams (2008), *Wikinomics: How Mass Collaboration Changes Everything*, New York: Portfolio Trade.

Williamson, Oliver E. (1985), *The Economic Institutions of Capitalism*, New York: Free Press.

Williamson, Oliver E. (1991), 'Comparative economic organization: the analysis of discrete structural alternatives', *Administrative Science Quarterly*, 36, 269–296.

Williamson, Oliver E. (1996), *The Mechanisms of Governance*, Oxford: Oxford University Press.

Winter, Sidney G. (2003), 'Understanding dynamic capabilities', *Strategic Management Journal*, 24, 991–995.

Winter, Sidney G. and Gabriel Szulanski (2001), 'Replication as strategy', *Organization Science*, 12(6), 730–743.

Wruck, Karen H. and Michael C. Jensen (1994), 'Science, specific knowledge, and total quality management', *Journal of Accounting and Economics*, **18**, 247–287.

Yonekura, Seiichirō and Michael J. Lynskey (eds) (2002), *Entrepreneurship and Organization: The Role of the Entrepreneur in Organizational Innovation*, Oxford: Oxford University Press.

Zeckhauser, Richard (2006), 'Investing in the unknown and unknowable', *Capitalism and Society*, **1**, 1–39.

23. The four functions of corporate personhood
Margaret M. Blair

In this chapter I argue that the legal device of creating separate juridical 'persons' for certain business activities serves at least four functions that became especially important to business organizers during and after the industrial revolution, and that those functions are still important to most large, publicly traded corporations. These are, first, providing continuity, and a clear line of succession in the holding of property and the carrying out of contracts. Second, providing an 'identifiable persona' to serve as a central actor in carrying out the business activity. Employees and investors in the enterprise, as well as customers of the enterprise, recognize and perhaps identify with this persona, which serves as the bearer of important intangible assets such as goodwill, reputation and brand. This persona is the counterparty to all contracts that the corporation enters into with its various participants (employees, customers, suppliers, and investors), and can sue and be sued in its own name. Third, providing a mechanism for separating pools of assets according to which assets are dedicated to the business, and which assets are the personal assets of the human persons who are participating in the business. The ability to partition assets in this way makes it easier to commit specialized assets to an enterprise, and lock those assets in so that they remain committed to the enterprise and can realize their full value (Blair 2003; Hansmann & Kraakman 2000). Fourth, the separateness of the corporate entity, once the corporation is created, requires a legal mechanism for self-governance, at least with respect to the undertakings of the entity. The governance structure prescribed by corporate law since the early nineteenth century is a managerial hierarchy topped by a board of directors that is distinct from shareholders, managers and employees, and that has fiduciary duties to the corporation itself as well as to shareholders.

These four functions of entity status in corporations, all of which have been associated with the concept of corporate personhood, are important sources of value in organizing business activities that involve a substantial number of people using dedicated assets over long periods of time. All four of these functions have been important since the industrial revolution, and continue to be important in business activities today. In large corporations with many shareholders and ongoing business activities, the four functions come as a package and are connected to each other, although the corporate form can be deployed to achieve as few as one of these purposes. These functions would be very difficult, if not impossible, to accomplish using only transactional contracts.

Careful analysis of the functions of 'personhood' or 'entity status' can shed light on policy questions about what constitutional rights should be recognized for corporations.

INTRODUCTION

The essence of what happens when a corporation is formed is that the law subsequently recognizes the existence of a legal entity that is separate from the organizers and investors, but that can carry out certain business activities like a 'person'.[1] Centuries ago, courts recognized that institutions like a church or university could hold property, sue and be sued, and enter into contracts in their own name, apart from any of the individuals who were members of or affiliated with the institution, if the institution had a charter from the King or Parliament, or possibly the Pope (Angell & Ames 1832; Canfield 1917). Importantly, property held by the chartered entity would continue to be held by the entity upon the death or departure of any of the natural persons associated with the entity (Blumberg 1993). Organizations which had these features were called 'corporations', from the Latin word *corpus*, meaning 'body', because the law recognized that the group of people who formed the corporation could act as one body or one 'legal person'.

Despite the importance in law of what is often called 'corporate personality', 'corporate personhood' or 'entity status',[2] scholarly work on corporate law since the 1980s has been dominated by a narrow contractarian view of corporations which holds that it is misleading to think of corporations as separate persons. Instead, scholars who adopt this view argue, a corporation is nothing more than a nexus through which all of the human persons involved in an enterprise arrange to contract with each other (Jensen & Meckling 1976; Alchian & Demsetz 1972; Easterbrook & Fischel 1991; Bratton 1988–89).[3] The standard contractarian approach is to assume that a corporation is just the 'legal fiction' through which shareholders, as principals, contract with directors and managers, who are regarded as agents of shareholders. Framed this way, the corporation is not seen as having a separate existence, but is simply an aggregate of the interests of shareholders. This version of contractarian thinking about corporations, as it has been developed by legal academics in the United States (US), supports the normative claim that corporations should be run in the interest of shareholders, and that it is inappropriate to believe or claim that a corporation has any interests that are separate or different from those of the shareholders.[4] Moreover, according to this line of argument, the job of managers and directors is to maximize the value of the shares owned by shareholders, and any other social or economic goal for corporations is illegitimate (Friedman 1962; Jensen & Meckling 1976; Chen & Hanson 2004).

In this chapter I argue that the legal device of creating separate juridical 'persons' for certain business activities serves at least four functions that became especially important to business organizers during and after the industrial revolution, and that those functions are still important to most large, publicly traded corporations. The focus on agency costs in the standard contractarian model obscures these functions, and thus may lead to misleading policy prescriptions. If corporations are merely nexuses of contracts, what distinguishes them from other collaborative approaches to carrying out business activities, such as partnerships, or alliances, or just ordinary contracts? And why have business organizers been so eager, over the last 200 years, to use the corporate form rather than one of these other arrangements? Attention to the role played in the law by the concept of corporate personhood, by contrast, illuminates important ways that the use of the corporate form for organizing business activities contributes to economic value, and helps to explain why this form continues to be the most widely used organizational form for business activity around the world.

The four functions that legal entity status serves would be very difficult, if not impossible, to accomplish using only transactional contracts.[5] The first of these is providing continuity, and a clear line of succession in the holding of property and the carrying out of contracts. This is because the separate legal entity continues to exist over time (and continues to hold the property, and be liable for performance under its contracts) even if the individual humans involved die or simply withdraw from the enterprise.[6]

The second is providing an 'identifiable persona'[7] to serve as a central actor in carrying out the business activity. Participants in the enterprise recognize and perhaps identify with this persona, which serves as the bearer of important intangible assets such as franchises or monopoly rights, special knowledge, competencies, reputation, image, and brand. Such intangible assets are sources of substantial value to the participants in corporate enterprises that would be difficult to develop, sustain and use by a group of people if the only thing holding the group together were transactional contracts or market exchanges.[8] This persona is the counterparty to all contracts that the corporation enters into with its various participants (employees, customers, suppliers and investors), and can sue and be sued in its own name.

The third function is providing a mechanism for separating pools of assets according to which assets are dedicated to the business, and which assets are the personal assets of the human persons who are participating in the business. The ability to partition assets in this way makes it easier to commit specialized assets to an enterprise, and lock those assets in so that they remain committed to the enterprise and can realize their full value (Blair 2003; Hansmann & Kraakman 2000). This is because assets that are locked in to the corporate entity also help to bond the entity's commitments to creditors and other stakeholders (Blair 2003; Hansmann & Kraakman 1999). Separation of assets also makes it easier for investors and other participants in an enterprise to limit their exposure to losses if the enterprise fails, a feature commonly called limited liability.

And fourthly, entity status requires a legal mechanism for self-governance, at least with respect to the undertakings of the entity.[9] Internal self-governance facilitates efforts by a large group of individuals, some of whom may not even know each other and may never meet, to coordinate their contributions and activities toward a common end, without requiring numerous separate contracts (Blair & Stout 1999; Radner 1992).[10] The governance structure prescribed by corporate law since the early nineteenth century is a managerial hierarchy topped by a board of directors that is distinct from shareholders, managers and employees (Gevurtz 2004: 108). The board has fiduciary duties to the corporation itself (MBCA §8.01 and §8.30), as well as to shareholders. The fact that a corporation is a separate entity requires that some legal mechanism be adopted to make decisions for the entity,[11] and the logic of team production makes an independent board an attractive solution to the problem (Blair & Stout 1999).

These four functions of entity status in corporations, all of which have been associated with the concept of corporate personhood, are important sources of value in organizing business activities that involve a substantial number of people using dedicated assets over long periods of time. All four of these functions have been important since the industrial revolution, and continue to be important in business activities today. In large corporations with many shareholders and ongoing business activities, the four functions generally come as a package and are connected to each other. Building and accumulating intangible assets such as a reputation for technological competence, for example, would be difficult if these assets were not linked to a separate entity, and if there were no assurance that the entity would continue in existence, and the assets would not be split up or dissipated if a key individual dies or separates from the firm (Blair 2003).[12] The death of

Apple Corp. founder Steve Jobs in October 2011 provides a particularly salient example of this. It is the separateness of Apple the entity, from Jobs the person, that provides assurance to Apple customers, employees and business partners that the firm will continue to exist and continue to produce innovative products. In words posted on Apple's website after Jobs' death, 'Steve leaves behind a company that only he could have built . . . [but] his spirit will forever be the foundation of Apple.'[13]

Separating assets used in the enterprise from the personal assets of the entity's participants is clearly easier if the corporation has a separate legal status. Moreover, administration of the separate entity is easier if creditors of the entity have access only to the assets of the entity to satisfy entity debts (limited liability), and if creditors and investors in the entity, and their heirs, cannot individually withdraw assets from the firm or compel dissolution (capital lock-in) (Blair 2003; Hansmann and Kraakman 2000).

Moreover, the separateness of the entity also makes it necessary for the law to specify who will have authority to make decisions and take actions for the entity. In corporations, that legal rule takes the form of a requirement that they are to be governed by a board of directors (MBCA §8.01). Governance by a board of directors is a solution that is particularly useful in solving the inevitable problems that arise in team production, in which numerous participants contribute complex inputs and produce a joint output that is more than the sum of the inputs (Blair and Stout 1999).

While all four functions are valuable for enterprises that involve a large number of individual persons, the corporate form can be used to take advantage of only one or two of these purposes.[14] In particular, in corporations whose shares are entirely owned by another corporation, it will often be the case that only one of these functions is particularly useful. Usually, this is the ability to partition assets, especially the limited liability feature (Mendelson 2002). Such enterprises already have the benefit of perpetual succession, board governance and an identifiable persona – through the parent corporation – to bear the reputation and other intangible assets. Indeed, a subset of such wholly owned corporations – corporations formed as 'special purpose entities' (SPEs) to facilitate securitization of financial assets – are formed solely to take advantage of limited liability. For such corporations, the contractarian model, which reduces corporations to little more than a contractual nexus, or a bundle of assets that belongs to shareholders, may be an adequate characterization, and legal rules or policy prescriptions based on that model may well be valid.

But for corporations in which corporate personhood or entity status is serving all four functions – which is surely true of the largest and most important corporations in modern economies today – entity status creates value for numerous participants in addition to shareholders, value which is often at risk in the enterprise just as shareholder capital is at risk. For such firms, there may be many situations in which the interests of the corporation as a whole diverge from what is in the best interests of any one set of constituents, such as shareholders. For example, it might be in the interest of diversified shareholders for the corporation to pursue risky but potentially high-return projects, but the value provided by longevity and continuity in property ownership and contracts, as well as the value of reputation and other intangible assets tied to the corporation's persona, may depend to some extent on the relative stability of the corporation, and may be put at risk if the firm pursues high-risk projects. To the extent that the value created from continuity and from holding and accumulating reputational assets is a source of wealth for other participants in the firm, such as employees, customers or suppliers, we can think of the interests of the corporation as a whole as substantially broader than the interests of shareholders alone.

Despite the use of the phrase 'corporate personhood' as a summary expression to indicate that a firm has the full package of corporate characteristics, all four characteristics actually distinguish corporations from human persons. This could have significant implications for the debate over policy questions such as whether corporations should have rights protected by the US Constitution,[15] and if so, what is the extent of such rights. Although it goes beyond the scope of this chapter to do so, it would be useful, for example, to consider whether a particular right is important to the effectiveness of one or more of the four functions that 'personhood' performs. For example, granting corporations the right to due process before property can be taken away is consistent with the function of continuity in property ownership, and thus it may make sense that corporations should be protected by such rights.

In this chapter, I explore these four functions to show why they are important in modern business enterprises, and why they would be difficult to achieve purely through transactional contracts. All four, however, are achieved easily when the law recognizes corporations as legal entities separate from any of their participants. Attention to these functions of entity status make it clear that, generally, a corporation should be regarded as more than simply a nexus of contracts.

First I review the history of the corporate form and the origins of the concept of corporate legal personality. Next I show how the concept of legal personality serves the four functions outlined above, and why it would be difficult to achieve the same results using contracts. I then argue that corporations in which all four of these functions are important will, from time to time, have interests that are different from those of their shareholders, interests that sometimes are and should be recognized in various ways by the law. Thus, analysis of the four functions of entity status points to a more nuanced answer to corporate governance questions such as what it means that directors of a corporation have fiduciary duties to act in the best interest of 'the corporation'.

HISTORICAL EVOLUTION OF CORPORATE PERSONHOOD

The earliest corporations were not organized for business purposes. Corporate law as we know it today evolved out of laws and practices governing municipalities, churches and religious institutions in the Middle Ages in Europe.[16] Such institutions were often granted charters by the local lords or kings. Charters gave religious institutions the authority to operate as separate entities for purposes of holding property. The ability of the institutions to hold property in their own names assured that the property would not be handed down to heirs of individual persons who controlled and managed the property on behalf of the institutions (such as bishops or abbots), nor would the property revert to the estate of the lord or be heavily taxed when those controlling persons died or were replaced. In other words, the charters granted to religious institutions gave them 'the power of perpetual succession' (Mark 1987: 1450; Angell & Ames 1832: 4).

The idea that a group of people could act together, in law, as a single entity with an indefinite life, at least for the purpose of holding property, was subsequently applied to boroughs, municipalities and guilds. By the sixteenth century, corporations were being used in a wide range of institutions, including 'the King himself, cities and boroughs, guilds, universities and colleges, hospitals and other charitable organizations, bishops, deans and chapters, abbots and convents, and other ecclesiastical bodies' (Harris 2000: 16–17). Notably absent from this list are businesses or commercial organizations. The purpose of incorporation, for all of these entities, was primarily perpetual succession, so that a succession of different individuals would be recognized as a single 'legal person', while the property and wealth of that 'person' could be accumulated and held over time for the relevant public or quasi-public purposes, and neither be taxed, revert to the state, nor be subject to division and distribution to heirs upon the death or departure of any of the administrators of the property or members of the corporation.[17]

A few categories of corporations involved only a single individual, such as the King, or a bishop. These corporations were called 'sole corporations', and their purpose was simply to make it clear that the property they held and controlled did not belong to them personally, but to the institution or public function they served, and the contracts they made were not entered into on their personal behalf, but only in their official capacity (Carter 1919: 14). This would ensure that the property, contract rights and liabilities would pass to successors in that office when the office-holder died or otherwise vacated the office.

All of the other categories were called 'aggregate corporations', and as to these, another important purpose of the corporate form was self-governance among a group of people. Charters granted to municipalities in the Middle Ages, for example, explicitly provided for self-governance (Angell and Ames 1832). For purposes of their external relations, the incorporated group was able to act as a single individual in buying, selling or holding property or entering into contracts. Within the group, they had to work out their own mechanisms and rules of governance and resolve their own disputes (Gevurtz 2004). Importantly, decisions about internal governance would not be subject to interference by the state or sovereign, except perhaps to enforce governance rules that were specified in their charters.[18]

In the seventeenth century, in England and on the Continent, charters also came to be issued to trading companies (Harris 2000). Trading companies were initially organized as 'companies', which were essentially partnerships, a legal category that was recognized as contractual at common law, and that did not require a charter. These partnerships were usually between a merchant sea captain and one or more passive partners who would provide financing for a fleet of ships that would sail to some faraway place to purchase spices or other goods. When the ship returned, the merchandise acquired would be sold, the proceeds would be divided, and the partnership dissolved (Gevurtz 2004). Successive missions were organized as new partnerships (Hansmann et al. 2006). Hence, these organizations did not have the features of perpetual succession, identifiable persona and asset separation, although such features may not have been needed given the nature of their business model.[19]

These trade missions were inherently extremely risky, and the risks of shipwreck, piracy and disease were compounded by the risk that if too many ships returned with too much spice, spice prices could collapse and even an otherwise successful venture could lose money (Harris 2000). So in 1600, Elizabeth I in England granted a charter to a group of merchants organized as the East India Company, along with monopoly rights to control the spice trade on behalf of England. Two years later, the Netherlands did the same thing, chartering the Dutch East India Company. These companies initially were formed for a limited number of years (which suggests that their initial purpose was not perpetual succession in the holding of property, as it was with churches and charitable organizations), but they were reorganized at the end of each term, and eventually, they were granted charters in perpetuity (Hansmann et al. 2006).

Because of their origins in partnership law, these early trading companies were generally governed like partnerships, with major decisions made by vote of investors on a one person, one vote basis. But trading companies that had received franchises from Parliament or from a monarch were sometimes governed like partnerships, and sometimes governed by councils that may have included individuals appointed by the King.[20]

By the end of the seventeenth century, numerous European chartered trading companies were building, populating, and governing colonies around the world, as well as controlling international trade between the colonies and Europe. For these organizations, the most important purposes of the charter may have been the franchises that came with the charters. Perpetual succession became important, however, after the organizations ceased to be dissolved at the end of each voyage and were given charters in perpetuity.

Just as guilds, towns and church organizations could have a changing membership over time, so it became useful for trading companies that continued in existence from one trade mission to the next to have different investors over time. This was made possible when the chartered companies issued investment 'shares' in exchange for financial capital, and investors began trading these shares among themselves (Werner 1981: 1631). Such companies were called joint-stock companies. Joint-stock companies might have evolved rather quickly into modern corporations in the eighteenth century after this development, except that English courts considered them to be a species of partnerships (Blair 2003; Warren 1929; Seavoy 1982). Moreover, the English Parliament and the King began to jealously protect and hoard the special franchises that had come with early charters, issuing them rarely. Then in 1719, Parliament passed the so-called Bubble Act, which made it illegal to trade in the shares of unincorporated joint-stock companies. From that time until Parliament repealed the Bubble Act and passed the first general incorporation Act in England in 1844, England had a two-tier system of business organizations in which only chartered companies had the primary characteristics we have come to associate with corporations, including entity status (but not necessarily limited liability; Angell & Ames 1858; Harris 2000; Hansmann et al. 2006), while unchartered joint-stock companies could not (legally) have tradable shares, and were treated as partnerships by English courts.[21]

The Joint Stock Companies Act of 1844 gave many more firms access to charters, and the Joint Stock Companies Act of 1856 streamlined the chartering process and served as the basis of modern company law in the UK. As a result of travelling this path, modern company law in England can be seen as having evolved out of partnership law rather than out of the law governing eleemosynary institutions. Some scholars have argued that this helps explain why some corporate law features in Britain are more contractual and partnership-like (Moore 2010; Dignam & Lowry 2010) than corporate law is in the US.

In the American colonies, most business activities were carried out either by individual proprietorships, or by partnerships, through the end of the eighteenth century, but the joint-stock company was a well-known organizational form because such companies had in many cases helped to establish, settle and govern the colonies. Business people would have encountered the corporate form frequently in other contexts too, because it was used by churches, libraries, universities other eleemosynary institutions, and for some public works projects such as canals, bridges, water works and turnpikes.[22] Most corporate charters in the colonies in the early eighteenth century had actually been granted by the governors of each colony, which granted charters much more liberally than did the King or Parliament in England. So this form was more readily available in the colonies than in England, and its status less ambiguous than that of joint-stock companies (which would probably have been considered partnerships by local courts). After the Revolution, however, when the authority of the English monarch and Parliament were no longer recognized, state legislatures took over the task of issuing charters, and did so with greater frequency, and for more different types of organizations (Blumberg 1993) than had the King or Parliament. Nonetheless, it was still costly and time consuming to organize a business as a chartered corporation rather than as a partnership or unchartered joint-stock company because, throughout the eighteenth century, each corporate charter required its own special Act of the legislature. By 1800, there were only about 335 business corporations existing in all of the states.[23]

Partnerships and unchartered joint-stock companies, while easier to establish, had a substantial drawback for industrial enterprises relative to chartered corporations. Assets accumulated by a business organized as a partnership were subject to being withdrawn at any time if a partner decided to pull out of the business, and if a partner died, the partnership had to be dissolved and reformed after paying out an appropriate share of assets to the heirs of the deceased (Blair 2003). By contrast, courts recognized that any business organized with a corporate charter obtained from the state was a separate legal 'person', that could hold the property in perpetuity, even as a stream of investors and managers came and went in the enterprise. Investors could sell their shares to another investor, but could not demand that their share of the assets be paid out of the corporation to them (Blair 2003). Thus, by early in the nineteenth century, business people began seeking corporate charters for a wider variety of businesses, and especially for any businesses that required a substantial commitment of long-lived capital. As a consequence, the law governing business corporations developed in the US more rapidly than it developed either in England or in other European countries.[24]

Despite the cost and difficulty of obtaining a charter, demand for charters increased rapidly, and by 1850 there were thousands of business corporations in existence in the US, and 14 of the 31 states either had general incorporation statutes, or state constitutional amendments or provisions that provided that any group who met certain requirements and filed the appropriate papers could form a corporation (Creighton 1990). As many as half of all corporations in existence by then were business enterprises (Creighton 1990). By 1890, there were 500 000 business corporations in existence in the US (Votaw 1965), substantially more than existed in any other country, and almost every state had a general incorporation statute.

Incorporation statutes did not always provide for limited liability for corporate shareholders, especially early in the nineteenth century (Blumberg 1986, 1993; Mendelson 2002).[25] So while this feature of corporations later became important, it was not initially the feature that caused so many business people to seek out and adopt this organizational form (Blair 2003; Creighton 1990).

What was compelling and attractive, however, was the legal standing that chartered corporations had as separate entities.[26] In particular, separate legal entity status provided continuity by assuring a clear line of succession in the holding of property and the carrying out of contracts, as it had traditionally done for eleemosynary or public purpose corporations. It also provided an identifiable persona that business people could contract with, and that could hold important intangible assets, such as monopoly rights (prior to the late nineteenth century), special knowledge, competences, reputation and brand. Such assets emerged as extremely important in the late nineteenth century to support mass production and mass marketing. And the corporate form provided a mechanism for partitioning assets and committing them to a particular enterprise while protecting those assets from creditors or heirs of the corporation's participants (Blair 2003), as well as protecting investors in the corporation from creditors of the corporation (Hansmann et al. 2006). By the mid-nineteenth century, an emerging body of corporation law provided that the entities created when a charter was issued by a state were to be governed by boards of directors. I discuss each of these purposes in the next section.

THE FOUR FUNCTIONS

Continuity through Perpetual Succession

The earliest corporate charters were granted to enable a 'perpetual succession of individuals . . . [to be] capable of acting for the promotion of a particular object, like one immortal being', according to Angell and Ames (1832: 2). The purpose promoted by these institutions was to accumulate property for a specific quasi-public use, such as religious buildings, monasteries or universities, in a way that would protect the property from division, confiscation or taxation by the King each time it came under the control of a new person, and to make it clear that the assets could not be handed down by inheritance to the heirs of such control persons.

The granting of a charter to a corporation had the effect of creating a separate legal entity that would continue in existence over time. If the entity held the property, then the property could continue to be dedicated to the purpose for which that entity was formed as long as the entity existed. The ability to commit property in this way was important for assets that would be dedicated to a specialized purpose, a function that became quite valuable in business as the industrial revolution generated scale economies in the nineteenth century and business people began building railroads, large refineries, mills and factories that could not be readily redeployed to some other purpose. For reasons I have explored at length elsewhere, business organizers prior to the late twentieth century could not achieve perpetual succession for the enterprise through the standard partnership form of organization without, as Angell and Ames (1832: 2) put it, 'perplexing intricacies, the hazardous and endless necessity of perpetual conveyances for the purpose of transmitting it from hand to hand'.[27]

The ability to commit specialized assets to a common purpose over time is still one of the most important functions of incorporation. Although today it may seem that corporations buy and sell assets and turn their properties over much more readily than they might have in the early twentieth century, business corporations continue to be substantial owners of specialized capital, both physical and intangible, that is more valuable if it can be committed to its specific function over a period of time, even though a succession of individuals may have management responsibility over the assets.

Identifiable Persona to Serve as a Contractual Party and Bear Reputational and Other Intangible Assets

Perpetual succession in the name of an identifiable persona was also important to assure counterparties that contractual obligations would be carried out by the entity, even if the individuals who negotiated and signed the contracts were no longer around. Entity status thus provided continuity that made it feasible for business organizers to enter into long-term contracts with suppliers that could assure that specialized assets such as a steel mill, for example, would have continuous access to raw materials, or that made it reasonable to build communities along the path of a railroad to provide services, supplies and equipment to the railroad and its passengers and crews.[28]

The idea that a corporation could stand in the place of a group of people who wanted to act collectively, so that they could own property, enter into contracts, sue and be sued as if they were a single person, is also fundamental to the corporate form, and its roots are deep in the history of corporate law. One of the main reasons for incorporation, according to Angell and Ames (1832: 1), was to make it possible for a group of individuals to unite 'under a common name, the members of which succeed each other, so that the body continues the same, notwithstanding the change of the individuals who compose it, and which for certain purposes is considered a natural person'. As corporations came to be used extensively to organize large-scale businesses in manufacturing, transportation, and wholesale and retail trade, business people learned to market their products to customers across great geographic, social and economic distances (Chandler 1977). But this meant that the customer no longer had personal relationships with the people who produced the goods. How could a customer be sure that the product would be well made, or that the producer or seller would stand behind the product? One solution to this problem turned out to be the development of the idea of 'branded' goods, such as Coca-Cola and Quaker Oats.[29]

Firms that produced factory-made machinery in the mid-nineteenth century, such as guns, sewing machines and farm equipment, for example, had to convince potential customers that the manufacturer would stand behind the product, and provide for repairs and maintenance. In the late 1850s and early 1860s, sewing machine maker I.M. Singer & Co. – originally organized as a partnership – developed a network of distributors in local communities who were direct employees of the firm (rather than independent distributors), who could sell the machines, teach women how to use them, provide financing for households to buy the machines, and repair the machines if they broke (Chandler 1977; Blair 2003). This network of employees helped to build a reputation for quality, reliability and service that made it possible to sell sewing machines to customers who never met Isaac M. Singer, the inventor of the machines, or his partner Edward Clark. The Singer sewing machine thus became one of the first branded factory-made machines to be used in many households.

By 1860, the reputational value that I.M. Singer & Co. (the partnership) had built up since its founding in 1851 was vulnerable to the extent that it was tied to Singer the person, because Singer was growing old, and became increasingly eccentric and flamboyant as he aged. Singer's partner Clark intuitively understood that it was crucial to the long-run success of the business that it have an identity separate from Singer, the person, that could be the bearer of the reputation for quality products. So he convinced Singer to reorganize the business as a corporation, the Singer Manufacturing Co. This had the effect of transferring all of the tangible assets of the business into a separate corporate entity, with its own persona, and helped to link the intangible reputational assets to that persona, which could be distinguished from Singer the person, and would continue in existence for more than a century after Singer was gone (Blair 2003).[30]

Having a corporate entity that serves as the identifiable persona, the bearer of reputational and organizational capital, results in a significant change in the relationships among customers and employees of the firm. In a market of individual producers and shops, customers trust the quality of the meat, bread and candles because they trust the competence of the individual butchers, bakers and candlestick makers. Where corporations make and sell mass-produced branded products in many markets, however, the customer often comes to trust the branded product first, and trusts the competence of individuals involved in making and selling the products without knowing them personally because they are employed by the corporation and identified with its brand.[31] In this way, the use of the corporate form of organization makes it possible to extend the reputational value created in the firm across time and space, so that numerous firm employees can share in the reputation of the firm, and so that the reputational value reaches many more possible customers.

This phenomenon was evident in the evolution of the various Du Pont family businesses in the late nineteenth century. From the 1870s through the end of the century, Henry du Pont and his nephew Lammot (operating as a partnership) were the faces and reputations behind the various explosives and gun powder products that were produced at plants owned by the partnership. Zunz (1990: 17) tells us 'Old Henry busily corresponded with an extensive network of independent agents' in the effort by the firm to serve a national market. These agents were often men of prominence in their communities who could vouch for the quality of the Du Pont products. But after Du Pont was incorporated as the E.I. Du Pont de Nemours Powder Co., independent agents were either brought into the company as managers, or the relationships were generally severed, so that, over a relatively short period of time, the company came to be seen as the entity behind the products, not the individual sales people, nor any specific DuPont family member. As such, the brand creates value for customers by reducing the transaction costs associated with identifying reliable sources for products, and reliable people with whom to do business.

If the brand is attached to the corporate entity rather than to any of the individual investors, managers, board members or employees, this makes it easier for the workforce of a firm to identify with the firm, and with each other, which in turn creates value because employees who identify with each other and with the firm have been shown to be more productive (Akerlof & Kranton 2005; Chen & Chen 2011; Boivie et al. 2011).

Asset Partitioning: Capital Lock-In and Limited Liability

The legal recognition of corporations as separate entities makes it much easier to separate pools of assets according to which assets will be available to which heirs or creditors for settlement of debts (Hansmann & Kraakman 2000; Blair 2003). Other scholars have written extensively about the benefits to business organizers of one aspect of partitioning assets, limited liability.[32] Limited liability means that the corporation itself, and only the corporation, is responsible for debts of the corporation, and equity holders and creditors cannot be held personally liable for the corporation's debts.[33] Limited liability makes it easier for corporations to raise equity capital from widely dispersed shareholders, or from shareholders who prefer to invest passively, leaving the management of the company to others. Limited liability and separate entity status for corporations may even provide efficiencies for creditors of corporations because they make it much clearer which assets back any loans to the corporation.

Separate entity status also facilitates capital lock-in. Corporate law makes it easier to commit capital to an enterprise because, under corporate law, the assets of the corporation belong to the corporation itself, and may not be pulled out by shareholders without a decision by the board of directors to make a distribution to shareholders. If shareholders want to get out of their investment for any reason, they have no right to have their interest bought out by the corporation individually (as partners would have in a partnership), nor do they have any authority to order a pro-rata distribution to all shareholders.[34] Instead, shareholders are generally entitled to sell or transfer their shares, which gives the purchaser of the shares the rights to any distributions, when and if they are made subsequently.

Moreover, if a shareholder dies, the corporation will not be broken up so that assets can be distributed to the heirs of the deceased shareholders (as would happen in a common law general partnership). Instead, the estate of the deceased is left with shares in the corporation that can be distributed to heirs without changing anything about the financing or management of the corporation. And, similarly, creditors of individual shareholders (or other investors) may not claim corporate assets or compel a distribution of corporate assets to satisfy their claims against the shareholders. Shareholders could, however, transfer their shares to the creditors as payment for the debts.

Hansmann and Kraakman (2000) use the phrase 'asset partitioning' to refer to the combination of these two functions: limited liability of shareholders for corporate obligations, and the protection of the firm from liability for debts of its shareholders or from having shareholders unilaterally pull assets out. They argue that it might have been possible to arrange for limited liability for shareholders through contracts in the nineteenth century and early twentieth centuries, but that it would be difficult or impossible to protect the firm from creditors of the shareholders by contract. Separate entity status for the corporation achieves these results however. Thus they assert that asset partitioning is the quintessential feature of legal entities such as corporations that distinguishes them from other contractual arrangements. Moreover, until the mid-twentieth century, full entity status was available in the US, the UK and parts of Europe only via incorporation.

While asset partitioning is undoubtedly a very important function of separate entity status, in the large corporations that emerged in the nineteenth century and came to dominate the industrial economy of the twentieth century, perpetual succession, an identifiable persona to bear reputational assets, and asset partitioning were all three important, and generally came as a package. Legal recognition of separate entity status neatly and cleanly accomplishes all three functions.

Governance Structure

From its earliest days, the corporate form was a mechanism for organizing the affairs of a group of people acting together, either in succession or contemporaneously, or both. In the US, as states began to pass general incorporation statutes in the first half of the nineteenth century, these statutes all required that there be at least three, or sometimes five or even seven, incorporators or members.[35] The corporate form was not available, as it is today, for use by a single individual (or another corporation) to carve their assets into separate pools, some available for business creditors and others available for personal creditors.[36] The requirement that at least three or more individuals were needed to form a corporation was still in place in nearly all states as late as 1950.[37] This was not considered controversial in the early development of corporate law because a corporation, according to Kyd, is 'a collection of many individuals . . . vested by the policy of the law, with a capacity of acting . . . as an individual, particularly of taking and granting property, contracting obligations, and suing and being sued' (Kyd 1793; as cited in Angell and Ames 1832: 1).

With multiple people involved, the participants in the enterprise must have some method of governing their relations. In firms organized as partnerships, the law views partners as having contractual relationships with each other. These relationships are supposed to be largely self-governed, but if a dispute arises among partners that they cannot resolve themselves, they can turn to a court of law to weigh the equities, consider the contract terms and determine the appropriate outcome.

Corporate law, by contrast, provides that corporations must have a board of directors, and that the board has sole authority to act for the corporation.[38] Although corporations are subject to regulations concerning their business activities and their public disclosures, as to internal questions about such matters as the choice of ventures to pursue, the allocation of resources within the firm to one project or another, or the distribution of wealth created by the firm as between bonuses and dividends, these matters are left to the business judgment of boards of directors, and courts will not second-guess them unless there is evidence that the directors breached their fiduciary duties in some way.[39]

Although the requirement of having a board appears to have emerged early in the history of corporate law, there has been relatively little scholarship on the origins of this requirement.[40] Gevurtz (2004) speculates that chartered associations formed for commercial purposes copied the organizational structure of chartered townships, which were governed by town councils, and that when states were drafting general incorporation statutes they incorporated this feature, which had become quite a common feature of corporate charters (Gevurtz 2004).[41]

Corporate law clearly separates the role of directors from that of shareholders. Although this separation of roles makes it easier for investors in corporations to be passive investors, it has also been troubling to legal scholars at least since Berle and Means (1932) documented the extent to which the ownership of shares in corporations had migrated to investors who were almost completely disconnected from corporate management. The concern is that separating ownership from control in corporations gives management free rein to run the corporation in pursuit of their own personal agenda, rather than to create value for shareholders.

Lynn Stout and I have argued elsewhere, however, that one of the important benefits of the corporate form is precisely that it takes power away from the individual participants, and vests all powers of action in the board, a governance arrangement that helps support 'team production' (Blair & Stout 1999). 'Team production' refers to productive activity carried out by a group of people who contribute complex inputs that are difficult to measure or specify, and in which the output is a joint output in the sense that it is not possible to determine which portion of the output is attributable to which input provider. Team production requires team members to cooperate. But if inputs are complex and difficult to specify in advance, it can be impossible to write complete contracts *ex ante* that can elicit this kind of cooperation without creating incentives for one or more team members either to shirk, or to attempt to 'hold up' the other participants in an effort to extract a larger share of the benefits *ex post* (Holmstrom 1982).

One solution to such a contracting problem is that all of the team members agree to give up control rights over the enterprise and its output to an outside third party who has the authority to hire and fire, as well as to allocate the surplus created by the team (Rajan and Zingales 1998). Boards of directors play this role in corporations. Since they exercise 'all corporate powers' (Model Business Corporation Act, §8.01(b)), all other participants can credibly commit not to use power over corporate assets to hold each other up.

Among some of the earliest corporations, it was clear that board governance helped to balance the competing interests of different participants in the firm. For example, the charter of the Farmers' and Mechanics' Bank of Philadelphia (incorporated in 1809) required that 'a majority of the directors be farmers, mechanics, or manufacturers actually employed in their respective professions' (Blair 2003: 436, n.196). This requirement suggests that the directors of the bank would be expected to represent the interests of the borrowers from the bank as well as of investors in the capital stock of the bank. Similarly, investors in early railroads included people who lived along the route of the railroad, who were interested in how the railroad affected their lives, in addition to earning a financial return, and who attended shareholder meetings and presumably elected directors sensitive to those issues (Werner 1981: 1637). In more recent times, a common pattern in high-tech firms financed with venture capital is that the boards of such firms consist of a representative or two of the entrepreneur, a representative or two of the venture fund that is providing financing, and several prominent individuals who are involved in and knowledgeable about the industry but have little or no direct investment in the firm (Liebeskind 2000). This pattern suggests that the board is expected to play a role as neutral mediator among the various interests in the corporation, rather than just representing one set of interests.

While it would be possible to vest control rights in a board without creating a separate legal entity, board governance and entity status complement each other. Board governance makes it clear who can act for the entity, and entity status provides a mechanism for embodying and expressing any interests of the group as a whole that may conflict with or at least not be shared with the interests of any of a firm's individual participants. Importantly, both statutory law and case law require that directors act 'in the best interest of the corporation', a requirement that makes much more sense if the corporation is recognized as a separate entity from its shareholders or managers, as well as from the board itself.

THE BEST INTEREST OF THE CORPORATION

Both statutory and case law of corporations in the US regard a corporation as an entity separate from its managers, employees, creditors and directors, and even from its shareholders. Statutory law provides that corporate directors owe their fiduciary duties to the corporation (MBCA §8.30(a)), and courts often describe the duties of directors as being owed either to the corporation, or to the corporation and its shareholders, clearly implying that the corporation is something different from its shareholders (Elhauge 2005; Dalley 2008). But advocates of shareholder primacy generally argue that it is dangerous and misleading to treat a corporation as having interests that are different from those of shareholders. They take the position that a corporation should be regarded as just a mechanism for aggregating the interests of shareholders, and that those interests can be succinctly summarized in one metric: the value of the shares (Gilson 2005).

Analysis of the four functions of separate entity status suggests that there might be some contexts in which the value of the equity shares may indeed be a complete measure of the interests of the corporation. An example would be in corporations formed as 'special purpose vehicles' for the limited purpose of partitioning assets and protecting the sponsoring corporation from liability in securitization transactions. In these corporations, there are essentially no employees and no suppliers, so the only interests are those of debt holders and equity holders. The holders of the securitized debt, moreover, are likely to be very sophisticated investors who carefully bargained (or should have bargained) for all the protection they needed.

But in most publicly traded business corporations, the separateness of the legal entity serves multiple functions, and the interests of the corporation cannot be so neatly summarized. Continuity in the ownership of assets and carrying out of contracts, combined with capital lock-in, makes it possible to dedicate assets to the pursuit of a business idea or to carry out an enterprise; having an identifiable persona to serve as a contractual counterparty, to which reputation can attach, facilitates building and accumulating reputational capital and other intangible assets. These are functions that support the building, preserving and sustaining of human institutions. As Larry Page and Sergey Brin (founders of Google) recognized and discussed in the initial public offering (IPO) filings for Google, large corporations nearly always have broader purposes than just the enrichment of shareholders: purposes such as providing safe and reliable products, good jobs for employees, new treatments for diseases, investment options for small investors, financing for housing or college, or access to communication networks that link individuals around the globe, make vast amounts of information available to them and give them an outlet for self-expression.[42] While investors in these institutions expect, and deserve, to get a return on their investment, profits for shareholders are clearly not the only value being created by such enterprises.[43] In these cases, the 'best interest of the corporation' can be interpreted to mean that the corporation is supposed to serve (or at least not harm) these other interests.[44] Governance by a board of directors can be useful in striking a balance that sustains the larger purpose.

But not all corporations have such interests. Since the mid-twentieth century, business organizers have discovered ways of using the corporate form solely for the purpose of asset partitioning, particularly for assuring that the organizers of the corporation are protected by limited liability. This occurs especially in two contexts: (1) in the creation of corporations in which a single corporation owns all the shares of another corporation; and (2) in the creation of 'special-purpose entities' (SPEs[45]) by financial firms for the purpose of 'securitizing' financial assets. When the shares of corporation A are owned in their entirety by corporation B, the incorporation of A as a separate entity adds little or no further 'perpetual succession' or 'identifiable persona' benefit that could not have already been achieved by the incorporation of the parent corporation.[46] Similarly, little governance purpose is served by A having a separate board of directors. Thus the primary function of the corporate form in the case of a wholly owned subsidiary of another corporation is to make sure that creditors of the subsidiary corporation do not get access to assets of the parent corporation to settle its debts (Mendelson 2002; Thompson 2003).[47] Special-purpose entities formed by financial firms for the purpose of securitizing financial assets are likewise created for the sole purpose of isolating the assets that would be available to pay the claims of purchasers of securities issued by the SPEs, and attempting to protect the parent corporation from liabilities associated with those securities.

When the corporate form is used in these limited and stylized ways, the resulting corporations come closer to conforming to the model that US contractarian scholars seem to have in mind, in which corporations are understood to be just a nexus of contracts that separates the property used in the business from property owned directly by shareholders. For corporations formed solely for such purposes, it might well be the case that there is no distinction between the interests of shareholders and the interests of the corporation. In such corporations, it is reasonable to believe that the only duty of boards of directors is to maximize share value. But in corporations that exist solely to partition assets, it is less clear that any purpose is served by the other features of personhood, especially the requirement of governance by a board of directors.

In conventional business corporations, however, where business people use the form to achieve continuity, to bear reputation, and to build an institution that lasts beyond the vision of the founder, separate identity, longevity and the accumulation of institutional assets such as reputation and brand are important. Actions needed to protect these sources of value might, from time to time, conflict with actions that might maximize value for current shareholders. In these corporations, where potentially competing interests must from time to time be reconciled, board governance provides a mechanism for balancing such competing interests: faced with such a potential conflict, the legal requirement on boards to act in the 'best interest of the corporation' serves to grant them vast discretion to try to build and preserve institutional capital that can create value for all of the corporation's constituents over time.

NOTES

1. 'What were the consequences of incorporation? Incorporation involved the creation of a new personality, distinct from that of individual human beings', according to Harris (2000: 18). Similarly, Berle (1947:

344) observed that 'the state's approval of the corporate form sets up a prima facie case that the assets, liabilities, and operations of the corporation are those of the enterprise'. Mark (1987) traces the history of how business corporations were 'personified' in American law.

2.   I will use these terms interchangeably in this chapter, although I think the terms 'entity status' or 'legal entity' are less emotionally and politically charged than calling a corporation a 'person', and therefore more likely to facilitate clear thinking about legal questions involving corporations.

3.   Bratton (1988–89: 424) asserts that the nexus of contracts view was an explicit attempt by theorists to 'dispel the tendency to regard organizations as persons'.

4.   Grandori (2010: 360), referring to the European Union (EU) juridical form of 'contracts of society', and in particular to 'societies of assets' which includes 'corporations', observes that in this broader contractarian view, '"entities" are themselves founded on contract . . . The fact that a contract is recognized, stylized, and regulated by law as a juridical form does not nullify its contractual nature.' This suggests that one can understand the entity status or 'personhood' of corporations within a broader, overarching contractarian framework.

5.   In recent decades, a growing variety of new organizational and contractual forms that adopt various combinations of corporate and partnership characteristics have become available in legal jurisdictions around the world so that the lines that historically distinguished corporations from partnerships may no longer be so clear. Some of these forms achieve full entity status. But the traditional business corporation was the first widely recognized form that incorporated all of the features discussed in this chapter.

6.   The corporate form makes it possible for 'a perpetual succession of many persons [to be] considered the same, and [to] act as a single individual', according to Chief Justice Marshall in *Trustees of Dartmouth College* v. *Woodward*, 4 Wheat. (17 U.S.) 518 (1819). See also Mark (1987: 1450) and Harris (2000: 19). Other scholars have emphasized the fact that the corporate form permits 'perpetual existence' (Blumberg 1986: 588) but I argue that the important aspect of this is that the entity can hold the property and be liable under contracts even as the people associated with the entity come and go.

7.   The phrase comes from Friedman (2000: 846), as cited in Pollman (2011: 26, n.167).

8.   Creighton (1990) observes that a corporate charter grants 'to an organization or collectivity . . . *the right to act in law under some common name*'. Angell and Ames (1832 [1858]) state that a corporation 'is an intellectual body, created by law, composed of individuals united under a common name'. Kogut and Zander (1996) argue that firms are social communities that exist because the shared identity within the firm facilitates communications and reduces its costs. Ashforth and Mael (1989) note that people can attribute characteristics to a group or an organization even if individual members of the organization do not embody those characteristics. Akerlof and Kranton (2005) argue that people form their self-identity in part on the groups to which they belong. Grant (1996) lays out a knowledge-based theory of the firm in which he stresses the role of organizational capabilities. Rodriques (2011) uses the idea of organizational identity to formulate a theory of non-profit corporations.

9.   Angell and Ames (1832 [1858]) note that the model of self-governance established in early municipal corporations 'contributed to the formation of those elective governments of towns which were the foundation of liberty among modern nations' (Angell & Ames, 1832[1858]: 12).

10.   Angell and Ames (1832 [1858]) report that Kyd enumerates five 'powers and capacities . . . which are considered inseparable from every corporation', the fifth of which is 'To make by-laws, which are considered as private statutes for the government of the corporate body' (Angell & Ames 1832 [1858]: 100, citing to 1 Kyd, 69).

11.   Hansmann and Kraakman (1999) observe that a corporation 'must have at least two attributes. The first is well-defined decision-making authority.' The second, according to these authors, is a pool of assets dedicated to use by the firm.

12.   This is similar to the argument that Ayotte and Hansmann (2009) make that entity status for corporations makes it possible to bundle contracts, so that none of the contracts can be transferred without all of the contracts being transferred together. 'The counterparties to the firm's contracts – the firm's employees, suppliers, creditors and customers – want protection from opportunistic transfers that will reduce the value of the performance they've been promised', they observe (Ayotte & Hansmann 2009: 1).

13.   http://www.apple.com/stevejobs/ last accessed 7 January 2012.

14.   Certain new organizational forms available in the US and in other countries can provide some of the benefits of the corporate form without incorporation.

15.   The US Supreme Court first recognized corporations as 'natural persons' in 1886, in *Santa Clara County* v. *S. Pac. R.R. Co.*, 118 U.S. 394 (1886). In a controversial decision in early 2010, the US Supreme Court found that Congress may not impose limits on the amount of money that corporations may donate to political campaigns, on the grounds that, because corporations are 'persons', they have constitutional rights to freedom of speech (*Citizens United* v. *Federal Election Commission* 130 S. Ct. 876, 906 (U.S. 2010)).

16.   Avi-Yonah and Sivan (2007: 155) claim that 'the corporation as a legal person separate from its owners is

a uniquely Western institution'. Some scholars have argued that there were antecedents to the corporate form in the traditions, practices and law of business people in the Roman Empire and in medieval Italy (Hansmann et al. 2006) but for my purposes in this chapter, we need not go back beyond the charters granted to municipalities and religious institutions in Europe in the Middle Ages.

17. Harris (2000) notes that the 'legal personality of a corporation did not terminate with the death of any individual', but, because the kings tended to oppose land-holding by 'immortal legal persons such as corporations', a corporation generally had to have a special license in the charter of incorporation to hold land, or be permitted to hold land by special statutes called 'mortmain' (Harris 2000: 19).

18. The internal hierarchy and board of directors of a corporation have long been regarded as a 'court of last resort' regarding decisions about the management of corporate assets. Gevurtz (2004) suggests that an early precursor to modern corporate boards were the governing boards elected by groups of merchants who banded together in the fifteenth and sixteenth centuries into 'Companies' to secure monopoly trading rights for their member merchants. 'The boards of the Company of Merchant Adventurers and the Company of the Merchants of the Staple existed to resolve disputes and to pass ordinances regulating the conduct of the members', he reports (Gevurtz 2004: 126). 'Corporate boards developed as a governance mechanism for merchant societies . . . or merchant cartels (like the Dutch East India Company) and only later evolved into the governance mechanism for large business ventures with passive investors' (Gevurtz 2004: 129). Today, courts will not hear a case involving a dispute between two managers of the same corporation over division of a bonus pool, for example. Blair and Stout (1999: 284) cite Williamson (1991: 274) for the proposition that 'courts . . . refuse to hear disputes between one internal division and another'.

19. Hansmann et al. (2006) argues that the asset-partitioning function on successive voyages was largely carried out by the physical separation of assets loaded onto each ship.

20. The Dutch East India Company, for example, was originally organized as a combination of smaller, city-based trading companies, and managed by directors who were appointed by governors of the cities in the combination (Dalley 2008; Gevurtz 2004).

21. From 1700 to 1800 in England, only about a dozen corporate charters were issued, and of these, only six were for manufacturing firms (Blumberg 1993: 14). So business people used the joint-stock company form, which flourished in England despite confusion over whether partnership law would apply to them, or whether they would be treated as entities like religious and educational institutions. Blumberg (1993) observes that 'modern English business law . . . developed as company law – or the law applicable to joint stock companies – not as corporation law' (Blumberg 1993: 15). Blumberg (1986: 579–580; as cited in Mendelson 2002: 1209) asserts that limited liability was not considered 'among the essential attributes of the corporation' in the early nineteenth century.

22. Creighton (1990: 30) reports that prior to the Revolution, only seven corporations were chartered for business purposes (other than public works, banks and insurance companies) in the American colonies.

23. And 88 percent of the charters for these business corporations had been issued after 1790. See Davis (1917: 3, 24, tbl.I).

24. By 1673, France had developed an organizational form called a *Société en commandite*, which was equivalent to a limited partnership (Angell & Ames 1832 [1858]: at 40), and this form was also used in many parts of Europe, though not in England. The limited partnership form permitted some participants to be passive partners, protected the passive partners from liability for the business, and permitted the shares of the passive partners to be transferrable. In the US, New York and Connecticut passed limited partnership statutes in 1822 (Lamoreaux 1998).

25. Angell and Ames (1832 [1858]) observed that 'corporations of our own time . . . are those which have been created in different parts of the United States by charters, that impose upon each member a personal responsibility for the company debts, and in that respect, resemble an ordinary copartnership' (Angell & Ames 1832 [1858]: 45). Hovenkamp (1988: 1651) asserts that 'during the first third of the nineteenth century, American states experienced a general legislative and judicial reaction against limited liability'. Limited liability became a standard feature of business corporations in the second half of the nineteenth century. California corporate law did not provide for limited liability until 1931 (Weinstein 2005).

26. The legal recognition of corporations as separate entities eventually led courts to absolve shareholders of liability for corporate debts, at least after they had paid in their full initial capital, so limited liability came to be associated with entity status. But entity status preceded limited liability.

27. See also Blair (2003: 421; citing Eyre 1823), and Williston (1888) on the difficulties of holding and transferring property held by a firm such as a partnership that did not have clear entity status.

28. Altoona Pennsylvania, for example, was founded as repair center in 1849 by the Pennsylvania Railroad, and came to have a population of over 30000 by 1893 (Zunz 1990).

29. 'Campbell Soup, Coca-Cola, Juicy Fruit gum, Aunt Jemima, and Quaker Oats were among the first products to be "branded", in an effort to increase the consumer's familiarity with their products' (Wikipedia,

http://en.wikipedia.org/wiki/Brand, last visited 21 November 2011). Aaker (1991) explores how brands add value to businesses, their products and services.

30.   In the context of modern business enterprises, Crain (2010: 1182) observes that 'brands allow a firm to separate itself and its reputation from the people who make the products or provide the services'.

31.   Social identity theory argues that individuals define and identify themselves partly in terms of the social groups to which they belong (Taylor & Moghaddam 1994). Empirical research has shown that most individuals have strong needs to identify with social groups (Ashforth & Mael 1989). Numerous scholars have studied how employees tend to identify with the firms that employ them, as well as with groups within the firms (Ashforth & Mael 1989; Akerlof & Kranton 2005).

32.   Mendelson (2002: 1209, n.14) cites articles and cases dating from 1927 through 2000 for the point that other scholars and jurists have deemed limited liability to be one of the most important corporate characteristics.

33.   Courts can 'pierce the veil' of the corporation and hold shareholders liable in exceptional circumstances, such as when a controlling shareholder abuses the privilege of limited liability by pulling assets out of the corporation, leaving it unable to pay its debts. But this is a clear exception, and courts are reluctant to take this step unless the abuse of the corporate form has been egregious.

34.   Delaware General Corporation Law §170(a), for example, provides that 'directors' must determine whether dividends can or should be paid, and Kehl's treatise on dividends (Kehl 1941) noted that, once limited liability became a standard feature of corporations, 'it soon became apparent that the original capital should be permanently devoted to the needs of the corporation', and that 'if the creation of a capital fund was not to defeat its purpose, safeguards against its withdrawal by repayment to shareholders in the guise of dividends, or otherwise, were indispensible' (Kehl 1941: as cited in Eisenberg 2005: 861).

35.   As late as 1960, according to the notation to Model Business Corporation Act, §2.01, 'all but nine states specified that the incorporators must be three or more natural persons', and the comment to the 1960 MBCA stated that the Act 'follow[ed] the traditional concept of several individuals combining to form a corporation'. The MBCA was changed in 1962 to permit incorporation by a single person, or by another corporation (MBCA 2011: 2–5).

36.   Case law going back at least to 1871 suggests that when, on occasion, a single individual came to hold all of the shares of a corporation, courts would still recognize that the corporation was a separate entity from the owner of its shares. See, for example, *Newton Mfg. Co.* v. *White* 42 Ga. 148, 1871. But it appears that corporations could not be formed for this purpose prior to the changes in state corporate law that took place in the 1950s and 1960s.

37.   Model Business Corporation Act Annotated, 2008: §2.01, Annotation, pp. 2–5.

38.   MBCA §8.01 ('each corporation must have a board of directors. (b) All corporate powers shall be exercised by or under the authority of the board of directors of the corporation, and the business and affairs of the corporation shall be managed by or under the direction, and subject to the oversight, of its board of directors'). The board may delegate authority to managers, but the board may not thereby avoid responsibility.

39.   Courts refer to this doctrine as the 'business judgment rule', which is 'a presumption that in making a business judgment, the directors of a corporation acted on an informed basis, in good faith and in the honest belief that the action taken was in the best interests of the company. Absent an abuse of discretion, that judgment will be respected by the courts' (*Aronson* v. *Lewis*, Delaware Supreme Court, 1984, 473 A.2d 805).

40.   Gevurtz (2004) is a significant exception.

41.   Blair (2003) reviews some of the evidence in the historical record that boards of managers or directors were a common feature of early business corporations.).

42.   Google's mission statement from the time it was founded was 'to organize the world's information and make it universally accessible and useful' (http://en.wikipedia.org/wiki/Google, last accessed 11 February 2012), and the company's S-1 filings associated with its initial public offering in 2004 included a letter from Page and Brin that said: 'We believe strongly that in the long term, we will be better served – as shareholders and in all other ways – by a company that does good things for the world even if we forgo some short term gains' (Google, Inc., Form S-1, Registration Statement, 29 April 2004, Letter from the Founders).

43.   Facebook founder Mark Zuckerberg similarly announced to potential investors in the S-1 filings for Facebook's IPO: 'Facebook was not originally created to be a company. It was built to accomplish a social mission – to make the world more open and connected.' Moreover, he added, 'we don't build services to make money; we make money to build better services' (Facebook, Inc., Form S-1, Registration Statement, 1 February 2012, Letter from Mark Zuckerberg).

44.   Bratton (1988–89: 427) makes a similar claim about the role of entity status in building institutions: 'The entity idea exists and matters because of a heightened interdependence among the parties participating in

corporate ventures and institutions. Their positions demand ongoing cooperation, and the entity reification embodies and strengthens common goals, such as the preservation of the relationship, that enhance cooperation.'

45. Such financing vehicles are also called special-purpose vehicles (SPVs) or structured investment vehicles (SIVs).
46. There may be benefits from maintaining separate brand identities for different parts of an enterprise; Procter and Gamble sells products under at least 50 different brand names, for example. But there is no compelling identity reason why the activities associated with each brand would need to be carried out under separately incorporated companies.
47. In *United States* v. *Bestfoods*, 524 U.S. 51 (1998), the US Supreme Court found that the parent company of a firm that owned and operated a hazardous waste facility would not be held liable for clean up costs associated with the facility unless the parent company itself actually operated the facility.

REFERENCES

Aaker, David A. (1991), *Managing Brand Equity: Capitalizing on the Value of a Brand Name*, New York: Free Press.
Akerlof, George A. and Rachel E. Kranton (2005), 'Identity and the economics of organizations', *Journal of Economic Perspectives*, **19**, 9–32.
Alchian, Armen A. and Harold Demsetz (1972), 'Production, information costs, and economic organization', *American Economic Review*, **62**, 777–795.
Angell, Joseph K. and Samuel Ames (1832), *A Treatise on the Law of Private Corporations Aggregate*, 1st edn, Boston, MA: Little, Brown & Co.
Angell, Joseph K. and Samuel Ames (1858), *A Treatise on the Law of Private Corporations Aggregate*, 6th edn, Boston, MA: Little, Brown & Co.
Ashforth, Blake E. and Fred Mael (1989), 'Social identity theory and the organization', *Academy of Management Review*, **14**, 20–39.
Avi-Yonah, Reuven S. and Dganit Sivan (2007), 'A historical perspective on corporate form and real entity: implications for corporate social responsibility', in Yuri Biondi et al. (eds), *The Firm as an Entity: Implications for Economics, Accounting, and the Law*, London: Routledge, pp. 153–185.
Ayotte, Kenneth and Henry Hansmann (2009), 'Legal entities as transferable bundles of contracts', working paper, November.
Berle, Adolf A. (1947), 'The theory of enterprise entity', *Harvard Law Review*, **47**(3), 343–358.
Berle, Adolf A. and Gardiner C. Means (1932), *The Modern Corporation and Private Property*, New Brunswick, NJ: Transaction Publishers.
Blair, Margaret M. (2003), 'Locking in capital: what corporate law achieved for business organizers in the nineteenth century', *UCLA Law Review*, **51**(2), 387–455.
Blair, Margaret M. and Lynn A. Stout (1999), 'A team production theory of corporate law', *Virginia Law Review*, **85**, 247–328.
Blumberg, Phillip I. (1986), 'Limited liability and corporate groups', *Journal of Corporation Law*, **11**, 573–632.
Blumberg, Phillip I. (1993), *The Multinational Challenge to Corporation Law: The Search for a New Corporate Personality*, Oxford: University Press.
Boivie, Steven, Donald Lange, Michael McDonald and James D. Westphal (2011), 'Me or we: the effects of CEO organizational identification on agency costs', *Academy of Management Journal*, **54**(3), 551–576.
Bratton, William W., Jr. (1988–89), 'The "nexus of contracts" corporation: a critical appraisal', *Cornell Law Review*, **74**, 407–465.
Canfield, George F. (1917), 'The scope and limits of the corporate entity theory', *Columbia Law Review*, **17**(2), 128–143.
Carter, James Treat (1919), 'The nature of the corporation as a legal entity, with especial reference to the law of Maryland', Dissertation, Johns Hopkins University, USA.
Chandler, Alfred D., Jr. (1977), *The Visible Hand: The Managerial Revolution in American Business*, Cambridge, MA: Belknap Press of Harvard University Press.
Chen, Ronald and Jon Hanson (2004), 'The illusion of law: the legitimating schemas of modern policy and corporate law', *Michigan Law Review*, **103**, 1–149.
Chen, Roy and Yan Chen (2011), 'The potential of social identity for equilibrium selection', *American Economic Review*, **101**, 2562–2589.
Crain, Marion (2010), 'Managing identity: buying into the brand at work', *Iowa Law Review*, **95**, 1179–1258.

Creighton, Andrew Lamont (1990), *The Emergence of Incorporation as a Legal Form for Organizations*, PhD Dissertation, Stanford University.

Dalley, Paula J. (2008), 'Shareholder (and director) fiduciary duties and shareholder activism', *Houston Business and Tax Law Journal*, **8**, 301–336.

Davis, Joseph Stancliffe (1917), 'Eighteenth century business corporations in the United States', *Essays in the Earlier History of American Corporations*, Cambridge: Cambridge University Press.

Dignam, Alan and J. Lowry (2010), *Company Law*, 6th edn, Oxford: Oxford University Press.

Easterbrook, Frank H. and Daniel R. Fischel (1991), *The Economic Structure of Corporate Law*, Cambridge, MA: Harvard University Press.

Eisenberg, Melvin Aron (2005), *Corporations and Other Business Organizations, Cases and Materials*, 9th edn unabridged, New York: Foundation Press.

Elhauge, Einer (2005), 'Sacrificing corporate profits in the public interest', *New York University Law Review*, **80**, 733–869.

Eyre, Manuel et al. (1823), *Remarks and Observations Showing the Justice and Policy of Incorporating 'The Schuylkill Coal Company'*, Philadelphia (Pamphlet in collection of Hagley Library).

Friedman, Lawrence (2000), 'In defense of corporate criminal liability', *Harvard Journal of Law and Public Policy*, **23**, 833–858.

Friedman, Milton (1962), *Capitalism and Freedom*, Chicago, IL: University of Chicago Press.

Gevurtz, Franklin A. (2004), 'The historical and political origins of the corporate board of directors', *Hofstra Law Review*, **33**(Fall), 89–173.

Gilson, Ronald J. (2005), 'Separation and the function of corporation law', Stanford Law and Economics Olin Working Paper No. 307.

Grandori, Anna (2010), 'Asset commitment, constitutional governance, and the nature of the firm', *Journal of Institutional Economics*, **6**(3), 351–375.

Grant, Robert M. (1996), 'Toward a knowledge-based theory of the firm', *Strategic Management Journal*, **17**, 109–122.

Hansmann, Henry and Reinier Kraakman (1999), 'Organizational law as asset partitioning', Working Paper No. 252, September.

Hansmann, Henry and Reinier Kraakman (2000), 'The essential role of organizational law', *Yale Law Journal*, **110**, 387–440.

Hansmann, Henry, Reinier Kraakman and Richard Squire (2006), 'Law and the rise of the firm', *Harvard Law Review*, **119**, 1335–1403.

Harris, Ron (2000), *Industrializing English Law: Entrepreneurship and Business Organization, 1720–1844*, Cambridge: Cambridge University Press.

Holmstron, Bengt (1982), 'Moral hazard in teams', *Bell Journal of Economics*, **13**(2), 324–340.

Hovenkamp, Herbert (1988), 'The classical corporation in American legal thought', *Georgetown Law Journal*, **76**, 1593–1689.

Jensen, Michael C. and William H. Meckling (1976), 'Theory of the firm: managerial behavior, agency costs and ownership structure', *Journal of Financial Economics*, **3**, 305–350.

Kehl, Donald (1941), *Corporate Dividends*, New York: Ronald Press Company.

Kogut, Bruce and Udo Zander (1996), 'What firms do? Coordination, identity, and learning', *Organizational Science*, **7**, 502–518.

Kyd, Stewart (1793), *A Treatise on the Law of Corporations*, London: Butterworth.

Lamoreaux, Naomi R. (1998), 'Partnerships, corporations, and the theory of the firm', *American Economic Review*, **88**(2), 66–71.

Liebeskind, Julia Porter (2000), 'Ownership, incentives, and control in new biotechnology firms', in Margaret M. Blair and Thomas A. Kochan (eds), *The New Relationship: Human Capital in the American Corporation*, Washington, DC: Brookings, pp. 299–326.

Mark, Gregory A. (1987), 'The personification of the business corporation in American Law', *University of Chicago Law Review*, **54**, 1441–1483.

MBCA (2011), *Model Business Corporation Act Annotated*, 4th edn, Vol. 1, ABA, Business Law Section.

Mendelson, Nina A. (2002), 'A control-based approach to shareholder liability for corporate torts', *Columbia Law Review*, **102**, 1203–1303.

Moore, Marc T. (2010), 'Private ordering and public policy: the paradoxical foundations of corporate contractarianism', Nov. 9, University College, London, available at http://ssrn.com/abstract=1706045.

Pollman, Elizabeth (2011), 'Reconceiving corporate personhood', *Utah Law Review*, **4**, 1629–1675.

Radner, Roy (1992), 'Hierarchy: the economics of managing', *Journal of Economic Literature*, **30**, 1382–1415.

Rajan, Raghuram G. and Luigi Zingales (1998), 'Power in the theory of the firm', *Quarterly Journal of Economics*, **113**, 387–432.

Rodriques, Usha (2011), 'Entity and identity', *Emory Law Review*, **60**, 1257–1321.

Seavoy, Ronald E. (1982), *The Origins of the American Business Corporation 1784–1855*, Westport, CT, USA and London, UK: Greenwood Press.

Taylor, Donald M. and Fathali M. Moghaddam (1994), *Theories of Intergroup Relations*, 2nd edn, Westport, CT: Praeger Publishers.

Thompson, Robert B. (2003), 'Agency law and asset partitioning', *University of Cincinnati Law Review*, **71**, 1321–1344.

Votaw, Dow (1965), *Modern Corporations*, Englewood Cliffs, NJ: Prentice Hall.

Warren, Edward H. (1929), *Corporate Advantages Without Incorporation*, New York: Baker, Voorhis & Co.

Weinstein, Mark (2005), 'Limited liability in California 1928–1931: it's the lawyers', *American Law and Economics Review*, **7**(2), 439–483.

Werner, Walter (1981), 'Corporation law in search of its future', *Columbia Law Review*, **81**, 1611–1666.

Williamson, Oliver (1991), 'Comparative economic organization: the analysis of discrete structural alternatives', *Administrative Science Quarterly*, **36**, 269–296.

Williston, Samuel (1888), 'History of the law of business corporations before 1800. II. (concluded)', *Harvard Law Review*, **2**(4), 149–166.

Zunz, Oliver (1990), *Making America Corporate, 1870–1920*, Chicago, IL: University of Chicago Press.

24. Worker cooperatives and democratic governance
John Pencavel

Research on the economics of worker-owned cooperatives once took two forms. One form was highly abstract and offered theoretical models that claimed to characterize certain aspects of the behavior of co-ops. The second form described the experiences of a particular co-op and offered at most anecdotal evidence of co-op behavior. The last two decades has seen a flowering of a new class of empirical research exploiting information over time on a number of individual co-ops and on comparable conventional capitalist enterprises. These studies allow for the determination of key empirical differences between the two types of organizations: co-ops and capitalist firms. This chapter explains and evaluates this new literature.*

INTRODUCTION

When presented with shocks to their economic environments, do firms behave differently when workers control decisions in the organization in which they work? There is a vast empirical literature addressing this question when the workers are organized in a body such as a union and when the union bargains with the owners or with the owners' agents in a conventional firm. In these circumstances, the firm's outcomes reflect the mixed and possibly conflicting objectives and constraints of the owners, the managers, and the production workers (or their representatives). The impact of the workers' preferences and constraints on the outcomes of firms are likely to be most salient when the workers own and manage the firm in which they work. The behavior of such firms, worker cooperatives, is the subject of this chapter.

Some argue that the prevalence of the capital-owned and capital-managed firm in market economies is testament to the superiority of this form of organization, the survival and proliferation of the fittest.[1] Certainly, the success and ubiquity of the capitalist firm as an economic organization calls for explanation. Yet the enduring attraction of worker-owned and worker-managed firms also asks for an understanding. Such organizations, where permitted and not discouraged or impeded, are found all over the world and some have demonstrated an ability to survive inhospitable environments. Indeed, worker co-ops are common in certain professions (such as accounting, law, medicine, investment banking),[2] in exchanges for stocks and securities including futures, and in particular types of jobs (taxis, trucking).

A careful study of worker cooperative organizations reveals considerable variety in their capital ownership arrangements. Most palpably, there are co-ops in which the workers use their own savings to provide the organization's capital and in which labor incomes are not separated from capital incomes. There are co-ops in which workers borrow financial capital from financial intermediaries and in which interest payments on these borrowed funds constitute a regular expense. Thus 'the' worker co-op is something of a fiction.[3] However, a key feature of this type of enterprise is that those who work in the firm hold two classes of rights: one right is ownership that includes the right to enjoy any positive residual of gross revenues over costs and the right to exchange this entitlement to another individual; the second right is that of making crucial workplace decisions, decisions that are associated with the firm's supervisors or controllers or directors. In short, the worker co-op combines worker ownership and worker management.

One or other of these two rights are often found in other firms in modern market economies.[4] For instance, through employee stock ownership plans (ESOPs), many workers in the United States (US) have become part owners of the firms in which they work, so the dimension of worker ownership in worker co-ops is found, at least in part, in many other enterprises.[5] The right to contribute to decision-making within an organization also exists in firms where workers sit on employee-involvement committees or health and safety panels or union–management work bodies. The operation of ESOPs and of employee participatory programs has been a vigorous area of research in its own right and the behavior of worker co-ops may be relevant to an assessment of the effectiveness of these other ventures too.

Given existing authoritative surveys of research on worker co-ops,[6] this chapter concentrates on recent research and on the scholarship of a few key issues. These issues concern the volatility of employment and earnings, the long-term viability of co-ops, the comparative production efficiency of co-ops, and problems of democratic governance within co-ops.

MODELS

Our understanding of the behavior of the conventional capitalist firm has been enriched by basic purposive models that strip particular and idiosyncratic elements from the firm's activities and that concentrate on generalizable and fundamental aspects. The principal workhorse among these purposive models has been that which ascribes to the capitalist organization the object of profit maximization: the firm's responses to changes in its economic environment are not serendipitous but are best understood as if the firm's decision-makers were deliberately and consciously pursuing the goal of maximizing net revenues or profits. There have been constructive modifications of profit maximization to take up issues such as discrimination, managerial discretionary behavior and other factors, but these have been understood as refinements of a model to deal with special circumstances and concerns and not as overturing wholesale the central characterization of net revenue maximization. What is the corresponding model to describe the worker co-op's responses to changes in its economic environment?

This question was taken up by Ben Ward in a seminal article in 1958. He proposed that a worker co-op's behavior is best understood as deriving from the maximization of net revenues per co-op member where wage payments to members are not counted in the computation of net revenues. I label this the 'income maximization hypothesis'. What does it imply?

In the simplest of characterizations, it assumes a congruence of members and workers: all co-op members are workers in the co-op and all workers are members of the co-op. Let E denote the co-op's employment which, in turn, equals the co-op's membership.

By virtue of being an owner and by virtue of the overarching principle of equal treatment, each member receives an equal fraction of total net revenues. The co-op employs a second input in production – call it M for raw materials. Assume capital is fixed at a level set by past decisions. The co-op has incurred debts on its loans and its regular payments on these loans are C. It operates in a product market environment in which its output (the level of which is given by X) is sold at an exogenous price of p per unit. Its raw materials are purchased at an exogenous price r. A smooth, continuous, strictly quasi-concave production function $X = f(E, M)$ regulates the transformation of inputs, E and M, into output X. The production function has the property that, for any input prices, the co-op's average cost curve is U-shaped with respect to output.[7]

The co-op's maximand is D defined as:

$$D = E^{-1} (pX - rM - C)$$

which is sometimes named the dividend rate. The variable inputs, E and M, are selected such that D is maximized given the fixed price environment and given the production function. The relationship between each endogenous variable and all predetermined variables are embodied in the following equations:

$$E = g_1 (p, r, C)$$
$$M = g_2 (p, r, C)$$

and, by substituting these in the production function, the co-op's output supply function is derived:

$$X = g_3 (p, r, C)$$

Each of these functions is homogeneous of degree zero in p, r and C. An increase in fixed costs, C, can be shown to induce an increase in employment as the co-op distributes these higher fixed costs over more workers, but otherwise these three g (·) equations are devoid of unambiguous sign implications except for those listed below.[8] Substituting these three equations into the maximand D yields the maximized value of D, call it D^*:

$$D^* = g_4 (p, r, C) \tag{24.1}$$

The maximum value function (24.1) is homogeneous of degree one in p, r and C. It is non-decreasing in p and non-increasing each in r and C. The envelope theorem implies:

$$\frac{\partial D^*}{\partial p} = \frac{X}{E}; \quad \frac{\partial D^*}{\partial r} = -\frac{M}{E}; \quad \frac{\partial D^*}{\partial C} = -\frac{1}{E} \tag{24.2}$$

The convexity of D^* implies:

$$\frac{\partial^2 D^*}{\partial p^2} > 0 \implies \frac{\partial (X/E)}{\partial p} > 0 \tag{24.3}$$

$$\frac{\partial^2 D^*}{\partial r^2} > 0 \implies \frac{\partial(M/E)}{\partial r} < 0 \tag{24.4}$$

$$\frac{\partial^2 D^*}{\partial C^2} > 0 \implies \frac{\partial E}{\partial C} > 0 \tag{24.5}$$

Increases in p and r induce changes in output–labor and materials–labor ratios and, as has already been noted, increases in fixed costs increase employment. By Young's Theorem (the irrelevance of the order of differentiation), there is a symmetry condition:

$$\frac{\partial(\partial D^*/\partial p)}{\partial r} = \frac{\partial(\partial D^*/\partial r)}{\partial p} \implies \frac{\partial(X/E)}{\partial r} = -\frac{\partial(M/E)}{\partial p}$$

These homogeneity, symmetry and sign implications were confronted with panel data on worker cooperatives in the US Washington state plywood industry and, by conventional statistical criteria, these implications could not be rejected.[9] An especially attractive feature of the study of the plywood co-ops in the Pacific North-West of the US is that there were a number of conventionally organized capitalist mills operating there too. Each of the mills (conventional and co-ops) was too small in relation to aggregate output to be anything but price-takers with respect to the purchase of their input of timber and the sale of their output of plywood. Hence we have the opportunity of observing how the two types of mills responded to the large fluctuations in the prices of timber inputs and the prices of plywood.[10]

There were marked differences between the two types of organizations in their responses. When plywood output prices dropped in a recession, the conventional mills responded by substantially reducing their employment and their hours per worker whereas the co-ops changed their labor input little and cut their hourly wages: the elasticity of worker-hours with respect to real plywood prices was 1.100 (0.205) in the conventional firms while it was 0.096 (0.131) in the co-ops; the elasticity of real hourly wages with respect to real plywood prices was 0.153 (0.151) in the conventional firms and 0.978 (0.160) in the co-ops.[11]

In answer to the question that opened this chapter, these results suggest the following hypothesis: an important difference between the prototype capitalist firm and the co-op is that, in response to shocks in its environment, the capitalist firm adjusts quantities – employment, hours, other inputs and output – while the co-op adjusts earnings per worker. In these plywood co-ops, the definition of earnings per worker includes any periodic dividends to members based on the mill's net revenues in excess of payments to reserves.

Qualitatively, these findings were replicated in a study of very many Italian enterprises:[12] in response to product market shocks, conventional capitalist firms adjusted employment much more than Italian co-operatives which were more inclined to adjust wages to these shocks. With respect to the income-maximizing model above, there was no persuasive evidence in these Italian co-ops that employment was a negative function of fixed costs (as measured by long-term debt payments) although wages paid in the co-ops tended to be negatively related to fixed costs (as implied by equation (24.2) above).

An analysis resembling the aforementioned Italian study was undertaken with Uruguayan firms.[13] The monthly panel data compiled by Burdín and Dean embrace the entire population of Uruguayan worker co-ops and conventional firms in 31 sectors from April 1996 to December 2005. They estimate annual first-difference equations for wages and employment allowing for responses to changes in predetermined variables to differ between co-op firms and conventional capitalist firms. Indeed, the wages paid to workers in the Uruguayan co-ops were more responsive to exogenous variations in its economic environment than the wages paid to workers in capitalist firms. Furthermore, the response of employment to output price shocks was estimated to be noticeably larger in capitalist firms than in worker co-ops.

This class of research has broadly been supportive of Ward's income maximization hypothesis. This may surprise many supporters and members of worker co-ops who do not view the co-op as simply a monetary venture and who extol the participatory dimension of worker co-ops. Expressed differently, whereas the owners of the capitalist firm will claim that consumers' wants are placed at the center of its mission, members of the co-op place the well-being of the workers at the core of its ideals. For the typical capitalist enterprise, the well-being of its workers is achieved as a by-product of the firm's activities; for the co-op the well-being of its member-workers is a distinct and categorical goal. The master–servant relation that predates the employer–employee association in the capitalist firm is replaced in the co-op by one of self-employment and the democratic determination of issues. Ward's income maximization hypothesis does not recognize this transformation of the workplace and yet the model still appears to perform creditably.

DEGENERATION

An enduring concern among proponents of worker co-ops has been that the co-op would evolve over time in such a way as to lose its distinctive participatory and democratic character. The process has been called 'degeneration' and it is often associated with the writings of Beatrice Potter and Sidney Webb who drew these inferences from the study of British worker co-ops.[14] Different explanations for degeneration have been offered. For example, some have seen in worker co-ops the operation of Robert Michels' 'iron law of oligarchy' in democratic organizations: a tendency for an elite within the co-op to assume a growing and commanding role that results in the effective capture of the enterprise.

Another argument turns on the nature of the co-op's financing. In meeting the enterprise's capital requirements, some advocates of the co-op organization have expressed a preference for external financing over self-financing. Drawing upon the experience of co-ops, Vanek (1977) felt that self-financing inclines the co-op's founders to regard themselves as the firm's aristocrats and subsequent members tend to be viewed as subordinate, something that undermines cooperation and work effort.[15] Self-financing is said to encourage a focus on the monetary returns of the enterprise whereas external financing is conducive to the broader vision of the co-op in which the community's well-being figures in its concerns. As workers retire from the co-op, the internally financed co-op will tend to replace them with capital and a privileged class emerges.

Perhaps the most common expression of the degeneration argument has been that the owners of a financially successful co-op would be induced to capitalize (pun intended) on their venture and hire non-member employees in place of departing member-workers. Over time, the organization would diverge from the principle that all workers are members and all members are workers; an increasing fraction of workers would be non-member employees. Eventually the firm would be indistinguishable from many conventional firms with ownership concentrated in the hands of a few and with key decisions taken by a small number of remaining owners.[16]

This worry is by no means fanciful. Thus the Olympia Veneer Company, the inspiration for the various plywood co-ops in the Pacific North-West, started operations in 1921 with 125 member-workers and, after initial difficulties, it prospered for many years. As founding member-workers left the mill, the co-op bought back the shares of the departing members and hired non-member workers in their place. By 1952, there were fewer than 50 working members and in 1954 the company was sold to the United States Plywood Corporation at prices that gave the remaining members a handsome return. The exemplar of the successful plywood worker co-op had 'degenerated' into a capitalist firm.[17]

Even the group of enterprises long esteemed by the proponents of worker ownership – Mondragon – has exhibited signs of such degeneration. Thus, at 'the average co-op', non-member workers constituted 10 percent in 1990 and 70 percent in 2007 of Mondragon's total workforce. Among the industrial group of co-ops at Mondragon, non-member workers reached 29 percent of total employment in 2000, but measures to address this dilution of the co-op caused this to decline to 12 percent by 2008.[18] The Israeli kibbutzim provide another example: their contraction in recent decades has been traced to several factors, one of which has been the increasing use of hired labor.[19]

The 'pure' co-op involving the complete congruence of workers and members is not common; many co-ops hire non-member workers. For instance, in those professions in which the organization is owned by the participating partners, ownership is generally restricted to the practicing attorneys or doctors or accountants; their support staff are usually employees. The income-maximizing model of the worker co-op can easily accommodate hired employees. Indeed, this model implies that, when non-member workers do work that is similar to or substitutable for the work performed by member-workers, an improvement in the co-op's product market will lead to an increase in the employment of non-member employees and a decrease in member-workers.

By contrast, when the work done by the non-member employees is complementary with that undertaken by the member-workers, this replacement of member-workers by non-member employees may not occur.[20] Hence, in a growing product market, the process of degeneration (an increase in the employment of employees relative to worker-members) is more likely where employees and worker-members do the same or similar work; degeneration is less likely when hired workers and worker-members are complements and do dissimilar work. This is a testable prediction. In the Uruguayan co-ops, Burdín and Dean (2009) report no meaningful statistical association between changes in output prices and changes in the employment of hired workers as a fraction of all workers. The authors indicate that hired workers often perform functions (such as various managerial activities) distinct from those performed by member workers so the absence of degeneration in these co-ops is consistent with the argument in the previous paragraph. Furthermore, in Uruguay, co-ops face the loss of tax benefits if hired workers pass a certain threshold and this further discourages their employment in co-ops.[21]

The concern about degeneration relates to the evolution over time of the employment structure of the co-op. A different issue pertains to differences across co-ops in the membership-to-employment ratio at the same stage of the life cycle of co-ops. Such differences will be associated, *inter alia*, with the nature of the skills of the workers. Given the investments they have sunk into the employment relationship with the current co-op, workers with firm-specific skills are more likely to be members of the co-op. By contrast, workers with general human capital have transferable skills that provide job opportunities at other firms and this reduces these workers' dependence on the fortunes of the firm with whom they are currently employed. Such workers are less likely to be co-op members. Does this help to explain why the attorneys in law firms are often members, while the para-legals and support staff are employees?[22]

In short, there is a good deal of evidence to support the notion that worker co-ops are apt to evolve over time into non-cooperative organizations. The complicated question is whether this testifies to their success or is a deficiency. Conventional firms often go through transformations that change their organizational form and yet the changes are usually not identified as some sort of inherent failure of the capital-owned enterprise.

COMPARATIVE PRODUCTION EFFICIENCY OF WORKER CO-OPS

The models of the profit-maximizing capitalist firm and the income-maximizing co-op are silent about the internal operations of firms. Yet important claims have been made about the internal activities of the worker co-op compared with the conventional firm. A number of these claims make directly opposing assertions.

For instance, in the co-op, the equal division of net revenues among many worker-members is said to provide weak work incentives.[23] With a manager whose job lasts only so long as the worker-owners being supervised approve of his oversight, it is argued that the co-op membership is prone to excessive malingering. The co-op workers become shirkers. Others claim that the capitalist firm creates an adversarial 'us versus them' mentality as supervisors try to extract more effort out of workers who see no benefit to them from working harder. In other words, different work incentives are identified in the two types of firms and completely opposite claims are made about work effort.

Similarly, opposing claims have been made regarding plant, machinery and raw materials. In their efforts to maintain employment for their members, co-ops are said to be slow and reluctant to adopt advances in labor-saving equipment and they cling to outdated technology and to inadequate capital. In other words, worker co-ops are alleged to underinvest in physical capital. On the other hand, workers in capitalist enterprises do not own the machines they work with nor the plant they occupy, and they see little reason to care for the capital with which they work. Supervisors in capitalist firms need to be alert for maltreatment of plant and equipment by workers. This induces greater use of supervisors in capitalist firms who are also told to watch for theft and sabotage. Similar to these arguments about plant and machinery, suggestions have been made that worker-members in co-ops are less wasteful and more careful with raw materials in the value-added process.[24]

These and other arguments are hypothesizing, firstly, that faced with the same prices, capitalist firms and co-ops will select different levels of inputs to produce output. Secondly, these arguments maintain that at the same levels of measured inputs, one type of firm will produce more output than the other. These issues have been taken up by researchers in a number of papers who have used information on inputs and outputs to determine whether factor proportions are different in the two types of firms, and whether one type of firm extracts more output from its measured inputs than the other. There have been important differences in these researchers' methods and specifications.

The claims above are not assertions about neutral differences in the firms' production functions. By neutral, I mean production functions that differ only by an intercept and that leave marginal products (or input–output elasticities) unaltered. The arguments about work effort are focused on the effectiveness of labor as an input with the suggestion that the measured work hours of one type of firm correspond to a greater level of effective labor input than that of the other type of firm. The arguments about plant, machinery and raw materials are conjecturing that typical measures of capital stock and the use of raw materials may miss the different vintages or the different depreciation and wastage rates in the two types of firms.

Investigation of these claims requires fitting production functions separately to worker co-ops and to conventional firms, not fitting a common production function to both types of firms save for an intercept shift term distinguishing one type of firm from the other. Hence the most relevant research is those investigations that permit the entire production functions for co-ops and capitalist firms to differ.[25] Perhaps the ideal set of observations to pursue these issues is a data set of inputs and outputs of the same firms or plants, some of them conventional or capitalist firms and others worker co-ops, in a given industry over time. To address the issues raised, a production function is envisaged for the set of input–output observations on the co-ops and a production function is envisaged to describe the input–output patterns for the capitalist firms.[26]

Before turning to this literature, I pause to consider whether observations on inputs and outputs identify a common production function. Without addressing this troublesome issue, it is unclear what the scatter of input–output observations describe. Consider a group of worker co-ops in an industry and suppose each co-op has the same goal as the others. Perhaps this goal is the maximization of net revenues per member-worker. At a given moment, suppose all the co-ops face the same prices for inputs and output. They operate in the same industry and, if a common production function is assumed for these co-ops and if the goal of each firm is the same as that of every other firm, why is each co-op not producing the same level of output with the same levels of inputs as all the other co-ops at that time? From where does the variation in inputs and outputs derive that allows us to fit a 'line' to these inputs and outputs at a given moment and to call this a production function?

The same issue arises in the identification of the production function for the capitalist firms in the industry, provided each capitalist firm has the same goal such as profit maximization. If input and output prices vary over time, this will generate variations in inputs and outputs over time, but some other source of variation is needed to generate differences in inputs and outputs at a given moment.

One response to this identification problem is to recognize that measured inputs at a given moment diverge from the 'true' inputs. Consider the input of labor which is commonly measured by the number of workers or by the number of worker-hours. Neither of these usual ways to measure labor input accounts for variations in work effort or in diligence or in cooperativeness or in other attributes associated with labor as an input to the production process. Similar mis-measurement applies to conventional indicators of raw materials, of machines, and of plant. In fact, convenient simplifying assumptions about the nature of the relationship between the 'true' values of the inputs and the 'measured' values of the inputs may allow the recovery of the common production function. To show this, suppose the input–output relations of all worker co-ops in an industry over time have a Cobb–Douglas production function of the following sort:

$$X_{it} = exp\,(A_i)\,.\,(L_{it}^T)^\alpha\,.\,(K_{it}^T)^\beta\,.\,exp(u_{it}) \qquad (24.6)$$

where the subscript *i* denotes each co-op and *t* denotes each period of observation, say a year. The particular results that follow do not generalize to all other forms of production functions.[27] My purpose here is to illustrate some general issues with the most popular of specifications for the production function. Particular results depend on production function specifications.

The error-free labor and capital inputs in co-op *i* at time *t* are L_{it}^T and K_{it}^T respectively and they are not observed. The superscript *T* denotes 'true'. The multiplicative equation error term is u_{it} and it stands for latent shocks to output out of the control of the co-op. Examples of such shocks are the weather or economy-wide disturbances linked to the state of the business cycle and macroeconomic public policy. Each co-op in the industry is assumed to have the same elasticity of output with respect to the true labor input (α) and the same elasticity of output with respect to the true capital input (β), but among the co-ops there are neutral productivity differences A_i that may be related to the production experience (learning-by-doing) of the plant or to its location. Differences in *A* across co-ops implies that, even at the same input and output prices, different co-ops will produce different outputs from given measured inputs.

Assume, conveniently, that the 'true' inputs are proportional to the measured inputs, L_{it} and K_{it} as follows:

$$L_{it}^T = (\lambda_{it}^L)\,L_{it} \qquad\qquad K_{it}^T = (\lambda_{it}^K)\,K_{it} \qquad (24.7)$$

where the factors of proportionality λ_{it}^L and λ_{it}^K are not constants but vary across firms and over time. Equations (24.7) embody the assumptions that the true-to-measured input ratios are systematically greater in one co-op than in another and that the true-to-measured input ratios are higher in some years for all co-ops than in other years. Differences in λ^L and λ^K across firms and over time cause different co-ops to use different levels of measured inputs to produce different levels of outputs. Substituting these expressions (24.7) in equation (24.6) and taking logarithms:

$$ln(X_{it}) = A_i + \alpha\,lnL_{it} + \beta\,lnK_{it} + \alpha\,ln\lambda_{it}^L + \beta\,ln\lambda_{it}^K + u_{it}. \qquad (24.8)$$

Suppose differences and movements in A_i, $ln\lambda_{it}^L$ and $ln\lambda_{it}^K$ may be characterized by firm (or plant) effects μ_i and time effects η_t and an 'error-components' model results in which measured outputs are related to measured inputs as:

$$ln(X_{it}) = \mu_i + \eta_t + \alpha \, lnL_{it} + \beta \, lnK_{it} + u_{it}. \tag{24.9}$$

Alternative methods are available to estimate the parameters of this equation depending upon assumptions about the distributions of μ_i and η_t. If μ_i and η_t are random components and distributed independently of the inputs lnL_{it} and lnK_{it}, a generalized least-squares estimator is consistent. However, this conditional independence is unlikely and the components μ_i and η_t are likely to be correlated with the inputs. On the other hand, if μ_i and η_t may be treated as parameters, then a fixed effects estimator is often applied. Nevertheless, the inputs may not be independent of u_{it}: for instance, if u_{it} embodies the effects of the weather or business cycle influences on output, then these effects are likely to be correlated with lnL_{it} and lnK_{it}. If appropriate instrumental variables are available (perhaps input and output prices), estimation by instrumental variables needs to be considered.[28]

This general approach was pursued by Craig and Pencavel (1995) in a study of the relative productive efficiency of worker co-ops and capitalist enterprises in the Pacific North-West plywood industry.[29] Among those firms producing approximately the same quantity of output, the input levels of capitalist firms and of co-ops were not the same but the differences were not stark. The possible exception was the use of raw materials, logs: the average input of logs among the capitalist firms was sixteen percent higher than the average among the co-ops. Given their similar output levels, this difference in raw material inputs implies that the average ratio of output to log inputs was higher for the co-ops than for the capitalist firms. This, in turn, was related to the estimated Cobb–Douglas production functions of the co-ops and capitalist firms: the estimated elasticity of output with respect to logs was larger in the production function for the capitalist firms than the corresponding production function elasticity fitted to the co-ops. Given that both types of firms faced the same prices for logs and for their plywood output, this difference in the elasticities of output with respect to logs in the production function means that the optimizing first-order condition for logs implies a higher ratio of output to raw materials for the co-ops than that for the capitalist firms.[30]

In terms of overall production efficiency, when the estimated production functions were simulated, at given inputs, the implied output of the co-ops averaged between 6 and 14 percent more than that of conventional capitalist firms of approximately the same size. This does not mean that co-ops actually produce more than conventional firms and are prone to overproduction. How much they produce will depend on their goals and on input and output prices. It means that they are capable of producing a given output with fewer inputs than comparable capital-owned firms.

A major investigation into the production functions of capitalist firms and co-ops in French industry has recently been undertaken by Fakhfakh et al. (2010). They compile two data sets on annual observations on the inputs and value added of individual firms. In the earlier data set, there are 431 co-ops and 5856 capitalist firms in seven industries over the years from 1987 to 1990. In the later data set, there are 166 co-ops and 2266 capitalist firms in four manufacturing industries over the years from 1989 to 1996. They specify augmented translog production functions to describe the patterns of inputs and value added across firms within each major industry where the parameters of the production functions for the co-ops are permitted to differ from those of the capitalist firms.[31] For the 1987–90 data set, they allow for time-invariant firm-specific effects which they treat as random and they apply a generalized method of moments (GMM) estimator to the observations within each industry and for co-ops and capitalist firms separately. For the 1989–96 data set, the translog specification is time-differenced (one year's observations subtracted from the subsequent year's observations) and the first differences of the inputs and the variables measuring the composition of the labor force are treated as endogenous using the lagged values of the variables expressed in levels as instrumental variables. This is estimated jointly with the equation specified in levels and using lagged differences in inputs as instrumental variables.

The authors report that tests of the null hypothesis of no difference between the production technologies of the co-ops and those of the capitalist firms are rejected 'in all cases'. They then simulate the outputs of the two production technologies at the same input levels. For the 1987–90 sample, in most industries, the co-ops' estimated technology yields higher output for given inputs than the technology estimated to capitalist firms. Results are less easily summarized for the 1989–96 sample and one wonders whether a problem of 'weak' instruments lies behind 'insignificant' differences. The authors conclude that, with respect to the production functions of co-ops and capitalist firms, 'the two groups of firms are more similar than is usually thought'. All in all, it is a thorough study and largely convincing.

The methods of Defourny et al.'s (1992) analysis of French cooperatives are different. They study production differences among co-ops, not between co-ops and capitalist firms. They posit a Cobb–Douglas production function[32] and restrict the error term to take the form of a truncated normal to permit the interpretation of their fitted equation as a production frontier. Their estimating methods are treated as maintained hypotheses. They fit their equation to observations on 143 co-ops in four industries over two years. Again output is measured as value added. They allow for the effects on production of variations in non-member workers to differ from those of variations in member workers.[33] Also the effects on production of variations in externally raised capital are allowed to differ from those of internally-provided capital.

In most of their estimates, the null hypothesis of no meaningful difference in the productivity of the two types of workers and the two types of capital cannot be rejected. They report important neutral efficiency differences across their co-ops. Explanations for these differences are not offered. They also conclude that conclusions about production efficiency that rest on production functions estimated with different assumptions about the nature of the errors and omitting indicators of membership among the workers may be 'very misleading'. However, results from applying different estimating methods are not presented, so the 'misleading' conclusions are not demonstrated. Also, the production function estimates that omit the distinction between members and non-members appear little different from those that incorporate this distinction.

A similar study is that of Jones (2007) who uses annual observations on 26 worker co-ops and 51 conventional firms in the Italian construction industry over time in the 1980s. There are 374 firm-year observations in all, about one-third of which are on the co-ops. Over the observation period, the workers in the co-ops enjoyed only small additions to their basic compensation from the distribution of net revenues, a feature Jones attributes to the financially difficult period in Italian construction. The typical size of the conventional firms (measured by real value added or by capital input or by labor input) is noticeably larger (by some 20 to 60 percent) than that of the co-ops.

To describe the input–output patterns of these enterprises, Jones specifies a translog production function with fixed firm and fixed year effects and also adding terms that measure the extent of participation among the co-op workers.[34] These participation indicators include variables in a given co-op in a given year measuring the proportion of members among the co-op's workforce, the average distributed profits per worker, and the average collectively owned reserves per worker-member. The interest in whether such variables bear an association with output is understandable, but there is an 'included variables problem' as well as the more familiar 'omitted variables problem': the more such performance-related indicators are included, the less likely it is that the fitted relation corresponds to a production function which is supposed to be restricted to inputs and output.

Moreover, in the equation that Jones estimates, the second-order terms in the translog function are constrained to have the same coefficients for co-op and conventional firms, so the notion of fitting two entirely different production technologies for the two classes of firms is not really applied. Furthermore, in one set of estimates, after first differencing the equation, the capital and labor inputs are treated as endogenous using lagged values of the endogenous variables as instrumental variables. The equation's error term is permitted to be heteroskedastic and serially correlated. In the first-difference instrumental variable estimates, almost 100 parameters are estimated, a somewhat courageous specification given 293 total observations.

Jones' results are not easily summarized, but it seems that a consistent pattern favoring either the co-ops or the conventional firms is not apparent. This is not surprising given the attempt to use these data to explore many different hypotheses: not merely that one form of organization produces output more efficiently than the other, but also that output is affected by the degree of financial participation, by the importance of membership in employment, by the size of each co-op's reserves, by distributed profits, by the amount that members have loaned to their co-op, in addition to unidentified firm-specific effects and time effects. A great deal is being asked of the data so that the absence of statistically significant differences from instrumental variable estimation is not surprising.

A general conclusion about the production efficiency of worker co-ops compared with conventional firms is difficult to draw. It would be remarkable if one organizational form dominated the other in every setting. There are enough instances in which co-ops seem no less efficient than capitalist firms that a presumption of co-ops' relative inefficiency is not warranted.

DEMOCRATIC GOVERNANCE

To this point, this chapter's focus has been on the worker co-op as an organization for production and issues of employment governance have not been addressed. Of course, the questions about worker co-ops concern more than production and employment. As an organizational form, the worker co-op has appealed to some with democratic capitalist sympathies and to some with contrasting democratic socialist sympathies. To the former, the worker co-op is sometimes viewed as a mechanism by which capital ownership is extended to a wider section of the community: workers become capitalists. The interest of these capital owners is in protecting and furthering their investments which induce them to take an active part in the management of their firm. To some democratic socialists, the worker co-op is seen as the mechanism to give workers effective authority in guiding production and employment decisions. It is the extension of the political franchise to the economic realm.[35] But how effective are workers in their capacity of making democratic decisions regarding the enterprise?

The type of governance problems that tend to characterize worker co-ops are illustrated by the recently published account of Oregon's Burley Design Cooperative. Schoening (2010) describes how Burley was set up in the 1970s selling bicycle accessories such as panniers, cycling clothing and trailers. Initially, all workers were co-op members and all co-op members were workers. Hourly pay was the same for all individuals and profits were distributed in proportion to each member's share of aggregate work hours. In the early years, all members engaged in decision-making in the manner of direct democracy.

As the firm grew in production and employment, non-member workers were taken on and, in the attempt to avoid the classic degeneration problem of members becoming a diminishing privileged minority, a rule was introduced that required membership to be offered to a hired worker who worked more than 1500 hours in a year. However, some of these new members did not share the same values as the original members and the organization's distinctive participatory culture suffered. The quality of decision-making deteriorated and a hired general manager assumed more responsibilities for determining issues. By 2006, to deal with continued losses, the remaining active members voted to turn their enterprise into a joint-stock company and then to sell it to a private investor who promptly cut the work force by one-half.

The experience of Burley Design Cooperative is a reminder that worker-owned firms require workers to assume critical costs of control and oversight and some workers resist taking on those costs.[36] The collective interest is often difficult (costly) to determine and the member-workers may have to be sufficiently similar or to devote resources to become similar along many dimensions to arrive at agreeable policies. The relevance of the homogeneity of workers has been emphasized by Hansmann (1996) and by Abramitzky (2011) in their studies of American and Israeli communes. It figures also in Rothschild and Whitt's (1986) investigation of cooperatives in California. They write, 'Efforts to develop democratic workplaces often run into difficulties if they have a very heterogeneous work force' (p. 96).

Why is homogeneity important? Perhaps because the lubricant of trust is more easily engendered among like individuals.[37] Or is it because consensus decisions are more easily reached and implemented? On the other hand, homogeneity 'narrows the membership base of the collective and it makes it less representative of the surrounding community' (Rothschild and Whitt (1986: 97). Others have suggested that heterogeneous decision-makers make better decisions when faced with complex problems. In capitalist organizations, most shareholders are concerned simply with monetary returns and problems arising from heterogeneous preferences are avoided, or so it is argued. However, owners have different time horizons and time preference rates and these sometimes result in opposing attitudes toward alternative income streams in capitalist enterprises.

A more systematic empirical analysis of these decision-making issues in the context of the organization of the firm would be valuable. A propitious direction for research may be the development of ingenious experiments that recreate the decision-making environment and that engineer the variables believed to affect behavior. For example, Mellizo et al. (2011) devised an experiment that indicated that, when individuals were allowed to design their own payment mechanism, their subsequent work effort increased. The authors refer to the relevance of their results for workplace democracy.

CONCLUSION

Behind the claims that co-ops are more efficient work organizations are two distinct classes of argument. One is that the compensation mechanism – the sharing of net revenues – among member-workers provides incentives for greater or more effective work effort. Such a compensation system may also attract individuals who are less averse to work effort and who are attracted to the possibility of augmenting their income through superior work effort, a selection effect. A second class of argument concerns the participatory dimension of a worker co-op: an organization works more effectively when individuals are engaged in activities that they have helped to define and that they control. In principle, organizations that involve workers extensively in decision-making need not be organizations that use profit-sharing or revenue-sharing as a wage payment mechanism. In fact, firms that involve workers in decision-making within the organization tend also to be firms that use some sort of revenue-sharing mechanism to compensate their workers.

The worker co-op is the limiting form of such a firm. It means that any productivity differences between capitalist firms and worker co-ops should distinguish among types of capitalist firms: if it is the profit-sharing element that matters most for productivity, then capitalist firms that use some sort of revenue-sharing mechanism for compensating their employees may be similar in productivity to the worker co-op; if it is the participation of workers in decision-making that matters most for productivity, then capitalist firms with employee-involvement programs or works councils may have similar productivity levels as worker co-ops. Or perhaps revenue-sharing payment schemes complement participatory mechanisms and it is the interaction of these two factors that matters most for productivity and there is little effect of one without the presence of the other.[38]

The literature on worker co-ops used to be characterized by theoretical speculation on how worker-owned enterprises behave and by particular case studies where generalization was avoided. The last 20 years or so has witnessed an increasing use of modern empirical methods applied to large numbers of observations to form empirical generalizations about the behavior of worker co-ops. As a result, much has been learned about worker-owned and worker-managed enterprises. As a generalization, it does not seem accurate to describe worker co-ops as technically less efficient operations than the capitalist firm. Co-ops do face governance problems arising perhaps from the differences among worker-owners, but when workers remain sufficiently homogeneous they may look forward to a long life.

There remain enduring claims about co-ops that have not been thoroughly examined and yet they are repeated over and over again when the topic of worker-owned firms arises. One old chestnut is that incentive problems inhibit co-ops from realizing a rapid rate of technological change. A second is that co-ops are ineffective in taking on outside unemployed workers when a local labor market is ailing. Thirdly, in empirical research that evaluates the performance and evolution of the worker co-op, little attention has been directed to issues of financing. Yet, as noted above, some have suggested that the co-op fares better and resists degeneration when it relies on external financing. It would be heartening to think that the next 20 years would bring empirical research to bear on these neglected issues.

NOTES

* Comments on an earlier version of this chapter by Ran Abramitzky, Anna Grandori, Derek Jones and Virginie Pérotin are acknowledged with thanks.
1. A well-written summary and evaluation of the arguments for the dominance of the capitalist enterprise is Dow and Putterman (1999).
2. Levin and Tadelis (2005) account for the frequency of co-ops in many professions in terms of information asymmetries. The net revenue-sharing feature of these partnerships prompts them to be unusually sensitive to the quality of the people with whom the profits will be shared. They are better able to identify high-quality individuals than consumers who, in turn, come to recognize the superior product of the co-op organization.
3. This is consistent with Lamoreaux's (1998) historical analysis of corporations and partnerships which stresses the continuum of arrangements rather than distinct and discrete categories of organizations.
4. Thus a recent volume introduces itself with the following claim: 'Almost half of American private-sector employees participate in "shared capitalism" – employment relations where the pay or wealth of workers is directly tied to workplace or firm performance. In many of these firms employees also participate in employee involvement committees or workplace teams that help management make decisions regarding the economic activities of the firm' (Kruse et al. 2010: 1).
5. Because workers tend to fear the employment consequences of new owners, firms threatened by takeovers have sometimes placed more of the firm's stock in the accounts of employees through ESOPs to repel predators. Examples have been provided by United Airlines and Weirton Steel. In these cases, the firm's shares are placed in a trust for employees who can access them upon retiring or upon leaving the firm. Then the firm often buys back the shares to retain ownership among the employees. Corresponding information for Europe is found in Pérotin and Robinson (2003) and for Japan in Jones and Kato (1995).
6. See especially Dow (2003) and Bonin et al. (1993).
7. This assumption guarantees satisfaction of second-order conditions and is discussed in Estrin (1982) and Ireland and Law (1982: 27–30, 182–85).
8. This means the effect of an increase in p has ambiguous implications for the sign of changes in X. When labor is the only input, a higher output price induces a fall in employment which, in turn, is associated with a fall in output, a comparative static result that has absorbed a remarkable amount of interest. In the general case, however, the sign of the output–price relationship (the income-maximizing co-op's output supply function) cannot be signed unambiguously, as Ward noted.
9. See Pencavel and Craig (1994). Information on C, fixed costs, was lacking in these data. However, in some specifications, the equations were fitted allowing for fixed effects for each co-op. The estimates of these co-op fixed effects may be interpreted as holding constant the effects of differences among these plywood mills in their fixed costs.
10. These prices are, indeed, volatile and the prices of logs reached remarkably high levels in the early 1980s. This brought many purchasers of logs (who often contracted on futures markets) to the brink of bankruptcy. Rescue came in the form of the Timber Contract Buyout Act of 1984 in which the federal government took over some debts of the timber buyers. See Mattey (1990).
11. These values are from the top two panels of Table 4 of Pencavel and Craig (1994). The numbers in parentheses are estimated standard errors.
12. See Pencavel et al. (2006).
13. See Burdín and Dean (2009).

14. See Potter (1891, especially Ch. V) and Sidney and Beatrice Webb (1921, especially pp.472–487). Of course, Beatrice Potter (Webb) (1858–1943) should not be confused with Beatrix Potter (1866–1943). Different versions of the degeneration hypothesis are investigated in Cornforth (1995).

15. Ellerman (1990) has expressed a similar concern with self-financing. His argument is that ownership of capital by the workers is no more to be encouraged than capital ownership by conventional capitalists. He writes, 'The villain of capitalist production is not private property or free markets (far from it), but the whole legal relationship of renting, hiring, or employing human beings. It was the employment relation that allowed some other party to hire the workers so that together with the ownership of other inputs, that party would be the residual claimant . . . Only the democratic firm – where the workers are jointly self-employed – is a genuine alternative to private or public employment' (1990: 208–209).

16. Various evolutionary paths taken by worker co-ops are described by Ben-Ner (1988).

17. This process of 'degeneration' for the co-op resembles a tontine in which members purchase a share in a fund that pays out an annuity whose value increases as a member leaves or dies. This process continues until the final surviving member or members receive the entire fund.

18. The information in this paragraph is drawn from Arando et al. (2011). In Mondragon's case, part of the reason for the growth in the employment of non-members has been that Mondragon has opened capitalist enterprises and joint ventures in Spain and overseas. However, there has been a growth in employees within the co-ops also.

19. See Satt (2007). More economic analysis on the evolution of the kibbutzim is found in Abramitzky (2010).

20. It is straightforward to demonstrate this. Suppose, in terms of the notation given above, that non-member employees are given by M and each is paid a wage of r. Suppose an increase in p signals an improvement in the co-op's product environment. What does this model imply for $\partial M/\partial p$ and for $\partial E/\partial p$? The answer turns on how the marginal product of member-workers is affected by an increase in non-member workers. In other words, it turns on the sign of $(\partial^2 X)/((\partial E)(\partial M))$. If $(\partial^2 X)/((\partial E)(\partial M))$ is negative, hired employees do work similar to and substitutable for that of member-owners in which case a higher product price (indicating a more favorable product market) induces more employment of hired workers and a lower level of member-worker employment:
$\partial M/\partial p > 0$ and $\partial E/\partial p < 0$. If the work done by non-member workers is different from and complementary with that of member-workers so $(\partial^2 X)/(\partial E)(\partial M)$ is positive, the marginal product of member-workers rises with the employment of more non-member workers. In this case, the signs of $\partial M/\partial p$ and of $\partial E/\partial p$ are ambiguous.

21. In a subsequent analysis of Uruguayan firms, Burdin (2012) uses longitudinal observations on firms over 12 years and finds that the rate at which co-ops close is lower than the corresponding rates for capitalist enterprises.

22. A recent report described the development at 'the nation's biggest law firms' of 'a second tier of workers' who do the same work as traditional legal associates but at half the pay. These 'career' or 'permanent' associates 'will never make partner' status (Rampell 2011).

23. Some of the literature on the productivity effects of profit sharing in conventional firms is reviewed in Bloom and Van Reenen (2010).

24. For instance, Dahl (1957: 33) observed of the plywood co-ops of the Pacific North-West that they 'try to get the maximum recovery out of the logs which is a very important factor [in affecting productivity]'.

25. This is not a new argument. For instance, the same conclusion was reached by some who have studied the consequences of profit-sharing schemes on various aspects of the performance of firms (e.g., Cable and Wilson 1989).

26. Although the analysis of input and output data on co-ops only may help to answer some questions about the internal organization of co-ops, such data will not aid in addressing the topic in this section, the comparative production efficiency of worker co-ops.

27. Indeed, if the production function is the translog (transcendental logarithmic or a second-order Taylor series expansion in the logarithms of inputs and outputs), the reasoning that follows in the text will not parse so conveniently into measured inputs and firm- and time-specific components. Instead, there will be interactions between the measured inputs and the error components.

28. These issues harken back to a vigorous literature several decades ago. See, for example, Hoch (1962), Mundlak (1963) and Nerlove (1971). There is, of course, an active contemporary literature on these issues. For instance, see Blundell and Bond (2000) and MaCurdy (2007).

29. Though equation (24.9) was estimated, it was found that a more restrictive specification could not be rejected by conventional statistical criteria. This more restrictive specification replaced the estimated fixed time effects with a time trend (one trend for the co-ops and one for the capitalist firms) and replaced the firm-specific fixed effects with a co-op dummy. The results reported below refer to this specification when fitted by instrumental variables (using input and output prices and year and firm dummy variables as instrumental variables) to co-ops and to the unionized capitalist firms separately and to those mills producing only plywood.

30. The argument here may be stated a little more formally. Let γ^j be the elasticity of output with respect to log inputs in the production function estimated for firms of type j where $j = \Pi$ for capitalist firms and $j = D$ for co-ops. For both types of firms, suppose the first-order condition for the optimal use of raw material logs, G, is $p\,(\partial X/\partial G) = r$ where p is the price of output and r is the per unit price of logs. Because $\gamma = (\partial X/\partial G).\,(G/X)$, the first-order condition for logs may be written $(X/G)^j.\,\gamma^j = r/p$ and, as r/p is virtually the same for both types of firms, differences in γ^j must be offset by differences in $(X/G)^j$. If γ^D is lower than γ^Π, then the first-order condition for logs requires $(X/G)^D$ to be higher than $(X/G)^\Pi$.
31. The word 'augmented' means that, in addition to labor and capital inputs, the equations include variables measuring the fraction of workers who are women and the fractions who are managers and supervisors. Also included is a variable measuring the firm's share of its product market. The authors write that this is designed to absorb the prices embedded in the dependent variable which is the logarithm of value added.
32. The data sources for the research of Defourny et al. seem to be the same as those of Fakhfakh et al. (2010) and they share at least one industry in common (printing), yet they report different results regarding their estimated production functions. Whereas Defourny et al. report that their estimation of the translog production function 'rarely works', Fakhfakh et al. (2010) write, 'the translog specification fits the data best'.
33. The fraction of all workers who are members varies across the four industries from an average of 57 percent in public works, 74 percent in furniture, 77 percent in printing and 85 percent in architecture. Some firms have no member-workers.
34. Jones writes, 'translog production function estimates are preferred to Cobb–Douglas estimates' though the reader is not shown this and the criteria determining 'preference' are not described.
35. For robust statements in this vein, see Bowles and Gintis (1996), Dahl (1985), and Ellerman (1990). Ellerman writes, 'Today's economic democrats are the *new abolitionists* trying to abolish the whole institution of renting people in favor of democratic self-management in the workplace' (Ellerman 1990: 210). Dahl writes, '*If* democracy is justified in governing the state, then it must *also* be justified in governing economic enterprises; and to say that it is *not* justified in governing economic enterprises is to imply that it is not justified in governing the state' (Dahl 1985: 111).
36. Bowles and Gintis (1993) refer to these problems as constituting a 'democratic capacities' constraint.
37. See Jones and Kalmi (2009).
38. See, for instance, Pendleton and Robinson (2010).

REFERENCES

Abramitzky, Ran (2010), 'Lessons from the kibbutz on the equality–incentives trade-off', *Journal of Economic Perspectives*, **24**(4), 1–24
Abramitzky, Ran (2011), 'On the (lack of) stability of communes: an economic perspective', in Rachel McCleary, (ed.), *Oxford Handbook of the Economics of Religion*, Oxford: Oxford University Press, pp. 169–189.
Arando, Saioa, Fred Freundlich, Monica Gago, Derek C. Jones, and Takao Kato (2011), 'Assessing Mondragon: stability and managed change in the face of globalization', IZA DP No. 5711, May.
Ben-Ner, Avner (1988), 'The life cycle of worker-owned firms in market economies: a theoretical analysis', *Journal of Economic Behavior and Organization*, **10**, 287–313.
Bloom, Nicholas and John Van Reenan (2010), 'Human resource management and productivity', National Bureau of Economic Research Working Paper 16019, May.
Blundell, Richard, and Steve Bond (2000), 'GMM estimation with persistent panel data: an application to production functions', *Econometric Reviews*, **19**(3), 321–340.
Bonin, John P., Derek C. Jones and Louis Putterman (1993), 'Theoretical and empirical studies of producer cooperatives: will ever the twain meet?' *Journal of Economic Literature*, **31**(3), 1290–1320.
Bowles, Samuel and Herbert Gintis (1993), 'A political and economic case for the democratic enterprise', *Economics and Philosophy*, **9**(1), 75–100.
Bowles, Samuel and Herbert Gintis (1996), 'Is the demand for workplace democracy redundant in a liberal economy?', in Ugo Paganao and Robert Rowthorn (eds), *Democracy and Efficiency in the Economic Enterprise*, London: Routledge, pp. 64–81.
Burdin, Gabriel (2012), 'Does workers' control affect firm survival? Evidence from Uruguay', unpublished manuscript.
Burdín, Gabriel and Andrés Dean (2009), 'New evidence on wages and employment in worker cooperatives compared with capitalist firms', *Journal of Comparative Economics*, **37**(4), 517–533.
Cable, John and Nicholas Wilson (1989), 'Profit-sharing and productivity: an analysis of UK engineering firms', *Economic Journal*, **99**(396), 366–375.

Cornforth, Chris (1995), 'Patterns of cooperative management: beyond the degeneration thesis', *Economic and Industrial Democracy*, **16**, 487–523.

Craig, Ben and John Pencavel (1995), 'Participation and productivity: a comparison of worker cooperatives and conventional firms in the plywood industry', *Brookings Papers on Economic Activity Microeconomics*, 121–160.

Dahl, Henry G., Jr (1957), 'Worker-owned plywood companies in the state of Washington', First National Bank of Everett, mimeograph, April.

Dahl, Robert (1985), *Preface to Economic Democracy*, Berkeley, CA: University of California Press.

Defourny, Jacques, C.A. Knox Lovell and Aké G.M.N'gbo (1992), 'Variation in productive efficiency in French workers' cooperatives', *Journal of Productivity Analysis*, **3**(1–2), 99–113.

Dow, Gregory K. (2003), *Governing the Firm: Workers' Control in Theory and Practice*, Cambridge: Cambridge University Press.

Dow, Gregory and Louis Putterman (1999), 'Why capital (usually) hires labor: an assessment of proposed explanations', in Margaret Blair and Mark J. Roe (eds), *Employees and Corporate Governance*, Washington, DC: Brookings Institution Press, pp. 17–57.

Ellerman, David P. (1990), *The Democratic Worker-Owned Firm*, Boston, MA: Unwin Hyman.

Estrin, Saul (1982), 'Long-run supply responses under self-management', *Journal of Comparative Economics*, **6**, 363–378.

Fakhfakh, Fathi, Virginie Pérotin and Mónica Gago (2010), 'Productivity, capital and labor in labor-managed and conventional firms', manuscript, April.

Hansmann, Henry (1996), *The Ownership of Enterprise*, Cambridge, MA: Harvard University Press.

Hoch, Irving (1962), 'Estimation of production function parameters combining time-series and cross-section data', *Econometrica*, **30**(1), 34–53.

Ireland, Norman J. and Peter J. Law (1982), *The Economics of Labor-Managed Enterprises*, New York: St Martin's Press.

Jones, Derek C. (2007), 'The productive efficiency of Italian producer cooperatives: evidence from conventional and cooperative firms', *Advances in the Economic Analysis of Participatory and Labour Managed Firms*, **10**, 3–28.

Jones, Derek C. and Panu Kalmi (2009), 'Trust, inequality, and the size of co-operative sector: cross-country evidence', *Annals of Public and Co-operative Economy*, **80**(2), 165–195.

Jones, Derek C. and Takao Kato (1995), 'The productivity effects of employee stock-ownership plans and bonuses: evidence from Japanese panel data', *American Economic Review*, **85**(3), 391–414.

Kruse, Douglas L., Richard B. Freeman and Joseph R. Blasi (eds) (2010), *Shared Capitalism at Work*, Chicago, IL: University of Chicago Press.

Lamoreaux, Naomi (1998), 'Partnerships, corporations, and the theory of the firm', *American Economic Review, Papers and Proceedings*, **88**(2), 66–71.

Levin, Jonathan and Steven Tadelis (2005), 'Profit sharing and the role of professional partnerships', *Quarterly Journal of Economics*, **120**(1), 131–171.

MaCurdy (2007), 'A practitioner's approach to estimating intertemporal relationships using longitudinal data: lessons from applications in wage dynamics', in James Heckman and Edward Leamer (eds), *Handbook of Econometrics*, Vol. 6A, Amsterdam: Elsevier B.V., pp. 4057–4167.

Mattey, Joe P. (1990), *The Timber Bubble That Burst*, New York: Oxford University Press.

Mellizo, Philip, Jeffrey Carpenter and Peter Hans Matthews (2011), 'Workplace democracy in the lab', IZA Discussion Paper No. 5460, January.

Mundlak, Yair (1963), 'Estimation of production and behavioral functions from a combination of cross-section and time-series data', in *Measurement in Economics: Studies in Mathematical Economics and Econometrics in Memory of Yehuda Grunfeld*, Stanford, CA: Stanford University Press, pp. 138–166.

Nerlove, Marc (1971), 'A note on error components models', *Econometrica*, **39**, 359–382.

Pencavel, John and Ben Craig (1994), 'The empirical performance of orthodox models of the firm: conventional firms and worker cooperatives', *Journal of Political Economy*, **102**(4), 718–744.

Pencavel, John, Luigi Pistaferri and Fabiano Schivardi (2006), 'Wages, employment, and capital in capitalist and worker-owned firms', *Industrial and Labor Relations Review*, **60**(1), 23–44.

Pendleton, Andrew and Andrew Robinson (2010), 'Employee stock ownership, investment, and productivity: an interaction-based approach', *Industrial and Labor Relations Review*, **64**(1), 3–29.

Pérotin, Virginie and Andrew Robinson (2003), 'Employee participation in profit and ownership: a review of the issues and evidence', European Parliament Working Paper SOCI 109 EN.

Potter, Beatrice (1891), *The Co-operative Movement of Great Britain*, London: Swan Sonnenschein.

Rampell, Catherine (2011), 'At well-paying law firms, a low-paid corner', *New York Times*, 23 May.

Rothschild, Joyce and J. Allen Whitt (1986), *The Cooperative Workplace: Potentials and Dilemmas of Organizational Democracy and Participation*, Cambridge: Cambridge University Press.

Satt, Ehud (2007), 'Introducing differential wage rates in the kibbutz economy: is it the end of the kibbutz?

Theory and new data', in Sonja Novkovic and Vania Sena (eds), *Cooperative Firms in Global Markets: Incidence, Viability and Economic Performance*, Vol. 10 of Advances in the Economic Analysis of Participatory and Labor Managed Firms, Bingley: JAI Press, pp. 79–107.

Schoening, Joel (2010), 'The rise and fall of Burley Design Cooperative', *Oregon Historical Quarterly*, **31**(3), 312–341.

Vanek, Jaroslav (1977), 'Some fundamental considerations on financing and the form of ownership under labor management', *The Labor-Managed Economy*, Ithaca, NY: Cornell University Press, pp. 171–185.

Ward, Ben (1958), 'The firm in Illyria: market syndicalism', *American Economic Review*, **48**(4), 566–589.

Webb, Sidney and Beatrice Webb (1921), *The Consumers' Co-operative Movement*, London: Longmans.

25. Internal and external hybrids and the nature of joint ventures

Jean-François Hennart

The literature on alliances is vast and diffuse. They have been studied by economists, strategists, sociologists and international business scholars, each following their own particular approach and setting up their own typologies and theories. In this chapter I develop a comprehensive framework to try to provide clearer definitions for the terms 'hybrids', 'networks' and 'joint ventures' and to show the relationship between these concepts. Specifically I will argue that: (1) within alliances a distinction should be made between external hybrids, which are a type of market relationship, and sharing agreements, which include equity joint ventures; (2) equity joint ventures are not hybrids but a type of firm; (3) networks are not a third organizing method, in addition to the price system and hierarchy, but instead the context of relationship-based governance.[1]

THE LITERATURE ON ALLIANCES, HYBRIDS, NETWORKS AND JOINT VENTURES

Starting in the early 1980s, a large number of theoretical and empirical studies have taken alliances as their unit of analysis. The term has been used to describe a wide variety of organizational and legal forms. Gulati (1998) defines an alliance as 'a voluntary resource exchange arrangement between firms engaged in the co-development or provision of services, products or technologies'. For Contractor and Lorange (2002), alliances cover 'several governance modalities ranging from relational contracting, to licensing, to logistical supply-chain relationships, to equity joint ventures'. These definitions are too broad to be useful because they include very different institutions: the empirical evidence shows, for instance, that equity joint ventures and formal and informal contracts have very different properties and are used to perform different tasks; they have been shown, for example, to transfer different types of knowledge (Davies 1977, 1993). I intend to go beyond this catch-all category and develop a more theoretically grounded taxonomy.

There is also considerable ambiguity in the literature about the precise meaning of hybrids, networks, and equity joint ventures. Firstly, there is no agreement over what is covered by the term 'hybrid'. Carter and Hodgson (2006: 468) remark that 'many different phenomena are described as hybrids, and what constitutes a hybrid relationship is open to dispute'. Oliver and Ebers (1998: 550) describe the literature on hybrids as 'a cacophony of heterogeneous concepts, theories and research results'. For example, Williamson (1996: 51), along with many other scholars (e.g. Kreps 1990; Gulati & Singh 1998: Oxley 1997; Boerner & Macher 2003) consider equity joint ventures to be hybrids. Indeed Oxley (1997: 390) calls joint ventures 'the classic form of hybrid organization'.

Secondly, it is not clear what hybrids themselves are and how they relate to markets and to firms. Williamson (1991) and Menard (2004), for example, consider hybrids to be a distinct type of organizing method, an intermediate form between pure market and pure hierarchy, and argue that they are used in situations of medium asset specificity, while firms are chosen when asset specificity is high and markets when it is low. In the words of Menard (2004: 347), hybrids 'rely neither on markets nor on hierarchies for organizing transactions'. I will show that hybrids do not constitute a third organizing method, alongside the price system and hierarchy, but rather that they are institutions that use both organizing methods simultaneously (Hennart 1993). Furthermore, equity joint ventures are not hybrids, but a type of firm, and hence they are not chosen when asset specificity (or more generally the level of transaction costs) is at an intermediate level but instead when it is simultaneously high for at least two interacting parties (Hennart 1988, 2008).

And what about networks? The concept has generated a vast literature (Grandori & Soda 1995). Powell (1990: 301) argues that a network transaction is 'neither a market transaction nor a hierarchical governance structure, but a separate, different mode of exchange, one with its own logic'. While in market transactions 'the benefits to be exchanged are clearly specified, no trust is required, and agreements are bolstered by the power of legal sanctions . . . network forms of exchange . . . entail indefinite, sequential transactions within the context of a general pattern of interaction. Sanctions are typically normative rather than legal' (Powell 1990: 301). Powell cites as examples of networks the web of subcontracting practices in the construction, publishing and film industries, and in the industrial districts of Germany and Italy, but he also includes equity joint ventures. For him, networks are not 'some mongrel hybrid' of market and hierarchy, but 'a distinctly different form' alongside the market and hierarchy (Powell 1990: 299). So are networks a third generic organizing method? I will argue that this is not the case, and that networks are a particular type of market relationship.

In this chapter I use a common framework to study the relationship between markets, contracts, alliances, hybrids, networks and equity joint ventures. I strive for breadth, not depth, and hence I do not offer an exhaustive survey of the relevant literature. I start by arguing that there are only two generic methods to organize cooperation: the exchange of outputs guided by prices and the direction of behavior under hierarchy. The question of which of these two methods one should choose would be moot if individuals had unlimited intellectual abilities and were perfectly honest (Williamson 1975; 1985). However, humans are boundedly rational and can be opportunistic, and this will cause problems regardless of the organizing method chosen. But because each organizing method uses a different recipe, each obtains a different level of rent from the organization of any specific interdependency. Institutions – that is, markets, hybrids and firms – combine these two generic organizing methods in variable proportions, with markets using mostly price incentives, but also some behavior constraints; firms using mostly behavior constraints, but also some price incentives; and hybrids using a more equal mix of both.

The first generic organizing method I consider is the exchange of outputs guided by prices. I identify the circumstances under which this organizing method breaks down. In that case it makes sense to correct its weaknesses with some behavior constraints, and this leads to external hybrids. I then argue that external hybrids can be enforced through the parties themselves or through third parties, and that what has been called 'networks' are webs of external hybrid relationships and hence not a third generic organizing method. When external hybrids incur high costs, organizing the interdependence with hierarchical processes may be the answer. But this solution also has weaknesses, and to correct these weaknesses some features of the price system can be reintroduced. The result is a firm which uses both the price system and hierarchy, that is an internal hybrid.

To add concreteness to these abstract concepts, I use the example of trademarked restaurants. I show that the choice between: (1) outlets owned by restaurateurs who contract for the use of a trademark; (2) outlets owned by a trademark owner employing restaurateurs; and (3) equity joint ventures between trademark owners and restaurateurs, depends on the relative level of transaction costs on the market for labor versus that for reputation, The model shows clearly that equity joint ventures are not hybrids, but a particular type of firm, and that they do not correspond to cases of intermediate asset specificity.

TRANSACTION COSTS

Individuals differ in their capabilities and talents, and hence can benefit from mutual exchange because it allows them to concentrate on what they do best. When they are not able to perform a task by themselves, pooling their efforts with those of others may be efficient. Hence there are potential rents to be had from organizing these two types of interdependencies.

But these rents do not accrue spontaneously. Interdependencies must be organized. Interdependent parties must be made aware of the potential gains of pooling and exchange; a way must be found to avoid excessive bargaining over the distribution of the rents; and the terms of the bargain must be enforced. Information, bargaining and enforcement costs are unavoidable. They are present in market transactions (market transaction costs) and in firms (internal organization costs) (Hennart 1982). They arise because humans are limited in their intellectual capabilities – they suffer from bounded rationality – and because they are opportunistic (Williamson 1975). Opportunistic agents cannot be expected to always live up to their promises. This does not mean that all human beings are fundamentally dishonest, but that it is often difficult to predict *ex ante* who will turn out to be honest or dishonest. The propensity of agents to indulge in opportunistic behavior depends on the legal and social constraints imposed by the social group to which they belong.

Bounded rationality and opportunism jointly give rise to transaction costs. If agents were all-knowing they would be able to distinguish *ex ante* between honest and dishonest traders, and would refuse to transact with the latter. Agents would also be able to perfectly assess *ex ante* the characteristics of the goods and services to be exchanged. Absent opportunism, bounded rationality would not be a problem, since parties would not take advantage of the difficulty that their transacting partners have in measuring goods and services and in anticipating all contingencies. Promises would be honored without the need for safeguards (Williamson 1975, 1985).

TWO GENERIC ORGANIZING METHODS: THE PRICE SYSTEM AND HIERARCHY

Hennart (1993, 2008) starts from the assumption that there are only two generic organizing methods that can be used to organize interdependencies: the exchange of outputs and the coordination of behavior. Real-world institutions, firms and markets, use both of these organizing methods, but in variable proportions. Hence 'hierarchy', which describes an organizing method, and 'firm', which defines an institution, are not synonymous, since, as I will show, some firms use very little hierarchy. Likewise I will argue that there are substantial differences in what we call markets, with some markets infused with more behavior constraints than others. The exchange of outputs guided by prices (the price system) and the coordination of behaviors by an employer (hierarchy) constitute two fundamentally different ways of solving the three basic tasks of informing parties, reducing bargaining, and enforcing the terms of the bargain. Hence they produce different levels of rent for a given interdependence. As institutions, such as markets, firms and hybrids, use different mixes of the two basic organizing methods, they also achieve different levels of rent for a given interdependence. So it is important to have a clear understanding of how the two generic organizing methods inform parties, enforce transactions, and reduce bargaining. The following summarizes the argument developed in Hennart (1982, 1993, 2008).

A perfectly functioning price system could solve the information, enforcement and bargaining problems. In a price system agents collect by themselves information on potential interdependencies and on the rents that may accrue from organizing them. That information is provided by prices. This is efficient if prices encapsulate all the information necessary to guide mutually beneficial action, that is, if prices are 'sufficient statistics'. When output is relatively easy to measure in all of its relevant dimensions, prices can efficiently enforce transactions by rewarding agents in proportion to their market-measured output. For the price system to function efficiently, parties must also have full knowledge of the good and service being put on sale. If there is information asymmetry between buyers and sellers in that regard, they may not agree on a price. In perfectly efficient markets, the large number of buyers and sellers spreads information about the product and service, reducing information asymmetry, and curbing bargaining by making prices exogenous.

I use the term 'hierarchy' to denote a specific organizing method. 'Hierarchy' is not synonymous with 'firm', since a firm is an institution, while hierarchy is an organizing method. Firms vary in their use of hierarchy as an organizing method, with small entrepreneurial firms and partnerships characterized by very flat information structures and high output incentives, and large firms by highly centralized information structures and tight behavior constraints.

Hierarchy, as an organizing method, relies on different means than the price system to organize interdependencies. It uses a centralized information structure. Agents collect a subset of the information necessary to make decisions and forward it to a central coordinator, the boss, who processes it and sends back directives for execution. This specialization in information gathering is efficient if the information needed is too complex for any individual agent to collect it in its entirety. Then it makes sense to separate the collection of information from its processing, and to have all information centralized and processed by a central party who coordinates the behavior of agents, for otherwise agents would fail to autonomously reach a coordinated response – they would suboptimize. While the hierarchical solution solves the problem of prices being 'insufficient statistics' and hence poor guides to action, it has nevertheless a number of limitations: (1) in contrast to the market solution, those who gather information are not those who use it, and this weakens their incentives for diligent and accurate information collection; this is particularly problematic if it is important to collect timely and local information (Hayek 1945); (2) the transfer of information up and down the chain of command may lead to involuntary or willful information distortion; (3) the centralized treatment of information by the boss may result in information overload. As a result, employees may have better information than that received from the boss. Decentralization is a possible solution here, but it can recreate suboptimization, the very thing it aimed to avert in the first place (Williamson 1975; Hennart 1982).[2]

Hierarchy rewards actors based on their behavior. Appropriate behavior is obtained through external means – personal supervision, bureaucratic rules and peer pressure – or internal ones, that is, having employees internalize appropriate behavior through indoctrination or socialization. When output is difficult to measure, directing behavior may be a more efficient way to organize interdependencies if behavior is a good guide to performance. However, given bounded rationality and opportunism, perfect monitoring of performance is impossible. Hence not all employees can be expected to always fully abide by the letter and spirit of their employment contract; those who do not can be said to be shirking (Hennart 1982, 1993).[3] Lastly, hierarchy uses managerial fiat to solve potential bargaining about what needs to be done and how to do it. The extent to which agents are willing to accept such fiat depends on their zone of acceptance (Simon 1951), but there are reasons to believe that the zone will be larger for employees than for contractors because, in contrast to contractors, the remuneration of employees is not linked to their market-measured output but depends rather on their obedience to managerial directives.

In the next section I use these building blocks to look at the different institutions that can be used to organize the interdependencies between owners of reputation and food service providers. This allows me to contrast three possible ways to organize these interdependencies: pure markets, hybrids (internal and external), and sharing agreements such as equity joint ventures. The emphasis will be predominantly on enforcement costs rather than on information and bargaining costs. The model will be shown to have wider applicability, for example in professional service firms, agriculture and high-technology business.

THE EXPLOITATION OF REPUTATION

Take 18 carat gold or grade A butter. These goods are easy to measure in all of their dimensions because they are sold according to product standards, and are not customized to particular buyers. The price of these products is a good measure of their value, the transaction requires only minimum monitoring, and the identity of the transactors is irrelevant. Any attempt on the part of sellers to mislead buyers would lead to buyers switching sellers and hence to cheaters losing business. In that case markets work well. This is the situation described by classical market contracting (Williamson 1979).

In most other cases, however, consumers incur substantial costs to evaluate products prior to purchase. Most products have many attributes (Lancaster 1966). A fast food meal, for example, can be described by the taste of the food, the care taken in its preparation, the quality of its presentation, the cleanliness and stylishness of the premises, the professionalism and friendliness of the staff, and so on. Some of these attributes are hard to ascertain *ex ante*: one cannot know how food tastes until one has started to eat it, while the consequences of eating spoiled food are only felt some time after it is consumed. Hence the price of food is not always a good predictor of its attributes.

In situations like these buyers must exert considerable effort to ascertain the quality of the product they intend to buy. One way to reduce such effort is through branding. By branding all of its products, a producer posts a bond that will be lost if any product sold does not live up to its advertised quality. This reassures consumers and allows them to economize on their search effort. Owners of valuable trademarks can transfer them to restaurateurs who do not have an established reputation.

In that case, two parties collaborate to supply food to customers, a trademark owner and a restaurateur. They can bundle their services in two basic ways: (1) independent restaurateurs can rent trademarks from their owners and keep whatever is left after such payment (the residual); or (2) trademark owners can hire restaurateurs for a salary that does not depend on the residual and keep the residual for themselves.

The first solution minimizes shirking by restaurateurs. Since they are remunerated in proportion to their output, they can be expected to self-monitor their tendency to shirk, since indulging in shirking will result in lower output, and hence lower income.[4] In other words, restaurateurs are subject to output constraints imposed by consumers. But because their reward varies with their output, they will have the incentive to increase their income by altering their output. They can take advantage of the fact that consumers cannot easily evaluate the quality of the food pre-purchase and lower the quality – but not the price – of the trademarked products below that promised by the trademark. This cheating, or free-riding, is more likely when consumers cannot cheaply ascertain quality pre-purchase, when at least some of the consumers are non-repeat, and when it is costly for the trademark owner to detect lapses in quality. In these cases, restaurateurs can pass on the reputation cost of substandard quality to all the other users of the trademark. If enough restaurateurs behave in this way, the brand will lose its value and the chain will lose customers (Brickley and Dark 1987; Michael 2000).

The pure market solution in which the use of trademarks is sold on anonymous markets to a restaurateur corresponds to cell 1 in Table 25.1. Because in this case restaurateurs have title to the profits, they will exert maximum effort, and hence this solution will be optimal when two conditions are met: (1) a high level of shirking would be expected, for example because the outlets are small and dispersed; and (2) the level of free-riding is likely to be low, for example because the clientele consists mostly of repeat customers (Brickley and Dark 1987). If this is not the case, restaurateurs will free-ride on quality and a pure trademark rental to restaurateurs without additional behavioral constraints will lead to the demise of the chain. Hence this solution results in a high level of effort but low quality.[5]

When this is the case, the alternative solution may be chosen: instead of renting the trademark to restaurateurs remunerated by the sale of the trademarked product, why not give title to the profits to trademark owners and have them pay restaurateurs an amount

Table 25.1   A typology of institutions: the case of trademarked restaurants

	Cost of transferring reputation (expected level of free-riding)		
	Column 1: Low	Column 2: Moderate	Column 3: High
Cost of monitoring restaurateurs (expected level of shirking) — Row 1: Low			Cell 3: Outlets owned by trademark owners hiring restaurateurs
Row 2: Moderate			Cell 4: Internal hybrids: outlets owned by trademark owners paying output-linked bonuses to restaurateurs
Row 3: High	Cell 1: Restaurateurs rent trademark on the market (usually not feasible)	Cell 2: External hybrids: trademark owners constrain the behavior of restaurateurs through franchise or relational contracts	Cell 5: Residual sharing agreement between trademark owners and restaurateurs

based on their obedience to managerial directives? This solution (cell 3 in Table 25.1) is that of outlets owned and operated by trademark owners. Trademark owners are now subject to the output constraints imposed by consumers. Because they own the brand, they are not able to pass on the cost of free-riding to others, and hence are less likely to free-ride. Because the pay of restaurateurs is now unrelated to their output – they are now employees – they have fewer incentives to free-ride by reducing quality and can be told to behave in such a way that all the standards promised by the brand are respected. But because their reward is no longer directly linked to their output, they have lower incentives to maximize it if doing so requires effort, and if exerting effort reduces their utility. When trademark owners find it costly to monitor the level of effort of their employees, the latter may shirk. Hence this solution is efficient if the expected level of free-riding on quality is high but that of shirking is low, for example because it is possible to serve the market with few outlets and observing behavior provides reasonable information on performance.[6] More generally, from an enforcement perspective, the price system will be used when the cost of measuring output in all of its relevant dimensions and the consequences of failing to do so are less than the cost of constraining employee behavior and the consequences of failing to do so.

HYBRIDS

A third solution besides the two polar extremes of full price incentives and full behavior constraints is to use both simultaneously. This is the essence of hybrids (Eccles 1981;

Hennart 1993; Grandori 1997). There are two types of hybrids, internal and external. In internal hybrids, agents are mostly constrained through behavior constraints, but selective price incentives are also introduced. In external hybrids, the price system is complemented by the selective use of behavior constraints.

Internal Hybrids

Under hierarchy, firm owners, or their delegated agents, that is, the firm's managers, tell employees what to do and observe and reward their behavior. This incurs high costs whenever: (1) employees know better than managers how to produce the requisite output; and (2) observing behavior is difficult or costly, or is a poor index of the quantity and quality of output. In these cases, firms can selectively introduce some aspects of the price system. They can give decision rights to subordinates and can motivate them with rewards linked to output.

Decentralization transfers some decision rights to subordinates, who can then be evaluated and rewarded based on the results of the subunits they head. This allows headquarters to access the local information held by these subordinates and to motivate them not to shirk. One example of such a strategy is the multidivisional structure (Chandler 1962; Williamson 1975), which consists in: (1) separating the firm into subunits (profit centers) which can interact with other subunits at market prices; (2) giving decision rights to subunit managers to allow them to maximize the profits of the subunits; and (3) rewarding them in function of these results. This solution will only be efficient if all interactions between subunits can be correctly priced. This is unlikely to be the case, for otherwise the subunits would be run as separate firms. Similarly, rewarding managers on the basis of current subunit profits may cause inter-temporal suboptimization. Headquarters (HQ) will therefore have to curb the most deleterious effects of these price incentives with behavior constraints. Hence the delegation of decision rights to subordinates and their remuneration based on the results of their units will necessarily be limited (Hennart 1991b, 1993; Foss 2003).

The price system may also be enlisted to reduce individual shirking. Piecework and commission schemes link a part of an employee's reward to their individual output. For instance, managers can be given stock options which tie their pay to the performance of the firm as a whole. All of these output-based rewards free management from having to know how workers should best perform their task and from monitoring them. We would expect employees paid through piecework to achieve higher output than those paid on salary, and there is empirical evidence to support that (Petersen 1991). When trademark owners own outlets, they may grant their managers bonuses linked to outlet performance (cell 4 in Table 25.1). This solution will be used when the cost of curbing shirking is moderate, but that of controlling free riding is high.

As in the case of decentralized units, the efficiency of individual output-based rewards depends on the extent to which all aspects of output can be measured. For example rewarding salespeople in function of their sales is likely to elicit higher sales, but can also lead them to neglect other aspects of their performance; the more crucial these aspects, the less efficient it is to reward them through commissions (John and Weitz 1989). Rewards linked to output tend also to make employees less cooperative, since cooperation is usually difficult to measure (Foss 2003).

External Hybrids: Contracts and Networks

In external hybrids (cell 2 in Table 25.1), restaurateurs are paid in function of their output, but because their tendency to free-ride is not effectively constrained by consumers, it is instead curbed by using behavioral constraints. There are basically two ways to impose such constraints in external hybrids: mutual enforcement and enforcement through third parties. Third-party enforcement can either be performed by public authorities such as courts, or through reputation effects within tight social groups, that is, within networks.

Rule-based third-party enforcement
The most discussed – if not necessarily the most common – way to impose behavior constraints on agents is rule-based third-party enforcement, in other words explicit contracts based on a published body of law and enforced by third parties, either public courts or private arbitrators, with the power to force parties to alter their behavior and/or pay compensation.

Lenders, for example, typically ask borrowers to sign loan covenants which force them to adopt certain measures to maintain loan quality, such as taking insurance on the assets financed by the loan. In franchising, franchisees are asked to follow specific behavioral rules devised by trademark owners to guarantee minimum quality levels. Domino's Pizza, for example, asks its franchisees to buy all product ingredients from approved suppliers and to respect corporate standards as to the quality and quantity of ingredients, manufacturing procedures, overall pizza aspect and taste, and delivery time. These guidelines are enforced by impromptu visits by inspectors. Repeated failure to adhere to guidelines may result in franchise cancellation (Dussauge 1998). Courts are the ultimate enforcement mechanism for all these clauses.

Rule-based enforcement has some limitations, however. Firstly, it requires being able to specify in writing the specific behavioral rules necessary to achieve the desired outcome (for example upholding quality in the franchising case) and to prove to the courts or arbitrators that they have not been respected. This is possible in the case of fast food, but may be difficult in other contexts, such as in consulting, auditing or higher education. More generally, constraining behavior through contracts requires anticipating all possible contingencies and their remedies, a difficult task in the presence of uncertainty (Williamson 1975). Recourse to the courts may also be costly because judges may not have sufficient knowledge of the context to set up appropriate remedies in case of breach. Court proceedings may divulge information that the parties would rather keep private (Peerenboom 2002).[7] More fundamentally, there must be an efficient and impartial court system with the power to enforce contracts.

Relationship-based enforcement
An alternative to rule-based third-party enforcement is relationship-based third-party enforcement in which parties protect themselves not by written contracts enforced through courts or arbitrators, but instead by doing business with parties they know, and from which they can expect cooperative behavior. The system works because parties can rely on shared values and on social norms of reciprocity, established through personal relationships, to assure non-opportunistic behavior. This offers a number of advantages

over rule-based third-party enforcement. As argued above, written contracts offer protection only to the extent that they can be enforced. Firstly, there must be efficient and unbiased courts with the power to enforce their judgments. Even when this condition is met, court enforcement has clear limits. One must be able to specify desired behavior in writing, and deviations from such behavior must be observable by third parties. That behavior, as well as the appropriate remedies in case of breach, must also be specified *ex ante* for all future contingencies. A clause specifying 'best efforts', for example, is difficult to enforce in court, as deviations from best efforts are hard to detect and to prove to third parties. As a result, contracts offer only limited protection in many cases. Parties in relationship-based exchanges who share common values are more likely to behave in a desired manner and more likely to handle unforeseen contingencies in a flexible and cooperative way. Relationship-based governance also facilitates the fine-grained information exchange necessary for quick adaptation (Uzzi 1997; Dyer and Singh 1998). This is likely to be particularly advantageous when parties locked into bilateral exchange need to make quick and frequent adjustments in their exchange terms (Jones et al. 1997).

Relationship-based governance can be bilateral or multilateral. Bilateral relationship-based governance, as the name implies, involves two parties. The range of agreements it can enforce is greater than in the case of third party enforcement since agreements that are mutually observable but not observable by third parties can also be enforced through tit-for-tat strategies (Li 1999). However, tit-for-tat requires recurring business. Because enforcement is based on personal bonds, partners must be chosen with care, and one must nurture personal relationships with them (Li et al. 2004). These two conditions imply repeated business with a limited number of partners, preferably individuals with whom one has pre-existing social relationships, such as family members, neighbors and classmates (Li 1999: 13).

Multilateral relationship-based governance has been called 'network governance' (Jones et al. 1997). It relies on a select and stable group of autonomous parties to communicate information and enforce transactions. The group has a macroculture, a set of 'widely shared assumptions and values . . . that guide actions and create typical behavior patterns among independent entities' (Jones et al. 1997: 929). Information on individuals who break these norms will be shared among group members, and the defaulters risk losing reputation and being ostracized. For this to work the group must be relatively small, homogeneous and stable. This makes it possible for group members to interact repeatedly with one another, thus building up common norms, facilitating the spreading of both good and bad reputation, and making it possible to collude to impose sanctions.[8] Consequently, it is crucial that the group be able to restrict entry (Jones et al. 1997). Hence multilateral relation-based governance will be particularly effective in tight social groups with stable membership, that is, in what sociologists have called networks. This is the case in European industrial districts, such as the knitwear district in Modena or the German textile center of Baden-Wurttemberg, which are made up of small family firms in business for generations whose owners have extensive personal relationships with one another (e.g. Brusco 1982; Lazerson 1988; Sabel et al. 1987); in craft industries such as film, music, publishing and fashion, which also tend to be geographically concentrated (Powell 1990; Saxenian 1990); in construction, which is typically local (e.g. Eccles 1981; Jones et al. 1997; Powell 1990); and in ethnic groups, and more generally in Asian societies such as Japan and China (e.g. Dore 1983; Li 1999).

Rule-based third-party enforcement and relationship-based governance

Rule-based third-party enforcement and relationship-based governance are not mutually exclusive. Individuals may use relationship-based governance for some transactions and rule-based governance for others (Zhou et al. 2008). They may also elect to use both mechanisms concurrently. Relationship-based governance, because it encourages more consummate cooperation and more flexible adaptation to unforeseen changes in the environment, may be a desirable complement to rule-based third party governance (Dyer and Singh 1998; Heide and John 1992). Relationship-based governance is, for example, often used by trademark owners to constrain the behavior of restaurateurs. Trademark owners foster social relationships with franchisees and between franchisees to facilitate the development of a set of implicit rules to govern behavior. In fast food chains this is typically done through training (e.g. McDonald's University). The goal is to facilitate the curbing of free-riding whenever behavior that damages reputation is difficult to specify and to detect, or when abrupt changes to the environment makes frequent adaptation necessary.

SHARING AGREEMENTS

When trademark-owners own the outlets (column 3 of Table 25.1), they have title to the profits jointly generated by the trademark and the restaurateur. They are therefore motivated to maintain the consistent quality of the products bearing their trademark. On the other hand, they must control shirking by restaurateurs who are paid either a straight salary or a salary plus bonus, but who do not have title to the profits of the chain. When restaurateurs own the outlets, they have title to the profits jointly generated by themselves and the trademark owners. They can be expected to curb their shirking, for which they now bear the full cost, but to indulge in cheating, that is, to reduce the quality of the products bearing the brand. The decision as to who should take title to the profit then depends on which aspect of performance is hardest to monitor. If shirking by restaurateurs is harder to monitor than their free-riding, then they should be given title to the profits (row 3 in Table 25.1); if free-riding by restaurateurs is harder to monitor than their shirking, then trademark owners should be given title to the profits of the joint product so they can curb free-riding (column 3 in Table 25.1). More generally, these two solutions arise when transaction costs in one of the two markets – the market for reputation or that for labor – are higher than in the other: franchising when it is more costly to monitor and constrain shirking by restaurateurs than to curb their free-riding (cheating); and outlets owned by the trademark owner hiring restaurateurs in the reverse case. In both these solutions one of the parties specializes in information gathering, decision making, and monitoring. Under franchising it is restaurateurs while under trademark-owners owned outlets, it is trademark owners.

But what happens when the costs of curbing shirking and free-riding are about the same? Then it makes sense to give title to the residual to both input providers: both the trademark owner and the restaurateur will have a claim on the result of their joint output. In other words, the solution will be a residual-sharing agreement between the trademark owner and the restaurateur (cell 5 of Table 25.1). Under this solution, both restaurateurs and trademark owners are subject to output constraints imposed by customers, since both parties are owners. Trademark owners will have an incentive to uphold the quality of the products they produce because, as co-owners, they will benefit from doing so; restaurateurs will be motivated to exert effort since this will increase total profits, in which they share. The strength of sharing agreements, as opposed to the arrangements displayed in cells 1, 2, 3 and 4 of Table 25.1, is that both input suppliers self-monitor because they both are rewarded by the outcome of their efforts. Note, however, that the incentive both have to self-monitor is weaker than in cells 1, 2, 3 and 4 because their share of the profit is less than 100 percent. More generally, sharing agreements are optimal when the performance of at least two cooperating parties is equally difficult to monitor, or, to put it another way, when the markets for the inputs contributed by at least two parties incur high transaction costs (Hennart 1988).

In contrast to franchised and trademark owner-run outlets where one party specializes in information gathering, decision making and monitoring, in sharing agreements all parties (trademark owners and restaurateurs) share responsibility for gathering information, making decisions and monitoring each other's behavior. Sharing agreements involve joint decision making by members of the firm (partners in partnerships, members in cooperatives, parent firms in joint ventures).[9] While this may increase the information available to make decisions, it also requires agreement by the members, which complicates decision-making. Second, in cells 1, 2, 3 and 4 the contribution of the party who does not self-monitor is generally well defined, at least in the case of rule-based solutions. In an employment contract (cells 3 and 4), the employer assigns explicit tasks to the employee. In a franchise contract, the franchisor sets up explicit behavioral rules to be followed by the franchisor. In contrast, sharing agreements only specify which inputs will be contributed and leaves unspecified the tasks to be performed and the specific outputs to be obtained (Grandori 2010). This is efficient when it is costly to specify and evaluate the outputs *ex ante*, but it also makes it possible for the parties to come up short on their *ex ante* commitments. Lastly, because sharing agreements typically pool inputs with weak property rights, it is possible for the parties to transfer the inputs contributed by their partners for use outside the arrangement. This causes problems if these uses compete with the parents or with the profit-sharing agreement itself (Hamel 1991). These potential problems can be alleviated by thoughtful design of the sharing agreement and careful choice of partners (Hennart and Zeng 2005).

There are many different types of sharing agreements. Some are between individuals while others are between firms. Some involve the joint ownership of assets while others do not. The goal of some is to maximize profits while others minimize costs.

Sharing Agreements between Individuals

Cooperatives, partnerships and share tenancy (sharecropping) are three types of sharing agreements between individuals. Cooperatives differ from partnerships insofar as outcomes in the former are typically shared equally between the members, while this is not necessarily the case in the latter. In cooperatives and partnerships, both assets and outcomes are shared, while in sharecropping only outcomes are shared.

Partnerships and cooperatives are firms which use hierarchy only to a limited extent, insofar as most members gather their own information, make their own decisions, and are rewarded for their efforts in a way which is more or less directly linked to their individual output.[10] Partners and cooperators have the following bundle of rights (Pejovich 1992): (1) decision rights; (2) a claim on the firm's cash flows and assets; however, the rights specified under (1) and (2) are not transferable and are contingent on employment with the firm. In short, members own their firm as long as they work for it. When does this arrangement make sense? Consider the case of accounting and legal partnerships. Value in accounting and law firms is created by combining the human capital of the partners with the brand name capital of the firm (van Lent 1999). Giving brand name owners the full right to the residual created by the combination, as in the case of outlets owned by trademark owners and operated by their employees, would reduce the incentives that partners have to make investments which contribute to the value of the brand, and would increase their incentive to free-ride on it. In contrast to our fast food restaurant example, it is difficult in accounting and law firms to use contracts to prevent partners from free-riding on the reputation of the brand because it is difficult to specify contractually what actions they need to take to uphold it. Hence franchising the brand name to partners would be risky. An alternative is to have brand owners take title to the profits and hire the partners. Two factors make this costly. Firstly, auditing and legal work both require skills which are hard to standardize. It is therefore difficult to direct behavior and to infer performance from the observation of that behavior.[11] Secondly, face-to-face contact is required in these two professions, and hence offices must be set close to the customer. This results in a large number of geographically dispersed offices (Malhotra and Morris 2009), making supervising employees costly. For these reasons, giving partners rights to the profit is likely to elicit more effort than paying them a straight salary and monitoring their behavior. Given the high cheating costs that would be incurred if audit firms were run as franchises, and the high shirking costs that would result if trademark owners hired accountants and lawyers as employees, the best solution is to give partners rights to the profit generated by the bundling of their human capital with the brand name of the firm. Accounting and law firms are therefore organized as partnerships. Rather than being monitored by the trademark owner, partners will self-monitor and monitor each other, since they have a stake in the firm's profits. Because they share in the firm's profits, partners have decision rights. Decisions are taken by vote, with major ones requiring unanimity (van Lent 1999).

Raising finance is often a problem in partnerships and cooperatives (Hendrikse and Feng's Chapter 26 in this volume; Pejovich 1992; Bonin et al. 1993). In such firms, the right to share in the firm's profits cannot be sold upon leaving the firm. Hence the firm's owners are not able to capture the returns to those investments which will yield returns after they have left the firm; they are therefore likely to underinvest in the firm. The inability of outside investors to have decision rights in the firm also reduces their willingness to lend to it. This may explain why partnerships are generally of small size, and if large, operate in labor-intensive businesses with a relatively small asset base, such as professional services.

Share tenancy differs from partnerships and cooperatives insofar as the assets are not held in common by the parties. Share tenancy is an output-sharing agreement in which a farmer obtains the use of land owned by a landowner in exchange for a share of the output thus obtained. Share tenancy can be explained by the same logic as legal and accounting partnerships. Agricultural output results from the combination of land and labor. Three types of arrangement are possible: (1) landowners can hire labor;

(2) landowners can rent their land to tenant farmers; (3) share tenancy. Landowners will hire labor if shirking can be cheaply controlled. Farmers who rent land will self-monitor their effort, and hence this solution is efficient when shirking is hard to control. On the other hand, tenant farmers have a greater incentive than employees to reduce land quality so this solution will not be chosen when landowners have difficulty preventing tenants from running down the land. Share tenancy will be efficient when both land abuse and shirking are hard to monitor (Roumasset 1995).[12]

Sharing Agreements between Firms

Joint ventures, capital ventures, partial acquisitions and consortia are sharing agreements between firms. These agreements come in many forms: they may or may not result in a separate legal entity; the entity may or may not own assets; the arrangement may maximize profits or minimize costs. All of these agreements have a common rationale: high transaction costs in the markets for complementary or similar inputs held by two or more parties.

Equity joint ventures involve the creation of a new firm which is jointly owned by two or more parent firms.[13] The parents have a claim on the output or profits of the new firm in proportion to their equity shares which are determined by the relative input contribution of the partners. Joint ventures often have their own managers, who report to a board of directors typically made up of delegates from the parent companies in proportion to their equity shares. Since, as seen above, this contribution is difficult to precisely ascertain *ex ante*, there is evidence that the division of equity in joint ventures is somewhat arbitrary, with a preponderance of 50:50 arrangements.[14] In the absence of clear *ex ante* measure of the expected contributions, a 50:50 split assures that neither of the two parents can unilaterally make decisions that may harm the other (Hauswald & Hege 2003).

Equity joint ventures are of two main types: scale joint ventures and link joint ventures (Hennart 1988). Scale joint ventures result from the simultaneous vertical integration forward or backward of two or more firms. The goal is to take advantage of scale economies that make integration by either party too costly. The bauxite and alumina joint ventures set up by aluminum companies are examples. Given the economic benefits of vertically integrating across the industry's first three stages – bauxite mining, alumina refining and aluminum smelting – and given differences in minimum efficient scale across these stages, joint ventures make it possible to integrate vertically while avoiding diseconomies of scale (Stuckey 1983). In 'take or pay' joint ventures, parents pay a share of the costs which is proportional to the share of the output to which they are entitled, whether or not they actually use that output.

The goal of link joint ventures is to bundle complementary inputs. These inputs can be quite varied. Some joint ventures are set up to combine two types of complementary knowledge. Siecor, a joint venture of Siemens and Corning, combines Siemens's knowledge of the electrical industry and Corning's expertise in glass to make fiber-optic cable. The typical market entry joint venture bundles technological knowledge held by a foreign firm with a local firm's distribution network and local market knowledge (Hennart 1988).

Joint ventures can be either set up from scratch, leading to the creation of a new firm (a greenfield joint venture), or result from a partial acquisition. An example of the latter is the capital venture. In this arrangement a venture capital firm provides an entrepreneurial firm with finance and advice in exchange for an equity stake. This is efficient when both the market for ideas and that for finance are subject to high transaction costs. Consider first the market for finance. New ventures, especially those in high technology, need capital. They often have difficulties obtaining loans because they cannot offer collateral, as their main asset is a still unproven business concept, and because their founder may not have a history of successful ventures. In contrast to lending, equity investing allows fund providers to closely monitor the use of their funds, and is therefore less risky. Potential lenders will therefore ask for an equity stake in the company and a voice in running the business (Williamson 1988; Hennart 1994). The market for new business models is also highly imperfect. Entrepreneurs cannot sell their idea to owners of financial capital due to imperfections in the market for intellectual property; financiers could potentially hire entrepreneurs, but given the difficulty of monitoring their behavior, this might result in too much shirking. The solution offered by capital ventures is to have suppliers of financial capital take a stake in the firm.[15] While capital ventures have received much attention, many partial acquisitions follow the same logic: acquirers leave an equity stake to the founders or top managers of the acquired firm to enlist their initiative and effort (Hennart 1988).

CONCLUSIONS

A number of disciplines have addressed the diversity of institutional forms which scholars see as neither pure market nor pure firm and which they have called 'alliances'. This has led to a variety of partially conflicting taxonomies and terminologies. In this chapter I try to make sense of this 'cacophony of . . . concepts and . . . theories' (Oliver & Ebers 1998: 550) by using a consistent theoretical approach based on transaction cost, institutional and property rights theories. To provide an intuitive feel for the concepts, I use the case of trademarked services. The analysis, however, is not limited to this special case but is applicable to many other different settings.

I start this chapter by distinguishing between organizing methods and institutions. I posit that there are only two generic organizing methods: one that rewards individuals for their behavior and the other that rewards then for their output. These two basic methods can be used in various proportions, and this yields a variety of real-world institutions. In traditional bureaucracies agents are rewarded for appropriate behavior, while in pure markets they are rewarded on the basis of their output valued at exogenously determined market prices. Hybrids can be defined as institutions that use a more balanced mix of the two generic organizing methods: internal hybrids add some output controls (i.e. price incentives) to an employment contract based on behavior constraints; while external hybrids add some behavior constraints to a base of output incentives. Thus internal hybrids are a type of firm, while external hybrids are a type of market exchange. This view is in contrast to the positions taken by Williamson (1996: 51) and Menard (2004) for whom hybrids constitute a third generic organizing method halfway between markets and firms.

Williamson (1996: 51) has argued that markets and firms can be placed along one dimension, usually called hierarchical intensity, and that equity joint ventures are in the middle of that continuum (Oxley 1997; Gulati and Singh 1998). For him and others (e.g. Boerner and Macher 2003; Kreps 1990), equity joint ventures are hybrids of market and hierarchy and are chosen in conditions of moderate asset specificity, while hierarchy is chosen when asset specificity is high, and markets when it is low (Williamson 1991). I have shown, however, that equity joint ventures are not hybrids. In hybrids, the right to the residual – what remains after all *ex ante* fixed commitments have been met – is granted to one of the interacting parties. For example, in Table 25.1, it is allocated to the trademark owner in internal hybrids and to the restaurateur in external hybrids. By contrast, the right to the residual in equity joint ventures is shared by both parties. Equity joint ventures, like all other residual-sharing agreements, are not a third governance form between market and firm, they are a type of firm. Because they are not in-between market and firm, the choice between full and partial ownership – for example between a fully owned foreign subsidiary and an equity joint venture – does not depend on the level of asset specificity, as argued by Williamson (1991), Erramilli and Rao (1993) and Brouthers et al. (2003), but rather on how the benefits of aligning the incentives of input providers balance the costs of joint decision making and of the potential conflicts this may entail (Hennart 1991a).

Looking at equity joint ventures as one type of sharing agreement also highlights the arbitrariness of some of the definitions in the alliance literature. Equity joint ventures have been defined as 'new legal entities that are created separately from but jointly owned by the partner firms' (Das and Deng 2002: 453; see also Oxley 1997: 390). This is a legal definition, but not a theoretical one, because what distinguishes equity joint ventures from other types of alliances is the fact that in equity joint ventures input suppliers are residual claimants, that is, they get paid from a share of the venture's residual. Since this is also the case in partial acquisitions and in capital ventures, there are no reasons to exclude them from the equity joint venture category, even though no new legal entity is formed.

Equity joint ventures are also qualitatively different from external hybrids. Equity joint ventures are chosen when two or more interacting parties would have difficulty monitoring each other, whereas situations where the behavior of one party is easier to monitor or measure than that of another result in external hybrids: that is, in arrangements where one party takes the title to the profits – and hence self-monitors – and enlists the behavior of the other, or others, through market contracts. In contrast to external hybrids, outputs and residual rights of control are shared in equity joint ventures, which are a type of sharing agreement. This results in both specific advantages and costs and makes sharing agreements qualitatively different. Lumping both types of arrangements into an alliance category obscures these differences.

I also show in this chapter how the sociological concept of networks fits within transaction cost theory. Sociologists (Powell 1990; Uzzi 1997) have shown that exchange within networks consists of repeated trades between parties who have close social relationships with one another, with the behavior of the parties guided by social norms rather than by written contracts, and with enforcement relying on reciprocity and reputation loss rather than on legal sanctions. While such exchange may seem a long way from pure market transactions where the identity of the parties is irrelevant (Williamson 1979: 236), it is still fundamentally market exchange, in the sense that parties coordinate their interdependence through outputs and hence are driven by output incentives. Hence exchange within networks does not constitute a third generic organizing method alongside the price system and hierarchy, as claimed by Powell (1990), but is one form of external hybrid in which behavior is not constrained by legal rules enforced by third parties such as courts and arbitrators but by social rules internalized by the parties and enforced by reputation effects.

As sociologists, legal (Macneil 1978) and management scholars (e.g. Boisot and Child 1996) have pointed out, relationship-based governance is much more common than assumed by economists. It flourishes in specific contexts (Hollywood and Silicon Valley, the construction sector) even in countries with reasonably efficient legal infrastructure such as the United States. Hence it is not solely determined by culture, nor is it an attribute of less-developed countries. The comparative advantage of rule-based govern- ance may be also less than generally thought (Peerenboom 2002). Further research on this topic is likely to enrich transaction cost theory and to improve its ability to predict governance choices.

NOTES

1. Acknowledgements: I thank Anna Grandori for stimulating comments and useful suggestions.
2. Socializing employees may make it possible to decentralize and yet avoid suboptimization.
3. Beyond loafing, shirking may also mean lack of initiative. Williamson and his followers (e.g. Williamson 1985; Zenger et al. 2011) call these behavior constraints 'low-powered incentives'. This is misleading, because behavior constraints can be very effective in eliciting desired behavior (e.g. in military organiza- tions). Behavior constraints have low power for the maximization of output, but high power to attain appropriate behavior, and since controlling behavior allows one to indirectly control output, the behavior constraints used by hierarchy are not low-powered in an absolute sense.
4. Outlets which are restaurateur-owned tend to be more efficiently run than franchisor-owned outlets. In February 1996, for example, the average cash flow of franchised McDonald's outlets in the United States was 13.7 percent of sales, versus 10.4 percent for McDonald's-owned outlets (Gibson 1996).
5. Michael (2000) shows that product quality in chains with franchised outlets is lower than that in chains with company-owned outlets.
6. Brickley and Dark (1987) find that outlets that are geographically close to the franchisor's headquarters, and hence easier to monitor, tend to be owned, while those located further away tend to be franchised. Fladmoe-Lindquist and Jacque (2005) find that US franchisors have a higher probability to own outlets which are located in geographically and culturally close countries.
7. For these reasons arbitration may be preferred to judicial enforcement, even though arbitration judg- ments may be harder to enforce.
8. Dyer and Ouchi (1993: 54) note that Japanese car assemblers, which have used multilateral relation-based governance to obtain the parts they need, use two suppliers for electrical wiring, whereas their US com- petitors use 20. Similarly, the membership of Kyohokai, the association of Toyota parts suppliers, has been remarkably stable: only three out of 156 dropped out between 1973 and 1984 (Asanuma 1989: 5).
9. Because in sharing agreements members share in the tasks generally assigned to top managers, top man- agers of such firms generally earn less and enjoy fewer perquisites than their peers in investor-owned firms (Hendrikse & Feng 2012).
10. 'Most' because partners in accounting and legal partnerships work with a significant number of employ- ees. How tightly a member's earnings are linked to their individual output varies across firms.
11. This is easier to do in engineering, hence the lower incidence of partnerships in engineering than in law and accounting (Malhotra and Morris 2009).
12. The production-sharing arrangements used in the oil industry can be explained by the same logic.
13. Sharing agreements between firms do not always feature the joint ownership of assets. Sometimes the partners supply the services of assets and share the resultant profits, but the assets are not pooled.
14. Moskalev and Swensen (2007) report that 50:50 joint ventures accounted for 71 percent of all two-party joint ventures in a sample of 20 785 joint ventures listed in the SDC database.

15. Free-standing firms, the dominant form of foreign direct investment before World War I, can be explained by the same logic (Hennart 1998).

REFERENCES

Asanuma, Banri (1989), 'Manufacturer–supplier relations in Japan and the concept of relation-specific skill', *Journal of the Japanese and International Economies*, **3**(1), 1–30.
Boerner, Christopher and Jeffery Macher (2003), 'Transaction cost economics: an assessment of empirical work in the social sciences', working paper, Georgetown University.
Boisot, Marc and John Child (1996), 'From fiefs to clans and network capitalism: explaining China's emerging economic order', *Administrative Science Quarterly*, **41**(4), 600–628.
Bonin, John, Derek Jones and Louis Putterman (1993), 'Theoretical and empirical studies of producer cooperatives: will ever the twain meet?' *Journal of Economic Literature*, **31**(3), 1290–1320.
Brickley, James and Frederick Dark (1987), 'The choice of organizational form: the case of franchising', *Journal of Financial Economics*, **18**(2), 401–420.
Brouthers, Keith, Lance Brouthers and S. Werner (2003), 'Transaction-cost enhanced entry mode choice and performance', *Strategic Management Journal*, **24**(12), 1239–1248.
Brusco, S. (1982), 'The Emilian model: productive decentralization and social integration', *Cambridge Journal of Economics*, **6**(2), 167–184.
Carter, Richard and Geoffrey Hodgson (2006), 'The impact of empirical tests of transaction cost economics on the debate on the nature of the firm', *Strategic Management Journal*, **27**(5), 461–476.
Chandler, Alfred (1962), *Strategy and Structure*, Cambridge, MA: MIT Press.
Contractor, Farok and Peter Lorange (2002), 'Preface', in F.J. Contractor and P. Lorange (eds), *Cooperative Strategies and Alliances*, Amsterdam: Pergamon.
Das, T.K. and B.S. Deng (2002), 'A social exchange theory of strategic alliances', in F. Contractor and P. Lorange (eds), *Cooperative Strategies and Alliances*, Amsterdam: Pergamon, pp. 439–460.
Davies, Howard (1977), 'Technology transfer through commercial transactions', *Journal of Industrial Economics*, **26**(2), 161–175.
Davies, Howard (1993), 'The information content of technology transfers: a transaction cost analysis of the machine tool industry', *Technovation*, **13**(2), 93–100.
Dore, R. (1983), 'Goodwill and the spirit of market capitalism', *British Journal of Sociology*, **34**(4), 459–482.
Dussauge, Pierre (1998), *Domino's Pizza International*, ECCH case 398-048-1.
Dyer, Jeffrey and William Ouchi (1993), 'Japanese style partnerships: giving companies a competitive edge', *Sloan Management Review*, **35**(1), 51–63.
Dyer, Jeffrey and Harbir Singh (1998), 'The relational view: cooperative strategy and sources of interorganizational competitive advantage', *Academy of Management Review*, **23**(4), 660–679.
Eccles, Robert (1981), 'The quasi-firm in the construction industry', *Journal of Economic Behavior and Organization*, **2**(4), 335–357.
Erramili, M. and C. Rao (1993), 'Service firms' international entry mode choice: a modified transaction cost analysis approach', *Journal of Marketing*, **57**(3), 19–38.
Fladmoe-Lindquist, Karin and Laurent Jacque (2005), 'Control modes in international service operations: the propensity to franchise', *Management Science*, **41**(7), 1238–1249.
Foss, Nicolai (2003), 'Selective intervention and internal hybrids: interpreting and learning from the rise and decline of the Oticon spaghetti organization', *Organization Science*, **14**(3), 331–349.
Gibson, R. (1996), 'McDonald's, US franchisees are on the rise', *Wall Street Journal*, June 26.
Grandori, Anna (1997), 'An organizational assessment of interfirm coordination modes', *Organization Studies*, **18**(6), 897–925.
Grandori, Anna (2010), 'Asset commitment, constitutional governance, and the nature of the firm', *Journal of Institutional Economics*, **6**(3), 351–375.
Grandori, Anna and Guiseppe Soda (1995), 'Inter-firm networks: antecedents, mechanisms, and forms', *Organization Studies*, **16**(2), 183–214.
Gulati, Ranjay (1998), 'Alliances and networks', *Strategic Management Journal*, **19**(4), 293–317.
Gulati, Ranjay and Harbir Singh (1998), 'The architecture of cooperation: managing coordination costs and appropriation concerns in strategic alliances', *Administrative Science Quarterly*, **43**(4), 781–814.
Hamel, Gary (1991), 'Competition for competence and inter-partner learning within international strategic alliances', *Strategic Management Journal*, **12**(S1), 83–103.
Hauswald, Robert and Ulrich Hege (2003), 'Ownership and control in joint ventures: theory and evidence', CEPR discussion paper 4056.

Hayek, Frederic (1945), 'The use of knowledge in society', *American Economic Review*, **35**(4), 519–530.

Heide, Jan and John, George (1992), 'Do norms matter in marketing relationships?' *Journal of Marketing*, **56**(2), 32–44.

Hennart, Jean-François (1982), *A Theory of Multinational Enterprise*, Ann Arbor, MI: University of Michigan Press.

Hennart, Jean-François (1988), 'A transaction cost theory of equity joint ventures', *Strategic Management Journal*, **9**(4), 361–374.

Hennart, Jean-François (1991a), 'The transaction costs theory of joint ventures: an empirical study of Japanese subsidiaries in the United States', *Management Science*, **37**(4), 483–497.

Hennart, Jean-François (1991b), 'Control in multinational firms: the role of price and hierarchy', *Management International Review*, **31**(Special Issue), 71–96.

Hennart, Jean-François (1993), 'Explaining the swollen middle: why most transactions are a mix of market and hierarchy', *Organization Science*, **4**(4), 529–47.

Hennart, Jean-François (1994), 'International capital transfers: a transaction cost framework', *Business History*, **36**(1), 51–70.

Hennart, Jean-François (1998), 'Transaction cost theory and the free-standing firm', in M. Wilkins and H. Schroter (eds), *The Free Standing Company in the World Economy*, London: Oxford University Press, pp. 65–98.

Hennart, Jean-François (2008), 'Transaction costs perspectives on inter-organizational relations', in S. Cropper, M. Ebers, C. Huxham and P. Smith Ring (eds), *Oxford Handbook of Inter-Organizational Relations*, Oxford: Oxford University Press, pp. 339–365.

Hennart, Jean-François and Ming Zeng (2005), 'Structural determinants of joint venture performance', *European Management Review*, **2**(2), 105–115.

John, George and Barton Weitz (1989), 'Salesforce compensation: an empirical investigation of factors related to use of salary vs. incentive compensation', *Journal of Marketing Research*, **26**(1), 1–14.

Jones, Candace, William Hesterly and Stephen Borgatti (1997), 'A general theory of network governance: exchange conditions and social mechanisms', *Academy of Management Review*, **22**(4), 911–945.

Kreps, David (1990), *A Course in Microeconomics Theory*, Princeton, NJ: Princeton University Press.

Lancaster, Kevin (1966), 'A new approach to consumer theory', *Journal of Political Economy*, **74**(2), 132–157.

Lazerson, M (1988), 'Organizational growth in small firms: an outcome of markets and hierarchies?' *American Sociological Review*, **53**(3), 330–342.

van Lent, Lawrence (1999), 'The economics of an audit firm: the benefits of partnership governance', *British Accounting Review*, **31**(2), 225–254.

Li, Shaomin, Seung-Ho Park and Shuhe Li (2004), 'The great leap forward: the transition from relation-based governance to rule-based governance', *Organizational Dynamics*, **33**(1), 63–78.

Li, Shuhe (1999), 'The benefits and costs of relation-based governance: an explanation of the East Asian miracle and crisis', unpublished manuscript, Department of Economics and Finance, City University of Hong-Kong.

Macneil, I. (1978), 'Contractual adjustments of long-term relations under classical, neoclassical, and relational contract law', *Northwestern University Law Review*, **72**(6), 854–905.

Malhotra, Namrata and Timothy Morris (2009), 'Heterogeneity in professional service firms', *Journal of Management Studies*, **46**(6), 895–922.

Menard, Claude (2004), 'The economics of hybrid organizations', *Journal of Institutional and Theoretical Economics*, **160**(3), 345–376.

Michael, Steven (2000), 'The effect of organizational form on quality: the case of franchising', *Journal of Economic Behavior and Organization*, **43**(3), 295–318.

Moskalev, Sviatoslav and R. Bruce Swensen (2007), 'Joint ventures around the globe from 1990–2000: forms, types, industries, countries and ownership patterns', *Journal of Financial Economics*, **16**(1), 29–67.

Oliver, A and M. Ebers (1998), 'Networking network studies: an analysis of conceptual configurations in the study of inter-organizational relationships', *Organization Studies*, **19**(4), 549–583.

Oxley, Joanne (1997), 'Appropriability hazards and governance in strategic alliances: a transaction cost approach', *Journal of Law, Economics and Organization*, **13**(2), 387–409.

Peerenboom, Randall (2002), 'Social networks, rule of law, and economic growth in China: the elusive pursuit of the right combination of private and public ordering', *Global Economic Review*, **31**(2), 1–19.

Pejovich, Svetozar (1992), 'A property rights analysis of the inefficiency of investment decisions in labor-managed firms', *Journal of Institutional and Theoretical Economics*, **148**(1), 30–41.

Petersen, Trond (1991), 'Reward systems and the distribution of wages', *Journal of Law, Economics and Organization*, **7**(Special Issue), 130–158.

Powell, Walter (1990), 'Neither market nor hierarchy: network forms of organization', *Research in Organizational Behavior*, **12**, 295–336.

Roumasset, J. (1995), 'The nature of the agricultural firm', *Journal of Economic Behavior and Organization*, **26**(2), 161–177.

Sabel, C., R. Hellrigel, R. Kazis and R. Deeg (1987), 'How to keep mature industries innovative', *Technology Review*, **90**(3), 26–35.

Saxenian, A. (1990), 'Regional networks and the resurgence of Silicon Valley', *California Management Review*, **33**(1), 89–112.

Simon, Herbert (1951), 'A formal theory of the employment relationship', *Econometrica*, **19**(3), 293–305.

Stuckey, John (1983), *Vertical Integration and Joint Ventures in the Aluminum Industry*, Cambridge, MA: Harvard University Press.

Uzzi, Brian (1997), 'Social structure and competition in interfirm networks: the paradox of embeddedness', *Administrative Science Quarterly*, **42**(1), 35–67.

Williamson, Oliver (1975), *Markets and Hierarchies: Analysis and Antitrust Implications*, New York: Free Press.

Williamson, Oliver (1979), 'Transaction-cost economics: the governance of contractual relations', *Journal of Law and Economics*, **22**(2), 233–261.

Williamson, Oliver (1985), *The Economic Institutions of Capitalism*, New York: Free Press.

Williamson, Oliver (1988), 'Corporate finance and corporate governance', *Journal of Finance*, **63**(3), 567–598.

Williamson, Oliver (1991), 'Comparative economic organization: The analysis of discrete structural alternatives', *Administrative Science Quarterly*, **36**(2), 269–296.

Williamson, Oliver (1996), 'Economic organization: the case for candor', *Academy of Management Review*, **21**(1), 48–57.

Zenger, Todd, Teppo Felin and Lyda Bigelow (2011), 'Theories of the firm-market boundary', *Academy of Management Annals*, **5**(1), 89–133.

Zhou, Kevin, Laura Poppo and Zhilin Yang (2008), 'Relational ties or customized contracts? An examination of alternative governance choices in China', *Journal of International Business Studies*, **39**, 526–534.

26. Interfirm cooperatives
*George Hendrikse and Li Feng**

An interfirm cooperative is an enterprise collectively owned by many other firms. The insights regarding its efficiency are organized based on the transaction and ownership relationship of the members with the cooperative enterprise. Evidence is grouped into aspects relating to the members, transactions, and the cooperative enterprise.

INTRODUCTION

Worldwide cooperatives are prominent in sectors such as agriculture and food, financial services, wholesale and retail. To illustrate, the European Union (United States of America, India, China) has 300 000 (29 000, 580 000, 525 000) cooperatives. About one-third of world food production passes through cooperatives (Patisson 2000). Cooperatives are also present in other industries, such as communications, consumer goods, day care and nurseries, handicrafts, housing, health care, memorial societies, rural electric systems, rural telephone systems and student housing (Hoyt 1989). Cooperatives are not only present in a variety of industries, but they are also very different from one another. For example, a bakery can be run by a consumer cooperative, a labor cooperative, a farmer cooperative, an investor cooperative, and perhaps others. Even fairly large manufacturing firms may be cooperative. For example, Spain's largest producer of refrigerators and other kitchen appliances is a cooperative. Worldwide, they provide 100 million jobs, 20 percent more than multinational enterprises. It is therefore not surprising that the United Nations (UN) has declared 2012 the International Year of Cooperatives.

An economic organization analysis of cooperatives has to identify its source(s) of competitive advantage compared to other organizational forms. An efficient organizational form maximizes total surplus by taking into account the costs and benefits of decisions for all stakeholders. Each stakeholder has various options, such as voice or exit (Hirschman 1970), available to express their preferences regarding decisions. Voice is often cumbersome and costly because collective decision making will elicit substantial influence efforts due to not all stakeholders being affected in the same way. Enterprises are therefore usually characterized by ownership of one stakeholder group (Hansmann 1996), such as investors, workers, suppliers, consumers, families, the government – or nobody. This raises the question of the optimal allocation of ownership. Ownership should be assigned to the group of stakeholders that can most effectively and responsibly make use of voice and that cannot be protected as cheaply by exit options (Holmström 1999). Particular relevance will be given here to comparative economic organization (Williamson 1991) as it entails that the benefits and costs of various organizational forms are compared, theoretically as well as empirically.

An interfirm cooperative (IFC) is defined as an enterprise collectively owned by many other firms staying in a specified relation for a specific purpose. We focus in this chapter on the case of a cooperative governing the vertical transactions in a value chain, in particular a suppliers' owned IFC, in particular in the case of agribusiness. An IFC is therefore an enterprise collectively owned (vertical relationship) by an association of many independent upstream parties (horizontal relationship). A distinction is often made between a cooperative firm and a cooperative association. If an IFC is characterized as a cooperative firm, then the object of study is the enterprise at the downstream stage of production.[1] A cooperative association consists of many parties. It does not have a formal connection with a downstream party, and therefore does not have a formal vertical relationship with an adjacent production stage. The object of study is the association.[2] One of the functions of a cooperative association is to bargain or negotiate with parties in an adjacent stage of production for better terms of trade. The advantage of our definition of an IFC is that we can address issues at the downstream cooperative enterprise as well as issues at the upstream association of members.[3]

Owners of an IFC are usually referred to as members. The guiding principle regarding understanding an IFC is that a member advances the interests of their own firm portfolio in an IFC. Members of an IFC have two roles. On the one hand, a member is a patron (buyer, supplier, borrower, investor, etc.). It implies that the members of a suppliers' IFC have a transaction relationship with the enterprise by providing inputs. On the other hand, a member is an owner. Members are owners collectively possessing the residual rights over the IFC and take decisions regarding it. The difference between an IFC and an investor-owned firm (IOF) is therefore the transaction relationship. It entails that the IOF is owned by investors outside the chain of production, while the IFC is owned by parties in an adjacent stage of production. The essence of the IFC is that members commit only certain issues to group decisions (Robotka 1947). Meanwhile, members are independent in the sense that they do not necessarily collaborate with each other on other aspects of their individual firms.

The main challenge of an IFC is that it has to address two audiences. An IFC has to serve member interests and to generate maximum value in processing. It is designed for the former task and is expected to have an impact on the latter task. The next sections show that this feature makes an IFC the efficient organizational form in various circumstances.[4] We show not only that various standard aspects of IFCs make it an efficient organizational form, but also that several other aspects of IFCs, which are often perceived as weaknesses, are actually strengths.

The research themes regarding IFCs are classified in Table 26.1 according to the three main aspects in the definition of an IFC: the member firm(s), the transaction relationship, and the joint ownership of an enterprise. The table is not exhaustive, but it reflects a large number of themes being prominent in the scientific literature regarding IFCs. This chapter addresses most of the themes in Table 26.1.

This chapter is organized as follows. It first formulates rationales for the existence and efficiency of IFCs originating at the transaction relationship, then highlights rationales due to the collective ownership of the enterprise by many independent suppliers. Evidence regarding IFCs is organized around members, transactions and the IFC enterprise. A final section concludes.

Table 26.1   Classifying research themes

Themes originating at		
Member firms	Transaction relationship	IFC enterprise
Portfolio problem	Double monopoly mark-up	Control problem
Horizon problem	Countervailing power	Influence problem
Single origin constraint	Asset specificity	Free-riding
Coordination (horizontal)	Market access / assurance	Tax benefits
Member satisfaction	Contracts	Formal/real authority
Social capital	Trust	Member involvement
Competition policy	Selection	Finance
Cooperative principles	Price volatility	Pooling
	Product quality	Inertia
	Coordination (vertical)	Diversification
	Complementarities	Board model
	Member commitment	Exit and voice
	Competition policy	Incorporation law
	Cooperative principles	Cooperative principles

TRANSACTION RATIONALES

Competition in markets has many beneficial effects, but markets are not without problems. Examples of the problems faced by small firms are the formation of prices in markets, price instability, the provision of high-quality inputs, lack of support services, exploitative grading practices and lack of access to markets (Dunn et al. 1979). Forming an IFC may solve these market failures (to a certain extent). We address the double monopoly mark-up, countervailing power, assurance of sale, competitive yardstick, coordination, information provision and providing member services.

Double Monopoly Mark-up

An advantage of vertical integration compared to a setting with independent upstream and downstream firms is that the double-marginalization problem is eliminated (Spengler 1950). An IFC is able to procure inputs from members 'at cost', because the economic functions of an IFC are ultimately the economic functions of the member-farms performed through the IFC. This results in improved allocative efficiency, and substantially higher profits for the IFC. It is one of the reasons why an IFC is expected to have a higher output level than an IOF. An additional advantage is that an IFC is taxed only once in a number of countries, while the net income of an investor-owned enterprise is taxed twice (once as corporate profits, once as dividend income).

Countervailing Power

It matters for the price level in a market whether a monopolistic seller is facing a fragmented demand side or many small sellers are facing a few large buyers (processors or retailers). The latter situation is increasingly representative for many agricultural markets due to the massive consolidation of retailers (Reardon et al. 2004). This provides large buyers with many opportunities to play one seller off against the others to elicit price concessions. IFCs have been, and are, formed by many small sellers, to build countervailing power (Galbraith 1952) in order to avert the power of large processors as well as to exploit power on their own. Many small sellers joining forces in an IFC seems like the formation of a cartel, but many countries provide a partial antitrust exemption for IFCs in their competition laws. IFCs are often instrumental in starting new markets. For example, the market for life insurance did not start until mutuals began to offer these policies (Holmström 1999).

Assured Market Outlet

A farmer has often a weak bargaining position due to the perishability of the harvest. The fear of the farmer is that there will be hold-up in the *ex post* negotiation process because the investment costs have been made and cannot be recovered elsewhere; that is, investment costs are sunk. The farmer anticipates that the other party may take advantage of the specificity of his investments and decides not to invest in surplus generating activities. This is the (inefficient) hold-up problem (Klein et al. 1978). The desire to obtain a more certain demand has been an important driving force in the emergence of IFCs. For example, Nourse (1922: 581) observes about 'a small fruit-producing section' that 'the salvaging of their investment, or the continuance of their life work may be at stake on the part of growers. Hence it is argued (and demonstrated in practice) that the cooperative association of producers frequently achieves results where private outside entrepreneurship fails.' One of his arguments (p. 593) is that 'the agricultural producer can advantageously avail himself of the same cooperative form to open and maintain a channel from his farm to the factory or the wholesale or even the retail market'.

Competitive Yardstick

Many small firms may form an IFC to mitigate the adverse effects of a few powerful buyers. They enter at the next stage of production as a competitor and compete directly with these buyers. This is called the 'competitive yardstick strategy' (Nourse 1922), and it is implemented by forming an IFC. This may result in more competitive prices and quantities. When the market has become sufficiently competitive, the IFC may take a standby position but maintain the organizational capacity to re-enter the market, if necessary. The IFC thus recaptures economic losses – for example, the deadweight loss of monopoly – and becomes the source of differential member returns. Sexton and Sexton (1987) and Sexton (1990) justify favorable public policy towards (open-membership) IFCs based on this argument.

Coordination

In many production and supply chains, coordination is the primary concern, ensuring that value is created through joint actions throughout the entire chain. Coordination problems arise when there are (positive) externalities between different organizational units. Shaffer (1987) argues that the characteristics of an IFC provide the potential for advantages in coordination for IFCs over IOFs since the coordination between the parties in an IFC internalizes the vertical externality. One advantage is that coordination generally increases price stability (Dunn et al. 1979). Another advantage is that coordination with suppliers may be more smooth in an IFC than in an IOF. Many crops require a dedicated processing plant, but inputs are provided only during a limited period of the year. Examples are sugar beet and peas. Horizontal coordination between many independent members reduces idle capacity at the cooperative enterprise by extending the period of the deliveries. Many IFCs use quantity (e.g. a delivery requirement) as a vertical coordination mechanism to obtain control over members' volumes. Feng and Hendrikse (2011b) identify the circumstances when this is efficient.[5]

Information Provision

IFCs provide many possibilities for horizontal as well as vertical information exchange. Many IFCs create a territorial-based forum for horizontal information exchange between the members (LeVay 1983). Shared information about safe pest control and other environmental concerns is an example (Peterson and Anderson 1996). This is often facilitated by the local nature of the membership. The vertical flow of information to the IFC can be superior for various reasons. Firstly, there are stronger incentives for voice in an IFC because 'exit' is a more expensive option for the IFC members than for the suppliers of an IOF (Cook 1994). Secondly, members as owners are more assured that the IFC would not use the information to act opportunistically towards them than an IOF (Staatz 1987a). An IFC usually has a list of members and collects a substantial amount of information about members' preferences, needs and production practices, and advice about products and services through periodic member surveys (Cook 1994). The result may be higher-quality, more frequent and more truthful information provision by the members to the IFC than they would to an IOF. For example, IOF American Crystal Sugar went bankrupt due to supplier protests of price differentiation, but as the firm became a cooperative there was trust among the membership (Balbach 1998). Another example is that the success of the Danish pig slaughterhouse cooperatives is due to the farmer-members being willing to let themselves be directed and controlled by the leadership (Søgaard 1994). Thirdly, members transact frequently with the IFC. This voices the preferences of the members well (Cook 1994). Finally, members of an IFC are significantly more independent to question management decisions and to reject its recommendations than the owners of an IOF (Hendrikse 1998; USDA 2002).

Providing Member Services

Members join the IFC primarily for economic reasons, such as prices and other business terms as well as transaction costs. They benefit also in terms of services, which affect the profitability of their individual farm enterprise. For example, when an individual farmer cannot afford to do consumer research related to the characteristics of farm commodities, it may be feasible for an IFC to do so. An investor-owned marketing agency has little incentive to provide this service because it cannot capture the benefits that accrue to farmers (Shaffer 1987). Other examples are field services, risk management services, farm business consulting services, operating capital and facility capital financing, insurance programs and lobbying. Members also pursue non-economic objectives, such as deriving value from being a member of an association, a broader business education, leadership training, legislative influence, personal stature in the community and a greater sense of achievement (LeVay 1983; Barton 1989; Cropp and Ingalsbe 1989). An IFC may therefore take on auxiliary activities that an IOF would inefficiently forego. Feng and Hendrikse (2011a) model this feature in a multi-task principal–agent setting with three activities. An IFC elicits valuable downstream activities not reflected in the public listing of an IOF. The statistical evidence on diversification by IFCs seems consistent with this case (Caves and Petersen 1986).

GOVERNANCE STRUCTURE RATIONALES

A governance structure delineates ownership rights, decision rights and income rights regarding (physical or financial) assets (Baker et al. 2008; Hansmann 1996).[6] Ownership rights specify the formal rights regarding the use of assets. These rights reside with the suppliers in an IFC. Decision rights address the question: 'Who has control (regarding the use of assets)?' They specify who directs the firm's activities; that is, the allocation of real authority. Finally, income rights address the question: 'How are benefits and costs allocated?' thereby creating the incentive system faced by decision makers.

Ownership Rights

Enterprises are not only part of the market, but are also an alternative to the market (Coase 1937). The crucial feature of an IFC is that the ownership rights of the enterprise are allocated to many firms in an adjacent stage of production. This is attractive for solving the hold-up problem at the adjacent stage of production. Hold-up explanations are relevant in various sectors, such as dairy, fruit and vegetables (Staatz 1987b).[7] Assigning more power upstream is efficient, and therefore the IFC is the most efficient governance structure only when the level of asset specificity required at the adjacent stage of production is relatively high compared to the level of asset specificity at the other stage of production (Grossman and Hart 1986; Hendrikse and Veerman 2001a; Hendrikse and Bijman 2002). This favors the incorporation of the IFC as a separate legal form.[8]

Shares of an IFC cannot be traded publicly without restrictions because the majority of the shares have to stay with the membership. Member dominance therefore poses restrictions on the tradability and transferability of IFC shares. This transferability problem is at the root of a number of specific issues in IFCs which will be addressed later, such as the horizon problem, the portfolio problem and the control problem. Another implication is that an IFC receives less favourable terms on outside equity than an IOF because the ownership rights regarding new investments face restrictions for the providers of funds. IFCs are therefore expected to be at least as leveraged as IOFs, given the level of asset specificity. Williamson (1988) shows that debt (equity) is efficient for investments with the level of asset specificity below (above) a certain level. It entails that IFCs may be efficient for intermediate levels of asset specificity (Hendrikse and Veerman 2001b).

Decision Rights

The distinguishing feature of an IFC is member dominance. This seems rigid in terms of tailoring the organization to a specific environment, but the many possibilities for structuring the bylaws, in terms of decision and income rights, often provide the flexibility to elicit efficient behavior. Several decision rights aspects will be addressed, such as delivery rights, collective choice rules, the organization of voice, the relationship between the owner and the management, and the incompleteness of laws.

Each member in an IFC is usually granted the right, and sometimes also the obligation, to deliver a specified quantity of the commodity each season. Nilsson (1998: 42) observes that: 'The delivery obligation for members is the dominating practice everywhere; in some countries it is even an obligation by law'. The right to patronage is crucial for members because it provides them with control over, and access to, the infrastructure at the downstream stage of production.[9] It mitigates or even eliminates the hold-up problem at the upstream stage of production by allocating most of the bargaining power regarding the (quasi-) surplus to the members (Bonus 1986).[10]

Member firms pool some of their assets in an IFC – that is, collective ownership – while retaining complete autonomy with respect to all their other activities. Collective ownership requires a method for collective decision-making. However, Arrow's impossibility theorem indicates that this causes problems. Most commonly a collective decision-making procedure of some sort is used to come to a group choice. Zusman (1992) relates the efficient collective decision rule to characteristics of the issue to be addressed. A presidential system is efficient for operational issues, a simple majority system is efficient for policy issues, while an unanimity system is efficient for constitutional amendments. This result is driven by the change in the member's expected utility and the change in decision costs. Both variables increase with the number of members required to accept a proposal, but the ratio of the member's expected utility to decision costs increases faster when issues become more important.

The general rule is that all members have equal voting rights. Some countries prescribe the principle of one member, one vote by law, but there are also countries where this is not specified in the law and one member, multiple votes schemes have been adopted. A problem with collective decision-making procedures characterized by simple majority is that they may yield inefficient decisions due to voting power being allocated independently of quantity and/or quality. An IFC is more likely to be efficient when the membership becomes more homogeneous (Hart and Moore 1996).

One way to reduce the costs of collective decision making is to delegate decision rights to another party. Enterprises assign their formal rights of control to their owners, but the decision rights are generally exercised by them in an indirect way through voting for the board of directors, which then selects the management of the firm. Real authority is therefore delegated by the members to the management (Aghion and Tirole 1997; Baker et al. 1999; Hendrikse 2005). IFCs and IOFs differ regarding the importance of the formal owners in the decision process. The chief executive officer (CEO) in an IOF often has a large, if not dominant voice in selecting the board of directors (Bebchuk and Fried 2003), despite that the board of directors has the legal power. The CEO often has substantial control over setting, ratifying and implementing company policy. In an IFC, the CEO usually has significantly less influence over who sits on the board. Members have a substantial number of seats in the board of directors and they are not dependent on the CEO for their position. They are sufficiently independent to question management decisions and to reject its recommendations. An IOF may therefore be conceived as consisting of one bureau, while an IFC consists of two bureaus with each bureau having veto power (Sah and Stiglitz 1986; Hendrikse 1998). This may account for some of the conservative decision making by IFCs. The veto power of each bureau in an IFC is efficient in environments with a relatively high percentage of poor projects or relatively high costs of adopting poor projects.

Having a law recognizing an IFC as a separate legal form facilitates the emergence of IFCs. However, there is less agreement about the specification of the bylaws. Laws between countries differ substantially regarding the freedom allowed to structure their bylaws. There is no law on cooperatives in Denmark, while the law is comparatively permissive in the Netherlands. The impression is that IFCs thrive when there is a law that on the one hand recognizes them as a distinct legal entity, and on the other hand is not very detailed regarding the bylaws. Another legal aspect is the essential role of organizational law (Hansmann and Kraakman 2000). Some enterprises, including IFCs, partition their assets into distinct pools of assets by creating separate legal entities in the enterprise to reduce the costs of business contracting, such as monitoring costs and isolating risks. Legal separation may also serve as a commitment that the members do not interfere too much with the daily activities of the management, and it may facilitate the distribution of rents over the various classes of members.

Income Rights

Ownership of the IFC is important for the members, but the actual payments are often more important for them. There are many degrees of freedom to structure the income rights in an IFC. LeVay (1983: 5) even states that 'IFCs may behave no differently from other types of enterprise'. It turns out that the income rights in informal, repeated relationships can be structured in such a way that exactly the same distribution of power results in an IFC as in other enterprises (Baker et al. 2002; Hendrikse 2007a). However, the actual composition of income rights often reflects that an IFC is collectively owned by many independent suppliers. Important issues regarding the structuring of income rights are geared towards the timely payment for deliveries, the quantity control problem, dealing with the tension between pooling and member heterogeneity, and the control problem.

Firstly, an important feature of an IFC is not only the assurance of sale for the members, but also the assurance of payment for deliveries. Ownership by the members guarantees that the time and method of payment for deliveries is tailored to the interests of the members, which reduces the bargaining problems regarding the terms of exchange experienced with other governance structures, such as independent processors or intermediaries.

Secondly, an IFC has several features in its design which makes it likely to produce more than an IOF. An IFC is expected to have lower marginal costs than an IOF due to the elimination of the double mark-up. Members receive for the inputs that they supply 'at cost' a market price plus a per-unit share of any rent obtained by the IFC. Another feature is that IFCs allocate revenues often proportional to deliveries. This payment scheme has attractive properties, but it often sends the wrong signal to members about revenues (Sen 1966; Bogetoft and Olesen 2007).[11] Members will therefore often over-produce due to the IFC's average revenue exceeding its marginal revenue. Additionally, the output policy of an IFC is driven by the average rather than the marginal member (Helmberger and Hoos 1962; LeVay 1983). Finally, the practice of accepting all member deliveries by most IFCs, due to the production orientation of member firms, provides IFCs with a strategic advantage (Albæk and Schultz 1998). Individual members enjoy the benefits of their overproduction, while the loss in profits is shared with the entire membership. This lack of input control provides a commitment to overproduce in the competition with an IOF.

Thirdly, member firms are often faced with various production uncertainties. Pooling practices by the IFC perform a beneficial insurance function for risk-averse farmers. Pooling entails also that revenues and costs are to a certain extent allocated indepen-dent of quantity and/or quality. Members benefit from their membership in proportion to their volume of transactions with the IFC, not in relation to their capital invest-ment. This may result in free-riding as well as adverse selection problems. Free-riding and underinvestment problems are to be expected when the transfer price paid to the member firms does not entirely reflect the benefits or the costs of deliveries by members. Adverse selection is due to the heterogeneity of the membership in terms of quantity and/ or quality of the deliveries. Cross-subsidization of one group of members by another group of members may result in the latter group leaving the IFC (Hendrikse 2011). It may also mask market signals (Fulton and Hueth 2009). However, the flexibility of income rights allows for dealing with these problems by tailoring financial incentives to specific member characteristics (Staatz 1984; Sexton and Iskow 1988; Bontems and Fulton 2009). For example, Sexton and Iskow (1988) argue that membership fees have to be made roughly proportional to a member's expected patronage in order to prevent these problems.

Finally, the owners of enterprises are facing control problems due to the delegation of decision responsibilities to managers. The precise agency problem depends on the type of enterprise, due to differences in the available information. For example, an IFC lacks a source of information compared to an IOF, but it has also an additional source of information. An IFC does not have a public listing. This makes the provision of incen-tives and the monitoring of the managers different than in a publicly listed IOF. Feng and Hendrikse (2012) show in a multi-task principal–agent model that the interactions between the downstream and upstream activities may make the IFC the unique effi-cient governance structure. The absence of public listing, and the IFC CEO having to bring the downstream enterprise to value as well as to serve upstream member interests, prevents the CEO from choosing the level of the downstream activities too highly. The IFC internalizes externalities to a certain extent by putting a positive weight on serving member interests and generating maximum value in processing. IFCs are efficient in sectors where the marginal productivity at the downstream stage is below a certain level, which is determined by the upstream and downstream marginal product and the chain complementarities.

The IFC has an additional source of information compared to an IOF. It arises from the owners also being users of the IFC (Peterson and Anderson 1996). The frequent trans-actions with the IFC allow for smaller monitoring costs and fewer losses from improper managerial decisions in IFCs than in other enterprises. The involvement of the member firms in the IFC limits the power of the top management. Peterson and Anderson (1996: 373–374) observe: 'Cooperatives appear to have a significantly lower pay structure than non-cooperatives, especially at the upper management levels. Cooperative managers receive fewer emoluments and firm sponsored benefits, for example, limos, country club memberships, etc. Cooperatives also appear to operate with leaner staffs and lower costs structures than many non-cooperative firms'.

EVIDENCE

This section is focused on the behavior of IFCs. It is organized around members, transactions and the IFC enterprise.

Members

Stylized facts are presented regarding characteristics of the membership and some of the repercussions of the membership composition for the incentive to invest in the IFC.

Multiple memberships
Many farmers in the same area have similar product portfolios consisting of various products. These products could be handled by one IFC, but each product is often handled by a different IFC; that is, many IFCs are one product IFCs. One explanation is the costs of voice. Reducing the heterogeneity of the membership by constraining the activities of the enterprise to narrow business lines decreases the costs of voice (Hansmann 1996). This facilitates collective decision making. On average, US farmers hold memberships in 2–6 IFCs (Dunn et al. 1979).

Local
Most IFCs have a membership located in a specific geographic area. They are typically located near the member firms. Cropp and Ingalsbe (1989) identify several advantages of these local IFCs. Firstly, communicating with members is simpler because members are more likely to know one another and have close personal relationships. Secondly, members have similar marketing and production problems and thus less chance of disagreement. Thirdly, there may be greater member support and loyalty due to voting directly for the board of directors and on major business decisions. Finally, members may have more confidence in the local manager whom they know personally and meet regularly. However, an important disadvantage of local IFCs is their relatively small business volume. This limits their bargaining power and their ability to take advantage of economies of scale. The number of local agricultural IFCs is declining.

Portfolio problem
The portfolio problem of IFCs captures that the diversification decision of an IFC is influenced by the farm portfolio of members. Members often tie a substantial fraction of their farm portfolio to one IFC because they have usually a limited number of crops and each crop is handled by one IFC. Members will try to establish their desired farm port-

folio by influencing the diversification decisions of an IFC. However, the special features of IFCs, such as the lack of public listing and therefore the very limited transferability of ownership shares, prevent the members from diversifying their farm portfolio (in terms of risk and return) in an optimal way. Cook (1995: 1157) observes that members 'will pressure IFC decision makers to rearrange the IFC's investment portfolio, even if the reduced risk portfolio means lower expected returns'. Caves and Petersen (1986: 5) report that the statistical evidence seems to support the portfolio problem argument. Notice that this may be attractive. An IFC may take on auxiliary activities that an IOF may inefficiently forego.

Horizon problem

A prominent argument is that IFCs will underinvest is the horizon problem, which is due to the limited transferability of ownership rights. Old members have a disincentive to contribute to long-term investment strategies because the productive life of an asset is longer than their remaining membership period. They will therefore support investment opportunities with a shorter productive life of assets than the efficient one; that is, projects that will pay off quickly. This entails a tendency to underinvest in long-term strategies, such as brand promotion, market research and new product development. Jensen and Meckling (1979) label this the 'horizon problem'. Other underinvestment arguments are formulated based on the portfolio problem, collective ownership, patronage rights, patronized-based financing, pooling practices, expensive outside equity, lack of public listing, upstream ownership, and so on. However, the flexibility of the bylaws in terms of the allocation of income and decision rights allows for dealing with these issues efficiently. Olesen (2007) is an example. Caves and Petersen (1986: 4) review the evidence and conclude that 'the behavioral evidence on local cooperatives reveals few signs of underinvestment. If anything, it supports a contrary hypothesis that members gain utility from seeing their cooperative have a "first class" plant, more capital-intensive and durable than optimal investment criteria might suggest'. Fahlbeck (2007) reports also no support for a horizon problem in agricultural cooperatives.

Transaction

This section highlights stylized facts relating to the inputs and outputs of the IFC being supplied by its owners. We address the market share of IFCs, the quality of products supplied, and contracts.

Market share of IFCs

Most agricultural markets show coexistence of IFCs and IOFs. For example, 26 percent of all major farm purchases were purchased through IFCs in the USA in 1989, while farmers marketed 28 percent of their products through IFCs (Cropp and Ingalsbe 1989). Most agricultural sectors in the European Union also exhibit the coexistence of IFCs and IOFs (Hendrikse 1998). Explanations have been formulated, such as supply assurance (Carlton 1979a, 1979b), competitive yardstick (Sexton 1990), differential screening (Hendrikse 1998) and contractual externalities (Hendrikse 2007b).

The incidence of IFCs varies between countries and over time. Hansmann (1999: 387) observes that: 'More generally and more strikingly, the overall share of economic activity accounted for by IFCs is larger in advanced economies than it is in less-developed economies. And, more striking still, the market share of IFCs in economic activity has grown throughout the 20th century'. For example, Sexton (1986: 1170) reports that IFCs' farmgate market share has been rising from 20 percent of marketing sales in the 1940s to about 30 percent in the 1980s and from 12 percent to 27 percent of farm input sales over the same period. Feng and Hendrikse (2011a) explain these developments by the rise of ICT, and its applications in the management of chain complementarities in supply chains.

Another observation is that the IFC share of business activity at the farm level is considerably larger than at subsequent levels of the food system. For example, Dunn et al. (1979: 243) report that local IFCs handle 40 percent of the grain moving off the farm, but only 21 percent of the initial volume moves to the next step in the IFC marketing system by the regional IFCs. By the time the grain leaves the export elevators, the IFC share is down to about 5 percent of the initial off-farm volume. There are a number of explanations for the limited ownership of activities much beyond the member firms, such as the member orientation on direct interests and experience (Caves and Petersen 1989), reduced information advantages of working closely with member firms (Ling 2010), reduced investment incentives (Hendrikse and Bijman 2002), and the increasing capital requirements of industrialized agriculture (Fulton and Hueth 2009).

Finally, there are considerable market share differences between sectors. Five commodities account for 90 percent of the marketing volume handled by IFCs (Cropp and Ingalsbe 1989). Two-thirds of the volume is accounted for by grain and dairy products. The other three commodities are fruits, vegetables and nuts as a group; livestock; and cotton. Membership percentages differ between sectors. For example, 87 percent of the farmers are in IFCs in the dairy sector, while livestock producers were least involved, with 48 percent in 1989. Dairy cooperatives have major shares in making hard products, 71 percent of butter, 96 percent of non-fat and skim milk powder, 26 percent of cheese, and 42 percent dry whey products, while their shares are less significant in sectors that are capital-, technology- and service-intensive and that carry high product and market risks: 7 percent of fluid milk, 4 percent of ice cream, 11 percent of yoghurt, and 14 percent of sour cream (Ling 2010). The same pattern is observed in IFCs' share of marketing activity. The IFC's share of total marketing activity is 78 percent in dairy, while it is 8 percent in livestock. Europe shows also substantial variation (Hendrikse 1998). The dairy, grain, and fruit sectors usually have the largest market share for IFCs. Caves and Petersen (1986) provide support for a number of explanations, such as local concentration and specialization, countervailing power and short-term hold-ups, and capital-intensive activities which are organizationally not complex.

Product quality

Some of the traditional IFC business practices may cause problems regarding product quality of upstream deliveries by member firms as well as the output of the IFC enterprise. The composition of upstream deliveries may be vulnerable to adverse selection for various reasons. Firstly, an IFC is traditionally a 'home' for member production: that is, all member deliveries are accepted. The price in a niche market may be undermined by the practice of accepting all deliveries by members. Secondly, the pooling practices of IFCs often fail to sufficiently reward the members delivering the highest-quality products.[12] Thirdly, many IFCs have an open membership policy: that is, a new member is accepted when the entry requirements are satisfied. Finally, the horizon problem entails that there are reduced incentives to invest in long-run activities to enhance quality. Cook (1995) observes that IFCs tend to operate in first-stage food manufacturing industries and that these industries are low-value-added industries. This is in line with Sexton and Iskow (1993) and Royer (1999), where the latter states that 'cooperatives ... tend to operate in the low value-added fluid milk segment of the industry'.[13] However, an IFC may also facilitate product quality due to various possibilities for superior horizontal as well as vertical information exchange.

Contracts

MacDonald and Korb (2011) distinguish three methods for transferring commodities from farms to the next stage of production: spot markets, vertical integration (including IFCs) and contracts. A farmer often has a portfolio of exchange mechanisms due to different transactions having different risks, such as biological risks, price risk, institutional risk and behavioral uncertainty.[14] Exchange mechanisms differ between agricultural products. For example, contracts are extensively used in poultry, hog, sugar beet and tobacco production, but are much less prevalent in corn, soybeans and wheat. Bogetoft and Olesen (2002, 2004) observe that the presence of coordination clauses in contracts depends on the perishability of the crop. Peas, fruit and broilers are coordinated through instructions, while storable products such as potatoes, sugar beet, and grass and clover seed are not coordinated in contracts.

Contracts are embedded in a governance structure, and the details may therefore differ between a market setting and an IFC. Balbach (1998) observes regarding the beet sugar industry in the USA that only IFC processors use contracts with clauses based on the extractable sugar content of the beets. He provides a measurement cost explanation. Non-IFC processors have an incentive to under-report quality, and the costs of monitoring a processor's quality measurements are too high for farmers. These contracts are attractive for the IFC processor because they give member firms an incentive to produce higher-quality beets and their processor has been able to reduce processing costs. Similarly, Bogetoft and Olesen (2002) observe regarding the contracts for the production of grass and clover seed that the authority to order reploughing is allocated to the processor in the IFC, whereas this right is not allocated to the private processors.

IFC Enterprise

This section addresses some stylized facts at the level of the IFC enterprise: pooling, conservative investments, production orientation, diversification, single-origin constraint, governance structure changes, inertia and Gibrat's law.

Pooling

Most IFCs use a pooling arrangement in which members share equitably on a per-unit basis in the revenue stream that has been created. Nilsson (1998: 43) observes that: 'The principle of equal treatment within agricultural IFCs is traditionally strong. This involves things as pricing, for example prices are not always differentiated based on quality and quantity, and member control, for example the general rule is that all members have equal voting rights'. Fruit and vegetable IFC The Greenery has experienced adverse selection processes with high-quality members leaving the IFC and forming grower associations due to pooling practices, but they came back after adjustments in the bylaws to provide sufficient compensation for members with high-quality deliveries (Hendrikse 2011).

Conservative investments

Members of an IFC often favor a conservative investment strategy in order to stabilize member returns (Staatz 1987a). Peterson and Anderson (1996) claim that the conservative investment strategy entails that only the most secure projects are considered as investment options. They report, based on a CEO survey, that 'CEOs were nearly unanimous (95 percent of those interviewed) in citing very conservative investment strategies within their cooperatives' (1996: 380). Feng and Hendrikse (2011c) formulate an explanation based on the upstream focus of agricultural cooperatives.

Production orientation

Nilsson (2001) observes that IFCs in most agricultural markets do have large production volumes and large market shares in the collection and primary processing of the raw produce. Bogetoft and Olesen (2007: 37) observe that problems of overproduction typically occur in cooperatives selling in 'thin markets'.

Diversification

Various ideas have been formulated which may be relevant for the diversification choices of IFCs, such as the portfolio problem, the horizon problem, conservative decision making, and the single-origin constraint. The approach in empirical research is usually to investigate the portfolio differences between IOFs and IFCs. Diversification choices of an IOF aim to maximize the net returns of the investors, while the diversification choices of an IFC are guided by bringing to value the portfolio of members. Hendrikse and Van Oijen (2004) establish that publicly listed enterprises diversify more in unrelated activities (two-digit industries) as well as related activities (four-digit industries).

Single-origin constraint

The diversification activities of an IFC are geared towards bringing the portfolio of the members to value because members may suffer substantial capital losses if their farming activities are not adequately supported. IFCs continue their efforts on behalf of their member-producers even during extended periods when economic and financial conditions would call for exit by other enterprises (Dunn et al. 1979). An IFC provides a 'home' for the output of members. The possibilities for diversification by IFCs are therefore constrained, especially when activities are involved far removed from the direct interests and experience of the IFC members. Cook (1997: 87) labels the member focus in the diversification activities of IFCs as the single-origin constraint. An illustration is the sugar industry in the Netherlands. It consisted of two enterprises: the publicly listed CSM (Centrale Suiker Maatschappij) and the IFC SuikerUnie, nowadays called Royal Cosun. CSM started to diversify into bakery ingredients, with sugar as an important ingredient. It nowadays has a leading position in the world market for bakery products, and has divested its sugar activities. Cosun maintains its sugar activities, and has diversified into potatoes and a few vegetables.[15]

Governance structure changes

The characterization of a governance structure in terms of ownership, decision and income rights allows for various governance structure responses to new circumstances. Firstly, a different allocation of ownership rights may be needed in order to deal effectively and efficiently with the increasing heterogeneity between members and/or increasing price competition and increasing concentration at the retail level. Examples of changing ownership rights are mergers between IFCs, the emergence of grower associations, and forward integration (Hendrikse 2011). Another response is demutualization by switching to the governance-structure IOF (Royer 1999; Fulton and Hueth 2009). The typology of Chaddad and Cook (2004) illustrates that there is substantial variety in the allocation of decision and income rights between IFCs.

Secondly, IFCs may respond to changing market conditions by changing the allocation of decision power between the various bodies inside the IFC, such as the general assembly, the board of directors, the supervisory committee and the management. Bijman et al. (forthcoming) present substantial board structure variety. Three IFC board models are demarcated: the traditional model, the management model and the corporation model. The general assembly appoints the board of directors as well as the supervisory committee in the traditional model, where the supervisory committee supervises the board of directors. The board of directors appoints the management. The management model is the same as the traditional model except for the management of the firm and the board of directors being merged into one body. The main characteristic of the corporation model is that the board of directors and the supervisory committee are one body. The firm has been legally separated from the society of members. The latter two models move decision power closer to the final product markets. They reflect four tendencies in IFCs: (1) a shift of decision rights from the board of directors to management, and therefore changes in the role of the supervisory committee; (2) a tendency of professionalization of the board of directors and supervisory committee, and therefore changes in the composition of these bodies; (3) a legal separation between the society of members and the IFC enterprise; (4) IFCs partition their assets by creating legal entities within the IFC.

Thirdly, the bylaws allow also for substantial variety in terms of the income rights. Differentiation and innovation in agricultural and horticultural markets has the tendency to increase member heterogeneity. This poses a challenge for a traditional IFC because various aspects are tailored towards homogeneous members (Hansmann 1996). Collective decision-making procedures and pooling arrangements are less likely to be efficient in a situation with a heterogeneous membership. Highly innovative growers demand a different treatment than the less innovative growers. IFCs have responded in terms of changing their income rights by specifying less uniform transaction requirements, cash payments and capital titles. A number of examples illustrate this development. Many IFCs have responded to changing market conditions by changing member incentive schemes. Different classes of members emerge based on meeting certain transaction requirements, such as transaction volume, delivery time, and quality. Financial innovations in IFCs are introduced, such as the introduction of transferable equity shares, appreciable equity shares, minimum upfront equity investments and payments partially based on investments levels. Related to this is the introduction of tradable delivery rights. IFCs with strong incentive structures are characterized by 'individualized' rather than collective capital structures. The introduction of individual member shares and proportional voting are examples. The 'new generation' IFC model (Cook 1995) is an illustration of IFCs allowing for more differentiation in the treatment of the members.

Finally, Krogt et al. (2007) study the effect of governance structure on the direction of interfirm consolidation and collaboration strategies. They argue that specific IFC attributes, such as democratic decision making and limited access to equity capital, imply that IFCs prefer strategies which involve relatively low risks and limited amounts of capital. Their data show that IFCs prefer mergers, collaboration agreements, joint ventures and licensing, while IOFs have a tendency to choose acquisitions and strategic shareholdings.

Inertia

I have argued above that there are many aspects of an IFC which may make it an efficient organizational form. However, these possibilities are often not exploited. For example, the provision of information in IFCs may be better than in an IOF. But information systems are needed to collect, process and use this information. Peterson and Anderson (1996) observe that these are often missing in IFCs. Another example is the flexibility allowed by the law to structure the bylaws. Again, these possibilities are often not used. Mérel et al. (2009: 206) observe that: 'Although cooperatives are free to specify their criteria for membership in bylaws, such criteria are usually general, encompassing, and outdated'. It results in frequent descriptions of the free-rider problem, horizon problem, portfolio problem, control problem and influence cost problem in IFCs (Vitaliano 1983; Staatz 1987a; Cook 1995). Fulton and Hueth (2009) indicate that these problems are due on the one hand to poor management such as in IOFs, and on the other hand are due to specific features of IFCs such as lack of capital, property rights problems and portfolio problems.

Gibrat's law

IFCs differ in scale and scope. Some IFCs consist of five or six members, while others consist of more than 10000 members. Some perform only one or two marketing functions, while others store, grade, process, package, brand, distribute and merchandise products. Many IFCs handle only one product. Some of them limit themselves to plain processing of the input, while others have developed a large product portfolio based on the input by the members. Dunn at al. (1979: 244) state that in many commodity markets: 'In value of products sold, the largest four cooperatives are considerably smaller than their noncooperative counterparts'. So, IFCs and IOFs seem to differ in terms of Gibrat's law: that is, the size distribution of enterprises (Simon and Bonini 1958).

CONCLUSION

Member firms are owners and users of an IFC. This feature is the driving force behind the efficiency and strategic explanations for the worldwide existence and persistence of IFCs. IFCs are usually founded to provide critical and valuable services to the member firms. Several aspects of an IFC make it an attractive organizational form, such as procuring inputs 'at cost' due to eliminating the double monopoly mark-up, establishing a fair price by organizing countervailing power, reducing hold-up by creating an assured market outlet, promoting competitive prices and quantities by creating a competitive yardstick to mitigate the effects of a few powerful buyers, facilitating (horizontal and vertical) coordination, improving information provision and providing member services.

Several other aspects of IFCs, which are often perceived as weaknesses, can also be strengths, such as the overproduction tendency, (partial) pooling, conservative decision making and the lack of public listing. The overproduction tendency endows the IFC with a strategic advantage in the competition with rivals by making it more aggressive. (Partial) pooling insures risk-averse farmers and counteracts the tendency of competitive enterprises to overproduce high-quality products. Conservative decision making is attractive when the incidence of poor investment projects is relatively large. Finally, the lack of public listing elicits valuable activities not reflected in the public listing.

These reasons imply that IFCs are to be expected in a number of sectors. IFCs prevent hold-up by downstream enterprises regarding upstream outputs. They are therefore expected when the asset specificity of member firms is relatively important compared to that of the cooperative enterprise. IFCs are also expected in environments with a relatively high percentage of poor projects or relatively high costs of adopting poor projects. Stringent screening reduces the likelihood of adopting poor projects. Value chains where the marginal productivity of member firms is relatively high compared to that of the cooperative enterprise is attractive for an IFC because it prevents the CEO from choosing the level of the downstream activities too high.

Studying IFCs is not only important for understanding and improving these enterprises, but it serves also as a counterfactual for the much-studied investor-owned firm, and to enhance our understanding of the institutional structure of production. Further research is desirable due on the one hand to conceptual developments, and on the other hand to the evolution of markets in terms of communication technologies, genetics, robotics, laws, and so on. This will enhance our understanding regarding the circumstances when an IFC is a desirable governance structure.

NOTES

* Comments by Anna Grandori, Constantine Iliopoulos and Jerker Nilsson are much appreciated.
1. A prominent example of a definition taking this perspective is Dunn (1988: 85). He defines an IFC as 'a user-owned and controlled business from which benefits are derived and distributed on the basis of use'.
2. A prominent example of a definition taking this perspective is provided by the International Cooperative Alliance (2007). It defines a cooperative as 'an autonomous association of persons united voluntarily to meet their common economic, social, and cultural needs and aspirations through a jointly-owned and democratically controlled enterprise'.
3. The nature of an IFC has been debated frequently. An important contribution is Emelianoff (1942), triggering the debate in the 1950s and 1960s. Three views are distinguished in the debate (Feng and Hendrikse 2008). The 'extension of the firm' view maintains that the IFC is just an association of firms, not a new firm per se; it has no entrepreneurial unit (Phillips 1953; Trifon 1961). The 'vertical integration' view advocates that member firms are integrated with the downstream production stage. It entails that several stages in the production process are brought under unified control (Phillips 1953). The 'firm view' suggests that an IFC is itself a business enterprise and an economic entity; a new decision-making body is created by the formation of an IFC (Helmberger and Hoos 1962; Robotka 1947). An IFC is viewed as a special type of firm capable of making entrepreneurial decisions just as any private corporation (Savage 1954).

4. The focus on the efficiency of the IFC is in line with the conclusion of the review by Lafontaine and Slade (2007: 680) regarding the findings of empirical studies that 'under most circumstances, profit-maximizing vertical-integration decisions are efficient, not just from the firms' but also from the consumers' point of view'.

   The efficiency of an IFC is usually determined by comparing it with the IOF, where the IOF is active in the downstream stage of production, such as the cooperative enterprise. Other governance structures than the IOF could serve as a benchmark, and are informative regarding an IFC. For example, we agree with Sexton (1984: 429) that 'Labor-managed firms are closely analogous to agricultural marketing cooperatives. Cooperatively processing and marketing the raw labor input is conceptually very similar to processing and marketing a raw agricultural commodity such as milk or grain.' However, identifying important similarities may neglect important differences. Pencavel (2001) is an eloquent overview about the unique aspects of labour compared to other inputs.

5. Various agricultural markets are governed by marketing orders (Babb and Bohall 1979). They regulate legally the terms of exchange for commodities.

6. These three rights are already distinguished in the agricultural economics literature. Dunn (1988) characterizes an IFC by 'user-owner, user-control, and user-benefits'. The labels 'formal/legal' authority, 'real' authority and 'incentives' are also being used.

7. Other aspects of transactions than asset specificity, such as complexity or uncertainty, may have more explanatory power in other sectors. For example, the complexity of the logistics process in the flower industry seems to be a more prominent concern than asset specificity in the organization of the economic activities regarding flowers.

8. The quadrupling of the number of IFCs in China since 2007 illustrates the importance of incorporation.

9. Carlton (1979a, 1979b) has investigated the value of outlet assurance in an uncertain market environment.

10. Hendrikse (2011) shows that countervailing power and the hold-up problem are intertwined and identifies the circumstances when countervailing power is required to provide the efficient incentives to invest in specific assets by farmers.

11. Zusman (1982) shows that this can be remedied by an appropriate choice of cost distribution rule, and that it is attainable through majority voting.

12. Saitone and Sexton (2009) show that partial pooling may be optimal because it insures risk-averse farmers and counteracts the tendency of competitive enterprises to overproduce high-quality products in order to maximize industry profit.

13. Feng and Hendrikse (2011a) show that IFCs are uniquely efficient in such settings.

14. Hendrikse (2007b) investigates the relationship between spot and contract markets. Suppliers contract with the high-reservation-price buyers when the contract is characterized by a delivery requirement and a contracting benefit. These relationships procure the high probability demand, while the spot market serves to supply inputs when the upstream party is not able to produce.

15. Hendrikse and Smit (2007) analyze the implications of an IFC never abandoning the activities of its members for product portfolio evolution in an agent-based simulation model. The product portfolio of the IFC evolves in one cluster around the single-origin constraint, while the product portfolio of the IOF disperses and disintegrates into a random pattern of diverging small clusters.

REFERENCES

Aghion, P. and J. Tirole (1997), 'Formal and real authority in organizations', *Journal of Political Economy*, **105**(1), 1–29.

Albæk, S. and C. Schultz (1998), 'On the relative advantage of cooperatives', *Economic Letters*, **59**, 397–401.

Babb, E.M. and R. Bohall (1979), 'Marketing orders and farm structure', in *Structure Issues of American Agriculture*, USDA ESCS Agricultural Economics Rep. 438, Washington DC: US Department of Agriculture, pp. 249–254.

Balbach, J.K. (1998), 'The effect of ownership on contract structure, costs, and quality: the case of the US beet sugar industry', in J.S. Royer and R.T. Rogers (eds), *The Industrialization of Agriculture: Vertical Coordination in the US Food System*, Aldershot: Ashgate Publishing, pp. 155–184.

Baker, G., R. Gibbons and K.J. Murphy (1999), 'Informal authority in organizations', *Journal of Law, Economics, and Organization*, **15**(1), 56–73.

Baker, G., R. Gibbons and K.J. Murphy (2002), 'Relational contracts and the theory of the firm', *Quarterly Journal of Economics*, **11**(1), 39–84.

Baker, G.A., R. Gibbons and K.J. Murphy (2008), 'Strategic alliances: bridges between islands of conscious power', *Journal of the Japanese and International Economies*, **22**, 146–163.

Barton, D.G. (1989), 'What is a cooperative?' in D.W. Cobia (ed.), *Cooperatives in Agriculture*, Englewood Cliffs, NJ: Prentice Hall, pp. 1–20.

Bebchuk, L.A. and J.M. Fried (2003), 'Executive compensation as an agency problem', *Journal of Economic Perspectives*, **17**(3), 71–92.

Bijman, W.J.J., G.W.J. Hendrikse and A.A.C.J. van Oijen (forthcoming), 'Accommodating two worlds in one organization: changing board roles in agricultural cooperatives', *Managerial and Decision Economics*.

Bogetoft, P. and H.B. Olesen (2002), 'Ten rules of thumb in contract design: lessons from Danish agriculture', *European Review of Agricultural Economics*, **29**(2), 185–204.

Bogetoft, P. and H.B. Olesen (2004), *Design of Production Contracts*, Copenhagen: Copenhagen Business School Press.

Bogetoft, P. and H.B. Olesen (2007), *Cooperatives and Payment Schemes*, Copenhagen: Copenhagen Business School Press.

Bontems, P. and M.E. Fulton (2009), 'Organizational structure, redistribution and the endogeneity of cost: cooperatives, investor–owned firms and the cost of procurement', *Journal of Economic Behavior and Organization*, **72**, 322–343.

Bonus, H. (1986), 'The cooperative association as a business enterprise: a study of the economics of transactions', *Journal of Institutional and Theoretical Economics*, **142**(2), 310–339.

Carlton, D.W. (1979a), 'Vertical integration in competitive markets under uncertainty', *Journal of Industrial Economics*, **27**, 189–209.

Carlton, D.W. (1979b), 'Contracts, price rigidity, and market equilibrium', *Journal of Political Economy*, **87**, 1034–1062.

Caves, R.E. and B.C. Petersen (1986), 'Cooperatives' shares in farm industries: organizational and policy factors', *Agribusiness*, **2**(1), 1–19.

Chaddad, F.R. and M.L. Cook (2004), 'Understanding new cooperative models: an ownership-control rights typology', *Review of Agricultural Economics*, **26**(3), 348–360.

Coase, R.H. (1937), 'The nature of the firm', *Economica*, **4**, 386–405.

Cook, M.L. (1994), 'The role of management behavior in agricultural cooperatives', *Journal of Agricultural Cooperation*, **9**, 42–58.

Cook M.L. (1995), 'The future of US agricultural cooperatives: a neo-institutional approach', *American Journal of Agricultural Economics*, **77**(5), 1153–1159.

Cook, M.L. (1997), 'Organizational structure and globalization: the case of user oriented firms', in J. Nilsson and G. van Dijk (eds), *Strategies and Structures in the Agro-food Industries*, Assen: Van Gorcum, pp. 77–93.

Cropp, R. and G. Ingalsbe (1989), 'Structure and scope of agricultural cooperatives', in D. Cobia (ed.), *Cooperatives in Agriculture*, Englewood Cliffs, NJ: Prentice Hall, pp. 35–67.

Dunn, J.R. (1988), 'Basic cooperative principles and their relationship to selected practices', *Journal of Agricultural Cooperation*, **3**, 83–93.

Dunn, J.R., G. Ingalsbe and J.H. Armstrong (1979), 'Cooperatives and the structure of US agriculture', in *Structure Issues of American Agriculture*, USDA ESCS Agricultural Economics Rep. 438, Washington, DC: US Department of Agriculture, pp. 241–248.

Emelianoff, I.I. (1942), *Economic Theory of Cooperation: Economic Structure of Cooperative Organizations*, Ann Arbor, MI: Edward Brothers.

Fahlbeck, E. (2007), 'The horizon problem in agricultural cooperatives – only in theory?' in K. Karantininis and J. Nilsson (eds), *Vertical Markets and Cooperative Hierarchies*, Dordrecht: Springer, pp. 255–271.

Feng, L. and G.W.J. Hendrikse (2012), 'Chain interdependencies, measurement problems, and efficient governance structure: cooperatives versus publicly listed firms', *European Review of Agricultural Economics*, **39**(2), 241–255.

Feng, L. and G.W.J. Hendrikse (2011a), 'Performance measurement and the efficiency of marketing cooperatives versus publicly listed firms', Rotterdam School of Management.

Feng, L. and G.W.J. Hendrikse (2011b), 'Coordination and governance structure: the case of cooperatives versus IOFs', Rotterdam School of Management.

Feng, L. and G.W.J. Hendrikse (2011c), 'Cognition and governance structure', Rotterdam School of Management.

Fulton, M.E. and B. Hueth (2009), 'Cooperative conversions, failures, and restructurings: an overview', *Journal of Cooperatives*, **23**, i–xi.

Galbraith, J.K. (1952), *American Capitalism: The Concept of Countervailing Power*, Boston, MA: Houghton-Mifflin.

Grossman, S.J. and O.D. Hart (1986), 'The costs and benefits of ownership: a theory of vertical and lateral integration', *Journal of Political Economy*, **94**(4), 691–719.

Hansmann, H.B. (1996), *The Ownership of Enterprise*, Cambridge, MA: Belknap Press of Harvard University Press.

Hansmann, H.B. (1999), 'Cooperative firms in theory and practice', *Finnish Journal of Business Economics*, **4**, 387–403.

Hansmann, H. and R. Kraakman (2000), 'The essential role of organizational law', *Yale Law Journal*, **110**, 387–440.

Hart, O.D. and J. Moore (1996), 'The governance of exchanges: members' cooperatives versus outside ownership', *Oxford Review of Economic Policy*, **12**(4), 53–69.

Helmberger, P.G. and S. Hoos (1962), 'Cooperative enterprise and organization theory', *Journal of Farm Economics*, **44**, 275–290.

Hendrikse G.W.J. (1998), 'Screening, competition and the choice of marketing cooperative as an organizational form', *Journal of Agricultural Economics*, **49**(2), 202–217.

Hendrikse, G.W.J. (2005), 'Contingent control rights in agricultural cooperatives', in T. Theurl and E.C. Meijer (eds), *Strategies for Cooperation*, Aachen: Shaker Verlag, pp. 385–394.

Hendrikse, G.W.J. (2007a), 'Two vignettes regarding boards in cooperatives versus corporations: irrelevance and incentives', in K. Karantininis and J. Nilsson (eds), *Vertical Markets and Cooperative Hierarchies*, Dordrecht: Springer, pp. 137–150.

Hendrikse, G.W.J. (2007b), 'On the co-existence of spot and contract markets: the delivery requirement as contract externality', *European Review of Agricultural Economics*, **34**(2), 257–282.

Hendrikse, G.W.J. (2011), 'Pooling, access, and countervailing power in channel governance', *Management Science*, **57**(9), 1692–1702.

Hendrikse G.W.J. and W.J.J. Bijman (2002), 'Ownership structure in agrifood chains: the marketing cooperative', *American Journal of Agricultural Economics*, **84**(1), 104–119.

Hendrikse G.W.J. and A.A.C.J. van Oijen (2004), 'Diversification and corporate governance', in G.W.J. Hendrikse (ed.), *Restructuring Agricultural Cooperatives*, Rotterdam: Erasmus University Rotterdam, pp. 51–64.

Hendrikse, G.W.J. and R. Smit (2007), 'On the evolution of product portfolio coherence of cooperatives versus corporations: an agent-based analysis of the single origin constraint', working paper ERS-2007-055-ORG, Rotterdam School of Management, Erasmus University Rotterdam.

Hendrikse G.W.J. and C.P. Veerman (2001a), 'Marketing co-operatives: an incomplete contracting perspective', *Journal of Agricultural Economics*, **52**(1), 53–64.

Hendrikse G.W.J. and C.P. Veerman (2001b), 'Marketing cooperatives and financial structure: a transaction costs analysis', *Agricultural Economics*, **26**(3), 205–216.

Hirschman, A.O. (1970), *Exit, Voice, and Loyalty, Responses to Decline in Firms, Organizations, and States*, Cambridge, MA: Harvard University Press.

Holmström, B. (1999), 'Future of cooperatives: a corporate perspective', *Finnish Journal of Business Economics*, **4**, 404–417.

Hoyt, A. (1989), 'Cooperatives in other industries', in D. Cobia (ed.), *Cooperatives in Agriculture*, Englewood Cliffs, NJ: Prentice Hall.

International Co-operative Alliance (ICA) (2007), http://www.ica.coop/coop/principles.html, 26 May.

Jensen, M.C. and W.H. Meckling (1979), 'Rights and production functions: an application to labor-managed firms and codetermination', *Journal of Business*, **52**, 469–506.

Klein, B., R.G. Crawford and A. Alchian (1978), 'Vertical integration, appropriable rents and the competitive contracting process', *Journal of Law and Economics*, **21**, 297–326.

Krogt, D. van der, J. Nilsson, V. Høst (2007), 'The impact of cooperatives' risk aversion and equity capital constraints on their inter-firm consolidation and collaboration strategies – with an empirical study of the European dairy industry', *Agribusiness*, **23**(4), 453–472.

Lafontaine, F. and M. Slade (2007), 'Vertical integration and firm boundaries: the evidence', *Journal of Economic Literature*, **45**(3), 629–685.

LeVay, C. (1983), 'Agricultural co-operative theory: a review', *Journal of Agricultural Economics*, **34**(1), 1–44.

Ling, C. (2010), 'What cooperatives do', *Rural Cooperatives*, **77**(2), 4–7.

MacDonald, J.M. and P. Korb (2011), 'Agricultural contracting update: contracts in 2008', US Department of Agriculture, *Economic Information Bulletin* No. 72, February.

Mérel, P.R., T.L. Saitone and R.J. Sexton (2009), 'Cooperatives and quality-differentiated markets: strengths, weaknesses, and modelling approaches', *Journal of Rural Cooperation*, **37**(2), 201–224.

Nilsson, J. (1998), 'The emergence of new organizational models for agricultural cooperatives', *Swedish Journal of Agricultural Sciences*, **28**, 39–47.

Nilsson, J. (2001), 'Organizational principles for co-operative firms', *Scandinavian Journal of Management*, **17**, 329–356.

Nourse, E.G. (1922), 'The economic philosophy of co-operation', *American Economic Review*, **12**(4), 577–597.

Olesen, H.B. (2007), 'The horizon problem reconsidered', in K. Karantininis and J. Nilsson (eds), *Vertical Markets and Cooperative Hierarchies*, Dordrecht: Springer, pp. 245–253.

Patisson, D. (2000), 'Agricultural co-operatives in selected transitional countries', http://www.agricoop.org/resources/resources.htm.

Pencavel, J. (2001), *Worker Participation*, New York: Sage.

Peterson, H.C. and B.L. Anderson (1996), 'Cooperative strategy: theory and practice', *Agribusiness*, **12**(4), 371–383.

Phillips, R. (1953), 'Economic nature of the cooperative association', *Journal of Farm Economics*, **35**, 74–87.

Reardon, T., C.P. Timmer, and J. Berdegue (2004), 'The rapid rise of supermarkets in developing countries: induced organizational, institutional, and technological change in agrifood systems', *Electronic Journal of Agricultural and Development Economics*, **1**(2), 168–183.

Robotka, F. (1947), 'A theory of cooperation', *Journal of Farm Economics*, **29**(1), 94–114.

Royer, J.S. (1999), 'Cooperative organizational strategies: a neo-institutional digest', *Journal of Cooperatives*, **14**, 44–67.

Sah, R.K. and J.E. Stiglitz (1986), 'The architecture of economic systems: hierarchies and polyarchies', *American Economic Review*, **76**(4), 716–727.

Saitone, T.L. and R.J. Sexton (2009), 'Optimal cooperative pooling in a quality-differentiated market', *American Journal of Agricultural Economics*, **91**(5), 1224–1232.

Savage, J.K. (1954), 'Comment on economic nature of the cooperative association', *Journal of Farm Economics*, **36**, 529–534.

Sen, A.K. (1966), 'Labour Allocation in a cooperative enterprise', *Review of Economic Studies*, **33**(4), 361–371.

Sexton, R.J. (1984), 'Perspectives on the development of the economic theory of cooperatives', *Canadian Journal of Agricultural Economics*, **32**, 423–436.

Sexton, R.J. (1986), 'The formation of cooperatives: a game-theoretic approach with implications for cooperative finance, decision making, and stability', *American Journal of Agricultural Economics*, **68**(2), 214–225.

Sexton, R.J (1990), 'Imperfect competition in agricultural markets and the role of cooperatives: a spatial analysis', *American Journal of Agricultural Economics*, **72**(3), 709–720.

Sexton, R.J. and J. Iskow (1988), 'Factors critical to the success or failure of emerging agricultural cooperatives', Giannini Foundation Information Series No. 88-3, Division of Agriculture and Natural Resources, University of California, June.

Sexton, R.J. and J. Iskow (1993), 'What do we know about the economic efficiency of cooperatives: an evaluative survey', *Journal of Agricultural Cooperation*, **8**, 15–27.

Sexton, R.J. and T.A. Sexton (1987), 'Cooperatives as entrants', *Rand Journal of Economics*, **18**(4), 581–595.

Shaffer, J.D. (1987), 'Thinking about farmers' cooperatives, contracts, and economic coordination', US Department of Agriculture, *ACS Service Report* No. 18.

Simon, H.A. and C.P. Bonini (1958), 'The size distribution of business firms', *American Economic Review*, **48**, 607–617.

Søgaard, V. (1994), 'Farmers, cooperatives, new food products', Aarhus Business School.

Spengler, J.J (1950), 'Vertical integration and antitrust policy', *Journal of Political Economy*, **58**, 347–352.

Staatz, J.M. (1984), 'A theoretical perspective on the behavior of farmers' cooperatives', PhD thesis, Michigan State University.

Staatz, J.M. (1987a), 'The structural characteristics of farmer cooperatives and their behavioral consequences', US Department of Agriculture, *ACS Service Report* No. 18.

Staatz, J.M. (1987b), 'Farmer's incentives to take collective action via cooperatives: a transaction cost approach', US Department of Agriculture, *ACS Service Report* No. 18.

Trifon, R. (1961), 'The economics of cooperative ventures: further comments', *Journal of Farm Economics*, **43**, 215–235.

USDA (2002), 'Agricultural cooperatives in the 21st century', *Cooperative Information Report* 60, Rural Business-Cooperative Service.

Vitaliano, P. (1983), 'Cooperative enterprise: an alternative conceptual basis for analyzing a complex institution', *American Journal of Agricultural Economics*, **65**, 1078–1083.

Williamson, O.E. (1988), 'Corporate finance and corporate governance', *Journal of Finance*, **43**(3), 567–591.

Williamson, O.E. (1991), 'Comparative economic organization: the analysis of discrete structural alternatives', *Administrative Science Quarterly*, **36**, 269–296.

Zusman, P. (1982), 'Group choice in an agricultural marketing cooperative', *Canadian Journal of Economics*, **15**(2), 220–234.

Zusman, P. (1992), 'Constitutional selection of collective-choice rules in a cooperative enterprise', *Journal of Economic Behavior and Organization*, **17**, 353–362.

27. The governance of franchising networks
Josef Windsperger

The aim of the chapter is to provide an overview and comparison of major research results regarding the governance structure of franchising networks based on different theoretical perspectives. In addition, I focus on the contribution the property rights theory can make to the franchise literature. Although franchising has been dealt with extensively in the organisational economics and management literature, the relation between residual decision and ownership rights in franchise firms remains largely unexplored. Most studies have focused on the explanation of the incentive structure (fees, royalties and other contractual restrictions) and the proportion of company-owned outlets (e.g. Rubin 1978; Brickley & Dark 1987; Norton 1988; Lafontaine 1992; Dnes 1992, 1996; Lafontaine & Kaufmann 1994; Bradach 1997; Combs & Ketchen 1999; Dahlstrom & Nygaard 1999; Dant & Kaufmann 2003; Lafontaine & Shaw 1999, 2005; Blair & Lafontaine 2005; Bürkle & Posselt 2008; Castrogiovanni et al. 2006a, 2006b; Combs et al. 2009; Barthélemy 2011; Hendrikse & Jiang 2011; Gonzalez-Diaz & Solis-Rodriguez 2012) without investigating the governance structure of the franchise firm as an institutional entity that consists of two interrelated parts: decision rights and ownership rights, the latter of which includes both residual income rights of franchised outlets and company-owned outlets. The franchisor therefore has to set up an efficient network architecture, consisting of contractual relations between the franchisor and the franchisees and hierarchical relations between the headquarters and the managers of the company-owned outlets. Since ownership rights are diluted in franchising network through the division of residual income stream between the franchisor and franchisees, ownership surrogates are used to simulate the incentive effect of undiluted residual income rights in franchise contracting (Windsperger 2003). For instance, the franchisor's diluted residual income rights under franchised outlets may be compensated by using the following contractual provisions as ownership surrogates: tying arrangements, resale price maintenance, lease control, exclusive dealing clauses and buy-back arrangements.

I start with the description of the governance structure of the franchise firm. Next, I present and compare major research results on ownership and contract structure of franchising networks. Finally, I discuss research strategies for the future.

CHARACTERISTICS OF THE GOVERNANCE STRUCTURE OF FRANCHISING NETWORKS

The governance structure of a firm refers to the structure of decision and ownership rights (Baker et al. 2008). In franchising, decision rights refer to the transfer of authority over the use of system-specific assets and local market assets through franchise contracts. Ownership rights refer to outlet ownership (proportion of company-owned outlets, multi-unit versus single-unit ownership) and residual income rights (royalties),

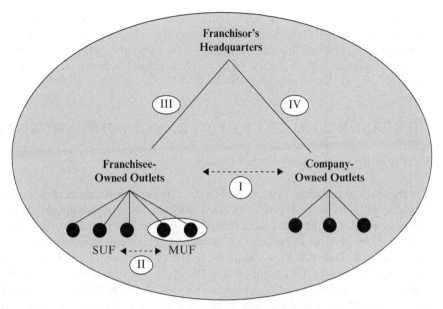

Figure 27.1   Organizational characteristics of franchising networks

as well as ownership surrogates. Ownership surrogates are contract provisions that help to compensate both franchisees and the franchisor for the dilution of residual income rights (Windsperger 2003). Ownership surrogates that increase the franchisees' investment incentives are exclusive territory and exclusive customer clauses, as well as lease and alienation rights; ownership surrogates that increase the franchisor's investment incentives are tying arrangements, resale price maintenance, lease control, exclusive dealing clauses and option rights, such as buy-back arrangement and approval rights and termination rights.

What are the main organisational characteristics of the franchising network (see Figure 27.1)? Most of the franchise systems are characterised by a dual ownership structure as a mix of company-owned and franchised outlets (see I, Figure 27.1). Under a given proportion of company-owned outlets (PCO), the franchisor can assign single- and multi-unit ownership rights to the franchisees (see II, Figure 27.1). In addition, the contract relations between the franchisor and franchisees regulate the allocation of decision rights, residual income rights and ownership surrogates (see III, Figure 27.1). Furthermore, the relations between the franchisor and the managers of company-owned outlets are regulated by employment contracts with performance-based incentives (see IV, Figure 27.1). As a result, when the franchisor sets up a franchise system they have to make the following governance decisions: what is the optimal ownership structure –

that is PCO and ratio between multi-unit franchising (MUF) and single-unit franchising (SUF), and what is the efficient contract structure? The latter refers to the allocation of decision rights, residual income rights and ownership surrogates between the franchisor and franchisees as well as the use of incentive contracts between the franchisor and the managers of company-owned outlets.

OWNERSHIP STRUCTURE OF FRANCHISING NETWORKS

The Proportion of Company-Owned Outlets

The majority of franchise systems have a dual ownership structure, that is, they consist of both company-owned and franchised outlets. The coexistence of franchised and company-owned outlets was examined from different perspectives. Starting from the ownership redirection hypothesis in marketing (Oxenfeldt & Kelly 1968; Dant et al. 1996; Baker & Dant 2008), an increase in the proportion of company-owned outlets was predicted during the organisational life cycle, because scarcity of the franchisor's resources (managerial and financial resources and local market knowledge) declines in later stages of the cycle. According to this resource scarcity view, the mix of franchised and company-owned outlets arises because it allows firms to gain access to scarce financial, managerial and information resources (Caves & Murphy 1976; Norton 1988; Minkler 1992; Baker & Dant 2008).

Since the 1980s, agency-theoretical explanations have been developed and tested (e.g. Brickley & Dark 1987; Brickley et al. 1991; Lafontaine 1992; Affuso 2003; Lafontaine & Shaw 2005; Castrogiovanni et al. 2006a; Combs et al. 2011; Penard et al. 2011). Agency theory offers the following explanation: under low monitoring costs company-owned outlets as low-powered incentive mechanism are more efficient than franchised outlets. When the monitoring costs rise due to local market uncertainty and opportunism, franchised outlets are more efficient, due to their high-powered incentive effects. Therefore, monitoring costs can be reduced through transferring residual income rights to the franchisees, because franchisees as residual claimants have higher incentives to use the specific market knowledge (e.g. Norton 1988; Lafontaine & Slade 2002; Vazquez 2007). Recently, Castrogiovanni et al. (2006b) integrated the resource-based and agency-theoretical perspective in order to explain the proportion of company-owned outlets.

Since the 1980s, transaction cost explanations of the ownership structure of franchise firms have been developed (Williamson 1985; Manolis et al. 1995; Klein 1980, 1995; Bercovitz 1999). The transaction cost explanation is based on the assumption that differences in asset specificity and uncertainty may explain the ownership of the individual outlets. Primarily, the influence of transaction specificity on the tendency toward vertical integration by company-owned outlets was investigated. Due to the hostage effect of the outlet-specific investments, the franchisor's opportunism risk is reduced, resulting in a lower proportion of company-owned outlets (Dnes 2003). On the other hand, franchising as a high-powered governance mechanism may increase free-riding costs (Klein 1995; Dnes & Garoupa 2005). The franchisor will choose franchised outlets when the shirking costs of company ownership exceed the free-riding costs of franchising (Bercovitz 2004).

According to the property rights theory (PRT) (Grossman & Hart 1986; Hart 1995;

Maness 1996; Windsperger & Dant 2006), the contractual mix between franchised and company-owned outlets depends on the distribution of non-contractible (intangible) assets between the franchisor and the franchisees. What are the intangible assets in franchising? Franchisees' intangible assets refer to the outlet-specific know-how in local advertising and customer service, quality control, human resource management and product innovation (Sorenson & Sorensen 2001). The franchisor's intangible assets refer to the system-specific know-how and brand name assets (Klein and Leffler 1981). They include knowledge and skills in site selection, store layout, product development and procurement. The higher the franchisor's fraction of intangible system-specific assets relative to the franchisees' intangible local market assets, the more ownership rights should be transferred to the franchisor and the higher the percentage of company-owned outlets (PCO) should be. Therefore, if the intangible system-specific assets are relatively more important for the creation of the residual surplus (compared to the intangible local market assets), the PCO should be relatively high. Conversely, if the local market assets of the franchisees are relatively more important compared to the system-specific assets, the PCO should be relatively low. Data from the Austrian franchise sector provides evidence that non-contractible system-specific and local market assets influence the contractual mix between company-owned and franchised outlets (Windsperger 2004a).

In addition, the PRT can also offer an explanation for ownership redirection in franchising networks, specifically for a decrease of the PCO during the initial stages of the organizational life cycle. The ownership-redirection hypothesis was first proposed by the resource scarcity view of Oxenfeldt and Kelly (1968). According to this view, during the initial stages of the organizational life cycle, the mix of franchised and company-owned outlets arises, because it allows entrepreneurial-minded franchisors to efficiently and quickly obtain access to scarce financial, managerial and informational resources by partnering with franchisees. This need is expected to decrease as the franchise systems grow and mature, thereby fostering a tendency toward a higher proportion of company-owned outlets during the later stages of the organisational life cycle. Empirical results provide little evidence that franchising follows the pattern described by the resource scarcity theory (Dant et al. 1996; Combs et al. 2004). The PRT provides a solution to the theoretical and empirical problems of the resource scarcity view. According to the Windsperger and Dant (2006), the differentiation between contractible and non-contractible resources is critical for the explanation of asset ownership. As Baker and Hubbard (2004) have argued, increasing the contractibility of assets may explain changes in the ownership structure. Ownership redirection is expected to result from an increase in contractibility of the franchisee's local market assets (local market knowledge and financial assets), and hence from the increase of franchisor's bargaining power during the contract period.

Multi-Unit versus Single-Unit Franchising

When the franchisor sets up a franchise system, they have to determine the proportion of company-owned outlets and decide if the franchisees receive single-unit or multi-unit outlet rights. The growth of franchising networks by opening up franchised outlets can be therefore based upon two ownership strategies: single-unit franchising (SUF) and multi-unit franchising (MUF). Under SUF, a franchisee operates only one outlet, while in the case of MUF arrangement a franchisee operates two or more outlets at multiple geographical locations in the same franchise system (Kaufmann & Dant 1996; Grünhagen & Mittelstaedt 2005).

Previous research primarily focuses on resource scarcity and agency cost perspectives to explain MUF. According to the resource scarcity view, the franchisors do not possess enough financial and managerial resources at the beginning of the franchise life-cycle (e.g., Kaufmann & Dant 1996). Financial resources scarcity of the franchisor may result in higher tendency towards MUF to finance the expansion of the system. MUF offers additional growth opportunities for the franchisor compared to the SUF, because the multi-unit franchisees are less constrained in financing the local investments compared to the single-unit franchisees. Agency cost explanations focus mainly on moral hazard, free-riding and adverse selection problems that can be mitigated by using MUF. The findings of these studies suggest that MUF can address a number of agency problems in a more effective way, compared to SUF (Bercovitz 2004; Garg & Rasheed 2003, 2006; Kalnins & Lafontaine 2004; Kalnins & Mayer 2004; Weaven 2009; Weaven & Frazer 2007; Gillis et al. 2011; Gomez et al. 2010; Chen 2010; Jindal 2011). Geographical contiguity of franchised units is one of the important factors that plays a role in the adoption of MUF. The franchise systems with a higher number of geographically contiguous units are more likely to use a higher proportion of MUF. The franchisor especially prefers MUF to SUF when the firm has a strong brand name, which reduces the risk of free-riding (Bercovitz 2004; Brickley 1999; Kalnins & Lafontaine 2004; Vázquez 2008). Recently, Gomez et al. (2010) show that franchisors use MUF as an incentive mechanism to help reduce the adverse selection and moral hazard risk involved in SUF. In addition, Jindal (2011) argues that franchisors use MUF to reduce the cost of internal hierarchy, hence shifting the burden of monitoring to the multi-unit franchisees, as they are better motivated to reduce monitoring costs than company-employed monitors. Gillis et al. (2011) argue that franchisors use multi-unit franchising as a reward in a tournament to reduce agency problems. The prospect of rewarding franchisees with additional units mitigates adverse selection and monitoring problems.

According to the PRT (Hussain & Windsperger 2010a, 2010b), the franchisor's choice between SUF and MUF depends on the contractibility of assets. Local market knowledge can be more efficiently acquired by SU franchisees when compared to the employees of the mini-chains of MU franchisees, because SU franchisees as residual claimants have higher entrepreneurial capabilities (Bradach 1995, 1998) and are more motivated to exploit the profit opportunities at the local market. Conversely, MUF offers additional growth opportunities for the franchisor when compared to SUF, because MU franchisees are less constrained in financing local investments compared to SU franchisees. Since MU franchisees have easier access to financial resources from external lenders than SU franchisees, they help to alleviate the financial scarcity problem of the franchisor, especially when the local market know-how is tacit and hence less contractible. Data from the German franchise sector (Hussain & Windsperger 2010b) provides some support for these hypotheses.

Comparison of the Different Perspectives

Compared to the PRT, agency theory does not distinguish between performance incentives and ownership incentives, because it implicitly assumes that 'a contract that provides full incentives to an individual is fundamentally the same as selling the firm to this individual' (Hubbard 2008: 349). According to Hart (1995, 2003), agency theory therefore cannot explain the allocation of ownership rights as residual rights of control, due to the complete contracting assumption. Furthermore, in contrast to the agency theory, PRT does not require the assumption of heterogeneous outlet characteristics. Moreover, Whinston (2003) criticised the transaction cost theory developed by Williamson (1979, 1985) and Klein et al. (1978; Klein 1980), because it does not differentiate between the various types of specificity that matter for integration decisions, for instance between contractible and non-contractible specific assets. Similarly, the resource scarcity perspective that focuses on information, managerial and financial resources as determinants of the ownership structure does not differentiate between contractible and non-contractible resources. According to the resource scarcity view, the PCO varies negatively with the franchisor's restraints in financial, managerial and informational resources. The empirical results of Windsperger and Dant (2006) are supportive of the information scarcity hypothesis measured by the impact of the franchisee's innovation assets on the PCO. However, they do not support the managerial scarcity hypothesis measured by the impact of the franchisee's operation assets on the PCO, because these assets show a relatively high degree of contractibility and, as predicted by the PRT, do not influence asset ownership. In addition, the data partially supports the financial scarcity hypothesis. According to the property rights interpretation, financial assets only influence asset ownership if the underlying operating assets (informational and managerial resources) are non-contractible. To summarise, the differences between the resource scarcity interpretation and the property rights results are due to the fact that, contrary to the property rights approach, the resource scarcity view does not differentiate between intangible (non-contractible) and tangible (contractible) resources.

CONTRACT STRUCTURE IN FRANCHISE RELATIONSHIPS

In addition to the ownership structure, the franchisor has to set up an efficient contract design that supports the combined use of the franchisor's system-specific know-how and the franchisee's local market know-how to maximise the residual income stream. Franchise contracting regulates not only the allocation of decision and residual income rights, but also ownership surrogates to mitigate the disincentive effect of diluted residual income rights (Windsperger 2003) (see Figure 27.1).

The Structure of Residual Income Rights

Franchisees have to pay initial fees when entering a franchise system and royalties (based on sales) during the contract period. Agency theory predicts a negative relationship between initial fees and royalties. According to the agency theory (e.g. Mathewson & Winter 1985; Lafontaine & Shaw 1999; Lafontaine & Slade 2002), royalties are chosen as a function of risk and incentives and the initial fees extracts rents left downstream by the royalty rate. With the exception of the work of Vazquez (2005), many of the findings do not support the negative relationship between royalties and initial fees (e.g. Lafontaine 1992; Scott 1995; Lafontaine & Shaw 1999; Brickley 2002).

According to the PRT, initial fees are the remuneration for the brand name assets transferred to the franchisee at the beginning of the contract period (Klein & Leffler 1981). The higher the franchisor's intangible brand name assets at the beginning of the contract period, the higher the rents generated by their system-specific know how, and the higher the initial fees. This reasoning is consistent with the view that the franchisor may recover their sunk investments through the initial fees, as high sunk investments may arise when the system-specific know-how is very important for the success of the franchise system (Dnes 1993). In addition, the more important the franchisor's system-specific investments are relative to the franchisee's intangible local market investments during the contract period, the higher the fraction of residual income created by them, and the higher should be the royalty rate (Rubin 1978). Therefore, PRT predicts a positive relationship between initial fees and royalties (Windsperger 2001). Many of the findings provide support for a positive relationship (Baucus et al. 1993; Kaufmann and Dant 2001; Rao and Srinivasan 1995).

The Structure of Decision Rights

In addition to residual income rights, franchisors use contracts to transfer decision rights across firm boundaries (Baker et al. 2008). For instance, they transfer authority to franchisees to make local advertising and training decisions. Although franchising has been treated extensively in organisational economics, management and marketing in the last two decades, the problem of the allocation of decision rights between the franchisor and franchisees remains largely underexplored (Arrunada et al. 2001, 2005; Azevedo 2009). Arrunada et al. (2001, 2005) and Azevedo (2009) derive hypotheses from an agency-theoretical framework. Arrunada et al. (2001, 2005) investigate the allocation of specific rights in contracts between car manufacturers and their dealers, such as completion rights, monitoring, and enforcement rights. Arrunada et al. (2001) argue that contracts assign more rights to manufactures when the costs of dealer opportunistic behaviour are high and when manufactures have a high reputation. Azevedo (2009) investigates the impact of brand name value and externality on the allocation of authority in franchising networks.

Windsperger (2004b) examines the allocation of decision rights between the franchisor and franchisees from the property rights perspective. According to Jensen and Meckling (1992), two ways for allocating decision rights exist: either knowledge must be transferred to those with the right to make decisions, or decision rights must be transferred to those who have the knowledge. This means that decision rights tend to be centralised in the franchising network when the costs of transferring local knowledge to the franchisor are relatively low. This is the case when the franchisor's portion of intangible assets is relatively high compared to the franchisee's intangible local market assets. On the other hand, residual decision rights have to be delegated to the franchisee when their local market know-how is very specific and consequently knowledge transfer costs are very high. In this case, the bargaining power of the franchisee is relatively strong due to their non-contractible local market assets. The results obtained from the survey of the Austrian and German franchise sector support this property rights view (Windsperger 2004b; Mumdziev & Windsperger 2011). In addition, Mumdziev and Windsperger (2011) disaggregate the structure of decision rights by applying Porter's value chain concept (Porter 1980). Decision rights are disaggregated according to the major value chain activities at the local outlets (such as product decision, procurement decision, advertising decision, price decision, human resources decision, investment decision and accounting system decision).

To conclude, complementary to the agency-theoretical view (e.g. Arrunada et al. 2001; Azevedo 2009), non-contractibility of system-specific and local market assets explains the allocation of decision rights in franchising networks from a property rights perspective. In addition, Mumdziev and Windsperger (2011) extend this view by disaggregating decision rights according to the major value chain activities at the local outlet.

Complementary and Substitutability in Franchise Contracting

The franchise contract regulates the assignment of decision rights, residual income rights and ownership surrogates between the franchisor and franchisees (see Figure 27.1). Although the existing literature investigates interactions between various contract provisions in franchise relations (e.g. Wimmer & Garen 1997; Brickley 1999; Berkovitz 1999; Arrunada et al. 2001; Lafontaine & Raynaud 2002; Vazquez 2008), the PRT focuses on the explanation of the contract design as a bundle of rights consisting of decision rights, residual income rights and ownership surrogates. Windsperger (2003) argues that the contract design is characterised by substitutability between residual income rights and ownership surrogates as well as complementarity between decision and ownership rights (residual income rights and ownership surrogates).

Firstly, the question to answer is which ownership surrogates can be included in franchise contracts and what are their incentive effects. In a survey of 153 German and (83 Austrian) franchise systems, Windsperger (2002, 2003) found that the following contract clauses were used: 61 per cent (68 per cent) non-binding resale price maintenance, 42 per cent (39 per cent) exclusive customer clauses, 36 per cent (49 per cent) tying arrangements, 44 per cent (52 per cent) franchisors' lease control rights, 67 per cent (56 per cent) buy back and approval rights, 79 per cent (63 per cent) exclusive dealing clauses, 72 per cent (73 per cent) alienation rights and 78 per cent (73 per cent) exclusive territory clauses. Due to the division of residual income rights between the franchisor and franchisees, ownership surrogates serve as incentive mechanism to compensate the franchisor and franchisees for the dilution of residual income rights. For instance, the disincentive effect of franchisee's diluted residual income rights due to high royalties may be compensated by territorial restraints, exclusive customer clause or alienation rights. On the other hand, tying arrangements, resale price maintenance, lease control, exclusive dealing clauses and buy-back arrangements, as well as approval and termination rights, may compensate the franchisor's diluted residual income rights. Therefore, ownership surrogates and residual income rights are substitutes. Secondly, based on the complementarity view of organisational design (e.g. Milgrom & Roberts 1990; Brickley et al. 1995; Grandori & Furnari 2008; Van den Steen 2010), decision and ownership rights are complements, because the residual income-generating effect of the allocation of decision rights to the network partners is enhanced by transferring ownership rights (i.e. residual income rights and ownership surrogates) to those that are best able to maximise the residual income stream. Windsperger (2003) provides some evidence for the substitute and complement relationship.

In conclusion, Windsperger (2002, 2003) extended the concept of property rights in contractual relations. Property rights between contract partners (e.g. franchisor and franchisees) refer to decision rights, residual income rights (e.g. royalties) and ownership surrogates. Since these contract provisions are closely intertwined, the franchisor can only set up an efficient contract design by considering the interactions between the different components of the network architecture. Recently, Grandori (2010) proposed such a view of theory building that focuses on the interactions between the different elements of a governance structure.

IMPLICATIONS FOR FUTURE RESEARCH

Finally, this chapter addresses the question about how to apply the property rights view and other theoretical perspectives in organisational economics and strategic management to new research questions on the governance of franchising networks.

Open Issues and Implications for the Economic Organisation of Franchising

The governance structure of the franchise firm

Since the network architecture of a franchise firm consists not only of contractual relations between the franchisor and franchisees but also of hierarchical relations between the headquarters and the manager of company-owned outlets (see Figure 27.1), the franchisor can only set up an efficient governance structure of the franchise firm by considering the interactions between decision and ownership rights. Previous research on the institutional structure of franchising networks has not investigated the governance structure of the franchise firm as an institutional entity consisting of decision and ownership rights. A first attempt is the study of Windsperger and Yurdakul (2007). They show that the governance structure of Austrian franchising firms is characterised by complementarity between decision rights and ownership rights (i.e. PCO and royalties) and substitutability between PCO and royalties. The substitute relationship between royalties and PCO is compatible with the view of Rubin (1978) and Scott (1995). Penard et al. (2003) provide evidence of a positive relationship. Research is needed to examine the relationship between ownership and decision rights in franchising networks by using a larger sample of franchise firms from different countries.

Relationship between multi-unit franchising and proportion of company-owned outlets

According to Fama and Jensen (1983), the decision structure of the firm consists of decision management and decision control rights. Whenever the decision management rights are divided between partners, due to their specific knowledge, control rights are installed to counter agency problems associated with the dilution of decision rights. For instance, the franchisor's decision rights are more diluted under MUF than under SUF.

Under MUF, the franchisees have more decision rights regarding monitoring of local outlets, local human resource management and knowledge transfer between headquarters and local outlets (Hussain & Windsperger 2010a). In this case, the franchisor may compensate the dilution of decision rights under MUF by an increase of control through a higher percentage of company-owned outlets (PCO). As a result, future research has to investigate the relationship between MUF and PCO.

Governance modes of international franchise firms

Franchise firms that enter foreign markets use non-equity and equity relations as governance modes, such as master franchising, area development franchising and joint venture franchising (Konigsberg 2008; Mumdziev 2011). Under master franchising, the sub-franchisees have residual income rights and decision rights mainly over operational activities, but they have no outlet ownership rights. On the other hand, regarding area development and joint-venture franchising, the local partners have both outlet ownership and decision rights and therefore a higher level of control over the local outlets. The application of PRT may offer new explanations of the relationship between ownership and control patterns in international franchise firms (Dant et al. 2011).

Decision structure and knowledge transfer mechanisms

In a recent study in the Austrian franchise sector, Windsperger and Gorovaia (2011) found that knowledge attributes (degree of tacitness) influence franchisor's choice of knowledge transfer mechanisms. High tacitness of system-specific knowledge requires more knowledge transfer mechanisms with high information richness (such as meetings, visits, workshops and training), and low tacitness requires more knowledge transfer mechanisms with low information richness (such as data bases, intranet, manuals). Since tacitness results in low contractibility of knowledge, the choice of knowledge transfer mechanisms is closely related to the question of allocation of decision rights between the franchisor and franchisees. For instance, if the decision rights are centralised under non-contractible system-specific knowledge, the franchisor has to use more face-to-face knowledge transfer mechanisms to facilitate the transfer of system-specific knowledge to the network partners. Future research should examine the relationship between the choice of knowledge transfer mechanisms and the allocation of decision rights in franchising networks.

Firm strategy and governance structure

Few studies focus on strategy issues of franchise firms (Muris et al. 1992; Michael 2000; Yin & Zajac 2004; Stanworth et al. 2004; Garg et al. 2005; Barthélemy 2008; Gillis & Combs 2009; Bordonaba-Juste et al. 2010). One very important and underexplored research question concerns the relationship between strategy and governance of the franchise firms. For instance, what is the impact of standardisation versus adaptation (Kaufmann & Eroglu 1999) on delegation and ownership structure? Standardisation implies the existence of more contractible system-specific know-how, which enables the franchisor to transfer more decision rights to local partners without high knowledge transfer and monitoring costs. Research is needed to explain the relationship between strategy and governance of franchise firms.

Relationship between uncertainty and incentives

According to the standard prediction of agency theory, royalties (as performance-based incentives) and risk should be positively related. Empirical results do not confirm this relationship (e.g. Lafontaine & Slade 2002, 2007; Prendergast 2002). In addition, recent theoretical results in organisational economics also question the risk–incentive trade-off (Rantakiri 2008; Shi 2011). How can the PRT offer a solution to this problem in the context of franchising? Based on James (2000), the relationship between risk and incentives in contract relations depends on the underlying governance mechanism (i.e. internal governance versus market or network governance). Under an employment contract between headquarters and outlet managers with more contractible assets, it is more likely that the relationship between risk and performance-based incentives is negative. On the other hand, under a franchise contract with more non-contractible assets of franchisees, it is more likely that the relationship between risk and incentives (royalties) is positive (negative). Therefore, it is expected that the governance mechanism (internal hierarchy versus network relationships) will influence the relationship between risk and incentives in contract relations. Future research has to address this question in the context of franchise contracting.

Relational and formal governance in franchising networks

Transaction costs, property rights and agency models can be enriched by research results from the relational governance perspective. According to the relational view of governance (e.g. Gulati 1995; Zaheer & Venkatraman 1995; Dyer 1997; Dyer & Singh 1998; Gulati & Nickerson 2008), trust as an informal or relational governance mechanism may influence franchisor's use of formal governance mechanisms, such as decision and ownership rights as well as knowledge transfer mechanisms. Trust reduces relational risk and increases information sharing, thereby enabling the franchisor to reduce formal control over operational decisions. For instance, considering trust in the transaction cost theory could supplement the explanation offered by the transaction cost theory on the allocation of decision rights in franchising networks (Mumdziev & Windsperger forthcoming; López-Fernández & López-Bayón 2011). In addition, trust influences the franchisor's choice of knowledge transfer mechanism (Gorovaia & Windsperger 2011). As a result, future research should examine the impact of trust on the use of formal governance mechanisms in franchise networks.

Implications for the use of empirical methods

Investigating complementary and substitute relations in franchising networks is not only a challenge for theory building but especially for empirical testing (Milgrom and Roberts 1990; Fiss 2007; Ennen and Richter 2010). Depending on the number of organisation design variables and their interactions, different methods must be used to examine complementarities and substitutabilities in intra- and inter-organisational relations (e.g. Arora & Gambardella 1990; Ichniowski et al. 1997; Poppo & Zenger 2002; Cassiman & Veugelers 2006). Therefore, the question for future research is how to apply adequate empirical methods to examine the network architecture of the franchise firm.

The Relations between Organisational Economics and Resource-based Perspectives

Resource scarcity versus resource-based view

The resource scarcity view attempts to explain the use of franchising as a means to overcome the scarcity of resources, that is, financial, managerial and informational resources. For instance, size and age of the franchise system are indicators of resource scarcity. The larger the size and the older the franchise system, the easier and less costly is the access to resources. This reasoning is compatible with the market failure explanation due to high transaction costs. From a methodological perspective, based on the 'structuralist view' of theories (Stegmueller 1979), the resource scarcity approach must be criticised, because hypotheses are formulated without defining the 'core' of the theory from which they are derived.

The resource-based view argues that knowledge sharing and creation through firm-specific resources and capabilities result in competitive advantage (or strategic rents) (e.g. Barney 1991; Madhok 1996; Teece et al. 1997). When applied to governance mode decisions, the resource-based view states that governance modes create strategic rents by efficiently sharing and creating knowledge. For instance, contrary to the resource scarcity view, empirical studies show that size and age may be more valid indicators of firm-specific resources and organisational capabilities to create a competitive advantage (e.g. Combs et al. 2004; Weaven and Frazer 2007). We can therefore conclude that the resource scarcity view and the resource-based view are not interrelated, because they address different research questions.

In franchising research, the resource-based theory is seldom applied to explain governance mechanisms (e.g. Thompson 1994). Therefore, future research has to focus on resource-based explanations of governance modes (Combs et al. 2004; Gillis & Combs 2009). For instance, one important application is the explanation of the plural network form (Bradach 1997; Cliquet 2000; Cliquet & Penard 2012). Plural franchise networks have higher organisational capabilities than pure forms, due to the synergy effects between company-owned and franchised outlets. Complementarities between higher exploitation capabilities of company-owned outlets and higher exploration capabilities of franchised outlets increase the governance capabilities and hence the residual income stream of the network (Sirmon et al. forthcoming). Recently, Hendrikse and Jiang (2011) explained these positive externalities in franchising networks with an incomplete contracting model.

Relationship between organisational economics theories and resource-based theory

Organisational economics theories refer to the explanations of governance modes using agency theory, transaction cost theory and PRT. Transaction cost and agency theory examine the impact of environmental and behavioural uncertainty and performance measurement difficulties, as well as asset specificity on the choice of governance modes in franchising. Consequently, the governance modes aim at reducing agency and transaction costs by setting up control and incentive mechanisms. For instance, if the risk of free-riding in the network is high, the franchisor increases control over decision making in the network. PRT focuses on analysing the residual income effect of the governance structure of franchise firms by assigning ownership and decision rights to the agents according to the distribution of intangible (non-contractible) assets. Therefore, governance modes aim at increasing the residual income by assigning decision and ownership rights to the agents with intangible assets. For instance, if the franchisees' local market know-how is more intangible relative to the franchisor's system-specific know-how, it generates a higher proportion of residual income of the network; hence the franchisor delegates more decision rights to the franchisees.

On the other hand, the resource-based view is a strategic theory of the firm (Rumelt 1984). It focuses on the explanation of governance modes as knowledge creation and sharing mechanisms to generate strategic rents by increasing the governance capabilities (Madhok & Tallman 1998; Mayer & Salomon 2006). Governance forms aims therefore at increasing competitive advantage by creating and exploiting firm-specific resources and capabilities. For instance, MUF may increase a franchise firm's organisational capabilities and hence its competitive advantage compared to an SUF-system (Hussain & Windsperger 2010a, 2012).

Consequently, organisational economics theories and the resource-based view of governance focus on fundamentally different research questions: On the one hand, which governance modes reduce transaction and agency costs (agency and transaction cost theory) or increase residual income (PRT), due to uncertainty/information asymmetry or non-contractibility of assets? On the other hand, which governance modes increase competitive advantage (strategic rents) through knowledge sharing and creation? In conclusion, organisational economic theories focus on the choice of governance modes as coordination and incentive mechanisms under given firm-specific resources and capabilities (Barney & Hesterley 1996), while resource-based theories focus on the choice of governance mechanisms to create firm-specific resources and organisational capabilities. Future research on governance structure issues of the franchise firm has to consider these fundamental differences when applying organisational economics and resource-based views.

CONCLUSION

Researchers from different fields in economics and management have examined the governance structure of franchising networks in the last three decades. In this chapter, I have attempted to make three contributions. Firstly, I provide an overview of major research results on the governance structure of franchise firms from different theoretical perspectives. Secondly, I compare the research results from agency theory, transaction cost theory and resource scarcity view with the results based on PRT. Thirdly, I discuss research strategies for the future, specifically new directions for the application of property rights theory, resource-based theory and the relational governance view to explain governance issues in franchising. In addition, I compare the different theoretical perspectives used in franchising and show that organisational economics applications address fundamentally different research questions compared to resource-based applications.

REFERENCES

Affuso, L. (2003), 'An empirical study on contractual heterogenity within the firm: the "vertical integration-franchise contracts" mix', *Applied Economics*, **34**, 931–944.

Arora, A. and A. Gambardella (1990), 'Complementarity and external linkage: the strategies of the large firms in biotechnology', *Journal of Industrial Economics*, **38**, 361–379.

Arrunada, B., L. Garicano and L. Vazquez (2001), 'Contractual allocation of decision rights and incentives: the case of automobile distribution', *Journal of Law, Economics, and Organization*, **17**, 256–283.

Arrunada, B., L. Garicano and L. Vazquez (2005), 'Completing contracts ex post: how car manufacturers manage car dealers', *Review of Law and Economics*, **1**, 19–173.

Azevedo, P.F. (2009), 'Allocation of authority in franchise chains', *International Studies of Management and Organization*, **39**, 31–42.

Baker, B.L. and R.P. Dant (2008), 'Stable plural forms in franchise systems: an examination of the evolution of ownership redirection research', in G. Hendrikse, M. Tuunanen, J. Windsperger and G. Cliquet (eds), *Strategy and Governance of Networks: Cooperatives, Franchising, and Strategic Alliances*, Heidelberg: Springer Verlag, pp.87–112.

Baker, G., R. Gibbons and K.J. Murphy (2008), 'Strategic alliances: bridges between "islands of conscious power"', *Journal of the Japanese and International Economies*, **22**, 146–163.

Baker, G.P. and T.N. Hubbard (2004), 'Contractibility and asset ownership: on-board computers and governance in US trucking', *Quarterly Journal of Economics*, **119**, 1443–1479.

Barney, J. (1991), 'Firm resources and sustained competitive advantage', *Journal of Management*, **17**, 99–120.

Barney, J. and W. Hesterly (1996), 'Organizational economics: understanding the relationship between organizations and economic analysis', in S.R. Clegg, C. Hardy and W.R. Nord (eds), *Handbook of Organization Studies*, London: Oxford University Press, pp.115–147.

Barthélemy, J. (2008), 'Opportunism, knowledge, and the performance of franchise chains', *Strategic Management Journal*, **29**, 1451–1463.

Barthélemy, J. (2011), 'Agency and institutional influences on franchising', *Journal of Business Venturing*, **26**, 93–103.

Baucus, D.A., M.S. Baucus and S.E. Human (1993), 'Choosing a franchise: how base fees and royalties relate to the value of the franchise', *Journal of Business Management*, **31**, 91–104.

Bercovitz, J.E.L. (1999), 'An analysis of the contract provisions in business-format franchise agreements', in J. Stanworth and D. Purdy (eds), *Proceedings of the 13th Conference of the International Society of Franchising*.

Bercovitz, J.E.L. (2004), 'The organizational choice decision in business format franchising: an empirical test', in J. Windsperger, G. Cliquet, G. Hendrikse and M. Tuunanen (eds), *Economics and Management of Franchising Networks*, Heidelberg: Springer, pp.38–65.

Blair, R. and F. Lafontaine (2005), *The Economics of Franchising*, Cambridge: Cambridge University Press.

Bordonaba-Juste, V., L. Lucia-Palaciosa and Y. Polo-Redondo (2010), 'Influence of franchisors' competitive strategies on network size: the impact of entry timing decision', *Journal of Marketing Channels*, **17**, 33–49.

Bradach, J.L. (1995), 'Chains within chains: the role of multi-unit franchisees', *Journal of Marketing Channels*, **4**, 65–81.

Bradach, J.L. (1997), 'Using the plural form in the management of restaurant chains', *Administrative Science Quarterly*, **42**, 276–303.

Bradach, J.L. (1998), *Franchise Organizations*, Boston, MA: Harvard Business School Press.

Brickley, J.A. (1999), 'Incentive conflicts and contracting: evidence from franchising', *Journal of Law and Economics*, **42**, 645–774.

Brickley, J.A. (2002), 'Royalty rates and upfront fees in share contracts: evidence from franchising', *Journal of Law Economics and Organization*, **18**, 511–535.

Brickley, J.A. and F.H. Dark (1987), 'The choice of organizational form: the case of franchising', *Journal of Financial Economics*, **18**, 401–420.

Brickley, J., F. Dark and M. Weisbach (1991), 'An agency perspective on franchising', *Financial Management*, **20**, 27–35.

Brickley, J.A., C.W. Smith and J.L. Zimmerman (1995), 'The economics of organizational architecture', *Journal of Applied Corporate Finance*, **8**, 19–31.

Bürkle, T. and T. Posselt (2008), 'Franchising as a plural system: a risk-based explanation', *Journal of Retailing*, **84**, 39–47.

Cassiman, B. and R. Veugelers (2006), 'In search of complementarity in innovation strategy: internal R&D and external knowledge acquisition', *Management Science*, **52**, 68–82.

Castrogiovanni, G.J., J.G. Combs and R.T. Justis (2006a), 'Resource scarcity and agency theory predictions concerning the continued use of franchising in multi-outlet networks', *Journal of Small Business Management*, **44**, 27–44.

Castrogiovanni, G.J., J.G. Combs and R.T. Justis (2006b), 'Shifting imperatives: an integrative resource scarcity and agency reasons for franchising', *Entrepreneurship Theory and Practice*, January, 23–40.

Caves, R.E. and W.F. Murphy (1976), 'Franchising: firms, markets, and intangible assets', *Southern Economic Journal*, **42**, 572–586.

Chen, H.-H. (2010), 'The explanations of agency theory on international multi-unit franchising in the Taiwanese marketplace', *International Journal of Organizational Innovation*, **3**, 53–71.

Cliquet, G. (2000), 'Plural forms in store networks: a model for store network evolution', *International Review of Retail Distribution and Consumer Research*, **10**, 369–387.

Cliquet, G. and T. Penard (2012), 'Plural form franchise networks: a test of Bradach's model', *Journal of Retailing and Consumer Services*, **19**, 159–167.

Combs, J.G. and D.J. Ketchen (1999), 'Can capital scarcity help agency theory explain franchising: revisiting the capital scarcity hypothesis', *Academy of Management Journal*, **42**, 196–207.

Combs, J.G., D.J. Ketchen, C.L. Shook and J.C. Short (2011), 'Antecedents and consequences of franchising: past accomplishments and future challenges', *Journal of Management*, **37**, 99–126.

Combs, J.G., S.C. Michael and G.J. Castrogiovanni (2004), 'Franchising: a review and avenues to greater theoretical diversity', *Journal of Management*, **30**, 907–931.

Combs, J.G., S.C. Michael and G.J. Castrogiovanni (2009), 'Institutional influence on the choice of organizational form: the case of franchising', *Journal of Management*, **35**, 1268–1290.

Dahlstrom, R. and A. Nygaard (1999), 'Ownership decisions in plural contractual systems', *European Journal of Marketing*, **33**, 59–87.

Dant, R.P. and P.J. Kaufmann (2003), 'Structural and strategic dynamics in franchising', *Journal of Retailing*, **79**, 63–75.

Dant, R.P., M. Grünhagen and J. Windsperger (2011), 'Franchising research frontiers for the twenty-first century', *Journal of Retailing*, **87**, 253–268.

Dant, R.P., A.K. Paswan and P.J. Kaufmann (1996), 'What we know about ownership redirection in franchising: a meta-analysis', *Journal of Retailing*, **72**, 429–445.

Dnes, A.W. (1992), '"Unfair" contractual practices and hostages in franchise contracts', *Journal of Institutional and Theoretical Economics*, **148**, 484–504.

Dnes, A.W. (1993), 'A case study analysis of franchise contracts', *Journal of Legal Studies*, **22**, 367–393.

Dnes, A.W. (1996), 'The economics of franchise contracts', *Journal of Institutional and Theoretical Economics*, **152**, 297–324.

Dnes, A. (2003), 'Hostages, marginal deterrence and franchise contracts', *Journal of Corporate Finance*, **9**, 317–331.

Dnes, A.W. and N. Garoupa (2005), 'Externality and organizational choice in franchising', *Journal of Economics and Business*, **57**, 139–149.

Dyer, J.H. (1997), 'Effective interim collaboration: how firms minimize transaction costs and maximize transaction value', *Strategic Management Journal*, **18**(7), 535–556.

Dyer, J.H. and H. Singh (1998), 'The relational view: cooperative strategy and sources of interorganizational competitive advantage', *Academy of Management Review*, **23**, 660–679.

Ennen, E. and A. Richter (2010), 'The whole is more than the sum of its parts – or is it? A review of the empirical literature on complementarities in organizations', *Journal of Management*, **36**, 207–233.

Fama, E.F. and M.C. Jensen (1983), 'Agency problems and residual claims', *Journal of Law and Economics*, **26**, 327–348.

Fiss, P.C. (2007), 'A set-theoretical approach to organizational configuration', *Academy of Management Review*, **32**, 1180–1198.

Garg, V. and A. Rasheed (2003), 'International multi-unit franchising: an agency-theoretic explanation', *International Business Review*, **12**, 329–348.

Garg, V. and A. Rasheed (2006), 'An explanation of international franchisor' preference for multi-unit franchising', *International Journal Entrepreneurship*, **10**(1), 1–20.

Garg, V.K., A.A. Raheed and R.L. Priem (2005), 'Explaining franchisors' choices of organization forms within franchise systems', *Strategic Organization*, **3**, 185–217.

Gillis, W.E. and J.G. Combs (2009), 'Franchisor strategy and firm performance: making the most of strategic resource investments', *Business Horizons*, **52**, 553–561.

Gillis, W., E. McEwan, T. Crook and S. Michael (2011), 'Using tournaments to reduce agency problems: the case of franchising', *Entrepreneurship Theory and Practice*, **35**(3), 427–444.

Gomez, R., I. Gonzalez and L.Vazquez (2010), 'Multi-unit versus single-unit franchising: assessing why franchisors use different ownership strategies', *Service Industries Journal*, **30**(3), 463–476.

Gonzalez-Diaz, M. and V. Solis-Rodriguez (2012), 'Why do entrepreneurs use franchising as a financial tool? An agency explanation', *Journal of Business Venturing*, **27**, 325–341.

Gorovaia, N. and J. Windsperger (2011), 'Determinants of the knowledge-transfer strategy in franchising: integrating knowledge-based and relational governance perspectives', *Service Industries Journal*, 11/2011, DOI: 10/1080/02642069.2011.632003.

Grandori, A. (2010), 'Asset commitment, constitutional governance and the nature of the firm', *Journal of Institutional Economics*, **6**, 351–375.

Grandori, A. and S. Furnari (2008), 'A chemistry of organization: combinatory analysis and design', *Organization Studies*, **29**, 459–485.

Grossman, S.J. and O.D. Hart (1986), 'The costs and benefits of ownership: a theory of vertical and lateral integration', *Journal of Political Economy*, **94**, 691–716.

Grünhagen, M. and R.A. Mittelstaedt (2005), 'Entrepreneurs or investors: do multi-unit franchisees have different philosophical orientations', *Journal of Small Business Management*, **43**, 207–225.

Gulati, R. (1995), 'Does familiarity breed trust? The implications of repeated ties for contractual choice in alliances', *Academy of Management Journal*, **38**, 85–112.

Gulati, R. and J.A. Nickerson (2008), 'Interorganizational trust, governance choice and exchange performance', *Organization Science*, **19**(5), 688–708.

Hart, O. (1995), *Firms, Contracts, and Financial Structure*, Oxford: Clarendon Press.

Hart, O. (2003), 'Incomplete contracts and public ownership: remarks and application to public–private partnerships', *Economic Journal*, **113**, C69–C76.

Hendrikse, G. and T. Jiang (2011), 'An incomplete contracting model of dual distribution in franchising', *Journal of Retailing*, **87**(3), 332–344.

Hubbard, T.N. (2008), 'Viewpoint: empirical research on firm boundaries', *Canadian Journal of Economics*, **41**, 341–359.

Hussain, D. and J. Windsperger (2010a), 'Multi-unit ownership strategy in franchising: development of an integrative model', *Journal of Marketing Channels*, **17**, 3–31.

Hussain, D. and J. Windsperger (2010b), 'A property rights view of multi-unit franchising', *European Journal of Law and Economics* (forthcoming).

Hussain, D. and J. Windsperger (2012), 'Multi-unit franchising: organizational capability and transaction cost explanations', Proceedings of the 26th ISOF Conference, Fort Lauderdale, Florida.

Ichniowski, C., K. Shaw and G. Prennushi (1997), 'The effects of human resource management practices on productivity: a study of steel finishing lines', *American Economic Review*, **87**, 291–313.

James, H.S. (2000), 'Separating Contract from Governance', *Managerial and Decision Economics*, **21**, 47–61.

Jensen, M.C. and W.H. Meckling (1992), 'Specific and general knowledge and organizational structure', in L. Werin and H. Wijkander (eds), *Contract Economics*, Oxford, pp. 251–274.

Jindal, R. (2011), 'Reducing the size of internal hierarchy: the case of multi-unit franchising', *Journal of Retailing*, **87**(4), 549–562.

Kalnins, A. and F. Lafontaine (2004), 'Multi-unit ownership in franchising: evidence from the fast-food industry in Texas', *RAND Journal of Economics*, **35**(4), 747–761.

Kalnins, A. and K. Mayer (2004), 'Franchising, ownership, and experience: a study of pizza restaurant survival', *Management Science*, **50**(12), 1716–1728.

Kaufmann, P.J. and R.P. Dant (1996), 'Multi-unit franchising: growth and management issues', *Journal of Business Venturing*, **11**, 343–358.

Kaufmann, P.J. and R.P. Dant (2001), 'The pricing of franchise rights', *Journal of Retailing*, **77**, 537–545.

Kaufmann, P.J. and S. Eroglu (1999), 'Standardization and adaptation in business format franchising', *Journal of Business Venturing*, **14**, 69–85.

Klein, B. (1980), 'Transaction cost determinants of "unfair" contractual arrangements', *American Economic Review*, **70**, 356–362.

Klein, B. (1995), 'The economics of franchise contracts', *Journal of Corporate Finance*, **2**, 9–38.

Klein, B., G. Crawford and A.A. Alchian (1978), 'Vertical integration, appropriable rents, and the competitive contracting process', *Journal of Law and Economics*, **21**, 297–326.

Klein, B. and K.B. Leffler (1981), 'The role of market forces in assuring contractual performance', *Journal of Political Economy*, **89**, 615–641.

Konigsberg, A.S. (2008), *International Franchising*, New York: Juris Publishing.

Lafontaine, F. (1992), 'Agency theory and franchising: some empirical results', *RAND Journal of Economics*, **23**, 263–283.

Lafontaine, F. and P. Kaufmann (1994), 'The evolution of ownership patterns in franchise systems', *Journal of Retailing*, **70**, 97–113.

Lafontaine, F. and E. Raynaud (2002), 'Residual claims and self enforcement as incentive mechanisms in franchise contracts: substitutes or complements', in E. Brousseau and J.M. Glachant (eds), *The Economics of Contract in Prospect and Retrospect*, Cambridge: Cambridge University Press, pp. 315–336.

Lafontaine, F. and K.L. Shaw (1999), 'The dynamics of franchise contracting: evidence from franchising', *RAND Journal of Economics*, **36**, 131–150.

Lafontaine, F. and K.L. Shaw (2005), 'Targeting managerial control: evidence from franchising', *RAND Journal of Economics*, **36**, 131–150.

Lafontaine, F. and M.E. Slade (2002), 'Incentive contracting and the franchise decision', in K. Chatterjee and W. Samuelson (eds), *Game Theory and Business Applications*, Dordrecht: Kluwer Academic Press, pp. 133–188.

Lafontaine, F. and M. Slade (2007), 'Vertical integration and firm boundaries: the evidence', *Journal of Economic Literature*, **45**, 629–685.

López-Fernández, B. and S. López-Baýon (2011), 'Delegation and autonomy in franchising', in M. Tuunanen, J. Windsperger, G. Clique and G. Hendrikse (eds.), *New Developments in the Theory of Networks: Franchising, Alliances and Cooperatives*, Heidelberg: Springer Verlag, pp. 31–44.

Madhok, A. (1996), 'The organization of economic activity: transaction costs, firm capabilities, and the nature of governance', *Organization Science*, **7**, 577–590.

Madhok, A. and S. Tallman (1998), 'Resources, transactions and rents: managing value through interfirm collaborative relationships', *Organization Science*, **9**, 326–339.

Maness, R. (1996), 'Incomplete contracts and the choice between vertical integration and franchising', *Journal of Economic Behavior and Organization*, **31**, 101–115.

March, J.G. (1991), 'Exploration and exploitation', *Organization Science*, **2**, 71–87.

Manolis, C., R. Dahlstrom and A. Nygaard (1995), 'A preliminary investigation of ownership conversions in franchised distribution systems', *Journal of Applied Business Research*, **11**(2), 1–8.

Mathewson, F. and R. Winter (1985), 'The economics of franchise contracts', *Journal of Law and Economics*, **28**, 503–526.

Mayer, K.J. and R.M. Salomon (2006), 'Capabilities, contractual hazards, and governance: integrating resource-based and transaction cost perspective', *Academy of Management Journal*, **49**, 942–959.

Michael, S. (2000), 'Investments to create bargaining power: the case of franchising', *Strategic Management Journal*, **21**, 497–515.

Milgrom, P. and J. Roberts (1990), 'The economics of modern manufacturing: technology, strategy and organization', *American Economic Review*, **80**, 511–528.

Milgrom, P. and J. Roberts (1995), 'Complementarities and fit: strategy, structure and organizational change in manufacturing', *Journal of Accounting and Economics*, **19**, 179–208.

Minkler, A.P. (1992), 'Why firms franchise? A search cost theory', *Journal of Institutional and Theoretical Economics*, **148**, 240–259.

Mumdziev, N. (2011), 'Allocation of decision rights in international franchise firms: the case of master and direct franchising', in M. Tuunanen, J. Windsperger, G. Cliquet, G. Hendrikse (eds), *New Developments in the Theory of Networks: Franchising, Alliances and Cooperatives*, Heidelberg: Springer Verlag, pp. 45–58.

Mumdziev, N. and J. Windsperger (2011), 'The structure of decision rights in franchising networks: a property rights perspective', *Entrepreneurship Theory and Practice*, **35**, 449–465.

Mumdziev, N. and J. Windsperger (forthcoming), 'An extended transaction cost model of decision rights allocation in franchising: the moderating role of trust', *Managerial and Decision Economics*.

Muris, T.J., D.T. Scheffman and T. Spiller (1992), 'Strategy and transaction costs: the organization of distribution in the carbonated soft drink industry', *Journal of Economics and Management Strategy*, **1**, 83–128.

Norton, S.W. (1988), 'An empirical look at franchising as an organizational form', *Journal of Business*, **61**, 197–219.

Oxenfeldt, A.R. and A.O. Kelly (1968), 'Will successful franchise systems ultimately become wholly owned chains?' *Journal of Retailing*, **44**, 69–84.

Pénard, T., E. Raynaud and S. Saussier (2003), 'Dual distribution and royalties in franchised chains', *Journal of Marketing Channels*, **10**, 5–31.

Pénard, T., E. Raynaud and S. Saussier (2011), 'Monitoring policy and organizational forms in franchised chains', *International Journal of the Economics of Business*, **18**, 399–417.

Poppo, L. and T. Zenger (2002), 'Do formal contracts and relational governance function as substitutes or complements?' *Strategic Management Journal*, **23**, 707–725.

Porter, M.E. (1980), *Competitive Strategy*, New York: Free Press.

Prendergast, C. (2002), 'Uncertainty and incentives', *Journal of Labor Economics*, **20**, 115–137.

Rao, R.C. and S. Srinivason (1995), 'Why are royalty rates higher in service-type franchises?' *Journal of Economics & Management Strategy*, **4**, 7–31.

Rubin, P. (1978), 'The theory of the firm and the structure of the franchise contract', *Journal of Law and Economics*, **21**, 223–233.

Rantakiri, H. (2008), 'On the role of uncertainty in the risk–incentives trade-off', *The B.E. Journal of Theoretical Economics*, April.

Rumelt, R.P. (1984), 'Towards a strategic theory of the firm', in R. Lamb (ed.), *Competitive Strategy Management*, Englewood Cliffs, NJ: Prentice-Hall, pp. 556–570.

Scott, F.A. (1995), 'Franchising vs. company ownership as a decision variable of the firm', *Review of Industrial Organization*, **10**, 69–81.

Shi, L. (2011), 'Respondable risk and incentives for CEOs: the role of information-collection and decision-making', *Journal of Corporate Finance*, **17**, 189–205.

Sirmon, D.G., M.A. Hitt, R.D. Ireland and B.A. Gilbert (forthcoming), 'Resource orchestration to create competitive advantage: breath, depth, and life cycle effects', *Journal of Management*.

Sorenson, O. and J.B. Sorensen (2001), 'Finding the right mix: organizational learning, plural forms and franchise performance', *Strategic Management Journal*, **22**, 713–724.

Stanworth, J., C. Stanworth, A. Watson, D. Purdy and S. Heleas (2004), 'Franchising as a small business growth strategy: a resource-based view of organisational development', *International Small Business Journal*, **22**, 539–559.

Stegmueller, W. (1979), *The Structuralist View of Theories*, Berlin: Springer Verlag.

Teece, D.J., G. Pisano and A. Shuen (1997), 'Dynamic capabilities and strategic management', *Strategic Management Journal*, **18**, 509–533.

Thompson, S.R. (1994), 'The franchise life cycle and the Penrose Effect', *Journal of Economic Behavior and Organization*, **24**, 207–218.

Van den Steen, E. (2010), 'Disagreement and the allocation of control', *Journal of Law, Economics and Organization*, **26**, 385–426.

Vázquez, L. (2005), 'Up-front franchise fees and ongoing variable payments as substitutes: an agency perspective', *Review of Industrial Organization*, **26**, 445–460.

Vazquez, L. (2007), 'Proportion of franchised outlets and franchise system performance', *Service Industries Journal*, **27**, 907–921.

Vázquez, L. (2008), 'Complementarities between franchise contract duration and multi-unit propensity in franchise systems', *Service Industries Journal*, **28**, 1093–1105.

Weaven, S. (2009), 'An empirical examination of the reasons governing multiple unit franchise adoption in Australia', *Asian Journal of Marketing*, **3**(2), 52–64.

Weaven, S. and L. Frazer (2007), 'Expansion through multiple unit franchising: Australian franchisors reveal their motivations'. *International Small Business Journal*, **25**(2), 173–205.

Whinston, M.D. (2003), 'On the transaction cost determinants of vertical integration', *Journal of Law, Economics and Organization*, **19**, 1–23.

Williamson, O.E. (1979), 'Transaction costs economics: the governance of contractual relations', *Journal of Law and Economics*, **22**, 233–262.

Williamson, O.E. (1985), *The Economic Institutions of Capitalism*, New York: Free Press.

Wimmer, B.S. and J.E. Garen (1997), 'Moral hazard, asset specificity, implicit bonding and compensation: the case of franchising', *Economic Inquiry*, **35**, 544–554.

Windsperger, J. (2001), 'The fee structure in franchising: a property rights view', *Economics Letters*, **73**, 219–226.

Windsperger, J. (2002), 'The structure of ownership rights in franchising: an incomplete contracting view', *European Journal of Law and Economics*, **13**, 129–142.

Windsperger, J. (2003), 'Complementarities and substitutabilities in franchise contracting: some results from the German franchise sector', *Journal of Management and Governance*, **7**, 291–313.

Windsperger, J. (2004a), 'The dual network structure of franchising firms: property rights, resource scarcity and transaction cost explanations', in J. Windsperger, G. Cliquet, G. Hendrikse and M. Tuunanen (eds), *Economics and Management of Franchising Networks*, Heidelberg: Springer Verlag, pp. 69–88.

Windsperger, J. (2004b), 'Centralization of franchising networks: evidence from the Austrian franchise sector', *Journal of Business Research*, **57**, 1361–1369.

Windsperger, J. and R.P. Dant (2006), 'Contractibility and ownership redirection in franchising: a property rights view', *Journal of Retailing*, **82**, 259–272.

Windsperger, J. and N. Gorovaia (2011), 'Knowledge attributes and the choice of knowledge transfer mechanisms in networks: the case of franchising', *Journal of Management and Governance*, **15**, 617–640.

Windsperger, J. and A. Yurdakul (2007), 'The governance structure of franchising firms: a property rights view', in G. Cliquet, G. Hendrikse, M. Tuunanen and J. Windsperger (eds), *Economics and Management of Networks: Franchising, Strategic Alliances, and Cooperatives*, Heidelberg: Springer Verlag, pp. 69–95.

Yin, X., E.J. Zajac (2004), 'The strategy/governance structure fit relationship: theory and evidence in franchising arrangement', *Strategic Management Journal*, **25**, 365–383.

Zaheer, A. and N. Venkatraman (1995), 'Relational governance as an interorganizational strategy: an empirical test of the role of trust in economic exchange', *Strategic Management Journal*, **16**, 373–392.

28. Subcontracting relationships
Ruth Rama and Adelheid Holl

In this chapter we review the literature on subcontracting relationships with a focus on organisational structures, antecedents and the spatial dimension in such relations. We argue that subcontracting can not be explained well as a general phenomenon but requires distinctions among different forms, dimensions, and relations. We point to major questions that research in this area should address in the future.[1]

INTRODUCTION

Recent decades have witnessed substantial changes in the organisation of production, leading towards interconnected production and the contracting out of activities at an increasingly global scale. In this context, firms are perceived as part of networks of interlinked businesses, and thus there is a growing current interest in subcontracting networks, as organisational forms which affect, firstly, company performance; and secondly, local, regional and national economic competitiveness.

Today there exists a very broad body of literature on the general phenomenon of outsourcing of activities and to a somewhat lesser degree on subcontracting as a specific type. The issue of subcontracting started to gain increasing interest in the academic literature in the 1980s following the introduction of flexible production systems in manufacturing in advanced economies. The issue has been addressed in a range of academic fields such as economics, geography, management and sociology, among others. Given that the literature on subcontracting and other types of outsourcing practices today is broad and in many different academic fields, a comprehensive review of all aspects of subcontracting relationships would be beyond the scope of this chapter. We, nevertheless, aim to draw a picture of the current state of knowledge with reference to recent key issues regarding more specifically organisational structures in subcontracting relations, their antecedents and spatial dimension. We also review part of the relevant empirical literature concerning the outcomes of subcontracting. In doing so, we point to major questions that research in this area should address in the future.

We have organised the chapter as follows. In the next section we provide an overview of how the concept of subcontracting has been used in the literature. We then review different types of subcontracting. We go on to review properties of subcontracting and company motives for subcontracting. Next we review literature regarding the spatial dimension of subcontracting, and the literature on subcontracting outcomes. A final section concludes.

SUBCONTRACTING – WHAT IT IS CONCEPTUALLY

In general terms, subcontracting is a contractual agreement whereby firms contract out specific tasks and processes to an external provider. Mere procurement activities are not considered to be subcontracting (Díaz-Mora 2008; Gilley and Rasheed 2000; Strange 2011). More specifically, however, subcontracting has been viewed as a mode of organising production which involves close inter-firm relationships and cooperation.

Subcontracting differs from the mere market transactions of ready-made parts or components in that the products supplied by subcontractors (suppliers) are based on specifications (quality, design, drawings, etc.) issued by the contractor (client firm) (Bala Subrahmanyan 2008). It may involve the outsourcing of parts, components, subassemblies, industrial processes or services supplied by the subcontractor according to the pre-established instructions of the contractor (EIM and IKEI 2009). The latter often provides the subcontractor with product specifications, materials and machines, technical and financial assistance, quality control or training (Kranton and Minehart 2000; Larsson 1999; Oman et al. 1989; Rama and Ferguson 2007; Whitford and Zeitlin 2004).

Amesse et al. (2001: 562) define subcontracting as 'a relationship whereby a firm, named the main contractor (or the prime contractor) places an order with another firm, named the subcontractor, for the manufacturing, transformation, assembly and/or finishing of a component incorporated into a good to be sold by the main contractor'. In turn, research and development (R&D) subcontracting takes place when a firm orders another to develop or test a technology according to detailed specifications (Dhont-Peltrault and Pfister 2011). To summarise, it is generally agreed that the underlying essence of any definition of subcontracting is customisation (Rama et al. 2003). Logically enough, the degree of coordination between firms is significantly higher for made-to-order products than for the purchase of ready-made products.

As noted by Amesse et al. (2001: 561), the subcontracting term is 'multifaceted and potentially heterogeneous'. Academics may use terms such as 'subcontracting networks' or 'production networks' for contracting out relationships involving collaboration. Common foci of such work are 'make-or-buy decisions', 'externalities', 'vertical disintegration' or 'strategic alliances'. Certain authors refer to the 'quasifirm', 'an organizational form with characteristics of both markets and hierarchies' (Eccles 1981). Other academics have also used the term 'outsourcing'[2] to refer to subcontracting relationships. Others refer to 'integrated outsourcing', as defined by close interaction between a buying plant and its providers, and by co-production of products, services and knowledge (Bengtsson and Dabhilkar 2009); or to 'transformational outsourcing', which implies collaboration and the possession of networking competences (Hätönen and Eriksson 2009). Certain academics refer to 'outsourcing to strategic alliance partners' or to 'contractual outsourcing' when they study specifically subcontracting relationships (Varadarajan 2009).

Since terms are often used loosely in the literature, a brief review of theory may help to further clarify the notion of subcontracting relationships. Work in institutional economics classifies subcontracting as a 'non-standard' form of organisation, a hybrid form unambiguously distinct from hierarchies and markets. According to Ménard (2006), hybrids do business together with little help from the price system and they share or exchange technology, capital, products and services without unified ownership.[3] Authors working from a sociological perspective challenge this view and see networks, including subcontracting networks, as unique forms of organisation with efficiency advantages to be found neither in pure markets nor in pure hierarchies (Podolny and Page 1998). One of the defining elements of networks, they claim, is an ethic of trust, while markets and hierarchies are better defined by more adversarial postures. Very few studies, however, analyse what companies actually understand for trust in subcontracting relationships.[4] In organisational studies, the notion of coordination 'through a mix of mechanisms not limited to price, exit and background regulation' is considered a hallmark of inter-firm networks (Grandori 1999: 2). As is evident from the preceding discussion, these different perspectives have in common the idea that subcontracting networks clearly differ from markets and hierarchies.

Another fundamental question is that subcontracting relationships do not emerge in a social vacuum as may be the case of mere commercial relationships. Networks of firms, including networks of subcontractors, are viewed as new forms of industrial structures and as the result of a social process (Cohendet and Llerena 2009). Social networking and institutional embeddedness within a country or region are often associated to business networking (including subcontracting networking), ensuring a smoother inter-firm transmission of information (Grandori and Soda 1995). More recently, certain authors emphasized the resurgence of social bonds as the underpinning of economic relations (Gilson et al. 2009; Lamoreaux et al. 2003). The sociological literature was among the first to propose this idea (Granovetter 1985).

However, there are other types of hybrids and networks than subcontracting networks (for typologies of networks, see Casson 2010; Grandori and Soda 1995). This circumstance adds ambiguity to our topic. Clarification of the terminology used is, therefore, essential. However, given the diversity that the concept embraces, the problem is not so much in the lack of a precise single definition. Instead, we argue that subcontracting cannot be explained well as a general phenomenon but requires distinctions among different forms, dimensions and relations.

TYPES OF SUBCONTRACTING RELATIONS

Different types of subcontracting relations can be distinguished according to their economic content, the degree of coordination, the nature of partners, the importance of subcontracted activity in firms' business portfolio, or the degree of dependence and distribution of power in subcontracting networks.

Subcontracting may first of all involve different activities such as production processes, support services, as well as research and design activities. While subcontracting started with production activities, in recent years subcontracting of services, and research and design activities, are becoming increasingly important (Olsen 2006; Varadarajan 2009). Today, subcontracting as a form of organisation has been adopted in all sectors (EIM and IKEI 2009). Taking also into account the content of contracts, some authors note that subcontracting can refer to the management of a phase of the production process (e.g. assembling), a component or a finished product (Razzolini and Vannoni 2011).

Secondly, the literature distinguishes most frequently between standard, capacity and specialised subcontracting (Rama et al. 2003). Blenker and Christensen (1995) categorise these three types according to two important dimensions: the degree of coordination required, and the task complexity involved in the inter-firm relationship. As noted by Grandori and Soda (1995) the literature on networks points actually to similar relevant variables: that is, the complexity of activities and the intensity of inter-firm interdependence. Standard subcontracting involves little coordination and little task complexity (Blenker and Christensen 1995). It is characterised by the presence of large investments, and task or product standardisation. In this type of relationship, it is difficult to distinguish a subcontractor from a supplier, except that the former need to follow the client's specifications. When we move up the scales of coordination and complexity, we find capacity subcontractors. In this case subcontractors act as a kind of buffer against unpredictable fluctuations in demand; at the same time, the contractor avoids the risk of excess capacity. Finally, further up the scale of task complexity are specialised contractors. Contractors may seek the specialised knowledge of other firms. They may deliberately choose not to develop a specific part of the industrial process and call for a specialized subcontractor, selected due to its knowledge or specialized equipment (EIM and IKEI 2009). This strategy permits contractors access to higher-quality inputs and services, and to use their core resources to focus on essential products and R&D. While specifications are still set up by clients, these relationships require greater information exchange and mutual adaptation. The degree of coordination should also be considered. For instance, modular subcontracting (systems subcontracting), common in the defence industry, involves highly specialised suppliers; however, inter-firm relationships are close to those characterizing arm's-length markets. In modular production, each module can serve many purposes and fit a variety of different products (Gilson et al. 2009).

Thirdly, subcontracting relations vary according to the importance of the outsourced activity in the firm's business portfolio. The literature often points to non-core business as a prime candidate for subcontracting (EIM and IKEI 2009; Imrie 1994). By contrast, other academics rank the activities of firms according to their distance from core activities; prime candidates for networking forms of production are 'intermediate' activities, neither core nor peripheral (Cohendet and LLerena 2009). In this case, it is argued, firms retain some knowledge but need to complement it by knowledge held by other companies. Other authors refer to core skills, such as expertise in supply networks management, rather than to core products (Arnold 2000; Gilley and Rasheed 2000). As noted by Hendry (1995), the emphasis Prahalad and Hamel (1990) place on core competencies has been used to justify the subcontracting of non-core activities. In the view of Hendry (1995: 197), however, core competencies are related with informal aspects of corporate culture and this nucleus may be disrupted by the 'breaking of the organisation' sometimes implicit in subcontracting and other forms of outsourcing. The general literature on outsourcing shows that even small firms may simultaneously outsource and produce in-house the same product, probably to acquire technical expertise (Parmigiani 2007). This finding suggests that some core activities might be simultaneously developed in-house and outsourced. This issue needs to be investigated in the specific context of subcontracting relationships owing to its important practical and theoretical consequences.

Arnold (2000) analyses the dematerialised company, which subcontracts all manufacturing. Though his research is based on case studies of modularised systems, evidence suggests that 'manufacturers without factories' may also emerge in more traditional subcontracting arrangements. For instance, some US firms which market at brand level in apparel seem to take no part in manufacturing activities, concentrating instead on design, marketing and retailing; manufacturing is left to subcontractors, under the supervision of the contractor or an independent agency (Christerson and Appelbaum 1995: 1363). In this context, Hätönen and Eriksson (2009) argue that questions such as what to outsource, either by subcontracting or other arrangements, are becoming increasingly important.

Fourthly, there are also major differences regarding the degree of contractual and organisational integration in the arrangement. Most academics, governments and international institutions define subcontracting as an economic and legal relationship taking place exclusively between independent firms (EIM and IKEI 2009). In practice, however, subcontracting relationships may take place within company groups. At the same time, the subcontracting relationship itself may be formalised through a contractual agreement between contractor and subcontractor (EIM and IKEI 2009). Such contracts are sometimes required to regulate iterated processes of continuous collaboration and innovation, instead of the usual *ex ante* specification of the desired product (Gilson et al. 2009). However, as noted by Grandori and Soda (1995), the literature also provides examples of subcontracting relationships governed by social and cultural networks. Surveying French engineering firms, Lorenz (2000), for instance, found no written contracts but a set of normative rules, determining what behaviour was permissible and what behaviour was a violation of trust. In similar vein, more recent analyses of subcontracting suggest that governing mechanisms are actually the long-term, repeated nature of interactions between partners as well as shared understandings and expectations (Gilson et al. 2009; Lamoreaux et al. 2003).

Fifthly, focusing on network relations in subcontracting, Sachetti and Sudgen (2003) distinguish two types according to the degree of dependence between companies. In networks of mutual dependence partners are able to participate in decision-making (even if their weight of opinion differs), but in networks of direction, they are not. As is also evident from the empirical literature, the shape of subcontracting networks may vary from single- to multiple-tiered networks. In the star-shaped structure, subcontractors have direct contacts with a contractor while indirect ties are limited (EIM and IKEI 2009). Pyramidal organisations, by contrast, have a multi-tier structure: first-tier subcontractors deliver the product to the contractors and, at the same time, outsource parts and components to second-tier subcontractors, usually small and medium-sized enterprises (SMEs).

The literature also offers some typologies which combine several dimensions of the subcontracting relationship. Amesse et al. (2001) propose a typology which combines the contractor's objectives, the nature of the performed work, the organizational structure, management style and technology. Three classes emerge. Subcontracting of economy involves simple, customized work (e.g. assembly). Subcontracting of specialization involves specialized suppliers. Finally, in subcontracting of supply, subcontractors perform the design and own the rights or property of goods delivered.

Empirical analyses suggest that classifications are not immovable (Amesse et al. 2001; Innocenti and Labory 2004); however, we are still in need of studies that analyse how these processes take place. Moreover, subcontracting networks are becoming progressively more complex, and subcontractors often also produce final goods or services, or themselves subcontract production or services to others. They may participate in different networks led by different client firms, some of them located abroad; this is, for example, increasingly the case of Japanese or Spanish subcontractors (Bala Subrahmanyan 2008; Cámaras de Comercio 2008); or they may request exclusive relationships with the client (Cambra de Comerç de Barcelona 2008). Again, the difficulty to find reliable longitudinal data limits our understanding of network evolution. Most empirical studies provide snapshots of the situation at two different dates or even compare the current situation with a qualitative description of the previous situation.

Consequently, subcontracting has been approached by and measured in different ways. Since more accurate data are often unavailable, some studies measure subcontracting by whether or not it occurs, not by the magnitude of the contracts themselves. Another approach has been to select the breath or depth of relationships (or both) as significant variables for analysis. As noted by Grandori and Soda (1995), the resource dependence theory distinguishes among types of dependence as possible predictors of networks. The breath of relationships, they observe, has been pinpointed as a predictor of the complexity of networks. A measurement for the breath of relationships could be, for instance, the number of activities which are subcontracted. To analyse the depth of linkages, authors have taken into account, for instance, the ratio of subcontracted tangible materials over production value (Bala Subrahmanyan 2008), while others calculate the proportion of work subcontracted out by the firm, by volume (Imrie 1994), or use perceptual measures (Gilley and Rasheed 2000).

Typologies based on the degree of inter-firm coordination and task complexity, in spite of their theoretical appeal, are difficult to quantify (Rama et al. 2003). These authors propose, therefore, to explore the principal motives clients have for externalizing production (e.g. temporarily expanding capacity, lack of equipment, cost-cutting), which closely identify with the above mentioned capacity and specialization categories. Then, they combine this information with information on the incidence and directionality of subcontracting. (Motives for subcontracting will be analysed below.)

The diverging measurement and conceptual techniques between industries or countries reduce the usefulness of their comparison, however. In practice, this makes it difficult to transfer results and findings from one context to another. The diversity of phenomena, definitions and measurements suggest that generalisations should only be made with great caution. Moreover, certain studies do not indicate the type of arrangement to which they are referring.

EXPLAINING SUBCONTRACTING

Properties of Subcontracting

The literature on subcontracting is related to the literature on vertical integration, since vertical divestiture may be associated with an increase in subcontracting practices and more precisely with an increase of the importance of subcontracting relationships; although this is not always the case.

The transaction cost (TC) approach has been most influential in the field of vertical integration (Hätönen and Eriksson 2009). Building on Coase's (1937) notion of transaction costs, this approach predicts that subcontracting (and other hybrid forms) are superior to both market and internal governance when the transactional parameters raising the sum of transaction and production costs on the market (asset specificity, uncertainty and frequency of transactions) assume intermediate values or point in different directions (Williamson 1991b).

Within a principal–agent framework, Ethier (1986) and Ethier and Markusen (1996) argue that in-house production takes place when information exchanges between the principal and the agent are complex and subject to incomplete contracting. The incomplete contract problem has been principally analysed within the context of international outsourcing, but this is a problem particular to the contracting out of R&D activities in general where the leakage of key information might imply the loss of competitive advantage for the principal (Lai et al. 2009).

Attractive as it was, the TC approach has not always been corroborated by empirical research. Notably, the quick rise of subcontracting has been an unexpected development given the organizational limitations of the TC approach associated with it (Dhont-Peltrault and Pfister 2011; Gilson et al. 2009).

Certain conceptual aspects of the TC are also controversial. One of the most hotly contested notions is the concept of opportunistic behaviour, a pillar of this theoretical approach. Arnold (2000) synthesises the opinion of other authors when he criticises the TC approach on the grounds that it is a very short-term, cost-based approach. The firm's engagement in social networks and its managers' expectations concerning future contracts with other companies may actually reduce opportunistic behaviour in subcontracting relationships (Eccles 1981; Gilson et al. 2009).

Trust in subcontracting is mostly based on past and future collaborations (Thorelli 1986). Learning about the qualities of a potential partner is a time-consuming and expensive 'investment' in understanding a partner's capabilities, as it increases switching costs and prevents firms from exiting from a previous relationship (Gilson et al. 2009).

Critics have also raised doubts regarding the usefulness of the 'asset specificity' construct; this refers, in the TC approach, to the 'ease with which an asset can be redeployed to alternative uses and by alternative users without loss of productive value' (Williamson 1991a: 80). Specific assets are locked-in investments which cannot be redeployed to other uses without incurring a financial loss (Lazonick 2001; Ménard 2009). The TC approach predicts that firms which use specific assets in their transactions with other companies may be vulnerable to contractual hazards resulting from unscrupulous partners (Williamson 1991a), and will thus avoid subcontracting with other companies for inputs, parts, R&D services, and so on. In practice, Japanese subcontractors, for instance, invest heavily in skills which are specific to their relationship with a specific client (Aoki 1988).

Academics have approximated the asset-specificity construct in several ways. In theory, the unit of analysis to be studied should be the transaction (not the firm), but data on specific transactions and the technology-related use of specific assets are difficult to obtain. Moreover, although some authors propose analyses at the product level (Gilley and Rasheed 2000), most analyses of subcontracting relationships are at the company or even industry level.

Consequently, academics have constructed alternative approximations of asset specificity, such as the costs required to convert the tooling to its next best use (Monteverde and Teece 1982) or managers' perceptions of the 'degree of non redeployability of the technology' (Delmas 1999: 635). Alternative measures of asset specificity include information on the firm's involvement in: (1) product markets where its regional competitors are few (Mazzanti et al. 2009); (2) high-tech industries (Acemoglu et al. 2010); or (3) 'thin' markets for intermediate inputs (Parmigiani 2007). The variety of ways used to measure this construct (for a review, see Klein 2005) indicates the need for caution when generalising findings.

Critics also note that the economic and social context are modifying factors, crucial to explain a company's decision to subcontract but not included in the original formulation of the TC approach.[5] Other authors believe that institutions may play an important role in deterring opportunistic behaviour or reducing the risk associated to asset specificity. In the Japanese production model, the presence of supplier associations may impose reputational sanctions on powerful client firms and limit, therefore, opportunistic behaviour (Gilson et al. 2009). The literature on agglomerations attributes a similar role to industrial districts and local production systems. Trust among partners (De Propris 2001; Liu and Brookfield 2000; Morroni 2006; Sacchetti and Sudgen 2003) or the active participation of unions in the company's decision to subcontract (Mazzanti et al. 2009) may induce firms to engage in subcontracting relationships involving highly specific investments. The multiplicity of modifying factors may, according to some studies, weaken the usefulness of the TC theoretical constructs in analyses of subcontracting relationships, given that their empirical results appear to differ as their sectoral and geographical context change (Mazzanti et al. 2009). Another limitation of most empirical studies is that they establish correlations, not causal relations, between asset specificity and governance (Klein 2005). The discussion suggests that asset specificity alone is not such a strong predictor of subcontracting as the TC approach posits.

New phenomena, such as international subcontracting, for instance, pose new theoretical questions. Christerson and Appelbaum (1995) note that the TC does not account, for instance, for the phenomenon of large apparel firms dispersing subcontracted production to low-wage locations. Instead of internalising transactions as a consequence of high TC, as predicted by the theory, the companies subcontract overseas. These authors claim that the companies successfully engage in international subcontracting thanks to their market power, high-volume orders and preferential access to the most reliable overseas subcontractors. Christerson and Appelbaum (1995) conclude that the TC insufficiently takes into account the variety of factors which influence subcontracting, notably international subcontracting. For Hätönen and Eriksson (2009), it is not that the theory has become obsolete but rather that the evolution of practice has complicated the theoretical base; and the TC approach, in their view, is now insufficient to explain the phenomenon into which outsourcing has evolved. Subcontracting relationships ('transformational outsourcing' in their terminology) are better explained, they argue, by organizational theories, evolutionary and learning theories, and network theory. The adoption of the TC as a single theoretical view, they claim, would probably lead to an oversimplified analysis.

In addition to the TC approach, other lines of thought attempt to explain subcontracting relationships. In the resource-based view (RBV) of the firm, subcontracting depends not only on the transaction and production costs, as in the TC approach, but also on the fact that different capabilities contribute to the improvement of a set of different tasks (Madhok 1996; Argyres 1996).

A perception of interdependence with potential partners may induce companies to collaborate (Gulati 1995). According to a review of the literature (Hätönen and Eriksson 2009), the RBV explanation emerged historically when subcontracting moved beyond occasional collaboration and cost reduction arrangements to become specialized sub-contracting. As noted by Klein (2005), however, the RBV literature on firm boundaries has not yet produced much empirical research. Nevertheless, the mainstream subcon-tracting literature now integrates the TC approach and the RBV view (Kotabe and Mol 2009). Following a literature review which includes all types of outsourcing procure-ment, Spencer (2005) concludes that there are no overarching explanations. This conclu-sion might be extrapolated, more specifically, to subcontracting relationships.

Agency theory maintains that conflicting goals and interests between firms and their workforces may induce the former to subcontract activities to external providers. According to the literature published in the 1970s, firms subcontracted with each other to reduce the power the trade unions had acquired in Western Europe by that time (Sacchetti and Sudgen 2003). Peoples and Sudgen (2000) argue that a multinational enterprise (MNE) may produce in different countries in order to weaken the bargaining power of its national workforce; international subcontracting, they argue, is an attrac-tive option for the company.

Authors in the network theory tradition base their approach to subcontracting rela-tionships on issues related to power distribution within the subcontracting network (Easton and Araujo 1992; Sacchetti and Sudgen 2003). Although based on consensus between partners, certain authors argue, subcontracting relationships are always sym-metrical to a degree, since financial planning remains concentrated in the hands of one or more actors within the network (Sacchetti and Sudgen 2003). Sources of power may be principally economic (e.g. supplier size) or mainly technological (superior technology) (Easton and Araujo 1992; Thorelli 1986). Certain authors, however, maintain that the concept of power in studies of subcontracting deserves more theoretical refinement and empirical validation (Strange 2011).

Company Motives Related to the Subcontracting Decision

Studies focusing on the 'why' firms contract out activities have not been developed spe-cifically in relation to subcontracting, but mainly in relation to the general phenomenon of contracting-out of activities (outsourcing). This literature offers alternative explana-tions of why companies choose to contract out part of their activities.

Firstly, cost reductions. Relative to in-house production, the contracting out of activi-ties to lower wage producers can produce labour cost savings. Specifically, high-wage firms that are unable to pursue different wage strategies internally may take advantage of lower wages elsewhere and contract out unskilled labour-intensive production tasks. Labour cost saving was one of the principal motives behind subcontracting in its earlier phases and continues to be an influential reason specifically for international outsourcing to low-wage countries. Cost savings can also be achieved where outside suppliers benefit from economies of scale, especially where individual production processes require differ-ent levels of minimum efficient scales. Secondly, another traditional explanation comes from the demand side. Firms may try to smoothe the workload of their core workforce by contracting out tasks during peaks of demand. Particular bottlenecks, such as tempo-rary demand fluctuations or seasonal upward trends, may encourage capacity subcontracting (EIM and IKEI 2009). Thirdly, contractors may seek the specialised knowledge of other firms. In this context, Bartel et al. (2009), for example, show that the outsourcing of production activities becomes more advantageous the faster technology changes. Acquiring the latest technology to produce intermediate inputs in-house involves a sunk cost in technology adoption; companies can save such costs by outsourcing the inputs to firms already using the latest technology. The faster technology changes, the less time firms have to amortise the sunk costs of new technology adoption and the more profitable is the outsourcing of the production of these inputs.

THE SPATIAL DIMENSION OF SUBCONTRACTING

The literature analysed so far has mainly been concerned with the degree of subcontracting and the determinants that influence firms' subcontracting decisions. To date, few studies have analysed the spatial dimension of subcontracting (Hätönen and Eriksson 2009). The question of where to subcontract is, however, important and of particular interest to policy-makers concerned about 'where jobs go'.

In this context, international subcontracting, together with offshoring,[6] has become increasingly debated in recent years. Some literature exists on the choice between domestic and international subcontracting, but little is known about its quantification. The few available studies suggest that, at least in Japan and the European Union, the proportion of firms which subcontract internationally is still very small, despite having increased recently (EIM and IKEI 2009; Holl et al. 2012; Mol et al. 2005; Tomiura 2007). It also appears that operations outsourced globally are currently highly mobile (Hätönen and Eriksson 2009). International contractors are firms with specific characteristics and resources such as higher organisational capabilities in coordinating geographically distant activities (Tomiura et al. 2010). Using the example of the German automobile industry, Bade et al. (2011) furthermore argue that domestic outsourcing precedes international outsourcing and that a better understanding of the domestic dimension of outsourcing can shed light on the future patterns of international outsourcing.

Grossman and Helpman (2002, 2005) show in a general equilibrium model that if search for outsourcing partners is expensive, outsourcing is more likely to be viable where firms find more potential outsourcing partners. Lower search costs are one aspect of positive agglomeration effects. There are however a number of other mechanisms through which geographic concentration can promote vertical disintegration and the rise of subcontracting arrangements. Helsley and Strange (2007) show how geographic concentration encourages vertical disintegration, by reducing opportunism through increasing mutual visibility and reciprocal trust. They argue that in this sense agglomeration serves as a substitute for vertical integration. Ono (2007) argues, in the context of service outsourcing, that bigger markets attract more suppliers, and these in turn induce greater competition. This can reduce the price of the subcontracted activity and increase the propensity to subcontract. Harrigan and Venables (2006) show, in a theoretical model, how the need for punctuality in delivery encourages proximity between supplier and customer. Proximity provides greater flexibility, reduces demand-related risk and guarantees delivery times for intermediate inputs. Proximity not only reduces distance costs and permits greater flexibility, since inputs can be more easily obtained in smaller quantities or on an as-needed basis, but also facilitates close contact between clients (contractors) and suppliers (subcontractors) in collaborative arrangements which require frequent face-to-face contact. Indeed, as Marshall (1920) showed in his seminal work, agglomeration allows for the sharing of inputs and facilitates the emergence of specialised intermediate input producers. Similarly, Stigler (1951) argued that increasing local market size leads to greater vertical disintegration. There exists some recent empirical evidence in this regard (see, for example, Holmes 1999; Ono 2007; Holl 2008; Li and Lu 2009; Figuereido et al. 2010).

While there is some empirical evidence on the positive relation between agglomeration and vertical disintegration, a key question is whether the spatial proximity of economic activities actually reflects the strength of subcontracting linkages among the neighbouring firms. Co-location of firms with a higher propensity to subcontract may occur without subcontracting relations being produced among proximate firms (Gordon and McCann 2000; Torre and Rallet 2005; Yeung et al. 2006). Holl and Rama (2009) and Cusmano et al. (2010) show, however, for Spain and Italy respectively, that subcontracting processes are indeed strongly regionally embedded.

Understanding the spatial extent of inter-firm linkages is important for policy-makers and academics, as it also provides an idea of the degree of integration of regions into the national and international economies and of the regional embeddedness of specific types of companies (e.g. multinational enterprises). Little research, however, has examined the destination of domestic outsourcing. This question is closely related to the literature that analyses the decision to fragment firms' operations (manufacturing, distribution, R&D) in space or to integrate them in the same location (Pais and Pontes 2008).

Why would firms want to separate tasks in space? From the urban economics literature we know, firstly, that urban costs rise with city size; and secondly, that skilled workers are more productive in larger cities. Given these factors it is more efficient to keep skilled workers within the city and to move less-skilled jobs to suburban locations or smaller-sized cities. How clients and suppliers are distributed in the urban system then becomes a pertinent question regarding subcontracting relations. Some recent evidence on the spatial organisation of firms has shed some light on this question. Duranton and Puga (2005) show that lower communication costs facilitate remote management and therefore have enabled firms to separate different tasks at different locations. They argue that this changes the clustering of firms by sectoral specialisation to a pattern of functional specialisation. Management functions are kept in bigger cities while production functions are concentrated in smaller cities.

Similar evidence is also provided by Rossi-Hansberg et al. (2009), who show that as cities grow, firms tend to locate their headquarters in the urban centre and settle their production plants in the suburbs. In their model, higher land rents resulting from increasing city population encourage firms to split up their operations, keeping only those functions that benefit most from interactions in central city locations within the city. In this context, Liao (2009) studies specifically where outsourced jobs go and why certain localities are popular destinations for domestic outsourcing. He shows for the United States (US) that office support jobs are increasingly outsourced to small cities for cost savings, and further demonstrates that increased mobility for workers would mean support workers are better off, as they would live in smaller cities without the costs of urban congestion. However, as Liao points out, if positive neighbourhood effects exist in larger cities, then the overall welfare effects for support workers moving to small cities would not be as clear-cut.

An important question concerns the conditions under which the constraints of distance are overcome. Holl and Rama (2009) show that proximity is important for subcontracting relations, but that subcontracting relations within company groups are much less spatially constrained.[7] In general, subcontracting relations that span regional boundaries are more common among larger and more R&D-intensive firms, companies with a greater presence in the rest of the country, and enterprises with more experience of cooperation and more stable relationships. A large firm may be able to support extensive quality-control staff over quality and delivery in its international subcontracting activities; moreover, it tends to obtain better prices from overseas subcontractors owing to large subcontracted volume (Christerson and Appelbaum 1995; Evans and Smith 2006). These authors also argue that the social embeddedness school of economic organisation may contribute to explaining how it is possible for apparel firms to subcontract production over large physical distances. They find that ethnicity and family ties may facilitate international subcontracting; the use of personal networks spanning the world may minimise the risks of such arrangements.

Together, these factors provide support to the concept of organised proximity and its importance in overcoming geographical distance. As Sacchetti and Sudgen (2003) suggest, analyses of the geographic scope of subcontracting relations should take into consideration the governance style prevailing in relationships. The separation of tasks across space requires service links such as transportation, logistics services, insurance and telecommunications. An open question in this context is the relation of supply chain management to subcontracting.

Subcontracting has profound impacts on the relocation of economic activity both domestically and globally. From the side of policy-makers, there is great interest specifically on international subcontracting. The research on domestic and international outsourcing has developed largely separately; but there are commonalities that can help to increase our understanding of the role of space in subcontracting relationships. Further research will also need to pay more attention to the role of global value chains and the organisational structures of transnational companies in international outsourcing relations. At the same time, an agenda for future research will also need to include small and medium-sized companies, and the way they may be included in international outsourcing networks. There is also a need for more research about the relative importance of organisational proximity versus physical proximity in different subcontracting contexts.

EMPIRICAL RESEARCH ON SUBCONTRACTING OUTCOMES

More than three decades of empirical research on subcontracting relationships have offered a wealth of empirical results. However, interpretation of these results and deduction of robust empirical patterns still pose a number of difficulties. Firstly, as mentioned above, research is often hampered by confusion about the definitions of subcontracting practices and lack of consensus on the variables chosen for analysis. This difficulty is not easily solved since different national statistics may adopt different conceptualizations of subcontracting practices (see, for instance, Taymaz and Kiliçaslan 2005). Nevertheless, a better definition of the nature of firms and types of subcontracting is essential to advance in empirical research on subcontracting relationships.

Secondly, as will be seen below, most of the models of industries which rely on inter-firm linkages have been built on examples taken from a few industrialised countries and have concentrated on specific sectors. They might not be generalisable to other countries or sectors.

With these limitations in mind, we turn now to some of the most important findings of the empirical literature on the outcomes of subcontracting. We concentrate on effects on the firms involved in the subcontracting relationship, though subcontracting also affects the working force and other agents. Although there exists 'a general widespread pro-network bias' (Grandori 1999: 2), opinions are not always sufficiently informed by facts. Systematic research into the possible advantages and, especially, the disadvantages offered by subcontracting relationships remains scarce.

In the 1970s and 1980s, the main idea behind the support for subcontracting was the potential benefits a small subcontractor may obtain from a large contractor through a guaranteed market, secured raw materials and technical assistance (Taymaz and Kiliçaslan 2005). In the last few years, there has been a resurgence of academic interest on a related issue: the dimension and benefits of MNEs' local sourcing (Crone 2002). Study cases on large firms which subcontract production, such as Toyota, Nissan, Sony and Telefonica, certainly suggest that large contractors may proactively engage in supplier development both at home and abroad (Dyer and Nobeoka 2000; López et al. 2002; Rama and Ferguson 2007; Morris and Imrie 1993). In theory, SMEs may obtain advantages over similar companies not engaged in subcontracting (Kelley and Harrison 1990). Nevertheless, the empirical literature also shows that, even in developed countries, subcontracting may pose difficulties for some smaller subcontractors. In the European Union (EU), these companies sometimes report power asymmetries in the subcontracting relationship and overdependence on contractors (EIM and IKEI 2009). According to certain authors, however, information decentralisation and the involvement of suppliers in knowledge creation are likely to promote a more balanced distribution of power within networks (Innocenti and Labory 2004). According to this view, such governance patterns, typical in networks of small firms, are now expanding also to networks led by large firms.

Effects of subcontracting on small subcontractors have been especially important as a topic in the literature dealing more specifically with subcontracting in developing or transition countries (for a review, see UNCTAD 2001). Results on the effects of subcontracting on the productivity of local partners are not conclusive (see, for instance, Batra et al. 2003; Hayashi 2002). By contrast, there is more consensus concerning the positive effects of subcontracting on technology transfers to local subcontractors. According to the United Nations Conference on Trade and Development (UNCTAD 2001) report, linkages of MNEs to domestic suppliers through long-term subcontracting may lead to the transmission of technological knowledge and skills to local partners. More recently, an analysis of affiliates confirmed this view in the case of Malaysian subcontractors (but not in the case of Vietnamese subcontractors) (Giroud 2007). The benefits of subcontracting concerning technology transfer do not seem limited to the industry of developing countries, as shown by a study on the linkages between multinational agribusinesses and their Latin American subcontractors (Oman et al. 1989).

On the other hand, as noted by the UNCTAD (2001) review of the literature, exclusive linkages with large, monopsonistic affiliates may weaken the bargaining power of local suppliers and promote unfair terms.[8] Also, within developing or transition countries, different types of subcontracting relationships may coexist (Taymaz and Kiliçaslan 2005); in some industries, large, advanced contractors may prefer to subcontract production to other advanced firms which possess complementary assets and technology, rather than to SMEs. Therefore, the suggestion that large companies should lead and modernise networks of SMEs subcontractors is not always feasible. From a practical point of view there is a need to identify the types of contractors, networks and local environments more conducive to promoting innovation and development in SME subcontractors in developing and transition countries (and elsewhere). From a scientific point of view, it should be stressed that we lack a well-defined theory of local procurement (Belderbos et al. 2001), not to speak of procurements taking place through subcontracting relationships.

Upgrading of products and transfers of technology to subcontractors are, perhaps, some of the benefits of subcontracting more often cited in the literature. The sociological literature was among the first to highlight quality advantages rather than costs as the primary economic benefits of networked forms (Podolny and Page 1998). The British subcontractors interviewed by Morris and Imrie (1993) reported, for instance, that the transfer of quality systems was probably the most beneficial aspect of partnership with Nissan, a Japanese MNE. Since subcontracting often entails specialisation, it may help contractors to reduce their costs and, instead, use their resources to finance R&D (Dhont-Peltrault and Pfister 2011; Suarez-Villa and Rama 1996). However, a trade-off may exist between the corporate need to reduce costs in the short run and the strategic importance of directly controlling R&D activity in the long run, especially for firms in high-tech sectors (Suárez-Villa and Walrod 2003). Studying the French industry, other authors argue that contractors are likely to subcontract standardized R&D tasks (rather than novel technology) because the TCs associated with these routine tasks are probably low (Dhont-Peltrault and Pfister 2011). Therefore, they contest the idea of a transfer of technology from the contractor to the subcontractor, at least concerning the most valuable technology. A question seldom investigated is whether subcontracting may limit the development of the subcontractor's innovative capabilities. A study suggests that excessive reliance on offshoring subcontracting, though commercially lucrative for Indian subcontractors of software, may discourage them from taking more complex projects at home (D'Costa 2002). As reported by another study, the high-tech subcontractors of a large telecom company complain that almost exclusive reliance on subcontracting limits their creativity (López et al. 2002).

The literature has also been concerned, though to a lesser degree, with the outcomes of subcontracting relationships for contractors. The general observation is that these companies benefit most from subcontracting when they operate in uncertain or risky environments. A shift to subcontracting seems to have allowed French SMEs operating in the engineering industry to avoid investment in up-to-date machine tools and, often, reduce capacity (Lorenz 2000). In a period of slow growth and uncertain markets (in the early 1980s), this author claims, it would have been impossible for these firms to amortise investments. Contractors were able to launch such strategy, he argues, because subcontractors could aggregate the demand of several clients. Reviewing the literature on French industrialisation, Innocenti and Labory (2004) confirm this point of view.

They note that most authors consider subcontracting as the main factor behind the competitiveness of the French industry.

In similar vein, Kranton and Minehart (2000), studying the Japanese electronics industry and the US apparel industry, opine that subcontracting networks are more efficient than vertically integrated firms when client firms face a recession and production capacity is costly. In other circumstances, they claim, networks are 'second-best industrial structures' because return to investments depends on the types of links and *ex post* distribution of surplus; and the latter depend, in turn, on the presence of cooperation or competition between agents. In agriculture and agribusiness, subcontracting relationships may help the contractor to control geographically dispersed production and, especially, to transfer unpredictable risks, such as droughts, to subcontractors (Oman et al. 1989; Prudham 2002).

This literature has advanced our understanding of the outcomes of subcontracting relationships. However, several elements may have inhibited progress in the field. Firstly, there are unobservable or difficult-to-measure factors related to historical series, line of business statistics and costs. Both advantages and disadvantages of subcontracting may be revealed in the long run rather than in the short run (Gianelle and Tattara 2010). We still know very little about how networked forms of organisation, and more specifically subcontracting networks, fail or evolve (Podolny and Page 1998). For instance, capacity or economy subcontractors can, with time, become specialised subcontractors (Amesse et al. 2001; Innocenti and Labory 2004). One of the few studies which span a long period of time found that Finnish subcontractors improved their relationship skills and increased their ability to plan capacity (Lehtinen 1999). These findings point to an upgrading of subcontractors. Since the expertise of firms may improve with time, a related issue affecting the outcomes of subcontracting deals with the development of specific organisational and bargaining skills within the networked company (Doh 2005; Meccheri and Morroni 2010). This brief discussion shows the importance of the time dimension, usually neglected by the empirical literature on subcontracting.

Also, the outcomes of subcontracting may be better evaluated at the business level, rather than at the company level as is usual. Raised by the general literature on outsourcing (Gilley and Rasheed 2000) this issue is probably extrapolable to studies on subcontracting relationships. Also, hidden costs of subcontracting (e.g. increased technology transfer costs or longer delivery times in the case of international subcontracting) probably need to be weighed against cost reductions in the client firm. The disruption of organisational life and of corporate culture caused by subcontracting in the client firm also needs to be weighed against the benefits of subcontracting. Though these issues have also been raised by the general outsourcing literature (see, respectively, Bengtsson 2008; Hendry 1995), they probably need to be investigated in the specific context of subcontracting relationships. Moreover, costs themselves are rarely studied although, as stated, they are considered among the main drivers of the contractor's decision to subcontract production or services. Finally, some benefits of subcontracting may be quite subtle and difficult to capture. Studies on high-tech industries in Canada and Europe found, for instance, that one of the most important outcomes of subcontracted activities were unexpected technology results which may arise from cooperation (Amesse et al. 2001: 562). As the sociologists have pointed out, actors may gain legitimacy or status from network affiliation (Podolny and Page 1998). For instance, a study found that suppliers subcontracted by multinational agribusiness were more likely to obtain credit from banks than were other Mexican farmers (Rama 1985). Statistical data on these factors which modify the outcomes of subcontracting are seldom available. Therefore, case studies, qualitative studies and typologies could be a step forward even if results were not generalisable.

Secondly, another factor which may limit progress in the field is the lack of comparative analyses. The literature suggests that different types of subcontracting relationships may have different effects. In Italy and the United Kingdom (UK), for instance, international subcontracting has generated immediate and strongly negative consequences for domestic subcontractors and regional industries (Evans and Smith 2006; Gianelle and Tattara 2010). Studying the Canadian aeronautical industry, Amesse et al. (2001) found that subcontracting of economy was strongly limited to organisational and managerial transfers of expertise to subcontractors, while other types of subcontracting also involved design and development, and manufacturing transfers. By the same token, the firm's positioning in different segments of subcontracting networks may also affect its international competitiveness or its productivity (Minetaki and Motohashi 2009; Razzolini and Vannoni 2011).

Thirdly, the benefits of subcontracting seem to be mediated by many different variables. For instance, some locations may facilitate specialisation and, consequently, better performance from both subcontractors and contractors (Rama and Calatrava 2002; Suarez-Villa and Rama 1996). A clear picture of the outcomes of subcontracting would require more in-depth study of interactions between subcontracting, size of the firm, strategy and location. Also, studies spanning multiple industries which control for industry effects would be a useful avenue for future research.

Fourthly, certain authors argue that the benefits of subcontracting relationships are better captured at the network than at the company level (Easton 1992). In similar vein, Powell et al. (1996) observe, in networks of biotechnology companies, that the locus of innovation is the network, not the firm. These authors make the case for the network as the appropriate unit of analysis in the biotechnology industry. Since the 1990s, when these studies were published, very little progress has been made. A stronger focus on networks would be another promising direction for future research in the field of subcontracting.

Moreover, a review of the literature concludes that a fundamental question has not yet been addressed, namely that of how success in subcontracting relations should be evaluated (Hätönen and Eriksson 2009). While specific benefits of subcontracting are difficult to identify, surveys which focus on general levels of contractors' satisfaction mostly report positive answers. This consideration is important, since certain authors maintain that outsourcing performance is not determined by a single factor alone (Hätönen and Eriksson 2009).

With some exceptions, the effects of subcontracting beyond the firms immediately involved in the contract have tended to be neglected (Hätönen and Eriksson 2009). Notably, subcontracting relationships may also have implications for the workforce.

CONCLUSIONS

Over the last few decades, the organisation of production has witnessed important changes. One of the core changes has been the rapid rise of subcontracting. Generally, subcontracting has been defined as a contractual agreement whereby firms contract out specific tasks and processes to an external provider according to specifications made available. This general definition, however, embraces quite different forms of subcontracting relations involving different economic contents, different degrees of coordination, different types of partners, and different degrees of dependence and distribution of power. We argue that subcontracting can not be explained well as a general phenomenon but requires distinctions among different forms, dimensions and relations. Moreover, subcontracting itself has changed over the last decades as regards what firms subcontract, how they subcontract and where they subcontract, depending on the type of industry as well as the institutional, cultural, technological and economic conditions under which subcontracting is developed. Thus, in order to advance our understanding of subcontracting relations, research needs to view subcontracting as differentiated process and pay much more attention to its differentiated nature.

In explaining subcontracting relations, research has mainly drawn on the transaction costs approach. However, the complexity that the phenomenon has recently acquired and the unforeseen evolution of different forms of subcontracting has encouraged the emergence of explanations combining this view with others, notably the resource-based view of the firm. More empirical research is needed to substantiate this line of thought. The literature has expanded now from inquiries which primarily investigated why firms choose to subcontract, emphasising the importance of cost reduction, to studies interested in questions such as what to subcontract or how to subcontract and where to subcontract.

Subcontracting involves the separation of tasks and in general this implies a separation in space. An important question in this respect concerns the spatial extent of subcontracting relations and the overcoming of their distance constraints. Here, further research could benefit from combining recent insights from economic geography and industrial organisation; two literatures that have so far developed largely separately. The international dimension of subcontracting relations has attracted much policy interest in recent years. Yet, studies which first of all quantify firms' domestic and internationally subcontracted production relations are still a necessity. In this area, we also need more in-depth studies on international subcontracting relations. Data constraints have so far limited research in this area, particularly as far as services are concerned. The study of the evolution of domestic subcontracting relations can help to shed light on the future patterns of international subcontracting. Furthermore, the overcoming of spatial distance constrains cannot be isolated from issues of organisational proximity and the rapid advancement in information and communication technology (ICT). A better understanding of the role of space in subcontracting relations is not only important from an academic point of view to explain shifts in economic activities across space, but will also help to clarify issues in the current 'delocalisation' debate.

Systematic research into the possible advantages and, especially, the disadvantages of subcontracting relationships remains scarce. How can subcontracting benefits be measured? And how long will the possible competitive advantages of subcontracting last? In any case, certain authors advise using more than just one indicator to measure success. More longitudinal studies, analyses at the business level, investigations of hidden costs and of the possible disruption which subcontracting may cause to informal relationships within the contractor, are needed to clarify these questions. More studies which compare different types of subcontracting arrangements will help us to identify 'best practices'. This will enable researchers and policy-makers to understand better the internal organisation of companies and the nature of inter-firm linkages which may promote success. By the same token, we need to understand better the mechanisms which facilitate transfers of knowledge within networks.

Other enquiries concern industries and countries where firms prefer to organise through subcontracting relationships rather than vertical integration. Such industries tend to grow rapidly and display fast technological change; at the same time, these companies face 'thick' markets for intermediate goods. Certain authors point to the influence of cultural and institutional characteristics as a possible explanation; however, more empirical research is needed to clarify reasons for differences in the extent of subcontracting relationships across countries. The legal system and the wider social and institutional environment in which business relationships are embedded may facilitate the formation of inter-firm cooperative linkages. Norms guiding subcontracting relationships are also likely to differ across countries and research in this area would be welcome.

Future research on the evolution of subcontracting relationships will also need to clarify whether there is a continued radical shift from the vertically integrated firm to the subcontracting networking. Or, by contrast, will globalisation erode the collaborative inter-firm relationships common in some countries? We are still in need of international comparisons and longitudinal analyses at the national industry level. The prevalence of companies which subcontract production within an economy, however, does not necessarily imply homogeneity of organisational forms.

Not only has research focused on an insufficient number of countries and sectors, but in addition divergent measurement tools currently provide only limited answers to these questions, which remain open.

NOTES

1. We are grateful for very helpful comments and suggestions from Anna Grandori.
2. Note, however, that the term 'outsourcing' has also been used in a purchasing perspective in trade studies, international business (IB) studies and a considerable part of the management literature. This perspective sees outsourcing as trade in parts, components and tasks deriving from the fragmentation of (national or international) production, whatever relationship exists between the buyer and the supplier. Outsourcing practices analysed by this line of research often consist of the purchase of a non-customised input through a spot market transaction (Spencer 2005). In this vein, the concept of offshoring (i.e. international outsourcing) has been employed as the importation of intermediate goods, parts or tasks (Grossman & Rossi-Hansberg 2008; Jones et al. 2005). Certain academics attempt to complement trade theory with concepts of industrial organisation and contract theory (for a review, see Spencer 2005).
3. Other hybrid forms of organisation include franchising, agricultural cropsharing and alliances (Klein 2005).
4. An exception is Lorenz (2000). Surveying French engineering firms, he finds that when contractors say that a subcontractor is trustworthy they have in mind prompt delivery, quality and price. For subcontractors, a reliable client is one who ensures a certain level of work; disclosure of relevant information is also considered essential.
5. An example could be the presence of 'thick' markets for subcontracting, that is, many suppliers who are able to provide an input.
6. Under offshoring, firms locate parts of their activities abroad via the setting up of subsidiaries while retaining the ownership of the whole of the production process.
7. The possibility of intra-group subcontracting relations is accepted by some authors (Sako 2005).

Nevertheless, their vision is contested by most authors and governments, as indicated above. According to most of the literature, subcontracting is exclusively defined by relations between independent firms.

8. Moreover, foreign firms may not be interested in establishing subcontracting relationships with local partners (Taymaz & Kiliçaslan 2005; Javorcik 2004; UNCTAD 2001). High transaction costs in the host country and insufficient social capital could limit their ability to construct subcontracting networks; or affiliates might find some of the resources they need within the multinational network (not in independent local firms).

REFERENCES

Acemoglu, D., P. Aghion, R. Griffith and F. Zilibotti (2010), 'Vertical integration and technology: theory and evidence', *Journal of the European Economic Association*, **8**(5), 989–1033.

Amesse, F., L. Dragoste, J. Nollet and S. Ponce (2001), 'Issues on partnering: evidences from subcontracting in aeronautics', *Technovation*, **21**, 559–569.

Aoki, M. (1988), *Incentives and Bargaining in the Japanese Economy*, New York: Cambridge University Press.

Argyres, N. (1996), 'Evidence on the role of firm capabilities in vertical integration decisions', *Strategic Management Journal*, **17**, 129–150.

Arnold, U. (2000), 'New dimensions of outsourcing: a combination of transaction costs economics and the core competencies concept', *European Journal of Purchasing and Supply Management*, **6**, 23–29.

Bade, F.J., E. Bode, E. Cutrini (2011), 'Does domestic offshoring precede international offshoring? Industry-level evidence', Kiel Working Paper No. 1699.

Bala Subrahmanyan, M.H. (2008), 'Manufacturing SMEs in Japan: more subcontracting intensive versus less subcontracting intensive industries', *Int. J. of Management and Enterprise Development*, **5**, 554–572.

Bartel, A., S. Lach and N. Sicherman (2009), 'Outsourcing and technological change', IZA DP No. 4678.

Batra, G., J. Morisset and K. Saggi (2003), 'Vertical linkages between multinationals and domestic suppliers: whom do they benefit and why?' Washington, DC: Foreign Investment Advisory Service, International Finance Corporation, http://rru.worldbank.org/Documents/PapersLinks/Vertical%20linkages%20May%2009.pdf.

Belderbos, R., G. Capannelli and K. Fukao (2001), 'Backward vertical linkages of foreign manufacturing affiliates: evidence from Japanese multinationals', *World Development*, **29**, 189–208.

Bengtsson, L. (2008), 'Outsourcing manufacturing and its effect on engineering firm performance', *International Journal of Technology Management*, **44**, 373–390.

Bengtsson, L. and M. Dabhilkar (2009), 'Manufacturing outsourcing and its effect on plant performance – lessons for KIBS outsourcing', *Journal of Evolutionary Economics*, **19**, 231–257.

Blenker, P. and P.R. Christensen (1995), 'Interactive strategies in supply chains – a double edged portfolio approach to small and medium-sized subcontractors position analysis', *Entrepreneurship and Reg. Develop.*, **7**, 249–264.

Cámaras de Comercio (2008), *La subcontratación industrial en España. Tecnología y competitividad*, Madrid.

Cambra de Comerç de Barcelona (2008), *La subcontratación industrial en Cataluña*, Barcelona.

Casson, M. (2010), 'Networks in economic and business history: a theoretical perspective', in P. Fernández Pérez and M.B. Rose (eds), *Innovation and Entrepreneurial Networks in Europe*, New York, USA and Oxford, UK: Routledge-Fundación BBVA, pp. 14–39.

Christerson, B. and R.P. Appelbaum (1995), 'Global and local subcontracting: space, ethnicity, and the organization of apparel production', *World Development*, **23**, 1363–1374.

Coase, R.H. (1937), 'The nature of the firm', *Economica*, **4**, 386–405.

Cohendet, P. and P. LLerena (2009), 'Organisation of firms, knowing communities and limits of networks in a knowledge-intensive context', in M. Morroni (ed.), *Corporate Governance, Organization and the Firm: Co-operation and Outsourcing in the Global Economy*, Cheltenham, UK and Northampton, MA, USA: Edward Elgar, pp. 104–120.

Crone, M. (2002), 'Local sourcing by multinational enterprise plants: evidence from the UK regions and the implications for policy', *Environment and Planning C: Government and Policy*, **20**, 131–149.

Cusmano, L., M.L. Mancusi and A. Morrison (2010), 'Globalization of production and innovation: how outsourcing is reshaping an advanced manufacturing area', *Regional Studies*, **44**, 235–252.

D'Costa, A.P. (2002), 'Software outsourcing and development policy: an Indian perspective', *Int. J. of Technology Management*, **24**, 705–724.

De Propris, L. (2001), 'Systemic flexibility, production fragmentation and cluster governance', *European Planning Studies*, **9**, 739–753.

Delmas, M.A. (1999), 'Exposing strategic assets to create new competencies: the case of technological acquisition in the waste management industry in Europe and North America', *Industrial and Corporate Change*, **8**, 635–672.

Dhont-Peltrault, E. and E. Pfister (2011), 'R&D cooperation versus R&D subcontracting: empirical evidence from French survey data', *Economics of Innovation & New Technology*.

Díaz-Mora, C. (2008), 'What factors determine the outsourcing intensity? A dynamic panel data approach for manufacturing industries', *Applied Economics*, **40**, 2509–2521.

Doh, J.P. (2005), 'Offshore outsourcing: implications for international business and strategic management theory and practice', *Journal of Management Studies*, **42**, 695–704.

Duranton, G. and D. Puga (2005), 'From sectoral to functional urban specialization', *Journal of Urban Economics*, **57**, 343–370.

Dyer, J.H. and K. Nobeoka (2000), 'Creating and managing a high-performance knowledge-sharing network: the Toyota case', *Strategic Management Journal*, **21**, 345–367.

Easton, G. (1992), 'Industrial networks: a review', in B. Axelsson and G. Easton (eds), *Industrial Networks: A New View of Reality*, London, UK and New York, USA: Routledge, pp. 3–27.

Easton, G. and L. Araujo (1992), 'Non-economic exchange in industrial networks', in B. Axelsson and G. Easton (eds), *Industrial Networks: A New View of Reality*, London, UK and New York, USA: Routledge, pp. 40–51.

Eccles, R.G. (1981), 'The quasifirm in the construction industry', *Journal of Economic Behaviour and Organization*, **2**, 335–357.

EIM and IKEI (2009), 'EU SMEs and subcontracting', report prepared for the Commission of the European Communities, under the Competitiveness and Innovation programme 2007–2013, Brussels.

Ethier, W. (1986), 'The multinational firm', *Quarterly Journal of Economics*, **101**, 805–834.

Ethier, W. and J.R. Markusen (1996), 'Multinational firms, technology diffusion and trade', *Journal of International Economics*, **41**, 1–28.

Evans, Y. and A. Smith (2006), 'Surviving at the margins? Deindustrialisation, the creative industries, and the upgrading of London's garment sector', *Environment and Planning A*, **38**, 2253–2269.

Figueiredo, O., P. Guimarães and D. Woodward (2010), 'Vertical disintegration in Marshallian industrial districts', *Regional Science and Urban Economics*, **40**, 73–78.

Gianelle, C. and G. Tattara (2010), 'Manufacturing abroad while making profits at home: the Veneto food-twear and clothing industry', in M. Morroni (ed.), *Corporate Governance, Organization and the Firm. Co-operation and Outsourcing in the Global Economy*, Cheltenham, UK and Northhampton, MA, USA: Edward Elgar, pp. 206–234.

Gilley, K.M. and A. Rasheed (2000), 'Making more by doing less: an analysis of outsourcing and its effects on firm performance', *Journal of Management*, **26**, 763–790.

Gilson, R.J., C.F. Sabel and R.E. Scott (2009), 'Contracting for innovation: vertical desintegration and inter-firm collaboration', *Columbia Law Review*, **109**, 431–502.

Giroud, A. (2007), 'MNEs vertical linkages: the experience of Vietnam after Malaysia', *International Business Review*, **16**, 159–176.

Gordon, I.R. and P. McCann (2000), 'Industrial clusters: complexes, agglomerations and/or social networks', *Urban Studies*, **37**(3), 513–532.

Grandori, A. (1999), 'Interfirm networks: organisational mechanisms and economic outcomes', in A. Grandori (ed.), *Interfirm Networks. Organization and Industrial Competitiveness*, New York: Routledge, pp. 1–14.

Grandori, A. and G. Soda (1995), 'Inter-firm networks: antecedents, mechanisms and forms', *Organization Studies*, **16**, 183–214.

Granovetter, M. (1985), 'Economic action and social structure: the problem of embeddedness', *American Journal of Sociology*, **91**, 481–510.

Grossman, G.M. and E. Helpman (2002), 'Integration versus outsourcing in industry equilibrium', *Quarterly Journal of Economics*, **117**(1), 85–120.

Grossman, G.M. and E. Helpman (2005), 'Outsourcing in a global economy', *Review of Economic Studies*, **72**, 135–159.

Grossman, G.M. and E. Rossi-Hansberg (2008), 'The rise of offshoring: it's not wine for cloth anymore', *American Economic Review*, **98**, 1978–1997.

Gulati, R. (1995), 'Social structure and alliance formation patterns: a longitudinal analysis', *Administrative Science Quarterly*, **40**, 619–652.

Harrigan, J. and A.J. Venables (2006), 'Timeliness and agglomeration', *Journal of Urban Economics*, **59**, 300–316.

Hätönen, J. and T. Eriksson. (2009), '30+ years of research and practice of outsourcing: exploring the past and anticipating the future', *Journal of International Management*, **15**, 142–155.

Hayashi, N. (2002), 'The role of subcontracting in SME development in Indonesia: micro-level evidence from the metalworking and machinery industry', *Journal of Asian Economics*, **13**, 1–26.

Helsley, R.W. and W.C. Strange (2007), 'Agglomeration, opportunism, and the organisation of production', *Journal of Urban Economics*, **62**(1), 55–75.

Hendry, J. (1995), 'Culture, community and networks: the hidden costs of outsourcing', *European Management Journal*, **13**, 193–200.

Holl, A. (2008), 'Production subcontracting and location', *Regional Science and Urban Economics*, **38**(3), 299–309.

Holl, A., R. Pardo and R. Rama (2012), 'Comparing outsourcing patterns in FDI and manufacturing plants: empirical evidence from Spain', *European Planning Studies*, **20**(8), 1335–1357.

Holl, A. and R. Rama (2009), 'The spatial patterns of networks, hierarchies and subsidiaries', *European Planning Studies*, **17**(9), 1261–1281.

Holmes, J.T. (1999), 'Localisation of industry and vertical disintegration', *Review of Economics and Statistics*, **81**(2), 314–325.

Imrie, R. (1994), '"A strategy of the last resort"? Reflections on the role of the subcontract in the United Kingdom', *Omega Inernational Journal of Management Science*, **22**, 569–578.

Innocenti, A. and S. Labory (2004), 'Outsourcing and information management: a comparative analysis of France, Italy and Japan in both small and large firms', *European Journal of Comparative Economics*, **1**, 107–125.

Javorcik, B.S. (2004), 'Does foreign direct investment increase the productivity of domestic firms? In search of spillovers through backward linkages', *American Economic Review*, **94**, 605–627.

Jones, R., H. Kierzkowski and C. Lurong (2005), 'What does evidence tell us about fragmentation and outsourcing', *International Review of Economics and Finance*, **14**, 305–316.

Kelley, M.R. and B. Harrison (1990), 'The subcontracting behaviour of single vs. multiplant enterprises in US manufacturing: implications for economic development', *World Development*, **18**, 1273–1294.

Klein, P.G. (2005), 'The make-or-buy decision: lessons from empirical studies', in C. Ménard and M.M. Shirley (ed.), *Handbook of New Institutional Economics*, Dordrecht: Springer, pp. 435–464.

Kotabe, M. and M.J. Mol. (2009), 'Outsourcing and financial performance: a negative curvilinear effect', *Journal of Purchasing and Supply Management*, **15**, 205–213.

Kranton, R.E. and D.F. Minehart (2000), 'Networks versus vertical integration', *RAND Journal of Economics*, **31**, 570–601.

Lai, E., R. Riezman and P. Wang (2009), 'Outsourcing of innovation', *Economic Theory*, **38**, 485–515

Lamoreaux, N.R., D.M.G. Raff and P. Temin (2003), 'Beyond markets and hierarchies: toward a new synthesis of American business history', *American Historical Review*, **108**(2), 404–433.

Larsson, A. (1999), 'Proximity matters? Geographical aspects of changing strategies in automotive subcontracting relationships: the case of domestic suppliers to Volvo Troslanda assembly plant', pp. 1–305, http://hdl.handle.net/2077/2508, edited by Meddelanden från Göteborgs Universitets Geografiska Institutioner. Serie B, Göteborg: Göteborg University. School of Business, Economics and Law, Department of Human and Economic Geography.

Lazonick, W. (2001), 'The theory of the innovative enterprise', Fontainebleau: INSEAD.

Lehtinen, U. (1999), 'Subcontractors in a partnership environment: a study on changing manufacturing strategy', *Int. J. of Production Economics*, **60**, 165–170.

Li, B. and Y. Lu (2009), 'Geographic concentration and vertical disintegration: evidence from China', *Journal of Urban Economics*, **65**(3), 294–304.

Liao, W.C. (2009), 'Outsourcing, inequality and cities', National University of Singapore, mimeo.

Liu, R-J, and J. Brookfield (2000), 'Stars, rings and tiers: organisational networks and their dynamics in Taiwan's machine tool industry', *Long Range Planning*, **33**, 322–348.

López, S., A. Pueyo and G. Zlatanova (2002), 'Colaboración bajo incertidumbre: La formación de un "grupo tecnológico" en el sector de las telecomunicaciones', *Economía Industrial*, **1**(34), 81–96.

Lorenz, E.H. (2000), 'Neither friends nor strangers: informal networks of subcontracting in French industry', in D. Gambetta (ed.), *Trust: Making and Breaking Cooperative Relations*, Oxford: Department of Sociology, University of Oxford, pp. 194–210; electronic edition http://www.sociology.ox.ac.uk/papers/lorenz.

Madhok, A. (1996), 'The organization of economic activity: transaction costs, firms capabilities and the nature of governance', *Organization Science*, **7**, 577–590.

Marshall, A. (1920), *Principles of Economics*, 8th edn, London: Macmillan.

Mazzanti, S., S. Montresor and P. Pini (2009), 'The general profile of the outsourcing firm: evidence for a local production system of Emilia Romagna', in M. Morroni (ed.), *Corporate Governance, Organization and the Firm. Co-operation and Outsourcing in the Global Economy*, Cheltenham, UK and Northampton, MA, USA: Edward Elgar, pp. 148–180.

Meccheri, N. and M. Morroni. (2010), 'Incentive-based and knowledge-based theories of the firm: some recent developments', *Journal of Industrial and Business Economics*, **37**, 69–91.

Ménard, C. (2006), 'Hybrid organization of production and distribution', *Revista de Analisis Economico*, **21**(2), 25–41.

Ménard, C. (2009), 'Oliver Williamson and the logic of hybrid organizations.' in M. Morroni (ed.), *Corporate Governance, Organization and the Firm. Co-operation and Outsourcing in the Global Economy*, Cheltenham, UK and Northampton, MA, USA: Edward Elgar, pp. 87–103.

Minetaki, K. and K. Motohashi (2009), 'Subcontracting structure and productivity in the Japanese software industry', *Rev Socionetwork Strat*, **3**, 51–65.

Mol, M.J., R. van Tulder and P.R. Beije (2005), 'Antecedents and performance consequences of international outsourcing', *International Business Review*, **14**, 599–617.

Monteverde, K., and D.J. Teece (1982), 'Appropriable rents and quasi-vertical integration', *Journal of Law and Economics*, **2**, 321–328.

Morris, J. and R. Imrie (1993), 'Japanese style subcontracting – its impact on European industries', *Long Range Planning*, **26**, 53–58.

Morroni, M. (2006), 'Innovative activity, substantive uncertainty and the theory of the firm,' *Economia e Politica Industriale*, **3**, 45–75, ISBN-ISSN 0391-2078.

Olsen, K.B. (2006), 'Productivity impacts of offshoring and outsourcing: a review', in *Statistical Analysis of Science, Technology and Industry*, Technology and Industry (STI) OECD Directorate for Science: OECD, pp. 1–35.

Oman, C., F. Chesnais, J. Pelzman and R. Rama (1989), *New Forms of Investment in Developing Country Industries: Mining, Petrochemicals, Automobiles, Textiles, Food*, Paris: OECD.

Ono, Y. (2007), 'Outsourcing business services and the scope of local markets', *Regional Science and Urban Economics*, **37**(2), 220–238.

Pais, J. and J.P. Pontes (2008), 'Fragmentation and clustering in vertically linked industries', *Journal of Regional Science*, **48**(59), 991–1006.

Parmigiani, A. (2007), 'Why do firms both make and buy? An investigation of concurrent sourcing', *Strategic Management Journal*, **28**, 285–311.

Peoples, J. and R. Sudgen (2000), 'Divide and rule by transnational corporations', in C. Pitelis and R. Sudgen (eds), *The Nature of the Transnational Firm*, London, UK and New York, USA: Routledge, pp. 174–192.

Podolny, J.M. and K.L. Page (1998), 'Network forms of organization', *Annual Review of Sociology*, **24**, 57–76.

Powell, W.W., K.W. Koput and L. Smith-Doerr. (1996), 'Interorganizational collaboration and the locus of innovation: networks of learning in biotechnology', *Administrative Science Quarterly*, **41**, 116–147.

Prahalad, C.K. and G. Hamel (1990), 'The core competence of the corporation', *Harvard Business Review*, May–June, 2–15.

Prudham, W.S. (2002), 'Downsizing nature: managing risk and knowledge economies through production subcontracting in the Oregon logging sector', *Environment and Planning A*, **34**, 145–166.

Rama, R. (1985), 'Some effects of the internationalization of agriculture on the Mexican agricultural crisis', in S.E. Sanderson (ed.), *The Americas in the New International Division of Labor*, New York, USA and London, UK: Holmes & Meier, pp. 69–94.

Rama, R. and A. Calatrava (2002), 'The advantages of clustering: the case of Spanish electronics subcontractors', *Int. J. Technology Management*, **24**, 764–791.

Rama, R. and D. Ferguson (2007), 'Emerging districts facing structural reform: the Madrid electronics district and the reshaping of the Spanish telecom monopoly', *Environment and Planning A*, **39**, 2207–2231.

Rama, R., D. Ferguson and A. Melero (2003), 'Subcontracting networks in industrial districts: the electronics industries of Madrid', *Regional Studies*, **37**, 71–88.

Razzolini, T. and D. Vannoni. (2011), 'Export premia and subcontracting discount: passive strategies and performance in domestic and foreign markets', *World Economy*, **34**(6), 984–1013.

Rossi-Hansberg, E., P.D. Sarte and R. Owens (2009), 'Firm fragmentation and urban patterns', *International Economic Review*, **50**, 143–186.

Sacchetti, S. and R. Sudgen. (2003), 'The governance of networks and economic power: the nature and impact of subcontracting relationships', *Journal of Economic Surveys*, **17**, 670–691.

Sako, M. (2005), 'Outsourcing and offshoring: key trends and issues', Oxford: Said Business School Emerging Market Forum.

Spencer, B.J. (2005), 'International outsourcing and incomplete contracts', *Canadian Journal of Economics*, **38**, 1107–1135.

Stigler, G.J. (1951), 'The division of labour is limited by the extent of the market', *Journal of Political Economy*, **59**, 185–193.

Strange, R. (2011), 'The outsourcing of primary activities: theoretical analysis and propositions', *Journal of Management and Governance*, **15**(2), 249–269.

Suarez-Villa, L. and R. Rama (1996), 'Outsourcing, R&D and the pattern of intra-metropolitan location: the electronics industries of Madrid', *Urban Studies*, **33**, 1155–1197.

Suárez-Villa, L. and W. Walrod (2003), 'The collaborative economy of biotechnology: alliances, outsourcing and R&D', *Int. J. of Biotechnology*, **5**, 402–438.

Taymaz, E. and Y. Kiliçaslan (2005), 'Determinants of subcontracting and regional development: an empirical study on Turkish textile and engineering industries', *Regional Studies*, **39**(5), 633–645.

Thorelli, H.B. (1986), 'Networks: between markets and hierarchies', *Strategic Management Journal*, **7**, 37–51.

Tomiura, E. (2007), 'Foreign outsourcing, exporting, and FDI: a productivity comparison at the firm level', *Journal of International Economics*, **72**, 113–127.

Tomiura, E., B. Ito and R. Wakasugi (2010), 'Offshoring and corporate headquarters: evidence from Japanese firm-level data', RIETI Discussion Paper Series 10-E-032.

Torre, A. and A. Rallet (2005), 'Proximity and localization', *Regional Studies*, **39**(1), 47–59.

UNCTAD (ed.) (2001), *World Investment Report 2001. Promoting Linkages*, New York, USA and Geneva, Switzerland: United Nations Conference on Trade and Development.

Varadarajan, R. (2009), 'Outsourcing: think more expansively', *Journal of Business Research*, **62**, 1165–1172.

Whitford, J. and J. Zeitlin (2004), 'Governing decentralized production: institutions, public policy, and the prospects for inter-firm collaboration in the US manufacturing', *Industry and Innovation*, **11**, 11–44.

Williamson, O.E. (1991a), 'Strategizing, economizing, and economic organization', *Strategic Management Journal*, **12**, 75–94.

Williamson, O.E. (1991b), 'Comparative economic organization: the analysis of discrete structural alternatives', *Administrative Science Quarterly*, **36**(2), 269–296.

Yeung, H. Wai-chung, W. Liu and P. Dicken (2006), 'Transnational corporations and network effects of a local manufacturing cluster in mobile telecommunications equipment in China', *World Development*, **34**(3), 520–540.

29. Public economic organisation
Jan-Erik Lane

The organisation of the public household, delivering a set of public services in a wide sense, is based upon a fundamental requirement for *quid pro quo*: the money provided the government(s) in the form of taxes and charges must at the end of the day correspond to the allocation of a set of valuable services, both quantitatively and qualitatively. But how is this to be achieved, in both a transparent and an effective way? At the root of the problematic of allocating public services is how to handle various modes of principal–agent interactions, where government can chose between alternative mechanisms: the bureau, incorporated units, ad hoc or statutory agencies, outsourcing, tournaments or auctions, tendering or bidding, public–private partnerships and multi-level governance. The overall trend in organisation change is the move away from hierarchy and formal organisation towards externalisation and networking. Public economic organisation is less the rule of authority, as with the classical Weberian model of the state, than the handling of massive numbers of contracts between government as the principal and a diverse set of agents.

INTRODUCTION

Public sector reform during the last 20 years has much been driven by the ambition to replace the monolithic bureaucracy with various forms of post-Weberian organisation. On the one hand, there are the 'atomistic' reforms such as agencification, incorporation and outsourcing, reducing the multiple functions of the traditional bureau. And on the other hand, there is holistic governance with, for example, joined-up and multi-level governance, adapting to interdependencies and social complexity with networking, regionalisation, and so on. The theory of public management attempts to cover basic types of governance forms, spelling out their implications for costs and value in the public sector.

Focusing here on the management of public services, one may approach public economic organisation as based upon deliberations or strategies of how governments at different levels in the political system can handle costs and organisational forms in order to receive value. All other things being equal, one may assume that government wants to maximise the difference between value and costs for each public service delivered, using organisational alternatives – or governance forms – when resolving this management task. Given the increasing relevance of social security (how shall governments fulfil their promises?), this chapter also looks at some options in the management of transfer payments, that is, the sending out of pay cheques.

The public sector in well-ordered societies amounts to somewhere between 35 and 55 per cent of gross domestic product (GDP) (Eurostat 2010). Much effort has been devoted to explaining the country differences in the relative size of public expenditures, without arriving at one established theory (Castles et al. 2010). But one may say generally that the variation in public sector size is a matter of both policy differences – the size of the welfare state – and accounting practices: whether for example all kinds of publicly determined social security outlays are included.

ON THE NATURE OF PUBLIC ECONOMIC ORGANISATION

The provision of public goods, merit goods and transfer payments presents a set of management tasks that are structured by the principal–agent mechanisms, linking the population with its government, that are inherent in democratic governance in well-ordered societies with a rule-of-law regime. The demand for public policies resulting in the provision of services and goods is basically handled by means of the democratic process or electoral politics. The supply of public goods, merit goods and social security payments is channelled through contracts between government and its agents. Thus, public management harbours principal–agent gaming involving self-centred strategies, asymmetric information and opportunism.

The recent immense financial crisis has shown beyond doubt the importance of the public sector; that is, public economic organisation complementing the market economy or the private sector. The neo-liberal philosophy that became so strong for a few decades led to a transformation of the structure of public economic organisation from the model of public administration (bureaucracy) to models of market decision-making (New Public Management (NPM)). However, neither classical bureaucracy nor the market offers a correct picture of public economic organisation.

It is true that public economic organisation has evolved out of bureaucracy with the modern state, but recent public sector reform has changed all that, allowing governments to draw upon other organisation models. However, one can never conclude that public economic organisation is merely business, or a gigantic set of markets driven by the logic of tendering and bidding. The logic of public sector management derives from public economics, aiming at social value, and it is heavily constrained by rule-of-law requirements as well as budgetary accountability. The public sector has two parts: the soft sector that is mainly tax financed and the business sector where user fees are employed fully.

Nested Principal–Agent Relationships

Public economic organisation is a vast nested set of principal–agent interactions, from elections to policy implementation. This web of interactions is heavily infused by politics, from the levying of taxes to the making of budgets. In well-ordered societies, the rule-of-law framework for the operations of the state infuses a heavy dose of public accountability upon the operations of public management in order to minimise the risks of patronage, embezzlement and corruption. Public economic organisation, for instance, does not typically run a 'bonus culture'.

Efficiency and Equity

The principal–agent problematic of finding suitable agents to do the work as well as providing them with incentives to operate efficiently is very much at the core of private sector organisation, especially in large corporations with a limited-liability legal structure (Jäger 2008; Macho-Stadler & Perez-Castrillo 2001). The owners of the organisation need to find chief executive officers (CEOs), and the CEOs in turn have to hire labour. Typical of recent developments in private sector contracting for CEOs is the immense increase in the compensation paid to them, compared with other employees or public officials. The difficulties in hiring and monitoring agents may be alleviated in other organisational forms such as the co-op, partnerships and business trusts.

Now, public economic organisation is in several aspects different from private economic organisation. On the one hand, principal–agent relationships are more complicated; and on the other hand, the objective function has at least two elements: efficiency and equity. As only parts of the public sector can be measured in terms of profitability – the business sector with user fees – the evaluation of performance and goal attainment becomes much more complex. In addition, equity considerations play a profound role in both the politics and the management of public programs.

Public services are handed down to the population by governments, seeking to combine efficiency in provision with a distributional structure of these services that agree with notions of equity. Thus, all citizens have legitimate expectations about receiving certain services *gratuit*, and to be treated equally, whatever differences there may be in terms of capacity to pay. In well-ordered societies with a democratic regime, elections tend to underline the value to the population of a large public sector comprising the allocation of numerous free or subsidised services as well as a plethora of entitlements.

In addition to the provision of goods and services, government also has the role in relation to private economic organisation of regulation; that is, to hand down and monitor a system of rules that structure the legality of private sector operations. Public regulation is a chief task for government, but its problematic is slightly different from the provision of goods and services, as oversight can be handled by a small set of regulatory agents in different agencies. Yet, there is a constant principal–agent problematic, as the politicians may not trust the regulators in prohibiting fraud (Enron) or bubbles (subprime).

BRIEF SKETCH OF THE THEORY OF PUBLIC MANAGEMENT

Given sharp public sector growth after World War II, the classical public finance framework focussing upon optimal taxation and the allocation of a small set of public goods was expanded to cover the millions of items of expenditure or policies that were subsumed under labels such as 'welfare state', 'great society' and 'mixed economy'. The theory of public economic organisation has passed through three major stages since the 1960s, involving shifts between the following paradigms.

Firstly, the planning approach: using linear programming, several attempts were made at a rational approach to public management at the macro level. Various budgetary frameworks in combination with cost–benefit analysis were launched in order to derive an optimal public economic organisation (Dror, 1968), e.g. zero-based budgeting.

The planning approaches did not fare well, either theoretically or practically. Although the players deciding and managing public sector programmes may engage in rational decision-making at the micro level, macro-level rationality is an elusive concept, bypassing all the evidence suggesting policy mistakes, inefficiencies, rent-seeking, and patronage and corruption. Budgeting is more than simply the calculation of algorithms (Wildavsky, 1986). A school of thought – marginalism, or incrementalism – emerged in order to vindicate the theory that public management was merely 'muddling through' (Lindblom 1959; Wildavsky & Caiden 2003). However, bounded rationality is hardly in agreement with basic game theory concepts, especially Bayesian updating.

Secondly, the market approach: the disillusionment with 'big government' in the early 1980s started an inquiry for the insertion of more of market mechanisms into public economic organisation, no doubt inspired by the public-choice school and Chicago school economics.

Looking at public management as basically business, NPM steered away from public resource allocation as planning and optimisation, favouring market-like mechanisms such as tendering and bidding, incorporation, and outsourcing and privatisation. Reducing the weight of bureaucracy with its long-term contracting, NPM implied that short-term contracting could be employed in order to reduce costs and X-inefficiency. The NPM philosophy had the most impact in the restructuring of the traditional public enterprise, which was basically eliminated as a governance form, to be replaced by public or semi-public joint-stock companies unless completely sold off. Yet, in the soft sector of public economic organisation, financed by means of taxation and not user fees, NPM had limited import, as government and its public sector involves more than markets. When put in practice with ideological zest for neoliberalist ideas, NPM has sometimes tended to result in policy pathologies as well as the hollowing-out of the state (Pollitt 2008; Suleiman 2003).

Thirdly, the network approach: bypassing the distinction between plan and voluntary coordination as competition, or state versus market, a number of organisational reforms suggested that there is a third way to provide public services, namely networking on the basis of trust. The search for social capital and the public domain together with the increasing relevance of civil society reinforced the relevance of such governance forms (Thynne & Wettenhall 2010).

As a matter of fact, some scholars had consistently argued that public economic organisation, however hierarchical, was always permeated by relations of reciprocity, both vertically and horizontally (Rhodes 1997; Kooiman 2003). In any case, turning to networks involving cooperation with stakeholders and civil society helped to heal the wounds, especially among public sector employees, from excessive contracting out and in. It may also reduce the often massive transaction costs in performance contracting.

Summing Up

Intense public sector reform has resulted in a host of governance forms that government may employ. There is no single mechanism that results in superior performance, as government needs to consider the use of different governance forms in relation to various public services. In the provision of public services, government hires teams or agents to do the job for it, thus running into principal–agent interaction and its basic difficulties (Laffont 2001). What, then, constitute the public goods and services, allocated in a mixed economy?

WHAT IS A PUBLIC SERVICE?

Public economic management targets the allocation of a set of public services. It also includes income maintenance, redistribution and social security. Transfer payments may be the result of entitlements, or they may include management, as with the workfare approach.

Public finance theory has delivered a set of criteria that identify what is public about a service (Musgrave 2008a, 2008b). Although these criteria were elaborated more than 100 years ago, they still retain their relevance for the separation between the public and the private sectors; that is, state and market. First and foremost, public resource allocation basically targets two forms of market failure:

- Non-excludability: the allocation of the good or service cannot be restricted to the group of people who are willing to pay for it; there is the possibility of free-riding, resulting in an undersupply of the good or service under market allocation.
- Non-subtractability: the enjoyment of the good and service is not restricted to any particular consumer, as in principle everybody can use the good or service.

Public services display various degrees of these two characteristics, as one may speak about pure public goods as well as semi-public goods. Moreover, one may also speak of national, regional and local public goods. Semi-public goods involve either excludability (toll goods) or rivalry (common pool goods).

Looking at the stylised facts about the government budget in a well-ordered society, one observes that the pure public goods only account for a small portion of the public expenditures. The semi-public goods, especially infrastructure in various forms such as roads, communications, harbours, electricity, water and sewage, constitute a much larger portion of the public expenditures. It should be pointed out that often not all public enterprises – traditional or joint-stock type – are included in the system of public expenditures. In a few countries, defence spending amounts to some 10 per cent of the budget or more.

Secondly, public economic management may provide so-called merit goods, as with the welfare state: education, health care and social care. The bulk of public expenditures relate to these types of items. In a full-sized welfare state regime they clearly make up the largest spending items.

Now, all other things being equal, governments would wish to provide more value at less cost for each item of public service concerned. This is the well-known rationality assumption in all forms of organisation (Thompson 2003). But how is this to be done?

The provision of public services can be organised in multiple ways. The fact that it is a matter of public resource allocation does not entail that the state must somehow be the producer. A number of alternative forms of public service provision have been developed in public sector reforms since the 1970 in a search for public sector improvement through governance reforms.

PRINCIPAL–AGENT FRAMEWORK FOR THE ANALYSIS FOR PUBLIC ECONOMIC ORGANISATION

Public management is hardly radically different from private sector management. Three things are distinctive of public management. Firstly, costs are often covered by taxes that are paid without a relationship to the consumption of a public service. Secondly, the ultimate judge of value from public services is the electorate, which delivers its verdict on the election day. Demand is thus expressed through the channel of politics. Finally, the set of organisational alternatives in public management is restrained by rule-of-law considerations, as the allocation of public services has to meet requirements in public law such as transparency as well as access to complaint and redress – the rule-of-law regime.

Public sector reforms during the last 20 years have resulted in new organisation structures, aiming at reducing costs and increasing value, including: bureaucracy, public enterprises, joint-stock companies, outsourcing through tendering and bidding; insourcing and performance contracting; tournaments and auctions; non-profit organisations; networking; multi-level governance; and joined-up government. The management problem in the public sector at any level of government is to choose the organisational forms that are most efficient in relation to a set of public services. Thus, public services may be provided in several alternative forms, which is the subject of public management theory, examining for example the cost and value implications of bureaucracy, traditional public enterprises, incorporated public enterprises, outsourcing, tendering and bidding in public procurement, and networking with the inclusion of non-governmental organisations (NGOs) as well as multi-level governance forms.

Public economic management is in principle directed towards maximising the equation: value of outputs minus costs of inputs, in theory. In practice, governments as principals do not have sufficient information or enough control power to achieve a maximum at a given time and place. Not only do they often face asymmetric information, but they also have to deal with the implications of opportunistic behaviour among the teams of agents that they contract with. Public sector organisation is prone to suboptimisation, displaying at times glaring inefficiencies due to lack of leadership and poor management as well as rent-seeking.

TEAM PROVISION: ASYMMETRIC INFORMATION AND OPPORTUNISM

The provision of public services is first and foremost a contractual question, as teams of employees must be contracted for the delivery of certain outputs at some specified cost (Laffont & Martimort 2001). Since these service contracts will be of some duration – from perhaps two years to 10–20 years – there arise the problems of asymmetric information between the principal (the government) and the service providers (the agents). Assuming that agents are much interested in the remuneration for their work, the problem of opportunism surfaces too, as effort is not observable and costly to verify.

The two main problems are adverse selection and moral hazard. The government –

local, regional or national – can only get its policies implemented by hiring a team of people, whether its own employees or external people. The service provision contract can be general as with insourcing, or specific as in outsourcing. Different opinions are bound to surface about the performance of the team under the contract, which may be handled either through internal procedures or through complaints and litigation in court.

The principal may employ long-term contracts or short-term contracts. Under long-term contracts, the team is in principle the employees of the principal, working under their supervision and accepting the normal terms of command in employer's authority. The difficulty with long-term contracting is that it involves post-contractual opportunism. In a long-term contract it becomes extremely difficult to verify effort with the inherent risk of shirking. The principal may monitor team performance but a strategy of opportunism may pay off handsomely, as low effort may be the hidden action under asymmetric information (moral hazard). Asymmetric information applies to both the team as a whole and to individual team members.

Short-term contracting became popular with NPM. It is basically a generalisation of public procurement as in, for instance, the model of internal markets. NPM resolves the problem of post-contractual opportunism by reducing the length of the contract, providing the principal with the possibility of terminating the contract when performance is judged insufficient. Thus, the agent has no incentive to shirk as the contract will not be renewed. However, running tournaments or auctions in order to score a winner for a short-term contract opens up the possibility of adverse selection, meaning that the principal cannot clearly establish the type of the agent. Perhaps they are a so-called lemon? Correcting after the contract has been signed could lead to high switching costs. The contract may have to be abandoned by means of court action leading to compensation claims. And the same problem – adverse selection – arises when a new contract is to be made, replacing the old agent with a new one (hidden information).

Asymmetric information in combination with opportunism results in inefficiency, meaning higher than necessary costs for the government as principal. Strategic public management includes a theory about the occurrence of agency costs in alternative organisational structure for the provision of public services.

SUPPLY: PRODUCTION VERSUS TRANSACTION COSTS

When government hires agents to deliver public services, then costs arise. The agents have to be paid somehow – production costs. But it also takes time and effort to reach an agreement with the agents as well as to monitor this contract – transaction costs. It holds generally for public economic management that one cannot simultaneously minimise both production and transaction costs. This sets up the basic management dilemma of whether to employ short-term contracting or long-term contracting when hiring the agents who are supposed to do the job.

Speaking generally, short-term contracting reduces production costs, all other things being equal. But it incurs transaction costs, as tournaments or auctions have to be staged within relatively short periods of time. The basic model of short-term contracting is that of public procurement (Laffont and Tirole 1993). What the NPM movement did was to expand the application of public procurement to almost any public service or good. Transaction costs can become staggering; especially if government changes the organisation structure too often – as with the British experience.

Production costs tend to be higher in long-term contracting than in short-term contracting, all other things being equal. But transaction costs do not present a major problem, as the principal has a rather broad scope of authority in relation to their agents. The main problem is increasing inefficiency, as the agent engages in post-contractual opportunism, such as shirking.

What, then, to choose in state management: lower production costs + higher transaction costs, or higher production costs + lower transaction costs? Before the arrival of the NPM approach, the standard preference was for long-term contracting, but now government need not commit itself to either one of these two modes of management but instead combine them on the basis of pragmatic considerations. It has been argued that the more standardised the public service is, the more advantageous short-term contracting would be, when compared with long-term contracting.

DEMAND: SIGNALLING THROUGH POLITICS

Typical of the public sector in well-ordered societies is the dominant role of government on the demand side. Demand may, however, be revealed in other ways than in the public budget by different governments at various levels in the political system, as for instance by the use of 100 per cent user fees in infrastructure or through the employment of the referendum in certain countries.

The allocation of public services is fraught with demand revelation difficulties, such as free-riding and preference distortions. In well-ordered societies, the value of public services is first and foremost estimated through the political process, with politicians or political parties offering various packages of services and tax prices to the electorate. Yet, the political process is fraught with ambiguity, opacity and self-seeking strategies. One may look upon the electoral process as the sending of signals from the principal to the political agents, but these signals are seldom crystal clear or received with clarity. In addition, political agents always want a piece of the pie for themselves somehow – the agency costs on the political arena (Besley 2007).

In public budgeting, government amasses financial resources from a lot of different sources: taxes, charges and borrowing. Although earmarking may occur, typical of public budgeting is the large amount of discretion of government as to how to spend its revenues. Even when activities are supposed to be funded to 100 per cent, government still faces the agency problem of finding people who will deliver the services in question as well as the problem of how to monitor their performance.

The political process sends ambiguous and often contested signals about the demand for public programmes. Whereas market reactions to change tend to be swift and encompassing, it may take years to change items in the public sector, as the political channel is not only about sending signals to politicians but also attracts the attention of other players such as, for instance, interest groups.

STRATEGIES IN PUBLIC MANAGEMENT: HOW TO ELICIT GOOD PERFORMANCE?

In public economic management, government faces a number of crucial strategic options concerning governance forms or alternative ways of organising the people who will deliver the public services. Governments in various countries have increasingly decided to combine them in different ways with a view to eliciting the best possible performance (Pollitt & Bouckaert 2004; Wettenhall & Thynne 2005, 2011). Here we mention the key options:

- long-term contracts or short-term contracts;
- insourcing or outsourcing;
- formal organisation: the bureau, the trading department (classical public enterprise) or the incorporated firm (partially or completely public);
- agencification: use of so-called executive agencies;
- networking;
- employment of non-profit organisations (NPOs);
- intergovernmental forms: joined-up government and multi-level government.

Governments may wish to reflect upon what alternatives they have when organising the provision of public services. If government pursues a clear philosophy over time with regard to choosing between organisational forms, one may speak of a strategy of public management. Governments often engage in the systematic elaboration of reform policies, based upon a philosophy with a strategy – at least to some extent. Logically speaking, government at any level in the political system would face the following strategic options in public economic management

Insourcing or outsourcing
Public sector reform has led to a sharp rise in outsourcing, as governments turn to tendering and bidding mechanisms to contract with producers from the private sector – firms or NPOs – or with individual entrepreneurs. If governments know how to run tournaments, then outsourcing may reduce costs considerably. This enlargement of the scope for public procurement may become institutionalised as governments cooperate to create a unified system of tendering and bidding; for example the European Union (EU) regime for public works. It has even been suggested that various government authorities be allowed to compete in such tournaments although the services to be provided are not located in their jurisdiction (Frey and Eichenberger 1999).

The evaluation of performance in alternative governance forms under insourcing or outsourcing has given mixed results. On the one hand, when public and private supply of the same service can be compared in all aspects of quality and quantity, then private supply appears to be cheaper (Mueller 2004). On the other hand, when outsourcing is done in an indiscriminate manner, then the outcome is uncertainty and sometimes confusion or pathology.

Incorporation
Of all the public sector reforms, the change from traditional public enterprises to joint-stock companies has been the most consistent, applied with almost 100 per cent coverage

to the business sector of government (Wettenhall & Thynne 2005). There are hardly any traditional trading departments – classic public enterprises – left in well-ordered societies, having gone through the combined process of incorporation, deregulation and sometimes privatisation. However, the employment of the incorporated governance form in the soft sectors of government, for instance health and social care, has not met with success in terms of outcomes, whether consumer or employee satisfaction.

Agencification

In an atomistic approach to public sector provision government could employ on a grand scale so-called executive agencies, that is, small units or teams with clear but limited tasks. The outcomes of agencification depend upon the function, namely how separable it tends to be. Government tasks that involve coordination among units do not fit this governance form.

Networking – micro or macro

A third alternative to bureaucracy and NPM, the network model has attracted serious attention in relation to public services where information is dispersed in many hands and individual motivation to engage in collective effort counts for much. It is a proper response to interdependencies where different service providers may draw upon collaboration.

On the one hand, there are micro networks in various localities. People from various bureaux may create ad hoc teams collaborating for some common purpose, cross-cutting various services such as education, health care or social care. On the other hand, whole administrative units may enter networks at the macro level, as when local governments set up regional organisations, sometimes across state borders.

Summing Up

In public economic organisation, government has to tackle two basic problems:

1. Information. How to ensure that the teams or agents it employs uses most recent technology when providing services? A team may employ strategies that limit access to new knowledge, if it can capture a rent in doing so, such as promoting X-inefficiencies. With asymmetric information, there is no way government can be sure a team updates its information base.

2. Motivation. How to communicate to the teams or agents that they need to try hard? Effort is the key element in the principal–agent model of public management besides asymmetric information. It is not enough for government to be able to identify effort *ex ante*, as even high-performance agents may resort to shirking *ex post*.

In public management, government basically employs alternative institutions to handle these two problems, searching for better results: more value and less costs. Empirical research has provided evidence to the effect that the various governance forms handle the typical problems in principal–agent interaction differently. One may suggest that:

- The bureau is prone to shirking.
- The classical public enterprise is inefficient: too many employees and too small output.
- The incorporated company mimics the private firm.
- Excessive agencification hollows out the state.
- Massive performance contracting in combination with tendering and bidding generates high transaction costs.
- The networking teams may resolve principal–agent difficulties – but how can they be held accountable?
- The NPOs constitute a mechanism of their own, besides bureaucracy and NPM. They feed on social trust, both internally and in their external relations. But perhaps not for a long time, as opportunism is bound to emerge.

Thus, there is no one single mechanism for the provision of public services. Government may wish to employ all of them, but in a pragmatic fashion.

SOME NEW PROBLEMATICS IN PUBLIC ECONOMIC ORGANISATION

The transformation of public economic organisation from mainly bureaucracy to the various mechanisms employed under NPM has thrown up a set of problems that remain unresolved. They exemplify the tensions inherent in public management, where the ultimate principal is the *demos*.

Stakeholder Influence

One often meets various calls for public management to somehow include so-called stakeholders in the provision of public services. Such a demand is based upon a variety of considerations: efficiency, equity, deliberative democracy, and so on.

The idea of stakeholder influence sits well with the model of public management as networking. But it really does not fit well into either bureaucracy or NPM. On the positive side, stakeholder participation may increase efficiency by removing asymmetric information and allowing government to draw upon spontaneous motivation. On the negative side, it may open up the implementation of public law to the capture of private interests and strategies.

The NPOs and Civil Society

Also the non-profit organisations offer governments a way to overcome moral hazard and adverse selection, but only in the short run. NPOs may undercut the costs of the bureau or outside contractors under NPM, given that they capitalise on voluntary work and altruistic leadership. However, once the NPOs receive the contracts, they will be more protective of their special interests.

Engaging with the NPOs and civil society offers government one more mechanism for getting the job done. In some contexts it works very well, as for instance when international assistance and donor aid does not want to rely upon the bureaux in a dictatorship country. In other contexts, the outcomes may not be so positive, because NPOs cannot really be held accountable in accordance with rule-of-law precepts. It is often complained that the early enthusiasm of the NPOs is rapidly replaced by the typical problems in any principal–agent interaction, that is, moral hazard.

The involvement of NPOs in public service delivery has increased since public sector reforms were initiated in around 1990. Operating in the implementation of government policies, domestically or internationally, they have to resolve two challenges to their existence: (1) elicit commitment from governments and other donors; (2) receive involvement from volunteers in their projects. Partly, the NPOs solve these two problems through emotions and future projections. Partly, the success of NPOs stems from the inspirational style of leadership in these organisations. Leadership style in NPOs is of the utmost importance for both government commitment and volunteer involvement. Third-sector participation in public policy implementation can only be understood if one ventures into the new economics of altruism (Kolm and Ythier 2006).

Redress and Complaint

Given the special features of much of public economic organisation – monopoly, hierarchy, no exit, limited voting by the feet, obligatory payment – the theory of public administration has always paid lots of attention to failures in service provision. The NPM revolution did not share this interest in how voice can be made to matter for citizens, as NPM strategies only targeted efficiency in allocation.

The key institution for enhancing voice is the Ombudsman. It is as relevant today for public economic organisation as it was before the onslaught of the neoliberal ideology. If it is true that exit is more effective than voice, there must be avenues for complaint and redress in relation to public management. The Ombudsman, nowadays a global institution, provides voice with an outlet that in many countries works well, not only in Scandinavia or the EU but also in India and other poor Asian countries.

Public Morality: *Fiscus*

Public money as well as public assets in general have certain special qualities that are not always respected, not even in well-ordered societies. Whereas looting the public purse has been the standard strategy in the new states in Africa after independence, corruption – patronage, embezzlement and bribes – has been heavily restricted in advanced countries. However, morality has decreased, according to much evidence. Public economic organisation cannot thrive or even survive without strict protection of the *fiscus*; that is, public assets of various kinds, such as capital and tax revenues, but also currencies, domestic and foreign. Looting in almost all African states spelled disaster for their states and their survival capacity, but it is one strategy available in all principal–agent gaming.

Decentralisation or Regionalisation

The most persistent reform trend of public economic organisation is the decentralisation of tasks and competencies from central government to lower levels of government in the political system. Delivering public services is basically a bottom-up process where the quality of what is provided is decided by the 'street-level bureaucrats': doctors, nurses, teachers, policemen, fire fighters, and so on.

Instead of relying upon huge bureaux in the capital, tasks and competences have been devolved, either to other tiers of government or to independent agencies or joint-stock companies. Knowledge about the conditions for service provision and the motivation to make an effort are to be found within regional or local teams, who can monitor results quicker than the central governments. The trend towards decentralisation and deconcentration has been profound since the 1970s, especially in unitary states.

At the same time as tasks and competences have been devolved, some governments have taken to regionalisation: that is, moving competencies upwards to an intergovernmental or supranational body, such as the EU.

Fiscal Federalism or Economic Structure of Unitary States

The state in a well-ordered society normally has three levels of government. The theory of fiscal federalism outlines a few basic principles for the structure of government with a distribution of tasks, competences and financing between these three levels. However, this normative theory about an optimal structure for the provision of public goods and services is equally applicable to unitary states as to federal ones. The basic idea is that services that are to be allocated generally and in the same manner for a whole country are best supplied by the federal or central government, whereas goods and services that may reflect local and regional variation in either preferences or conditions of production are best allocated by lower tiers of government.

SOCIAL SECURITY: HOW TO REDUCE THE RISK OF INSOLVENCY?

Public economic organisation comprises a huge sector of transfer payments; that is, the sending out of pay cheques to people. It is not really public management, at least not when these payments are considered as entitlements. In a workfare state framework, social security also becomes public management.

The steady increase in the so-called dependency ratio forces every government to develop a strategy in order to contain the costs in social security. Whatever the basic system for funding social security may be, governments attempt to delay payments and increase individual contributions. The problem of funding social security has implications for both current deficits and the overall size of public sector debt. Governments fearing the risks involved in a sovereign debt crisis may engage in drastic spending cuts, hurting social welfare – as in the fiscal austerity policies of several countries in Europe and the United States (US) in 2010–11.

It should be pointed out that the turn to austerity policy-making in some of the advanced capitalist democracies has now reached a scale that effectively threatens the traditional European welfare state. Whatever attitude one may harbour towards austerity policies – necessary adjustment, market surrender or globalisation-induced – it is more important than before that government has a clear and comprehensive overview of the pros and cons of alternative ways of structuring the supply of public services.

CONCLUSION

In well-ordered societies, from one-third to half of the economy enters public economic organisation somehow, comprising both public resource allocation and income maintenance. Delivering a huge set of goods and services, government faces the principal–agent task of contracting with teams, paying them as well as monitoring their effort in getting the job done as effectively as feasible. Government disposes of certain degrees of freedom when deciding about policies and moving to their implementation, namely a set of governance forms. The key question in public management is to use the governance forms that are most suitable in relation to the variety of public goods and services.

The comparative evidence emerging from several comprehensive public sector evaluations (e.g. Ferlie et al. 2007; Pollitt 2008) strongly suggests that there is no doctrinaire answer to the problem of how to structure public organisation, such as for instance compulsive tendering and bidding (Niskanen 1968), encompassing networking (Kooiman 2003), incorporation (Thynne 1994) or a massive return to bureaucracy (Olsen 2011). Governments as the principal for the delivery of public services may wish to reflect over the comparative advantages and disadvantages of alternative governance forms when approaching agents and setting up interaction mechanisms with them. A contingency approach appears most promising, as each ministry faces its own problematic of finding, motivating, instructing, monitoring and evaluating agents to get the job done; that is, the allocation of public services in a broad sense.

REFERENCES

Besley, T. (2007), *Principles Agents?* Oxford: Oxford University Press.
Eurostat (2010), *Government Finance Statistics 2010*: http://epp.eurostat.ec.europa.eu/cache/ITY_OFFPUB/KS-EK-10-001/EN/KS-EK-10-001-EN.PDF.
Castles, F.G., S. Leibfried, J. Lewis and H. Obinger (2010), *The Oxford Handbook of the Welfare State*, Oxford: Oxford University Press.
Dror, Y. (1968), *Policy Making Re-examined*, San Francisco: Chandler.
Ferlie, E., L.E. Lynn Jr. and C. Pollitt (eds) (2007), *The Oxford Handbook of Public Management*, Oxford: Oxford University Press.
Jäger, C. (2008), *The Principal–Agent-Theory within the Context of Economic Sciences: Summary*, Norderstadt: Herstellung und Verlag, Books on Demand Gmbh.
Kolm, S-C. and J.M. Ythier (eds) (2006), *Handbook of the Economics of Giving, Altruism and Reciprocity: Foundations: 1*, Amsterdam: North-Holland.
Kooiman, J. (2003), *Governing as Governance*, London: Sage.
Laffont, J-J. (2001), *Incentives and Political Economy*, Oxford: Clarendon.
Laffont, J-J. and D. Martimort (2001), *The Theory of Incentives: The Principal–Agent Model*, Princeton, NJ: Princeton University Press.
Laffont, J-J. and J. Tirole (1993), *A Theory of Incentives in Procurement and Regulation*, Cambridge, MA: MIT Press.
Lindblom, C. (1959), 'The science of muddling through', *Public Administration Review*, 19(2), 79–88.
Macho-Stadler, I. and J. David Pérez-Castrillo (2001), *An Introduction to the Economics of Information: Incentives and Contracts*, Oxford: Oxford University Press.
Mueller, D. (2004), *Public Choice III*. Cambridge: Cambridge University Press.

Musgrave, R.A. (2008a), 'Public finance', *The New Palgrave Dictionary of Economics*, 2nd edn, Steven N. Durlauf and Lawrence E. Blume (eds), Basingstoke: Palgrave Macmillan.

Musgrave, R.A. (2008b), 'Merit goods', *The New Palgrave Dictionary of Economics*, 2nd edn, Steven N. Durlauf and Lawrence E. Blume (eds), Basingstoke: Palgrave Macmillan.

Niskanen, W. (1968), 'The peculiar economics of bureaucracy', *American Economic Review*, **58**(2), 293–305.

Olsen, J.P. (2011), 'Maybe it is time to rediscover bureaucracy', *Journal of Public Administration, Research and Theory*, **16**(1), 1–24.

Pollitt, C. (2008), *Time, Policy, Management*, Oxford: Oxford University Press.

Pollitt, C. and G. Bouckaert (2004), *Public Management Reform: A Comparative Analysis*, Oxford: Oxford University Press.

Rhodes, R. (1997), *Understanding Governance*, Milton Keynes: Open University Press.

Suleiman, E. (2003), *Dismantling Democratic States*, Princeton, MA: Princeton University Press.

Thompson, J.D. (2003), *Organisations in Action*, Edison, NJ: Transaction Publishers.

Thynne, I. (1994), 'The incorporated company as an instrument of government: a quest for a comparative understanding', *Governance*, **7**(1), 59–82.

Thynne, I. and Wettenhall, R. (2010) (eds), 'Symposium on ownership in the public sphere', *International Journal of Public Policy*, **5**(1), 59–82.

Wettenhall, R. and I. Thynne (eds) (2005), 'Symposium on public ownership and enterprise management', *Asia Pacific Journal of Public Administration*, **27**(2), 111–290.

Wettenhall, R. and I. Thynne (eds) (2011), 'Dynamics of public ownership and regulation', Special Issue of *Policy Studies*, **32**(3), 179–301.

Wildavsky, A. (1986), *Budgeting*, Edison, NJ: Transaction Publishers.

Wildavsky, A. and N. Caiden (2003), *The New Politics of the Budgetary Process*, New York: Longman.

CONCLUSIONS

Integrating economic and organization theory: products, problems and prospects
Anna Grandori

The integrated approach between organizational economics and organization theory offered in this volume yields various theory extensions and a number of reconciliations between the common divides and contrapositions of concepts that are increasingly under strain. The main achievements of this type are highlighted in the first section of these conclusions ('Beyond divides').

The subsequent sections highlight some notable substantive and methodological advances emerging from the *Handbook* in terms of 'new' elements that are gaining importance in the analysis of economic organization (EO). These elements are 'new' in the sense that they have been traditionally neglected or underconsidered, and emerge as gaining importance here due to the combined effect of two methodological options and concerns: not only the effort of integrating relevant economic and organization theory, but also the effort of taking the challenge of an 'empirically based' economic science seriously (Simon 1997) that is capable of predicting and prescribing EO structures and behaviours in the modern economy, usually characterized as increasingly dynamic and uncertain, knowledge intensive and differentiated. These new elements include new variables, both in the role of *explanans* and *explananda*; new practices and systems that can enrich the typically contemplated portfolio of EO governance mechanisms; and new methods contributing results that would otherwise be difficult to achieve.

Some (examples of) new questions for future research are posited at the end of each section or subsection, in addition to those highlighted by the authors in the conclusions of each chapter, and among the many questions that researchers will hopefully put forward, independently and creatively, from the rich and original material contributed by the authors in this book.

BEYOND DIVIDES

Economic, Administrative or 'Enlighted' Man?

The 'mother of all the divisions' lies in the foundations of EO on assumptions about human rationality. The notion of rationality emerging from the reviews and revisiting of EO micro-foundations in Part I is extended, and the divide between bounded and non-bounded rationality is reduced in various ways. In contrast with the common characterization of bounded rationality as a weaker form of thought, the positive sides of bounded rationality and heuristic reasoning are stressed especially in Grandori's and in Foss's chapters. Those strengths do not reduce to decision efficiency and the reduction of cognitive effort, as they have been conceived in the part of the cognitive tradition emphasizing the positive rather than negative sides of bounded rationality (e.g. by Gigerenzer and associates). The aspiration is to define a form of reasoning capable of generating new knowledge through logically sound discovery processes. An underlying conceptual operation is a disentanglement of the notion of knowing or foreseeing (everything), from the notion of proceeding rationally (perhaps a return to the 'Austrians', including not only Hayek but also Popper).

Lindenberg, and Osterloh and Frey, extend the conventional view of rationality and cognition especially on the motivational side. They underscore and document the 'plasticity of preferences', and the possibility, even the likelihood in many conditions, of non-selfish interests (reciprocating or even altruistic). For these reasons, it may also be said that another neglected part of Simon's legacy is positioned center-stage: the difference between interest and self-interest, or even opportunistic self-interest (Simon 1997).

As a result, an expanded 'model of man' emerges from Part I, with respect to the two dominant traditions in economic and organizational theories respectively. This is an actor who is much more illuminated than the 'behavioural actor' and much less selfish than the 'economic actor'.

Most chapters in Part I also develop some broad governance implications of these extended and renewed assumptions. These implications converge in pointing towards at least one common direction: the need for governance mechanisms designed not only to bring greater utility to economic players, but also to reduce errors and mispredictions about what their own utility might be in the first place, as well as about the causal texture of the world in which they act. If and when these judgments are difficult to make and are confronted with uncertainty, governance mechanisms that enable participation, knowledge exchange and knowledge sharing are indicated as critical. In those conditions, it is also argued that highly powerful incentives, leveraging heavily on instrumental and extrinsic motivation, have many undesirable and unintended effects which make them most often counterproductive. By contrast, the selection of appropriate partners and collaborators becomes more important, along with the transparency of the procedures of team formation.

A further innovative way of analyzing the relation between micro-foundations and governance is that the behavioral assumptions are to a large extent endogeneized. Firstly, the state of knowledge and the configuration of interests are typically treated as variables, not as assumptions: knowledge is not assumed as complete or incomplete; nor actors as opportunist or fair. Configurations of knowledge and interests vary, and not in an unpredictable way. Secondly, the governance and organizational arrangements adopted greatly influence what knowledge will be produced and how actors will define their interests. The implications of this reverse causation seem clear: it would be very risky, and very costly, to design EO as if these effects could safely be ignored. This point may be taken as a criticism of the usual approach of economics as applied to organization, designing EO 'as if' all players were selfish and opportunistic (given that it is deemed impossible to discern *ex ante* who is who). Following Lindenberg, and Osterloh and Frey, the problem is precisely that these organization designs are likely to foster opportunistic frames and to further raise the costs of coordination and monitoring. Likewise, following Foss, the reverse causal nexus, whereby structure generates knowledge, implies that arrangements designed only for production and transaction cost reduction purposes are likely to be suboptimal for knowledge generation purposes.

The Reconciliation of Contract and Organization

Part II gathers contributions on the foundations of EO in interactions and agreements between different players. The notion of contract is therefore central in this part. This core notion for EO attains a broader scope in the treatments offered in the various chapters. Goldberg examines the core problems of finding binding agreements between economic players, noting that they have much the same nature within and between legal entities. In addition, he reproposes and elaborates on his view that at the opposite extreme of the option represented by short-term or spot contracts there are constitution-like, condominium agreements. This view is compatible with the idea that contracts could regulate, even establish, communities and not only regulate exchanges. Masten's analysis goes in the same direction, further highlighting some fundamental similarities, along with the much analyzed governance dissimilarities, between different types of communities and entities such as firms, universities and municipalities. Taken together, these two contributions can be interpreted as indicating that the various forms of entities we observe may have more in common than is usually acknowledged, and that these commonalities may be closer to such things as constitutional and representative orders than to the usually stressed alternatives of power and authority, or even of relational games and trust. More than one chapter in this *Handbook* takes a converging stance and elaborate on the core issue of governance thus intended – how constitutions are selected (Sacconi), and who should be entitled to which right (Blair, Pagano, and Grandori's Chapter 15).

The notion of contracting is also broadened to include social and communication dimensions by Sacconi and by Warglien. These analyses go well beyond the now commonly accepted observation that contracts can be relational (regulating an ongoing relation) and not only transactional (regulating the terms of an exchange). The 'social' in the notion of social contracts is not just a surrounding atmosphere or a shadow of the future and a game of reputation (as in most organizational economic views). The 'social' is the very matter of contracting. A social contract is a contract that founds societies, as in Rousseau and Rawls. As a consequence, Sacconi's argument states that ethical rules are not an arbitrary or embedding addendum to EO, but an intrinsic and necessary component in defining any Pareto-efficient form of EO.

Warglien further enriches our view of contracting by analyzing its linguistic texture. Agreements, organizational documents and contracts, as well as all informal information and communication, are inevitably expressed through language, whereby the degree of codifiability of matters into language becomes a central variable in understanding the different types of agreements on which EO can be based. The lower the codifiability, and the wider the scope and need for interpretation, the more parties have reasons to prefer agreements that are not too precise, detailed and predefined. To live (safely) under ambiguity, therefore, they may see fit to shift from single exchanges to an ongoing relation in which it is possible to continuously negotiate and renegotiate the meaning and spirit of the agreements.

This point may be connected to new emerging interpretations (or revisions) of the notion of incomplete contracts. Firstly, the 'incompleteness' of contracting, similarly to the 'boundedness' of reasoning, becomes an endogenous design matter. However, and in addition, it does not reduce here to a matter of calculating an optimal degree of incompleteness, given the cost of writing and enforcement, as done in emerging strands of the economics of contracts. The contributions by Warglien, Goldberg, Masten, Foss and Grandori in this *Handbook* all imply that there are knowledge reasons, and not only cost reasons, for not specifying details. The outcome is perhaps not even to be called an 'incompleteness', but a shift to a qualitatively different type of contracting, designed not for regulating the exchange of goods and services, but the association of actors. In those views, the 'relational' is not some extra-contractual component that complements incomplete contracts, but the very matter of contracting. The implication of those analyses is then to see much more continuity, if not consubstantiality, between contract and organization, where much contraposition is usually seen.

Hybrids Beyond Continua and Discreteness

The reduction of the contract versus organization divide is reinforced and made more applied and precise, rather than contradicted, in various other chapters that have to pass through the internal versus external, market versus organization divide for dealing with their topic. The reinforcements and refinements in this direction that can be derived from the various chapters can be summarized as follows.

Hennart observes that joint ventures – being firms constituted and owned by 'mother firms' – are firms, not hybrids, as they are usually considered. Similarly, Hendrikse and Feng make clear that 'inter-firm cooperatives', being cooperative firms constituted and jointly owned by other firms, are again firms, not a type of network or inter-firm association, as has been sometimes argued.

Franchising contracts emerge as much closer to firms than usually thought, from Windsperger's analysis: in fact, they are documented to include proprietary agreements on residual rewards, residual decision rights and 'ownership surrogates', as a wide array of exclusivity clauses and tying arrangements, accompanied both by authority and agency relations. Rama and Holl point out that subcontracting can occur between independent firms or also inside firms (among firms in the same company group); and that even when it is external it can be hierarchical (even involving the acceptance of authority).

The notion of hybrids is therefore also put under strain and emerges as a construct in need for rethinking. A clear effort in this direction is present in this *Handbook* in Hennart's chapter, which goes much further than analyzing joint ventures, revisiting hybrids in more general terms. He starts with an abstract alternative between governing on inputs or on outputs, and arrives at the conclusion that combining these two types of mechanisms is possible and indeed frequent. These combinations give rise to various forms of external and internal hybrids: price-like coordination is used within firms in pay-for-performance or pay-for-service systems; hierarchy is ubiquitous within and across firms (although it may be based on authority or on other mechanisms, such as agency (as in franchising), or election (as in public economic organization, cooperatives and associations), or third-party arbitration (as in contractual agreements).

In sum, the conventional notions of where the boundaries between internal and external forms of EO lie and how they should be defined are put under strain. The limitations of the notion of discrete structural alternatives that informed many of the analyses of boundaries among forms of EO in the past decades have, in general terms, been noted for some time (Ménard 1995; Grandori 1997). These contributions highlighted, as does Hennart's chapter here, that one of the underlying problems is that there is a difference – often overlooked – between forms of EO intended as complex multi-mechanism arrangements, even codified and legitimized as institutions (as the market, the firm); and the component mechanisms or organizing methods (as prices and hierarchy). A precise comparative analysis is possibly attainable at the level of governance mechanisms, while it is perhaps hopeless at the level of complex institutions that inevitably apply almost all mechanisms albeit in different doses and combinations.

Some chapters in this *Handbook* explicitly address those problematic aspects of a discrete and mutually exclusive notion of economic organization forms as unboundable or even institutionalized packages of internally homogeneous mechanisms, and also propose innovative solutions to these problems, as illustrated in what follows.

Internal Organization beyond 'Coherence'

In their analysis of the internal organization structure of firms, Argyres and Zenger note in unambiguous terms that 'the discrete organization forms available are simply unable to match the dimensionality of performance required'. Their solution acknowledges that there are limits to the combinability of mechanisms, and indicate in the 'oscillation' among arrangements a possible way for a dynamically optimized structure, particularly among centralized/integrated and decentralized/disaggregated arrangements. They also acknowledge, however, that this solution may live alongside a static expansion of forms to include a more varied portfolio of mechanisms, to the extent that they entail positive rather than negative complementarities. In fact, in organization theory – under specified conditions of uncertainty and interdependence – the possibility that effective organization forms are simultaneously integrated and differentiated, centralized and decentralized, rich in teamwork and in incentives, has been highlighted in both classic and more recent contributions to organization design.

The difficult issue, however, to a large extent yet to be addressed, is to understand where the positive versus negative complementarities among (which) governance and organization mechanisms lie, and what is their origin. This question, of paramount importance to enable undertaking any design of economic organization, has been left considerably unanswered by those who are merited with introducing the analysis of complementarity among organizational practices in the EO agenda (Milgrom and Roberts 1995). Some chapters in this *Handbook* offer advances on this terrain.

At a general governance system level, Lindenberg maintains that organizational arrangements can be characterized by a 'core' – inspired by alternative governance logics, namely 'incentive alignment' or 'goal integration' – and by a 'belt' of mechanisms that 'protect' the functioning of the core. Interestingly, and I think convincingly, the mechanisms in the belt protect the core precisely because they are different in kind from those in the core. As much as rules and antitrust authorities are needed to protect competitive markets, internal courts of last resort, negotiation, forbearance, reputation and job security can protect the otherwise fragile governance through incentives and the alignment of interests. Conversely, governance by communitarian goal integration needs to be complemented and protected by individual accountability, balanced performance evaluations and authority based on functional competence.

At a 'micro' organization of work level, the so-called 'high-performance work practices' packages have often been empirically demonstrated as sustaining performance, as Leoni's chapter illustrates. Leoni also stresses that, nevertheless, there is considerable variance in the mechanisms that may compose those packages. In addition, if we examine the content of those configurations often, if not typically, we find practices and mechanisms that should be classified as different in kind according to standard views in economics of organization (using Williamson's terminology). For example, an array of mechanisms including horizontal communication, teamwork and knowledge-sharing systems coupled with pay-for-performance, structured and transparent performance evaluation and high specialization, can be said to include communitarian as well as bureaucratic as well as market-like mechanisms. In sum, the idea (common in economics of organization but to some extent also in organization theory) that discrete structural alternatives or organization forms should be composed by 'syndromes of attributes' and mechanisms that are coherent in the sense of 'similar in kind', seems to be in need of revision.

The Purpose-Independence of Structures

A need for revision of other important and common partitions among forms of EO is also directly or indirectly implied by other chapters. This is the case of the partitions between public and private economic organization (Lane) and between capitalistic and co-operative (Pencavel) forms of enterprise.

These modes are definable in two different ways: a structural functionalist way – different forms allocate various rights (ownership, decision, residual rewards) to certain categories of actors differently and perform different functions; or a teleological way – different types of entities are assumed to pursue different goals.

I think that all contributions in this volume contribute to a structuralist definition of forms, and imply a healthy critique of subjective and teleological definitions. In fact, despite the latter definitions still being very common, it can be observed that objectives and purposes are very malleable and very poorly verifiable. Consequently, the 'purpose' of a firm is very slippery terrain on which to found any distinction among forms. As clearly emerges from the chapters on different types of firms in Part VI, private firms may pursue various missions and goals. For example, in co-operatives, economic objectives are usually stylized as if they were the maximization of net income per worker (Pencavel). However, in principle (and in law) they are defined as governance structures that 'can' pursue any economic, social or cultural interest of members (and these substantive missions may be set by statute). Knowledge growth objectives could lie behind the 'provision of judgment' by entrepreneurs (Foss & Klein), as much as other and more instrumental objectives may lead to the establishment of entrepreneurial firms. Research on the 'motives of attachment' in emerging firms empirically support the proposition that intrinsic motivation based on passion for the task or love for co-workers and partners (Baron & Kreps 1999) are even more important than other objectives. Corporations themselves have distinctive features and functions (clarified in Blair's chapter) – such as asset partitioning and shielding, identifiability of responsibility, the possibility but not the obligation to distribute dividends – that can define that form precisely without any recourse to goals.

Furthermore, arguments in other chapters converge in suggesting that, in the contemporary highly imperfect and Schumpeterian competitive world, if firms behave 'as if' they were pursuing multiple goals (rather than 'as if' they were maximizing profit) they would be operationalizing the actually relevant performance parameters in a more valid way (Argyres & Zenger; Burton & Obel; Grandori's Chapter 1). Some contributions also highlight, based on simulation research, that there are limits to the proliferation of goals (Burton & Obel). Hence, rather than partitioning types of firms on the basis of a single and assumed goal, it would be more fruitful to identify the objectives that can more parsimoniously operationalize performance in different fields of action and sectors; taking into account that they are likely to be manifold, but, as in any good model, they should be reduced to a few key dimensions that make a difference in terms of being effective in guiding action.

Even if we define EO forms in terms of structural features rather than referring to any goal or ultimate motive, the possible effective configurations seem far from being captured by two opposed configurations: not only, as already argued, in the case of the market versus hierarchy opposition; but also in the case of public versus private, and in the case of capitalist versus collective EO.

According to Lane's excursus, the governance mechanisms employed in public EO include mechanisms and arrangements that are hardly distinguishable from those applied within and between private firms: joint-stock companies, outsourcing, internal performance-based contracting, tournaments, auctions, agency relations and alliances. The variables used to explain these arrangements are also similar to those employed for private ones: standard production and transaction cost considerations apply. The main difference stressed by Lane reduces to the identity of the principals who have the right to elect or nominate the managers: citizens or partners/investors. Lane also highlights that public EO faces specific problems due to the number and the dispersion of principals and difficulties in measuring performance. On the other hand, it can also be noted that these two problems are by no means absent in the private sphere; the difference seems one of degree rather than kind.

Pencavel explicitly notes that some features considered typical of worker co-ops, such as the allocation of various property rights to workers, are also increasingly diffused in capitalistic firms; and vice versa, hired work as well as many governance systems and mechanisms that used to be typical of capitalistic firms can be, and are, also applied in co-ops, whereby a continuum of arrangements rather than distinct and discrete categories of organizations is envisaged.

The implications of such a reassessment should not of course be a theoretical confusion or reduced to the simple observation of a blurring of boundaries among forms. It should instead lead to a more precise understanding of forms, asking where and which the commonalities and differences are, rather than assuming that there are only differences. In addition, this clarification may guide design and illuminate the extent to which and the direction in which mechanisms may be selectively transferred across forms and domains. Otherwise transfers are declared either as 'impossible selective interventions' (as occurred in theory), or anything that seems to work in another form or setting is declared as transferable (as has often occurred in practice). For example, in reality, the transfer of practices has mostly occurred from the private to the public field, and from corporations and capitalistic firms to collective or entrepreneurial firms in the cost managing domain (Lane, Pencavel). The chapters in Part VI, especially those just cited, can be interpreted as signaling that, conversely, the governance of private capitalistic firms may also have something to learn from public EO and from entrepreneurial and collective firms in terms of how to manage distributed knowledge and multiple interests. Hence, the reduced divides among forms can be intended as enabling and guiding more intense, fruitful and reasoned reciprocal learning between the forms, under the shadow of a unified theory of governance; taking into account that the canons of good science consider a more general theory better than different theories explaining different types of objects.

Human Resources (Re-)Meet Human Relations

Another significant recomposition is offered by the chapters that consider work governance practices and mechanisms (Kaufman, Leoni). The main recomposition is here between the rather divorced fields of human resources (HR) and industrial relations (IR). Thanks to this broad approach, these treatments also contribute to rendering EO theory in this area less idiosyncratically linked to the specificities of the United States versus Europe. In fact, in Europe, the governance of the employment relation is conceived and practiced as an intensely negotiated relation (albeit through different institutions in Germany, the United Kingdom and Mediterranean Europe). In addition, the models of these relations were developed primarily with the problem of the entire workforce in mind. By contrast, the human resources management (HRM) toolkit has for a long time been intended as a unilateral firm design of evaluation, reward and mobility systems, and developed primarily for 'managing the managers'. However, as highlighted by Kaufman, HRM research and practices have progressively broadened to include further dimensionalities evolving towards a wider and negotiated approach both to individual employment relations (as in the 'free actor' approach) and to collective employment relations (as in 'strategic HR' and human and social capital-based approaches). Both Kaufman and Leoni convincingly indicate that an analysis of the complementarities between HR and IR practices, and cross-fertilization between the underlying theoretical approaches, is a fruitful direction for future research.

All in all, these analyses seem to call for a different approach to the assessment and design of EO forms in which practices, mechanisms and rights are 'unbundlable' and recombinable with higher degrees of freedom than usually admitted in the comparative institutional assessment of given, discrete, internally homogeneous and mutually exclusive bundles or institutional alternatives. The subsequent chapters, dedicated to organizational design and evolution, as well as to specific forms of EO, but with a strong concern with design as well, provide methodological advances capable of enriching the traditional repertory of analytic methods applied to the study of EO in such a way as to contribute in addressing some of these and other substantive challenges.

METHODOLOGICAL ADVANCES IN EO EVOLUTION AND DESIGN

Evolution Meets Design

How is EO shaped and how can it be shaped into forms? Two main broad alternative approaches have inspired the possible answers to this question: evolution and design. Here again, the alternative has often been cast as a contraposition between two mutually exclusive processes. The chapters in Part III reconduce the difference to its proper and sound nature of a methodological option for analysis rather than a factual proposition on how EO does take form and change. In fact, in a methodological and conventional stance, the possibility of an intentional modification of structure is suspended for analytical purposes, so as to study only evolutionary dynamics; without excluding that, in reality, both intentional choice and selection actually exist, and normally coexist. The chapters dedicated to evolutionary dynamics in this *Handbook* take further steps in analyzing the two processes jointly.

Hodgson has forcefully argued here and elsewhere that the Lamarkian and intentional adaptation of structures and behaviors can be (and needs to be) nested in a wider generalized Darwinian selection model. In fact, not only has it been pointed out that Darwinian selection can act upon any variation, whether intentional or not (see also Bonifati & Villani), but it is also argued that Lamarkian evolution requires inheritable (genotype-like) instructions for the transmission of acquired characteristics.

The contrast between evolution and design is downplayed even more when the underlying process is not limited to adaptation but also considers the possibility of 'exaptation' (Bonifati & Villani): a process in which an artifact or feature may be selected for any of its multiple functions with respect to many environments (as in the famous example of the selection of bird plumage for its flying function, beyond its basic function of warming the body). An intelligent actor, knowing that this is how selection could work, may intentionally design multifunctional action to increase its robustness (Grandori's Chapter 1).

Hence, these types of analyses suggest a notion of evolutionary processes where design is nested in ecological processes, rather than the thus far prevailing adversarial view that the two processes are mutually exclusive. Furthermore, the emerging approach may liberate the design implications of evolutionary analysis, which would otherwise be denied and remain unexploited.

Other chapters are specifically dedicated to, or have strong implications for, EO design.

Generative and Generalized Design

A design logic has to specify some rules generating possible organizational solutions (Burton & Obel). Design is about 'the world as it might be' (Simon 1969): hence, design rules should be able to generate organization forms, only part of which may be observable (already applied). This stance, albeit anticipated by Simon, is not so common, as Burton and Obel aptly stress. What is usually called 'organization design', both in organization theory and in organizational economics, is most often only a comparative assessment of existing forms. The chapters by Burton and Obel, and Puranam and Raveendran, instead offer a specification of design rules as 'if-then' propositions linking some premise or condition to some efficient or effective organizational attribute or element. This is per se a step forward, with respect to the current and common state of the art. In addition, the fact that those rules are specified taking into account a wide and interdisciplinary basis of study leads to defining design rules that are more general than in most available organization design works taken separately.

In particular, Puranam and Raveendran provide here an accurate translation between the notion (and types) of interdependence in organization theory and the notion (and types) of complementarity in organizational economics. This type of inter-theoretical integration effort, conducted by these authors on interdependence and complementarity, converges with that by a few others (Grandori 2001) on other core design variables used in both organization theory and economics – such as uncertainty, coordination costs and substitutability – in heading toward a generalized approach to design; not only because it takes into account a wider set of variables, but also because it is applicable at different levels, from the micro level of job design to the level of macro-structure design, to the design of the boundaries and coordination mechanisms among firms.

The applicability of the same design principles at different levels is aptly termed 'recursivity' by Warglien in his chapter. Recursivity is the constancy of design principles or rules at different levels of generality, as in fractal design. The core message is that the basic problems of division of labor, interdependence and coordination, and some basic features of their solutions, are essentially the same at the micro, meso and macro levels. In each design 'round' these principles and rules are applied to the results of the previous round (e.g., elementary operations are aggregated in tasks, tasks in positions, positions in units, units in firms, always according to the same rules). Warglien's chapter, discussing the possible contribution of seeing organizations as languages, highlight that a grammar-like view of organization may help in identifying the 'combinative rules' of organizing (how attributes and practices can be combined, as grammar specifies how letters and words can be combined in constructing phrases) in addition to the 'contingency rules' emphasized in the Puranam and Raveendran and the Burton and Obel chapters.

Approaches to design based on experimental research designs are particularly conducive to analyses focused on precise properties of specific structural components or traits of EO and to design-oriented research, particularly of a generative kind. In fact, behavioral experiments are notoriously powerful in isolating the expected and unexpected consequences and the evolution of real behavior in response to precise treatments; and economic laboratory experiments exploit this strength to study the relation between structural and economic treatments, and behavior in particular (Kriss & Weber). The strength of computer-based simulations, as applied to EO, lie in their capacity to explore the consequences of alternative combinations of structural components, especially if and when these combinations are not (yet) commonly observable in practice (Burton & Obel). Both methodological approaches are thus particularly suited in different ways to sustaining design proper – the study of the 'world as it might be' – going beyond the mere assessment of what it is.

Reconciling Contingency and Universalistic Design Approaches

The latter point raises an issue and a question about what precisely are the 'degrees of freedom' that we may have in the design of EO. An interesting question indeed in an age of crisis and 'reforms' of EO. On this terrain, some divides seem to (re-)emerge, rather than being resolved. It is the case of a contrast between universalistic and contingency approaches: that is, between design intended as finding the best way of organizing, or design as the specification of 'if-then' rules linking contingencies to solutions.

The rejuvenated appeal of a universalistic approach may be ascribable to some extent to the circumstance that the 'one best way' of reasoning appeals to many economists. In fact, there are important areas of EO design that have been addressed with a universalistic approach in economics, such as corporate governance in an agency theory perspective; or the empirical search for 'the' high-performance work system. In these areas of EO design, the core question has largely been: what is the best way of organizing? Instead of the question: which way is better under what circumstances?

This dilemma surfaces in this *Handbook* especially in the chapter by Leoni on work systems. His analysis also offers food for thought for solving the tension between unconditionally and conditionally superior EO. In fact, he highlights that the 'new organizational configuration' 'is composed by innovative bundles of different "ingredients"' and by different weights of each ingredient. Hence the new and superior configuration is actually a set of possible (and equifinal) configurations.

This observation suggests that a two-tiered approach to organization design may be a possible conciliation of universalistic and contingent approaches in a wider configurational approach to design. Such an approach would build, first of all, on the observation that some organizational aspects may be contingently effective, while others may be universally desirable – such as practices and procedures guaranteeing accountability, or right of appeal. Hence, an organizational arrangement may be designed in two steps: firstly, by including those ingredients that are (singularly or in combination) universally effective and excluding traits that are (singularly or in combination) universally ineffective. This design rule does not lead necessarily to homogeneity, as there are usually multiple attributes that perform similar functions and multiple equilibria in their combination. Secondly, an organizational form may be further designed and differentiated by infusing other elements that are contingently effective as fit to particular conditions.[1]

These advances on organization design, taken together, can therefore contribute to developing a much-invoked renewed approach to the design of economic organization: and there is promise that it can be a more general approach, including a much better understanding, or even theory, of structural heterogeneity than currently available. Clearly defining what the structural elements are, and how they can combine into forms, seems to be territory in need of a great deal of further empirical and theoretical development.

From Static to Dynamic Design

Traditional organization design models in organizational economics and organization theory are predominantly static models. Many chapters and results in this *Handbook* in fact concur in calling for dynamic design approaches and in signaling the relevance of time and change in any attempt to optimize structure. There are various ways of constructing dynamic models, though, and different contributions in this volume suitably represent the different modes of rendering analyses dynamic as well as illustrating the different types of results that can thereby be achieved.

A first way of constructing dynamic models is by observing or simulating the variation of structure (or aspects of it) over time, usually in relation to the variations of some conditions or contingency variables. The notion of temporary optimal organizational regimes examined in Burton and Obel's chapter (drawing on Levinthal and Siggelkow's simulations) is of this type; and an example of a substantive proposition reached is that temporary decentralization is effective if the landscape changes in a 'rugged' mode.

A second and stronger sense in which a model can be dynamic is to be 'genetic': the state of a system in previous configurations is a cause of the state of that system in subsequent configurations. Here, a link is established between a prior state of an evolving system with its further states, and not only between a time series of explanatory variables and a time series of structural configurations. There were some genetic models with implications for design in early organization theory, mainly based on stages of growth; but they have for a long time been absent, possibly partly due to the lack of reliable and rigorous methods for testing those dynamic processes. Now the methods are ripe and dynamic design has returned to the research agenda in new, much more sophisticated ways than through simple analogies with growing living organisms.

A model of this type is Argyres and Zengers's model of oscillating structural change. The substantive proposition is also more radical: any regime, decentralized or centralized, may be temporary, as its very adoption generates forces and reasons for reverting (oscillating) towards the other.

Another genetic model of organization is incorporated in the experiments on organization formation reviewed by Kriss and Weber, where the effects on performance of the attachments of marginal members are analyzed. The interesting and substantive insight reached in this way – particularly useful in times of an unconditional celebration of growth – is that after 'slow food' there may be a need for a 'slow growth' movement (fast-expanding groups are less effective).

A third way of achieving dynamic rather than static organization design models is to evaluate EO solutions according to their own dynamic rather than static properties. In the realm of contract design, for example, Goldberg positions change governance properties center stage as a criterion for evaluating EO solutions in contract design. He observes that this criterion has been underused in the economics of contracts, in which the static optimization of contractual structure contingently to asymmetric information, moral hazards, hold-up and risk aversion has been privileged. As to organizational structure design, Burton and Obel offer a typology of structural properties defined in terms of managing change, such as static stability (resistance of a structure with respect to performance, to external shocks); dynamic stability (how safely and timely a structure returns to the same desired performance after a shock); and manoeuvrability (the capacity and speed of an organization in moving towards the new desired performance).

These contributions open the way to and invite investments in further research oriented to more systematically and precisely define a set of change-based performance criteria: what are the specific differences and consequences of all these properties of structures deemed important under change and stress, such as flexibility, resilience, adaptability, exaptability, robustness, manoeuvrability . . .?

NEW KEY DIMENSIONS AND MECHANISMS

What are the key variables that are fundamental in explaining and designing effective EO? Does the changing specification of these variables and/or the changing weight attributed to them also change the specification and configuration of EO? In the picture of the field offered by the analyses gathered in this *Handbook*, it can be noticed that some variables gain importance and others lose relevance with respect to their current use. These variables will be highlighted here together with the type of relationship that they (are conjectured to) have with organizational attributes.

The Knowledge Revolution

Knowledge in all its forms and dimensions stands out among the factors gaining importance. In a sense, the *Handbook* as a whole responds to the extant authoritative invitations to go beyond the consideration of costs only, and to pay more attention to knowledge considerations: how knowledge can be acquired and constructed (Demsetz 1991), and how different EO architectures affect knowledge performance (Sah & Stiglitz 1985). In other words, economic models, traditionally focused on issues of scarcity and possible conflict of interests, have been marked by a 'knowledge neglect' problem. Not surprisingly, a contribution of the dialogue with organization science, traditionally focused on information and knowledge processing, brings about advancements on this terrain.

On the other side, knowledge-based organizational perspectives have been enriched by the dialogue with economic theory. In organization theory and design (neglecting here merely descriptive work), knowledge dimensions have been employed mostly as exogenous 'contingency' variables for organization; secondly the considered dimensions have been emphasizing the impediments and limitations in knowledge production and transfer (e.g. tacitness, stickiness, paradigmatic incommensurability, etc.) (Grandori & Kogut 2002).

By contrast, the analyses of knowledge in this *Handbook* are much more concerned with the prescription of 'good methods' for governing knowledge growth. In addition, as highlighted in particular by Foss and by Pagano, knowledge – incorporated both in human assets and in technical assets – is also treated as an endogenous variable, a result of EO architectures, and not only as an exogenous determinant of them.

In accordance with these two methodological options, new knowledge dimensions achieve center stage and new implications are highlighted.

The lack of a priori knowledge and its fallibility does not lead to distorsions or impediments or deviations from some perfect world, but to situations of Knightian uncertainty that may be addressed rationally through epistemic rationality (Grandori's Chapter 1), sound entrepreneurial judgments (Foss & Klein), and coordination mechanisms able to manage epistemic interdependence (Puranam & Raveendran).

States of knowledge in which interpretation and discretionary judgment are necessary are contrasted with conditions in which language and knowledge codification is possible. In turn, the latter condition is seen as enabling more 'automatic action' and greater appropriability of knowledge (Warglien; Lakhani & Tushman; Colombo & Rossi Lamastra).

The 'knowledge intensity' of human, social and technical assets is a further knowledge dimension of emerging importance and significant consequences, in particular for the efficient allocation of decision and property rights. For example, the choice between partnership-based versus salaried work-based employment relationships is examined in this light (Pencavel; Grandori's Chapter 15; Colombo & Rossi Lamastra), as well as the relative superiority of alternative HR architectures (Kaufman).

It can be argued that it is mostly thanks to their knowledge component that human capital and social capital have acquired a much more important role both in real economic organization and in our models of it. More precisely, it is mostly the knowledge component that makes the difference between people, human resources and human capital; where only the latter is a category of assets that may be invested at varying degrees into firms and other entities (Grandori's Chapter 15). Similarly, it is mostly their knowledge ('know-whom') component that transforms social ties from a contextual atmosphere and social embeddedness variable into a category of assets, a form of capital.

The diffusion or distribution of knowledge assets, finally, plays a major role in understanding which EO architectures are effective (Lakhani, Lifshitz-Assaf & Tushman; Foss & Klein; Grandori's Chapter 15). In particular, the principle of co-location of decision rights with relevant knowledge leads to predicting that decentralized arrangements should be superior in conditions of distributed knowledge, albeit more or less (horizontally) integrated according to asset separability versus interdependence (Lakhani, Lifshitz-Assaf & Tushman; Sanchez & Mahoney; Puranam & Raveendran).

The knowledge component of assets, both human and technical, greatly affects important properties of assets, such as (to use the notations now common in organizational law) the possibility of partitioning and protecting (shielding) them. Asset separability is in fact emerging as another complementary and key variable. Separability is often seen in economics as a problem that can always been expressed in terms of costs. By contrast, most contributions in this *Handbook* consider separability between various types of assets as a problem of knowledge and technical feasibility more than a problem of cost. This makes a difference, because it means that some partitions or separations can just not be made, at any cost. For example, 'tacit knowledge' is defined precisely as knowledge that cannot be separated from the person through expression (a person does not know how to express what they know, no matter what the cost). In this same sense, some technical assets may or may not be technically separable from other technical assets or 'modularizabile' (Tushman, Lifshitz-Assaf & Lakhani; Sanchez & Mahoney). In addition, further problems of separability are highlighted in some contributions: to what extent assets that differ in kind, in particular technical and human assets, are separable (Colombo & Rossi Lamastra); and to what extent assets can be partitioned from the actors holding them, protected with property rights from expropriation and invested into firms (Grandori's Chapter 15; Pagano).

The implications of knowledge intensity and asset separability for EO structures are pervasive.[2] To start with, some forms of enterprise, such as the corporate form, are distinctively based on asset partitioning from actors (Blair); hence, they actually require the separability of assets from actors.

Worker co-operative forms were already considered as a response to the inseparability between human and technical assets, in conditions of criticality of human assets (Hart & Moore 1990). The effectiveness domain of the latter form emerges as actually wider in Pencavel's assessment of the cooperative form. They include situations of knowledge-intensive human capital that is inseparable from persons (as in professional firms) rather than from technical assets only, whereby the co-operative form emerges as a possible and effective arrangement even in the absence of inseparabilities and specificities between human and technical assets (and even in the absence of any relevant technical asset).

Entrepreneurial governance, intended as an arrangement where the providers of judgments and of human capital are entitled to property rights, is explained in terms of epistemic complexity leading to failing markets for judgment (Foss & Klein) and the partial separability of people from their knowledge assets, so that the latter can be invested 'into' a firm (Grandori's Chapter 15).

Rediscovering Democratic Governance

An important consequence of introducing or attributing more weight to the above key variables is that new attributes and dimensions of organization and governance also emerge. Among governance mechanisms, incentives and prices, hierarchy and command, and communitarian practices, have been thus far emphasized, in both organizational and economic fields. Various chapters in this *Handbook* concur in highlighting – via both experiments (Kriss & Weber) and analytical tools (Sacconi; Lindenberg) – the serious limitations in effectiveness, the likely vicious circles, and the actual tendency toward overuse, and even abuse, of authority and incentives.

In addition, it has been argued that the portfolio of governance mechanisms included in the 'markets, bureaucracy and clans' dominant view is narrower than it could be (Grandori 2004). In particular, one important group of mechanisms that is entirely missing are democratic governance mechanisms. This mode is significantly re-evaluated by many contributions here. Various authors have in fact found it necessary to consider democratic governance mechanisms to solve the governance problems addressed in their chapters. Those mechanisms include practices such as political alternance, collective ownership, community governance, voting and negotiation: in a sense, a return to the basic Hirshmanian insight that the alternative to exit is not only 'loyalty' and clan-like control, but also, and most prominently, 'voice' in all its forms (not only in the form of authority and 'fiat') (Masten; Grandori's Chapter 15).

Relatedly, a number of chapters indicate that the governance of entry may be as (and perhaps even more) important than the governance of exit, as in any democracy, and indicate criteria through which participants in EO can effectively accept or reject each other as partners or collaborators; which participants are entitled to enter as (or to become) principals in the democracy and to what extent (through which right holding); which voice right is efficient and fair to assign to other participants joining through employment contracts (Kriss & Weber; Kaufman; Lindenberg; Osterloh & Frey; Sacconi; Pencavel; Colombo & Rossi Lamastra).

Actually, an even more profound implication of reappraising the role of democratic governance in economic organization may lead to state that the matter is not even just one of infusing democratic mechanisms into firms under particular conditions, but that economic organization entities, firms included, 'are', legally and constitutionally, democratic institutions (Grandori 2013). The issue is who has a vote or a voice in the democracy (Masten; Grandori's Chapter 15): only financial investors? or others as well: investors or holders of relevant knowledge? or anyone having a stake? and so on.

Another issue is why in the real practice of governance, democratic governance finds such a limited application in economic organization, and in firms in particular. Masten proposes the easiness of the exit alternative as an explanation of that fact. The studies reviewed by Kriss and Weber document with experimental precision that economic organization is far from immune from what has been recently called (by Fehr and colleagues) a 'lure of authority' (a taste for authority beyond its efficiency conditions), and has always been called plain power-seeking behaviour. Other analyses indicate that democratic arrangements are difficult to sustain, and vicious circles and 'degenerated' trajectories are possible or even likely in the absence of efforts and institutions dedicated to avoid them (as occurs for sustaining competition in markets). In that respect, Pagano envisages an emerging 'knowledge divide' or polarization between a world of reunification between physical persons, their human capital, physical technical assets, and the firm; and a world of increasing separation between persons and assets, where not only technical assets are separated from those who use them, but also human assets (such as intellectual capital and knowledge) are separated from those who provide them, and are appropriated (or expropriated) by 'intellectual monopolist' firms. Pencavel examines the phenomenon of the 'degeneration' of worker co-operatives into capitalist firms (due to internal dynamics, unrelated to the conditions of superiority of each form), judging this to be a significant risk. Lindenberg identifies various reasons that are likely to reinforce gain frames and incentive alignment arrangements rather than the alternative normative frame and goal-integration governance system.

In the light and awareness of these different possible trajectories, it seems more instructive and beneficial to address the evolution of the actual forms of EO in our future not so much as a matter of prediction (commonly, and I think excessively, asked of economic science) but mostly (returning to one of the leitmotivs of these conclusions) as a matter of design: designing a good world is possibly more important than predicting which world will obtain; and, as this *Handbook* as a whole testifies, also something that an economics and an organization science that reciprocally integrate, enlarge and enlighten seem to be better equipped to provide than other approaches.

NOTES

1. George Hendrikse, commenting on these Conclusions, observed that Milgrom and Roberts's (1995) system of attributes approach could be interpreted as compatible with a two-staged procedure in which 'first many compositions are excluded as being incoherent, second the contingencies determine which equilibrium cluster of attributes is efficient'. In fact, building on the complementarity approach a two-tiered analysis of that type has been explicitly developed by Grandori and Furnari (2013), specifying what

the sources of complementarity and the contingencies may be. Hendrikse also signalled that the 'bounds approach' adopted by John Sutton in the field of industrial organization is another example of a two-stage approach reconciling universalistic and contingency logics.
2.   It would seem possible to consider 'knowledge intensity' and 'asset separability' as extended and revised versions of the traditional narrower variables of 'uncertainty' and 'asset specificity'.

REFERENCES

Baron, J.N. and D.M. Kreps (1999), 'HRM in emerging companies', in J.N. Baron and D.M. Kreps, *Strategic Human Resources*, New York: Wiley.

Demsetz, H. (1991), 'The theory of the firm revisited', in O. Williamson and S. Winter (eds), *The Nature of the Firm: Origins, Evolution and Development*, Oxford: Oxford University Press, pp. 159–178.

Grandori, A. (1997), 'Governance structures, coordination mechanisms and cognitive models', *Journal of Management and Governance*, **1**(1), 29–47.

Grandori, A. (2001), 'The configuration of organization: a generalized model', in A. Grandori, *Organization and Economic Behavior*, London: Routledge, pp. 220–252.

Grandori, A. (2004), 'Reframing corporate governance: behavioral assumptions, governance mechanisms and institutional dynamics', in A. Grandori (ed.), *Corporate Governance and Firm Organization*, Oxford: Oxford University Press, pp. 1–27.

Grandori, A. (2013), *Epistemic Economics and Organization. Forms of Rationality and Governance for a Wiser Economy*, London: Routledge.

Grandori, A. and S. Furnari (2013), 'Configurational analysis and organization design: toward a theory of structural heterogeneity', in B. Cambré, P. Fiss and A. Marx (eds), *Research in the Sociology of Organizations: Configurational Theory and Methods in Organizational Research*.

Grandori, A. and B. Kogut (2002), 'Dialogue on knowledge and organization', *Organization Science*, **13**(June), 224–231.

Hart, O. and J. Moore (1990), 'Property rights and the nature of the firm', *Journal of Political Economy*, **98**(6), 1119–1158.

Ménard, C. (1995), 'Markets as institutions versus organizations as markets? Disentangling some fundamental concepts', *Journal of Economic Behavior and Organization*, **28**(2), 161–182.

Milgrom, P. and J. Roberts (1995), 'Complementarities and fit: strategy, structure and organizational change in manufacturing', *Journal of Accounting and Economics*, **19**, 179–208.

Sah, R.K. and J.E. Stiglitz (1985), 'Human fallibility and economic organization', *American Economic Review*, **75**(2), Papers and Proceedings 97th American Economic Association Meeting, 292–297.

Simon, H.A. (1969), *The Sciences of the Artificial*, Cambridge, MA: MIT Press.

Simon, H.A. (1997), *An Empirically-Based Microeconomics*, Cambridge: Cambridge University Press.

Index